An **International History**
of the **War for Peace** in **Vietnam**

# HANOI'S WAR

## Lien-Hang T. Nguyen

THE UNIVERSITY OF NORTH CAROLINA PRESS *Chapel Hill*

The paper in this book meets the guidelines for permanence and durability of the Committee on Production Guidelines for Book Longevity of the Council on Library Resources. The University of North Carolina Press has been a member of the Green Press Initiative since 2003.

Library of Congress Cataloging-in-Publication Data
Nguyen, Lien-Hang T., 1974–
Hanoi's war : an international history of the war
for peace in Vietnam / Lien-Hang T. Nguyen.
p. cm. — (The new Cold War history)
Includes bibliographical references and index.
ISBN 978-0-8078-3551-7 (cloth : alk. paper)
ISBN 978-1-4696-2835-6 (pbk. : alk. paper)
ISBN 978-0-8078-8269-6 (ebook)
1. Vietnam War, 1961–1975—Vietnam (Democratic Republic)
2. Vietnam War, 1961–1975—Peace.
3. Politics and war—Vietnam (Democratic Republic)
I. Title. II. Series: New Cold War history.
DS558.5.N467 2012
959.704′31—dc23    2011051976

Parts of this book have been reprinted with permission in revised form from the following works: "The War Politburo: North Vietnam's Diplomatic and Political Road to the Tết Offensive," in *Journal of Vietnamese Studies* 1, nos. 1–2 (February 2006): 4–55, © 2006 by the Regents of the University of California, published by the University of California Press; "Cold War Contradictions: Toward an International History of the Second Indochina War, 1969–1973," in *Making Sense of the Vietnam Wars: Local, National and Transnational Perspectives*, edited by Mark Philip Bradley and Marilyn B. Young (New York: Oxford University Press, 2008): 219–49; and "Waging War on All Fronts: Nixon, Kissinger, and the Vietnam War, 1969–1972," in *Nixon in the World: American Foreign Relations, 1969–1977*, edited by Fredrik Logevall and Andrew Preston (New York: Oxford University Press, 2008), 185–203, by permission of Oxford University Press, Inc.

# HANOI'S WAR

THE NEW COLD WAR HISTORY | Odd Arne Westad, editor

*To my parents,*

Nguyen Thanh Quang

*and*

Tran Thi Lien,

*whose love and support*

*sustain me*

# Contents

# Illustrations

# Acknowledgments

This book would not have been possible without the critical support of a small village of colleagues, friends, and family. Certain individuals at key institutions deserve special mention: Paul M. Kennedy, John Lewis Gaddis, Ann Carter-Drier, and Susan Hennigan at International Security Studies at Yale University; Lynn Eden and Scott Sagan at the Center for International Security and Cooperation at Stanford University; Stephen Rosen at the former John M. Olin Center for Strategic Studies at Harvard University; and Wm. Roger Louis and Miriam Cunningham at the National History Center. The Smith Richardson Foundation, Fulbright Program, and Colleges of Arts and Sciences at the University of Kentucky and at Yale University also provided key financial support. The staff at the Nixon and Ford presidential libraries, National Archives and Records Administration, National Security Archives, and Vietnam Archives at Texas Tech University made doing research in the United States an enjoyable experience. Correspondingly, Truong Xuan Thanh at the Vietnam Ministry of Foreign Affairs, Nguyen Tien Dinh and Pham Thi Hue at the Vietnam National Archives, Nguyen Vu Tung at the Diplomatic Academy of Vietnam, and most importantly Colonel Nguyen Manh Ha at the Military Institute of Vietnam made sure that I always felt at home in Vietnam, had documents to read, and had enough artichoke tea to drink. Finally, the staff at the French Foreign Ministry Archives, British National Archives, and Hungarian National Archives ensured that my research always proceeded smoothly.

I owe much to the higher institutions that have educated me and now make it possible for me to remain gainfully employed. The latter first: the Department of History at the University of Kentucky remains a tremendous place to pursue Vietnam War studies thanks to the legacy of George C. Herring. My colleagues and friends on the seventeenth floor of Patterson Office Tower presently make my workplace a wonderful place to teach and write. At my alma mater, the University of Pennyslvania, Walter McDougall and Drew Gilpin Faust sparked my initial interest in history, which continued to flourish during my graduate school years at Yale. In New Haven, Paul Kennedy created the ideal intellectual and social community, while John Gaddis acted as a superb mentor and role model. It is John's standard of approval that I sought for this book and will continue to seek for all future scholarship.

Two professional societies have become "homes" for me over the years, making their annual meetings more like reunions than conferences. My colleagues and friends in the Society for Historians of American Foreign Relations and the Vietnam Studies Group are too numerous to list, but I must name a few. They, along with my friends from various stages of life, have made the decade-long journey to complete this book an adventure and not an ordeal: Naveen and Faiz Bhora, David Biggs, Kate Black and Kathi Kern, Jennifer Boittin, Lady Borton, Bob Brigham, Kate Cambor, Jessica Chapman, Mei Chin, David Elliott, Kate Epstein, David and Thuy Hunt, George Herring and Dottie Leathers, Ryan Irwin, Pierre Journoud, Ben Kiernan, Jeffrey Kimball, Helen Kinsella, Yeewan Koon, Mark Lawrence, Adriane and Christian Lentz-Smith, Lorenz Luthi, Erez Manela, Vojtech Mastny, Steve Maxner, Cécile Menétrey-Monchau, Nguyen Hong Nhung, Jason Parker, Lorraine Paterson, Julie Pham, Jeremy and Beate Popkin, John Prados, Sophie Quinn-Judge, Daniel Sargent, Karthika Sasikumar, Sarah Snyder, Ronald and Dianne Spector, Balasz Szalontai, Michele Thompson, Hoang and Hanh Tran, Thanh and Phuong Truong, Tuong Vu, and last, but never least, Marilyn Young. One friend deserves special note: Susan Ferber played an integral role at every stage not only in the life of this book but also in my own life.

A few individuals who read and re-read this manuscript deserve special mention. Larry Berman, who is a dear friend and mentor, has shown me that being a scholar in Vietnam can reach rock star proportions. Peter Zinoman and Edward Miller read many chapters and gave me critical feedback at every juncture. Pierre Asselin, Mark Bradley, and Andrew Preston read the book cover to cover, and their big-picture comments as well as their line-by-line edits helped make it what it is now. I owe a significant debt of gratitude to Fred Logevall, Chris Goscha, and Jim Hershberg. Their friendship, support, and scholarship were essential to this book's completion. Their respective book series represent the cutting edge of war scholarship. One individual whose generosity and breadth and depth of knowledge continue to humble me is Merle Pribbenow. Merle is a generous scholar with an encyclopedic knowledge of the war, and the importance of his role in this book cannot be overemphasized. And finally, I owe much to George Herring. It is a delight when one meets a giant in one's field and discovers that he conforms to every expectation and more. The "father" of Vietnam War studies is a southern gentleman who found time to read and comment on an entire draft of the book as well as provide bourbon and basketball tickets at the right times.

I owe a debt of gratitude to Odd Arne Westad for believing in this manuscript and allowing it be in The New Cold War History series. His scholarship is the model for that of all international Cold War historians. Thanks to Arne and to my editor, Chuck Grench, and the talented team at the University of North Carolina Press for creating such a beautiful book.

My husband, Paul T. Chamberlin, a fellow traveler in international history, should share credit for this book since it bears his imprint as much as mine. With news that we were expecting a baby, Leila, we rushed to complete our respective manuscripts before life as we knew it changed. I look forward to expanding our family and our scholarship together.

Finally, my family. My parents; eight older siblings, Hung, Hai, Huong, Hiep, Hung, Hanh, Hien, and Ha, and their spouses; my nieces and nephews; my maternal aunt, Tran Thi Uyen; and my paternal uncle, the late Nguyen Khac Chinh, have been with me every step of the way. Although they might not have understood why I was researching painful past events, they nevertheless provided an endless supply of love and support. Since my paternal grandparents were casualties of the First Indochina War and my maternal grandfather died during the French colonial period, I only had the pleasure of knowing my maternal grandmother, Luu Thi Quy. She witnessed the tremendous changes of the twentieth century as a girl from rural Annam, fled to colonial Saigon as a young woman, and later lived out her final two decades in the United States.

This book is dedicated to my parents, Nguyen Thanh Quang and Tran Thi Lien, who bore the weight of history silently on their weary shoulders. Although they rarely speak about their lives before 1975 and took low-paying jobs and worked night shifts to put all nine children through college—a luxury they never enjoyed in Vietnam—their struggle for survival in the past ensured that our futures would flourish. To them, I owe my life, success, and happiness.

# Abbreviations

*The following abbreviations are used throughout the book.*

AAL   Association of Arts and Literature

ARVN   Army of the Republic of Vietnam (Quan Doi Viet Nam Cong Hoa)

ASEAN   Association of Southeast Asian Nations

BBC   British Broadcasting Corporation

CCP   Chinese Communist Party

CEC   Central Executive Committee (Ban Chap Hanh Trung Uong)

CIA   Central Intelligence Agency

CMAG   Chinese Military Assistance Group

CMC   Central Military Commission (Quan Uy Trung Uong)

COSVN   Central Office of South Vietnam (Trung Uong Cuc Mien Nam)

CPK   Communist Party of Kampuchea

CPSU   Communist Party of the Soviet Union

CRP   Committee to Re-elect the President (later nicknamed CREEP)

CWIHP   Cold War International History Project

DMZ   Demilitarized Zone

DRV   Democratic Republic of Vietnam (Viet Nam Dan Chu Cong Hoa)

FUNK   National United Front of Kampuchea (Front Uni National du Kampuchéa)

GDR   German Democratic Republic

GNR   Government of National Reconciliation (Chinh Phu Hoa Giai Hoa Hop Dan Toc; later named Hoi Dong Hoa Giai Hoa Hop Dan Toc)

GO-GU   General Offensive and General Uprising (Tong Tien Cong Va Noi Day or Tong Cong Kich, Tong Khoi Nghia)

GPD   General Political Department (Tong Cuc Chinh Tri)

ICC   International Control Commission

| | |
|---|---|
| ICP | Indochinese Communist Party (Dang Cong San Dong Duong) |
| ICSC | International Commission for Supervision and Control |
| IWC | International Works Committee (Ban Cong Tac Quoc Te) |
| MAAG | Military Advisory Assistance Group |
| MACV | Military Assistance Command, Vietnam |
| MALPHILINDO | Malaysia, the Philippines, and Indonesia |
| MOFA | Ministry of Foreign Affairs (Bo Ngoai Giao) |
| MR | Military Region |
| NAM | Nonalignment Movement |
| NCNRC | National Council of National Reconciliation and Concord |
| NDC | National Defense Council (Hoi Dong Quoc Phong) |
| NLF | National Liberation Front (Mat Tran Giai Phong Mien Nam) |
| NSC | National Security Council |
| NSSM | National Security Studies Memorandum |
| *NV-GP* | *Nhan Van–Giai Pham* |
| PAVN | People's Army of Vietnam (Quan Doi Nhan Dan Viet Nam) |
| PKI | Perserikatan Komunis di Indonesia (Communist Party of Indonesia) |
| PLAF | People's Liberation Armed Forces (Quan Giai Phong Mien Nam) |
| POW | prisoner of war |
| PRC | People's Republic of China |
| PRG | Provisional Reolutionary Government (Chinh Phu Cach Mang Lam Thoi) |
| PWD | Political War Department (Tong Cuc Chien Tranh Chinh Tri) |
| *QDND* | *Quan Doi Nhan Dan* (People's Army Daily) |
| RGNUK | Royal Government of National Union of Kampuchea |

RVN   Republic of Vietnam (Viet Nam Cong Hoa)

RVNAF   Republic of Vietnam Armed Forces (Quan Luc Viet Nam
Cong Hoa)

SALT   Strategic Arms Limitation Talks

SAM   surface-to-air missile

SRV   Socialist Republic of Vietnam (Viet Nam Xa Hoi Cong Hoa)

VC   Viet Cong

VVAW   Vietnam Veterans against the War

VWP   Vietnam Workers' Party (Dang Lao Dong Viet Nam)

WILPF   Women's International League for Peace and Freedom

# HANOI'S WAR

*During the dark years under the neocolonial system of the*
*U.S. imperialists in the south, he had a clear vision of the possibility of the*
*people winning victory through the masses' concerted uprising.*
*—Truong Chinh on Le Duan[1]*

# INTRODUCTION

Before the bombs fell, Hanoi was relatively quiet. Although the war had disrupted the frenetic pace of life in North Vietnam's largest city, the late fall and early winter of 1972 seemed even more desolate than seasons past. Between one-quarter and one-half of the population had been evacuated since early December, leaving empty such places as the bustling Dong Xuan market nestled in the maze of the Old Quarter and the tree-lined boulevard surrounding West Lake that had once provided a romantic backdrop for strolling young lovers.[2] *Mua phun*, the steady light rains of the winter months, enveloped Hanoi, shrouding the city in a damp cloak of despair.[3]

Four years had passed since the start of negotiations, yet the war's end seemed nowhere in sight. The dim prospect for peace sank the morale of war weary North Vietnamese to new depths in the latter half of 1972. In retrospect, it was the lull before the storm. At 7:15 P.M. on 18 December, an emergency warning rang out over the city's loudspeakers announcing the imminent arrival of U.S. bombers. Hanoi's remaining residents had twenty-five minutes to relocate to their bomb shelters before B-52s filled the night sky.[4] For twelve consecutive days and nights, with a brief pause on Christmas Day, the United States dropped nearly 36,000 tons of bombs over North Vietnam, while communist forces shot down more than two

1

dozen tactical aircraft and B-52s. The war for peace had reached its bloody climax.

Thousands of miles away in Paris, the fallout from Operation Linebacker II's B-52 bombing and the Vietnamese aerial defense known as Dien Bien Phu Tren Khong (Aerial Dien Bien Phu) would soon be felt. Near the close of January 1973, the four parties involved in the conflict—the United States and Republic of Vietnam (RVN or South Vietnam), on one side, and the Democratic Republic of Vietnam (DRV or North Vietnam) and the Provisional Revolutionary Government of South Vietnam (PRG), on the other—signed the Paris Agreement on Ending the War and Restoring the Peace. Yet no side believed the fight for control over southern Vietnam was over. Before the ink could dry on the peace settlement, Vietnamese forces were once again locked in battle; their guns would only fall silent two years later with the fall of Saigon as the few remaining Americans watched. Forged over four years of acrimonious negotiations and intense struggle, the 1973 settlement allowed the United States to exit the conflict, but it provided only a brief respite from fighting for the Vietnamese. Hanoi remained at war for a little while longer.

How did Hanoi's struggle, which began as a limited armed conflict against the RVN in 1960, lead it to become the target of America's heaviest bombing campaign in history a mere dozen years later? Under what conditions did the local Vietnamese communist war for national liberation transform into a major international contest in the Cold War? Although much is known about America's war in Vietnam, the "other" side's conflict remains a mystery. Questions endure over the configuration of the Hanoi leadership, its strategies during the "anti-American resistance struggle for reunification and national salvation," and the nature of its victory.

The key to unlocking these puzzles lies with one individual who has managed to escape scrutiny: Le Duan.[5] Despite being the architect, main strategist, and commander-in-chief of communist Vietnam's war effort, the former first secretary somehow resides on the historical margins of that conflict, the prodigious scholarship on which has centered overwhelmingly on the American experience.[6] Indeed, he served in this top Party position in Vietnam from 1960 until his death in 1986—the longest running reign in modern Vietnamese history. Overshadowed by more compelling characters such as Ho Chi Minh, Vo Nguyen Giap, and even Pham Van Dong, Le Duan remains an obscure figure. Much of his obscurity, however, was self-cultivated during the war. The quiet, yet stern, leader from humble origins in central Vietnam seemed to shun the spotlight and turned it over to comrades who were better suited for public leadership. Cutting a "bland figure," as one journalist described him on the occasion of his death, Le Duan knew he was not blessed with Ho's grandfatherly demeanor, Giap's military prowess, or Dong's gift for statesmanship.[7] However, he possessed the focus, administrative skill, and iron will that perhaps these others had lacked. Devoid of the charisma necessary to lead the most visible war for national liberation in the Third World and the most important struggle within the international proletarian movement against neoimperialist forces, Le Duan successfully cultivated the idea of collective leadership in the Vietnam Workers' Party (Dang Lao Dong Viet Nam, VWP) rather than promoting a cult of personality in Vietnam.[8]

Behind the calm facade of the VWP leadership, however, ran ideological divisions, personal rivalries, and power struggles that often intersected with the larger debates taking place in the communist world. The making of Hanoi's postcolonial grand strategy involved juggling multiple, at times conflicting, factors to maintain a critical balance in its internal and external policies—a fragile balance crucial to waging a successful revolutionary struggle within the wider Cold War. Nonetheless, this idea of comrades unified under the benevolent guidance of Ho Chi Minh has stood the test of time even though the reality was far different. Obscured by the impenetrable "bamboo curtain" that has concealed decision making in Hanoi since the war, Le Duan actually stood as the *primus inter pares* at the locus of power, the Political Bureau or Politburo (Bo Chinh Tri). Along with his right-hand man, the redoubtable Le Duc Tho, Le Duan managed to stymie domestic opponents, temper powerful foreign allies, and defeat the world's leading superpower in an epic struggle. However, little is known about who these two men were or how they waged and won a war of global and historic import. Although scholars have examined the Vietnam policies of U.S. leaders such as Dwight D. Eisenhower and John Foster Dulles, John F. Kennedy and Dean Rusk, Lyndon B. Johnson and Robert S. McNamara, Richard M. Nixon and Henry A. Kissinger—much remains elusive regarding the war leadership of Le Duan and Le Duc Tho.[9]

Using recently released materials from Vietnam, the United States, Europe, translated communist bloc documents, and firsthand interviews with former officials, this study attempts to part the bamboo curtain to present an international history of the Vietnamese communist war effort. It not only renders transparent the internal workings of America's most elusive enemy during the Cold War, it also exposes how the enemy's war effort unfolded in the global arena. Although studies on American involvement and defeat in Vietnam highlight contingency and human choices, depictions of the Vietnamese revolution and victory emphasize structural forces and inevitability. This book reveals that in fact the war and its outcome were shaped as much by individuals in Hanoi as by historical structures. It thus offers new answers to old questions: *who* was in charge of the communist war effort, *what* were their war aims and strategies, and *how* did they manage to defeat the United States and the RVN in the war for peace?

By placing Hanoi and not Washington at the center of an international history of the Vietnam War, this study also makes three important contributions to the nature and the role of Third World actors in the international postwar era.[10] First, it reveals how postcolonial leaders brought about and sustained superpower involvement in their struggles. Officials in Hanoi and Saigon not only played important roles in their nations' development, they also dictated the terms of American intervention and shaped the nature of the international Cold War system. Second, this study shows how divisions in the communist world derailed postcolonial development in the radical Third World. As polarizing as the East-West conflict, the zero-sum game of the Sino-Soviet split greatly complicated North Vietnam's socialist revolution. Third, the ability of Hanoi to frustrate Washington in the international arena demonstrates just how "small power" global politics managed to undermine superpower diplomacy at this pivotal juncture in the Cold War. A "diplomatic revolution" did indeed take place and the Vietnam War underscores its magnitude.[11]

Not just a study of Le Duan and Le Duc Tho's leadership and the war they waged, then, this book also pays ample attention to leaders in Washington and Saigon as well as Hanoi during the war for peace, when all sides conducted their diplomatic struggles on the world stage. Richard Nixon and Henry Kissinger, as well as RVN president Nguyen Van Thieu and PRG foreign minister Madame Nguyen Thi Binh, round out the cast of characters in this tragic drama. Although a dedicated international history, this study does not purport to give equal representation to all of the major parties involved in the war. Nor should it. The perspectives of the Vietnamese parties, including the DRV, the RVN, and the National Liberation Front (NLF)–PRG, constitute three-quarters of the story and the United States only one-quarter. Despite that obvious, albeit contrived, ratio we know much more about America's war than we do about the Vietnamese sides of the conflict.

A brief survey of the archival landscape explains this imbalance. To date, the collections that would reveal the most about high-level communist decision making during the war in Vietnam—the Party, Military, and Foreign Ministry archives—remain closed not only to foreign researchers but also to domestic Vietnamese scholars. Although historical preservation and record keeping has a long and venerable tradition in Vietnam, the state archives pertaining to the war period only opened their doors in the late 1990s. As for the Saigon regime, although copious amounts of material were ostensibly destroyed at the end of the war in 1975 as the few remaining Americans and hundreds of thousands of South Vietnamese fled the country, a relatively untapped archive on the former Republic of Vietnam exists in Ho Chi Minh City today. This collection—as well as the vast materials on the Saigon regime stored in America—sit more or less ignored; the vanquished never seem to attract the same level of attention as the victors. In contrast to the difficulties associated with Vietnamese sources, the materials that pertain to U.S. policy during the Vietnam War are not only open but vast. In fact, government records on U.S. decision making began appearing as the war was being waged.[12] After the conflict ended, executive orders and federal declassification policies ensured that the National Archives and Records Administration and the various presidential libraries, despite lawsuits by some estates threatening to withhold materials indefinitely, continued to churn out millions of pages of documents. Indeed, a scholar interested in writing a history of the Vietnam War would gravitate toward the American side based on availability of documents alone.

Based on unprecedented access to Vietnamese archival collections and texts, this study rectifies the imbalance in our understanding of that oft-studied war. For more than a decade, I was able to carry out extensive research in the Vietnam National Archives as well as in the various libraries and academic centers located in Hanoi and Ho Chi Minh City. In 2003, I managed to become the first scholar—Vietnamese citizen or otherwise—to gain access to the Archives of the Vietnam Ministry of Foreign Affairs (MOFA); I am still the only scholar who has received this honor. As archival doors began to open, I was able to conduct interviews, as well as participate in closed conferences and workshops, with former participants and officials both north and south of the seventeenth parallel. As a result, I have accumulated a wealth of high-level documents never before seen, including archival sources, strictly confidential and limited circulation texts, and interview transcripts. Combined with the seemingly endless yet never fully comprehensive Richard M. Nixon presidential material declassifications, especially after 2000, as well as the recently released *Foreign Relations of the United States* volumes on Vietnam, French and British archival documents, and translated Chinese, Russian, and East European sources, this book is a pathbreaking study of the Vietnamese communist war effort as well as an international history of American withdrawal from Southeast Asia and the struggle for peace in Vietnam set against the backdrop of the global Cold War.

Even with a new cache of documents from archives around the world, any history of the Vietnam War owes much to the impressive existing scholarly literature, particularly on U.S. policy toward Vietnam.[13] Despite the recent resurgence of studies that justify American intervention on moral or geopolitical grounds, the overwhelming interpretation of what one noteworthy historian of the conflict has called "America's longest war" is highly—and justifiably—critical.[14] The problematic roots of U.S. military intervention have garnered the most attention from scholars in the field.[15] From Truman to Johnson, presidents—and their advisors—led the United States deeper into war, prompting experts to describe this decision-making process as a "quagmire," "stalemate," or "flawed containment."[16] More recently, historians have begun to elaborate and even shift these old paradigms previously centered on decision making in the White House by injecting transatlantic pressure, domestic political considerations, intense bureaucratic infighting, and heterogeneous forces invested in modernization schemes as the foundation on which the shaky edifice of U.S. policy toward Vietnam was constructed.[17]

America's endgame in Vietnam, which is the focus of this book when it analyzes U.S. decision making in depth, has garnered less attention from scholars of the war.[18] Just as historians of the origins of American involvement ask whether escalation could have been avoided, scholars who grapple with the U.S. exit from Vietnam ponder whether peace could have been achieved earlier. The vast majority of Vietnam War scholars agree that Nixon and Kissinger, who held tight control over Vietnam policy, consciously set out to produce a flawed settlement. However, they disagree over the reasons why. The "decent interval" thesis argues that America only sought a fig leaf with which to leave Vietnam.[19] Convinced that the Saigon regime would eventually collapse if the Americans withdrew, Nixon and Kissinger produced an agreement aimed only to prevent the fall of Saigon on Nixon's watch. Conversely, the "permanent war" interpretation holds that Nixon, though perhaps not Kissinger, never intended to respect the terms of the settlement and sought instead to reintroduce B-52s at the earliest provocation.[20] Watergate, however, prevented Nixon from keeping his promises to Saigon. A third interpretation faults the Nixon administration for producing a stalemate in 1973 by consistently choosing the "middle option," as his predecessors had done vis-à-vis Vietnam, in pursuit of containment—neither exerting enough pressure on Hanoi to submit nor pulling out all the stops for peace.[21] All three interpretations, however, are in accord that peace was a sham and a negotiated settlement was impossible before 1973 because Nixon and Kissinger did not want an immediate end to America's war in Southeast Asia. Outside the Oval Office, scholars of America's end game in Vietnam have also begun to tackle the role that domestic politics played in policy making. These studies reveal simultaneously the constraints on, as well as the "imperial" heights of, Nixon and Kissinger's power, the lengths to which the White House went to shield decision making from the influence of the Washington bureaucracy, Congress, and public opinion, as well as the president's co-optation of disparate groups as a means to continue the war.[22]

The excellent literature on America's war effort thus provides a firm base on which to build an international history. Whether one sees U.S. actions in Vietnam from 1950 to 1975 as driven by the domino theory, misguided notions of credibility, realpolitik tendencies, imperialist modes of modernization, long-standing Open Door tenets, deep-seated anxiety and paranoia in the White House, or subterranean racist and gendered currents in U.S. policy making, there is general agreement that the American people were wrongly led to embark on a protracted and unwinnable war in Southeast Asia.

While scholars of America's war in Vietnam produce detailed monographs with alacrity, area studies experts have only slowly and episodically begun to take an interest in this violent period in Vietnam's development.[23] In direct response to the unparalleled attention that the war has garnered in contemporary American history, the field of Vietnam studies in the West opted to ignore the conflict in support of the dictum that "Vietnam is a country, not a war." However, the conscious neglect of the war has been challenged by a new generation of area studies scholars who, with the requisite linguistic capabilities and deep grounding in the country's history, politics, society, and culture, seek to reclaim that academic space from Americanists. What they have produced often challenges the portrayal of Vietnam and the Vietnamese in the dominant U.S.-centric literature, in addition to showing that Vietnam was neither just a war nor a monolithic country.

Of particular interest to me in writing this book was the area studies scholarship that has revolutionized our understanding of the Party leadership in Hanoi and the southern context of the war. Vietnam experts have begun to dissect the Communist Party by compiling studies of individual leaders to reveal that the ruling regime in Hanoi was neither static nor monolithic.[24] They expose the limits of Party power on daily life and emphasize the breadth of popular dissent that existed behind the banner of unified struggle.[25] Meanwhile, studies on South Vietnam have challenged the notion that revolutionaries south of the seventeenth parallel were devoid of agency and that the RVN lacked sovereignty. Instead, area studies experts have persuasively shown that South Vietnamese polities were active agents during the war and that they possessed civil societies that were at times both anticommunist and anti-American.[26] Just like their U.S. counterparts, however, Vietnam studies experts agree that American intervention exacerbated an already fractious and contentious scene to the detriment of the millions of Vietnamese who died in what turned out to be one of the most violent of all Cold War conflicts.

Finally, there is a growing body of scholarship that aims to bridge the two fields to present bilateral and international studies of the war. Since the late 1990s, the "internationalization" of the field has produced studies that analyze the war from both the American and Vietnamese perspectives as well as introduce important third-party players in the conflict. In the early stages of U.S.-Vietnamese interaction, there were clear indications of "missed opportunities" in Washington to avert war with Ho Chi Minh's government.[27] By the time war was under way, however, both Hanoi and Washington circumvented an early peace agreement.[28] The studies of relations between the United States and South Vietnam have revealed that Saigon was far from a puppet regime.[29] Instead, RVN leaders possessed their own modernization schemes and sought to carve out a sphere of autonomy within an Americanized war. In addition to the bilateral and bilingual scholarship, historians have begun to place the Vietnam War within an international Cold War and global twentieth-century context.[30] These scholars analyze the impact of the Vietnam War within the communist world by exploring relations between Hanoi and its allies in Beijing and Moscow, as well as Latin America and Eastern Europe.[31] At the same time, studies have placed the war within the regional Southeast Asian context.[32] These studies, as well as other international and transnational studies of the conflict, reveal that the war's far-reaching repercussions shook the foundation of the global world order.[33]

This book has profited from all of these trends in the historiography. It culls from the prodigious literature on America's war, contextualizes the newer findings in area studies, and contributes to the internationalization of the field to place the war in a global context while maintaining a focus on the major parties involved and forging a new interpretation based on new materials. I argue that Washington was not alone in prolonging the war; often, American leaders were at the mercy of actors in Hanoi and Saigon who had their own geostrategic reasons to extend the fighting and to frustrate the peace negotiations. I will show that leaders in Hanoi did not only operate on the defensive but instead possessed a grand strategy that included the construction of a police state in the North, the marginalization of indigenous revolutionaries in the South, and a policy of equilibrium in the Sino-Soviet split in order to conduct a total war for reunification that brought them to an epic battle with the United States. Finally, this book shows how Hanoi, Saigon, and Washington all possessed international strategies as they waged a war for peace in the global arena, but it was Hanoi's global campaign—more than its military battles or political struggle to win the hearts and minds of the South Vietnamese people— that proved victorious in the end.

Chapter 1 traces the rise of Le Duan and Le Duc Tho from their heady days in the Mekong Delta to the heights of Party power in the Red River Delta through their campaign to promote war in the South. The Party, far from being forced to sanction war by southern revolutionaries on the cusp of annihilation, saw its policy hijacked by Le Duan and Le Duc Tho for their own ends. As we see in chapter 2, in order to seal their authority in the North and their control over the war effort in the South, Le Duan and Le Duc Tho constructed a repressive Party hierarchy. Despite official exhortations to the contrary, the Vietnamese communist struggle was anything but a harmonious, unified effort; rather, it was the product of Le Duan's national security state.

The VWP's debates were not insular; they reflected the growing ideological tensions within the communist world. As the Sino-Soviet split threatened to further unravel Party politics in North Vietnam, Le Duan and Tho kicked their police state into full gear between 1963 to 1967 to deal with domestic opponents who condemned their war policies, southern revolutionaries who challenged northern authority over their liberation struggle, Chinese critics who pressured them to implement Mao's military strategy, and Soviet obstructionists who wanted them to end the war through negotiations. Chapters 3 and 4 reveal that strategy deliberation in Hanoi took into account not only the military picture in South Vietnam and the political situation in the United States but also DRV domestic politics and foreign relations, as Le Duan's war planning hinged on his controversial General Offensive and General Uprising strategy. In 1964, Le Duan's first bid for victory resulted in American intervention; in 1968, his second attempt facilitated the rise of more intractable enemies in Washington and Saigon.

Thus, the war for peace in the aftermath of the Tet Offensive ushered in new actors with new international strategies. Chapters 5 and 6 reveal how Le Duan and Nixon sought to find each other's breaking point in the battlegrounds of Cambodia and Laos rather than order their deputies, Tho and Kissinger, to compromise in Paris. Meanwhile, South Vietnamese leaders, RVN president Thieu and PRG leader Madame Nguyen Thi Binh, emerged as major players in the war for peace. While the former engaged in a battle of wills against both his allies in Washington and his enemies in Hanoi, the latter proved a formidable diplomat as the new embodiment of the Vietnamese revolution after the death of Ho Chi Minh in 1969.

The regionalization of the air and ground wars to all of Indochina was not the only way the Vietnam War extended beyond the geographic bounds of North and South Vietnam; chapters 7 and 8 explore how the war's diplomatic sphere went global in the 1970s. As Nixon sought to use détente with the Soviet Union and rapprochement with China to his advantage in Vietnam, Thieu promoted conservative regional relations to secure the RVN's place in the wake of American withdrawal from Southeast Asia. At the same time, Le Duan as well as Madame Binh garnered the support of the wider communist world, the revolutionary Third World, progressive segments of the West, and the global antiwar movement more generally. As Nixon's superpower diplomacy threatened Hanoi's war effort, however, Le Duan once again turned to his controversial plans for victory. Although the Easter Offensive failed to topple the Saigon regime in early 1972, Vietnamese communist diplomacy managed to blunt Nixon's triangular offensive as well as Thieu's obstructionist tactics by the end of the year. It was not enough, however, for Le Duan to win the war for peace. Instead, the endgame to American intervention witnessed the fashioning of an untenable agreement and cease-fire in early 1973.

Thus, stalemate prevailed in Vietnam until Vietnamese forces once again engaged in battle, as the United States became consumed with its own domestic struggle in the aftermath of Watergate. By the time peace returned to Vietnam in 1975, Hanoi—and indeed all of Vietnam—was a very different place than it had been three decades earlier in the wake of nominal independence or even two decades earlier following decolonization. This is a story, then, where there are no clear winners, only leaders who were willing to go to war over their contested visions for the future of Vietnam.

## NOTE ON SOURCES: A GUIDE FOR THE READER AND THE RESEARCHER

Given the challenges of archival research in Vietnam, a short description of the Vietnamese archives as well as Vietnamese-language publications on which this study is based is necessary. Since the "troika"—the Party, Military, and Foreign Ministry archives—is currently off limits to all researchers, one must access other sources to piece together the narrative. The Vietnam National Archives, overseen by the Ministry of the Interior, contain a wealth of materials on the war period. Currently, they include four centers located in Hanoi, Ho Chi Minh City, and Da Lat. Center 1 in Hanoi and center 4 in Da Lat contain French colonial period collections; center 3 in Hanoi holds the materials from the DRV (1945–76) and the SRV (post-1976), while center 2 in Ho Chi Minh City stores the files of the former RVN.

Center 3 is indispensable for any history of the DRV at war since it contains the important collections of the state bureaucracies. Even though it is less forthcoming for a high-level military, political, and diplomatic history, a resourceful scholar who understands Vietnamese and is grounded in the political configuration of the communist government can garner an indirect view of the troika's holdings from within the collections of the national archives. For example, the files of the National Reunification Committee and the Office of the Prime Minister provide a glimpse into the Foreign Ministry and the top Party leadership. In contrast, center 2, which houses the former RVN collections, contains top-level documents of the First and Second Republics. Scholars interested in Saigon's foreign policy can access the president's notes, Foreign Ministry cables, memoranda of conversations with foreign leaders, Defense Department reports, to name a few. An astounding amount of materials managed to escape obliteration in 1975. In short, the collections on the DRV as well as the RVN are abundant. Scholars who have carried out research in these two archives have revealed that it is no longer possible to write about Vietnamese perspectives on the war without consulting these materials or at least relying on the scholarship that has.

In addition to the national archives, the libraries affiliated with the Foreign Ministry and the Ministry of Defense are open to scholars and contain primary documents. In addition to these libraries, the troika have circulated texts that draw from their closed archives. Although most of these texts have been sanitized and published, others remain "for internal circulation only [*luu hanh noi bo*]" but nevertheless have managed to make their way into researchers' hands. This book is the first to incorporate these published, semicirculated, and closed texts of the Party, Military, and Foreign Ministry, which have proven essential to understanding Hanoi's war effort in lieu of full access to the archives. What are these texts and what do they contain?

*Van Kien Dang Toan Tap* (The Complete Collection of Party Documents), compiled by the Vietnamese Communist Party, is similar to the *Foreign Relations of the United States* in its inclusion of official documents from the governing apparatus.[34] These include such documents as Party resolutions, Secretariat directives, Central Executive Committee reports, and instructions from the Politburo to southern commanders, and communication between the Party center in Hanoi and the provinces. Published in hardback editions in red and gold, this open collection spans the period from the formation of the Communist Party in the 1920s to the present day, with each volume covering an individual year.[35] In fact, the volumes that address the period of the "Anti-American Resistance Struggle for Reunification and National Salvation" from 1959 to 1975 have been in print since the early 2000s. Although heavily sanitized and edited, these volumes stand as the only contemporaneous official documentation of the Party leadership during the war. A scholar equipped with the historical grounding and an ability to read the current political tea leaves can approach these volumes by utilizing the same tools that Kremlinologists employed to "read between the lines" (but with far greater accuracy).

*Dai su ky chuyen de: Dau Tranh Ngoai Giao va van dong quoc te trong nhung chien chong My cuu nuoc* (Special Chronology: The Diplomatic Struggle and International Activities of the Anti-American Resistance and National Salvation, *DTNG*) was undeniably the most valuable source for the second half of this study on the war for peace.[36] Daily chronologies are useful sources in Vietnam since many of these volumes and tomes introduce materials from the three closed archives.[37] Although *DTNG* is still classified and only two of the five volumes include entries that are more than perfunctory or culled from media outlets, the collection's significance can be compared to that of the *Pentagon Papers* for the diplomatic sphere of Hanoi's war. Volume 4 and part of volume 5 cover the years between 1968 and 1973, quoting directly from classified telegrams between the Politburo and the DRV delegation in Paris. In other words, it includes the correspondence between Le Duan and Le Duc Tho on the diplomatic struggle. Their telegrams discuss the Party's international strategy, North Vietnamese assessments of each secret meeting with Kissinger in Paris, evaluations of Nixon's triangular offensives, Hanoi's orders to southern diplomats, and frank reports on meetings with Chinese and Soviet leaders. In short, this source represents the "holy grail" for diplomatic historians interested in the war for peace.

These open, semicirculated, and classified primary sources along with archival collections still need to be buttressed by official histories, public speeches, memoirs, biographies, reminiscences, and other publications. Official histories of the war often reflect today's political battles in Vietnam; nonetheless, they include important historical insights that are not available in Western studies. The Institute of Military History has recently completed its eight-volume study of the war, including the official statistics of the People's Army of Viet Nam (PAVN).[38] In addition to national, regional, and provincial studies, publishers in the SRV have made available the public speeches and writings of top Party leaders.[39] Combined with the biographies and volumes of reminiscences and tributes to fallen leaders, these sources are helpful in piecing together the evolution of the lives, policies, and careers of Hanoi's ruling class. In short, they provide both a way to evaluate the contemporaneous primary sources and a three-dimensional rendering of the historical actors involved in high-level decision making in Hanoi.

One memoir deserves special note. The unpublished autobiography of Le Duan's second wife, Nguyen Thuy Nga, allowed me to present a fuller depiction of the elusive first secretary.[40] Nga's memoir provides both personal and professional details of Le Duan's life, including excerpts from their love letters and commentary on her husband's career. In addition, Nga's life and revolutionary activities are notable in their own right. As a southern communist who moved to Hanoi during the pivotal interwar years, spent a period in China during the advent of the Sino-Soviet split, and returned to the Mekong Delta on the eve of the conflict's Americanization, she provides great insight into her husband's handling of the war effort, and her movements reflect critical turning points in his war.[41]

Although *Hanoi's War* draws heavily from these Vietnamese sources, it does not incorporate diacritics in the post-1976 official SRV spelling due to publishing constraints. Regarding Vietnamese names, I have shortened most of them by using given names when appropriate (except for Ho Chi Minh, whom I refer to as "Ho" since that is more common, and Le Duan, whose name rarely gets shortened) to avoid confusion. I have also used the official Vietnamese spelling for geographical terms except in four instances where I adopt the Westernized spelling to avoid confusion: Hanoi, Saigon, Mekong, and Vietnam (unless it is part of a direct quote).

## NOTA BENE

The youngest of nine children, I was born in Saigon in November 1974 and had kin who served on both sides of the war.[42] My family's journey to the United States in the final days of April 1975, when I was five months old, meant that I do not have any direct memories of that war or what came after in Vietnam. Instead, I grew up in a working-class neighborhood in post–Vietnam War America during a time when that episode in the nation's past was being collectively suppressed. My family and I were shameful reminders of a war that should have never been fought. The war was both distant and proximate; I did not live it but who I am is a direct result of it. Rather than focus on the everyday lives of people who lived through the war and whose experiences should not be invalidated no matter what side of the Pacific, the seventeenth parallel, or the ideological divide they found themselves on, I have sought answers at the loci of power. This is not because I believe that leaders matter more than the people they ostensibly led or that the decisions they made behind closed doors are necessarily more important or definitive than the individual choices and actions of those on the ground. But to understand who is responsible for how and why whole nations go to war, a "top-down" approach is necessary. Thus, I have set out to understand how certain leaders made specific decisions in the corridors of power in Hanoi, Saigon, and Washington that led to the deaths of approximately 58,000 Americans and an estimated 2–6 million Vietnamese.

# part one

# THE PATH TO REVOLUTIONARY WAR

*Revolution is offensive. —Le Duan*[1]

## chapter one

# LE DUAN'S RISE TO POWER AND THE ROAD TO WAR

Under the cover of darkness on 22 January 1955, Le Duan, Party secretary of the Southern Territorial Committee, bid a hasty farewell to his second-in-command, Le Duc Tho, at the mouth of the Ong Doc River off the tip of Ca Mau province in the deep south of Vietnam. While Le Duan secretly descended the river on a rickety canoe back to the heart of the Mekong Delta, Le Duc Tho stayed onboard the larger ship headed for North Vietnam.[2] Earlier that day, the two Party leaders had boarded the Hanoi-bound Polish vessel *Kilinski* amid great fanfare in front of international observers tasked with overseeing the 300-day period of free movement stipulated in the 1954 Geneva Accords.[3] With the imminent closing of the border at the seventeenth parallel, Le Duan, otherwise known as "Comrade Three," clandestinely remained in the South, leaving Le Duc Tho, or "Six Hammer," to journey alone to Hanoi.

During the war against the French, the Party sent both men to operate in the Mekong Delta even though neither of them hailed from the region. Le Duan, a man with perennially sad eyes and protruding ears, was from Quang Tri province in the central region, while Le Duc Tho, with his high cheekbones and hair that would turn nearly all white decades later, came from Nam Dinh province in northern Vietnam. Their commitment to southern Vietnam, however, later earned them a reputation for being the "first to set foot in the South and the last to leave" during the struggle for decolonization.[4]

Their connection to the South would have a lasting impact on their leadership beyond the French-Indochina War. As the prospect of speedy reunification dimmed in 1956, "Ba" Duan and "Sau" Tho would find themselves occupying pivotal roles in Party history. As Hanoi's man in the South, Le Duan was in charge of the increasingly difficult task of exerting Party direction over the revolution as local insurgents, under attack by Saigon forces, took matters into their own hands and demanded support from the North to move the resistance to armed struggle. Rather than temper insurgent ambitions in the South, however, Le Duan fanned the revolutionary flames in the region in an attempt to force his reluctant comrades in the North to go to war. If the Party did not support the local insurgency, he warned, then the southern resistance either would be wiped out or, just as troublesome, would slip out of Hanoi's control.

His appeal, however, fell on deaf ears as the top-level leadership in Hanoi remained preoccupied with the travails of state building in the DRV in the mid-1950s; however, the opportunity for a policy shift emerged by the end of the decade. The fallout from the Party's costly campaigns during peacetime greatly compromised the communist leadership's standing as the North Vietnamese people stood up in defiance of the campaigns' excesses. Placed in a key position to oversee the fallout, Le Duan's deputy now in the North, Le Duc Tho, became the Party's most powerful apparatchik. As rivals in the Politburo fell into disgrace, Tho's authority allowed him to clean house in Hanoi, a crucial portfolio to possess on a fractious political scene. With the Party looking to rehabilitate its image by promoting a new leader and a cause that could rally the North Vietnamese people, Le Duan emerged as the obvious choice.

Thus, Le Duan and Le Duc Tho were the driving force behind Party policy during Vietnam's pivotal half century that witnessed revolution, war, and reunification set against the backdrop of the Cold War. Before the United States made Indochina a hot spot in the East-West confrontation, there were driven leaders heading warring factions with local agendas in Vietnam that shaped events in the region and eventually the world.

This chapter examines the early careers of Le Duan and Le Duc Tho from colonial Indochina to postcolonial Vietnam, the lessons they learned along the way, the Party they built in Hanoi, and their policies that led to war not only with the Saigon regime but also ultimately with the United States. Offering a complex picture of the communist leadership in North Vietnam, one that perhaps leads to more questions than it answers, this chapter sheds new light on the inner workings of the one enemy America could not defeat.

## THE REVOLUTIONARY EDUCATION
## OF LE DUAN AND LE DUC THO

Like those of many Vietnamese revolutionaries, Le Duan and Le Duc Tho's careers were forged in the actual and metaphorical prisons of colonial Indochina under French rule. Born in 1907 in Hau Kien village of Quang Tri province in the French protectorate of Annam, Le Van Nhuan was the second youngest of five children in a poor family. In 1928, Nhuan married Le Thi Suong from his home village, departed for Hanoi to assume work at the Indochinese Railway Office, and shortly thereafter changed his name to Le Duan. Like many young Indochinese of the era, Le Duan was caught up in the anticolonial fervor. He immediately participated in political agitation in the center of the French protectorate of Tonkin by joining the Tan Viet (New Vietnam) Revolutionary Party and later the Hoi Viet Nam Cach Mang Thanh Nien (Vietnam Revolutionary Youth Association), overseeing the mobilization of railway workers. With the establishment in 1929 of the Vietnamese Communist Party (VCP), which would become the Indochinese Communist Party (ICP) after its first plenum later in 1931, Le Duan's anti-French resistance deepened as the Party leaders designated him a member of the Committee for Education and Training.

Le Duan's second-in-command possessed a similar revolutionary résumé. Born on 10 October 1911 in what was known then as Dich Le village, My Loc hamlet of Nam Dinh province situated in Tonkin, Le Duc Tho entered the world as Phan Dinh Khai. He began his revolutionary career at the age of fifteen by taking part in school boycotts and other anticolonial activities organized by the famous patriot Phan Chu Trinh. In 1928, he moved closer to the communist faction of the resistance when he joined the Revolutionary Youth League in Nam Dinh province, and like Le Duan, he rose quickly through the ranks of the Party the following year.

For these two young men—and multitudes of other young nationalists—the excitement of anticolonial agitation of the 1920s gave way to the harsh realities of French colonial prisons in the 1930s. With the onset of the global depression and the upsurge in nationalist activity in Indochina,

French colonial forces grew more repressive, exemplified by their severe crackdowns against the Yen Bai uprising and the Nghe Tinh revolt.[5] During what historian Peter Zinoman describes as a period of mass incarceration with a deluge of "communists, nationalists, secret-society members, and radicalized workers and peasants" into the French prison system, Le Duc Tho was arrested in Nam Dinh in late 1930 and sentenced to ten years' imprisonment; a few months later in April 1931, Le Duan's revolutionary career took a decisive turn when French secret agents arrested him in the port city of Hai Phong.[6] Both men became not only prisoners of the French colonial regime but also, and more important, ardent communist revolutionaries by the end of their prison stints at Hoa Lo, Son La, and Con Dao.[7]

The advent of the Popular Front government in Paris in 1936 brought a relaxation in French colonial policies and amnesty for more than 1,500 prisoners, including Le Duan and Le Duc Tho, who were set free from the colonial gulags. Rather than give up revolutionary agitation after their grueling incarceration, they left the prisons even more ideologically and politically committed to the communist path to independence. Le Duan returned to the central region where he made contact with the Party organization and quickly rose to the top as secretary of the Party committee in Annam in March 1938 and a member of the Central Executive Committee (CEC) standing committee the following year. Likewise, Tho returned to his northern home province of Nam Dinh and reconnected with the local Party cell.

During the Second World War, the revolutionaries in Tonkin, Annam, and Cochinchina found themselves subject to two colonial masters: Vichy France and imperial Japan.[8] In late 1939, soon after rising to the top of Party ranks in the middle region, Le Duan transferred his area of operations to Cochinchina, where he took up residence in the heart of French power in Indochina, Saigon. A few months later, in early 1940, Le Duan's work for the revolution came to a stop once again when he was captured and imprisoned on Con Dao island. Meanwhile, Tho was also summarily arrested after his return to Nam Dinh and spent the war imprisoned in various jails in the North. During their incarceration, the ICP formed the Viet Nam Doc Lap Dong Minh Hoi (Vietnam Independence League), otherwise known as the Viet Minh, to fight both the French collaborators and the Japanese fascists.

It was not until nearly the end of the Second World War that Le Duan and Le Duc Tho were finally sprung from jail by their colleagues. Although they had missed out on most of the action during the war, their early involvement in the revolution and long prison records earned them high-ranking positions in the Party on their release.[9] Freed in time to take part in the Viet Minh–led August Revolution of 1945 that brought government institutions into Vietnamese hands after the Japanese surrender but before the arrival of Allied forces, Le Duan and Le Duc Tho—along with the communist leadership—witnessed what they perceived as the Party's organizational success in harnessing the seemingly limitless power of the masses to effect change.[10] Although the revolutionaries were prepared for violence, there was relatively little bloodshed in the Viet Minh seizure of power. While Ho Chi Minh, using the Nguyen Ai Quoc pseudonym for the final time, called on his countrymen to "stand up and rely on our strength to free ourselves," differing factions within the Party located in the three regions easily ensured that the August Revolution remained under communist guidance.

Although the desire for self-determination and liberation was strong in all of Vietnam, Party control over the revolutionary political scene varied; it dominated in Tonkin, operated adequately in Annam, but lacked strength in Cochinchina.[11] With Ho Chi Minh's historic proclamation of the founding of the Democratic Republic of Vietnam on 2 September 1945 in front of thousands gathered at Ba Dinh Square in Hanoi, the Party was in firm control of the new provisional government. While Ho assumed the presidency of the DRV, Truong Chinh held the reins of power in the ICP as the first secretary, a position he had occupied since 1941. Born Dang Xuan Khu in early 1907 in Nam Dinh province, Khu later changed his name to Truong Chinh, meaning "long march," in honor of Mao Zedong's ascent to power. A committed anticolonialist who participated in school boycotts in Nam Dinh city that called for the release of Phan Boi Chu in 1925 and that mourned the loss of Phan Chu Trinh in 1926, Khu eventually moved to Hanoi, where he helped establish the Communist Party in 1929. A year later, he was imprisoned by French authorities and sentenced to twelve years in Hoa Lo and Son La prisons. Freed halfway through his sentence in 1936, Khu—now a staunch revolutionary—was surveilled by the French colonial regime when he returned to Hanoi, where he worked openly as a newspaper editor and secretly as a leading member of the Tonkin Party Committee.

When the Second World War began, Khu rose to the top Party position of first secretary and officially became Truong Chinh. At the Eighth Plenum, held in a small hut in May 1941, Party leaders voted to shift their resources from land reform to national liberation. The historic plenum also witnessed the first meeting between Nguyen Ai Quoc, who would rise to greater fame as Ho Chi Minh, and Truong Chinh.[12] Hailing from two different factions within the Party that operated in different regions in the north during the Second World War—Ho along with Vo Nguyen Giap and Pham Van Dong were part of the Pac Bo contingent near the Chinese border, whereas Chinh led the Red River Delta group that boasted that they were never more than a bike ride away from Hanoi—the revolutionary leaders banded together to seize power in 1945.[13] The latter would prove more powerful.

After his release from prison, Le Duc Tho returned to Hanoi, where he followed in Le Duan's 1938 footsteps by being elected standing committee member of the CEC and being appointed head of the Party Organizational Committee. In this capacity, Tho's primary responsibility was to ensure the smooth operation of the Party bureaucracy, a position that would become increasingly important in this next phase of the communist revolution.

At the time, however, the Party's plans for state building would have to be put on hold as leaders in Hanoi dealt with two seemingly insurmountable obstacles to independence: occupying Chinese nationalist forces stationed in the northern half of the country and the return of French colonial forces, via the British, in the lower half. Although Franklin D. Roosevelt's insistence on international trusteeship under the United Nations in Indochina had waned in the days before his death, Harry S. Truman was less ambivalent in his recognition of French sovereignty over the region. At the Potsdam Conference in July 1945, the United States agreed that the Guomindang would oversee the surrender of Japanese troops in northern Vietnam and allowed the British Southeast Asia Command, sympathetic to the French, to oversee the southern half.[14] Although the ICP was in firm control of the political scene in Tonkin, the Guomindang forces pressured Ho Chi Minh to include their Vietnamese allies, non–Viet Minh officials from the Vietnamese Nationalist Party (Viet Nam Quoc Dan Dang) and the Revolutionary League, into the new government. Holding out the northern region to the French, Chiang Kai-shek also negotiated economic concessions from France at the expense of the Vietnamese. Events in the southern half of the country posed even greater challenges for the Party. Through British General Douglas Gracey, whose troops oversaw the surrender of Japanese forces in the south, France was able to regain a foothold in Cochinchina, where it intended to reconquer its colony and protectorates. In an effort to thwart France's attempts to restore its colonial empire, Ho needed to build a broad coalition of forces within the country and win support from countries abroad, particularly the United States.

In this situation fraught with difficulties and no clear solutions, Ho Chi Minh made two decisions that would compromise his position within the Party leadership. In November 1945, he dissolved the ICP into a Marxist-Leninist working group and replaced known communist members with leaders from other political parties in order to attract broad support for a united front and to garner foreign aid, particularly from the United States. At the same time, Ho undertook negotiations with French officials in Tonkin, including Jean Sainteny, who were cognizant of France's limited military capabilities and opted to negotiate the France's return peacefully. By signing the Preliminary Accord on 6 March 1946, Ho received French recognition of the DRV, which would form a part of the Indochina Federation under the French Union, in exchange for permitting 15,000 French soldiers to return to Indochina and for allowing the fate of Cochinchina to be determined by a popular referendum at a later date. Meanwhile, despite aid to the DRV cause from individual U.S. Office of Strategic Services (OSS) officials, Washington remained deaf to Ho's pleas for support. Nonetheless, despite his having no other viable alternatives in 1945–46, Ho's decisions to dissolve the Party and shelve the issue of Cochinchina were deeply unpopular among certain factions within the communist leadership.[15]

Although the Ho-Sainteny agreement was meant to be a starting point for further negotiations, French colonial authorities in Cochinchina sabotaged diplomacy at Da Lat and Fontainebleau. Following the French massacre at Hai Phong harbor in late November 1946, militant factions within the DRV disillusioned with diplomacy and impatient to strike back launched a nationwide counterattack on French forces on 19 December.[16] A short time after celebrating the end of World War II, the Vietnamese were plunged into yet another war, this one for decolonization.

## THE WILD SOUTH

When the French-Indochina War began, Le Duan sought to make a name for himself in the Party after languishing in prison during the Second World War. In late October 1945, he was elected temporary head of the Southern Territorial Committee at a conference held in My Tho province in the Mekong Delta, possibly after failing to land a higher-level position within the military leadership in Hanoi.[17] Le Duan's task of directing Party operations in southern Vietnam was an unenviable one, filled with tremendous dangers and professional pitfalls. Far from Party headquarters in Hanoi and close to the center of French colonial power in Saigon, Cochinchina was a region rich in revolutionary tradition that boasted manifestations of strong communist insurrections such as the 1940 Nam Ky Khoi Nghia (Southern Uprising). The region also possessed an array of local actors who vied with the communists for control over its tough terrain that included dense forests, boggy swamps, vertiginous waterways, and cavernous mountains to the west.[18] Religious sects including the Hoa Hao and the Cao Dai possessed powerful armies and committed followers who were much more comfortable in the southern countryside than were the city-based communists.[19] The Party's response was to send "Nam Tien" (Southward March) units from Hanoi to even out the numbers.[20]

Moreover, the communists in the Mekong Delta were not a monolithic force.[21] Although the Party needed to appeal to a broad array of forces to present a unified front against returning French colonial forces, the communist leadership, first under Tran Van Giau and then Nguyen Binh in 1946, often operated beyond the purview of Hanoi and worked against Party policy.[22] By unleashing revolutionary violence in the increasingly volatile scene in the Mekong Delta, these "rogue" leaders not only threatened Party control in Cochinchina but also incurred the wrath of rival groups in the Delta and exacted high casualty rates in confrontations with and battles against the French.[23]

In order to fortify Hanoi's control over the chaotic region, the Viet Minh leadership sent Le Duc Tho south in 1948. As a professional revolutionary who had begun to streamline operations in the DRV, Tho would do the same in the Mekong Delta. When Tho met Le Duan for the first time in 1948, he realized that he had met someone he could not push around.[24] Le Duc Tho thus became Le Duan's loyal deputy as vice secretary, and together the two men set out in the late 1940s to neutralize their communist and noncommunist opponents while waging war against returning French colonial forces.[25] Their endeavors in these heady days of the war for decolonization forged a partnership that would come to dominate the communist leadership for nearly the next half century.

An event deep in the U Minh Forest in 1948 sealed their friendship. Amid war, a maquis marriage took place between a young southern resistance fighter of the Women's National Liberation Forces based in Bac Lieu–Can Tho, Nguyen Thuy Nga, and the head of the Southern Territorial Committee, the formidable Le Duan. Earlier in the year, Le Duan met

Nga for the first time when her battalion attended a regional committee conference at his headquarters in Dong Thap Muoi. One morning, Nga's task, which was common given the gender inequity even in the revolutionary maquis, was to make sure that Le Duan enjoyed his sumptuous meal of chicken rice congee with two hard-boiled eggs. Captivated by Nga, Le Duan ordered the wait staff to prepare another seat at his table, and he even offered her one of his eggs. After their brief encounter at breakfast, Le Duan confided to his second-in-command that he was interested in Nga. He was already married, but Le Duan could not see his family since they were living in enemy territory. Losing little time, Le Duc Tho used a visit to Can Tho, where Nga's battalion was based, to arrange a marriage. "If you agree to marry him," Tho told Nga, "you are agreeing to a very important task since it would be your job to take care of him and to make sure that he has the health to carry through the revolution." Thanks to Le Duc Tho's *lam mai* (romantic setup), Le Duan and Nguyen Thuy Nga were married at a ceremony near the Southern Territorial headquarters presided over by Le Duan's and Le Duc Tho's close friend, colleague, and coconspirator, Pham Hung.[26]

Far from Le Duan's revolutionary marriage at Dong Thap Muoi, the key battles against the French eventually emerged at the opposite end of the country in the mountainous terrain in northern Tonkin with the onset of American and Chinese involvement in the French-Indochina War. The early years of the war had produced a stalemate of sorts, with colonial troops occupying the cities and towns by driving Viet Minh forces to the villages in the countryside and to mountain hideouts. With the hardening of positions in Washington and Moscow by 1947 and the founding of the People's Republic of China in 1949, the Cold War had arrived in full force in Asia and set the way for the internationalization of the French-Indochina War by 1950.[27] While Mao Zedong's China provided the foreign assistance that Ho Chi Minh and the DRV needed, the Truman administration came to the aid of France's Fourth Republic and its increasingly unpopular "dirty war."[28]

The PRC's diplomatic recognition of the DRV, which led the Soviet Union and its satellite countries to follow suit, allowed Ho Chi Minh to travel to Beijing and Moscow in pursuit of aid. Although Ho was less successful in the Soviet Union in procuring direct assistance, he reached an important agreement with Mao whereby Chinese advisors would train Viet Minh soldiers and help organize a campaign to clear French soldiers from the Sino-Vietnamese border. In January 1951, ties with China were further strengthened by the visit of the DRV's rising military star, Vo Nguyen Giap, to southern China. Most important, the establishment of the Chinese Military Assistance Group (CMAG) in the DRV (which carried out a task identical to that of the American Military Advisory Assistance Group [MAAG] in Saigon) ensured that the Viet Minh would continue to implement Mao's revolutionary strategy of warfare. Although the Vietnamese had adopted Mao's military doctrine prior to the victory of the Chinese communists in 1949, the direct involvement of Beijing in the French-Indochina War indicated that the Sino-Vietnamese alliance would be further strengthened—and ultimately tested—as Mao's three-stage strategy of warfare unfolded precariously on the Indochinese terrain.

With foreign support, Ho was also able to publicly reinstate the Communist Party following the Chinese model as the Vietnam Workers' Party, with himself as chairman, at the Second Party Congress in early 1951. Truong Chinh, however, retained the actual leadership of the Party when he was elected first secretary once again in 1951. Preoccupied with events in the Mekong Delta and unable to travel during wartime, the Congress also witnessed the elevation in absentia of Le Duan to the highest level of power within the Party: the VWP Politburo. Le Duan now joined the ranks of revolutionaries such as Ho, Giap, and Pham Van Dong, as well as Truong Chinh, who were already well known within the country.[29] Moreover, operations in the south were given a higher priority with the reclassification of the Territorial Committee of the South as the Central Office of South Vietnam (COSVN). As head of COSVN, Le Duan was now politically and militarily in charge of operations, placing him in direct confrontation with the popular and independent-minded commander of the armed forces, Nguyen Binh.

By 1951, Binh, a colorful "swashbuckling" character who commanded loyal troops in Saigon, had waged a costly war by undertaking a campaign of assassination against rival groups as well as shifting to a more proactive stage against the French by launching large-scale attacks against colonial forces in the south and in southwestern parts of Cochinchina.[30] Binh's costly offensives did not achieve the desired military results and thus came under fire from Party members who had long envied his popularity. In a series of publications, Le Duc Tho spoke out against Binh's reckless behavior, alluding to a "spirit of formalism" and cadres who were too aggressive.[31] Shortly after the Party inducted Le Duan into the Politburo, it recalled Binh to Hanoi. Binh, however, never made it back to his home region. Although Binh's fall from power and the conditions surrounding his death in late 1951 have been a matter of speculation, it is clear that Le Duan and Le Duc Tho, as well as their third-in-command, Pham Hung, greatly benefited at the time from his departure from the southern scene.[32]

Their first brush with political rivals, then, taught Le Duan and Le Duc Tho important lessons that they later applied in Hanoi when they encountered leaders less easily removed than Nguyen Binh. Ironically, they would adopt, to little avail, the same hard-driving military tactics against the Americans that Binh had against the French. Unlike Binh, however, Le Duan, Tho, and Hung were much better at protecting their flank from rival Party leaders who could exploit any missteps.

While Le Duan and his comrades dealt with southern rivals, war escalated in the north. Despite Chinese assistance and recognition and the Party's internal consolidation of power, the Viet Minh's military struggle in Tonkin continued to encounter difficulties on the ground. Subscribing to Mao's revolutionary war strategy, Viet Minh forces shifted from defensive war (*phong ngu*), which relied primarily on guerrilla tactics, to the equilibrium stage (*cam cu*), which incorporated large-scale attacks, at the beginning of the decade. The final stage, which would lead to certain victory, included the general counteroffensive (*tong phan cong*). Although the Viet Minh's 1950 victory over the French at Cao Bang provided forces with a much-needed morale boost, it also led Vietnamese military leaders to undertake foolhardy offensives in 1951–52, just as Nguyen Binh did in the south. These "human wave" offensives aimed at breaking through the French cordon sanitaire in Tonkin; however, they proved disastrous and were easily blocked by French forces at Vinh Yen and Mao Khe in January and March–April 1951.

The defeat at these two battles prompted a reassessment among the Viet Minh military brass. In early June 1951, Ho's close ally, Vo Nguyen Giap, who was both the commander-in-chief of the armed forces and the minister of defense, criticized Viet Minh training and military performance and called for a more effective mobilization campaign and greater propaganda efforts. By the late summer of that year, Giap urged greater attention to guerrilla war: a concerted step back to the defensive stage. In his postwar memoirs, Giap takes full blame for the premature shift to the equilibrium stage and claims that he had even disregarded warnings from his Chinese advisors, who had counseled against these offensives. At the time, however, he appeared to have blamed another military leader in northern Vietnam for the mistakes.[33]

The target of Giap's criticism was a rival high-ranking military officer by the name of Nguyen Chi Thanh. In 1951, Thanh served as the commissar of the army's General Political Department (GPD), which supervised the ideological aspects of the military. He thus may have directed the frontal assault campaigns that had failed so miserably in the north as the vice secretary of the Party's Central Military Commission (CMC).[34] Thanh, whose real name was Nguyen Vinh, was born in January 1914 in central Thua-Thien-Hue province. The two military men, Giap and Thanh, could not have been more different. While Giap was a cosmopolitan intellectual fluent in French who had taught in Hanoi at Tonkin's most prestigious school before becoming a full-time revolutionary, Vinh spent most of his childhood and teenage years as a peasant farmer who only completed primary school before joining the anticolonial movement in the imperial capital of Hue. When Vinh was arrested for his "illegal" anti-French activities in the 1930s, the judge at his hearing asked him why he chose to be a communist. Vinh, with his stern demeanor and square features, responded, "I fight for the people, for democracy, for our livelihood, so what is the sin? I haven't yet understood communism so how can I be a communist? But communists are patriots and fight for the masses so what is wrong with that?"[35] In July 1937, Vinh was inducted into the Indochinese Communist Party, and by September 1938 he was appointed secretary of the Central Regional Committee. Attending the historic Tan Trao meeting, which laid the groundwork for the August Revolution, Vinh met Ho, Giap, and Dong for the first time and adopted the name Nguyen Chi Thanh. By the Second National Congress in 1951, Thanh, like Le Duan, was elevated to the Politburo.[36]

As the army's political czar, Thanh was an obvious rival to Giap. Not only did Thanh's department answer to the Party and not to Giap's Ministry of Defense, but Thanh also promoted Party primacy and ideological adherence to Marxism-Leninism within the armed forces in contrast to Giap's preferred professionalism and modernization of the PAVN. The stage was set for a showdown between Giap and Thanh following the costly offensives in 1951 and 1952. While Giap called for temporary restraint in order to rebuild the forces, Thanh urged greater aggression in order to maintain momentum. More than a decade later, these two generals would argue precisely along these same terms during the war against the Americans. Although Giap emerged victorious in the military debates in the early 1950s during the struggle against the French, Thanh's more aggressive stance would prevail in the 1960s, thanks predominately to the support of Le Duan and Le Duc Tho.[37]

During the height of the Giap-Thanh debates on Viet Minh strategy, the Party recalled Le Duan to the DRV to attend the CEC plenum in 1952. After the plenum, Le Duan traveled to China for undisclosed medical reasons. While there, he saw firsthand the destructive nature of China's early preparation for what would become the Great Leap Forward, including agricultural collectivization. When he returned to the DRV in 1953, he was aghast to see some of these Chinese measures adopted in the northern Vietnamese countryside.[38] During his stint in northern Vietnam, he also met his long-time nemesis, General Giap, for the first time.[39] Since 1945, Le Duan may have been jealous of the general, who was four years younger but occupied a higher position and enjoyed closer relations with Ho Chi Minh. Subsequent events did little to lessen Le Duan's envy.

Despite the disastrous campaigns in 1951–52, Giap would gain international fame—and an enduring historical legacy—as the grand strategist behind the battle of Dien Bien Phu. While Giap and his committee prepared for the siege against General Henri Navarre's forces in northwestern Vietnam, Le Duan must have felt exiled when the Party sent him to train cadres in Viet Minh's Interzone 5 in the central province of Quang Ngai, far from the heroic siege that would help end the French-Indochina War. Fortunately for Giap, U.S. president Dwight D. Eisenhower failed to procure British support and congressional approval for intervention on behalf of the beleaguered French, sealing the fate of the French colonial empire in Indochina.

With the signing of the Geneva Accords and the return to peace, the Party sent Le Duan back to the Mekong Delta to explain the terms of the agreement, convey the orders of the CEC for postwar planning, and oversee the period of free movement in the run-up to the national elections for reunification set for 1956.[40] During Le Duan's absence, Tho took over as head of COSVN, where he used his position to tear down any remaining vestiges of Nguyen Binh's legacy in the region.[41] On the day of Le Duan's return, two rows of cadres lined the road and enthusiastically greeted their leader's arrival by holding up two fingers, the symbol for reunification of the country. Over the next few days in October 1954, however, during a regionwide conference of southern revolutionary leaders held in Bac Lieu province, Le Duan had to dispel the euphoria when he explained the terms of the Geneva Accords. Although the period from 1954 to 1960 witnessed the "golden era of peace," especially compared to what would come after, it was also marked by great violence for revolutionaries under the Diem regime.[42]

According to Vo Van Kiet, a Le Duan protégé who would become prime minister of Vietnam, he and his southern comrades were extremely troubled by Le Duan's rendering of the postwar situation and posed some difficult questions to the top Party leader at the conference: "Why, if Dien Bien Phu was such a massive victory, didn't the Party continue the struggle for a few more months in order to gain better terms at the negotiating table? Did the Soviet Union and China pressure us to sign the agreement? Why did we agree on a temporary division at the seventeenth parallel instead of cease-fire in place? And finally, why were national reunification elections scheduled for two years from now and would there even be any guarantee that the enemy will abide by these terms?"[43] Revisiting this troubled period, Kiet said he believes that "Uncle Ho and the CEC sent Le Duan to get southerners on board with Party policy, particularly concerning resettlement to the North." Kiet, who became one of Le Duan's trusted men in the South, recognized the difficulty of his chief's duty, later commenting that "this was going to be no easy task."[44] Keeping his opinions to himself, Le Duan only stated the obvious in his response to his comrades' questions. "There are two possible outcomes," Le Duan said. "Perhaps the 'U.S.-Diem' [My-Diem] clique will be obligated to carry out the Geneva Accords; just as likely, they may not. The southern revolution has to have a plan for either eventuality."[45]

Nga, Le Duan's southern wife, recalled waking one night in 1954 after their joyous reunion to see her husband pacing to and fro in consternation. After the war, the Party wanted Le Duan to return north, but he was convinced that he should remain behind and sent three telegrams requesting that he be allowed to stay below the seventeenth parallel. The Party held firm the first two times but relented with his third plea. Nga, who by 1954 had borne him a daughter, Vu Anh, and was carrying a second child, wanted to stay in the Mekong Delta alongside her husband. Le Duan, however, remained adamant that she and their children remain out of harm's way by relocating to Hanoi. Showing more resilience than his colleagues in Hanoi, Le Duan quieted Nga's pleas. "The upcoming situation in the South will be fraught with difficulties," he told her, "so if you stay back, you and our children will endure hardships and you will inevitably expose my work here."[46] A new, but no less bloody, era had arrived in Le Duan's revolutionary career.

## THE STATE OF PEACE AND THE ROAD TO WAR

Le Duan was reelected as Party secretary of the Southern Territorial Committee, formerly COSVN, at the October 1954 conference. There he divided the South into three interprovinces, eastern, central, and western, as well as one region covering Saigon–Cho Lon.[47] The shift from COSVN back to a territorial committee underlined the Party's commitment to political struggle rather than armed conflict to reintegrate the southern half of the country. Following the Geneva Accords, the period of resettlement witnessed some 200,000 people moving northward and 1 million in the other direction.[48] As secretary of the committee, Le Duan opted to remain covertly in the South, alongside approximately 10,000 other revolutionaries, and thus parted ways with northbound Le Duc Tho in early 1955 to travel secretly back to Ca Mau.

Nga, who had failed to convince her husband to allow her to remain in the South, was also on the *Kilinski*, where she hid in her cabin with their daughter until the Polish ship reached its final destination. In for a rude awakening, Nga, a revolutionary girl who hailed from the western Mekong Delta, was about to face a stern and ideologically rigid Hanoi society that refused to accept her officially—or even informally—as Le Duan's wife. Le Thi Suong, Le Duan's first wife, and their children had been separated from Le Duan for the duration of the war against the French, but in peacetime their home village was located in DRV territory. Suong and her children, then, would be considered the first secretary's family when he rose to power, not Nga and hers.

Far from the domestic squabbles that he created by marrying twice, Le Duan disembarked from the rickety canoe in early 1955 at Ca Mau, where he was greeted by Vo Van Kiet and other deputies. At the time, the Southern Territorial Committee's offices were divided into two divisions. The base dubbed "Territorial Committee 1" remained in the old headquarters in Tri Phai village, Tho Binh district, Ca Mau province, under Le Duan's control while "Territorial Committee 2" fell under Standing Member Hoang Du Khuong.[49] From Ca Mau, Kiet and Le Duan's other bodyguards escorted him northeast to Ben Tre.[50]

Although Le Duan's position has been portrayed in official histories as caught between a hesitant Party in the North and a hasty insurgency in the

*The Mekong Delta (Douglas Pike Photograph Collection,*
*Vietnam Center and Archive, Texas Tech University)*

South, recent evidence has shown that he may have secretly had a greater role in stoking the revolutionary fires. Moreover, his outwardly conservative position before 1956 in the face of southern demands to undertake military action most likely reflected his desire to exert control over the fractious situation before condoning rash policies that were too reminiscent of Nguyen Binh during the French-Indochina War. According to David Elliott, Le Duan's position had always been ambivalent after his return to the Mekong Delta, and it only grew bolder and less content with the Party line as the years progressed.[51] Official Hanoi policy during these years remained centered on political agitation primarily and political assassination only when necessary. Even when it became clear that reunification elections would not transpire, the Politburo under Truong Chinh would not budge from its policy of strict compliance with the Geneva Accords and of restricting revolutionary activities to political struggle. Traveling around the western Mekong Delta, the southern countryside, and even the cities, Le Duan undermined Hanoi's orders by mobilizing irregular and regular troops to prepare for an eventual war.[52] At the same time, he reined in more "hotheaded" southern comrades lest they destroy the resistance with their call to arms or, just as disconcerting, lest they—and not he— reap any rewards if the masses responded.

Caught in this dilemma, Le Duan decided to relocate the headquarters of the Territorial Committee to Saigon, ostensibly to ascertain the political mood of the capital city. Kiet and his crew were responsible for protecting Le Duan in the heart of the enemy's power, and they feared for his safety each day of his stay in Saigon.[53] These were indeed precarious times, and Le Duan's actions in Saigon would make them even more dangerous. Once firmly ensconced at the Territorial Committee headquarters at 29 Huynh Khuong Ninh Street in the heart of the city, Le Duan penned what would become his manifesto, *Duong loi cach mang mien Nam* (The Path to Revolution in the South), forging the way to liberation through both political and armed struggle. When the political heat became too much to bear, Le Duan headed for the cool environs of the former French mountain resort town of Da Lat, where he stayed for two months until events settled down in the RVN capital.[54]

This manifesto may have been Le Duan's attempt to simultaneously outflank any competitors in the South and state his campaign in the North. The timing was perfect. In mid-1956, the beleaguered Politburo was searching for a solution to its problems with northern reconstruction, and the situation in the South appeared the most promising distraction from those troubles. The Party announced that it could begin to broach the idea of revising its strict policy of political agitation since it now had a base of support.[55] At the same time that leaders in Hanoi started to reassess their policy below the seventeenth parallel, southern revolutionaries, who were being hunted down by enemy forces, had already begun to take matters into their own hands. In other words, they believed, "war was the only road to take."[56] Seeing the writing on the wall, Le Duan attempted to move to the forefront of the armed-conflict issue with his manifesto. With Party backing, the shrewd leader believed he could unleash the forces of revolution without losing control over them.

Although the manifesto stated his shared belief with southern revolutionaries that reunification would only be possible with the complete overthrow of the Diem regime, he could not yet sanction armed conflict. At the Second Plenum of the Southern Territorial Committee in late 1956 and early 1957 held in Phnom Penh, Le Duan "opposed efforts to incite war and demand peace and reunification. The most immediate demand," he claimed, "would be to demand that continued contacts between the two halves of Vietnam be allowed.[57] Immediately following the plenum in Cambodia, the Party recalled Le Duan to Hanoi.

Events in the North would soon bolster Le Duan's cause. While he snuck back to the Mekong Delta in early 1955, Le Duc Tho returned to Hanoi and assumed the position of secretary of the Reunification Commission, predicated on his experience below the seventeenth parallel during the French Indochina War. By the end of the year, however, Tho's attentions were drawn away from the situation in the South as domestic problems arose in the DRV. As a second-tier member of the Party leadership, Le Duc Tho benefited from the top rung's struggle with advancing socialist transformation of the economy during peacetime. In fact, Tho's personal fortunes rose in direct proportion to the difficulties encountered by the Politburo's nation-building efforts in the latter half of the 1950s.[58]

Many of the obstacles to North Vietnam's development were inherent in the transition from war to peace, as well as in the shift from colonial protectorate to independent nation. However, the Politburo under Truong Chinh also made unwise choices to implement policies that were detrimental to a large segment of the population. From December 1953 to July 1956, the VWP had carried out a land reform campaign and an organizational rectification program that aimed to abolish landlordism, placing the land in the hands of peasant smallholders while simultaneously elevating the role of the dispossessed within the Party. In the VWP's conception of its socialist revolution, the land issue was of utmost importance, since 80 percent of Vietnamese lived in rural areas. At the top, Hanoi leaders strove to consolidate Party control down to the village level and purify the VWP of bourgeois or capitalist elements who had to be tolerated during the exigencies of the French War. In the villages, however, the Party's policies created an atmosphere of fear, distrust, paranoia, and greed as neighbors turned against one another.[59]

As the top Party leader at the end of the French-Indochina War, Truong Chinh assumed control over land reform during peacetime. In order to bolster his position within the Politburo, the first secretary pushed for greater control of the agrarian issue by the mass organizations over the more established government administration. By 1956, however, the North Vietnamese people, who were subjected to the wave of terror in the countryside, rose up against the excesses of the campaigns, prompting the government to send its armed forces to quell the demonstrations. When soldiers fired on their own people, the VWP leadership understood that it had to make amends with the masses and undertake damage control within the Party.[60] In August 1956, Ho Chi Minh publicly acknowledged the mistakes of the land reform and Party organizational rectification campaigns, but he was powerless to stop the rebellions that ensued through the remainder of the year. Shortly thereafter, General Giap gave a lengthy speech in which he addressed the specific errors committed by the Party.[61]

Official apologies, however, were not enough. The investigation and subsequent reckoning, known as the "rectification of errors" campaign, brought down Truong Chinh and curbed the power of the mass organizations. However, the government (Ho Chi Minh and Pham Van Dong) and the armed forces (Vo Nguyen Giap) were also tainted in the process.[62] At the Tenth Plenum of the VWP Central Committee in late September 1956, Truong Chinh officially stepped down as first secretary, although he was not ousted from the Politburo.[63] The Party man who oversaw the rectification of errors was none other than Le Duc Tho. When it became clear that Truong Chinh's policies were wreaking havoc on Party control over the countryside, the CEC made Le Duc Tho head of the campaign and inducted him into the Politburo. After Tho cleaned house in this capacity in late 1956, he was appointed Party organizational chief, a position he had occupied from 1945 until he was sent to the Mekong Delta in 1948.[64] Regaining this portfolio in the late 1950s greatly expanded his powers during a vital period in the VWP's development.

One by one, then, Le Duan and Le Duc Tho's rivals to power in the North suffered major blows to their prestige and prominence. Although the rectification of errors was by far the most thorough campaign to destabilize the old power hierarchy within the Party and Politburo, Le Duan and Le Duc Tho could not yet force the VWP to adopt their campaign to launch a war for reunification in the South. Their position within the Party would receive a tremendous boost, however, from two other troubling developments in the DRV and from the inclusion in their clique of two other men—one in the military, the other in propaganda and culture. By the end of the decade, not only did they command a strong base of support within the Party, but the problematic state of the socialist revolution in the North also allowed them to push for war in the South from the top perches of leadership within the VWP.

Following on the heels of the land reform debacle, the Party's crackdown spread to the cities as the "reeducation of the capitalists [*cai tao tu san*]" and intellectual dissidents threw urban centers into disorder.[65] During the start of the rectification of errors campaign, there was a rise in literati dissent in the capital city of Hanoi, which led to the *Nhan Van–Giai Pham* (Humanism–Masterpiece) (*NV-GP*) affair. Named after two short-lived publications, this affair involved the intelligentsia—writers, historians, philosophers, musicians, journalists, critics, and lawyers—who chafed at Party regulation and demanded greater intellectual, cultural, and political freedom of expression, without calling for the overthrow of the entire system as other movements had in Eastern Europe.[66] During the French Indochina War, the Party and the state had beseeched their writers, many of whom joined the army, to produce propaganda and official literature (*tuyen truyen*) aimed at mobilizing the masses for the decolonization struggle.[67] In 1949, the PAVN established the Army Office of Art and Literature and created the journal *Van Nghe Quan Doi* (Army Art and Literature) to showcase the talents of its writer-soldiers for the anticolonial cause. Since the office fell under Nguyen Chi Thanh's department, the army's ideological watchdog known as the GPD, it also regulated the personal and professional lives of the writer-soldiers in an effort to curb any bourgeois tendencies.

The informal contract that existed between the state and intellectuals during the war broke down, however, as the latter began to feel betrayed in peacetime. When a group of disgruntled writer-soldiers complained about the lack of creative freedom in art and literature to the GPD in February 1955, Thanh dismissed their grievances and castigated the soldier-writers for allowing capitalist ideology to seep into their consciousness.[68] These intellectuals, many of whom believed their military service had earned them the right to speak, claimed that the Party's strict literary guidelines for socialist realism hampered their creativity. Now that the DRV was at peace, there was no longer a reason to subjugate art to the military, the state, or the Party.

After the unsuccessful meeting with Thanh, intellectuals focused their discontent on the Association of Arts and Literature (AAL), which was established and controlled by the Party. Writers argued that it curtailed intellectual expression and established a worrisome precedent for literary achievement. Here, Hanoi's dissidents would come up against To Huu, a rising member of the Party who, like Thanh, was in charge of policing ideological adherence to Marxism-Leninism in the North. Born in 1920 in Phu Lai village in the central region known then as Annam, To Huu, whose original name was Nguyen Kim Thanh, came from a middle-class family outside Hue and joined revolutionary activities in the imperial capital as a young man in the 1930s. During the French-Indochina War, To Huu served as the Viet Minh's information director, and in 1951 he was elected as alternate member of the VWP Central Executive Committee.

During peacetime, To Huu used his leadership position within the VWP to undercut more talented rivals in the literary community. On a broader scale, he reinforced Party control over the intelligentsia, which threatened to undermine the Party's status in the DRV. In March 1955, the AAL organized two events that further strained the already tense relationship between the writers and the Party. The first included a session to discuss a book of poetry by To Huu titled *Viet Bac* (North Vietnam), and the second involved the distribution of literary prizes for 1954–55. The literary community in Hanoi expressed near-universal disdain for the widely published *Viet Bac*, calling it "bland and small." Later, writers rallied against the awarding of prizes to substandard works that won for being ideologically correct rather than for any literary merit.[69] A group of these disaffected and disillusioned writers started two publications, a series of four books titled *Giai Pham Mua Xuan* (Masterpiece of Spring) and a weekly newspaper, *Nhan Van* (Humanism), both representing an attempt to reclaim the private, intellectual space from the Party's grip. The latter publication sought to connect North Vietnam's intellectual sphere to international, liberalizing tendencies seen in the Hundred Flowers Campaign in China, the Hungarian Revolution, and Poland's October, even though it never called for the same wide-reaching reform.[70] Nonetheless, the readership of both publications quickly extended beyond intellectuals.[71]

To Huu's response was severe. With the Party's support, he imprisoned the writers, shut down publishing houses, and launched a countercampaign. By early 1958, To Huu instituted even more extreme measures, subjecting the intellectual community to self-criticism sessions. The Party eventually suppressed the movement by sending the "counterrevolutionary" ringleaders to labor reform camps and refashioning the literati dissidence as a Trotskyist, reactionary plot.[72]

Within this oppressive environment, with apparatchiks like Thanh, To Huu, and Le Duc Tho ascendant, Le Duan returned to Hanoi in 1957. At that time, Ho Chi Minh, chairman of the VWP, took over as acting first secretary with Vo Nguyen Giap and Politburo member Nguyen Duy Trinh as his assistants following Truong Chinh's demotion in 1956. This arrangement was only temporary, since the Party leadership needed to promote a new first secretary who had not been involved with the disastrous decision making in the North. Moreover, the old guard—including Ho, Giap, Pham Van Dong, and the recently demoted Truong Chinh—wanted to promote a new acting head who would respect and practice the Vietnamese communist leadership's long-held tradition of collective decision making. Le Duan, who remained far from the troubles in the North and who appeared to lack a strong base of power within the Party, appeared the ideal candidate, but even then nothing was confirmed. Holding a fake Cambodian passport and traveling under a Chinese name, Le Duan set out from Saigon to neighboring Cambodia and from there to Hong Kong and through Guangzhou to reach Hanoi.[73]

When he arrived in the DRV, Le Duan had to resolve personal matters as well as professional ones. While Nga and her two children bounced around apartments and eventually settled with Pham Hung's family in Hanoi, Le Duan's first wife, Suong, and her children resided in their home village of Nghe An more than 100 miles to the south. After exchanging many letters, the two wives and their families met one Tet holiday when their husband was in the South. Nga later described this period as very stressful. Although Suong seemed to accept her as a "younger sister," her father-in-law was less embracing. Moreover, Nga's friends—many of whom attended her maquis wedding to Le Duan in the South—began to pressure her into divorce so that Le Duan would not face any criticism in Hanoi. Finally, the real obstacle to their marriage would come from Suong's adolescent children, who moved to Hanoi for school once their father assumed a leadership role in the Politburo. With the National Assembly's Family Decree delineating that a family could only consist of one husband and one wife, Nga believed her husband would have to make a choice.[74]

Le Duan, however, believed the law did not apply to him. One quiet afternoon after his return to Hanoi when he visited Nga's quarters to play with their infant son, Thanh, she broached the subject of dissolving their marriage. He railed against the idea: "I will become First Secretary so it mandates our divorce, but my heart breaks and I cannot rest easy with that decision. A communist must possess loyalty and compassion. If I abandoned you, it wouldn't sit well with me as a communist and so I cannot do it. I won't destroy a family."[75] Not everyone agreed with his stance, and Nga ostensibly faced the repercussions. Although this is hard to believe given Le Duan's status in the Party, Nga claims that when Le Duan beseeched the Women's Union to accept Nga and their situation, the women "vehemently opposed." Despite being a ranking communist official who devoted countless hours to studying Party doctrine in the western Mekong Delta, Nga saw that the Women's Union in Hanoi was able to negate her training and her accomplishments and instead make her an "object of their scorn [*doi tuong cac chi ghet bo*]."[76]

Powerful as he became in the Party, Le Duan may indeed have been powerless when it came to his children. One evening when Le Duan was tending to Nga and their baby son, the daughter of his first marriage, Hong, made a scene by banging against their door and wailing. Le Duan, not knowing what else to do, sent Nga away so he could calm his daughter down. On another occasion, when a southern comrade called on Nga to see if he could set up a meeting with her recently returned husband, the entire household forced her to hide while they pushed him away. Nor did the inhospitality extend only to fellow southern revolutionaries. Nga's eldest brother and youngest sibling were turned away when they came for a visit. During the engagement party of Le Duan's eldest son from his first marriage, the future bride's family made the mistake of calling Nga "Le Duan's wife," prompting Hong to wail in defiance. Unable to tolerate the stigma any longer, Nga, then three months pregnant with their third child, resolved to go to China to further her studies.[77]

As domestic bliss evaded Le Duan, he also soon discovered that his rival Vo Nguyen Giap still held the means to undermine him. In early 1957, Ho Chi Minh had entrusted Giap with drafting Resolution 15, which would dictate the Party's policy toward the southern resistance. Along with Tran Quang Huy and Hoang Tung, Giap consulted members of the Politburo and diligently worked on the resolution, which might have advised against armed struggle, or at least curtailed its use. In early 1958, when Giap gave Ho an update on the drafting of Resolution 15, the aged leader, most likely under pressure from Le Duan, told Giap to hand over the document to Le Duan, who would finalize the resolution and present it to the CEC plenum the following year.[78] At the same time that he sought to wrestle control over Resolution 15 from Giap, Le Duan faced the added pressure of having to put off two southern emissaries sent North by the resistance in the summer of 1957, Phan Van Dang and Pham Va Xo, to seek Party approval for armed conflict. Le Duan probably secretly cursed General Giap as he reluctantly locked the southern emissaries away in Hanoi, not allowing them to interact with other Party leaders until he had firm control over VWP policy. It has been speculated that Le Duan's deep-seated jealousy of Giap and the general's initial drafting of Resolution 15 were the key reasons Le Duan would devote himself to sidelining the general for the remainder of the war.[79]

The reason for Giap's reluctance to approve armed conflict may have been connected to the economic situation in the North by the late 1950s. As the dust began to settle in the countryside and in the cities following land reform and the intellectual dissident movements, the Party resolved to take concrete steps toward a centrally planned socialist economy by accelerating its agricultural collectivization and industrialization programs. In mid-February 1958, the National Assembly approved the Three-Year Plan for Economic Development and Transformation of Cultural Development (1958–60), which outlined the socialist transformation of the economy as well as the cultural and ideological campaign to mobilize the entire nation behind the revolution.[80] At the Fourteenth Plenum in November, VWP leaders decided to accelerate socialist construction. One month later, the National Assembly approved the accelerated Three-Year Plan. Party leaders hoped that collective farming cooperatives, as the bedrock of a socialist political economy, would increase production, control consumption, and direct agricultural earnings to building factories and strengthening other sectors of the economy.[81] In addition, the organizational element of collectivization would contribute to national defense, since the peasantry could easily be mobilized in armies and militias. During the land reform campaign, collectivization collapsed in many areas, but by 1957, cooperative experiments began to increase.[82] Once again, however, the North Vietnamese people resisted the Party's policies. Political scientist Benedict Kerkvliet describes villagers' use of "weapons of the weak" to hide their resistance by "shirking work" and "snitching grain" during this period.[83] Ignoring the recommendation of local leaders to avoid a rapid increase in cooperatives, the CEC hastened collectivization efforts in late 1958 with the accelerated Three-Year Plan, fearing that the peasantry would abandon the socialist revolution entirely.[84] "By late 1960 . . . the reform of agriculture in the North Vietnamese countryside had been virtually completed, using the form of low-level cooperatives. More than 85 percent of the peasant families had joined cooperatives that contained 68.06 percent of the land. Of that 85 percent, 11.81 percent joined high-level cooperatives. In the urban areas, 100 percent of industrial bourgeois families, 98 percent of commercial bourgeois families, and 99 percent of mechanized transportation facilities included in the area of reform were socialized."[85] Although the Party boasted success, with approximately 2 million people enlisted in the cooperatives from 1958 to 1960, according to Kerkvliet, the collectivization plan rested "uneasily on wobbly foundations."[86] In some instances, villagers openly resisted the accelerated col-

lectivization attempt even though news of the *NV-GP* crackdown had trick-
led to the countryside.[87]

In addition to agricultural collectivization, the VWP attached great
importance to urban reconstruction and industrial development.[88] The
Three-Year Plan stipulated the building of industrial sites throughout
Hanoi but with more emphasis on the outskirts of the capital.[89] East European sources reveal that the North Vietnamese leadership launched an
overly ambitious program, ignoring the fact that an agricultural country
could not be transformed into an industrial one overnight. By the early
1960s, the Hungarians were complaining that the "already chaotic conditions [that] existed in planning further worsened."[90]

Some of North Vietnam's difficulties could be attributed to the increasingly complex international environment. During the late 1950s, the fates
of postcolonial states were inseparable not only from the struggle between
capitalism and communism but also from the schisms that existed within
the two camps. In the case of the VWP, the emergence of what would become the Sino-Soviet split greatly complicated North Vietnam's reconstruction, socialist development, and path toward reunification. By the
late 1950s, Hanoi faced two alternative modes of revolution, as Moscow
and Beijing solidified their separate ideological positions: peaceful reunification through socialist development of the North and violent reunification through liberation struggle in the South.

The first cracks in the international proletarian movement appeared at
the Twentieth Congress of the CPSU in early 1956, where First Secretary
Nikita Khrushchev denounced Stalin's crimes and cult of personality. Following the historic congress, the Soviet Union decided to pursue a policy
of "peaceful coexistence" in competition with the capitalist world.[91] Khrushchev's line now posed a direct threat to Mao Zedong's China, ideologically as well as geostrategically, since Mao sought constant revolution
both at home and abroad in order to consolidate his authority within the
CCP.[92] Wanting to be treated as an equal partner in the Sino-Soviet alliance, the PRC also took offense at what Beijing saw as Soviet insistence
on perpetuating an unequal relationship. In particular, Soviet disapproval
of Mao's handling of the Quemoy-Matsu crises, Moscow's proposal of the
1958 joint naval arrangement that Mao considered unfair, and Soviet neutrality during the 1959 Sino-Indian dispute over Tibet contributed to Beijing's desire to break free of the patron-client relationship.[93]

Since China provided the bulk of the aid to Hanoi during the French-
Indochina War, Beijing wielded more influence over Hanoi's policies than

did Moscow. Moreover, Stalin, and even later Khrushchev, showed little interest in Indochina and, with the founding of the PRC, relegated the region to Mao. However, the Soviet Union continued to be considered by the Vietnamese communists as the ideological center of the world communist movement.[94] During this period of DRV state building, Sino-Soviet relations, though tense, were far from severed. As a result, following Saigon's cancellation of nationwide elections in 1956, both Beijing and Moscow approved Hanoi's decision to concentrate on political agitation rather than armed struggle in the South against the Diem regime. China's Bandung strategy and the Soviet Union's Asia policy pushed the same ideological line: to encourage neutralism rather than revolution among postcolonial states and nationalist regimes.[95] Both powers encouraged Hanoi to continue its political struggle, implying a de facto acceptance of the continued division of Vietnam. In 1957, Moscow had proposed that both Vietnams enter the United Nations. However, by the end of the decade, as the Soviets and Chinese began to part ideological ways, the growing resistance in the South grew more urgent in North Vietnamese estimation. As Beijing again changed its policy and began to welcome national liberation struggles, including the Iraqi revolution, the Algerian Front de Libération Nationale movement, and the Congolese struggle, to name a few, Moscow cooled to these violent movements. Just as the East-West conflict forced the postcolonial world to choose a side, the emergence of the Sino-Soviet split put communist, radical, and left-leaning revolutions in a bind.

As a result of these international debates, two contending factions began to emerge in the VWP, complicating the already existent power struggles in the Politburo. Although far from homogenous or static, these heterogeneous factions coalesced around the vital question of reunification. "North-firsters" wanted to continue concentrating the DRV's resources on state building: socialist development of the economy that would compete with and ultimately defeat the South. The "South-firsters" wanted to shepherd the DRV's resources into supporting the rising resistance in the South: reunification through war. The terms of the debate centered on the rate and methods of the agricultural revolution in the North but were intimately connected with the insurgency in the South. As the Sino-Soviet rift deepened and the conflict in the South intensified, the opposing factions invoked Khrushchev's peaceful-coexistence and Mao's anti-imperialist lines to advance their respective causes.

Until the Party archives are opened, it will be difficult to state definitively who was a "North-firster" and who was a "South-firster" in the

Politburo; however, reasonable estimations can be made. At the Eighth National Assembly in early 1958, Prime Minister Pham Van Dong reiterated the need to pursue reunification through peaceful means.[96] Alongside Dong, Giap might have also belonged to the "North-firsters," since he feared getting sucked into a war in the South at the expense of development in the North, especially with the lack of unified international support and the emergence of domestic divisions. A long-time advocate of modernizing the armed forces, Giap perhaps believed that the Party's support for armed struggle in the South would risk full-scale mobilization of his army, which required time to recuperate and rebuild after the war for decolonization. Given his conservative stance at the outbreak of the French-Indochina War, Ho most likely agreed with his Pac Bo companions that the DRV was not ready to launch a war for reunification. The positions of these men in the subsequent decade lend credence to this argument. For these leaders and other "North-firsters" in the Party, the diversion of men and matériel to the southern battlefield when the socialist revolution in the North remained so fragile was foolhardy. By 1959, asking more sacrifice of the people to support war in the South after so many failures in the North could push the masses to rebel against the Party.

Le Duan, Le Duc Tho, and their "South-first" faction, however, believed the opposite. War in the South could provide the rallying cry that the Party needed to reinvigorate the masses and bolster its position within the DRV—a lesson they drew from recent Vietnamese history. It was a gamble that Le Duan and Le Duc Tho were ready to take not only because they had dedicated their careers up to that point to the southern revolution but also because the promotion of war below the seventeenth parallel was the key to their eventual seizure of power within the Politburo.[97] By 1959, factors in both the North and the South converged, allowing them to seize the initiative. With Giap's relinquishing of Resolution 15 to Le Duan, the latter and his faithful southern deputy and close confidant Pham Hung began to draft a more militant resolution, one that would bind the Party to supporting armed conflict in the South.[98] In order to strengthen his case to promote Party support for war in the South, Le Duan embarked on a secret trip to the South some time following the Fourteenth Plenum in November 1958. There he found that Ngo Dinh Diem's anticommunist denunciation campaign of 1955 to 1958 had escalated to even more repressive measures with Decree 10/59 in May 1959, which subjected anyone suspected of political opposition—be they former Viet Minh, communists, or anyone undertaking antigovernment activities—to a sentence of life in prison or death. Although Diem's draconian law pushed more South Vietnamese villagers into the revolution, it also threatened to unleash an uprising that could slip completely from Party control in the North.

At the same time, Le Duan continued to firm up his base of power by promoting the power of apparatchiks within the Party. The Politburo had recalled Le Duan to Hanoi and made him de facto first secretary because key members believed he lacked a base, but it became apparent that they underestimated his organizational prowess. Giap's nemesis in the army, Nguyen Chi Thanh, and To Huu—men who had predicated their rise in the VWP on being agents of the apparatus—provided support within the Party that could challenge the other Politburo leaders. By promoting Party primacy to suppress any dissent within the armed forces and the intelligentsia, Thanh and To Huu became obvious allies with the top apparatchik, Party organizational chief Le Duc Tho, who remained Le Duan's second-in-command. Together, these VWP leaders who had built their careers on promoting the Party apparatus filled the void left by the decline of Truong Chinh's mass organizations, Ho Chi Minh and Pham Van Dong's state organs, and Vo Nguyen Giap's armed forces. Since the Party as a whole had been greatly compromised by the obstacles on the DRV's road to socialist revolution, Le Duan and his faction exploited the Party leadership's desire for a new cause that could rally the people behind the Party banner.

And so the die was cast for Le Duan's ascent to the top Party position as first secretary, thanks to the unsuspecting current heads of the Politburo who agreed to elevate him. In his reminiscences about Le Duan, Giap wrote that he had in fact floated the idea among his comrades within the Politburo that Le Duan should assume the position of first secretary a little while after the latter returned to Hanoi. At the time, according to Giap, Le Duan played coy, saying, "We should wait to see what the Third Party Congress wants to do."[99] During the Politburo convention that outlined the agenda for the upcoming Party Congress, the members of the top leadership body suggested that Le Duan head the delegation to prepare the Politburo's political report, a very important and high-profile task. Again, he demurred: "Since I haven't been in the North for the past ten years, I fear the responsibility of presenting the political report. I propose that comrades Truong Chinh and Vo Nguyen Giap be on the delegation to prepare the report instead."[100] In the end, the Politburo decided that Ho would head the delegation and Le Duan would be vice chair.

Le Duan abandoned this feigned reluctance to assume a position of leadership at the expanded plenary meeting of the CEC in late Decem-

ber 1958 and early January 1959. At this gathering Le Duan and the apparatchiks scored their first, albeit limited, victory. As the historic plenum
opened, Le Duan took the podium to emphasize the dire nature of the
situation below the seventeenth parallel: the southern insurgency was in
danger of being annihilated by Ngo Dinh Diem's troops unless the Party
intervened.[101] An unspoken message, which at least the ranking southern representatives present at the plenum understood, was that the lower
levels had already begun to take matters into their own hands, and that
if the Party refused to sanction their violence, it could lose control of the
resistance below the seventeenth parallel. After painting a dismal picture,
Le Duan closed his speech with what he thought offered a bright solution
to the Party's dilemma. Resolution 15, which drew from his 1956 southern
manifesto but which he and Pham Hung had shepherded through another
twenty-two drafts after seizing it from Giap, called for the Party to commit
to the overthrow of the Diem government through not only political agitation but also military means. Since the Diem regime refused to carry out
nationwide elections for unification, the replacement revolutionary government would have to be imposed by force.[102]

Although the CEC members at the January 1959 plenum had approved
Le Duan's Resolution 15, a question remained about which balance its
guidelines should strike between the act of political resistance and the
use of military force. To Le Duan's dismay, Party leaders opted to shelve
the issue and reconvene in May. Le Duan may have attempted to alleviate the concerns of the North-first moderate faction of the Party when he
stated to the CMC in March: "We won't use war to unify the country, but
if the United States and its puppets use war, then we have to use war, and
the war that the enemy has initiated will be an opportunity for us to unify
the country."[103]

The guidelines for the implementation of the Resolution went through
three more drafts before it was finally presented in May.[104] Although Party
records remain silent on the five months between the Fifteenth Plenum's
two sessions, Le Duan and his faction must have lobbied for the resolution
to state, in no uncertain terms, that the Party would move solidly toward
armed conflict. At the May meeting, Party leaders finally decided to go
ahead with the terms agreed on at the January meeting by establishing a
Special Military Operations Corps dubbed Doan 559 (Group 559), named
after its founding in May 1959, to maintain the logistical supply route that
ran through the Annamese cordillera (Truong Son) to the South, more
commonly known as the Ho Chi Minh Trail. In September, the Party cre-

ated Doan 959 (Group 959, later Front 959) in order to expand the supply routes running through southern Laos and to serve as headquarters for North Vietnamese military support of Pathet Lao troops.[105] Thus, after nearly a decade of mucking around in the backwaters of the South, Le Duan made the region and its armed struggle a priority for the Party, and perhaps even the solution to the VWP's domestic problems in the North.

His victory was only tentative, however, since Resolution 15 hesitated to approve the use of armed force in situations other than self-defense.[106] In addition to the internal divisions within the VWP regarding the balance between political resistance and armed conflict, the ambiguous state of relations between Beijing and Moscow contributed to a delay in the transmission and implementation of Resolution 15. According to the late historian Ralph B. Smith, "Until Sino-Soviet relations were clarified, they and their colleagues [Vietnamese Party leaders] decided not to take up a clear position of their own, and to delay publication of the 'hard line' 15th Plenum resolution."[107] Although the PRC's increasing support of national liberation struggles in the Third World allowed prowar leaders in Hanoi to broach the aim of overthrowing the Ngo Dinh Diem government by force, both Beijing and Moscow advised Hanoi to concentrate on the political struggle.[108] As a result, the contents of the resolution did not reach the South until 1960, when Beijing's radical stance grew more pronounced.[109] Hanoi's compromise strategy of caution toward the struggle in the South clearly reflected the burgeoning divisions at home and abroad and was not merely a response to the crisis in the South.

Nonetheless, the North-first moderates in the Party must have seen the May session as a major defeat even though the expanded Sixteenth Plenum, which took place before and after the May session, was devoted to domestic issues.[110] These initial steps toward war, like the establishment of Group 559, meant that northern resources would be funneled to the southern struggle at the expense of development in the DRV. The Party's campaign to liberate the South from the oppressive Diem regime and to foment a national people's democracy would delay the socialist revolution in the North, especially if the southern struggle proved to be an epic quagmire. Meanwhile, at the opposite end of the country, revolutionaries in the South could not await the return of their high-level leaders (who remained in Hanoi to attend both sessions of the Fifteenth Plenum) for the Party's approval for war. By the summer of 1959, when the plenum's delegates returned to their various zones below the seventeenth parallel, the revolution had already begun in some areas. In what the Party calls the

Concerted Uprising, peasant revolt had begun to shake the foundations of power in the South.[111]

## CONCLUSION

Le Duan and Le Duc Tho's first brush with anticolonial resistance and grueling incarceration in the 1930s and 1940s set them on a Marxist-Leninist path toward independence and national liberation. During the struggle for decolonization, both men sought to rise in the ranks of the Communist Party in the context of the violent and tumultuous south. Their experiences in the Mekong Delta would equip them with the tools to build a veritable empire during the Cold War and beyond. Although their revolutionary careers during these early decades were noteworthy, their postcolonial activities made the greatest mark on their nation's development. As they parted ways in 1955 in the delta moonlight, they enacted major events that would change the course of Vietnam's modern history, which would eventually include engaging the world's greatest superpower in war.

As rival leaders in the Politburo attempted and failed to bring about a socialist revolution in the DRV, Le Duan's reunion with Le Duc Tho amid the shambles of the Party's state building enterprise would seal the fates of North and South Vietnam. The two men engineered the greatest usurpation of power in the annals of the Vietnamese Communist Party. When Le Duan left Saigon in the late 1950s, he would not set foot in the southern capital for nearly two decades; but the South was never far from his mind. Shortly after he arrived in Hanoi, he quickly rose to the highest seat of power and championed a campaign that appeared to solve the Party's immediate woes not only in the North but also in the South: war for the liberation of the South and ultimate reunification of Vietnam.

Although Le Duan's Resolution 15 only sanctioned armed force to support the political struggle in the South, it constituted the first stage in Le Duan and Le Duc Tho's campaign for total war. Armed conflict would prove unsatisfying for the two Party leaders who had built their careers in the Mekong Delta; they wanted a full-scale war for reunification. The 1960s would witness the achievement of that goal.

*Le Duan and Le Duc Tho were behind the so-called Revisionist
Anti-Party Affair that kept me locked behind bars for most of my life for
doing nothing wrong. —Hoang Minh Chinh*[1]

chapter two

# POLICING THE STATE IN
# A TIME OF WAR

Walking through the halls of the Social Sciences Institute in 1963, Hoang Minh Chinh worried that he had not done everything in his power to re-balance VWP policy. A devotee of Soviet thinking, Chinh, head of the Marx-ist Institute of Philosophy, was convinced that the Party was veering dan-gerously close to the Chinese line and away from the accepted path of peaceful coexistence espoused by Moscow. Instead of devoting energy to industrialization and collectivization, North Vietnam was sending pre-cious manpower and matériel southward in an endless stream. When Hanoi's foremost theoretician, Truong Chinh, approached him to com-pile a report for the upcoming CEC plenum on the correct international line, Hoang Minh Chinh had no qualms about criticizing the apparent Chinese tilt in North Vietnam's external policy. Little did he know that Le Duan had already decided on Vietnam's international position. The first secretary, who had first viewed squabbles between Beijing and Moscow as worrisome, began to see the benefits of the Sino-Soviet split. With China's support of violent confrontations with neoimperalist forces in the Third World, Le Duan could now appeal to Chinese support for his southern war effort without fear of losing his autonomy to the Middle Kingdom. Not only would Hoang Minh Chinh's report prove futile in undoing a tilt in Hanoi's foreign policy, but it would also feed a domestic policy to stamp out any criticism of Le Duan's war in the South and police state in the North.

During the years between Le Duan's assumption of power in 1960 and the Americanization of the war, the DRV took firm steps in the direction of total war. For the first three years of the new decade, Le Duan and Le Duc Tho consolidated decision making into their hands in Hanoi and slowly marginalized dissenting voices within the Politburo and the Party who objected to the increasing diversion of DRV resources to the struggle in the South. They did this by creating a formidable police state. Although the Party had privileged the building of the northern economy internally and had officially subscribed to peaceful coexistence externally, by late 1963 Le Duan and Le Duc Tho were able to reorient the DRV's domestic and foreign policies to reflect their militant South-first objective of full-scale war for reunification. Exploiting the emerging split in the communist world and the increasing political volatility in South Vietnam, they were able to use China's patronage and Ngo Dinh Diem's assassination to sideline their opponents in the VWP. Meanwhile, below the seventeenth parallel, Le Duan was not about to let southerners command the war effort. Using the Central Office of South Vietnam, Le Duan and the Party center in Hanoi maintained control over decision making.

While battling these internal rivals, Le Duan and his militant faction attempted to dissuade the United States from directly intervening in South Vietnam by "going for broke" in 1964 using the strategy that Le Duan had devised: the General Offensive and General Uprising. When their gambit proved a dismal failure, as Lyndon B. Johnson dropped American bombs over North Vietnam and dispatched U.S. ground troops to South Vietnam, Le Duan and Le Duc Tho found themselves struggling on four different fronts. First, the peace faction of the Party had never approved of promoting armed conflict in the South. Instead, these midlevel "North-first" officials sought to promote the socialist revolution in the DRV that could compete, and ultimately defeat, the RVN economically and politically. As such, they called for an immediate end to the war through the neutralization of South Vietnam. Their calls, however, were drowned out as Le Duan marched a greater number of northern troops to the southern battlefield.

Second, the indigenous southern revolutionary leadership continued to challenge Hanoi's takeover of its war effort. With the buildup to total war, Le Duan directed COSVN to streamline operations in the South, reorganize the command structure, and build conventional main-force units. Southerners viewed many of these orders as foolhardy, especially after American intervention, and tried their best to resist the Party center's encroachment on their military and political affairs.

Third, the advent of American military intervention during the "long 1964" not only mobilized the "North-first" Party members into action, it also elevated Vietnam's importance in the zero-sum game of the Sino-Soviet split. With Vietnam's conflict the most visible one in the international proletarian movement against neoimperialist forces and the highest-profile struggle for national liberation in the Global South, Moscow and Beijing engaged in a fierce competition for Hanoi's favor by lavishing North Vietnam with aid but also demanding increasing influence. While Beijing pressured North Vietnam to avoid peace talks at all costs and to reject Soviet aid and advice, Moscow pushed North Vietnam to negotiate and to hold the PRC accountable for the disruption of aid transport.

Fourth, amid this cacophony of foreign advice and domestic criticism, Le Duan and Le Duc Tho were convinced that rivals within the Politburo threatened their control over the war effort as well. In particular, General Vo Nguyen Giap emerged as a potential threat who could undercut the "comrades Le" during these troubled times. By promoting Nguyen Chi Thanh in the military leadership, Le Duan and Le Duc Tho hoped to offset Giap's popularity within the armed forces. Although General Thanh was in charge of the southern war effort, as the conflict ground to a stalemate, Thanh and Giap began to butt heads over military strategy. While Thanh preferred big-unit war to maintain the initiative, Giap advocated a more decisive turn to protracted guerrilla war in order to reduce losses. As Hanoi leaders confronted the "fork in the road," Le Duan ensured that the DRV would pursue the more violent path. De-escalation was not an option.

Just as America's war in Vietnam stemmed from its long-standing containment policy and immediate choices made by hawkish leaders, so too was North Vietnam's revolutionary struggle for reunification and liberation a product of the Party's enduring goal of a unified Vietnam as well as the intervention of a militant leadership in Hanoi that chose war as the path to national reunification. This chapter examines how Le Duan and Le Duc Tho consolidated decision making into their hands and how they used their command over the Party apparatus to advance "bigger war" at the expense of the indigenous southern resistance. In doing so, it reveals that the communist leadership was wracked with division. For Le

Duan and Le Duc Tho, achieving their goals of total war in the South and silenced dissent in the war-weary North required using every weapon in the police state at their disposal.

## THE ESTABLISHMENT OF NORTH VIETNAM'S NATIONAL SECURITY STATE (1960–1963)

At the start of the new decade, Le Duan could be moderately pleased with himself. The Party had agreed to support military action in the South and elevate it to the same level of importance as development in the North. Set to ascend to the top Party position, Le Duan also had at his disposal loyal deputies within the Party leadership who could help him thwart any potential rivals in the Politburo and advance his militant South-first campaign throughout the lower rungs of the Party and, ultimately, the general populace. These deputies rose to the top by ensuring Party loyalty during the period of great volatility following the troubles with socialist development in the 1950s. Their ability to suppress criticism and create an atmosphere of repression was exactly what Le Duan needed to supplant state building in the North with revolutionary war in the South.

At the Third Party Congress of the VWP held in the DRV capital from 5 to 10 September 1960, Ho Chi Minh ceremonially oversaw the approval of Hanoi's war plans and welcomed a new and enlarged Central Executive Committee and Politburo as well as a new Party first secretary.[2] Although Ho's position as chairman of the committee—which he had held since 1951 and to which he was reelected in 1960—was considered the supreme position in the Party, real power had long resided with the first secretary, who oversaw the daily activities of the top decision-making body in the VWP, the Politburo.[3] In 1960, approximately 500 participants at the congress witnessed the start of a new era in Vietnamese communism as a new leader approach the dais. Le Duan, who had operated for more than a decade in the backwaters of the South, now emerged as the top Party man in the North.

Although Le Duan was chosen to head Politburo affairs, the Party agenda remained split. The title, Congress of Socialist Construction in the North and of Struggle for Peaceful National Reunification, underlined the dual nature of Party policy in 1960. After Ho's opening statement, Le Duan stepped up to the podium, put on his thick reading glasses, and read the Politburo's collectively written political report. The report must have taken hours to deliver, but its message was clear: "Our official line while we ad-

Left to right, front row: *Le Duan, Ho Chi Minh, and Truong Chinh
at the 1960 Third Party Congress (Douglas Pike Photograph Collection,
Vietnam Center and Archive, Texas Tech University)*

vance the socialist revolution in the North should be: *Develop the North to
give to the South* [*xay dung mien Bac, chieu co mien Nam*]" (italics in original). Although the report also elaborated the DRV's first Five-Year Plan
(1961–65), Le Duan would work behind the scenes to ensure that building
socialism served the purposes of waging war. Under his early stewardship,
the "communist revolution" in the North took a back seat to the "national-
democratic revolution" in the South.[4]

To ensure the veneer of a separate southern legitimacy, the congress
laid the foundation for the creation of the National Liberation Front (Mat
Tran Dan Toc Giai Phong, NLF). Southern revolutionaries, many of whom
had fought a long war against the French as Viet Minh soldiers or were
members of the younger generation who sought to mimic their elders, had
risen up in defiance of Diem's repressive policies before the Party in the
North sought to exert direct control over their affairs.[5] The creation of the
NLF in 1960 was a northern response to genuine peasant uprisings at
the village level in the southern countryside; it was a construct poised to
reap the success of the spontaneous agitation and portray it as a "concerted uprising [*dong khoi nghia*]" orchestrated by communist cells under
the direction of the VWP.[6]

Thus, Le Duan was able to create two levers with which to take over the resistance struggle, the first by co-opting southern leaders into an ostensible broad-based united front, the NLF, and the second by strengthening COSVN, which had been reestablished, at the Third Party Congress.[7] As a result, the relationship between revolutionaries in the South and the Party in the North had been fraught with tension, regardless of official exhortations to the contrary. More than any other VWP leader, Le Duan had long called for the Party to muster all of its resources to direct the revolution in the South. During the 1940s and 1950s, he had witnessed firsthand how noncommunist groups as well as rival communist forces in the Mekong Delta could slip entirely from the control of or even undermine the Party center in the Red River Delta. Although Le Duan was a "South-first" leader of the first order who early on campaigned for elevating the southern struggle to a nationwide emergency, he was not about to let southern liberation fighters oversee such an important war for national reunification. With the revitalization of COSVN, he and other Hanoi leaders intended to direct military activities in the South, even though it would take them many years to stamp out the final vestiges of southern autonomy. Nguyen Van Linh, who had served with Le Duan in the Mekong Delta, became chief of COSVN.[8] Meanwhile, Le Duan, Le Duc Tho, and Pham Hung served on the National Reunification Committee, which more or less filtered the Politburo's diplomatic-sphere directives southward, along with Nguyen Van Vinh, who would become the committee chair.[9]

While he laid the groundwork to usurp revolutionary power in the South, Le Duan constructed a solid foundation to bolster his leadership and gain support for his policies in the North. In order to become the "first among equals" in the Politburo, Le Duan needed to firm up his base of support within the Party so it would not crumble as easily as Truong Chinh's did in the wake of the land reform debacle. With the adoption of the Party's statute on 15 September 1960—one that would remain in place until reunification in 1976—the power hierarchy in the Party solidified: the Politburo remained situated at the top, but the role of the first secretary and his Secretariat, the executive arm charged with the specific responsibility of "[solving] the daily problems and [controlling] the carrying out of the Politburo's decisions," became even more important after 1960.[10] The Secretariat included Le Duan's loyal deputies who were either associated with his activities in the South or whose power derived from the Party apparatus (and sometimes both): Le Duc Tho, Pham Hung, Nguyen Chi Thanh, and To Huu. The first three were elected to the Politburo; all of them were voted onto the CEC.[11] As such, they possessed the same level of power as other Party leaders who also occupied important government posts such as chairman of the Standing Committee of the National Assembly (Truong Chinh), prime minister (Pham Van Dong), and minister of national defense (Vo Nguyen Giap). Finally, Le Duan astutely co-opted a key agency—the Ministry of Public Security—that would allow him to extend his power beyond the Party, the intellectuals, and the army, to police the lives of all citizens in North Vietnam.

By building a communist bureaucracy that answered to him and his deputies, Le Duan was able to accomplish what previous leaders of the Politburo could not. With the adoption of the 1960 Party Statute, Le Duan consolidated decision making under his leadership by expanding the jurisdiction of the Secretariat over such disparate sectors as propaganda and training, foreign affairs, finance, science and education, and industry and agriculture. Hence, the statute greatly expanded the sway of the head apparatchiks in the VWP. Le Duc Tho remained in the increasingly important post of chief of the Party Organizational Committee, which dictated the careers and livelihood of all Party cadres.[12] The General Political Department of the North Vietnamese Army, under Nguyen Chi Thanh, was one of the few staff agencies permanently established as a department by the statute.[13] Since 1950, Thanh had acted in this capacity as a light counterweight to Giap; ten years later, the balance tipped in Thanh's favor. Not only did the GPD ensure that the North Vietnamese armed forces remained under the watchful eye of the Party, Thanh was also promoted to full general in September 1959, rendering his rank equal to Giap's.[14] The Party's officially sanctioned intellectual, To Huu, continued his surveillance and repression of the intelligentsia as chair of the Education and Propaganda Department. Regarding military affairs, Le Duan made sure to appoint men to the Party's military decision-making group, the CMC, which had long eclipsed the State's National Defense Council. Actual decision making for the war, however, resided with the Politburo subcommittee that included Le Duan and Le Duc Tho.[15] Le Duan's Party leadership during the war was a complex structure that involved multiple committees nominally performing the same tasks. This arrangement allowed the first secretary to undercut his opponents by getting them mired in powerless committees while he stood at the center of the key decision-making bodies in Hanoi.

Holding positions of power, these prowar leaders were well situated to change the course of Party policy in Hanoi, but they also needed a mechanism to control the northern population. Indeed, one of the lessons of the land reform debacle was that the masses could rise up in defiance of Party policy. But just how would the prowar leaders extend Party control over the DRV? The answer lay neither in volunteerism and mass organization nor in reliance on the armed forces to maintain order but rather in the construction of a garrison state. Le Duan promoted the security forces, known as the Cong An (Security Police) and Bao Ve (Military Security), allowing the militants in power to surveil not only communist cadres, intellectuals, and high-level military officers but also the general population. In short, he created a police state by ramping up the dreaded Ministry of Public Security (Bo Cong An). Although the Ministry was a government body, it answered to the top Party apparatchiks under Le Duan's reign. Using fear tactics to beef up internal security in the DRV during a time of war, the Politburo tasked its security forces with stepping up the struggle against "counterrevolutionaries" and granted the security forces greater authority to apprehend suspects who threatened national security and the war for reunification.[16] Moreover, the Ministry of Public Security's Political Security Department (Cuc Bao Ve Chinh Tri) worked closely with the Party's own Domestic Affairs Committee (Ban Noi Chinh) and the army's Security Forces (Cuc Bao Ve), creating a web of security and intelligence personnel who served as watchdogs.[17] In effect, Le Duan laid the foundation for the sturdiest power structure the Party had ever seen, and whose vestiges continued to loom over Hanoi decades after the war ended.

Tasked with overseeing the internal security of the DRV, the Bao Ve and Cong An possessed near limitless power over the citizenry, making the short and stocky minister of public security, Tran Quoc Hoan, an integral player in the construction of Le Duan's empire. Born Nguyen Trong Canh in early 1916 to a poor peasant family in Nghe An province, Tran Quoc Hoan ran away in the early 1930s to Laos, where he worked in the mines of Ban Boneng. Shortly after he joined the Communist Party in 1934, the French colonial state arrested and exiled Hoan. When he returned to Vietnam later in the decade, he moved to Hanoi. Near the end of the Second World War, Hoan became head of the Northern Territorial Committee, and during the French-Indochina War he was responsible for Party activities in the capital. In 1951 Hoan became a member of the CEC, and the following year he was second-in-command of the public security forces, then part of the Ministry of Home Affairs (Bo Noi Vu). Hoan's fortunes continued to rise when public security became its own ministry in 1953 with Hoan at the helm. At the Third Party Congress, he was elected as an alternate member of the Politburo, and shortly thereafter Le Duan included Hoan in the CMC so the minister could also weigh in on defense matters.[18]

Hoan's speeches offer a fresh glimpse of North Vietnam from the perspective of a powerful state bent on crushing all opposition during a time of war. Unveiling his plans at the Third Party Congress, Minister Hoan spoke of the need to step up the struggle against counterrevolution (*dau tranh chong phan cach mang*) in the face of the enemy's "Northward March" (Bac Tien) plot. Hoan warned that the North faced innumerable dangers since the return of peace in 1954. In particular, the U.S.-Diem clique inserted spies and commandoes and had the allegiance of collaborators "disguised as religious leaders and reactionaries among the oppressor class," who together advanced a "war of aggression" to sabotage the people's revolutionary cause in the North.[19] Promoting "Directive No. 69VP/P4" (called "Plan 69") on "preparations of all types to deal with the U.S.-Diem plan to start a war," Hoan monopolized all resources, including other staff agencies and local governments, to carry out the requests that the Ministry of Public Security—now the "core force"—deemed necessary to "crush all acts of disruption and sabotage." Four years later, Plan 69 sent nearly 12,000 individuals deemed "dangerous to our security and social order" to reeducation camps.[20]

While Le Duan constructed his formidable empire in the early days of the new decade, Nga, his second wife and "true love," could not join in on the celebrations surrounding her husband's promotion at the Third Party Congress.[21] Instead, she was in another key Asian capital in the Cold War. Along with her three children—she had given birth shortly after she arrived in China—Nga pursued her studies in Beijing, where she was far from the judgmental eyes of Hanoi society. Her routine was rigorous. She awoke in the early morning hours, fed and dressed her elder children, roused the baby awake, and sent them off before going to the university. When she returned home in the early evening, she cooked dinner, bathed her children, and made sure they were snug in bed at a decent hour. She then studied Chinese until her eyelids grew heavy. Every so often, she received love letters from her husband, encouraging her to persevere in her roles as student, mother, and dutiful wife. But the load was too much for the single mother to handle, and she sent her two older children back to Hanoi. Eventually even her youngest joined his siblings after he fell ill, leaving her to question how she had wound up alone in a foreign country so far from her home in the Mekong Delta.[22]

Le Duan's visits to Beijing in 1960 at least dispelled some of the loneliness for Nga. Prior to the Third Party Congress, Le Duan made two trips to China alongside Truong Chinh and Ho Chi Minh. Both times Nga was given permission to stay with her husband, who was lodged at the magnificent Diaoyutai State Guest House (Dieu Ngu Dai), listed during the previous year as one of the Ten Great Buildings in time for the Tenth Anniversary celebrations of the PRC. For the first time in a long while, Nga felt like the first wife as she posed alongside the wives of Chinese leaders such as Zhou Enlai and Liu Shaoqi, at the prodding of Ho Chi Minh. "Come now," Ho said as he pushed a timid Nga to stand closer to her Le Duan for the official photo, "a husband and wife must be as close as birds in the air and branches of a tree [*vo chong phai nhu chim lien canh cay lien canh*]."[23]

On another occasion when Ho persuaded Nga to put away her books and join the delegation for a night out on the town, she donned her Chinese "student uniform," which consisted of a simple floral-print shirt and matching pants. When they arrived at the theater, the Vietnamese delegation was treated to a spectacular show before the performance. After waiting for fifteen minutes, anticipation rose as two young women slowly and dramatically parted red velvet curtains amid great fanfare for Mao Zedong to step through and make his grand entrance. When Nga was introduced to the chairman, she charmed the Chinese leader: "I hear that Chairman Mao has swum across the Yangtze River." To which Mao laughed and responded, "Well, something like that!" When other dignitaries decked out in their formal attire began to take their seats, Nga began to regret her choice of outfit and tried to stay back and blend in as much as she could. Mao, however, insisted that she take a seat in the front row.[24]

The backdrop to the festivities in Beijing, however, was the deepening Sino-Soviet rift. Hoping to gain approval for their southern policy, Le Duan and the delegation must have felt anxious during the visits not only to Beijing but also to Moscow in 1960 and 1961. For his part, Ho Chi Minh tried to use his personal capital to get his Chinese and Soviet comrades to mend their differences. His appeal, however, came to no avail; the depth of the rift doomed the diplomatic missions. Although the situation in the South and the response of the VWP's internal Party mechanisms looked promising for the southern war, VWP leaders still had to tread carefully on the fractious international scene.[25] With Mao's 1960 article in *Renmin ribao* (People's Daily), which denounced Nikita Khrushchev as a revisionist, and Khrushchev's retort at the Bucharest congress, where he denounced Mao as a deviationist, North Vietnam, like other small and middle powers in the communist camp, was sucked into the growing chasm.[26] Hanoi leaders, who desired support from both powers, avoided any issue that would deepen the rift between Moscow and Beijing. Moreover, neither ally wholeheartedly supported the resumption of war. Khrushchev and the CPSU had rejected the notion of "local wars," contending that any conflict between East and West could escalate into nuclear war, and so Moscow stressed its desire for peaceful reunification in Vietnam.[27] Although Mao and the CCP leadership were more receptive to the VWP's Resolution 15, Beijing still advised Hanoi to emphasize political struggle and avoid rapid escalation. A complete break with Moscow was undesirable, and the possibility of rapprochement with the CPSU was discussed by the CCP leadership.[28] Le Duan, then, still had to balance his discussion of Party strategy toward war in the South with socialist transformation in the North.[29]

The issue of support for wars of national liberation, however, became unavoidable in Sino-Soviet polemics after the VWP Congress. At the November 1960 Conference of Eighty-One Communist Parties, Le Duan must have warmly greeted the new Soviet line, which for the first time pledged to support revolutionary struggles in the Third World. Moscow finally read the writing on the wall: if it did not address liberation movements in Asia, Africa, and Latin America, it could lose the entire Third World to the Chinese.[30] In January 1961, Khrushchev specifically referred to South Vietnam as a place where conflict was inevitable, a statement endorsed by the CPSU. In practice, though, Moscow began to disengage from Indochina as Beijing became more involved.[31]

The Laotian crisis underlined the divergence in Soviet and Chinese policies toward the region. The Soviets and the British were cochairs of the International Conference to the Laotian Question, which began on 16 May 1961 in Geneva. Khrushchev, interested in seeking détente with the West, promised to cease Soviet support for the Pathet Lao, to guarantee international communist observation of the cease-fire, and to work toward neutralization at the conference.[32] He allowed his deputy foreign minister, Georgi Pushkin, to reach an agreement with U.S. representative W. Averell Harriman whereby the Soviets would ensure communist compliance while the Americans and British would do the same for their factions in Laos. Beijing, however, refused to make any promises of that nature. The PRC loudly increased its support for the Laotian communists and advocated stepping up the military struggle in order to negotiate from a position of strength.[33] Because North Vietnam was inextricably involved in the Laotian civil war—its supply route to the South ran through southeastern Laos—it found China's policy more appealing in Geneva.[34]

At the same time that the John F. Kennedy administration pursued a negotiated settlement in Laos, the United States toughened its stance against the insurgency in South Vietnam.[35] Moving slowly in the spring of 1961, the charismatic young president, who believed that defeating communist guerrillas in the Third World lay with counterinsurgency methods, increased the number of advisors and sent 400 Green Berets to train South Vietnamese soldiers. However, the American "bureaucratic machinery" could not stop at such limited measures, especially as officials within the administration urged greater American involvement. Kennedy's need to stand firm to the Soviets in the Third World allowed him to portray Ho Chi Minh as a communist first and foremost and present Ngo Dinh Diem's survival as dependent on increased American involvement. After Kennedy sent Deputy National Security Advisor Walt W. Rostow, along with the president's close military adviser, General Maxwell D. Taylor, on a mission to South Vietnam in the fall of 1961, the U.S. role would go from being an advisory one to a "limited partnership."[36]

Kennedy's actions served Le Duan's campaign to galvanize the southern war effort. Increased American involvement in and support for the RVN meant that Hanoi's existing strategy of political struggle and limited armed conflict against Diem's forces would not deliver a communist victory. In late 1961, Le Duan set Hanoi's war machinery into motion as nearly 5,000 PAVN soldiers—namely, the southern regroupees—traveled south along the overland trail as well as by sea to join 25,000 troops of the People's Liberation Army Forces (PLAF) alongside 80,000 communal guerrilla and self-defense fighters to wage war against 280,000 ARVN soldiers advised and facilitated by 3,000 U.S. troops in South Vietnam.[37] Le Duan's Politburo military subcommittee and the Party's CMC responded to Washington's acceleration of its "special war," fought with American money and arms but mostly Vietnamese blood, through a five-year military plan (1961–65). Although the military plan paid lip service to "ensur[ing] socialist construction in the North," it also aimed to "step up the armed struggle in combination with the political struggle" in the South as well as "to afford positive assistance to the Lao revolution."[38] The plan divided the southern war into three zones and assigned different modes of struggle to each zone: military in the mountains; equal parts military and political in the plains; and political in the cities.[39] The armed struggle, which had always been couched in terms of "self-defense," moved on the offensive with the expressed goal of attacking and annihilating the enemy's forces. Finally, the Party leadership projected sending approximately 30,000 to

40,000 PAVN soldiers down the Truong Son trail by 1963.[40] Meanwhile, in the South, the first COSVN conference took place in early October 1961. In addition to COSVN chief Nguyen Van Linh, the other figures elected to positions of leadership included trusted friends and former bodyguards of Le Duan, including Vo Chi Cong and Vo Van Kiet. The conference reaffirmed Hanoi's directives and laid out a ten-point mission for South Vietnam's Party chapters at all levels. The mission's aim was to increase political and military activities to undermine U.S.-Diem policies.[41]

To the dismay of the moderate faction in the VWP, which included even some CEC members such as Duong Bach Mai and Bui Cong Trung and possibly Politburo members such as Ho Chi Minh, Pham Van Dong, and Vo Nguyen Giap, peaceful reunification no longer remained a viable option, and socialist development of the northern economy seemed less urgent.[42] As fate would have it, one midlevel VWP official, Hoang Minh Chinh, left Moscow for Hanoi and walked straight into the maelstrom that would radically change the Party. Born Tran Ngoc Nghiem in 1922 in Le Duc Tho's home province of Nam Dinh, Hoang Minh Chinh joined the Communist Party in Vietnam when he turned nineteen. During the war for decolonization, Chinh led an attack on French planes at Bach Mai airport in Hanoi. His valor led the Party to send him to study in the Soviet Union from 1957 to 1960, precisely the years when Le Duan rose to power and Party policy shifted to support war in the South. When Chinh returned to Hanoi in 1961, he assumed the concurrent posts of head of the Philosophy Department of the State Social Sciences Committee and director of the Nguyen Ai Quoc Party School. In this capacity, the Soviet-trained Chinh emerged as one of the top Party theoreticians. Excited about the bright future that ostensibly lay ahead of him in 1961, Chinh was blissfully unaware that he would subsequently become the fall guy in the debates over Party policy.

Chinh's education and training, which emphasized northern economic development, would inevitably clash with the views held by the ascendant South-first militant faction. In Chinh's view, waging war in the South would neither benefit North Vietnam in the short term nor serve the interests of all of Vietnam in the long term. For moderates like him, peaceful reunification through economic and political competition offered the most viable path. As such, Chinh and other Moscow-trained scholars at the National Committee of the Sciences wanted to apply their Soviet education to facilitate the socialist transformation of the DRV's economy and cooperate with other communist nations to place it in a stronger position vis-à-vis the RVN.[43] War would only sap North Vietnam's resources and threaten its socialist revolution. Chinh watched with growing concern as the Party's attention and greater amounts of North Vietnamese resources flowed southward. In 1962, the Politburo allocated 15 percent of the total state budget to defense, even though agricultural collectivization and industrialization were not proceeding according to plan.[44] In fact, the DRV's 1962 economic plan had to be modified the next year because the original targets could not be met: "The modifications caused some disruptions (e.g., cancellation of industrial investments), and the chaotic conditions already existing in planning further worsened. The DRV was unable to meet either the demands of its own population or those of its socialist commercial partners (it imported more than it could export), and, as a consequence, its debts generally increased. On the other hand, loans given by the 'fraternal' countries for the year 1962 often remained unused."[45] Chinh and other moderates in the Party called for greater economic cooperation with the DRV's allies in order to advance socialist transformation of the northern economy, especially at this crucial juncture in the DRV's Five-Year Plan. They were on the losing side; Le Duan and his militants promoted a model of a self-sufficient North Vietnamese economy that could sustain the liberation struggle in the South.[46] With General Thanh overseeing agricultural affairs, in addition to his portfolio as chief political commissar in the army, Le Duan's trusted general held firm control over domestic policy.[47] Under their leadership, the DRV would become a strong rear base for the southern war effort.

Although these North-first moderates could not unseat Le Duan as first secretary, they could still pose obstacles to his ultimate objective of all-out war in the South. In fact, Le Duan struggled to maintain a balance not only in domestic politics but also in war strategy and foreign relations. With growing American involvement in South Vietnam, it was crucial for the first secretary to apply sufficient military and political pressure to defeat the Ngo Dinh Diem government without provoking full-scale U.S. military intervention. Despite Diem's Strategic Hamlet Program and the alarmingly growing presence of Americans in South Vietnam by early 1962, the Party concluded that the balance of power in the southern countryside remained the same as before 1961.[48] At the same time, Le Duan understood that he needed to maintain a policy of neutrality in the Sino-Soviet rift in order to garner much-needed aid from both allies to support both his southern war and northern development. Beijing's increasingly militant stance toward both "imperialists" and "revisionists" made it more difficult for the North Vietnamese to straddle the ideological fence.[49]

In 1963 the VWP ended its vacillation among promoting political struggle or armed conflict, practicing neutrality in the Sino-Soviet split or siding with the Chinese, and investing in the southern war or northern development as the path to reunification.[50] The year began with a communist battlefield success and ended with the political assassinations of North Vietnam's enemies, signs that pointed toward an imminent victory for Le Duan. On 2 January, the communist leadership interpreted the Battle of Ap Bac as a resounding triumph that proved the inherent weakness of the Saigon regime, since ARVN soldiers, equipped with modern weaponry and a numerical advantage, sustained heavy casualties but failed to inflict much damage on PLAF forces, who escaped largely intact. Party leaders now possessed a clear example of the fallibility of American-style counterinsurgency.[51]

By the summer, however, diplomatic calls to end the fighting presented a major challenge to Le Duan's desire to expand the war. On 29 August 1963, French president Charles de Gaulle called for the "neutralization" of Vietnam along the same model as the Laotian settlement.[52] Although aimed at forcing the Americans to withdraw and allowing the Vietnamese to settle their own affairs, De Gaulle's overture could have presented a thorn in the side of Le Duan and his militant leadership as well. When the Ngo brothers, particularly Diem's brother Nhu, expressed interest in this scheme and initiated talks with the NLF as a means to corner the Americans, who had grown more critical of their administration, they not only signed their own death warrants, but they also may have increased Le Duan's anxiety that the pro-Soviet "North-first" moderates' desired peaceful reunification was a real possibility.[53] Nhu even went as far as meeting with the head of the Polish delegation to the International Control Commission (ICC), Mieczyslaw Maneli, to discuss this scheme. Polish archives reveal that the "Maneli affair" did not constitute a serious attempt to initiate contact between Hanoi and Saigon—it appeared that the Ngo brothers were bluffing and that the Polish government never authorized Maneli to get involved—it nevertheless forced Le Duan to act.[54] In order to squash the moderates in the North and ensure that no rogue NLF representative met with high-level Saigon officials, Le Duan ordered his trusted friend, Pham Hung, to meet with Nhu. Unfortunately, there is no record of that meeting, which supposedly took place in the jungle somewhere between Bien Hoa and Da Lat.[55]

These secret contacts and neutralization schemes were smoke and mirrors, but they were rendered moot with the shooting of the Ngo brothers on 1 November 1963. On 22 November, President Kennedy was assassinated in Dallas. Whether their deaths represented the last chance to thwart war, we will never know definitively.[56] What we do know is that Le Duan was presented with a fork in the road at the end of 1963 similar to the one Kennedy's successor, Lyndon B. Johnson, faced a year later. The VWP first secretary could either negotiate with the new southern regime and consolidate the insurgency's military victories or he could accelerate the war to attempt a total military victory before the Americans, whose presence now numbered 16,000 advisors, could further intervene.[57] With the upcoming Ninth Plenum in late 1963, Le Duan set his sights on the latter option, just as his American counterparts would do during the "long 1964."[58] His success meant that the militant hawks achieved the categorical response in 1963 that they had wanted in 1959: mobilization of the entire country behind the war effort through a marked increase in the rate of infiltration of arms, matériel, and troops to the South.[59]

In order to secure passage of his policies at the plenum, Le Duan dispatched his loyal deputies to lay the groundwork for a major shakedown in Hanoi and to take over the reins of the expanded war in the South. Prior to the Ninth Plenum, the political atmosphere in the DRV capital remained conducive to free exchange over the relative merits of Chinese and Soviet policies and over the correct VWP position within the ideological split.[60] But as Le Duan's carefully appointed deputies brought the repressive machinery of their police state to bear on the DRV citizenry, dissent to war as the path to reunification and any anti-Chinese thought were no longer tolerated. The Ministry of Public Security's Directive No. 21/VP/P4, titled "Intensifying the Struggle against Counterrevolutionary Forces following the Coup against Diem and Nhu," passed on 23 November 1963, elevated threat levels to their highest peak to promote the ministry's movement to "preserve secrecy and defend against traitors."[61] Meanwhile, with the planned escalation of the struggle in the South from armed conflict to "bigger war," Le Duan appointed General Nguyen Chi Thanh as commander of COSVN. From that point onward, Le Duan and his faction simultaneously began to neutralize the moderate opposition in the North and to marginalize the indigenous revolutionary leadership in the South.

On the eve of the Ninth Plenum, when Party leaders made the decisions that would lead to American intervention, the political climate in Hanoi was extremely volatile. Reflecting on those dangerous times, the late Luu Doan Huynh told an interesting story to Vietnam expert Merle Pribbenow during a 2007 interview. Huynh, an old Foreign Ministry hand who later became a respected scholar-diplomat and welcome figure at international academic conferences until his recent death, recalled a 1963 debate on the Sino-Indian War organized by the DRV Foreign Ministry. Challenging a colleague's assertion that India was an expansionist power that had threatened China, Huynh, who had spent several years in New Delhi, intimated that perhaps Beijing was the expansionist power, since it had not respected the border between the two countries. Another colleague took an alternate track to defend Beijing's actions: "If socialist troops seized land that belonged to a capitalist country, that's good. There's no problem with that." Huynh, who remained unconvinced of China's morally superior position in the war, retorted, "No. No matter whether a country is capitalist or socialist, we must still respect the country's borders. We have to respect its territorial integrity." When the debate ended, Huynh recalled that a few of his coworkers took him aside and expressed concern for his welfare. "You had better be careful," they warned Huynh. "You may be disciplined for what you just said, because we are very close to China."[62]

Huynh, like many other midlevel officials, began to fear the consequences of expressing opinions that went against the majority in the days before the Ninth Plenum in December 1963. Huynh escaped punishment for his indiscretion, but the VWP's most outspoken advocate for peaceful coexistence, Hoang Minh Chinh, paid dearly for his views. Convinced that the Party should not devote any more resources to the struggle in the South at the plenum, Hoang Minh Chinh wrote a report for Truong Chinh, who asked him to draft a recommendation for the upcoming plenum on what the correct Party line should be, stating that the VWP should remain neutral between the CPSU and the CCP and adhere to peaceful coexistence, as the French, Czech, and Polish communist parties had done.[63] Truong Chinh had no intention of recommending this report for adoption; he had already decided to align himself with Le Duan and the militants in order to secure his position within the Politburo.[64]

Throwing Hoang Minh Chinh's report in the proverbial dustbin, Le Duan strode confidently into the Ninth Plenum of the CEC in December 1963 and enacted decisions that would elevate the Vietnamese civil war to an international Cold War conflict. At the plenum, Le Duan put forth

a military strategy that he believed would lead communist forces to sure
victory in 1964: the General Offensive and General Uprising (Tong cong
kich, Tong khoi nghia, or GO-GU). In formulating this master plan, the
VWP first secretary drew lessons from modern Vietnamese history. The
1945 August Revolution demonstrated the success of combining a military
offensive in the countryside with a political uprising in the cities, while
the 1954 battle at Dien Bien Phu showcased the immense power of the
masses to overcome military odds. Appropriating and subverting Mao's
military doctrine to suit Vietnamese needs, Le Duan intimated that victory
in the South could be achieved without having to progress through the
three-stage process of war of defense (*phong ngu*) to equilibrium (*cam cu*)
to general counteroffensive (*tong phan cong*), which the Viet Minh followed
to a tee in the previous war. The difficult "equilibrium" stage, which may
have proved Giap's undoing in the French-Indochina War, could be circumvented, Le Duan believed, through his ingenious strategy. Receiving
reports from COSVN throughout the year on the "political strength of the
masses," Le Duan was convinced that the Saigon regime sat on a tinder-
box ready to explode.[65] In the aftermath of the "American coup against
the Diem government," the Politburo ordered COSVN to "incite a mass
movement that will cooperate with our armed forces to conduct insurrections."[66] In the GO-GU scheme, then, the success of dramatic large-scale
attacks by revolutionary forces would spark a mass political uprising, combining the force of the troops with the power of the people to topple the
already fragile Saigon regime. In effect, Le Duan's strategy abandoned the
idea of winning the southern struggle through protracted warfare, particularly in the Mekong Delta where the heart of the insurgency lay. Instead,
it mandated a major buildup of conventional military force in the Central
Highlands and the area northwest of Saigon to bring the war to a speedy
end.[67] Attempting total victory over the RVN before the Americans could
intervene, Le Duan was essentially "going for broke" in 1964.[68]

After Party leaders approved the adoption of his GO-GU at the Ninth
Plenum, Le Duan instructed General Thanh, whose military career in the
North was based on ensuring total loyalty to the Party, to drop all of his
duties in agricultural affairs and pack his bags to take over the war effort
in the South. Meanwhile, the CMC and the Ministry of Defense brought
the DRV military to wartime strength, raising the standing army to approximately 300,000. The PAVN General Staff (Tong Tham muu) oversaw
the first transfer of complete regiments of main force units, including
the 101st, 95th, and 18th Regiments of the 325th Division, to the south-

ern battlefields. These soldiers joined the southern regroupees and high-ranking cadres already sent below the seventeenth parallel, bolstering the PLAF. In addition, weapons and supplies sent down the Ho Chi Minh Trail increased fourfold in 1964, while the navy shipped thousands of weapons and cadres south in late 1963 and throughout 1964. The DRV transformed into a great "rear base." Factories, warehouses, production facilities, repair stations, and hospitals were dedicated to serving the war effort.[69]

In his decision to set the DRV on the path to "bigger war," Le Duan also needed to curry favor with Beijing over Moscow. The VWP circulated two resolutions after the plenum: an official communiqué on 20 January 1964 addressing the "world situation" and the "party's international duties" and a secret resolution calling for the intensification of the armed struggle in the South.[70] Le Duan's speech at the plenum appeared in the February issue of the Party's theoretical journal, *Hoc Tap* (The Study), in February 1964.[71] Although he did not explicitly criticize Khrushchev at the plenum, his intimations concerning the "mistaken nature" of the "defensive posture" of the revisionists left no doubt as to whom the Vietnamese leader was criticizing. The first secretary claimed that those who placed peaceful coexistence with imperialists above all else were hampering the development of the revolution. In contrast, the Vietnamese leader applauded Mao's contribution to the development of Marxist-Leninist theory, in which the Chinese leader emphasized the role of the peasantry, the establishment of rural bases, the encirclement of cities by villages, and protracted armed struggle.[72] Although the VWP was now, if only temporarily, in the Chinese camp, its published resolution steered clear of overtly offending the Soviet Union by not explicitly calling Khrushchev or the CPSU revisionists.[73] With the acceleration and expansion of the war, Le Duan did not want to close off the option of more Soviet aid.

Le Duan and the militant faction of the Party made up for this external ambiguity, however, with internal repression. Hoang Minh Chinh, who was not present at the plenum, would serve as the sacrificial lamb. Since Le Duan, Le Duc Tho, and a now rehabilitated Truong Chinh had resolved to adopt violent Maoist revolutionary methods in order to expand the war in the South, peaceful coexistence became synonymous with revisionism.[74] According to Hoang Minh Chinh decades after the affair, Le Duan was the main architect of the resolution, even though nearly half of the Politburo supported peaceful coexistence.[75] The hardliners silenced the more moderate Politburo members with threats and blackmail, including sidelining President Ho Chi Minh at the Ninth Plenum by invoking

*Hoang Minh Chinh and author*

his past indiscretions. In fact, Le Duan presented Ho with the option of "following the Politburo line or standing aside" at the plenum.[76] Using the "theory of two mistakes"—Ho's wrongful capitulation to the French in 1945 and incorrect acceptance of the terms of the Geneva Accords in 1954—Le Duan was able to shame the aged leader into submission.[77]

Even though they were able to silence some individuals in the Politburo, the hardliners could not prevent less senior CEC members from voicing their opposition at the Ninth Plenum. Bui Cong Trung, vice chair of the National Scientific and Technological Commission, urged greater economic cooperation with other socialist countries and the abandonment of the chimera of a self-sufficient North Vietnamese economy, while former foreign minister Ung Van Khiem and others expressed vehement opposition to the adoption of a pro-Chinese policy.[78] Receiving letters from approximately fifty mid-ranking cadres who had exhorted their superiors to continue following a middle course between China and the Soviet Union, these moderate Committee members still lost the debate at the plenum.[79]

When Hoang Minh Chinh heard that his report had been rejected and labeled revisionist, he noted that the VWP was not only abandoning the principles it adopted at its own Third Party Congress but also going against the majority line adopted at the Conference of Eighty-One Communist Parties in Moscow.[80] The militant faction intended to make its message loud and clear by assembling 400 high- and midlevel cadres in Ba Dinh Square in January 1964 to study Resolution 9. At the gathering, Truong

Chinh announced that given the complicated state of the international communist movement, the most important aspect of the plenum's resolution could not be written down.[81] At the same time, Le Duan's second-in-command, Le Duc Tho, darkly warned the assembled crowd that the Party now had to be wary of "modern revisionists" who threatened the revolutions taking place in the North and the South.[82] One month later, the published resolution elaborated on Tho's comments:

> A small number of cadres have been influenced by modern revisionism. When the *Nhan Van–Giai Pham* clique took advantage of the fact that our party criticized its own shortcomings and errors during the application of the land reforms and the consolidation of its organizations and took advantage of the opposition to the cult of Stalin's personality to engage in sabotaging activities, a number of our cadres and party members sided with it. During the past few years, while a fierce ideological struggle broke out within the international communist movement, a number of cadres supported the erroneous views and stand of the revisionists.

Concerning the liberation struggle of the southern compatriots, Resolution 9 stated that "rightist" elements in the Party "feared that these struggles might be protracted and arduous; they have been afraid of sacrifices. . . . They have adopted a somewhat indifferent attitude."[83] The battle in Hanoi had begun.

### THE REVISIONIST ANTI-PARTY AFFAIR

Le Duc Tho's fearmongering at Ba Dinh Square and the Party's adoption of Resolution 9 unleashed what became known as the Revisionist Anti-Party Affair (Vu xet lai chong Dang). The investigation of supposed "revisionists" was headed by the military-security henchmen of the Ministry of Public Security, the Party's CMC, and the army's GPD. Their investigation included tasking the dreaded military security forces, the Bao Ve, with reviewing and screening all military cadres who were studying and working abroad in order "to gain a solid understanding of their ideological thinking."[84] While the Bao Ve oversaw the criminal targets within the armed forces, the equally feared Cong An under Hoan's Ministry of Public Security investigated civilian cases. Rather than answer to the Ministry of Defense and the government, both security forces answered to the Party

Secretariat.[85] The real masterminds behind the affair, then, were Le Duan and Le Duc Tho.[86]

The campaign to stamp out these "modern revisionists" in 1964 led to the marginalization and house arrests first of Moscow-trained military officials and then of those deemed "pro-Soviet" in the VWP, including high-ranking cadres, overseas students, intelligentsia, and journalists. "In order to limit the influence of erroneous thinking and to counter the efforts of revisionists to recruit or seduce our cadres as much as possible," the official history of the Bao Ve stated on the tumultuous mid-1960s, "we decided to recall a number of military cadres who were studying in the Soviet Union and bring them back home to Vietnam."[87] The interrogation of these Soviet-trained military men allowed the Bao Ve to identify many individuals who subscribed to "international dogmatism" and thus were discharged from the armed forces. While the Bao Ve ousted these dangerous pro-Soviet elements from the military, it also had to circumvent a planned "violent demonstration" by volunteer Chinese soldiers in front of their embassy who were in no doubt caught up in the radical spirit of the Cultural Revolution raging in China. DRV domestic politics began to fracture under the massive weight of the Sino-Soviet split.[88]

With the pressure mounting in Hanoi, some Vietnamese officers opted to stay in Moscow. Following the defection to the Soviet Union of Major General Van Doan, chief editor of the widely read *Quan Doi Nhan Dan* (People's Army Daily, *QDND*), the army's ideological police and security forces launched a full-scale investigation of the newspaper. "Secretive cadres who arrived in cars with their windows obscured," recalled one *QDND* staff member, paid multiple visits to the office and rounded up at least five staff members who not only lost their jobs but were permanently marked as suspect by the Bao Ve.[89]

The campaign to eradicate revisionism soon spread outside of military circles. The vocal CEC moderates who spoke up at the Ninth Plenum began to lose their positions and their prominence within the Party. Bui Cong Trung not only lost his seat on the committee but also was fired from his post as head of the National Committee of Science and Technology. Demotions and firings were not the only repercussions. Duong Bach Mai, a committee member and vice president of the Vietnamese-Soviet Friendship Association who had been an outspoken opponent, died under "mysterious circumstances."[90] Vietnamese students in the Soviet Union and Eastern Europe were called back to attend "reeducation" classes in

1964.[91] Drawing on his experience cracking down on the intelligentsia in the 1950s, To Huu, a Secretariat member and chairman of the Education and Propaganda Department, launched a new campaign against "revisionist" influences in Vietnamese literature. He warned against a "bourgeois humanism" propagated by modern revisionists.[92] Any individual who had any interaction with the socialist diplomatic corps in Hanoi, or who was exposed to peaceful coexistence ideas, was considered suspect and treated as a criminal by the militants in charge.

By the third quarter of 1964, the growing number of suspects prompted the Politburo to create the Special Case Committee (Ban Chuyen an) to carry out a major investigative criminal case. As was common within the Vietnamese communist bureaucracy, a shadowy higher-ranking body acted as "advisor" to the committee, known as the Investigation Guidance Committee (Ban Chi dao). The advisory committee was headed by none other than Le Duc Tho and Tran Quoc Hoan. They, in turn, appointed a subcommittee to help carry out the work and placed their top henchmen, such as Bao Ve director Tran Kinh Chi and other leaders in the Cong An, in positions of power. Tho and Hoan's security apparatus proceeded to "conduct investigations using various measures, including internal reconnaissance [spies/informants], external reconnaissance [physical surveillance], technical reconnaissance, and combined surveillance measures."[93] Working "night and day," the Bao Ve and Cong An doggedly pursued these revisionists criminals who "tried to sabotage the foreign policies of our Party and our Party's policy of fighting the Americans to save our nation, and [who] instead supported a policy of rightest compromise and conciliation."[94] The investigation, which marked the start of Hanoi's total war in the South, would "go public" three years later at the height of America's war in Vietnam.

## LE DUAN'S GAMBIT AND AMERICAN ESCALATION

After five long years away from her children, Nga returned to the DRV during these turbulent days under her husband's reign. She accepted a job on the editorial staff of the *Hai Phong Daily*, which allowed her to raise her three children in the coastal city about sixty-five miles from Hanoi. During her absence from the DRV capital, Le Duan's first wife and his father moved to Hanoi, but relations between the two families worsened despite Nga's distance and took a toll on Le Duan's health. Each time the first secretary paid a visit to his second family in Hai Phong, his "surly" daughter from his first marriage insisted on accompanying him. On an occasion when Nga had to stay overnight in Hanoi for work, she was run out of Le Duan's house by his first family. After a particularly bad visit when Nga stayed with his first family and fell ill afterward, Le Duan wrote her in Hai Phong, "Whenever I see my family behaving like this, I grow despondent. If I didn't have such strong compassion, I'd prefer to live without any of them." Sensing that her husband was losing patience with these domestic spats, Nga offered a way out. "Why don't I return to the South to aid the struggle? Even though we would be separated by greater distance," she wrote, "by working toward the same goal, it would be like we are close together again."[95] Le Duan consented, allowing Nga to return to the region of her birth and to take part in the expanded war effort in the South; however, she would once again have to leave her children to be raised by their father. Nga would keep her husband apprised of the situation in the South.

Although Le Duan was able to resolve his family problems, the brotherhood between Party militants and southern revolutionaries became more complicated. Now that he had a free hand in the North to oversee the escalation of the war, the VWP first secretary needed to ensure that command over the expanded war effort remained with the Party leadership in Hanoi and not with southern revolutionaries in the Mekong Delta. The mechanism through which he sought to exert his control over the southern revolution was his old outfit, COSVN. By 1964, however, Le Duan's protégé, COSVN commander Nguyen Van Linh, was able to make little headway. Southerners resisted many of the directives and orders that Hanoi issued and COSVN tried to enforce, particularly when they sought to reform the southern leadership structure.[96] Local commanders resented the influx of northern officers sent by Hanoi to assume positions of authority in the South, particularly the 1961 "Orient Group," which consisted of 500 high-ranking military and political cadres.[97] Behind the banner of unity lay tensions that had formed early in the struggle for reunification and were never fully resolved, even after war's end.

Colonel-General Tran Van Tra, a military officer-cum-scholar whose postwar writings shed the most light on regional tensions during the war, underscored the difficulties that the Party faced in the South in the early 1960s.[98] Tra, a southerner who oversaw the regrouping of his forces to the North following the 1954 Geneva Accords, remained in the DRV, where he became deputy commander of the PAVN General Staff. For the remainder of the 1950s and early 1960s, Tra spent his time studying in the Soviet Union. When he learned of Resolution 15 in 1959, Tra requested transfer to the South, but physicians deemed him too ill to undertake the journey. In 1963, he finally received the authorization and clean bill of health to return to the region of his birth. With the promulgation of Resolution 9 to launch "bigger war," the Party ordered Tra to establish the headquarters of the PLAF. When he arrived at the B2 Theater, however, he saw that his comrades who had stayed behind resisted northern Party encroachment in their military and political affairs. "Many of our people in South Vietnam," Tra later commented, "continued to cling to the concept of guerrilla warfare and armed insurrection by the civilian populations and said there was no need for a regular army, even though the United States had already started full-scale war."[99] Convinced that his southern comrades were wrong, Tra recommended to COSVN Commander Linh that he build up main force units by recruiting youth primarily from the lower Mekong Delta and sending weapons northwest to the jungle base area where COSVN headquarters was located. Although Linh approved Tra's recommendations in 1963, it was not until 1967 that Tra's southern comrades accepted Hanoi's military doctrine, including a sizeable role for a regular army.[100]

According to southern commanders, Hanoi's order to create division-size units in the South and for certain areas, particularly Military Region 9 (MR 9) in the B2 Theater known as "western Nam Bo," to send both men and matériel northward to the mountain jungle base area of COSVN's Party and military headquarters, were foolhardy moves that caused major logistical problems. Building a regular army and shifting operations away from guerrilla tactics were not the only steps to which some southerners—particularly those from MR 9—objected:

> We had formed main force regiments, the Military Region's powerful fists, with which we had attacked the enemy and scored a series of continuous victories. However, we had not carried out the guidance from the Central Military Party Commission to develop division-size units. At this time, with assistance, manpower, and weapons, provided by the Central level [Hanoi], we were capable of building large forces, and we needed to build such forces. Instead, the Military Region sent one entire regiment, along with thousands of recruits in separate, smaller groups, up to COSVN to serve there. This was a mistake in terms of basic policy. History demonstrated that for every man we sent away, the Central level later had to send back five or six

men as replacements. For this reason we were unable to exploit our opportunity in 1965 to win a great victory.[101]

With the appointment of Nguyen Chi Thanh as COSVN commander, the debate over building division-size COSVN main force units versus relying on local guerrilla operations was laid to rest, even if the conclusions of that debate were not universally accepted. After leaving his post in the Ministry of Agricultural Affairs in Hanoi, General Thanh set out for the South in mid-1964.[102] By October, he reached COSVN headquarters in Tay Ninh.[103] The stern general, who had risen through the Party ranks by policing ideological correctness within the PAVN, immediately set out to squash any southern opposition to Hanoi's policies. One admirer of Thanh's organization and military prowess chalks up the general's success to his patience:

> I remember that in 1964, a COSVN conference to study a resolution from the Center [i.e., Politburo] dragged out for twenty-one days arguing about our strategic formula, especially regarding the building up of our forces. Many attendees suggested that we continue to intensify our guerrilla warfare operations and said we should not concentrate our efforts on building up COSVN main force units. Some of the arguments became rather heated. However, with an attitude of patient persuasion, and by focusing his leadership efforts on building main force units and fighting large-scale battles of annihilation at Binh Gia, Dong Xoai, Dau Tieng, Bau Bang, etc., he gradually was able to build a high level of unanimity from COSVN and the COSVN Military Party Committee down through each individual military region down to each individual province and to successfully build powerful main force "fists" to fight on the battlefields of B2.[104]

When Pham Hung officially joined General Thanh in the South and replaced Linh as deputy chief of COSVN by 1965, this marked the beginning of the end of southern autonomy in military matters, a process that began only haltingly after the 1960 Third Party Congress.[105] Just as General Thanh had ensured that the PAVN answer to the Party in the North as head of the army's General Political Department, he now oversaw the subjugation of the NLF and the PLAF to COSVN.

One of the general's first tasks was to draft a COSVN resolution that reflected Le Duan's strategy outlined at the Ninth Plenum. Revolutionary troops were to intensify the military struggle in order to change the balance of forces in South Vietnam and prepare for a general offensive and uprising that would lead to ultimate victory. Under General Thanh's command, the escalation of the war produced results. In 1964, communist forces were able to expand the liberated zones from the Central Highlands all the way to the Mekong Delta, allowing them to control not only more than half of the total land area but also more than half of the population.[106] With General Thanh neutralizing any southern objection to the Party's go-for-broke military strategy and with Pham Hung ensuring that the general did not play the lone cowboy as commanders were prone to do, Le Duan hoped the combined effect of COSVN's attacks on such places as the Bien Hoa airbase, the American barracks at Pleiku, and the launching of Plan X (Ke hoach X) in the Saigon–Gia Dinh metropolitan area would topple the weak Saigon regime and dissuade the United States from committing its troops to a land war in Asia.[107] Le Duan in particular placed much stock in the Binh Gia Campaign of late 1964 and early 1965, since it constituted the first full-fledged campaign conducted by COSVN main force units. "The liberation war of South Vietnam has progressed by leaps and bounds," Le Duan noted at the time. "After the battle of Ap Bac the enemy knew it would be difficult to defeat us. After the Binh Gia Campaign the enemy realized that he was in the process of being defeated by us."[108]

Within less than a year, however, the military and international forces that had propelled Le Duan's Resolution 9 had become obsolete. Hanoi's gamble failed with American intervention, and the VWP's pro-China tilt ended with the advent of substantial Soviet aid.[109] On 2 August 1964, North Vietnamese patrol boats attacked the U.S. destroyer *Maddox* in the Gulf of Tonkin under the mistaken notion that the destroyer's presence was connected to ongoing South Vietnamese raids on the North under OPLAN-34A. Two days later, the United States falsely claimed more attacks at sea by communist ships, allowing the Johnson administration to launch reprisal air strikes against North Vietnamese installations.[110] These incidents set off the chain of events that brought the Gulf of Tonkin resolution, President Johnson's congressional approval for war. In the aftermath of the 1964 elections and into the beginning of 1965, the American president, a tough Texan with a grand domestic vision, increasingly committed himself to a foreign war, despite public apathy and allied resistance, since he saw his nation's—and his own—credibility on the line in Southeast Asia.[111] The communist attack on the U.S. Army barracks at Pleiku in February 1965, which Johnson's national security advisor, McGeorge Bundy, famously likened to a streetcar (meaning that it was a readily available pretext for escalation), was the unfortunate product of Le Duan's "go-for-broke" strategy.

This new level of American intervention, in turn, brought about a change in relations between Hanoi and its larger allies. Following the VWP's tilt toward China at the Ninth Plenum, Soviet frustration with the DRV led Moscow to decrease economic aid and exports to North Vietnam, while Chinese approval of Hanoi's policies led to an increase in support and the offer to send volunteer troops.[112] After the events of August 1964, however, Soviet policy toward Vietnam began to shift, with the confrontation between the United States and the DRV rendering aid to the fraternal socialist cause mandatory.[113] After the ousting of Khrushchev in October, newly appointed General Secretary Leonid I. Brezhnev made a concerted effort to improve ties with the North Vietnamese, culminating in Soviet premier Alexei Kosygin's visit to Hanoi in early 1965. The first substantial shipments of Soviet aid and military equipment arrived in February and March after Kosygin's visit.[114] In response, VWP leaders ceased their criticism of revisionism and once again practiced neutrality in the Sino-Soviet split.[115] Meanwhile, although Mao encouraged the Vietnamese war with the Americans and placed China on military alert after the Tonkin Gulf incidents, he sought to contain the war in Vietnam and exhorted Hanoi to fight a protracted war against the Americans. Mao signaled to Washington that Beijing would only enter the war if Chinese territory were attacked. The chairman was only willing to fight the Americans down to the last Vietnamese.[116]

Even before March 1965, when the first marines arrived on the beaches of Da Nang in central Vietnam to protect American airbases, Le Duan realized that his GO-GU strategy had failed to topple the Saigon regime and thwart American intervention, but he stubbornly held onto his ambitious military plans. At the Eleventh Plenum in March, the Party leadership resolved to increase the attacks to confront the Americanization of the war, but it remained ambiguous regarding how best to maintain the strategic initiative and achieve victory.[117] Le Duan's letters to General Thanh reveal that the two were in agreement on a communist strategy that would "increase [our] military forces, and match the enemy's growing numbers."[118] After Johnson approved Military Assistance Command, Vietnam (MACV), Commander General William Westmoreland's request for 100,000 U.S. ground troops in July 1965 in what Hanoi called America's "limited" or "localized war [*chien tranh cuc bo*]," General Thanh continued his aggressive strategy by directing large-unit warfare to match American escalation.[119] As the COSVN commander's military doctrine on defeating the Americans played out over loudspeakers in Hanoi, Le Duan supported his general by sending secret letters, urging him to continue "fighting hard."[120] Like Washington, Hanoi hoped for a speedy, military victory.

In the spring of 1965, the VWP enjoyed nationwide support for the anti-American struggle in the DRV. Le Duan must have felt vindicated by the outpouring of support, as men and women signed up to serve and the country prepared for an epic struggle. At the special session of the Tenth Plenum on 25–27 March 1965, Party leaders claimed initial success as the United States was forced to shift gears and land the first marines in Vietnam. Although the war had just begun, the resolution concluded with what would become an important slogan: "Chung ta nhat dinh thang [We will ultimately win]."[121] In April, the Party's Three Readiness Campaign (Ba san sang) called for "readiness to join the army, to partake in battle, to go wherever the fatherland deems necessary."[122] The North Vietnamese Army answered the call; mobilization drives more than doubled the ranks of the PAVN in the first few months of war.

However, the initial flush of war fever soon turned to weariness as casualties mounted under General Westmoreland's search-and-destroy missions and the expanded bombing, which covered more of the North by the end of the year. At no point, however, did Le Duan give up on his dreams of fomenting a general uprising in the cities. Citing the Cuban model, in which Fidel Castro attacked the cities three times before gaining power in Havana, Le Duan urged his forces to keep attacking. "If for some reason the uprisings in the cities run into trouble and we are forced to pull our forces out, that will not matter. That will just be an opportunity for us to practice and to learn lessons from experience in order to prepare to try again for a later date."[123] By the end of 1965, the United States had 184,300 military personnel engaged in the South, making a large attack on urban centers impossible.[124]

The massive onslaught of the U.S. war machine exacted enormous casualties and costs not only on the insurgency in the South but also on economic development in the North. Although U.S. strategists were disappointed that their sustained bombing campaign, which included 25,000 sorties over the DRV by late 1965, had little effect on the North's rate of infiltration, Operation Rolling Thunder did disrupt socialist development.[125] In 1966, Johnson ordered air strikes on industrial and transportation systems as well as petroleum storage facilities.[126] American bombs wreaked

havoc on the North's transportation infrastructure, led to the abandonment of factories and industries not contributing to the war machinery,
and prompted the relocation of the urban population to the countryside.[127]
For the North-first faction, Le Duan's proclamation must have been particularly hard to swallow: "We will emerge from this war not shattered but
stronger and more solid. An army of workers will take form and science,
technology, and engineering will be developed in the rural areas because
of our evacuation policy, for we are not evacuating and dispersing to flee
but in order to produce and to fight the enemy."[128] To the dismay of Party
cadres who had hoped to use their scientific education and expertise to develop the economy in North Vietnam, their efforts would be squandered in
an expensive, drawn-out war in South Vietnam.[129]

In this volatile environment, Le Duan and his faction found themselves
dealing with a two-pronged attack from within the Party. The first prong
came from vocal members of the North-first faction, which had been
stifled but not completely silenced after 1963. It demanded an immediate
negotiated end to the conflict. The Americanization of the war and the end
of Hanoi's China tilt had rejuvenated the moderates in the VWP who had
less to fear from being labeled "pro-Soviet" with the onset of substantial
aid from Moscow. Moreover, their cause had become even more urgent by
mid-decade. Prior to U.S. intervention, the southern struggle only diverted
resources and attention away from socialist construction, but now American bombing of the North threatened to destroy incipient DRV development completely. Using the opportunity of Johnson's thirty-seven-day
bombing pause in December 1965 and January 1966, the "peace" faction
redoubled its call for negotiations, but the militant members of the Politburo easily outmaneuvered them.[130] Nonetheless, their criticisms forced
the militants to respond publicly. In February 1966, Le Duc Tho addressed
the dissension in the Party, which he attributed to "pessimism over the
war in the North, doubts on the war in the South, concern over the international support for the DRV position, and disagreements over balance
between production and fighting."[131] But he portrayed the moderates as
naive, merely a "small number of comrades" who had failed to realize the
"deceptive nature" of the negotiations "plot."[132]

The "naive" North-firsters, however, may have begun to attract the sym-
pathies of higher-ranking Party members who worked behind the scenes
for a political settlement. By 1966–67, the "pronegotiations" faction, some
of whose members may have initially supported military means to victory but now sought to advance a diplomatic struggle to end American

intervention, represented a greater threat to Le Duan's leadership than the more vocal midlevel moderates. East European archives suggest that the desire for negotiations extended to Le Duan's comrades in the Politburo.[133] Although official Vietnamese accounts state that the Hanoi Politburo agreed in 1966 that pursuing negotiations with Washington was fruitless, new evidence reveals that unanimity may not have existed. According to historian James Hershberg's work on "Marigold," a serious peace attempt by the Poles in late 1966 involving Prime Minister Pham Van Dong, reveals that some influential Party leaders sincerely desired direct talks with the Americans and were able to advance their agenda internationally.[134] Dong, who was very popular within the Party and close to Ho Chi Minh, had been associated with diplomacy since the French-Indochina War and continued to take an active role in foreign affairs as prime minister during the anti-American resistance struggle.[135]

Le Duan, who had already marginalized Ho Chi Minh in the Party leadership by invoking his failed negotiation attempts with the French, remained apprehensive of a diplomatic solution and moved to block the powerful "peace" proponents. In other words, he drew a significant lesson from the First Indochina War: diplomacy without military superiority should be avoided at all costs. Particularly because his ambitious war strategy had placed communist forces at a disadvantage militarily in South Vietnam, Le Duan was convinced that peace talks with the Americans in 1965 would be akin to Ho's negotiations with the French in 1945. At the Twelfth Plenum in late 1965, the first secretary weighed in on the debate regarding the strategy of "talking while fighting [*dam va danh*]." He concluded that the necessary conditions were not yet present for the Party to engage in substantive peace talks since communist forces had not yet scored a major victory that would bring the universal support of the "fraternal socialist nations" for negotiations.[136] Treading carefully between China and the Soviet Union, Le Duan endorsed the pro-Chinese international line adopted in Resolution 9 and scolded a "number of comrades [who] have mistakenly concluded that our party's policy has changed," but at the same time, he reiterated Hanoi's neutral stance in the Sino-Soviet split. "The strategic policy of our party differs from the policies of the Soviet Communist Party and the Chinese Communist Party."[137] Internecine Party politics and complex foreign policies threatened to derail Le Duan's war in the South if he could not disentangle the two.

At the same time that the militant leadership encountered criticism from the North-first and pronegotiations factions in the Party, Le Duan and Le Duc Tho identified yet another challenge to the war leadership. General Giap, Le Duan's long-time nemesis, threatened to exploit their vulnerable position. In 1966, General Giap engaged General Thanh in a very public and blunt debate via print and radio in Hanoi over war strategy. It amounted to a show of military machismo between the two generals.[138] Although their feud may not have revealed what was actually at stake and definitely did not leak any state or military secrets, the timing of the "war of words" in 1966 may have placed Giap at the top of Le Duan's blacklist once again. By 1967, during the more secret—and thus very substantive—debates, Le Duan zeroed in on Giap and undercut his position in a way that General Thanh could not do publicly on the airwaves and in print against the hero strategist of Dien Bien Phu.

The importance of the "war of words" between Thanh and Giap in 1966 is heightened by the fact that another Politburo member, the ailing Ho Chi Minh, essentially echoed Giap's public position during the private debates of 1967. In addition, the 1966 public feud invoked the same themes as their high-profile debate a generation earlier during the war against the French. Giap, a proponent of modernizing the PAVN, believed that Thanh's strategy had wasted main force units in suicidal clashes where protracted warfare would have proven more successful, given superior U.S. firepower and mobility.[139] In defense of his tactics, Thanh insisted that Westmoreland's strategy of attrition would ultimately fail for lack of manpower and endurance. The COSVN commander reasoned that if communist forces switched to a defensive strategy, revolutionary morale would slip. Moreover, Thanh claimed, the critics in Hanoi were guilty of devising strategy in the abstract (*truu tuong*) since they were too far from the battlefields of South Vietnam.[140] This was a thinly veiled attack on Giap and his "armchair generals," who were safely ensconced in the North.[141] Invoking his firsthand military experience in the South, Thanh argued that the resistance must include an aggressive military strategy that allowed communist forces to engage the enemy in set-piece battles at will and that had the North's full support.

Although General Thanh "won" this first round of debates with his aggressive strategy for the 1965–66 winter–spring season, mounting casualties forced Le Duan to order the COSVN commander to incorporate aspects of protracted guerrilla warfare.[142] Although the summer of 1966 included raids and harassing tactics in addition to battles using main force units, criticism of General Thanh's refusal to rely predominately on guerrilla forces continued to increase.[143] By the 1966–67 dry season, General

Giap and his supporters dominated the publications and airwaves with pieces extolling the efficacy of the guerrillas, even in urban warfare, over the suicidal attacks of regular units.

In the late spring and early summer of 1967, even the debates that were merely posturing abruptly stopped. The flurry of peace activities and the sobering military stalemate in the South had the effect of bringing the military establishment together.[144] From April to June, Generals Giap and Thanh convened a series of meetings with the senior leadership of the PAVN General Staff and agreed that communist forces should attempt a "decisive victory" while the United States was preparing for the upcoming presidential election and a possible shift in its military strategy.[145] Even though Thanh and Giap agreed that their forces should attempt to break the stalemate, however, they disagreed on the best means to bring about that goal.

As the hardliners in the VWP dealt with domestic challenges, Hanoi's allies exerted unwanted pressure and offered conflicting advice on how the North Vietnamese should conduct the anti-American struggle. At the Twelfth Plenum in late 1965, Le Duan had reminded his comrades that their struggle for reunification would encounter difficulties since it was unfolding at a period of great turmoil within the internationalist movement.[146] Although Kosygin tried to convince Mao in early 1965 to combine their efforts to aid the Vietnamese, Mao rebuffed him, proclaiming that the Sino-Soviet split would last for another 10,000 years.[147] As a result, both key allies held separate leverage in North Vietnam. The PRC controlled transport logistics and stationed 170,000 Chinese troops at its peak in North Vietnam, consisting of engineering and antiaircraft units, while the Soviet Union provided antiaircraft artillery and heavy weaponry as well as approximately 1,165 advisors to operate surface-to-air missiles (SAM).[148] While Beijing pushed Hanoi to wage a Maoist-style conflict with emphasis on protracted, guerrilla war in the countryside and to resist talks with Washington, Moscow urged Hanoi to negotiate and equipped communist forces to fight a conventional war in order to test Soviet military hardware against the Americans.[149] In late 1966, the Party leadership undertook high-level trips to China and the Soviet Union, with Le Duan, General Thanh, and COSVN leader Linh traveling to Beijing in October, and Le Duc Tho and Foreign Minister Nguyen Duy Trinh leaving two months later for Moscow. It was clear to the Hanoi Politburo that its allies were not going to reconcile their divergent positions.[150]

As Soviet military and economic aid continued to increase, with Moscow eventually overtaking Beijing as the largest contributor to the DRV by 1967, China's fears reached a fever pitch. Conversations between Chinese and Vietnamese leaders from 1965 to 1967 reveal warnings and even thinly veiled threats to the Vietnamese regarding the "perfidy" of Soviet aid.[151] At the outset, the PRC was geographically able to control the valve of Soviet support to North Vietnam, but the disruption of transport due to the Cultural Revolution had by late 1966 weakened the already strained transport system.[152] In response to Soviet accusations that the Chinese were hindering Russian arms deliveries, Pham Van Dong went out of his way to "thank China" for its "help in the transit of aid from the Soviet Union and other fraternal East European countries according to schedule."[153]

The Soviets struck back by encouraging Vietnamese leaders to denounce Chinese hegemony and the Cultural Revolution. In addition to criticizing the Chinese, the Soviets also utilized their growing influence to urge the North Vietnamese toward a negotiated settlement.[154] The response from the Chinese was unequivocal. Mao and the CCP tried to foil the Soviet "peace talk plot" at every turn and even tried to enlist fraternal parties to denounce Soviet machinations.[155] In a conversation between the director of the National Reunification Committee, General Nguyen Van Vinh, and Soviet chargé d'affaires P. Privalov, General Vinh reportedly stated that holding talks then "would mean losing everything, and, first of all, friendship with China which is utterly opposed to negotiations."[156] Nevertheless, emboldened by a growing interest within certain segments of the VWP in establishing peace talks, the Soviet embassy in Hanoi advised Moscow to put all of its efforts into promoting Hanoi's newfound willingness to broach a political settlement to end the war.[157] Since the Chinese had been in North Vietnam longer than the Russians, Ambassador Ilya Scherbakov and the Soviet embassy sought to catch up by fostering a network of local contacts and friends in the Vietnamese capital.[158] Sensing the growing divisions in the VWP, Hanoi's allies were trying to use the factionalization to their advantage.

## CONCLUSION

Far from a unified effort, Hanoi's road to war was wracked with dissension and division. Le Duan steamrolled over his adversaries in the North as well as in the South. By strengthening the power of the apparatchiks in the Party leadership in 1960 and creating a veritable police state by 1963, he was able to change the course of VWP policy and, thus, modern Vietnamese history. Rather than continue the policy of paying equal attention to northern economic development and the southern liberation struggle, Le Duan subordinated the former to promote the latter. At the same time, he strengthened COSVN to take over direction of the southern war, displacing the indigenous leadership in the process. Southern revolutionary leaders objected to the Party center's realignment of their leadership structure and Hanoi's orders for "bigger war," but they were powerless to stop Le Duan's designs.

The domestic casualties of Le Duan's policies were numerous. While the socialist revolution in the North was set back indefinitely, southern autonomy over their revolution came to an end. VWP moderates who had hoped to avoid reunification through war lost their jobs and became targets of repression by the police state. Vietnamese men and women of the South who had long fought against the Saigon regime, and of the North who had dutifully answered the call to war, died in droves at the hands of a new foreign enemy. That enemy, equipped with weapons of mass destruction and an ideological resolve, radically altered the terms of the Vietnamese civil war.

The United States, however, was not the only foreign power to intervene in the Vietnamese conflict; the Soviet Union and China became increasingly involved as well. With the Americanization of the Vietnamese war, Sino-Soviet competition for influence over North Vietnam greatly increased. While Moscow hoped to see Soviet technology defeat American arms in Vietnam, Beijing wanted to showcase the power of Mao's military strategy on the Vietnamese battlefield. In addition to military matters, the Soviet Union and China also clashed over aid logistics as well as over the issue of negotiations. While the Soviet Union pushed Hanoi to engage in peace talks to ensure that the conflict not escalate into nuclear war, China advised Hanoi to avoid negotiations at all costs. In other words, both countries saw in the Vietnam War a chance to advance their international stature.

In addition to their direct involvement, the growing hostility between China and the Soviet Union also exacerbated political divisions within North Vietnam. The years between 1960 and 1966 reveal how great-power rivalry complicated North Vietnam's postcolonial development. While VWP officials trained in the Soviet Union advanced the line of peaceful coexistence and of socialist transformation and industrialization of the North as the means to reunification, other Party members influenced by Chinese thought urged for violent confrontation with the West and war for liberation of the South and reunification of the entire country. The divisions allowed leaders in Hanoi to exploit these internationalist debates for domestic gains.

With the stakes raised both domestically and internationally by late 1966, Le Duan and his militant deputies needed to break the will of their domestic opponents, reaffirm their autonomy vis-à-vis their allies, and break the military stalemate in the South. The cacophony of the "dovish" call for talks in the Party, doubts regarding war strategy within the military leadership, Chinese diatribes about Soviet perfidy, and Soviet pressure to negotiate needed to be silenced. Desperate to retain control over their war in the South and their leadership in the North, Le Duan and Le Duc Tho resolved to take extreme measures both militarily and politically. As America's war of attrition reached its second year and the conflict in the South entered its seventh by 1967, Le Duan drew from his revolutionary experiences in the Mekong Delta, where he had learned that in order to wage a successful revolution, one must always be on the offensive.[159]

# part two

# BREAKING THE
# STALEMATE

*These traitors have sowed dissension within the Party and*
*undermined the unity of our army. Their underhanded activities are evident.*
*Their purpose is to organize a faction to oppose our Party, the Workers' Party. . . .*
*They assumed that in the last 20 years our Party lines and policies have been*
*affected by dogmatism and that our plan of opposing the U.S. for*
*national salvation is shortsighted.* —Le Duc Tho[1]

chapter three

# THE BATTLE IN HANOI FOR THE TET OFFENSIVE

On 5 July 1967, one day before he was set to return South, COSVN Commander General Nguyen Chi Thanh had lunch with an ailing Ho Chi Minh. Lingering at his car before leaving, General Thanh worried it would be the last time he would be able to set eyes on the aged leader. Ho was thinking along the same lines. Asking Thanh to convey a message to the southern revolutionaries since he might not live to see victory and reunification, Ho wanted them to know that the South was always in his heart. Moved by Ho's parting words, Thanh made his way to his next appointment with his sometime nemesis, General Vo Nguyen Giap. On that day, however, the two generals seemed to get along well enough as they strolled around beautiful West Lake with their wives and later dined together without their wives at Giap's residence. After a hearty feast with heavy drinking—a proper sendoff meal before returning to the front—Thanh stumbled home around 11:00 P.M. to find his wife and four children awaiting his arrival.

That humid July night was made even more unbearable when an electricity outage hit Thanh's Ly Nam De neighborhood to the west of the Old Quarter in central Hanoi. After putting his kids to bed and telling them to behave in his absence, Thanh took an ice-cold bath to cool off, and around

1:00 A.M., he went to bed. An hour later, he woke his wife, Cuc, telling her that he felt as if water was rushing through his body. When Thanh's bodyguards rushed into the house to take him to the hospital, the proud general refused to be carried out and walked himself to the car. The show of strength belied his condition. General Thanh was pronounced dead of a heart attack at 9:00 A.M. on 6 July 1967 at Military Hospital 108. At the funeral the next day, as Ho Chi Minh moved everyone to tears by bidding an emotional farewell to the general who would be unable to deliver his message to the South, those gathered could not understand how the seemingly healthy general had died so suddenly. To Huu composed a poem that he read at the funeral, capturing the disbelief of those attending the wake with his first line, "Oh Thanh, are you really gone?"[2] Waiting until nightfall, when American bombs stopped falling, Party and military leaders held Thanh's burial service under the cover of darkness at Mai Dich Military Cemetery, but they did not lay to rest their doubts and suspicions.[3]

A few weeks after the general's funeral, Hoang Minh Chinh, the Party theoretician who found himself on the wrong side of the internationalist debate, was arrested by internal security forces. Upset at what he saw as the hijacking of VWP policy by South-first militants since the early 1960s, Chinh had called on North Vietnamese Party leaders to heed Soviet advice and engage in negotiations with the United States to end the destructive war. At the start of the wet season in July 1967, security forces silenced Chinh by arresting him along with several other academics and journalists as typhoon rains—and American bombs—pummeled Hanoi. Although large segments of the Hanoi populace, as with other major cities in North Vietnam, had been evacuated to the countryside as a result of American bombing, enough "treasonous" elements still managed to thrive in the capital to attract the attention of the police state. For the remainder of the year, as the military plans for the 1968 offensive took shape in the corridors of Party power, security forces in Hanoi rushed into people's homes in the dark of the night, kicked down doors, and incarcerated hundreds of supposed traitors.

General Thanh's death and Hoang Minh Chinh's arrest in 1967 set the stage for Hanoi's greatest strategic victory and gravest tactical defeat: the Tet Offensive. Although the 1968 surprise attacks represented a major turning point in the Vietnam War, much of North Vietnam's decision making surrounding the offensive remains unclear. Hanoi's strategy deliberation, which took place from the spring of 1967 to the beginning of 1968, is still shrouded in mystery.[4] In the absence of official documents relating to the Tet Offensive, many debates still abound regarding the origins, the timing of key decisions, and the aims of what the North Vietnamese leadership called the General Offensive and General Uprising (Tong cong kich, Tong khoi nghia, GO-GU). The current Vietnamese and Western historiography offers only limited answers.[5] According to David Elliott, "There is a curious reticence among Party and military historians about the decision-making process that led to the Tet Offensive, even decades after the event."[6]

Contemporaneous and postwar studies published in Vietnam assert that the military losses and political setbacks suffered by the United States and the RVN in 1966 and 1967 presented a key opportunity for the communist forces to undertake a major offensive in 1968.[7] Indeed, Vietnamese scholarship cites the inability of the United States to achieve its projected speedy victory over the insurgency as the *only* factor in Tet decision making.[8] In this view, the failure of Washington's war of attrition[9] and its bombing campaigns over North Vietnam,[10] compounded by the growing political disillusionment with the war in the United States, prompted the leadership of the VWP to shift the "revolution to a new stage, that of decisive victory."[11] With the U.S. presidential elections approaching in 1968, Hanoi made the decision in the spring of 1967 "to quickly prepare on all fronts to seize the opportunity to achieve a large victory and force America to accept a military defeat."[12] According to Vietnamese scholars, then, the Tet Offensive was strictly a result of the Party leadership's astute decision to exploit the favorable conditions, both militarily and politically, arising from the enemy's failing war effort in the South.[13]

Conspicuously absent from the literature is any mention of conditions within the DRV that played a part in the Tet strategy deliberation. To be sure, there were grave domestic and international concerns weighing on the minds of Le Duan's "War Politburo" as it devised its military plans in 1967.[14] After two costly years of war against the world's greatest superpower ground down to a stalemate, internecine Party struggles reached a feverish pitch in Hanoi. Even though Le Duan held firm control over the VWP leadership, his dogged persistence in winning the war militarily through big-unit warfare, rather than initiating negotiations or reverting to protracted guerrilla struggle, brought about challenges to his authority not only from rival Politburo members but also from Hanoi's allies, who coupled much-needed military and economic aid with unwanted and often conflicting advice. This chapter looks at the "incremental, contested, and improvisational" Tet strategy deliberation in 1967, which, like earlier decisions, took into account not only the U.S.-RVN war effort but also VWP politics and the Sino-Soviet split.[15]

In retrospect, the direction of the war could have gone in several directions in 1967; the decision to proceed with the Tet Offensive was far from written in stone at the beginning of the year. In January, the Party leadership adopted a military-political-diplomatic strategy, codified in Resolution 13, that appeared to offer a solution, since it split the difference between various factions.[16] The resolution not only advanced the diplomatic struggle but also called for a "spontaneous uprising in order to win a decisive victory in the shortest possible time."[17] A few days after the passage of the resolution, DRV minister of foreign affairs and Politburo member Nguyen Duy Trinh underlined the diplomatic aspect of the strategy by indicating that if the United States stopped bombing unconditionally, talks could begin.[18] To the dismay of the North-firsters and pronegotiations factions as well as the Soviet allies, Le Duan had secretly decided that peace talks could not begin until communist forces had fulfilled the other aim of Resolution 13: a "decisive victory" on the battlefield. By launching a major military action against the South Vietnamese forces during the upcoming U.S. presidential election year, Le Duan hoped to topple the Saigon regime, forcing any subsequent negotiations with the United States to reflect a victorious DRV over a vanquished RVN. Le Duan only had to look at Ho Chi Minh's marginalized position in the Party leadership since the French-Indochina War to be wary of premature negotiations.

Like most issues concerning military strategy, however, Party and military leaders were divided on how best to achieve a "decisive victory." Mirroring the debates taking place in Washington at the same time, the VWP leadership could not agree on the most effective way to break the stalemate. While Ho Chi Minh, General Giap, and Chinese leaders urged caution by preparing communist forces for a protracted war, Le Duan and his hawks strove for total victory through an ambitious and risky large-scale offensive aimed at the cities and towns of South Vietnam. Not only had the first secretary predicated his power on the southern cause in 1959–60, he became personally identified with the GO-GU strategy used in 1963–64. When his go-for-broke strategy not only failed to bring a clear victory but also triggered American military intervention, Le Duan bided his time until he could redeem his military approach. In 1967, Le Duan again became convinced that a concerted series of attacks on the urban centers of South Vietnam could bring total and complete victory.

In reality, Le Duan's costly strategy for victory was just another "roll of the dice."[19] Nevertheless, he succeeded in getting the Party leadership to approve plans for another GO-GU with the passage of Resolution 14 in January 1968, once again relying on his apparatchiks and utilizing the powers of his police state.[20] The first secretary and his militant faction thus emerged victorious in the struggles that gripped the leadership in 1967; the resultant Tet Offensive plans were a major blow to both domestic opposition and foreign obstruction. In order to understand the evolution of Party policy from Resolution 13 to Resolution 14, it is necessary to understand not only the battle waged in South Vietnam but also the one unfolding on the streets of Hanoi.

The Revisionist Anti-Party Affair—which has also been referred to as the Hoang Minh Chinh Affair, in recognition of its first and most vocal victim—reached its dramatic conclusion three years after it began.[21] Although the affair began as an internal Party debate over the international communist line, it ended as a means for Le Duan to launch the 1968 Tet Offensive without any obstructions. Prior to his incarceration in the summer of 1967, Hoang Minh Chinh had circulated a controversial 200-page report titled *Ve chu nghia giao dieu o Viet Nam* (Dogmatism in Vietnam) that criticized the lack of openness and democracy in the Party.[22] Not only was Chinh suspected of treasonous activities with this publication, he was accused of being part of a larger network of saboteurs including cabinet ministers, high-ranking PAVN officers, CEC members, National Assembly delegates, government leaders, distinguished veterans, intelligentsia, journalists, doctors, and professors who conspired to overthrow the government.[23] As spy fever spiked in the capital, the Secretariat kept secret these arrests as it assessed its Instruction 145 (Chi thi 145), promulgated by the Party in early March, which monitored any espionage activities and their effect in the North.[24]

The purges occurred in three waves. On 27 July, the Bao Ve rounded up Chinh as well as a small group of professors and journalists. In mid-October a second wave of arrests began. The security forces apprehended more Party members, but this time, the arrestees included more high-ranking and noteworthy figures, such as the well-known generals of Vo Nguyen Giap's staff, Le Liem, Deputy Defense Minister Dang Kim Giang,

Deputy Chief of the General Staff Lieutenant-General Nguyen Van Vinh, and the General Staff's military intelligence chief, Senior Colonel Le Trong Nghia, as well as Ho Chi Minh's former secretary, Vu Dinh Huynh. The third and largest wave of incarcerations, which took place on 25 December, involved Party members and non-Party professionals, including Vu Dinh Huynh's son, Vu Thu Hien, who later wrote their memoir based on the injustices they underwent.[25] With the testimony of Vuong Quang Xuan, a captain of the North Vietnamese Army and intelligence agent who defected to the RVN in early 1969, the outlines of the purge became known early on:

> In late 1967 and early 1968 several hundred people, including high-ranking party and government officials, were arrested for being against Lao Dong party war policies and plotting the overthrow of Ho Chi Minh. . . . The party had known of the group for a long time, and Le Duc Tho supposedly had talked with [Hoang Minh] Chinh and other members of the group about their beliefs before they were arrested. . . . A bulletin written by Chinh had been seized and was considered proof of his treason. The bulletin took a position against Resolution Nine which stated that the situation in South Vietnam was now favorable for the use of military means to overthrow the government of South Vietnam, and that the party would not repeat, not use political means only to achieve victory. It asked for the full support of all North Vietnamese cadres and people in this effort. . . . Chinh's bulletin opposed North Vietnamese military participation in the liberation of South Vietnam.[26]

The scope of the perceived threat to national security and the shift from a secret investigation begun in 1963 to an overt one by 1967 resulted in the mobilization of greater manpower for Le Duc Tho and Tran Quoc Hoan.[27] In addition to the various intelligence subcommittees and the personnel and staff under their direction since 1963, Le Duan's security apparatus and police state burst at their seams by 1967 with additional cadres drawn from regional committees, the navy, as well as the Communications and Engineering Departments.[28] In July, Minister Hoan gave a speech on how the Cong An were able to escape the pernicious influence of modern revisionism that had infected other cadres.[29] On 30 October, the Standing Committee of the National Assembly presided over by Truong Chinh promulgated a decree setting forth the terms of punishment for treason, espionage, and transmitting state secrets. By the end of the year, Le Duc Tho circulated two reports that warned of a plot in their midst. Although the suspects arrested were not formally accused until 1972,[30] Tho wrote the following report in late 1967:

> These traitors have sowed dissension within the Party and under-mined the unity of our army. Their underhanded activities are evi-dent. Their purpose is to organize a faction to oppose our Party, the Workers' Party. They have deliberately made inaccurate analyses, partial critiques, and mischievous evaluations in the Politburo with the intention of fomenting friction between Party leaders. They have gained the allegiance of a number of high-ranking cadres of various ministries, even those of a foreign country. They have sought meth-ods of stealing our confidential documents. They have taken advan-tage of our cadre's carelessness to collect classified information on our military plans, economic projects, and on foreign aid provided to us by friendly countries for our national salvation against the U.S. aggression. They have tried to hinder our counterattack of the enemy. They have tried to prevent COSVN from implementing Resolution 9. They assumed that in the last 20 years of our Party lines and policies have been affected by dogmatism and that our plan of opposing the U.S. for national salvation is shortsighted.[31]

The alleged traitors were imprisoned in central Hanoi at Hoa Lo, known to Americans as the "Hanoi Hilton."[32]

It is unlikely that these individuals posed an actual threat to national security. Although the Revisionist Anti-Party Affair had its origins in the controversial 1963 plenum and would have legal and political repercus-sions for the DRV beyond 1968 and even 1975, the immediate rationale for the arrests in 1967 rested squarely on the Politburo's choice of tactics and strategy for the Tet Offensive.[33] Nothing else would have prompted a purge of such proportions. By this point, theoretical arguments couched in seemingly dense but innocuous Marxist-Leninist terms actually sig-nified intense debates regarding the direction of the war in the South.[34] Under Le Duan's leadership, the decision to forgo substantive negotiations and to pursue a "decisive" military victory by launching large-scale attacks on the cities and towns across South Vietnam in pursuit of a GO-GU was highly controversial and hotly contested within the VWP. By integrating the timetable regarding decision making from above and the arrests on the ground, the pieces of the Tet puzzle begin to fall into place, revealing that as plans for the military offensive grew more ambitious, so too did the scope of the arrests.

As was the case when Le Duan led the Party to elevate the political struggle to armed conflict in 1959 and to go for broke in 1963, his ability to promote the adoption of the GO-GU strategy in 1967 must be situated at the intersection of Hanoi's foreign and domestic policies and be seen as a response to the military picture in South Vietnam or the political situation in the United States. In doing so, the Revisionist Anti-Party Affair and the Tet decision-making process can be understood on three interrelated levels: (1) the DRV's policy of equilibrium in the Sino-Soviet split; (2) personal power struggles in the Hanoi Politburo; and (3) political repression in the VWP. Drawing on their survivalist modes of leadership, garnered first during their experiences in the Mekong Delta battling multiple rival factions in the 1940s and 1950s and then strengthened during their steady climb to power in the Red River Delta in the 1960s, Le Duan and Le Duc Tho resorted to intrigue, double-dealing, and intimidation so that "darkness descended in midday" for hundreds of Hanoians in 1967.[35]

## SIGNALING THE ALLIES

For three years, Mao Zedong, Zhou Enlai, and other leaders in Beijing watched with consternation as North Vietnamese leaders seemingly moved away from the Chinese sphere of influence and into the Soviet one.[36] Recalling the early days of the French-Indochina War and even the beginning of Vietnam's war for reunification, when Moscow could not be bothered with the events in Indochina, Chinese leaders could not understand how the North Vietnamese were unable to see through the present Soviet ruse. According to Beijing, support from the revisionist Soviet regime always came with strings attached. Chinese leaders were convinced that Leonid Brezhnev, Alexei Kosygin, Nikolai Podgorny, and their cronies in the CPSU would sell out the Vietnamese revolution to the Americans when this served Soviet interests.

Although Moscow's military and economic aid to the DRV appeared in 1967 to be on the verge of eclipsing China's, Beijing leaders could take solace in two reasons the North Vietnamese remained beholden to the PRC: not only did Beijing control transport logistics, but there were also hundreds of thousands of Chinese troops in North Vietnam, even if they were only set to work on building roads and infrastructure.[37] Mao and other Chinese leaders felt they could make a few demands of their Vietnamese allies. They wanted Hanoi to reject both Soviet advice to engage in negotiations and Russian-style warfare as well as remain skeptical of all forms of Moscow's support. Beijing hoped instead to see Vietnamese leaders apply Chinese revolutionary strategy and prove to the world that Mao, rather than Brezhnev, could lead internationalist forces to defeat the world's leading neoimperalist power. To their dismay, however, the North Vietnamese not only gladly accepted Soviet aid and training as well as offers of technical assistance but also seemed to be heeding Soviet advice and mimicking Soviet warfare.

Le Duan and his colleagues in the VWP Politburo were all too familiar with Beijing's anti-Soviet thinking, and they tried their best to allay Chinese fears of a supposed VWP tilt toward the CPSU. In early April 1967, General Giap and Prime Minister Dong traveled to Beijing, where they praised Chinese military influence on Vietnam's revolutionary struggle. "Some of the strategies we are adopting on the battlefield in South Vietnam," Dong informed Zhou Enlai, "follow what you suggested to us in the past."[38] At a subsequent meeting, Giap said to Mao Zedong, "In our fighting against the Americans, we always remember your words: try to preserve and develop our forces, steadfastly advancing forward." After lavishing their hosts with praise, Dong and Giap informed their allies that Party and military leaders in North Vietnam had agreed to introduce "new" elements into their "strategic principle" for 1968.[39]

Despite such reassurances, however, Mao feared that the "new" elements in Vietnamese military planning would mean adopting a Soviet model of warfare, which included large-scale offensives aimed at urban centers in an attempt to win a quick victory. Such a strategy would increase North Vietnamese dependence on Russian aid and weaponry, and perhaps even push Hanoi further into the Soviet orbit. "We have a saying," Mao stated in his characteristically allegorical manner, "'If you preserve the mountain green, you will never have to worry about firewood.' The U.S. is afraid of your tactics. They wish that you would order your regular forces to fight, so they can destroy your main forces. But you were not deceived. Fighting a war of attrition is like having meals: [it is best] not to have too big a bite."[40] Although General Giap inwardly agreed with the Chinese leader regarding the necessity to wage protracted war at this juncture in the war, he was powerless to stop Le Duan and General Thanh from taking a big "bite."

Although the April 1967 meetings reveal that Beijing approved of Viet-

namese plans to escalate the war, Mao was right to be wary of North Vietnamese military aims for 1968. When the delegation returned to Hanoi in
the late spring, planning for the Tet Offensive began to take the form of
an ambitious nationwide attack on major cities and provincial towns—a
move the Chinese would later consider premature and a reflection of the
Soviet proclivity for urban warfare. In May and June, the VWP leadership
essentially rejected Mao's doctrine when it assessed the military picture
for 1968 and concluded that guerrilla war alone could no longer remain
the guiding principle for the resistance forces in the South.[41]

Although the Chinese were concerned about the rising Soviet influence
on Vietnamese military strategy, they were relieved that the Hanoi Politburo still rejected Soviet advice to enter negotiations. Arriving later in the
game than the Chinese and possessing no clear-cut allies in the Politburo,
the Soviet embassy in Hanoi under Ambassador Ilya Scherbakov tried to
cultivate contacts and allies among VWP officials who had studied in Moscow in order to increase the Soviet Union's influence in North Vietnam and
promote its negotiations agenda.[42] The culmination of Moscow's meddling occurred in late June when Premier Kosygin met President Johnson
in Glassboro, New Jersey, with private reassurance from Prime Minister
Pham Van Dong that if the United States stopped bombing, negotiations
could begin.[43] Between Dong's private reassurance and Foreign Minister
Trinh's public statement earlier in the year, Ambassador Scherbakov and
his bosses in Moscow believed that their influence had now reached beyond midlevel VWP officials all the way up to the Vietnamese Politburo.

As the Soviets increased their efforts to initiate peace talks between
Washington and Hanoi, thereby bolstering the moderates in the Party as
well as the Politburo, Le Duan and his faction launched a preemptive strike
against these forces and their Soviet benefactors. In doing so, Le Duan
sent a thinly veiled message to Moscow: the DRV would not be pressured
into negotiations. Essentially, the Revisionist Anti-Party Affair signaled to
the Soviet embassy in Hanoi that the arrests of its "eyes and ears" in the
VWP also meant the end of Moscow's hopes to push forward its agenda.[44]
Charged with "gain[ing] the allegiance of a number of high-ranking cadres
of various ministries, even those of a foreign country," and then passing on
state secrets and classified information, the arrestees were basically guilty
only of maintaining close ties with the Soviet Union. The Soviet embassy
in Hanoi understood the message loud and clear: exasperated reports to
Moscow indicated that North Vietnamese leaders were no longer interested in pursuing negotiations.[45]

The arrests of pro-Soviet officials who had "assumed that in the last 20 years [the] Party lines and policies have been affected by dogmatism" were intended as much to placate the Chinese as to deter the Soviets.[46] These so-called traitors had passed information to the Soviet embassy in Hanoi and abroad regarding the extent of *Chinese* activity and aid to the DRV.[47] Their arrests signaled to Beijing that the VWP would not fall into the hands of a pro-Moscow group. The victims of the 1967 purge were sacrificed in order to maintain North Vietnam's policy of neutrality and equilibrium in the Sino-Soviet split. As Hanoi's juggling act became trickier to maintain, the arrests sent a clear message to the allies without posing substantial risks to North Vietnam's diplomatic relations.

## POWER STRUGGLES IN THE POLITBURO

The arrests were also meant as unveiled threats to high-ranking members of the Politburo who had dared to challenge Le Duan's authority. By 1967, the first secretary identified multiple figures in the Party and military leadership who stood in the way of his goal of redeeming the GO-GU strategy. By arresting the loyal subordinates of their rivals, Le Duan and Le Duc Tho were able to undermine the positions of their detractors without disturbing the illusion of a unified leadership in Hanoi necessary to guide communist forces to victory.

During his colonial education, Le Duan must have stumbled across Georges Clemenceau's famous adage that war is too serious a matter to entrust to military men. Although it is difficult to assess the nature of civil-military relations in the DRV during the Vietnam War, there is tentative evidence that tension existed between Party leaders and the military brass. As high-profile commanders who possessed the allegiance of men both north and south of the seventeenth parallel, Nguyen Chi Thanh and Vo Nguyen Giap were extremely popular generals. Their popularity may have been a double-edged sword, since it inspired the jealousy of the first secretary. Although there is no proof that Le Duan had anything to do with the mysterious death of General Thanh—other than a postwar allegation by the defector and Politburo member Hoang Van Hoan in his memoirs—the circumstances surrounding Thanh's death on 6 July 1967 have produced much speculation.[48] At the time, Western observers believed that he had been killed in B-52 attacks.[49] The main source of Hanoi gossip after the war, Bui Tin, claims that General Thanh died the day before he was to return to the South via the Ho Chi Minh Trail after suffering a heart attack.[50]

According to Thanh's widow, Nguyen Thi Cuc, her husband became inexplicably ill after a full day of meetings and sumptuous meals, though she abstained from alleging poisoning.[51]

Whether due to natural or other causes, Thanh's death took place during an extremely important juncture in the planning for the 1968 offensive. Two months before, Thanh had convened COSVN's Fifth Plenum and confirmed his long-held position in various speeches that communist forces would maintain the strategic initiative by attacking enemy forces head on, rather than by reverting to defensive guerrilla war, and thus would score a decisive victory in 1968. He did not, however, elaborate a specific military strategy.[52] In June, Thanh's comrades in the Politburo recalled him to Hanoi in order to report on the military situation in the South. After three long years on the war front, General Thanh left the South on what would be his last journey. While in Hanoi, he ordered the Combat Operations Department (Cuc Tac chien) to "continue, in a systematic matter, to brainstorm the strategic direction and objectives that would lead to a decisive victory."[53] During the course of his stay in the DRV capital, General Thanh heard disparate viewpoints from members of the Politburo subcommittee for military affairs, the Party's CMC, and the PAVN General Staff. While some members of the Politburo were dubious that communist forces could achieve a decisive victory against American forces in 1968 through large-scale battles, Le Duan adopted a more militant position:

> It is impossible for the United States to maintain its current troop level, to expand the war, or to drag it out. The Americans have no option other than employing greater military strength. As such, we have to counter their strategy by ratcheting up our war effort to a new level—one that the Americans will not be able to endure, leading to their military defeat and their political isolation. If we can accomplish this, the Americans will surely have to withdraw from South Vietnam. Thus, I say we increase our military attacks so we can then seize the initiative to advance the diplomatic struggle in order to use world public opinion against the imperialist Americans and their bellicose puppets.[54]

In other words, Le Duan believed he could find America's breaking point. Resurrecting his bold strategy that had failed to win the war in 1964, Le Duan was convinced that the GO-GU would achieve that sought-after decisive victory in 1968. The Da Nang uprisings in 1966 offered Le Duan indisputable proof that the cities and towns were tinderboxes for general insurrection, which a spectacular military victory could spark.[55] Although the majority of the military leadership, led by General Giap, believed that revolutionary forces were not yet ready to launch large-scale attacks aimed at the cities and towns of South Vietnam, Le Duan was willing to take the chance in 1968. Whether General Thanh, who had staked his military credentials on big-unit warfare in order to maintain the initiative and uphold troop morale, disagreed with Le Duan, we will never know. Most likely he did not, since General Thanh was a hawk who had predilection for sending troops into battle and took pleasure in proving General Giap wrong.[56]

After weeks of contentious debate over military strategy, General Thanh scheduled his return to the front lines. Although Thanh's death the day before he was set to leave was a clear loss for the militants, Le Duan may have concluded that the peasant general had already served his purpose by maintaining the strategic initiative in the South and thwarting Giap in the North. Had he lived, Thanh could have either blocked Le Duan's military strategy for 1968, if they had disagreed, or threatened to eclipse the first secretary if the upcoming 1968 offensive proved successful. Despite the rising death toll and the public debate with Giap, Thanh's popularity rose in the South, possibly prompting comparisons in Le Duan's mind with the legendary Nguyen Binh of the French-Indochina War. Regardless of the cause of Thanh's death, Le Duan may have stood to gain from his premature demise during the planning stages for 1968.

Le Duan's personal animosity toward Vo Nguyen Giap is slightly better documented. The "comrades Le" continued to sideline Giap and saw to it that the general wielded significantly less power in the struggle against imperial America than he had in the war against colonial France.[57] With General Thanh's death, their main counterweight to Giap was gone, prompting the impetus for a preemptive strike against the popular general, who had objected to Le Duan's urban-centered plan for the upcoming offensive. Although Giap had agreed with the hawks that revolutionary forces had to strive for some sort of "decisive victory" in 1968, the general expressed doubts that any offensive should begin with the cities and towns of South Vietnam. At the 14–16 June 1966 meeting of the Politburo subcommittee for military affairs and the Party's CMC, at which Le Duan, Le Duc Tho, Pham Hung, and even General Thanh were present, Giap had agreed with his comrades that revolutionary forces must fight large-scale battles, but, he warned, "it was necessary to build up to attack on the cities."[58] "By mid-1967, although a number of revolutionary bases, commando and crack troop units had been deployed in cities and suburbs," one Vietnamese historian claimed, "no one could imagine a general offensive all over South Vietnam against the cities and towns, particularly when the U.S. war efforts were reaching a climax."[59]

With Thanh dead and Giap in disagreement, Le Duan needed a more pliant general to implement his risky military strategy. Vietnam expert Merle Pribbenow portrays the genesis of the 1968 Tet Offensive as a Faustian bargain between Le Duan and Senior General Van Tien Dung. Dung was born in 1917 to a middle peasant family from Ha Tay province, just south of Hanoi. Unlike most of his comrades in the senior leadership, Dung was actually a proletarian. As a young worker in the Cu Chung textile mills, Dung became openly involved in revolutionary activities, joining the ICP during the Popular Front period in the fall of 1937. Arrested on the eve of the Second World War, Dung escaped from a colonial prison a few years later and quickly climbed the communist ranks in Tonkin. During the French Indochina War, Dung became head of the Military Political Department, a precursor to Thanh's army watchdog outfit, the GPD, particularly for the Viet Bac region, which began to see most of the action after 1950. Friction between Dung and Giap might have arisen during this period, since Dung was in charge of policing Giap's troops, and probably came to the fore when Dung replaced Giap's friend Hoang Van Thai as PAVN chief of staff a little while later. Nonetheless, in 1954, the intellectual and the worker had to put their differences aside to carry out the siege at Dien Bien Phu. At the start of the southern war, Dung was promoted to senior general, elected to the CEC and to the Politburo as an alternate member, and served under Giap on the National Defense Council after the 1960 Third Party Congress.[60]

Seven years later, however, Dung seized an opportunity to advance his career after Thanh's death and at his boss's expense. Playing on Le Duan's desire to promote his brand of military offensive, Dung requested a private meeting with Le Duan behind General Giap's back. At their meeting, the ambitious Dung expressed support for the first secretary's position that revolutionary forces had no choice but to foment a general uprising in the towns and cities of South Vietnam even though communist soldiers did not possess a clear military advantage over enemy troops in urban centers. Although he more likely agreed with his boss, Giap, and fellow military commanders that communist forces were not yet ready to lead the masses to the final stage of people's war and to ultimate victory, Dung was ready to put his own career ahead of the revolution. By ingratiating himself to Le Duan and criticizing the military decision making under the direction

*Ho Chi Minh (left) and Vo Nguyen Giap (right) (Anonymous Collection [left] and Douglas Pike Photograph Collection [right], Vietnam Center and Archive, Texas Tech University)*

of Giap, Dung shrewdly positioned himself as a replacement for Thanh. Le Duan, recognizing that he now possessed an ambitious new counter-weight to Giap willing to do his bidding, promoted Senior General Dung to oversee the new and improved plans for the 1968 offensive.[61]

Not only was Giap's fate sealed during the private meeting between Le Duan and Van Tien Dung, but so too were the plans for what would become the Tet Offensive. On 18–19 July, nearly two weeks after Thanh's death, Le Duan and Dung unveiled their controversial strategy at a high-level meet-ing including Politburo members and the military brass. While main force units tied down American troops away from urban centers, they advocated, large-scale attacks on the cities and towns of South Vietnam would incite a mass political insurrection to topple the puppet regime in Saigon. Their strategy met immediate resistance from the assembled group of Party and military leaders, the most powerful of which came from none other than Ho Chi Minh. In his final attempt to exert authority over the revolution that he only symbolically led, Ho went on the attack. First, the aged leader questioned the "subjectivity" of Le Duan and Dung's plans, intimating that perhaps the first secretary and his senior general were being unreal-istic and overly optimistic in their goals for the upcoming offensive. The chairman then urged caution for the upcoming offensive. Although the Party and military were in agreement that the forces could *attempt* a decisive victory, they must prepare for a protracted war. As such, Ho resurrected General Giap's position, the "need to expand guerrilla warfare" over sole reliance on big-unit warfare.[62]

Despite Ho's sensible advice, Le Duan brushed aside this challenge to his command by ordering Dung to continue drafting the military plans based on large-scale attacks on urban centers. While Dung worked out the military details in Hanoi, Le Duan promoted Pham Hung to replace Thanh as head of COSVN. In August, Hung successfully completed what would have been Thanh's journey to the South, carrying not only the outlines of Le Duan's plans for an urban-centered offensive, but also the mandate that southern revolutionaries carry them out without question.[63] When it became clear that the upcoming 1968 offensive clearly bore Le Duan's GO-GU imprint, Giap left for Eastern Europe and did not return until well into 1968.[64] The defeated Ho Chi Minh followed suit and left for Beijing to convalesce, though he apparently never fully recovered from what had ailed him in 1967.

### SPY FEVER IN THE POLICE STATE

Although the purge indirectly served international purposes and became a proxy battle for Politburo members, it held very real ramifications for political life in Hanoi. While moderate Politburo leaders fled North Vietnam, Le Duan and Le Duc Tho removed any vestiges of Ho and Giap's influence in the lower rungs of the Party and thus paved the way for the adoption of the Tet Offensive strategy. Soon after the pivotal mid-July meeting, Le Duan and Tho applied their brand of ruthless revolution, culled from their dangerous days in the Mekong Delta, to the war-weary and bomb-saturated Red River Delta. The Revisionist Anti-Party Affair, begun three years earlier at the controversial 1963 plenum, reached its dramatic climax with the arrest of its first victim, Hoang Minh Chinh, on 25 July 1967, and ended only with the passage of Resolution 14 giving the go-ahead for the Tet Offensive.[65]

With the escalation of the air war over North Vietnam, Le Duan's police state placed the nation on high alert and declared a state of emergency. Minister of Public Security Hoan's tireless speeches and promulgations whipped up paranoia, creating spy fever as bombs rained down on the North. Hoan warned the ministry's staff and the security forces to be on guard against neoimperialist use of intelligence and espionage operations to instigate coups or incite "peaceful evolution." The United States conducted nefarious activities in other sovereign countries by unleashing the CIA even in ostensibly pro-American countries such as South Vietnam. At the start of Hanoi's "bigger war" in 1963, Hoan claimed, the United States sent individual spies into North Vietnam, but by the latter half of the decade it had infiltrated the DRV with commando teams tasked with carrying out acts of sabotage aimed at paralyzing logistics and fomenting insurrection. After the start of Rolling Thunder, the minister said, America redoubled its espionage activities and concentrated on four areas: (1) collection of strategic and tactical intelligence in all sectors of North Vietnamese life; (2) assassination and kidnapping of cadres and civilians to gather intelligence; (3) recruitment of agents to support operations; and (4) psychological warfare aimed at sowing fear and confusion within the DRV.[66]

Although the DRV foiled most of the South Vietnamese and American plots by 1967, Hoan advocated constant vigilance since the enemy proved very wily and adept. To be sure, the enemy's sources for information were diverse. The United States was able to garner intelligence through "careless revelation of state secrets in our own propaganda, press, and radio broadcasts," and at times through superior technology, including reconnaissance aircraft, radar, and electronic intelligence. Moreover, "delegations from capitalist and imperialist" countries, nations that had embassies, consulates, or trade missions in Hanoi, and regional powers such as Laos and Thailand, all supplied information to Washington. For example, Hoan claimed, de Gaulle's neutralization schemes were plots to buffer America's defeats in South Vietnam, while Japanese spies and British imperialists used their commercial ties and diplomatic missions to carry out long-term espionage operations for the Americans.[67]

However, Hoan warned, security forces had to be most wary of "spies hiding inside North Vietnam," who came from disaffected sectors of society. The minister laid bare these reactionary elements to his security forces, which now possessed the authority to trample North Vietnamese civil rights with impunity: "Currently the enemy still has a number of refuges, places where he can hide to carry out his activities in our society in North Vietnam. These refuges are reactionary elements utilizing the cloak of the Catholic religion; reactionary elements among former members of the puppet government and army; former members of ethnic minority bandit groups and former members of reactionary parties; the former upper classes in ethnic minority areas; former members of the exploitative classes; and those who are dissatisfied with society."[68]

Since these elements were either spies directed by the enemy or re-actionaries who wanted to establish contact with the enemy, Hoan claimed that "our fight against imperialist spies is intimately linked with the fight against reactionary elements inside our country, and vice versa."[69] In other words, there was absolutely no room for dissent within the DRV; opposition was either proof of espionage or reactionary. Hoan instructed his security forces to first establish the origins of individuals suspected of being spies or reactionaries (i.e., whether they were legally or illegally residing in North Vietnam) and then to detect contradictions in the sus-pects' lifestyles (when their spying ran counter to their professional cover). Spies and reactionaries were never capable of maintaining the ruse, Hoan observed, and identifying their inability to function in their cover profes-sions—even more than deciphering their origins—was the key to exposing traitors.

Despite being adept at their alleged cover jobs as successful Party cadres, military officers, lawyers, doctors, and teachers, the suspects of the Revisionist Anti-Party Affair were rounded up by Hoan's security forces and summarily labeled as traitors. In reality, Chinh and the other Party officials arrested after publicly opposing the war in the South and decrying the mounting repression in the North posed no threat to national security. Instead, their arrests demonstrated that Le Duan's Politburo would not tolerate any criticism of the southern struggle and the northern revolution and that it would go to any lengths to prevent the leak of war plans or state secrets to allied powers. With the strategy deliberation for the Tet Offen-sive under way, Le Duan could not allow Chinh and his publication of *Dogmatism in Vietnam* to go unpunished and his connections with Soviet officials to go unchecked. Since Chinh and other pro-Soviet Party officials had criticized the Party leadership's refusal to end the costly southern war through negotiations, their opposition to the upcoming 1968 offensive would be even more intense. Based on their challenge to Resolution 9 in 1963, which confirmed Hanoi's tilt toward Beijing and laid out the GO-GU plans for 1964, these "North-first" moderates would surely object to the resurrection of the same risky strategy for 1968, one that ran counter not only to Soviet advice to seek negotiations and to de-escalate the fighting but also to the VWP's own Resolution 13 in 1967 that ostensibly advanced the diplomatic struggle.[70] Moreover, the architects of the purge incarcer-ated the vocal antiwar members of the Party in July because they wanted to protect the element of surprise necessary for the Tet Offensive to suc-ceed in the midst of the spy fever that gripped Hanoi.[71]

In mid-October, the second wave of arrests began—this time of Party members and military officials more high-ranking than those caught in the July purge—as Le Duan and Van Tien Dung continued to forge ahead with their military plans for the 1968 offensive. Including elements of Thanh's favored big-unit warfare along Khe Sanh, in the mountains of the extreme northwestern corner of South Vietnam and along the DMZ, the Duan-Dung amendments included "big battle" strikes against the cities and provincial towns of South Vietnam to incite a general insurrection.[72] Shortly after the Politburo reviewed the revised plans from 20 to 24 October, the Bao Ve arrested Giap's loyal staff from the Dien Bien Phu campaign, including Lieutenant-General Nguyen Van Vinh and Senior Colonel Le Trong Nghia, who had been active in drafting the 1968 offensive as members of the General Staff and who had briefed the Politburo members at the October meeting. Although the official histories state that Vinh and Nghia presented favorable reports on the likelihood that large-scale attacks would incite a popular insurrection in the cities, the two officers disappear entirely from the historical record after the Politburo meeting, only to appear in the 1990s on the list of arrestees in 1967.[73]

These October arrestees who had served at Giap's side claimed that security officials under the control of Le Duan, Le Duc Tho, and Tran Quoc Hoan had hoped to implicate Giap in the Revisionist Anti-Party Affair. When these top military men arrived at Hoa Lo prison, the Bao Ve began to interrogate even Hoang Minh Chinh and the earlier July arrestees regarding any interactions they may have had with the famous general.[74]

Neither Giap nor Ho were able to fly back to Hanoi to spring their subordinates and staff from jail.[75] They thus also forewent an opportunity to voice their opposition to the direction of the Duan-Dung plan during the October Politburo meeting. Perhaps Giap and Ho had finally given up; not only had their objections proven unable to alter Le Duan's designs, but their continued opposition also kicked the first secretary's police state into full gear. In fact, the debate surrounding military planning had become so contentious that Le Duan refrained from attending the October meeting as well, leaving Truong Chinh, who had begun to take an avid interest in stamping out the Revisionist Anti-Party Affair, to preside over the Politburo's deliberations. Even though the members present postponed the approval of the "general uprising" section of the upcoming offensive, citing the absence of key leaders, Le Duan was confident that he had already won the battle for the Tet Offensive.[76]

The power struggle among these key Politburo members not only prompted a wave of political arrests in Hanoi but also caused a momentary breakdown of military leadership that had disastrous results for the Lunar New Year attacks. "One of the mysteries of the planning for the Tet Offensive," Vietnam scholar David Elliott writes, "is how much (and when) the lower levels . . . knew about the specific nature and extent of changes that may have taken place in the basic plan between June 1967, its formal transmittal to the South in October 1967, and the final Hanoi Politburo resolution of December 1967."[77] Although indoctrination sessions occurred in the southern theaters prior to October, the emphasis remained on protracted struggle, fighting while negotiating, and taking advantage of local environments. The events of October led to the de facto approval to target urban centers, what one military historian has called "a daring decision of Vietnam indeed because if we had simply considered the balance of military force at that time (October 1967), we would not have taken this audacious decision."[78] Tran Van Tra later criticized the northern leadership for not giving the southern resistance adequate time to prepare for the Tet Offensive.[79] Since many of the October arrestees included military commanders who were involved in the planning for the upcoming offensive, Le Duan's personal vendetta against Giap had finally spilled over into the war effort itself.

The final and largest round of arrests, on Christmas Day, did not involve figures associated with Giap or the moderates in the Politburo; rather, they were mainly of Party officials and Hanoi professionals who had become "suspect" under Minister Hoan's definition, as security thugs carried out their boss's instructions to crack down on potential leaks. Since the first arrestee, the purported Soviet spy Hoang Minh Chinh, had raised the banner for "reactionaries" to oppose the Party line with his publication, Bao Ve forces needed to round up the supposed adherents of Chinh's "revisionist ideology" in December. The urgency, of course, was the timing of the Politburo meeting in late December and the CEC plenum in early January to pass Resolution 14 that would codify Le Duan's GU-GO strategy for 1968. If Chinh and his associates, with "foreign" backing, leaked information regarding the upcoming offensive that relied on the element of surprise, all would be lost. By the end of the year, Party and non-Party members who had any contact with Chinh, or who had ever criticized the Party leadership after 1963, or who had any family members guilty of "bourgeois" sentiments, were summarily arrested.[80]

The 1967 purge thus represented the militant leadership's conflation of

ideological divisions in the internationalist movement with political repression at home so that the hawks could carry out their military policies
in the South. Although leaders in Hanoi, including Le Duan, Giap, and Ho,
may have adopted aspects of Chinese or Soviet policies, the ultimate goal
was always to promote Vietnamese interests and ambitions. Extreme pro-
Soviet or pro-Chinese inclinations may have existed among midlevel officials who had studied in either the Soviet Union or the PRC, but members
of the Politburo were never that partial.[81] The reasons for neutrality within
the highest strata of the VWP were twofold: the Hanoi Politburo needed
to steer a separate course not only for fear of alienating or displeasing one
ally over the other but also to instill a sense of patriotism and Vietnamese
identity within the Party and the people. However, neutrality in foreign
policy did not prevent the use of ideological divisions within the international proletarian movement to control domestic politics at home. Certain
leaders were not above accusing others of "revisionism" or "dogmatism"
for domestic political gain.

Le Duc Tho, Truong Chinh, and Tran Quoc Hoan, who received the majority of media coverage during and after the arrests, emphasized Party
control over all stages of the revolution and the need "to struggle against
opportunism from left or right."[82] These leaders delivered their speeches
and published their articles in an atmosphere of danger—as Red Guards
and radical thinking spilled over from China's Cultural Revolution—and
of intrigue—as spy fever heightened by American bombs gripped the DRV
capital.[83] It is conceivable, then, that Le Duan and his faction orchestrated
the arrests to capitalize on this fear by whipping up paranoia with accusations of espionage and treachery in order to ensure that the planning for
the Tet Offensive unfolded in the utmost secrecy it needed to succeed. Recalling the clamor that the pro-Soviet moderates had created in the wake
of Resolution 9 in 1963, Le Duan needed Resolution 14 to be passed without complications in 1968. By charging the arrestees with "sowing dissension" and "fomenting friction between Party leaders" in order to "organize
a faction to oppose our Party, the Workers' Party," the leaders who orchestrated the arrests finally removed their long-standing opponents in one
fell swoop.[84] The Politburo, however, remained intact, even though some
members were now fully aware of the lengths to which Le Duan would go
in order to get his way. It was in this environment that Hanoi made the decision to launch what would become the major event of the Vietnam War:
the Tet Offensive.

CONCLUSION

Since Hanoi was supposedly infested with spies and American bombs threatened the city, the Fourteenth Plenum took place outside the capital, in Hoa Binh province, in early January. In his opening speech, Le Duan formally elevated General Dung to the top military slot by allowing him to brief the plenum on behalf of the Central Military Party Commission. Although it would have been Giap's duty to provide the briefing as head of the CMC, he was conveniently out of the country. As for Ho Chi Minh, the frail leader had returned to Hanoi in December to make a final stand against the GO-GU strategy at the Politburo meeting in December, but to no avail. The Politburo approved forwarding the Tet Offensive resolution to the Central Executive Committee for a rubber stamp. With the Politburo's December blessing, then, the attendees of the Fourteenth Plenum in January 1968 reviewed and debated the risky strategy for 1968. Once again Ho abstained from the vote—just as he had for Resolution 9 in 1963—and silently watched as the revolution proceeded without him.[85]

Beset with problems from the start, military planners for the Tet Offensive delayed setting the date for the offensive nearly to the last minute. In order to maintain the element of surprise, war leaders in Hanoi gave local, regional, and provincial commanders in the South little more than two weeks to prepare their forces for battle. On 15 January 1968, D-Day was set for the night of 30–31 January, to coincide with Lunar New Year's Eve. The Year of the Monkey, however, proved inauspicious for communist forces. Due to calendar discrepancies, some of the central region provinces launched their attacks one day early, thereby giving away the element of surprise, while other headquarters received their instructions too late and thus failed to "*tien cong* [advance]."

Without contextualizing VWP strategy deliberation within the interplay of inner Party debates and Sino-Soviet-Vietnamese relations, it is impossible to understand the full weight of the decisions made by Le Duan and his hawks in 1967. Although the military picture in South Vietnam and the political climate in the United States were important factors in the calculations of the "War Politburo," they were not the only ones. The militants' gamble following the 1963 Ninth Plenum to go for broke through a General Offensive and General Uprising strategy succeeded in fatally weakening the Saigon regime, but it failed to prevent the arrival of American soldiers and bombs. Le Duan, though, saw it differently. He was convinced his strategy had succeeded, but the United States had snatched away his victory at the final moment.

As near victory in 1964 turned into a costly stalemate by 1967, Le Duan and Le Duc Tho identified a solution to deflect the multiple challenges to their leadership by the "North-first" moderates in the Party who called for negotiations to end the war, by figures in the Politburo and the military who called for a more conservative military strategy for 1968, and by opinionated Soviet and Chinese allies who promoted conflicting agendas. Relying first on General Nguyen Chi Thanh, and later Lieutenant-General Van Tien Dung, Le Duan found the instruments to redeem his strategy in 1967, when the Party leadership as a whole decided that its forces needed to attempt a decisive victory in 1968. Although the General Offensive and General Uprising was a risky strategy with little chance of success, Le Duan forged ahead and cut down his detractors (foremost among them Ho Chi Minh and Vo Nguyen Giap) by launching the largest purge in Party history, one that remains relatively unknown. With the successful conclusion of the Revisionist Anti-Party Affair and the passage of the General Offensive and General Uprising resolution by early 1968, Le Duan could look forward to reaping the fruits of his labor in the Lunar New Year.

*Diplomacy could never replace military strength. — Le Duc Tho*[1]

chapter four

# TO PARIS AND BEYOND

It was apparent to many Saigonese living in the labyrinth of pathways just off Justice Bridge (Cau Cong Ly) that something was afoot on the eve of the 1968 Lunar New Year. For weeks prior to the holiday, new cyclo drivers, street vendors, and itinerant peddlers positioned themselves in tucked-away corners and deep in ghetto alleys. Even during the busiest seasons these seemingly innocuous neighborhoods rarely attracted new faces, unlike the Paris-inspired boulevards of downtown Saigon where expensive restaurants, crowded cafés, and the bustling Ben Thanh Market maintained a constant buzz of activity. Busily preparing for the upcoming Tet festivities, however, average Saigonese families paid little attention to the strangers. It was only after the dust had settled that the residents near Justice Bridge realized that these peasants were actually PLAF soldiers positioned to launch the Tet Offensive.[2]

Outside of the busy capital city in the lush environs of the Mekong Delta, southern communists prepared themselves for what would become the fight of their lives. At 11:00 P.M. on the night before New Year's Eve, Nga and her comrades in the western Mekong received orders to proceed with their prepared plans. "D-Day, zero-hour [*ngay 'N' gio 'G'*] had arrived," just as they were roasting a thirty-pound pig and preparing caramelized pork in a hot pot, traditional dishes for the holiday season.[3] Jumping onto their boats with their half-roasted swine, Nga recalled, the soldiers traveled all night, as revelers along the banks wished them well on their way to defeat the Americans and topple Thieu. Admitting in retrospect that their preparations were not fully adequate, the western Mekong Delta forces still managed to strike at all nine cities and provincial towns in the region and forty-one hamlets and villages, sustaining substantial losses but arising victorious in world opinion.[4]

Far from Justice Bridge in central Saigon and the western Mekong Delta, Le Duan followed the progress of his military plans in the bomb-saturated North. Successful at every turn in his career, the first secretary requested and received war in 1959, "bigger" war in 1963, and the redemption of his GO-GU strategy in 1967. Sending his second-in-command, Le Duc Tho, to join his third, COSVN secretary Pham Hung, in the South, Le Duan trusted them to be his eyes and ears during the offensive. While General Vo Nguyen Giap stayed in self-imposed exile in Hungary to show his disdain for Le Duan's offensive, Senior Lieutenant-General Van Tien Dung had made the first secretary's plans operational. As communist forces began to tie down American troops in Khe Sanh, a district capital in the Central Highlands, in the late fall of 1967, Le Duan ordered a massive, coordinated attack on the cities and towns of South Vietnam to crush the Saigon army and incite the masses to join the soldiers in overthrowing the Thieu regime. However, the militant leader's hope for a general uprising did not occur after the first wave of attacks, nor did it materialize in the wake of the second or the third. At the time, however, the official line was positive. On 12 December 1968, the PLAF High Command proclaimed the GO-GU a resounding success; 630,000 enemy troops were allegedly killed in action in the South and 557 planes were shot down in the North.[5] Le Duan and the militants in his Politburo, however, knew that their roll of the dice had failed, just as it had in 1964.

The writing of history in present day Vietnam is the intellectual and political property of the government and thus tends to extol the policies of the Vietnamese Communist Party.[6] The history of the 1968 General Offensive and General Uprising is one of the few exceptions. Although the official studies claim that Tet Mau Than succeeded in its goal of delivering a major political and psychological blow to the United States, Le Duan's death has allowed more recent works to dampen their praise by citing the high casualty rates suffered by the southern resistance in pursuit of an elusive objective.[7] According to Vietnamese historian Ho Khang, "Tet Mau Than is still a subject that arouses controversial views. Looking from one angle, some think they have had a comprehensive grasp of Tet, but look-ing from another angle, others are perplexed and unable to explain the event."[8] Nonetheless, the majority of Vietnamese publications aver that the communist offensive achieved its primary aim of crippling the politi-cal will of the United States in a crucial election year.

This first half of this chapter questions whether Le Duan's primary ob-jective for the Tet Offensive was achieved and surveys how his 1968 bid for military victory radically altered the landscape of war. In addition to nearly destroying the southern communist infrastructure, Le Duan's costly strategy set back the revolution in three other ways. First, his de-termination to prove his GO-GU strategy successful by toppling the Sai-gon regime in a popular insurrection resulted not only in significant mili-tary losses but also in major diplomatic and political setbacks. The first secretary's refusal to advance the diplomatic struggle in any substantive way squandered the political capital accrued in the first wave of attacks. Second, the Tet Offensive and the initiation of negotiations threatened Hanoi's equilibrium in the Sino-Soviet split. Although Le Duan and Le Duc Tho launched the 1967 Anti-Party Affair to placate the Chinese and thwart the Soviets, the events of 1968 managed to reverse both of those trends. Finally, the failures of 1968 continued to be felt into 1969, which witnessed the nadir of the Vietnamese revolution. The victory of a hawkish Republi-can leader in the 1968 U.S. presidential election, the violent turn in the Sino-Soviet split in March 1969, and the revitalization of the Saigon regime posed substantial new threats to Le Duan's designs.

The second half of the chapter addresses the new stage of fighting in the wake of Le Duan's failed 1968 General Offensive and General Uprising. With the arrival of Richard M. Nixon and Henry A. Kissinger in the White House and an invigorated Nguyen Van Thieu at the Independence Palace in Saigon, Hanoi's war for peace would soon be elevated to the interna-tional arena. While Nixon and Kissinger employed the same methods to consolidate decision making in their hands as Le Duan and Le Duc Tho had done a decade earlier, the U.S. leaders began to take advantage of the violent turn in Sino-Soviet relations. Washington intended to use the contradictions in the Cold War to America's advantage in Vietnam. When Nixon realized he could not win the war during his first year in office, he and Kissinger prepared themselves for a protracted conflict. Meanwhile, the Saigon regime appeared to awake from its stupor as the Thieu regime began to reassert itself in the U.S.-RVN war effort. As Washington an-nounced its intention to withdraw from Vietnam, Saigon did everything in its power to prolong that process. In this "new war," Le Duan and Le Duc Tho found themselves battling these new enemies on a dangerous terrain, the diplomatic battleground where they had seen predecessors fall.

### PHASE 1: MOMENTOUS VICTORIES AND SECRET FAILURES

The General Offensive and General Uprising began with a bang amid Lunar New Year celebrations in South Vietnam on 30–31 January. This first and most noteworthy phase included a coordinated PAVN-PLAF surprise attack on thirty-six provincial capitals, five autonomous cities, and sixty-four district capitals in the South. Rather than inciting a general uprising in the urban centers, communist forces were only able to hold onto the former imperial city of Hue until 24 February, with disastrous results for the local population.[9] The rural uprising was more successful, but because of the continuing emphasis on towns and cities throughout the remainder of the offensive, NLF troops were forced to abandon their victory in the villages.[10] Nonetheless, the first wave of the offensive set off momentous changes in the war.

Even though Le Duan and his militant faction were not criticized within the Party for their costly and unsuccessful attempt at a decisive victory, the Hanoi Politburo as a whole still had to contend with feuding allies during the first wave of attacks. Chinese fears and paranoia concerning Soviet machinations in Vietnam, which had abated during the 1967 purge, rose once again in early 1968 with Tet. Beijing leaders saw the offensive, with its emphasis on the towns and cities across South Vietnam, as a total repudiation of Mao's protracted strategy and an embrace of more Soviet-style warfare. As late as February 1968, the Chinese tried to convince the North Vietnamese to scale down the Lunar New Year attacks, telling them that the shift to a General Offensive and General Uprising was premature.[11]

Chinese fears were unfounded. Although Hanoi received military aid and weaponry from Moscow for the 1968 offensive, VWP leaders did not collaborate with Moscow on Tet strategy.[12] More important, the ambitious scope of the first wave of attacks delivered a shock that, however slowly and haltingly, brought change in the United States. On 31 March, one month after the end of the first wave, President Johnson rejected Westmoreland's and JCS chairman General Earle Wheeler's request for 206,000 additional troops and promised to cease the bombing at the twentieth parallel, just north of the DMZ. Moreover, Johnson declared that if U.S. restraint were "matched by restraint in Hanoi," then he was prepared to send

*Saigon during the Tet Offensive (Douglas Pike Photograph Collection, Vietnam Center and Archive, Texas Tech University)*

W. Averell Harriman as his personal representative to peace talks in "any forum, at any time."[13] Faced with rising discontent and an antiwar challenge for the Democratic presidential nomination from Senators Eugene McCarthy and Robert Kennedy, Johnson then shocked his nation—and Le Duan in Hanoi—by announcing that he would neither seek nor accept another term in office.

Although the Lunar New Year attacks failed to induce the South Vietnamese masses to overthrow the Thieu regime in Saigon, they did manage to topple the Johnson presidency. Even though Johnson's fall proved a far greater triumph for Le Duan's strategy in many aspects, it did not result in an end to the war, which Thieu's ouster might have accomplished. The first secretary had no choice but to agree to direct talks with the Americans after Johnson's 31 March speech, even though the U.S. president had not met Hanoi's demand to cease unconditionally the bombing of North Vietnam. Diplomatic compromise, however, would never take over the role of battlefield victories in 1968. Le Duan was as determined to topple the Saigon regime as Johnson was to preserve it. Therefore, the first secretary moved hesitantly with the talking aspect of his "talking while fighting [*dam va danh*]" policy.[14] Just like Johnson, Le Duan did not abandon his objective in 1968, he merely changed his tactics to salvage a policy that had failed to produce immediate results.[15] Unlike Johnson, however, Le Duan was spared a domestic challenge in the aftermath of Tet. Even though he decided to enter direct discussions with the United States, Le Duan ordered communist forces to launch a second wave of attacks on urban centers to create the conditions for a mass insurrection.[16]

### PHASE 2: EMERGING DIPLOMATIC THEATER OF WAR

The second phase of the communist offensive began on 4 May with an attack on 119 southern bases, towns, and cities, and ended on 17 August with high casualties for the communists and the destruction of Saigon's eighth district.[17] Once again, a general uprising failed to materialize. Instead, more than a week later on 13 May, American and North Vietnamese representatives met at the Hotel Majestic in Paris to begin preliminary discussions. Even though the talks immediately encountered obstacles, their start fundamentally altered the nature of the conflict by forcing the warring parties to redefine victory in Vietnam from a military conquest on the battlefield to a favorable political settlement at the conference table. A "new war" had begun, noted official-cum-scholar Luu Van Loi, who participated in the Paris talks, "a war around a green carpet as bombs were still exploding on the battlefield."[18]

Before Luu Van Loi compiled Hanoi's history of the secret talks with Henry Kissinger and became the foremost historian of Vietnam's relations with the outside world, he conducted revolutionary diplomacy. Born on 1 July 1913 outside of Hanoi in the direction of Gia Lam, Loi managed to master the French language at the age of ten, though he never completed school since his parents' death left him and his five siblings destitute. In 1944, Loi joined the Viet Minh and became a journalist whose job was to work closely with defectors from the French Legionnaires. In 1945, he first met Ho Chi Minh when he helped organize the proclamation of the formation of the DRV at Ba Dinh Square. When the French war broke out, Loi was promoted to director of the Enemy Proselytizing Office, putting him in charge of propaganda aimed at enemy soldiers. His official career in diplomacy began near the end of that war when Loi acted as chief-of-cabinet of the Trung Gia conference, where France and the DRV arranged a prisoner swap. By 1960, he transferred to the Ministry of Foreign Affairs,

*Luu Van Loi and author*

attended the Geneva Conference on Laos in 1962, and accompanied Ho on many overseas trips. As the chief of MOFA's Second Asian Bureau (Vu A Chau II) and then as cabinet chief (*chanh van phong*) during the 1960s, he was in charge of drafting and reviewing Vietnamese- and French-language documents as well as witnessing the failed peace attempts by various third parties.

With the start of peace talks in 1968, Loi's job was to monitor all of the meetings in Paris, both public and private. Although his whereabouts remain ambiguous during this pivotal year—one source has him at the North Vietnamese Embassy in Moscow, another on a mission in Africa, and a third in Hanoi as assistant to the minister of foreign affairs—it is clear that he had a front-row seat to witness this new stage of war.[19] Over four years and nine months, Loi was Le Duc Tho's personal secretary, traveling between Paris and Hanoi with the "special advisor" twenty times over the course of the negotiations.[20]

In this new war, the Sino-Soviet split became increasingly difficult for the North Vietnamese leadership to handle. Hanoi's relationship with Beijing continued to sour in 1968, and the alliance never recovered to its pre-Tet level. While disagreement over military tactics during the first wave of attacks weakened the Asian alliance, Hanoi's decision to enter into negotiations with Washington exacerbated Sino-Vietnamese tensions. If large-unit operations aimed at urban targets made Beijing doubt Hanoi's loyalties in the Sino-Soviet split, Hanoi's decision to engage in direct talks with the Americans made the Chinese paranoid. Beijing's stern opposition to peace initiatives stood in stark contrast to Moscow's work for negotiations.[21] Following Hanoi's 3 April announcement that it would accept Washington's offer of preliminary discussions in Paris, Chinese criticism of supposed Soviet infiltration of Vietnamese strategy took on a markedly acerbic tone, while Soviet intervention in Hanoi's affairs increased to levels not witnessed since before the Revisionist Anti-Party Affair.

A series of meetings in April between Premiers Zhou Enlai and Pham Van Dong in Beijing reveal the extent to which Chinese leaders believed that the Hanoi Politburo committed a major mistake by accepting negotiations. On 13 April, the Chinese leader argued that there was a causal link between DRV's 3 April announcement and the assassination of Martin Luther King Jr. on 4 April: "Had your statement been issued one or two days later, the murder might have been stopped."[22] Apparently not satisfied with blaming the death of the civil rights leader on Hanoi's inept decision making, less than a week later Zhou Enlai accused North Vietnamese leaders of disappointing the "people of the world" by making two "compromises": first by accepting a meeting when Johnson only offered a partial bombing halt and second by acceding to Washington's rejection of Phnom Penh as the site of negotiations.[23] After a brief trip to the Soviet Union, Dong returned to Beijing, where he found his Chinese hosts still upset over Hanoi's policies. As the Cultural Revolution wreaked havoc inside China, Zhou Enlai found fault with Hanoi's revolutionary struggle. Invoking Mao's military doctrine, the Chinese premier pointed out that, far from dominating the battlefield, Vietnamese forces were in a "holding phase" known as the "equilibrium" stage. Zhou considered the VWP leadership's decision to join negotiations foolish, a move that put Vietnamese troops on the ground in a precarious situation.[24]

Although Beijing leaders never addressed Moscow's activities directly during the April meetings, the North Vietnamese were aware that China's greatest concern was Soviet influence over Hanoi's decision making. In fact, the DRV's decision to accept negotiations did create space for Soviet involvement but not to the extent that Beijing feared. Although Moscow played an integral role in ensuring that the U.S.-Vietnam peace talks overcame their initial obstacles, Soviet political influence with Hanoi leaders did not rise proportionally.[25] During a meeting between Le Duan and Soviet chargé V. Chivilev in Hanoi on 2 May, the first secretary sought Moscow's help in securing an acceptable locale for the peace negotiations. In particular, Le Duan needed the Soviet government to persuade the United States to accept the DRV's proposal, which was to be made the following day.[26] The next day, the DRV Ministry of Foreign Affairs suggested that Paris, like Phnom Penh and Warsaw, which Hanoi had suggested earlier, would be acceptable and that if such a site were accepted talks could begin on 5 May or a few days after.[27] The Soviet Union was ecstatic when the United States, which had independently begun to explore Paris as a possible meeting place, immediately accepted Hanoi's proposal. Russian optimism, however, soon turned to dismay. On 4 May, communist forces launched the second wave of attacks on South Vietnam. The VWP leadership had no intention of pursuing Moscow's desire for a speedy settlement in 1968; instead, Hanoi used the public meetings for "probing" purposes only.[28]

If the Soviets began to doubt North Vietnamese intentions of embarking on serious negotiations in early May, the Chinese were equally suspicious of their junior allies but for different reasons. While en route to Paris, Xuan Thuy, the DRV representative to the talks, met with Chinese leaders at the Great Hall of the People in Beijing on 7 May. Since Mao Zedong refused to meet with him, Thuy was subjected to a brief lecture from Zhou Enlai and Marshal Chen Yi.[29] After repeating Beijing's official line that Hanoi's decision to engage in talks with the United States was a major mistake that would cost Hanoi all of the military gains made up to that point, both Chinese leaders instructed the North Vietnamese to at least refrain from informing the Soviets of any further developments regarding negotiations. They warned their Vietnamese guest that Moscow could not be trusted; the Soviets would sooner or later sell out the Vietnamese cause to the Americans whenever it suited their interests. Citing the "disclosure" of military and diplomatic secrets by "revisionists" in Hanoi as examples of Soviet duplicity, Zhou Enlai tried to invoke the bogeymen of Vietnam's Revisionist Anti-Party Affair.[30]

Beijing's criticism of Hanoi's policies was not confined to the diplomatic realm; it began to spill over into Chinese assessment of Vietnam's military strategy as well. Words of caution during the first wave of attacks turned caustic by the second. Chinese fears once again rested on supposed Soviet influence on North Vietnamese strategy, particularly the attacks on urban centers. By the summer, the Chinese leaders did not attempt to soften their tone as they had in the winter and spring. In a June conversation between Zhou Enlai and Pham Hung, the Chinese premier stated:

> Your recent attacks on the cities were only aimed at restraining the enemy's forces, helping the work of liberating the rural areas, mobilizing massive forces in urban areas. Yet, they are not of a decisive nature. The Soviet revisionists are claiming that attacks on Saigon are genuine offensives, that the tactics of using the countryside to encircle the urban areas are wrong and that to conduct a protracted struggle is a mistake. In their opinion, only lightning attacks on big cities are decisive. But if you do [that], the US will be happy as they can concentrate their forces for counterattack thus causing greater destruction for you. The losses that you would suffer will lead to defeatism on your side.[31]

Whether Chinese or Soviet leaders had North Vietnam's best interests in mind is unclear. These conversations do confirm that Beijing and Moscow each sought to convince Hanoi to implement its brand of warfare (Soviet predilection for large-scale urban attacks versus Chinese inclination for protracted fighting in the countryside) and adopt its policy advice (to negotiate or not to negotiate). As the Sino-Soviet split increasingly became a zero-sum game, North Vietnam's war effort became a primary battleground in Beijing and Moscow's rivalry for leadership of the communist world.

While foreign policy posed significant challenges for Hanoi, domestic politics played a smaller role in 1968. Aside from incidents in the northwest region, the DRV was quiet.[32] Le Duan's quest for a mass insurrection in the late spring and in the late summer was extremely controversial, but the previous year's purge had silenced any dissent.[33] It was rumored that Vo Nguyen Giap, who had returned in February 1968 from self-imposed exile, did not agree with the second (or subsequent third) wave of attacks, but he knew better than to voice his objections. With members of his staff in prison, the general knew he was in the minority and that "others would not have listened to him."[34] With Giap cowed, Le Duan once again placed his key deputies in positions of power in the new war. In particular, Le Duc Tho's movements in 1968 reveal strategic shifts in Le Duan's strategy. During the first wave of attacks, the first secretary sent his most loyal subordinate south to oversee the offensive. Le Duc Tho was to "reinforce [*tang cuong*]" COSVN as Pham Hung's deputy and "bolster [*phat huy*]" the results of the Lunar New Year attacks.[35] Even though Tho outranked Hung, he had a tendency to adopt humble titles that did not indicate the full extent of his authority. When the offensive failed to incite a mass insurrection, Le Duan recalled Tho to Hanoi so that he could prepare his second-in-command to become the "special advisor" (another misleading title) to the DRV's chief delegate in Paris, Xuan Thuy. Although Pham Van Dong had the most experience conducting negotiations, second perhaps only to Ho Chi Minh, and seemed the more appropriate choice than Tho, Le Duan might not have trusted the moderate Dong.

Nonetheless, Le Duan's decision to send Tho to Paris must not have been an easy one. The first secretary deeply distrusted negotiations. Not only had he arrested those who had long called for a peaceful settlement to the war in 1967 and launched the Tet Offensive in 1968 in order to end the war through a military victory and not political compromise, Le Duan had also silenced Ho Chi Minh's objections to the expanding war effort by invoking the aged leader's failures on the diplomatic front during the French-Indochina War. In other words, Le Duan knew all too well the dangers of failed diplomacy and of opportunists who would try to exploit any miscalculations on his part. Moreover, Le Duan learned an important lesson from the 1954 Geneva Accords: gains on the battlefield were not always reflected at the negotiating table. Even though Le Duan was privy to how the Soviets and Chinese forced the war-weary North Vietnamese leadership into accepting less-than-stellar terms at Geneva, he also witnessed firsthand the revolt of the vast majority of Party members against the apparent capitulation of 1954. It is worth recalling that Le Duan had the unenviable duty of informing southern revolutionaries that the Geneva settlement surrendered their half of the country to capitalist powers.[36]

By sending his reliable deputy to Paris, however, Le Duan could ensure that the peace process would not thwart his military objectives. Moreover, if the Paris talks resulted in a Geneva-like failure, Le Duc Tho would take the blame. Tho later stated that he regretted having to leave his post as Party organizational director, since his work was vital to Party life.[37] In fact, Tho's most important responsibility, that of overseeing the committee tasked with investigating the Revisionist Anti-Party Affair, had been concluded successfully by the time of his departure from Hanoi. As Tho arrived in Paris to assume his new duties and as Le Duan exhorted his forces to continue the second wave of attacks in South Vietnam in mid-June, the arrestees of the 1967 purge who had refused to admit their guilt in return for pardon were transferred from Hoa Lo prison in central Hanoi to a labor camp in remote Son Tay province.[38] Throughout the rest of their five to eight years of imprisonment, they were never officially charged with specific crimes—other than being generally labeled as reactionaries and traitors—and their cases were never tried in court.[39] Even though North Vietnam's participation in the Paris talks seemed a victory for many of these arrestees, who had called for negotiations with the Americans to end the costly war in South Vietnam, they could not enjoy the fruits of their triumph.

When Le Duc Tho arrived at the negotiations, after first stopping in Beijing and Moscow, he oversaw both the public meetings and the simultaneous private contacts. Before Tho's arrival, Xuan Thuy along with his deputy, Ambassador Ha Van Lau, engaged Johnson's skillful veteran diplomat W. Averell Harriman and the U.S. deputy secretary of defense Cyrus Vance in "polemical posturing and propaganda."[40] Since the public meetings at the spectacular International Conference Center on the Avenue Kléber were all for show, Hanoi followed Moscow's advice to consent to private meetings that had a greater chance to produce substantive progress. One of the early obstacles that emerged at both the public and private meetings over the summer of 1968 was the debate over reciprocity and restraint.[41] Washington offered to stop bombing North Vietnam if Hanoi exhibited "restraint" during the bombing halt. This meant that North Vietnam would have to promise not to violate the DMZ by sending men and supplies to the South or by attacking major cities including Saigon, Hue, and Da Nang. The DRV refused since Washington's offer implied "reciprocity" and Hanoi insisted that the cessation of bombing had to be unconditional.

At the end of July, as the second wave of attacks resulted in high casualties for the communist forces and the Paris "talks about talks," both private and public, continued to drag, Hanoi leaders including Le Duan, Le Duc Tho, and General Dung met again to reevaluate strategy.[42] After hearing the results of the first and second waves from Senior General Dung, the first secretary again concluded that the resistance had to make one final stab at a general uprising in South Vietnam.[43] Le Duan reasoned that if the forces could rally the people to take the RVN capital, then the communists would be in a better position to open a stronger wave of attacks in the countryside. Prior to the Tet Offensive, the revolution was in a dominant position vis-à-vis Saigon's forces in the countryside. After the winter and spring waves of attacks focused on cities and towns, however, not only did the southern revolution give up its dominant position in the rural areas, but also the communist infrastructure was badly damaged throughout the RVN. In addition to seizing the initiative, Le Duan called for a third attempt to stir a general insurrection to offset Thieu's call for a general mobilization on 19 June. This call enabled the Saigon regime not only to replace the troops lost during the communist attacks but also to increase the number of its fighters from 552,000 in 1967 to 555,000 in 1968.[44] Moreover, Hanoi believed that the United States, far from winding down its involvement, was on the verge of expanding the war and increasing its forces in the region.[45] As a result, in early August, the Politburo approved launching a third—and final—wave of attacks on the cities of South Vietnam.[46]

### PHASE 3: TOWARD DAM VA DANH

The final phase of the 1968 offensive, and undoubtedly both the most costly and weakest effort of the resistance, began on 17 August and ended on 30 September, as communist forces shelled American installations and coordinated assaults throughout South Vietnam. With the U.S. presidential race in full gear and the negotiations in Paris facing various impasses and roadblocks, Le Duan ordered his communist forces to advance once again to rally the troops and the people to defeat the South Vietnamese Army and to topple the Saigon regime. Heavy and effective B-52 bombing, however, ensured that the RVN capital did not fall to the communists—a prospect that grew more improbable with each wave of attacks.

As communist troops died in vain to create conditions for a mass uprising in August, Le Duc Tho accepted Harriman's invitation for a private meeting.[47] More than two weeks later, that meeting took place at Vitry-sur-Seine on 8 September as communist forces took heavy casualties during the lengthy Tay Ninh–Binh Long campaign. Although Tho's presence at the private meetings signified the increasing importance of negotiations, Le Duan was not ready to advance talks past a certain stage until it was undeniably clear that his third wave of attacks had failed to win a major military victory over U.S.-ARVN forces. As a result, throughout September, the DRV representatives refused to give any ground. On 7 September, Tho completely avoided discussing any concrete issues with Harriman, instead lecturing him for nearly an hour on the history of American intervention in Vietnam.[48] At the subsequent two private meetings on 12 and 15 September, Tho continued to harangue and resort to other diversionary tactics to avoid engaging on substantive issues. A few days later, at the final private meeting of the month on 20 September, Harriman reiterated that the United States attached "great importance" to the participation of the Thieu administration at the talks, prompting the North Vietnamese negotiators to denounce the Saigon "puppet" regime.[49] Xuan Thuy further criticized Harriman for failing to present anything new on the American side after his brief trip to Washington, while Xuan Thuy's "special advisor" avoided committing the DRV to any position by stating that he was awaiting further instruction from Hanoi.[50]

However, Tho and Thuy's classified telegrams to the Politburo reveal a very different picture. After the 20 September meeting, the two North Vietnamese negotiators were far less critical of the American delegation. Harriman, they reported, had put forward an important new proposal: Washington was ready to accept the participation of the NLF or any other party that the DRV wanted to put forth as representative of South Vietnam on the DRV's side at the talks.[51]

Even though he could not move forward until Le Duan gave him the green light, Tho began to devise a negotiating strategy. In a telegram dated 28 September, Tho laid out what he believed should be the key elements in the fall round of discussions: objectives, composition, timing, and agenda. In the first section regarding objectives, Hanoi should aim to end the American "invasion [*xam luoc*]" by understanding the relationship between the three struggles: political (*chinh tri*), military (*quan su*), and international (*quoc te*). On the composition of the Paris talks, Tho suggested that while the United States agreed to any group that North Vietnam wanted to invite on its side, the DRV should refuse to accept any representative from the Thieu regime. In addition, Tho decided that only a representative from the NLF, and not any other political group, be invited to participate at the talks alongside the DRV. In the final two sections of the telegram on "timing" and "agenda," Tho recommended that the Party leadership continue its private meetings with the United States in the run-up to the American presidential elections, but important items of business should wait until four-party conference could be established.[52]

Tho's telegram, written two days before the official end of the third and final wave of the Tet Offensive, reveals that it was only after Hanoi war leaders exhausted their forces in the GO-GU that the VWP Politburo began taking the diplomatic sphere of the war seriously. By 30 September, when Le Duan ended the final attempt to incite a mass uprising, communist losses in the third wave of attacks were staggering. Luu Van Loi claims that the resistance could no longer keep up pressure through the DMZ, and that the enemy even managed to shrink the liberated zones by stepping up pacification and counteroffensives.[53]

With his hopes for military victory dashed, Le Duan grudgingly focused on the negotiations. Although the Lunar New Year attacks convinced key segments of U.S. society that intervention in Vietnam had failed, the losses sustained by communist forces in the second and third wave of attacks instilled renewed optimism within the Johnson administration. By autumn, it appeared to U.S. policy makers that Hanoi's war effort was on the verge of collapse. Not only did Le Duan's costly strategy breathe new life into Johnson's war policies, however, the first secretary also failed to capitalize on the political gains in the wake of Tet. By failing to follow up with a diplomatic offensive that could have made headway for the communists in Paris, Le Duan squandered the political capital accrued in the first—and most noteworthy—phase of attacks.

By early October, then, Hanoi was operating from a position of military weakness in the diplomatic struggle. Nonetheless, the VWP leadership sought to influence U.S. domestic politics through the negotiations in Paris. Recently declassified materials from Vietnam reveal that Le Duan's Politburo began to devote its attention to the 1968 presidential elections. In particular, the Hanoi leadership assessed the candidates and their attitudes toward the bombing halt and negotiations.

On 3 October, the Politburo sent a long telegram to Tho and Thuy stating that regardless of the November outcome, Johnson would still take de-escalatory steps while in office because he wanted to be viewed in history as a "peace" president.[54] The Politburo advised its negotiating team that Hanoi's sole aim should be to facilitate American de-escalation by adopting a more flexible position in Paris. As a result, Party leaders concluded that the green light should be given to a four-party conference, although U.S.-DRV contacts should continue independently, as long as the RVN agreed to recognize the NLF as the legitimate party to the talks.[55] Tho then relayed to Harriman on 11 October that serious talks could now begin. It appeared that the DRV was willing to accept the Saigon regime's participation in the Paris negotiations.[56]

However, a day before the meeting on 10 October, the Politburo sent a top-secret telegram to COSVN that suggests Le Duan had a change of heart. He no longer saw the need to adopt a more flexible attitude in Paris. The Politburo informed COSVN that it would order Tho and Thuy to put forward new demands: before four-party negotiations could begin, the Saigon regime and the United States would have to consent to talks with the NLF and the period between the bombing halt and the beginning of negotiations would have to be longer.[57] The United States wanted a two-side arrangement and only a twenty-four-hour period between the halt and negotiations. Luu Van Loi recalls that when Tho and Thuy received these new instructions on 13 October, they were dismayed at how rigid and unrealistic these new demands appeared, especially in light of the progress made during the 11 October meeting with the Americans.[58] The negotiators feared that Hanoi's new position would undo all of the gains made up to that point and wondered what prompted the shift in the Politburo's strategy. Although the Paris team understood that the VWP had to enhance the role and position of the NLF, the military balance of power did not support Hanoi's demands. The United States still had more than half a million troops in South Vietnam, while the Saigon army numbered 700,000. Moreover, the costly second and third waves and the enemy's counteroffensives meant that the Saigon administration controlled the greater part of South Vietnam. Staying up late into the night, the North Vietnamese delegation decided that the best way to disabuse the Politburo was for Le Duc Tho to make a hasty trip back to Hanoi and lend "perspective" to the situation.[59]

The Politburo's 10 October cable to COSVN may provide some explanation for Hanoi's sudden shift in strategy that seemingly vexed the North Vietnamese delegation in Paris. In the first section of the cable, titled "The Direction of U.S. Policy toward the Vietnam War," which appears before the section on Party strategy that called for a more rigid negotiating posture, Politburo leaders give a detailed analysis of the 1968 U.S. presidential candidates and their positions on the war. Regarding Democratic nominee Hubert Humphrey, Hanoi leaders asserted that the vice president's stance was less hard-line than Republican nominee Richard Nixon's. Humphrey's campaign emphasized peace, the complete cessation of bombing of the DRV, troop withdrawal, and negotiations with the NLF. Nixon, in contrast, campaigned on negotiating from a position of strength and opposed a bombing halt between the DMZ and the twentieth parallel and his position on the NLF was unknown. Politburo leaders described Nixon's position as "obstinate [*ngoan co*]" but still powerless to change the course of American de-escalation. However, Hanoi predicted that if Nixon were elected president, he would at some point and in some fashion complicate the withdrawal process. Nonetheless, Politburo leaders concluded the section on an optimistic note. Regardless of who emerged victorious at the polls, the next president of the United States would have no choice but to de-escalate the war. If Humphrey won, Johnson's policies and the Democratic Party's position on de-Americanization would prevail; if Nixon won,

Johnson would take steps toward peace in the final weeks of his administration that Nixon could not reverse.

This belief that the United States was certain to de-escalate gave way to a more pessimistic assessment of the VWP's policy options. Although eventual U.S. withdrawal from South Vietnam seemed inevitable after Tet, enduring American support for the Saigon regime necessitated a more stringent negotiating posture. Since South Vietnam was a neocolonial possession for the United States, Politburo leaders believed that American leaders—regardless of party affiliation—would continue propping up their Saigon "puppets." In order to avoid an ignominious defeat and not have U.S. soldiers' sacrifices be in vain, Johnson sought to secure Saigon's inclusion at the negotiating table and his successor would continue to bolster the "lackey" regime's diplomatic position in Paris. As a result, Le Duan concluded that it was more important to emphasize pinning down a date for the total cessation of bombing north of the seventeenth parallel. In essence, the Politburo ordered Tho and Thuy to put forth conditions at the negotiations that it knew Harriman and the Americans would not accept.

On 15 October, Xuan Thuy and Ha Van Lau met privately with Harriman and Vance. Harriman noted Le Duc Tho's absence and asked if "Mr. Tho" was going to meet with Soviet premier Alexei Kosygin. The two North Vietnamese representatives carried out the Politburo's instructions, but they tried to soften the blow by presenting Le Duan's demands as requests and not preconditions.[60] During that contact and the subsequent public talks, Thuy evaded Harriman and Vance's requests to set a date for "serious" talks, saying he needed further instructions from Tho and the Politburo.[61]

Meanwhile, "Mr. Tho" did make a brief stop in Moscow, as well as Beijing, on his way to Hanoi. There is no record of whom Tho met with while in Moscow, but we do know what transpired during his brief visit to Beijing.[62] During a meeting on 17 October, Tho heard this vitriolic condemnation of Hanoi's handling of the negotiations from Chinese foreign minister Chen Yi: "At present, Washington and Saigon are publicizing the negotiations, showing the fact that you have accepted the conditions put forward by the US. Your returning home for party instruction all the more proves it to the world's people. With your acceptance of the quadripartite negotiations, you handed the puppet government legal recognition, thus eliminating the National Liberation Front's status as the unique legal representative of the people in the South."[63]

Moreover, Chen Yi claimed, North Vietnamese acceptance of a four-party conference would only "help Johnson and Humphrey win their elections," and he invoked China's greatest bugaboo: "In our opinion, in a very short time, you have accepted the compromising and capitulationist proposals put forward by the Soviet revisionists. So between our two parties and the two governments of Vietnam and China, there is nothing more to talk about." Chen Yi did, however, blunt his invectives at the very end. Invoking Ho Chi Minh's statement about China and Vietnam being not only comrades but brothers as well, Chen Yi hoped that the situation in November would improve fraternal relations. Since Tho was purportedly heading back to Hanoi to soften the Politburo's negotiating stance and convince his comrades that their new demands were unreasonable, he responded ambiguously to Chen Yi's lecture. "On this matter, we will wait and see," Tho stated. "And the reality will give us the answer. We have gained experience over the past 15 years. Let reality justify." [64]

Arriving in Hanoi after these contentious meetings with the Chinese, and possibly after tense discussions with the Soviets, Tho debriefed his comrades in the Politburo on the situation in Paris. No records exist of these meetings on 17, 18, and 19 October; however, a telegram from the Politburo to Xuan Thuy as well as a cable from DRV foreign minister Trinh to Pham Hung's COSVN, both dated 20 October, reveal that Tho's exhortations succeeded in changing Le Duan's stance. The new demands were taken off the table and an approximate date was set for "serious" talks. In seven to ten days, after the cessation of bombing but before the U.S. presidential elections on 5 November, preparatory four-party talks could begin. In the telegram to Xuan Thuy, however, Hanoi leaders instructed the Paris delegation to remain vague and appear rigid regarding the date of the conference in order to avoid seeming too eager. [65] Trinh, on behalf of the Politburo, further elaborated on the NLF's role in the upcoming phase of the diplomatic struggle in his cable to Pham Hung. Appearing to be a response to COSVN leaders' cables 93 and 95 to Hanoi, the DRV foreign minister agreed with the Central Office that the NLF had to issue a public statement that accorded with North Vietnam's position at the talks. Interestingly, Trinh also reiterated that the division of labor between the Politburo and COSVN vis-à-vis the southern insurgency should remain the same. While COSVN should remain in charge of ideological leadership, military planning, and political agitation, the Politburo would maintain strict control of diplomatic issues and international work. As a result, Trinh informed COSVN that Politburo leaders would work on the NLF's public pronouncement. [66] If there ever was any doubt regarding who controlled the southern insurgency, the 20 October statement, along with many other newly declassified materials from Vietnam, should lay the debate to rest. Even in the new war, the NLF and the southern insurgency had no choice but to follow Hanoi's orders.

On 21 October, equipped with new instructions, Xuan Thuy met with Harriman at the private residence of the North Vietnamese delegation in the suburbs of Paris. With the question of South Vietnamese participation, both in terms of the Thieu administration as well as the NLF, for all intents and purposes resolved, only two issues regarding dates remained unsettled: the cessation of bombing and the start of the enlarged conference.[67] The Americans wanted a short interval between the announcement of the bombing halt and the start of four-party talks, while the North Vietnamese, presumably wanting to appear less eager, claimed that the NLF would need a few weeks to send its representatives to Paris.[68]

Hoping to break the impasse, the Soviets acted as intermediaries by brokering a "common sense solution," which included a compromise between a few days and several weeks.[69] In contrast to Chen Yi's warning to Le Duc Tho that North Vietnamese compliance in Paris would only bolster Johnson and Humphrey, the Soviets preferred to see Humphrey victorious at the polls since they considered Nixon too unpredictable and reactionary. In meetings with Americans and North Vietnamese, Soviet chargé d'affaires Valentin Oberemko, acting under the general instructions of his government, suggested an interval of seven days. Furthermore, on 25 October, Kosygin sent a letter to Johnson hoping that "third-rate details" concerning the Paris talks could be resolved.[70] Finally on 27 October, perhaps with Soviet persuasion, the North Vietnamese dropped all outstanding demands and proposed that the United States cease bombing on 30 October and that four-party talks begin on 3 November.

Although the Soviets welcomed the progress at the Paris peace talks, the Chinese seemed to make good on their threat that there was "nothing left to talk about" with the North Vietnamese. Johnson's 31 October announcement of a full bombing halt and the start of four-party talks in Paris prompted the Chinese to recall their troops from the DRV and reduce military aid.[71] Beijing claimed that its actions were aimed to ensure Vietnamese self-reliance. Now that the United States ceased bombing North Vietnam, Beijing claimed, there was no need for Chinese antiaircraft artillery units in the DRV. Hanoi leaders, however, read the gesture differently. North Vietnamese leaders believed that Beijing's policies were motivated by anger with the Vietnamese for choosing Soviet over Chinese guidance.

By late October, however, Hanoi's last-minute flexibility proved futile.

RVN President Thieu was able to undercut Humphrey's bid for the presidency as effectively as communist forces had shattered Johnson's ambitions for a second term. Through his ambassador in Washington, Bui Diem, Thieu received a steady stream of reports that South Vietnam would receive a better deal under the Republican candidate.[72] Using various channels, Nixon was able to pass along messages to Thieu to stand firm against Johnson's demands that Saigon send a delegation to Paris to participate in the upcoming four-party talks.[73] In the weeks preceding Election Day, then, intrigue permeated the corridors of power not only in the United States, but also in the two Vietnams, as leaders in Saigon and Hanoi both tried to manipulate American electoral politics to further their own objectives in the war. In the end, South Vietnamese interference proved more successful. Buoyed by receiving messages from the Nixon camp to "hold out," Thieu defied Johnson's 31 October announcement that four-party talks were imminent by delivering his own speech stating that he would not send a team to Paris.

To the extent that it aided Nixon's razor-thin election, Thieu's diplomatic coup managed to buy his regime at least four more years. For Le Duan, although the year began with a bang, it ended with a whimper. After Nixon's victory, American and North Vietnamese negotiators continued to squabble over the logistical and procedural issues, including the shape of the table, as they waited for their junior partners to arrive in Paris.

### 1969: THE NADIR OF THE REVOLUTION

If the Year of the Monkey did not prove as auspicious as Le Duan had hoped, the Year of the Rooster began downright ominously. With the arrival of Richard Nixon and Henry Kissinger in the White House in January 1969, Le Duan and Le Duc Tho confronted their equals. Like the "comrades Le," the two American leaders used their first year in office to consolidate decision making in their hands. Although they paid lip service to U.S. disengagement from Vietnam, in the form of Vietnamization, troop withdrawal, and "peace with honor," Nixon and Kissinger privately sought to win the war by dictating the terms of the peace.

With the failure of Le Duan's General Offensive and General Uprising strategy, the VWP first secretary advocated a "talking while fighting" policy, despite protests from Politburo members who wanted to put even less emphasis on the "fighting" aspect in 1969.[74] These moderate leaders, including the vindicated Vo Nguyen Giap, preferred a decisive return to protracted struggle. Although Le Duan eventually emerged victorious in these debates, as evidenced in the captured COSVN Resolution 9, which called for communist forces to be "relentless" in developing their strategic offensive, the setbacks from the Tet Offensive tempered the scope of attacks.[75] Phases X (22 February to 30 March) and H (11 May to 25 June) of the Spring–Summer Offensives sought to maintain the strategic initiative. Beginning with low-level attacks in the countryside in early 1969, communist forces did not approach the cities until March. Although Phases X and H bolstered the morale of the troops,communist forces could not maintain pressure on the cities, and by July the VWP more or less adopted Giap's more cautious strategy.[76]

After five fruitless attempts to capture the cities in 1968 and 1969, recalls Nga, who had become the regional deputy chief of propaganda, the Tet Offensive and its aftermath ushered in the darkest days of the revolution for the western Mekong Delta, second only to the period following the 1954 Geneva Accords. Soldiers from the provinces of Ca Mau, Rach Gia, Tra Vinh, and Vinh Long converged on the important city of Can Tho, leaving their position in the countryside weak. The ARVN, with its American commanders and superior Western weaponry, was able to take village after village as B-52 bombers stupefied villagers.[77] Those who had survived the unsuccessful attacks on the cities or managed to find cover from ARVN forces or American bombs were forced to go into hiding and barely had enough to eat. When news reached Nga that her brother, an officer in the Ninth Division, had been killed near the border with Cambodia, she did not even have the energy to weep.[78] Nonetheless, she continued to believe in her husband.

With reports reaching Hanoi of the deteriorating military picture in South Vietnam, the Party leadership had no choice but to advance the diplomatic struggle in Paris in order to provide much-needed support for the weakened military and political struggles in South Vietnam. On 1 January, the Politburo sent an upbeat cable to Le Duc Tho and Xuan Thuy in Paris to prepare the negotiating team for the upcoming four-party negotiations. Le Duan and his colleagues expressed confidence that the U.S. president-elect had no choice but to de-escalate the war in Vietnam even though he sought "peace with honor."[79] The Party's negotiating strategy should aim to force Nixon to withdraw all American forces from South Vietnam, and thus Tho and Thuy were ordered to appear cooperative at the talks but not overly eager in working toward a settlement.[80] In other words, the Politburo advised the negotiators to consider the Paris talks as another battleground where territory should not be given up without a fight. Nonetheless, the military struggle to topple the Thieu regime would remain the Party's most important objective.

As DRV leaders cobbled together a negotiating policy that aimed to buy time for the military struggle, Washington decision makers devised an international strategy to confront the conflict in Vietnam. Although Nixon and Kissinger inherited the Vietnam War when they assumed office, they undeniably made it their own. Even though much debate surrounds the actual intentions of the president and his national security advisor, the two men did succeed in creating more room to maneuver than the Johnson administration had left them. Elected on the promise of extricating the United States from Vietnam, Nixon spent his first term waging war on all fronts in order to prolong the conflict in Vietnam in hopes of winning ultimate victory. Although he could not reverse the process of de-Americanization, as North Vietnamese leaders had predicted, Nixon was convinced he could still win the war for peace by forcing Hanoi to accept American terms in Paris. Winning the war for peace meant finding Hanoi's breaking point. Like Le Duan and Le Duc Tho, Nixon and Kissinger adopted a combative approach toward international allies as well as domestic opponents who stood in the way of their policies. Initially, the American leaders were confident that they could end the war in short order.[81] By the end of 1969, however, with peace nowhere in sight, Nixon and Kissinger dug in for the long haul as they prepared for battle not only in Vietnam but also on the home front.

Although the president-elect had announced that he would quit political life in 1963, he re-entered the political arena in 1968 to win the highest seat in the land. Taking advantage of the Democratic Party's failures at home and abroad, Nixon campaigned on maintaining "law and order" and ending America's war in Southeast Asia. During the 1968 campaign, Nixon had promised to deliver peace with honor by terminating American military involvement in Southeast Asia while simultaneously preserving an independent, noncommunist South Vietnam. Vaguely hinting toward a "secret plan" that would bring the troops home without endangering the Saigon regime and thus American credibility, Nixon continued to base success on long-standing and unchanged U.S. objectives.[82]

Although far from concrete during the campaign or his first year in office, Nixon's complex strategy would eventually consist of diplomatic, military, and political components. The diplomatic centerpiece of this plan would include negotiations with the Soviet Union. Through the concept of linkage, Nixon intended to compel the Soviets to pressure their North Vietnamese allies to negotiate by using carrots—progress on arms control and détente—and later sticks—playing the "China card" and exploiting the Sino-Soviet split.[83] Eventually, Nixon would also work on improving relations with Beijing to pressure Hanoi as well. Nixon's triangular diplomacy (or quadrangular with Vietnam added) would strike at the heart of Hanoi's international strategy, which had allowed it to use the Sino-Soviet split to garner maximum aid while simultaneously maintaining its independence. Another important component of Nixon's strategy, one he never revealed to the wider public, was his intention to threaten to use and actually use "irresistible military pressure" to force Hanoi to accept a settlement on American terms.[84] Even though Johnson had failed to find Hanoi's breaking point, Nixon was convinced that he could succeed by exploiting his reputation as a hardline Cold Warrior who was willing to take irrational military measures to achieve his objectives. Confiding to his White House chief of staff, Harry "Bob" Haldeman, Nixon stated, "They'll believe any threat of force Nixon makes because it's Nixon."[85] Nonetheless, since certain aspects of U.S. de-escalation seemed more or less inevitable, Nixon spoke on more politically palatable issues to war-weary Americans about reducing the number of American troops and turning more responsibility for the fighting over to the South Vietnamese. Although disdainful of public opinion's potential to hamper policy, Nixon would become consumed with his public image.[86]

When Nixon narrowly triumphed at the polls in November, he hardly received the mandate to govern that he coveted.[87] Distrustful of a permanent bureaucracy under the control of Democrats, he began during the transition period to plot how to ensure ultimate control over foreign policy making in general and Vietnam policy in particular. In his selection of Kissinger as assistant for national security affairs, Nixon found a partner in policy making who was also convinced that America's best chance to "win" included employing great-power diplomacy and exerting major military pressure to force Hanoi's hand in Paris while staving off public disapproval with the war through de-Americanization and Vietnamization.[88]

On the surface, Kissinger appeared an unlikely partner for Nixon. As a German Jew who had fled Hitler's Third Reich, Heinz Alfred Kissinger—who would later go by "Henry"—rose to the top of academia in his adopted country.[89] Dissatisfied with scholarly life, Kissinger yearned to shape public policy and thus straddled the world of academia and politics by offering his services to the Kennedy and Johnson administrations and advising presidential hopefuls while maintaining his faculty position at Harvard. When Nixon asked Kissinger to join his administration, Kissinger finally received a ticket out of the academy. Although the two men appeared vastly different—Nixon had hailed from a small California town and had disdain for the ivory walls that had once contained Kissinger—they shared not only common objectives and beliefs but also similar anxieties.

Nixon and Kissinger's precarious partnership yet firm conviction that they alone knew what was best left no room for others to influence Vietnam policy. Convinced that they had to neutralize ostensible threats to their authority, Nixon and Kissinger did not want to be hindered by a cumbersome government bureaucracy, a shortsighted Congress, or the vagaries of public opinion.[90] To combat these domestic threats they consolidated foreign policy making into their hands by circumventing the State and Defense Departments, went on the offensive against the antiwar segment of Congress and society, and either lied to or kept uninformed the American people.

After commissioning the RAND Corporation to carry out a National Security Agency review during the transition period, Kissinger supplied Nixon with the bureaucratic road map they needed to revamp the foreign policy apparatus. With Nixon's blessing, Kissinger went to great pains to usurp the role traditionally played by the secretary of state in particular. Both men viewed the "leak-ridden" State Department as a major impediment to their designs and thus sought to conduct foreign policy directly from the White House. By revamping the National Security Council apparatus, Kissinger and his NSC were able to replace Rogers and the State Department to dominate policy making under Nixon's watch. By screening interdepartmental policy papers, setting NSC agendas, and chairing the important Senior Review Group, Kissinger became indispensible to Nixon's consolidation of foreign affairs in the Oval Office.

The possible impediments that Nixon and Kissinger saw to their designs included not just other Americans but the U.S. ally in South Vietnam.[91] In order to circumvent any possible obstruction by the Saigon regime, Nixon and Kissinger continued the Johnson administration's policy of holding bilateral talks with Hanoi alongside the less important four-party public negotiations. These bilateral talks would not be merely private; they would eventually be secret. What took place behind closed doors in the suburbs of Paris would not only be hidden from public view and even from other parts of the U.S. government; the full proceedings would be kept from Saigon as well.

In one of his first directives after inauguration, Kissinger ordered key national security agencies to respond to a series of questions regarding the negotiating environment, the military and political effectiveness of the South Vietnamese military and government, enemy capabilities, and U.S. military operations. In addition, the study directive also included questions regarding the role of Moscow and Beijing in Hanoi's war effort. The final result, National Security Studies Memorandum (NSSM) 1, completed in March 1969, showed general agreement among the different agencies. NSSM 1 revealed that neither Beijing nor Moscow had attempted to exert heavy pressure on Hanoi and were unlikely to do so now for various reasons. The CIA noted that "in competing for influence, Peking and Moscow tend to cancel out each other."[92]

Nixon and Kissinger did not use NSSM 1 to elicit agency proposals; rather, they used the memorandum to map the bureaucratic landscape as they had with the RAND Corporation study during the transition period.[93] The questions posed in NSSM 1 were meant to reveal where agencies stood on various matters so that the two strategists could better manipulate and control the bureaucracy. As a result, Nixon and Kissinger discounted the agencies' pessimistic responses regarding U.S. potential to exploit the contradictions in the communist world for American ends in Vietnam; they had, in any case, already decided to move forward with the Soviets. In early 1969, Nixon told Soviet ambassador Anatoly Dobrynin to discuss issues with Kissinger before making any contact with Rogers.[94] Opening a secret diplomatic channel to Moscow through Dobrynin on 21 February that ran through the White House and not the State Department, Kissinger seized the opportunity to sideline Secretary of State Rogers. The national security advisor could not allow Rogers to handle the delicate diplomacy required to link strategic armaments limitations talks with progress toward an acceptable settlement to the Vietnamese conflict.[95]

Nixon and Kissinger's China strategy, however, was slower to develop. The U.S. president originally aimed to use the threat of aligning with the Chinese against the Soviets to force Moscow to cooperate on international issues.[96] Although Nixon had broached the idea of normalizing relations with China prior to his presidency in 1967, once in office, he moved slowly toward rapprochement given the possible negative domestic and strategic repercussions of dealing with the radical Asian power. In fact, the Nixon administration used antagonistic rhetoric toward China up to March 1969.[97]

Equipped with their bureaucratic roadmap and confident of their great-power diplomacy, Nixon and Kissinger believed they could end the war within six months.[98] In order to achieve a negotiated settlement in Paris that reflected American terms, Nixon and Kissinger concentrated on the secret talks with Hanoi and getting the Soviets to impress on the North Vietnamese the need to compromise once at the table. Like the Johnson administration, they preferred closed meetings with Hanoi negotiators not only because progress proved impossible in the quadripartite plenums but also because secret bilateral talks would minimize the role of other government agencies and potential obstruction by the Saigon regime.

The form of these talks was not the only important matter to Nixon and Kissinger; the substance of the sessions was also paramount. While the United States preferred to work out military issues with the DRV and leave political issues for the RVN and NLF to hash out, Hanoi insisted that military and political terms could not be separated. In March, Nixon approved the first contact between Henry Cabot Lodge, former ambassador to the RVN and W. Averell Harriman's replacement as the lead negotiator in Paris, and Xuan Thuy. As with the U.S.-Soviet channel, however, Kissinger would soon take over the secret talks with the DRV. While Nixon wanted the Oval Office to maintain strict control over negotiations, Kissinger wanted to make himself indispensable—and Secretary of State Rogers peripheral—to Nixon.

In order to strengthen their bargaining position vis-à-vis North Vietnam and the Soviet Union, Nixon and Kissinger looked for opportunities to exert major military pressure in Indochina. Taking advantage of improved relations with Cambodia and claiming the need to strike back against Hanoi's attacks on Saigon in early 1969, Nixon ordered the secret, intensive bombing of Vietnamese communist sanctuaries in Cambodia on 22 February.[99] Militarily, Nixon reasoned that Operation Menu—consisting of "Breakfast," "Lunch," "Snack," and "Dessert"—limited Hanoi's ability to launch a large-scale offensive in the South. In addition to Menu, Nixon also ordered the resumption of maximum aerial reconnaissance over North Vietnam.[100] The real objective of these military measures was to show Hanoi and Moscow that Nixon was willing to escalate the war in ways Johnson had not been.

At the same time, Nixon resolved to keep these escalatory measures secret from Congress, the media, the American public, and even his own cabinet members. When Secretary of State Rogers and Secretary of Defense Laird discovered that the president was "contemplating" bombing Cambodia (when in fact he had already made the decision to proceed), they both expressed deep reservations. Laird doubted that the bombings could be kept secret and feared the public backlash if news got out, while Rogers objected to the bombing's potential adverse impact on the Paris negotiations. Nixon continued the charade by holding a meeting in the Oval Office on 16 March with Kissinger, Rogers, Laird, and Joint Chief of Staff Earle Wheeler in which he pretended that the "decision was still open."[101] For his part, Kissinger used the meeting to portray Rogers as an unhelpful recalcitrant.[102] The following day, 17 March, the secret bombing of Cambodia began, and although the *New York Times* broke the story about "Breakfast," Nixon and Kissinger moved quickly to squash the story and ordered wiretaps on the phones of government employees to track down the leak by working closely with FBI director J. Edgar Hoover.

While Nixon secretly escalated the air war, events in the communist world propelled his international strategy into action. Although he and Kissinger had only concentrated on the Soviet Union, their diplomatic efforts would ultimately aim at fostering a competition of sorts between the communist countries for America's favor by affecting the situation in Vietnam. Essentially, Moscow and Beijing were to demonstrate their desire for bettering relations with Washington by selling out Hanoi. The events that would allow Nixon and Kissinger's strategy to find fertile ground took place not in Southeast Asia but at the Sino-Soviet border in early March. Chinese and Soviet troops clashed on the island of Zhenbao (Damansky) in the Ussuri River, land claimed by both sides. Although Sino-Soviet alliance, as outlined by the 1950 treaty, had deteriorated in practically every aspect, the skirmishes on the border constituted the first military clash between the two nations.[103] Over the remainder of the year, no fewer than 400 clashes occurred between the two nations' border troops.[104]

Le Duan and Le Duc Tho immediately moved to reverse the damage that Sino-Soviet clashes could inflict on North Vietnam's war effort, particularly its negotiations with the Americans. Through various intermediaries including Jean Sainteny, a former French colonial official close to both Ho Chi Minh and Kissinger, North Vietnamese leaders knew that the Nixon administration wanted to continue bilateral, private talks. At the first private meeting in March 1969, Xuan Thuy warned Lodge, the new U.S. chief negotiator, that the United States would gain nothing from the divisions between the Soviet Union and China and that, despite the clashes, Moscow and Beijing would continue to aid Hanoi. Internally, North Vietnamese leaders were not as confident as they tried to appear at the 22 March meeting. The VWP realized early on that the border skirmishes would lead both Moscow and Beijing, particularly the latter due to the failure of the Cultural Revolution, to entertain thoughts of reconciling with the United States to counterbalance the other side.[105]

It was Moscow, however, that caved first. The Soviet Union approached the United States following the March border clash with China. "An emotional Ambassador Dobrynin raised the Ussuri incident with me," Kissinger noted in his memoirs, "when I tried to change the subject by suggesting it was a Sino-Soviet problem, Dobrynin insisted passionately that China was everybody's problem."[106] By April, however, little had changed; despite clashes with China, Moscow had not succumbed to American pressure. Nonetheless, on 14 April, Kissinger wielded the stick with Dobrynin. Unless there was a settlement in Vietnam, Kissinger warned the Soviet ambassador, "other measures would be invoked which could involve wider risk to U.S.-Soviet relations."[107] That same night, North Korean fighter jets shot down a U.S. reconnaissance plane, killing all thirty-one crew members onboard. Nixon and Kissinger wanted to respond with force, but at a National Security Council meeting on 16 April, Rogers, Laird, and Wheeler objected to military retaliation against the North Koreans. Despite the overwhelming opposition, Kissinger still tried to convince Nixon that a strong U.S. response would show North *Vietnam* that Nixon could be "irrational." Lacking a consensus among his advisors, the president decided to show restraint. He immediately regretted his decision and took out his frustrations in Cambodia.[108] Kissinger, meanwhile, took advantage of Nixon's regret to consolidate his control over policy making at the expense of the president's other advisors. The president was onboard with Kissinger's pursuits, having sent an angry memo to Secretary of State Rogers to rein in "disloyal" elements on the Paris negotiating team bent on "sav(ing) the President from himself."[109]

## SAIGON AGENCY

Nixon and Kissinger were not the only actors in the new war equipped with an international strategy. RVN president Nguyen Van Thieu began to revise his policies in 1969 when it became apparent that Washington would not always act in Saigon's best interests. The Thieu regime had come to power in June 1965, after wresting control from the final civilian government, and remained in place until a few days before the fall of Saigon in 1975. There were many changes and reshuffles of power in the military regime as well as a widely known rivalry between Nguyen Van Thieu and Nguyen

Cao Ky. Officially, power rested with the Armed Forces Council, and a directorate served as the council's executive body. In 1967, Thieu claimed the chairmanship of the directorate and thus outmaneuvered the more flamboyant but less politically adept Ky. Although military rule transformed into an ostensibly representative government with a constitutional assembly in 1966 and the promulgation of the constitution and democratic elections in 1967, intimidation and corruption pervaded the Saigon regime. During his near decade in office, Thieu acted in his own interests and not in those of his constituents. However, with the advent of U.S. withdrawal, Thieu, along with his cousin and advisor, Hoang Duc Nha, began to take an active role in shaping the RVN's destiny and to assert Saigon's independence vis-à-vis the Americans. Using the tools available to client regimes during the Cold War, including blackmail, foot-dragging, and manipulation, Thieu was able to force his superpower patron to do his bidding or at least frustrate Washington's aims whenever these ran counter to Saigon's interests. Although the Thieu regime was dependent on the United States to survive, it was an active, and relatively independent, agent in the post-Tet war.

In an early January 1969 report, RVN ambassador to the United States Bui Diem impressed on Thieu that since Nixon's war policy was still unclear, Saigon had to be proactive in convincing the Republican administration to pursue a policy most beneficial to the RVN. Otherwise, he warned, given the unswerving nature of the "American bureaucratic machinery [*bo may Hoa Ky*]," Saigon would be powerless to change U.S. policy once it began to pursue a course detrimental to the RVN. He urged President Thieu to order a comprehensive review of all spheres—political, military, diplomatic, economic—in the war to coordinate a new and improved South Vietnamese strategy.[110]

The most interesting aspect of Ambassador Diem's January report was his emphasis on winning, in a sense, the "hearts and minds [*tinh cam*]" of the American public and world opinion. In particular, he urged Thieu to publicly accept American troop withdrawal since it was a fait accompli and to appear committed to peace in Paris. Diem pursued an aggressive one-man public relations campaign while in France to ensure the world of Saigon's good faith at the Paris negotiations:

> Having a horde of journalists in one place was a bonanza for someone who wanted to make a public point. For starters, I accepted all interviews I could possibly fit in. One day I met with Andre Fon-

taine and Claude Julien of *Le Monde*, the next day with Roger Massif, Nicholas Chatelain, and Max Clos of *Le Figaro*. I did interviews for the *Times* with London, German, and Italian newspapers and television and what seemed almost daily background briefings with American journalists including Stanley Karnow, Marvin Kalb, Peter Kallisher, James Wilde, Takashi Oka, and Jessie Cook. . . . I was also able to clearly state our position. South Vietnam, I said, desired peace.[111]

The South Vietnamese ambassador was convinced that the diplomatic sphere of the RVN war effort could no longer be left to the Americans. Urging President Thieu to win over the U.S. public, Diem warned that if Thieu did not act quickly, popular opinion in the United States could work against the RVN, leaving Saigon in a position of having to accept any plan Nixon puts forth.[112]

On 14 May 1969, it was apparent that time was running out for the RVN. In response to the NLF's "Ten-Point Overall Solution" for peace in Paris, which included a demand for total, unreciprocated U.S. withdrawal and the abolition of the Saigon regime, Nixon turned to the public face of his strategy to bring peace with honor. Appearing on television, Nixon announced his eight-point plan for peace, including simultaneous withdrawal of American and North Vietnamese troops, and acknowledged the NLF's peace proposal by accepting the possibility of a neutral South Vietnam. In essence the May peace plans differed on two main points: on the one hand, the NLF demand for unilateral U.S. withdrawal and an interim coalition between cessation of hostilities and the holding of elections, and on the other, the U.S. call for simultaneous withdrawals and an international body to oversee these withdrawals and to supervise the elections. Although Nixon did not expect Hanoi to respond favorably to his speech, he had hoped for a positive reception at home, especially from the media. When it did not materialize, he fell into depression. It did not help that the antiwar movement, which had subsided since the tumultuous days of 1968, now began to stir again.

But if Nixon could not control domestic criticism of his policies, he could suppress dissent from South Vietnam. Following Nixon's speech, Kissinger informed the press that the it had been cleared by Saigon even though U.S. ambassador to South Vietnam Ellsworth Bunker gave Thieu the text on 12 May, two days before its intended delivery. The speech shook Saigon's confidence in the U.S.-RVN alliance. "The whole process was something of a shock," recalled Ambassador Diem. "There had been some informal exchanges on these subjects, but there was no real consultation or agreement, certainly nothing had ever been 'cleared' with Saigon." In fact, RVN leaders claimed that they were not given time to object to any of Nixon's proposals, prompting Diem to note, "The game of imposition and attempted finesse that would become the Nixon administration's trademark in dealing with its ally had begun with a bang."[113] Exactly one week after the speech, Thieu requested a meeting with Nixon.

When private talks stalled by late May[114] and with the United States and the RVN planning to show the world their solidarity in a meeting on Midway Island in early June, Hanoi stole the spotlight by orchestrating the creation of the Provisional Revolutionary Government (Chinh Phu Cach Mang Lam Thoi, PRG). Party leaders intended the PRG, founded in the same location as the NLF nearly a decade earlier, to appear as a broadbased administration that could garner international support and recognition as the true voice of the South Vietnamese people. With Nguyen Thi Binh as the PRG representative to the Paris talks and foreign minister, the Vietnamese communists possessed a powerful diplomatic tool against the Thieu regime. Madame Binh admitted after the war that even though she was the foreign minister and head delegate of the PRG in Paris, real "decision making regarding negotiations [*nhung nha lanh dao chu chot cua dam phan cua ta*]" rested with Le Duc Tho and Xuan Thuy.[115] While the "guerrilla diplomats" put forward Madame Binh, Nixon encountered problems convincing his head delegate, Lodge, to remain at the talks on the Avenue Kléber. The U.S. president was not that concerned since substantive negotiations would take place elsewhere.

When Nixon agreed to Thieu's request for a meeting, the South Vietnamese president was neither given the chance to win over the U.S. public on American soil nor able to sway Nixon to change the course of his policies toward Vietnam in 1969. Nixon rejected Thieu's request to hold a meeting in Honolulu and, fearing riots, concluded that Washington was out of the question. Instead, Nixon and Thieu met on 8 June 1969 against the "isolated and desolate" backdrop of Midway.[116]

The allies were clearly not on the same page during the uncomfortable private meeting. While Thieu spoke of his desire for the redeployment of American troops and increased aid, Nixon reiterated America's commitment to troop withdrawal and private negotiations with Hanoi. In exchange for Thieu's compliance, Nixon promised that Vietnamization would include four years of increased military aid during his first term, followed by four more years of economic support in his second, and that

America would insist on mutual troop withdrawal.[117] With no other options, Thieu accepted that the United States would pull out 25,000 troops starting in July and that private talks between the United States and the DRV on the future of South Vietnam would resume.[118] When the meeting adjourned and Nixon and Thieu stepped in front of White House correspondents, the reporters and their cameras failed to detect the cracks in the U.S.–South Vietnamese alliance.[119]

On his way back to Saigon, Thieu stopped in Taipei to meet with Chiang Kai-shek and further reflected on the Midway meeting. In an exchange that underlined the powerlessness and frustration felt by junior partners in the Cold War, Thieu related Saigon's quandary to his host: "You know when Nixon decides to withdraw, there is nothing I can do about it. Just as when Eisenhower, Kennedy, and Johnson decided to go in, there was very little my predecessors had to say about it."[120] Chiang commiserated by recalling his own experiences dealing with the United States on the eve of his escape to Taiwan and the American pressure to compromise with Mao Zedong's communist forces. Stressing his "Four No's"—no recognition of the enemy, no neutralization of South Vietnam, no coalition government, and no surrender of territory to the enemy—Thieu told Chiang that he would never allow a coalition government if North Vietnamese troops were allowed to remain in the South.

Disturbed by his meeting with Nixon at Midway and distressed by listening to Chiang's experiences, the South Vietnamese president returned to Saigon determined to implement major changes in the RVN's war policies. In particular, Thieu ordered the Foreign Ministry to coordinate a diplomatic strategy to enhance the war effort.[121] Given Washington's commitment to troop withdrawal and the initiation of four-party peace negotiations in Paris, Saigon realized the importance of devising its own international strategy.[122] In an attempt to shore up world support for its cause against the communists north and south of the seventeenth parallel, the RVN embarked on an accelerated diplomatic campaign in the latter half of 1969, including revamping its foreign service and promoting closer relations with regional powers.

RVN foreign minister Tran Van Lam's report written at the end of 1969 outlined the three goals of his ministry for that year: (1) establishing more diplomatic missions abroad; (2) opening more press offices in not just democratic nations but neutralist ones as well; and (3) making Saigon's voice heard in Paris.[123] The Political War Department (Tong Cuc Chien Tranh Chinh Tri, PWD) also issued a policy recommendation that urged the government to utilize world opinion to advance its diplomatic struggle as the Vietnamese communists had successfully done over the past year.[124] However, the department warned that "the issue is not just sending delegations to other countries, not just increasing the amount of staff in the foreign embassies, and not just establishing more press offices." The PWD proposed that the administration thoroughly study the enemy's diplomatic strategy in order to devise its own plan in waging a political war against the communists at the international level. In particular, the RVN needed to align itself more closely with Taiwan, South Korea, and West Germany, since those countries were undergoing similar partitioned experiences. Finally, the PWD recommended pushing forward economic and cultural exchanges with the democratic nations of Asia with the ultimate goal of establishing a viable economic bloc that would counter communist expansion.[125]

By the end of 1969, then, the amount of "international" work necessitated the revamping of the RVN Foreign Ministry. Thieu believed that a strong centralized system would vastly improve South Vietnam's foreign service. Outlining nine steps of varying degrees of importance, Thieu's meticulous pronouncements covered issues ranging from proper diplomatic conduct to the optimal number of staff at any given embassy.[126] The attention to detail underlined the importance of the war's diplomatic sphere for the RVN president. During the period from 1969 to 1973, the reports on the "international picture" broken down by regions and specific countries grew with every passing year. Juxtaposing the quantity of these reports against their absence from the Foreign Ministry in the early years of the war, one can conclude that by 1969 the RVN recognized the importance of the diplomatic sphere and the international level of the conflict.

### THE NIXON DOCTRINE AND KISSINGERIAN DIPLOMACY

As Saigon awoke from its complacency and began to reassert itself in the war against communist forces, Nixon grew weary of the public and private talks in Paris. With little progress on the negotiating front, and Lodge's resignation, Nixon decided to communicate directly with the DRV, sending Ho Chi Minh a letter that expressed his desire for peace but also issued a threat that if progress toward a settlement did not come by 1 November, he would have to resort to "measures of great consequence and force."[127] Following this letter, the first secret meeting took place between Kissinger and North Vietnamese negotiators on 4 August 1969.

*Richard Nixon and Nguyen Van Thieu, followed by Henry Kissinger,*
*Nguyen Cao Ky, and Ambassador Ellsworth Bunker, at the Independence Palace*
*in Saigon, July 1969 (Douglas Pike Photograph Collection, Vietnam Center*
*and Archive, Texas Tech University)*

In order to provide cover for Kissinger's secret meeting with Xuan Thuy in Paris, Nixon in mid-1969 embarked on a public relations campaign to shore up support for his policies with constituents at home and with allies abroad. In late July, the president departed on an around-the-world trip during which revealed to reporters what became known as the Nixon Doctrine. Short of war with a major power, he declared in Guam, the nations of Asia engaged in civil wars would have to fend for themselves.[128] At the end of his tour of Southeast Asia, Nixon took up Thieu's invitation to visit Saigon. As the first stay by an American president at the Presidential Palace, Nixon's visit sent the message to Thieu's allies and adversaries that he still enjoyed U.S. support.[129] Privately, though, Nixon sent more ambiguous messages to Thieu. On the one hand, he declared his intentions to escalate the war in order to force Hanoi to settle in Paris; on the other, he let the

South Vietnamese president know that additional American troop withdrawals would follow a systematic timetable.[130]

Meanwhile, Kissinger had less success intimidating the North Vietnamese.[131] "If by November 1, no major progress has been made toward a
solution," Kissinger warned Thuy, "we will be compelled—with great reluctance—to take measures of the greatest consequences."[132] The meeting
still yielded few results, as was evident in the response to Kissinger's question of whether there would be a reply to Nixon's letter to Ho Chi Minh. No,
Xuan Thuy answered. For the rest of the meeting neither side budged from
its position. When the reply finally came at the end of August, Nixon felt it
underscored the futility of making threats. The VWP, on behalf of Ho Chi
Minh, sent what Nixon considered a "cold rebuff."[133] In reality, it was Le
Duan who had rejected the offer; Ho Chi Minh might have been amenable
had he not been marginalized in the Politburo and nearing the end of his
life.[134]

By taking over the secret talks, Kissinger usurped the role that normally
would have been played by Rogers not only in regards to Vietnam but also
with the Soviet Union. Throughout the summer, the national security advisor met with Ambassador Dobrynin to convey America's position on
issues including U.S.-Soviet relations, Sino-American relations, and the
Vietnam War.[135] Kissinger acknowledged the positive role that the Soviets
had played in the negotiations in Paris up to that point, but he expressed
concern that the Soviets had not utilized their maximum leverage over
the North Vietnamese. Indeed, Moscow had overtaken Beijing as the main
supplier of military and economic aid to Hanoi, although Chinese assistance to the North Vietnamese was still significant. Although Kissinger
emphasized Washington's noninterference in the Sino-Soviet confrontation, he still dangled a threat by saying that the United States sought better
relations with China. In an "ironical" manner, Kissinger pointed out to
Dobrynin that the Soviet Union had replaced the United States as China's
"main object of attacks."[136]

Nixon and Kissinger eventually made good on their threat to the Soviet
Union by improving relations with China. In July, the United States began
lifting travel and trade restrictions, ending patrols by the Seventh Fleet in
the Taiwan Straits, and sending diplomatic messages via third parties that
the United States would not support Moscow's proposal for a collective
security system in Asia. Meanwhile in Beijing, Mao Zedong and the CCP
leadership confirmed Kissinger's observations; the Soviet Union posed a
bigger threat to China than the United States. Eventually, the four mar-

shals—Chen Yi, Ye Jianying, Xu Xiangqian, and Nie Rongzhen—proposed that the PRC resume Sino-American ambassadorial talks.[137]

Nonetheless, Nixon had reached a crossroads. His strategy to end the war within his first year had failed as his ultimatum to Ho and his comrades fell on deaf ears. Moreover, his advisors were split on how to proceed. Kissinger urged ending the war quickly by pushing for a settlement and, if Hanoi remained obstinate, forcing the North Vietnamese into submission through sharp military action. Rogers and Laird, in contrast, advised caution and feared that escalation would upset Congress and spark major unrest at home. Nixon, exhilarated by Neil Armstrong's walk on the moon in late July and incensed by North Vietnamese defiance, leaned toward toughness and thus Kissinger's plan. The national security advisor, exploiting the president's mood, figured out a way to isolate Nixon from alternate—and more moderate—points of view: he asked and received approval for the formation of a Special Vietnam Study Group, which he would chair.[138] Kissinger also tasked members of his NSC staff to explore military options that would lead to the crystallization of the contingency plan known as Duck Hook. Duck Hook constituted a revised version of the military plan formulated in April, before events in North Korea intervened. Kissinger's NSC staff, known as the September Group, examined the consequences of a four-day attack that would include massive bombing of twenty-nine major targets, mining ports, and harbors, and possibly even using tactical nuclear weapons.[139]

Throughout the rest of September and October, Kissinger moved aggressively to win Nixon's approval for the implementation of Duck Hook. In September, the national security advisor sent a bleak assessment of the situation in South Vietnam, had his staff prepare a presidential speech announcing the military plan, and worked on linkage by sending threats to Moscow via Dobrynin that the president considered the Vietnam War the crucial issue in U.S.-Soviet relations.[140] In fact, Nixon ordered the Pentagon to put U.S. nuclear forces on high alert to rattle the nerves of the Soviets so that they would place pressure on their North Vietnamese allies to be more cooperative in Paris. Although Nixon did not have any intention of pursuing the nuclear option, he liked the Eisenhower-brinkmanship nature of placing U.S. nuclear forces on alert to scare the Soviets into thinking that Nixon could use these weapons in Vietnam.[141] But when Rogers and Laird found out about Duck Hook and Nixon's 1 November deadline to Hanoi leaders, they increased their opposition to Kissinger's plan. Playing on Nixon's insecurities of mounting domestic criticism of his war effort and pointing out the flaws in Kissinger's military plans, these more moderate presidential advisors won the day: Duck Hook did not go forward in 1969.[142] In urging the president to stress long-range solutions like Vietnamization, Rogers and Laird were supported by the advice offered to Nixon by counterinsurgency expert Sir Robert Thompson, who gave an upbeat yet cautious assessment of the likelihood of American success in South Vietnam. Thompson, drawing on his experience gained in the British campaign in Malaya, convinced the president that it would take two years before Vietnamization would succeed.[143]

The persuasive arguments against Duck Hook and for Vietnamization put forward by Rogers and Laird were not the primary reasons that Nixon abandoned his "madman" military plans. In the fall of 1969 Nixon feared the first nationwide antiwar demonstrations under his presidency, Moratorium and Mobilization against the War, scheduled for mid-October and mid-November. Although his approval ratings rose with each troop withdrawal announcement in June and September, overall public support for the war continued to drop. As a result, he decided to attack opponents at home rather than the ones abroad in order to buy more time for his Vietnam strategy. Marshalling his hawkish and conservative forces in the administration, Congress, media, and general public, Nixon launched a counteroffensive to blunt the pressure for a hasty peace.

On 15 October, Moratorium Day witnessed average Americans across the country suspending their "business as usual" to participate in antiwar protests. Although Nixon believed he not only had weathered the storm but in fact had emerged stronger after Moratorium, he braced himself for Mobilization and once again contemplated taking major military action. Convinced that he should deliver a hawkish speech in early November before the demonstration, he once again considered placing Duck Hook on the table. But cooler heads prevailed, and Nixon, who convinced a dejected Kissinger and even himself that Duck Hook was only temporarily shelved, issued a different sort of speech. Appealing for support on Capitol Hill and delivering a television address on 3 November, Nixon targeted the "silent majority" of Americans who, he claimed, backed administration policy.[144] While Nixon basked in his 77 percent approval rating after his televised address, hundreds of thousands of demonstrators converged on Washington, carrying candles to commemorate the tens of thousands of lives lost during the war and to call for the end of death and destruction in Vietnam. Although the speech, and less ethical measures including the campaign to create fake grassroots or "astroturf" support for the speech, worked to increase both congressional and popular backing, the president was none-theless haunted by the decision to cancel Duck Hook.[145] Like Le Duan, Nixon would bide his time until he found a suitable opportunity to implement his military plans.

### A FUNERAL AND A REUNION

As Nixon wrestled with the public and private facets of his Vietnam strategy and as he balanced the militant and moderate forces in his cabinet and within himself, an event in Hanoi brought despair to the communist revolution. In the early morning of 2 September, on the twenty-fourth anniversary of the founding of the DRV and the August Revolution of 1945, Ho Chi Minh passed away.[146] Although by the time of his death he was more or less a figurehead, "Bac Ho" (Uncle Ho) still commanded international respect as a revolutionary who had devoted his life to liberating his country from the Japanese, French, and later the Americans. In addition, he had played a crucial diplomatic role that helped North Vietnam manage a policy of equilibrium between China and the Soviet Union. Following Ho's death, Hanoi leaders pressured Moscow and Beijing to suppress their own interests to honor the wishes their legendary comrade expressed in his published testament: "Being a man who has devoted his whole life to the revolution, the more proud I am of the growth of international communist and workers' movement, the more pained I am by the current discord among the fraternal Parties. I hope that our Party will do its best to contribute effectively to the restoration of unity among the fraternal Parties on the basis of Marxism-Leninism and proletarian internationalism, in a way which confirms to both reason and sentiment. I am firmly confident that the fraternal Parties and countries will have to unite again."[147]

Ho Chi Minh's posthumous appeal ensured that Moscow and Beijing would need to avoid any allegation of collaboration with the United States. The Soviet Union appeared to do an about-face while China stopped even its timid steps toward Washington.[148]

In addition to bringing an abrupt halt to the improvement of relations between Hanoi's major allies and the United States, Ho's death also brought about an attempt at reconciliation between the Chinese and the Soviets. At his funeral in Hanoi, the North Vietnamese pressured the allies to reconcile their differences. The Soviets sent a message to Chinese leaders requesting an end to the hostilities on the Sino-Soviet border. When they did not receive a response, Kosygin returned to Moscow via

Calcutta. While en route, he received word from the Chinese proposing a meeting, and on 11 September, Zhou Enlai and Kosygin met at the Beijing Airport, for the first time since February 1965. The meeting did not result in "the restoration of unity" Ho Chi Minh had wanted, but it nonetheless suggested the VWP's political power in the communist world, influence Hanoi would need in the new decade.[149]

CONCLUSION

As Vietnamese official histories begin to present the Tet Offensive as a tactical defeat but a strategic victory, it is important to explore the extent of that defeat and the tangibility of that victory. Le Duan's pursuit of the General Offensive and General Uprising in 1968 exacted enormous casualties on the Vietnamese resistance. The coordinated military attacks on all of the major cities and towns of South Vietnam during the first wave of the offensive failed to deliver a definitive military victory over ARVN forces or to incite a general political uprising of the masses. Instead, they brought about a public shift in U.S. war policy that resulted in the initiation of peace negotiations. Le Duan had never been predisposed toward ending the war through a political settlement, as the moderates had called for until their arrests in 1967, and he clung to his objective of toppling the Saigon regime through a general insurrection. Throughout the spring and summer of 1968, Le Duan ordered VWP forces to launch a second and third wave of attacks. With each successive wave, the first secretary led communist forces further from victory and deeper into military loss.

It would take the Vietnamese resistance three years to recover from Le Duan's disastrous strategy. On the twentieth anniversary of the Tet Offensive, the former political deputy of COSVN, General Tran Do, described this period in stark terms: "We had thrown all our forces into the general offensive . . . and when the enemy opened its counteroffensive, we had no force left, our position was weakened and we coped with the counteroffensive with great difficulty. We fell into a critical situation in the years 1969, 1970, and 1971."[150] At the start of this "critical situation" in 1969, the VWP implemented "talking while fighting" while continuing to exert military pressure on the Saigon regime, but the mounting casualties forced Hanoi to take stock of its situation. Sino-Soviet clashes, the arrival of a new U.S. president who sought to exploit the contradictions in the Cold War, a revitalized Saigon regime, and the death of the revolution's beloved leader made 1969 the most trying year for Hanoi's war effort. On the tenth anniversary of the start of Hanoi's national liberation struggle, VWP leaders felt no closer to victory.

For the United States, the 1968 Tet Offensive constituted a watershed, but it could have been more of a turning point. Although the Johnson administration stemmed the escalation of America's war after Tet, the Nixon administration in many ways reversed that trend beginning in 1969. Like Le Duan and Le Duc Tho, Nixon and Kissinger were confident that they could succeed where their predecessors had failed by streamlining policy making and introducing a three-pronged strategy that took into account the military, political, and diplomatic spheres of the war. Like North Vietnamese leaders, the president and his national security advisor sought to minimize both internal and external threats to their authority. While decision making regarding the Vietnam War rested solely in the White House, maintaining utmost secrecy in their policies would provide Nixon and Kissinger the protection they needed to thwart domestic political pressure to end the war. Just as Le Duan dealt firmly with the southern revolution, so too did Nixon act swiftly to put his Saigon ally in its place. The Thieu regime instantly realized that the U.S.-RVN alliance had entered a new stage, one in which Saigon and Washington did not necessarily share the same goals and objectives. Finally, Nixon sought to exploit the Sino-Soviet split for American ends in Vietnam, just as Le Duan had at the start of his war effort.

As Luu Van Loi noted, the stage was set for a new war as Hanoi leaders confronted their equally tenacious rivals in Washington, as relations between traditional Cold War allies began to shift, and as a new theater of battle emerged at the Paris negotiations. The diplomatic sphere of the war leveled the playing field, as the Saigon regime and the southern revolutionaries became more active in the international arena. The war for peace in the 1970s, however, would not only pit diplomats sparring on the world stage; instead, the fighting would reach new heights of violence and spread beyond the borders of Vietnam. As the conflict grew hotter throughout Indochina, tensions thawed in the wider Cold War, threatening to flood the Vietnamese resistance. At the start of the new decade, North Vietnam would find itself caught in the torrent of this dangerous realignment in great-power relations.

# part three

# THE PURSUIT
# OF A CHIMERIC
# VICTORY

*Le Duc Tho undoubtedly was the stuff of which heroes are made.*
*What we grasped only with reluctance — and many at home never understood —*
*is that heroes are such because of monomaniacal determination. They are*
*rarely pleasant men; their rigidity approaches the fanatic; they do not specialize*
*in the qualities required for a negotiated peace. —Henry Kissinger*[1]

chapter five

# SIDESHOWS AND MAIN ARENAS

Le Duc Tho met Henry Kissinger for the first time on a cold winter's day in a working-class suburb of Paris. Having sparred directly and indirectly with other American negotiators, including W. Averell Harriman and Henry Cabot Lodge, Tho quickly took stock of Kissinger, who appeared quite different from his patrician predecessors. Tho, and his colleagues in the Politburo, steeled themselves for this new type of American negotiator: a German Jew who had risen to the top in both academia and government in his adopted home country.[2] Recalling two lines from the Vietnamese epic poem *Truyen Kieu*, "Dan long cho doi it lau, / Chay ra thi cung nam sau voi gi [Wait a little while, / sooner or later the result will be the same the following year so why hurry]," Tho's guiding philosophy in negotiations disregarded the enemy's skill in argument since success rested on a single factor: one's own patience. The end result, Tho reasoned, would be the same whether he rushed or waited.[3]

Kissinger, who had dealt only with Xuan Thuy up to this point, also sized up his new opponent. Although the national security advisor seemed impressed with his interlocutor's dignified yet stern manner and "monumentally courageous exertions" as a revolutionary imprisoned under French colonial rule, Kissinger believed that Le Duc Tho's ideological zeal led him, like other Vietnamese, to extreme haughtiness and paranoia. Kissinger later concluded that negotiations with the man known as "Tho" never stood a chance. Speaking decades later at a State Department conference commemorating the war, Kissinger, who outlived Tho, walked up to the Vietnamese dignitaries from Hanoi and said, "It is Le Duc Tho's fault that I look this old. He aged me quite a bit during our negotiations."[4]

Stepping into the new decade, North Vietnamese leaders braced their population for what appeared an interminable war. As Tho and Kissinger sparred in Paris, Le Duan emerged from behind the curtains to rally the North Vietnamese people to continue the costly war. By 1970, the first secretary had no choice but to resort to an "economy of forces" policy in order to rebuild communist strength in the aftermath of the draining 1968 and 1969 military offensives. At the same time, his security chief, Tran Quoc Hoan, pulled out all the stops in his campaign to eradicate all opposition to the revolution.

As North Vietnam assumed a defensive position on the South Vietnamese battlefield, the fighting escalated in Cambodia and Laos. Instead of winding down the war and negotiating peace, the combatants expanded their conflict to all of Indochina. Although the fates of the Indochinese nations, and indeed all of Southeast Asia, were intimately intertwined at the outset, the start of the 1970s witnessed a major shift in the region's postcolonial development, including the deterioration of relations among the Indochinese nations. Not only did Saigon and Phnom Penh bicker over dwindling American funds for the war against the communists, but the latent antagonism between the VWP and the Khmer Rouge rose to the surface as well. The regionalization of the Vietnam War also attracted international concern: Why was the war expanding to Cambodia and Laos when the four parties involved in the fighting were ostensibly working toward peace in Paris?

Diplomacy offered each side a way to deflect criticism and buy time for its forces to regroup on the battlefield. While Nixon and Kissinger sought to pressure Hanoi during the secret talks and began to concentrate on the China card in their international strategy, Le Duan and PRG foreign minister Madame Nguyen Thi Binh reached out to other nations in the socialist sphere and the nonaligned world with great success. Meanwhile, RVN president Nguyen Van Thieu launched a diplomatic campaign to bolster his—and the RVN's—image on the regional stage. Le Duan's Politburo, as well as the Nixon administration and the Saigon regime, used diplomacy as a tool of warfare to the great detriment of the region's political development. As the diplomatic struggle grew more entrenched in Paris and the military battles in Indochina intensified, however, the chance for a viable peace agreement grew more remote.

### THE FORGOTTEN REVOLUTIONS

As the military and political situation in Indochina offered no respite to communist forces, Party leaders turned to new public relations initiatives to bolster their control over the war effort. Le Duan carried out the most significant campaign. Although Ho's death in late 1969 did not result in a power struggle since Le Duan had been in firm control of the Hanoi Polit-buro even when the president was alive, the first secretary may have de-cided to step out from behind the shadows to show the North Vietnamese people and the world that he was the man in charge. On 2 February 1970, Le Duan gave a speech commemorating the fortieth anniversary of the Party titled, "Duoi la co vang cua Dang, vi doc lap, tu do, vi chu nghia xa hoi, tien len gianh nhung thang loi moi" (Under the Glorious Banner of the Party for Independence, Freedom, Socialism, Advancing to New Victories), which was widely covered in all major Party and government newspapers and journals, including *Nhan Dan* (The People's Daily), *Quan Doi Nhan Dan* (People's Army), and *Hoc Tap* (The Study).[5] Although the first secre-tary stressed the importance of North Vietnam's support for the war, he also emphasized the need to build socialism in the DRV by advancing the "three revolutions," with the most important being the technological one.[6] In early March 1970, Le Duan distributed a Politburo resolution that in-augurated an elite year-long class designed to familiarize top Party cadres with the teachings of Ho Chi Minh. The resolution aimed to strengthen the ideological backbone of Party cadres by invoking the revered leader's life and legacy.[7] Perhaps to ward off a crisis in his war leadership, Le Duan sought to shift the people's attention to internal matters.

As Le Duan placed more emphasis on boosting the morale of North Vietnamese society, Minister of Public Security Hoan continued to crack down on disgruntled elements. In 1969, his security forces investigated an organization known as the Democratic Antiwar Peace Force (Mat tran hoa binh dan chu chong chien tranh) that was operating in Hanoi, Ha Bac, Ninh Binh, Tuyen Quang, and Lan Son. According to Hoan's report, this organization was in the process of reaching out to reactionaries in the Catholic strongholds of Bui Chu and Phat Diem. Although the group began in 1967 as a number of "young men [who] were frequently meeting to sing yellow music [*nhac vang*],[8] to discuss reactionary propaganda," it

*Le Duan and Nikolai Podgorny (Douglas Pike Photograph Collection,*
*Vietnam Center and Archive, Texas Tech University)*

soon began to "spread distortions about Party and state policies, and to discuss forming a reactionary organization." By late December of that year, security forces arrested all of the leaders, who they claimed were "children of former capitalists, landowners, puppet soldiers, etc. . . who lived lives of depravity and leisure and who harbored class hatred and hated our regime," and sentenced them to fifteen years in prison.[9]

Hoan's "disruption of this nascent reactionary organization" is important since it coincided with a reevaluation of the role of the Public Security Services in early 1970. In the minister's "concluding speech on investigative operations and determining suspected threats," he said he had moved too slowly against the leaders of this "yellow music" movement.[10] Fortunately, security forces had "nipped the reactionary organization in the bud, . . . prevent[ing] negative influences in a key, focal-point area where the national headquarters offices of our government and Party and a number of foreign embassies were located."[11] Contrasting this investigation with the ministry's handling of the Revisionist Anti-Party Affair, in which Hoan believed that he and his forces had moved too slowly, the minister emphasized pursuing suspected targets early and at the slightest provocation. Invoking the 1967 arrest of Dang Kim Giang, a high-ranking officer and protégé of Giap, Hoan admitted that Giang had expressed disagreement with Resolution 9 passed in 1963. "Initially he did not do anything," Hoan recalled, "and only when there was public debate did he begin to attack people." Had security forces arrested Giang in 1963 and not 1967, Hoan reasoned, the affair would not have become a significant movement. In other words, the Minister of Public Security indicated that the state had to be more vigilant of suspected "dissatisfaction" and "nip" any dissent at its incipient stage before it could blossom into full-blown counterrevolution.[12]

Hoan's circumspection paid off. In early 1970, he ordered his forces to gather reconnaissance intelligence on the People's Revolutionary Party (Dang nhan dan cach mang) operating around Hanoi. The objective of this group, according to Hoan's forces, was to disrupt security and public order and to oppose the revolution. Since the ministry caught wind of this group early on and arrested its ringleader, who was ostensibly fired from his job at Da Phuc Airport for "theft and illicit relations with members of the opposite sex," the organization quickly disbanded and only the leader needed to be sent to reeducation camp. In their records, security officials boasted that they "had blocked this organization in a timely fashion before anything unfortunate could occur."[13] As antiwar sentiment increased in the DRV, Hoan's police state went on the offensive with its campaign that rendered illegal even the slightest criticism of Le Duan's policies.[14]

Le Duan and Hoan were not the only Party members to concern themselves with stemming war-weariness in North Vietnamese society. At the CEC's Eighteenth Plenum in late January, Party leaders as a whole sought to address the past and look to the future by assessing the war in the aftermath of the Tet Offensive and to put forward new tasks for 1970.[15] The resolution promulgated by the plenum on 10 March outlined what Party leaders viewed as the four aims of Nixon's strategy: (1) protecting Vietnamization through only gradual de-escalation; (2) threatening the revolution's strength in the countryside through accelerated pacification; (3) strengthening the Saigon regime through increased military activity in Cambodia and Laos; and (4) reducing the prospects for real peace in Paris through diplomatic offensives aimed only to placate U.S. public opinion.[16] When they turned their focus inward to assess their own war effort, VWP leaders concluded that they had launched the General Offensive and General Uprising at an inopportune time since the enemy still had a substantial number of troops on the ground in 1968. As a result, they predicted that the new stage of the war was going to be "difficult, decisive, and complicated [*gay go, quyet liet va phuc tap*]" and that victory could be achieved only in increments.[17] Party leaders, however, did not advocate a return to guerrilla warfare but instead stressed the importance of maintaining the "strategic initiative." Nonetheless, Le Duan recognized that the losses sustained in his drive to redeem his ambitious strategy in 1968 would mean that General Giap's moderating influence would be apparent in 1970. Le Duan's worst fears were realized in the plenum's Resolution 18, which promoted an "economy of forces" strategy by elevating the political and diplomatic spheres of the war and by stepping up support for the revolutionary struggle in Cambodia and Laos.[18] The first secretary's goal of fomenting a mass uprising in South Vietnam through large-scale attacks on its cities and towns was put on hold indefinitely.

The first prong of the strategy put forward by Party leaders essentially called for the promotion of the diplomatic struggle. Not only would communist diplomacy aid the military struggle in South Vietnam and boost political morale in North Vietnam, but Hanoi's global offensives would also target domestic politics in the United States.[19] Although the Party claimed to have begun the diplomatic struggle in 1965, declared its advancement in January 1967 with Resolution 13, and rhetorically increased diplomacy's importance with the start of peace talks in May 1968, the VWP only upgraded the diplomatic struggle to the same level as the military and political struggles in 1970. Politburo leaders circulated a subsequent resolution describing the North's responsibilities in the new stage of war. Truong Chinh, whose duties included maintaining production levels in the DRV to support the war effort in the South, was the main architect of the Politburo resolution.[20]

At the same time that Party leaders convened the Eighteenth Plenum and elevated the importance of the diplomatic struggle, RVN president Thieu, like Le Duan, decided that his political image needed a makeover. Thieu sought to use a visit to Japan in 1970 to make a "deep impression on the world so that it can reverberate back home."[21] Interestingly, he never thought to do it the other way around. The RVN leader wanted to appear as an able leader with a clear grasp of international issues who promoted democracy and peace at home and abroad. However, the "kinder and gentler" Thieu continued to stand firm against any peace that would allow invading forces to remain in his country. Facing a future of reduced U.S. aid, Thieu put forward an economic proposal for the success and development of the Southeast Asian economy—starting with an integrated Cambodian-Laotian-Vietnamese-Thai economic bloc—that would link the entire region, from "Japan in the north to New Zealand, Australia, and Indonesia in the south."[22] His long-term economic, strategic, and geopolitical vision for the RVN and the region was key to the revitalization of his image as a leader.

As the U.S.–South Vietnamese alliance languished, strong regional ties became the highest priority in RVN foreign relations.[23] From the beginning of the U.S. intervention, Thai, South Korean, Filipino, Taiwanese, New Zealand, and Australian troops fought alongside American soldiers against communist forces in South Vietnam. During the Cold War, the region's small and middle powers collaborated not only on the battlefields of Vietnam, but also in the economic and political arenas to carve out a sphere of economic and political autonomy from heavy American and Japanese influence.[24] The Association of Southeast Asian Nations (ASEAN) was founded by Indonesia, Malaysia, Singapore, the Philippines, and Thailand on 8 August 1967 for this very reason.

Even though previous attempts at regional communities had failed, including the Association of Southeast Asia and MALPHILINDO (an acronym for Malaysia, the Philippines, and Indonesia), ASEAN managed to survive. Although the founding members denied that ASEAN was an anticommunist alliance, it was apparent to the RVN that ASEAN included like-minded countries which saw a common threat posed by the Sino-Soviet struggle, North Vietnam, and domestic communist insurgencies. Moreover, ASEAN's founding mission was to promote free trade and political stability in Southeast Asia. With the promulgation of the Nixon Doctrine and the British proclamation to pull out troops east of Suez, Southeast Asian nations steeled themselves for the long-term impact of Western withdrawal. Due to the growing interconnectedness of the region, Saigon aimed to promote closer relations with noncommunist nations in Asia to offset both the communist threat and de-Americanization of the war.

In order to bolster relations with ASEAN and other friendly nations, the Thieu administration sent Phan Quang Dan, one of four ministers of state (*quoc vu khanh*) who ranked below the deputy prime minister and above the minister of external affairs, on a "goodwill tour [*vieng tham thien chi cac quoc gia ban*]" of select nations in the region of South and Southeast Asia.[25] The tour, which took place in late 1969, included Thailand, Burma, India, Malaysia, Singapore, Indonesia, Philippines, Australia, and Laos. Prior to the tour, Saigon was worried about Dan's visit to New Delhi and Djakarta. In India, the Indira Gandhi government had been contemplating elevating the DRV diplomatic mission to embassy status. In light of this, Dan's visit to India would have to include warning New Delhi that such a move would harm South Vietnamese–Indian relations. In Indonesia, due to the lack of RVN representation in Djakarta, Dan's visit posed logistical and potential political problems for the Suharto regime. Saigon was concerned with diplomatic protocol and, given the status of Indonesia in Southeast Asia, the RVN could not afford to offend Djakarta.

On his return, Dan reported to RVN prime minister Tran Thien Khiem in early 1970 that he had been greatly encouraged by the desire the other nations expressed for the RVN to play a greater role in regional affairs. He claimed his visit had led Indonesia to withdraw its opposition to the participation of South Vietnam in ASEAN. Originally, Singapore had been reluctant to include the RVN, and Malaysia's Tunku Abdul Rahman had been obliged to take a strong stand against Saigon's inclusion. However, Dan reported that Lee Kuan Yew had become aware during his visit that a Saigon victory in the war was essential for Singapore. In Djakarta, Dan noted that Foreign Minister Adam Malik and Prime Minister Ali Moertopo were especially gracious and expressed interest in reestablishing close relations with Saigon. Since Dan's visit was not publicly announced, he did not meet with President Suharto; however, Dan claimed that it was widely known that Suharto and Malik held divergent opinions on Vietnam. Regarding the lack of diplomatic presence in Djakarta, Dan and his Indonesian hosts agreed that the two countries would open trade offices in each other's capitals and that although the representatives would be called trade commissioners, they would in effect have the authority to speak as ambassadors. In Laos and Thailand, Dan argued that the RVN must maintain close contact with its embassies in Vientiane and Bangkok given the level of Vietnamese communist troop activity in both countries. The only pessimistic evaluation Dan gave in his report was his analysis of the situation in New Delhi. Dan expressed his country's concern to the Indian Foreign Ministry that India's increasing partiality and apparent procommunist bias in the Vietnamese dispute could cost New Delhi its moral authority and influence in the area, especially since it chaired the ICC. However, given the high level of Soviet influence and the strong local communist presence in India, Dan could only recommend that Saigon increase its activities in New Delhi.[26]

While Thieu made some diplomatic progress with his strategy of "them ban, bot thu [more friends, fewer enemies]," Nixon paid more attention and poured more resources into Vietnamization, even though intelligence estimates reported increasing pessimism in Saigon regarding American strategy.[27] Early in the year, Nixon announced that 150,000 troops would be withdrawn from Vietnam by the spring of 1971. Knowing that the United States would still have 344,000 troops there at the end of 1970 and that Vietnamization would be in full swing by this point, Nixon believed that his diplomatic and military offensives would ultimately succeed in garnering a peace agreement that would ensure the survival of the anticommunist regime in Saigon. On the negotiating front, Nixon was less optimistic. Since the end of 1969, when Lodge had officially resigned from his post, Nixon had not appointed a replacement in order to show his dissatisfaction with the progress of the Paris talks.

Nonetheless, Kissinger, confident in his negotiating abilities, persuaded Nixon to let him reopen the secret talks with Hanoi. After his first private meeting with North Vietnamese leaders in the summer of 1969, five months had passed without a subsequent meeting. Although U.S. officials indicated that Kissinger desired another meeting with Xuan Thuy in late 1969, Le Duan declined the invitation, citing Washington's "demotion of the Paris conference."[28] On 14 January 1970, the U.S. defense attaché in Paris, General Vernon Walters, approached the DRV representative to the Paris talks, Mai Van Bo, to request another private meeting between Xuan Thuy and Kissinger.[29] In accordance with the promotion of the diplomatic struggle at the Eighteenth Plenum, the North Vietnamese were finally ready to accept the American invitation to another secret negotiating session. When Bo conveyed his government's approval on 16 February for a private meeting, General Walters told him that Kissinger desired to meet with Le Duc Tho, who had announced his intent to come to Paris for the French Communist Party Congress.[30] In fact, Tho had already planned to use the congress as a cover; his true mission was to participate in secret meetings with Nixon's national security advisor.[31]

The first encounter between the two men who would be awarded the Nobel Peace Prize for their negotiating efforts took place on 21 February at the residence of the DRV delegation in a Parisian suburb, Choisy-le-Roi, in what Kissinger later described in his memoirs as the "dingy living room" of a house "that might have belonged to a foreman in one of the factories in the district."[32] In these humble surroundings, Kissinger spent the first half of the meeting presenting his points and proposals. Hanoi had missed a golden opportunity to end the war, the U.S. national security advisor pointed out, when it refused America's proposal of mutual with-drawal and the maintenance of the existing political relationship made on 4 August 1969. Since then, Kissinger claimed, Nixon's position had only grown stronger, while the DRV's military and diplomatic fortunes had de-clined.[33] Putting forward the two proposals, the former Harvard professor offered either to negotiate based on the NLF's Ten-Point Overall Solution or Nixon's eight-point proposal, or to scrap both plans and draw up new set of general principles that could guide discussions.[34]

When the discussions resumed after a brief recess following Kissin-ger's fifty-five-minute exposition of the American position, the North Vietnamese launched into what would become their modus operandi: lengthy, castigating lectures intended to wear Kissinger down. Thuy first blamed the United States for allowing negotiations to deteriorate by fail-ing to offer anything new in late 1969. Hanoi, in contrast, had proposed two concrete terms, including U.S. withdrawal in five to six months and the establishment of a three-component coalition government. During the second half of the meeting in the late afternoon, Tho delivered a long lecture challenging Kissinger's assessment of the situation after August 1969. He pointed out that the United States had consistently underesti-mated the strength of the revolutionary forces and that Kissinger's current assessment was no exception. After listing four instances when the United States misjudged the military situation—propping up the Ngo Dinh Diem regime in the 1950s, supporting Diem's Strategic Hamlet scheme in the early 1960s, introducing American bombing and ground troops in 1965, and implementing Vietnamization in 1969—Tho warned that the United States was now committing yet another misstep with its increased bomb-ing of Laos.[35] Tho also found dubious Kissinger's claim that Nixon was in a stronger position since the previous meeting in August 1969. The formi-dable Vietnamese negotiator invoked the results from recent Gallup polls that showed how more Americans favored immediate troop withdrawal and quoted statements made by leading figures in the Democratic Party, members of the Senate Foreign Relations Committee, and even former government officials who demanded change in U.S. policy toward Viet-nam.[36] Although Kissinger deemed listening to his adversary talk about American domestic dissent as "not compatible with our dignity to debate," Tho's questions regarding U.S. chances for victory taunted the national security advisor. "Before, there were over a million U.S. and puppet troops, and you failed. How can you succeed when you let the puppet troops do the fighting? Now, with only U.S. support, how can you win?"[37]

INDOCHINA AT WAR: LAOS

Before adjourning the session and settling on a date for the next secret meeting, Kissinger made an astute comment regarding North Vietnamese policy toward Laos: "We have remarked that most of the Pathet Lao troops were speaking Vietnamese."[38] Even though the Party's Eighteenth Plenum earlier in the year had called for stepped up support of the Laotian revolution, Hanoi had already been firmly entrenched in Laotian territory since the French-Indochina War, when the Viet Minh worked closely with the Pathet Lao to defeat the colonial forces.[39] After 1954, North Vietnam increased its presence in Laos and contributed to the resumption of hostilities in the country at the end of the decade.[40] Although the 1962 Geneva agreements aimed to ensure Laotian neutrality, not only did the United States violate it but so did the North Vietnamese, who, with the acquiescence of the "Red Prince" Souphanavoung of the Pathet Lao and other Laotian communist leaders, maintained a military presence in southeastern Laos both to help the Laotian revolutionaries in their liberation struggle and to protect Hanoi's logistical supply route to the South.[41] By 1965, North Vietnam's ability to wage war in the South depended heavily on these infiltration routes over land and sea that cut through not only Laos but Cambodia as well.[42]

When Nixon entered office in 1969, he intensified what the Pathet Lao called America's "special war," increasing American bombing over the Ho Chi Minh Trail in Laos and building up Major General Vang Pao's Hmong forces in the northern and southern regions of the country. The U.S. president hoped to increase military activity in Laos in order to compel Hanoi to divert its main force units from staging attacks in South Vietnam and threatening Vietnamization.[43] General Giap, who appeared to recover some of his power in the VWP, personally directed North Vietnamese troops during the joint PAVN–Pathet Lao counteroffensive, "Campaign 139" to stop the enemy's advances in the region.[44] As a result, the Plain of Jars and the eastern section of Laos became a veritable free-fire zone. Of the 40,000 North Vietnamese troops stationed in Laos in 1969, 25,000 maintained the Ho Chi Minh Trail, while 15,000 remained in the northeast.[45] In October, General Giap's forces were unable to defeat the CIA-trained Secret Army under Major General Vang Pao, who managed not only to seize the Plain of Jars but communist-controlled Xieng Khoang as well.

Following the instructions put forward at the Eighteenth Plenum, Viet-

Left to right: *Faydang Lobliayao, Le Duan, Prince Souphanouvong, Pham Van Dong, Sithon Kommadam, and other Vietnamese leaders and Laotian guests before the departure of the Lao People's Delegation from Hanoi, May 1970 (Douglas Pike Photograph Collection, Vietnam Center and Archive, Texas Tech University)*

namese communist forces and Lao revolutionary troops launched an offensive on 11 February after three months of "road building, completing logistics preparation, and deploying campaign forces."[46] As a result, Kissinger's remarks were not off the mark; greater numbers of PAVN soldiers were fighting alongside the Pathet Lao to expel the Hmong forces from the Plain of Jars. By the end of the offensive, the joint communist force was able to threaten the Hmong major general's base in Long Tieng.[47] Nixon and Kissinger tried to salvage the situation by secretly bombing targets in the Plain of Jars, but they immediately faced domestic criticism. Intended to be hidden from the American public, the B-52 raids were leaked to the *New York Times*. In early March, congressional hearings forced Nixon to acknowledge the secret war in Laos, but he continued covertly to send allied troops from Thailand to aid Vang Pao's forces.[48]

Although Kissinger was able to jest about the situation in Laos at the February meeting, the discussion turned serious on 16 March.[49] After presenting the U.S. plan for troop withdrawal from South Vietnam over a sixteen-month timetable, Kissinger insisted that Vietnamese communist sanctuaries located in neighboring countries be dismantled as well.[50] Le Duc Tho refused to concede. Prior to the meeting, Tho had received an urgent telegram from the Politburo encouraging him to exploit Nixon's domestic problems over his Laos policy and to remain obstinate at the March meeting.[51] As a result, in addition to criticizing Kissinger's proposed timetable as a "step backward" from public statements made at the four-party talks on Avenue Kléber, Tho warned Kissinger that the United States would meet with failure in Laos.[52] Tho's prediction proved wrong in the short run. On 27 March, Thai and Royal Lao troops with American air support were able to rescue Vang Pao's Secret Army by staging an attack around the Hmong base in Long Tieng.[53] As the military situation deteriorated for the Vietnamese communists in Laos, political events in Cambodia posed an even greater threat to the VWP's war effort.

### INDOCHINA AT WAR: CAMBODIA

Like in Laos, Cambodia saw its postcolonial development complicated by the Vietnam War. Unlike Laos, however, Cambodia was able to maintain a neutral foreign policy for most of the war under the leadership of Prince Norodom Sihanouk. In the 1950s, the mercurial prince consolidated power by implementing an international strategy of neutrality abroad while co-opting segments of the Left and foiling the coup attempts of the Right within Kampuchea. Sihanouk's regional policy included using the PRC to balance the DRV, giving himself greater room for maneuver than his Laotian counterparts, who were squarely aligned with North Vietnam. By the early 1960s, however, Sihanouk began to lose his balance in domestic and foreign policy. Within Cambodia, the prince repressed the communist movement that had begun to step up its antigovernment activities. In May 1965, as hostilities escalated and greater numbers of American troops arrived in South Vietnam, Sihanouk broke off relations with the United States and moved closer to the socialist camp. As the Vietnamese communists increasingly used Cambodian territory as a sanctuary and as the United States began bombing the country in early October 1965, Sihanouk was powerless to prevent the Vietnam War from swallowing up his country.[54] By 1966, the prince's grip over Cambodia had further weakened. The Cambodian Right assumed more power following the National Assembly elections in September 1966, while the Communist Party of Kampuchea (CPK) grew more radical. Cambodian communist leaders considered the CPK's ideology more advanced than the VWP's, and perhaps equal to that of the CCP. In April 1967, the new radical leadership of the CPK combined armed conflict with political struggle to launch its first rebellion, sparking civil war in Cambodia. Using weapons provided by Beijing and Moscow, Sihanouk counterattacked CPK strongholds while the VWP tried to convince the CPK to refrain from provoking hostilities with Phnom Penh. Amid this chaos, Sihanouk still stood as the legitimate leader of Cambodia domestically and abroad.[55]

In Phnom Penh during 1969, however, Cambodian prime minister Lon Nol and deputy prime minister Prince Sisowath Sirik Matak began to significantly curtail Sihanouk's ability to control the cabinet, relegating the prince to ceremonial functions. As Sihanouk turned to producing and directing films, Sirik Matak and Lon Nol privatized banks and businesses and devalued the riel by nearly 70 percent.[56] Although these measures alleviated pressure on the Cambodian economy, anti-Vietnamese sentiment continued to rise among the Khmer elite and threatened Sihanouk's policy of neutrality in the Vietnam War, as did Nixon's escalation of U.S. bombing of Cambodian border areas. Right-wing factions blamed North Vietnamese occupation of border areas and Hanoi's support of the growing Cambodian communist insurgency for leading the country to sure war.[57]

With his powers as chief of state severely curtailed, Sihanouk traveled abroad in order to boost his position at home and to wrest back control of the government from Sirik Matak and Lon Nol. When Sihanouk left for medical treatment in France on 6 January 1970, however, Matak passed laws that further reduced Sihanouk's financial holdings in Cambodia, while Lon Nol enacted anti-Vietnamese measures that positioned Cambodia closer to the United States and South Vietnam. Lon Nol's policies had devastating consequences for the Vietnamese communists. Khmer troops began shelling PAVN-PLAF bases in February, and on 11 March demonstrators in Phnom Penh burned down the DRV and NLF embassies. In Paris, Sihanouk denounced the demonstrations as a right-wing plot to position Cambodia in the imperialist camp, but he was powerless to stop the growing anti-Vietnamese sentiment in Phnom Penh. Meanwhile, Matak canceled the Cambodian-PRG trade agreement, and Lon Nol demanded that all Vietnamese communists leave the country by 15 March.[58]

As anti-Vietnamese demonstrations increased in the capital, Sihanouk delayed his return to Cambodia by stopping in Moscow and Beijing. The Cambodian leader hoped to ease the tensions in his country by persuading the Soviets and Chinese to pressure the North Vietnamese to decrease their activities in Cambodia. During his meeting in Moscow, Sihanouk discovered that Soviet leaders were willing to support a campaign against the Cambodian Right, but they were unwilling to pressure the North Vietnamese to reduce the level of operations in Cambodia. As Sihanouk set out to board the Ilyushin 62 to Beijing in order to plead his case with the Chinese, however, he received unsettling news. On 18 March, Soviet leader Alexei Kosygin informed the Cambodian prince that the National Assembly had voted him out of office. When a worried Sihanouk arrived in Beijing, Premier Zhou Enlai received him and offered words of support on behalf of the Chinese government.[59]

VWP leaders were shocked and dismayed by the turn of events in Cambodia. Like Beijing, Hanoi did not report the coup d'état immediately but waited until 21 March.[60] However, unlike the Chinese and the Soviets, North Vietnamese leaders never contemplated hedging their bets in Cambodia by considering diplomatic relations with Lon Nol's government.[61] During a meeting with Zhou Enlai on 21 March, Pham Van Dong indicated that the VWP Politburo had already rejected negotiations with the Lon Nol government, since "they would eventually fight against us. . . . As for Sihanouk, our attitude is affirmative and our position on other issues will be based on that."[62] Zhou, however, was more ambivalent. Beijing would only "support Sihanouk for the time being," since Lon Nol had revealed that he did "not want to displease China and the Soviet Union" and had promised to protect their embassies in Phnom Penh after the coup.[63] Later that night, the Chinese leader met with Sihanouk but did not indicate that Beijing had any such misgivings about Chinese support for the prince.[64] Even though the CCP made private assurances to Sihanouk and had accorded the prince treatment befitting a head of state since his arrival in Beijing, Chinese leaders made no official announcement in support of the Cambodian leader.

Although the North Vietnamese pledged greater loyalty and offered more public support to Sihanouk than the Chinese did, the Cambodian prince was wary of depending solely on the DRV.[65] Sihanouk blamed Vietnamese communist military activity in Cambodia and the VWP's support of the CPK for his ouster.[66] On 22 March, he used China to offset North Vietnam when he told Premier Dong the terms of his cooperation: acceptance of Chinese aid; a summit for the Indochinese peoples; and military training in North Vietnam for his forces.[67] Within Cambodia, however, Sihanouk had to rely on his former enemies. Although the Khmer communists worked to undermine the prince's power before the coup, Sihanouk needed their help to regain power in Cambodia.

Even though the CPK suffered under Sihanouk's rule, the Lon Nol–Sirik Matak regime constituted a greater threat to the Khmer communist revolution in 1970. Although many factions existed within the CPK, its top leader was Saloth Sar, otherwise known as "Brother Number One" and later Pol Pot, who had eradicated his competition in the early 1960s before disappearing into the maquis.[68] With Sihanouk in command of a national front that included the CPK, Pol Pot's "Organization" (Angkar) gained more legitimacy among the Cambodian masses due to the prince's popularity in the countryside. Angkar, however, had an agenda very different from those of the prince and the other factions in the CPK. Even though Angkar benefited from the VWP's protection throughout the 1960s, Pol Pot detested his Vietnamese patrons.[69] In 1970, Pol Pot had three objectives: (1) waging armed struggle against the Phnom Penh regime; (2) augmenting his personal power in Cambodia and the CPK; and (3) containing the Vietnamese military presence and political influence in Cambodia. Waging war against Lon Nol's forces often took a back seat to the Khmer Rouge's other two objectives. Whether Le Duan and the Hanoi Politburo were fully aware of Pol Pot's anti-Vietnamese sentiments in the early 1970s did not really matter. As the war expanded into Cambodia, the Vietnamese were powerless to stop the rise of the Khmer Rouge.[70]

From the outset, then, Asian communist relations among the Chinese, Vietnamese, and Cambodians following the anti-Sihanouk coup were a tenuous alliance of convenience. In conversations with COSVN leader Pham Hung in 1968, Zhou Enlai asserted that the CCP had no direct relations with the CPK and had deferred to the VWP's assessment of the Cambodian revolution during the 1960s.[71] However, Beijing was already aware that tensions existed between the VWP and the CPK:

Recently our embassy in Cambodia reported that Khmer Communist Party complained that Vietnamese comrades did not supply them with weapons when the opportunity had been ripe for an armed struggle. . . . We have told Comrade Pham Van Dong and later President Ho that we did not have direct relations with Khmer comrades. It will be easier if Vietnamese comrades can directly exchange opinions with them. Comrade Pham Van Dong said that we should not interfere in the internal affairs of the Khmer Communist Party. However, I hear them complain that Vietnamese comrades have a chauvinist attitude, do not want to help, to discuss with them, or give them weapons.[72]

In 1970, Beijing saw an opportunity to interfere in the internal affairs of the Khmer Communist Party and to exploit Hanoi's "chauvinist" attitude toward the Cambodians. With Sino-Vietnamese disagreements over the Paris negotiations and continued North Vietnamese acceptance of Soviet aid and advice, Beijing began to view Sihanouk as a potential counterbalance to the North Vietnamese in Indochina. Le Duan immediately sensed the new threat. Although he and his colleagues in Hanoi focused on fighting the Americans and the Saigon regime in 1970, they could not help but fear a postwar Asia where China would dominate all of Indochina with the Khmer prince's help.[73]

Sihanouk thus played a key role in the formation of the Asian communist alliance in 1970, but he was immediately relegated to being a figurehead—a symbolic leader useful only to rally the masses yet given no real control.[74] The prince possessed no other viable option but to align with the Asian communists abroad and at home in order to reclaim power in Cambodia. On 23 March, Sihanouk issued a "Message to the Nation" from Beijing in which he called on the Khmer people to rise up against the Lon Nol regime. Although he did not announce his new alliance with the PRC and the DRV, Sihanouk called on the Khmer people to disregard the laws and decrees issued from Phnom Penh and instead offered a national unity government, a National Liberation Army, and a National United Front of Kampuchea (FUNK) to govern and defend the Khmer people. In Cambodia, the response to Sihanouk's declaration was mixed. In Phnom Penh, students demonstrated against Sihanouk and the Viet Cong, while in the countryside, thousands of people signed up to support the prince as Vietnamese and CPK forces helped propagate Sihanouk's 23 March call-to-arms.[75]

Sihanouk's declaration of war also evoked a range of responses abroad. Between 25 and 27 March, Hanoi issued formal statements that condemned the coup as an American plot, pledged support for Sihanouk's struggle to reclaim authority, and announced the withdrawal of DRV and NLF representatives from Phnom Penh.[76] The VWP Politburo could not have been more unequivocal in its support of the Cambodian prince. In contrast, Chinese leaders continued to hedge their bets. Beijing worked simultaneously to bring Sihanouk into the Chinese camp (and away from the Vietnamese), while maintaining relations with Lon Nol by keeping a diplomatic presence in Phnom Penh. It was not until 5 April that the PRC made its first official announcement condemning the U.S. role in overthrowing Sihanouk and not until 5 May that Beijing finally broke off relations with the Lon Nol regime by recalling its diplomats from Phnom

Penh. Possibly in order to deflect from China's dual-track policy, Zhou Enlai painted the Soviets as opportunists and fair-weather allies of Siha-nouk.[77] The Chinese leader was partially correct. After Kosygin became the bearer of bad news, the Soviets believed that they had lost Sihanouk to the Chinese when the Cambodian prince boarded the plane to Beijing rather than staying put in Moscow. Although Kosygin pledged his support to Sihanouk on the tarmac, the Soviets later avoided criticizing the United States for any alleged involvement in the coup and responded tepidly to Sihanouk's 23 March call-to-arms. Instead, the Soviets opted for an even more conservative stance toward Cambodia than the Chinese dual-track policy. In addition to maintaining relations with the Lon Nol regime (until 1975), the Soviet Union joined other third-party nations calling for an international conference to restore order in Cambodia and to guarantee its neutrality in the Vietnamese-American war. In doing so, the Soviets wanted to avoid either a U.S.- or a Chinese-controlled Cambodia. At first, Moscow favored France's 1 April declaration that called for a conference involving all interested parties—as opposed to governments—so that Sihanouk's party, the Pathet Lao, and the PRG could attend.[78] When it appeared unlikely that France's proposal would come to fruition, Moscow used its position as cochair of the Geneva conference along with London in order to suggest convening another meeting to ensure Cambodian neutrality.[79]

France's 1 April declaration and the Soviet-British offer to reconvene the Geneva conference were not the only international demands for diplomatic intervention; the question of Cambodia's neutrality and the expansion of the war to all of Indochina prompted regional calls for conferences as well. Sihanouk declared his intent to hold an Indochinese conference and Indonesian foreign minister Adam Malik proposed a meeting in Djakarta to provide a separate forum to solve the Indochina issue outside of the peace negotiations taking place in Paris. Of the four calls for international and regional conferences, only the ones proposed by Sihanouk and Malik actually took place.

In order to curry favor with Sihanouk and to undercut the Soviet proposal to reconvene another conference in Geneva, the PRC hosted the "Summit Meeting of the Indochinese Peoples" near Guangzhou from 24 to 25 April 1970.[80] At the Conghua hot springs resort, four representatives of the Indochinese parties attended including Sihanouk, Pham Van Dong, Prince Souphanouvong, and Nguyen Huu Tho of the PRG. Squabbles between the Indochinese allies immediately erupted, prompting Zhou Enlai to attend the summit on the evening of 24 April to smooth out disagreements between Pham Van Dong and Sihanouk.[81] To Dong's dismay, the Cambodian leader insisted that the revolutionary movements in Indochina retain their separate identities and areas of operations in their war against the U.S.-backed Lon Nol regime. The North Vietnamese prime minister and his colleagues in the Politburo did not want to rely on inferior Cambodian forces to protect Hanoi's western flank.[82] The joint statement that resulted from the conference included a unified Indochinese front against the United States and their right-wing "lackeys," China's promise to provide a "rear area" and support for the Indochinese struggle, and Sihanouk's formal approval for PAVN-PLAF forces to use Cambodian territory in the current war.[83] Sihanouk also decried the attempts by the great powers to further partition Indochina through international conferences. The prince singled out the upcoming Asia conference hosted by Indonesian foreign minister Malik as a blatant American plot that had nothing to do with Asia and even less to do with peace.[84]

Nearly one month later, on 16–17 May 1970, the Asia-Pacific Conference on the Cambodia Question took place in Djakarta. It was indeed hostile to the Vietnamese communists and to Sihanouk. When the Indonesian government proposed that conference in late April, Hanoi immediately denounced the idea.[85] Although Malik invited the foreign ministers of both the DRV and the RVN—in addition to ministers from Afghanistan, Australia, Burma, Ceylon, the PRC, India, Japan, North Korea, South Korea, Laos, Malaysia, Nepal, New Zealand, Pakistan, the Philippines, Singapore, Thailand, and Mongolia—to attend the meeting, the PRG was not invited to send a representative. Malik informed Saigon that the intention of the Indonesian government was to place pressure on Hanoi: "If the DRV wants peace, it will come, and if it rejects the invitation, then the world will see."[86]

Saigon's policy toward the Cambodia question was initially ambivalent. Sihanouk's popularity and the difficulties created by the guerrilla forces in the countryside made the future of the Lon Nol government less than secure. An international conference that would demand the total withdrawal of all foreign troops from Cambodian soil, then, would not be in Saigon's best interests. The RVN would benefit from either a truly neutral Cambodia where communist forces would not be allowed sanctuary or an anticommunist Cambodia that would join forces with the RVN to defeat the communists and thereby also receive aid. Neutrality, however, seemed too risky and impossible for a country neighboring Vietnam. Given Cambodia's instability, the South Vietnamese Foreign Ministry said that Saigon would only gain from attending an international conference if the Khmer Republic publicly aligned itself with the RVN.[87] Foreign Minister Tran Van Lam, however, told French diplomat Laurent Giovangrandi that although Saigon wanted peace, it could not accept neutralism as the solution for Cambodia.[88] Lam also stated that it would be to the RVN's advantage to attend the Djakarta Conference so that Saigon could demand that all foreign elements leave Cambodia, especially the Viet Cong. However, South Vietnamese troops in Cambodia should not be condemned since they fought to remove the foreign communist threat inside the country.[89]

If high-profile conferences did nothing to solve the problems confronting Cambodia, neither did a secret meeting between Le Duc Tho and Kissinger on 4 April. Since Cambodia was of utmost concern to the North Vietnamese, the Politburo advised its negotiators to adopt a "wait and see" attitude by forcing Kissinger to speak first regarding the situation there.[90] After disagreeing on the terms of withdrawal and political power in South Vietnam, the conversation quickly turned to the rest of Indochina.[91] Kissinger proceeded to outline the Nixon administration's position on Laos and Cambodia.[92] The United States was ready to reduce military operations in northern Laos if Hanoi stopped its military operations that had begun earlier that month in South Vietnam.[93] Regarding Cambodia, Kissinger indicated that the United States was prepared to work out arrangements to guarantee the "neutrality and inviolability of Cambodia."[94] Tho, however, refused to accept Kissinger's portrayal of the military and political situation in these countries. First, he accused the United States of escalating the hostilities in Laos by sending Thai mercenary troops to and dropping bombs on the Plain of Jars. Second, Tho charged the United States with masterminding the anti-Sihanouk coup and implementing the Nixon Doctrine, which called for "using Asians to fight Asians."[95] As such, the North Vietnamese were adamantly opposed to any international conference or neutralization scheme concocted by the United States or its client regimes. Instead, Hanoi leaders supported Sihanouk's five-point declaration, which called for the overthrow of the Lon Nol government and warned the Nixon administration that the peoples of Indochina would unite to defeat the United States just as they had the French more than a decade earlier.[96]

## THE FALLOUT FROM CAMBODIA

As Kissinger and Tho agreed to disagree on Cambodia, the violence reached new heights in the spring and early summer of 1970, deepening local, regional, and global concern for the precarious situation in Indochina. By late April, the ARVN had launched shallow border operations against communist bases, while Vietnamese communist forces shelled Lon Nol's government troops and positions. With pressure mounting to announce more troop withdrawals and little movement toward a negotiated settlement in Paris, Nixon resolved to move troops on Cambodia. Once again, however, the senior officials in his administration were split when Cambodian policy was discussed at an NSC meeting on 26 April. While the Joint Chiefs urged the most hawkish option of using whatever force was necessary to neutralize all base areas, Rogers and Laird counseled against an invasion and insisted on diplomacy instead. Kissinger preferred a middle option: using both American and South Vietnamese troops to attack the sanctuaries.[97] As was often the case, Nixon had already decided against Rogers and Laird before the meeting took place. After an encouraging briefing by Admiral John McCain, who extolled the option of a joint U.S.-ARVN operation that would save Cambodia from the communists and provide a boost to Vietnamization, Nixon ignored the warning from his more moderate senior advisors that any attack could incite antiwar opinion at home.[98]

On 30 April, Nixon launched the "Cambodian Incursion," referred to as Operation Toan Thang (Total Victory) in the RVN, when he sent U.S. ground forces alongside South Vietnamese troops in a joint offensive that aimed to locate and destroy the elusive COSVN and communist sanctuaries in Cambodia. After two days of heavy combat, Vietnamese communist troops withdrew deeper into Cambodia, fleeing to the northwest, where they had relocated their headquarters even before the joint U.S.-ARVN offensive began. The U.S.-ARVN operation thus failed to locate and destroy Pham Hung's base of operations.[99] Even though the joint incursion did not significantly change the military balance of power on the ground, it held great consequence for Nixon at home. Following swift criticism from Republican and Democratic senators of the first phase of Operation Toan Thang, Nixon delivered a televised address on 30 April explaining how the joint U.S.-ARVN "incursion" saved American lives and facilitated negotiations. Few were persuaded, and the invasion revitalized the antiwar movement. Throughout May, antiwar protests erupted in cities and on college campuses. At Kent State University in Ohio, four students were shot dead and nine were wounded when the National Guard opened fire on demonstrators after four days of intense confrontation that had begun as a peaceful protest against the Cambodian invasion. After Kent State, students across the country took part in demonstrations not only against the war in Southeast Asia but also against the killings at home.

Nor was the antiwar agitation confined to college campuses. It reached into newsrooms, Congress, and even the offices of senior advisers. On 29 April two of Kissinger's top staff, Anthony Lake and Roger Morris, resigned from the NSC staff, citing increasing alienation from the domestic and foreign policies of the Nixon administration. While Kissinger faced dissension in his ranks, Nixon had to contend with Capitol Hill. A few days into the joint U.S.-ARVN incursion, Republican Senator Sherman Cooper of Kentucky alongside Democratic Senator Frank Church of Idaho proposed an amendment that would essentially cut off all military funding for operations in Cambodia after 30 June. This was not the only bipartisan attack against Nixon. Democratic Senator George McGovern of South Dakota and Republican Senator Mark Hatfield of Oregon took their dissatisfaction with Nixon's war one step further, proposing an amendment that would terminate all funding for operations in Indochina by the end of 1970 and require the administration to pull out all troops by the end of 1971. In a symbolic act of defiance, the Senate overwhelmingly repealed the Tonkin Gulf Resolution of 1964 that had given Johnson the authority to use military force in Southeast Asia. Although the various amendments failed to pass both houses of Congress given the number of American soldiers still fighting in Southeast Asia, Nixon and Kissinger were on high alert. Time was running out at home for their war in Vietnam.

Nixon buckled under the weight of the public outcry. Calling his valet at four in the morning on 9 May to take him to the Lincoln Memorial, where student protestors had camped out, a less-than-lucid Nixon engaged these bewildered protestors in a strange conversation that jumped from one subject to the next. In addition to defending his Cambodia policy, he spoke of his service during World War II, the oppression against minorities, and even college football.[100] In the days and weeks that followed this bizarre encounter with student protestors, Nixon regained his wits and set out in a calculated manner to mount a counterprotest operation. Instead of reevaluating his strategy in light of the firestorm it created in America, Nixon instead struck back at his domestic enemies that summer. As he assuaged domestic opinion by announcing his intention to pull all American troops out of Cambodia by the end of June, he approved what became known as the Huston Plan, named after White House aide Tom Charles Huston, who drafted the forty-three-page report on proposed security options. Huston, who had worked with Nixon during the previous year to locate a connection between foreign communist support and domestic dissidence, was now allowed to resort to illegal measures for combating the antiwar movement.[101] In what historian George C. Herring has described as "one of the most blatant attacks on individual freedom and privacy in American history," Nixon expanded his arsenal against the antiwar movement to include opening mail, electronic surveillance, and even burglary.[102]

American college students and U.S. civil liberties were not the only collateral damage following the Cambodian debacle. Anti-Vietnamese sentiment continued to rise in Phnom Penh, and in early May the mood turned ugly. Lon Nol's army and police units in Takeo and elsewhere rounded up and shot thousands of Vietnamese civilians, including women and children. International condemnation of the massacres ensued.[103] A report from Saigon's director of the Overseas Vietnamese Committee described the situation as follows:

> Vietnamese are still being repressed cruelly and are kept under strict curfew. The Cambodian Security forces have rounded up the Vietnamese in the city and have seized their property. This month, droves of Vietnamese have been driven outside Phnom Penh and summarily executed. When all bullets have been fired, the executioners then resorted to chopping off the heads of the remaining victims. In one case, Vietnamese Catholics were killed behind their church. According to the foreign press, there are concentration camps outside Phnom Penh that the Khmer authorities won't allow Vietnamese delegations to see.[104]

Although Lon Nol allowed 300,000 surviving Vietnamese in Cambodia to emigrate to South Vietnam, relations between Saigon and Phnom Penh suffered.

Although American troops withdrew from Cambodia by June, the ARVN hoped to stay.[105] On 4 June, Vice President Ky visited Phnom Penh to stress the importance of maintaining cooperation between the two countries against the Vietnamese communists.[106] Received by Lon Nol and Sirik Matak with full honors and consideration appropriate for a head of state, Ky's visit was a major success and helped boost the legitimacy of the Phnom Penh government in Cambodia. More important for the RVN, Ky's visit set the basis for future military cooperation and joint planning as well as established priorities among urgent problems such as military assistance and longer-term problems including repatriation and economic cooperation. The most important issue discussed during Ky's visit was that of South Vietnamese troops in Cambodia. The RVN and the Khmer Republic agreed to a continued South Vietnamese military presence that would be left at Neak Luong, thirty miles southeast of Phnom Penh on the Mekong. In addition, South Vietnamese mobile task forces would be stationed near the border and could be deployed on short-term basis to meet specific threats in Cambodia. Action, then, would not necessarily be confined to sanctuary areas.[107]

However, joint military activity immediately encountered problems. As was the case between Americans and the South Vietnamese, the more interaction ARVN soldiers had with Cambodian civilians, the greater the opportunity for hostile exchanges and cultural insensitivity.[108] Tensions persisted not only between Vietnamese soldiers and Cambodian villagers but between the Saigon and Phnom Penh governments as well. The issue, though, was no longer about the behavior of South Vietnamese troops in Cambodia; rather, it centered on who was going to pay for the military operations.

In December 1970, Secretary of Defense Laird stated in an interview with the BBC that the RVN would not request money from the Cambodian government but would like to propose to Phnom Penh that it share in the cost of ARVN operations in Cambodia. On 6 January 1971, the Cambodian Foreign Ministry sent a note to the RVN requesting that Saigon reevaluate the military expenditure issue. From Phnom Penh's perspective, since South Vietnamese operations in Cambodia aimed to eradicate the Viet Cong threat, the Khmer Republic had the right to view those operations as unconditional aid under international law. Moreover, the Cambodian Foreign Ministry claimed that although these military operations were beneficial to both Saigon and Phnom Penh, they were *more* beneficial to the South Vietnamese. According to Saigon's version of the events, the RVN sent a friendly response on 18 January to reaffirm its goodwill toward Phnom Penh and to confirm Laird's statements. The RVN then shelved the issue of military expenditures and refrained from raising the issue with Cambodian foreign minister Koun Wick during his visit to Saigon. However, tempers began flaring by the spring. On 11 March 1971, the Cambodian Foreign Ministry raised the military expenditure issue on the eve of a South Vietnamese delegation's arrival in Phnom Penh. Foreign Minister Lam's classified report reveals that Phnom Penh's behavior meant one of two things. Either Cambodia was convinced that the RVN needed Cambodia more than the other way around or Phnom Penh leaders were trying to create bad press for the RVN in the United States.[109] Lam concluded that Cambodia should not be allowed to view South Vietnamese troop activity as unconditional aid and that Cambodia had benefited from those military operations as much as the RVN had. Foreign Minister Lam urged his superiors not to "let them go away with the incorrect notion that we need them more than they need us [*dung de ho co y niem sai lam la ta can ho hon ho can ta*]," since if it were not for the ARVN in Cambodia, Lam argued, the communists would annex the entire country before they would start any trouble for Saigon.[110] Both Prime Minister Tran Thien Khiem and President Thieu agreed with their foreign minister's assessment and ordered South Vietnam's ambassador to Cambodia to convey the message to Phnom Penh.[111] Diplomacy gave way to bullying as Saigon and Phnom Penh seemed to momentarily forget that the war was against the communists and not each other.

The RVN tried once again to raise the question of support for Vietnamese troops in Cambodia at an economic conference in which the two countries addressed issues such as bilateral trade, overland transit rights, delineation of boundaries, and security of water and land routes. By late 1971, the RVN continued to hope for a Cambodian contribution to South Vietnamese military operations in Cambodia that had amounted to $6.5 million. A British diplomat observing the disintegration of relations between Phnom Penh and Saigon over military expenditures at that point stated: "Cambodian resistance of this claim can scarcely be wondered at, and we have no reason to think that the Vietnamese will press their point as they are only too conscious of the security advantage to them of having their troops sweeping the area in Cambodia from which VC/NVA attacks on Saigon and the Delta can be mounted. . . . There have been suggestions that the Vietnamese adopted a bullying attitude toward the Cambodians, emphasizing Cambodia's dependence on Vietnamese military aid."[112] Compounding the military expenditure issue, the Lon Nol administration began taking measures to phase out the South Vietnamese military presence in Cambodia's war against the communists. Although the previous year's joint communiqué signed by Ky and Lon Nol agreed to delineate a free military zone, which included eight kilometers on either side of the border, allowing the ARVN and the Cambodian Royal Army to enter each other's countries at any time, the agreement was now in jeopardy. By the autumn of 1971, the Lon Nol administration decided to change the system of border operations since it believed that the original aims had been achieved and communist activity had decreased in the border areas. Sirik Matak told the press that during a meeting in Chadomuk on 4 September 1971, Lon Nol announced that he would end the agreement with the RVN that allowed for South Vietnamese and Cambodian troops to undertake operations in the sixteen-kilometer zone. A confidential report from South Vietnamese General Cao Van Vien to President Thieu described Cambodia's unilateral decision as potentially catastrophic. Vien urged Thieu to use diplomatic pressure to convince Phnom Penh to retract its statement before any damage could be done.[113]

Coinciding with the change in the system for military border operations was Cambodia's demand for the withdrawal of South Vietnamese soldiers from the Neak Luong base. Saigon concluded that the Khmer Republic would ask for the withdrawal of all ARVN troops in order to exact more military and economic aid from the United States. In light of the military burden and potential repercussions for Vietnamese-Cambodian relations if ARVN troops remained in Cambodia, Foreign Minister Lam suggested to his superiors that the ARVN transfer the fighting over to the Cambodian Army both to improve relations between the two countries and to show the world that the RVN respected Cambodian sovereignty.[114] By the end of the year, however, the South Vietnamese embassy in Phnom Penh sent telegrams urging Saigon to maintain its military presence in Cambodia since the withdrawal of ARVN troops would trigger an increase in communist troop activity that the Cambodian Army would be unable to put down. As a result, Lam changed his position and warned that although the Cambodian people and world opinion would use the opportunity to accuse the RVN of expansionist desires, the threat to Cambodia and South Vietnam would be far greater if ARVN troops withdrew from Cambodia.[115]

Although poor relations between the Khmer Republic and the RVN cannot be blamed entirely on Saigon, the South Vietnamese government did little to ameliorate the situation. By treating the Khmer Republic as a client rather than an ally, Saigon committed many of the mistakes that the United States committed in South Vietnam. The superior attitude displayed in the "they need us more than we need them" belief as well as the inability to transfer the war over to the Khmer Army resulted in poor relations between the RVN and the Khmer Republic at a time when a strong alliance was needed. Saigon's policy of "more friends, fewer enemies" rang hollow in Indochina.

The escalation of interethnic violence in Cambodia exacerbated tensions not only between the Nguyen Van Thieu and Lon Nol governments but also between the revolutionary parties in the summer of 1970. With the joint U.S.-ARVN offensive, the Hanoi Politburo stepped up its support for Sihanouk's newly created Royal Government of National Union of Kampuchea (RGNUK), founded in late April. On 2 May, the Secretariat sent out a circular to all of its cadres that the VWP must spare no effort in the new regionwide struggle.[116] On 19 June, the Hanoi Politburo released a resolution that officially called for the creation of a united Indochinese front.[117] As with most partnerships in this messy war, Cambodian suspicion—and under Pol Pot, deep-seated hatred—of the Vietnamese prevented a steady alliance. Equally to blame, as Vietnamese military officers have stated, was Vietnamese disdain for and superior attitudes toward the Cambodians, which they did not hide.[118]

Thus, Vietnamese communists encountered greater hostility and resistance from their Khmer allies after the anti-Sihanouk coup, particularly from Pol Pot's faction based in northeastern Cambodia. According to a 1978 publication of the Khmer Rouge regime, most likely written by Pol Pot, titled *Livre noir* (Black Book), the North Vietnamese tried to exploit the CPK. In return for military aid, the VWP demanded that Khmer revolutionaries agree to the establishment of a joint military command, to protect COSVN now relocated to Kratie in western Cambodia, and to provide logistics support along the trails running through the country to South Vietnam.[119] Pol Pot, who stayed in Hanoi until May 1970, claimed that he brushed Le Duan's proposals aside and forced his subordinates to do the same in country. When Le Duan instructed Region 5 Party secretary Vo Chi Cong to inform CPK leaders that the VWP wanted to send troops to northeastern Cambodia, Pol Pot's second-in-command, Ieng Sary, refused the troops and requested arms shipments only.[120] Cong relayed Ieng Sary's message to Hanoi but Le Duan ordered his deputy to disregard it and insisted that Vietnamese troops be stationed in northeastern Cambodia— the area was too important to leave in the hands of weak CPK forces in light of the joint U.S.-ARVN invasion and Lon Nol's subsequent operations in the region.[121] In the end, Angkar stood aside as large numbers of PAVN troops arrived in the northeastern zone. The anti-Vietnamese faction of the CPK did not possess enough troops and weapons to challenge North

Vietnamese forces at that time. Even Brother Number One was powerless against the VWP. After his return to Cambodia, Pol Pot moved his headquarters westward, closer to COSVN, in September 1970, revealing that he did anything but brush aside Le Duan's proposals for the establishment of a joint military command.[122]

Although Pol Pot's forces were too weak to resist North Vietnamese demands in 1970, they found other ways to display their hostility toward their patrons and limit Vietnamese strength in Cambodia. Le Duan was not oblivious to the situation. In July 1970, he wrote to Pham Hung and COSVN emphasizing the importance of improving relations with their Khmer allies. "On the road to liberation," Le Duan wrote, "it is impossible to avoid differences between us and our friends."[123] However, the "differences" soon turned bloody. When Lon Nol launched Operation Chenla I in September 1970 around Kompong Thom, eighty-five miles north of Phnom Penh, the Khmer Rouge used the "fog of war" to fire on Vietnamese troops from behind. The fighting between the friendly forces may have escalated, since a Vietnamese circular appeared one month later warning its troops not to fire on CPK forces.[124]

In addition to shooting unsuspecting Vietnamese soldiers, Pol Pot found another way to display his disdain for the Vietnamese and limit the VWP's influence in the Khmer revolution. In 1970, Pol Pot asked the VWP to send back the Vietnamese-trained Khmer communists so that they could join the unified front. After the Geneva Accords in 1954, 189 Khmer revolutionaries who fought alongside the Viet Minh regrouped to Hanoi. In subsequent years, 322 joined the original post-Geneva group in order to receive education at the Vietnamese-Khmer Friendship School.[125] According to historian Ben Kiernan's estimates, the number of Khmer revolutionaries who had received training in North Vietnam was closer to 1,000.[126] Their expertise in Marxism-Leninism and military combat might have made them attractive to Pol Pot, who had poorly trained and undisciplined troops. However, their exposure to Vietnamese culture and society rendered them suspect. After completing an arduous, three-month journey over the Ho Chi Minh Trail on which some perished, the Vietnamese-trained Khmer communists returned to Cambodia in groups of 100 at a time. Although the returnees were viewed with distrust, Pol Pot ensured that his forces benefited from their training. In mid-1971, however, the honeymoon between the Vietnamese and Cambodians ended when Pol Pot declared communist Vietnam "the long-term acute enemy of the Kampuchean revolution" during a two-week CPK conference in the Northern

Zone.[127] Confident that his anti-Vietnamese faction outnumbered those who preferred cooperation and collaboration with the VWP, Pol Pot began to kill off Hanoi's strongest link to the Khmer revolution. By 1975, nearly the entire 1,000 Vietnamese-trained Khmer communists had died at the hands of the Khmer Rouge, and not in battle against "reactionary forces" or from the treacherous conditions on the Ho Chi Minh Trail.

Although the northeastern zone continued to witness tense relations between Vietnamese and Khmer communist forces, the VWP was able to make headway in northern, eastern, and southwestern Cambodia.[128] Together, the Vietnamese and Khmer troops made significant gains throughout the country in 1970. Official military historians in Vietnam admit that the Indochinese revolutionary forces were unable to destroy American troops during the joint U.S.-ARVN incursion; however, they were able to liberate five northeast provinces in Cambodia by June 1970.[129] By the end of the year, communist forces claimed to control fourteen of eighteen provinces, but less than half of the population lived in liberated zones.[130] As U.S. bombs fell with more frequency and covered greater territory in Cambodia, the shift in the balance of power toward the Khmer Rouge would eventually favor neither Washington nor Hanoi.[131]

## WAR DIPLOMACY

As the regional picture appeared bleak for all sides, Hanoi, Washington, and Saigon advanced their international offensives. Alongside the media blitzkrieg that Le Duan launched at home during the Cambodia crisis, the first secretary undertook high-profile trips to the Soviet Union and the PRC to boost Hanoi's flagging war effort. On 18 April 1970, Le Duan departed for Moscow, where he met with Brezhnev on 5 May.[132] Six days later, the North Vietnamese leader flew to Beijing. Although there is no available record of Le Duan's meeting with Brezhnev, the CWIHP transcript of the conversation with Mao on 11 May reveals that the two Asian leaders began the meeting by remarking that they had not met since the mid-1960s. Since then, of course, both had battled and defeated supposed domestic adversaries in order to maintain control over their respective communist parties. Although the timing of the meeting took place as events in Cambodia reached a crucial juncture—Nixon and Thieu had just launched their joint U.S.-ARVN offensive and Vietnamese-Khmer revolutionary forces had formed a tenuous alliance alongside the Laotians in Indochina—little was said about Cambodia. Le Duan started the discussion by admitting that the "situation in Vietnam and in Indo-China is complicated, and there exist some difficulties." Even though Beijing had just thrown its full weight behind Sihanouk and recalled its diplomats from Phnom Penh on 5 May, Mao stated, "Now there is another person, Prince Sihanouk. He is not an easy person to deal with either. When you offend him, he will come out to scold you." In conveying this to Le Duan, the Chinese leader may have wanted to smooth over any differences between the Vietnamese and Cambodians that arose at the Summit Meetings of the Indochinese Peoples in late April but also to indicate that Prince Sihanouk was squarely in Beijing's corner.[133]

On the surface, the conversation followed the same protocol as it had in the early days of the war. Le Duan spoke as the grateful supplicant ("We Vietnamese keep Chairman Mao's great goodness always in our minds"), while Mao acted as the benevolent patron ("You have done a very good job, and you are doing better and better"). However, tensions lay beneath the surface. First, Mao apologized indirectly for the disruption that the Cultural Revolution caused to the North Vietnamese. Although Mao's direct comments about the Cultural Revolution have been struck from the existing record, the chairman did address the purging of Zhu Qiwen, who had been the Chinese ambassador to the DRV from August 1962 to 1968. Mao explained that Beijing did not know that Zhu Qiwen was a "Guomindang agent" but that CCP leaders were very concerned with his telegrams from the Chinese embassy in Hanoi that were critical of the North Vietnamese. Second, although Le Duan was a major proponent of large-scale urban battles as witnessed in his Tet Offensive strategy and his maintenance the "strategic initiative" after 1968, the Vietnamese leader paid lip service to waging a protracted struggle: "Why are we in a position to persist in fighting a prolonged war, especially in fighting a prolonged war in the South? Why dare we fight a prolonged war? This is mainly because we have been dependent on Chairman Mao's works." Mao, who probably realized that he was dealing with the main proponent of large-unit warfare, also met Le Duan halfway. The chairman urged the Vietnamese to "prepare to fight a prolonged war," but he also recognized that a short war would be "better" and that the Vietnamese had adapted his teachings to make their "own creations."[134] Although Le Duan's high-profile trips confirmed to the North Vietnamese people and communist leaders abroad that he remained in control of the VWP after Ho Chi Minh's death, he did not possess the charisma of Uncle Ho. Instead, Hanoi leaders, with Soviet help, seemed to cultivate the persona of Madame Nguyen Thi Binh, the PRG foreign minister and head delegate at the Paris talks, so that she would represent the Vietnamese struggle.[135]

Hailing from a long line of revolutionaries, including her grandfather Phan Chu Trinh, who operated as both antimonarchist and anti-French in the early twentieth century, Binh became the diplomatic embodiment of the Vietnamese struggle after Ho Chi Minh's death. Prior to 1969, Binh's revolutionary credentials were vast and impressive. During the French Indochina War, she formed the Women's Association in Saigon but was captured by enemy forces and not freed until 1955. After her release, she immediately began working for the Association for the Defense of Peace, under future NLF and PRG leader Nguyen Huu Tho, which sought to ensure that reunification elections take place as stipulated by the Geneva Accords. When it became clear that elections would not take place, she caught the eye of Party leaders, who sent for her in 1956 to become the secretary for Muoi Thap, president of the Women's Union and party secretary of the Women's Committee. Under Thap's tutelage, Binh, who used the name Yen Sa, attended classes at the Nguyen Ai Quoc Party school, where her focus on gender studies led her to analyze the role of women in collectivization as well of primary school education on the path to liberation. Her future seemed bright in Hanoi, but as southern regroupees began returning to the Mekong Delta in droves by the early 1960s, Muoi Thap suggested that Binh return to her home region, since the revolution needed her there.[136]

As she prepared to return south, however, the National Reunification Committee—the apparatus that enforced the Politburo's directives on the southern revolution in political and diplomatic matters—decided that she had another destiny to fulfill for the southern cause. Approaching Muoi Thap, the committee wanted to "borrow sister Yen (Binh)," since the NLF was about to begin its diplomatic struggle to win international support for the southern cause. Her talent at diplomacy ensured that her stint lasted beyond a few months. Binh recalled that the short staffing forced her and her colleagues to pull double, and at times triple, duty serving on the Liberated Students' Association, the Youth Party, the Committee for Afro-Asian Solidarity, and the Peace Committee of South Vietnam. When the Women's Association of South Vietnam was founded, Nguyen Thi Dinh, the author of the famous pamphlet *No Other Road to Take* and a southern guerrilla leader, became its president. However, Dinh and her staff lacked funds to travel abroad, so Binh and her colleagues assumed their duties as well. Alongside the North Vietnamese delegation, these women

*Nguyen Thi Binh (Douglas Pike Photograph Collection, Vietnam Center and Archive, Texas Tech University)*

diplomats attended the conference of the International Women's Movement and there—just as in other venues—won world support for the Vietnamese communist war effort.[137]

When peace talks began in 1968, Binh's stellar record earned her Xuan Thuy's recommendation to head the NLF delegation.[138] Arriving in Paris, Binh recalled feeling overwhelmed by the throngs of people assembled at the talks, in contrast to her small delegation, which had only six members. Everyone, she remembers, was shocked to see her—a petite woman— heading the NLF delegation. Shy by nature, Binh decided that she could no longer be timid; she would have to talk straight, pose for countless pictures, and grant numerous interviews. From that point forward, she was no longer the naive "Yen Sa." She officially became the indomitable Madame Nguyen Thi Binh.[139]

In 1970, Binh toured the world with her delegation of women, including long-time colleagues Do Duy Lien, Nguyen Thi Chon, Nguyen Ngoc Dung, Pham Thanh Van, and Phan Thi Minh, who referred to themselves as representatives of the "soldiers with long hair" on South Vietnam's diplomatic front.[140] In the summer, Binh set off on a world public relations campaign, in June visiting Algeria, where she was received by President Houari Boumediene and Foreign Minister Abdelaziz Bouteflika. That same month, the PRG foreign minister met with Premier Zhou Enlai in Beijing, where the Chinese leader prophesized an eventual Vietnamese victory over the Americans similar to the Chinese victory in the Korean War.[141] In July, she and her delegation visited India and Sri Lanka at the request of both governments led by women, Indira Gandhi and Sirimavo Bandaranaike, respectively. Binh's visit to India constituted a major diplomatic victory for the PRG since it took place over the protests of the RVN consul general in New Delhi.[142]

In September, Binh arrived in Lusaka, capital of Zambia, for the third conference of the Nonalignment Movement (NAM). Binh and the delegation of four, which included her fellow "long-haired" soldier Nguyen Ngoc Dung, viewed the PRG's invitation to attend the conference with the utmost importance. Being only one year old, the PRG was at a disadvantage vis-à-vis the United States and its legion of allies. Although ecstatic about the invitation, Dung recalls, the delegation could not figure out a way to travel to Lusaka, since the PRG did not have diplomatic relations with Zambia. The group arrived first in Dar es Salaam, Tanzania, where Prime Minister Julius Nyerere solved the PRG's dilemma. He invited Binh and her team to accompany him, along with Ugandan president Milton Obote, on Nyerere's private plane. Their dramatic arrival in Lusaka boded well for the PRG, as Madame Binh emerged on the tarmac flanked by two African presidents. Although Dung recalled that a few Southeast Asian delegates objected to the PRG's presence at the conference, claiming that "the PRG is not a government . . . and if it claims it is sovereign state, its capital is no place that any other nation recognizes." Other representatives from Algeria, Congo, Guinea, and Mali, however, jumped to the PRG's defense, saying that nations that allowed the United States to use their bases to attack other nations were the ones that had no reason to be present at this nonaligned conference.[143] Fidel Castro perhaps phrased it best in Dung's estimation when he stood up and declared, "Is not Vietnam the most excellent example of the soul and spirit of the nonalignment movement—we are honored to have them here. The Cuban delegation proposes that we make Vietnam a member, that we end this arguing now and immediately file the paperwork to invite Nguyen Thi Binh's delegation to participate."[144] Amid the clamor and applause following Castro's plea, Binh, dressed in an *ao dai*, the traditional Vietnamese tunic, with her hair in a demure bun, approached the dais and gave a powerful and stirring fifteen-minute speech. The next day the African press held up Binh's speech as the rallying cry of the summit. Two years later at the nonaligned conference in Guyana, the PRG became a full member of NAM, joining fifty-four other nations in Asia, Europe, Africa, and Latin America.[145]

As Binh won over the Third World, Hanoi's diplomatic campaign focused on fundraising efforts for the war. Although the most aid during this period came from Moscow and Beijing, smaller communist powers also furnished crucial economic and military support to Hanoi. For socialist aid to Vietnam, 1970 was a vital year. Given the acceleration of the fighting in all of Indochina, the DRV had to dispatch, for the first time in the war, two separate delegations of high-ranking officials to negotiate aid agreements. Nguyen Con, vice premier and secretary of the CEC, headed the first economic delegation, which left Hanoi in the fall of 1970. After completing trips to Beijing and Moscow, his delegation arrived in Eastern Europe and Northeast Asia in early November. Landing first in Prague on 2 November, the Hanoi delegation signed an agreement with Czechoslovakia that promised economic and military aid to the DRV and an agreement on goods exchange and payments for 1971. Leaving Prague, the North Vietnamese went to Pyongyang on 17 November and concluded similar aid and trade agreements with the North Koreans.

Throughout the summer of 1970, as Vietnamese communist troops fought alongside Khmer and Lao revolutionaries on the Indochinese battlegrounds and Party leaders traveled the world in pursuit of diplomatic recognition and aid, the negotiations in Paris languished. In fact, both the public sessions and the secret talks broke off after the joint U.S.-ARVN invasion of Cambodia and did not resume until the late summer.[146] After repeated harangues from the North Vietnamese, the Nixon administration finally appointed David K. E. Bruce, a veteran diplomat and former ambassador to various European nations, as the head of the American delegation.[147] With the recommencement of the four-party talks on 6 August, Hanoi leaders agreed to Kissinger's request to resume the secret meetings.

Le Duc Tho was not present for the scheduled 7 September private meeting since the Politburo was not ready to advance substantive negotiations in light of events in Cambodia. Instead, Kissinger met only with Xuan Thuy and Mai Van Bo to offer them a twelve-month schedule for troop withdrawal—a measure that the North Vietnamese read as a sign of weakness, deducing that the increased antiwar sentiment in the United States following the invasion of Cambodia had forced Nixon to change his policies.[148] The negotiators instantly realized this was the first time that Nixon and Kissinger had presented a timetable for U.S. troop withdrawal without making any similar demands on the North Vietnamese to remove their forces other than vague references to "reciprocity."[149] Kissinger's report of the meeting to Ambassador Bunker (and thus to RVN President Thieu) concealed this concession; he made no mention of the twelve-month timetable and stated only that he had emphasized American refusal to replace the Thieu administration.[150]

In response to the optimistic report from Xuan Thuy following the 7 September meeting, Tho and Foreign Minister Trinh devised a diplomatic strategy to take advantage of what the North Vietnamese saw as Nixon and Kissinger's urgent domestic problems.[151] The Hanoi Politburo ordered its negotiators to adopt a more rigid posture, exploit the peace movement, and stick to Hanoi's demands for the removal of all U.S. troops by 30 June 1971 and the overthrow of the Thieu-Ky-Khiem regime. Meanwhile, North Vietnamese leaders decided that the PRG would balance the DRV's rigid posture by introducing a new proposal to show their willingness to work toward peace and thus fool the Americans into presenting even better terms. In other words, the North Vietnamese used the carrot and stick approach to negotiating. On 17 September, Binh presented the PRG's "Eight-Point Clarification of the Ten-Point Overall Solution." Her proposal was significant because it was the first time that U.S. troop withdrawal was linked to the release of American prisoners.[152] Kissinger took the bait and interpreted Binh's peace proposal as a demonstration of Hanoi's flexibility.[153] He hoped that the PRG's eight points would be a starting point for North Vietnamese negotiators who would ultimately be willing to accept his offer of rapid American withdrawal for a cease-fire regardless of the long-term consequences for the RVN.[154] On 27 September, Kissinger was disappointed. Xuan Thuy followed Politburo orders and stuck rigidly to the terms set forth in Binh's eight-point proposal, leaving no room for compromise on any of her points. Kissinger knew that Nixon would never accept this bargain. In addition, Thuy not only demanded the removal of the Thieu-Ky-Khiem regime, but he also stated that Hanoi reserved the right to ensure that the two of the three components in the coalition government stood for "peace and neutrality." Both sides deemed the meeting so unproductive that they did not set a date for the next meeting.[155]

Meanwhile in China, Pham Van Dong met with Zhou Enlai and Mao Zedong in mid- to late September 1970. Although these meetings were cordial, they revealed that the PRC and DRV had long-standing problems including Sino-Vietnamese "misunderstandings" as a result of "chauvinist" behavior by Beijing's diplomats in Hanoi and past disagreements over North Vietnam's decision to advance its diplomatic struggle. During Dong's meeting with Zhou Enlai on 17 September and with Mao six days later, both Chinese leaders went to great lengths to show the Vietnamese prime minister that China would do its best as the "Great Rear" to aid the Vietnamese struggle and blamed any problems in the past on the "mandarin ambassadors" at the Chinese embassy in Hanoi.[156] Although Mao had purged former ambassador Zhu Qiwen, the chairman recommended that North Vietnamese leaders still go directly to Beijing whenever they needed anything rather than through the Chinese embassy in Hanoi.

As Zhou and Mao spoke of "bad diplomats" and "chauvinist policies" by the Chinese diplomatic corps in Hanoi, Dong spent most of his time discussing the importance and strength of the Vietnamese communist diplomatic struggle. On 17 September, the North Vietnamese leader outlined Hanoi's strategy to Zhou Enlai: "First, we have to win the sympathy of the people in South Vietnam, especially the ones in the urban areas. Furthermore, we have to influence the antiwar public opinion in the US that includes not only the people at large but also the political, business, academic, and clerical circles to ensure a stronger support by them. . . . From this calculus, we hold that the diplomatic struggle can serve as another front. Therefore, the NLF is conducting new diplomatic offensives."[157] Dong identified two aims for Hanoi's international strategy: the unconditional withdrawal of American troops according to a concrete timetable and the removal of the Thieu-Ky-Khiem regime. The Vietnamese premier indicated that these demands were not new, but that Hanoi wanted to "corner Nixon by influencing public opinion in the US and the rest of the world."[158] Nonetheless, Dong confided to his Chinese hosts that Hanoi leaders did not believe that the diplomatic struggle alone could win the war.

Chinese leaders finally conceded during the September 1970 meetings that Hanoi's negotiating posture and diplomatic struggle—points of contention since the initiation of peace talks in May 1968—had borne fruit. It is apparent from the records of conversation that Chinese leaders were kept abreast of the secret meetings between the United States and the DRV. Mao and Zhou remarked on Xuan Thuy's wit and humor, which they believed ran circles around Kissinger, during the 7 September secret meeting. Not only impressed with Thuy, Zhou Enlai heaped praise on Binh as well, describing her as "very sharp."[159] On 23 September, Mao Zedong finally spoke the words that North Vietnamese leaders had been waiting to hear since May 1968: "I see that you can conduct the diplomatic struggle and you do it well. Negotiations have been going on for two years. At first we were a little worried that you were trapped. We are no longer worried."[160]

What Dong and his comrades in the Hanoi Politburo did not know, however, was that China was on the cusp of making its own diplomatic move that would come at the expense of the Vietnamese war effort. Although Beijing leaders promised increased aid as the "Great Rear" to the Indochinese front and praised Hanoi's diplomatic struggle, the PRC also desired rapprochement with the United States. Since January 1970, the CCP had begun to pursue better relations with the Nixon administration with the resumption of ambassadorial talks in Warsaw.[161] Events in Cambodia, however, slowed down the process. The anti-Sihanouk coup and the joint U.S.-ARVN invasion of Cambodia had made it impossible for Mao to reach out to Nixon. However, by the fall of 1970, as Cambodia retreated into the background, Beijing perceived that Sino-Vietnamese competition in Indochina and increasing Soviet-Vietnamese cooperation would result in the encirclement of China. As a result, using the occasion of Chinese National Day on 1 October, Mao Zedong relayed to American journalist Edgar Snow at Tiananmen that he desired a meeting with Washington. Nixon, losing no time, followed up with a response via a Pakistani channel that the United States was prepared to send an envoy.[162]

The Soviets, whom the North Vietnamese also kept abreast of the secret meetings in Paris, weighed in on Hanoi's diplomatic struggle in late 1970.[163] During Kosygin's visit to Hanoi, the Soviet leader offered advice to his hosts. First, he suggested that the VWP promote the DRV's ten points and the PRG's eight points in a more unified fashion, since both proposals included the same two demands for a cease-fire: unconditional withdrawal of U.S. troops and the establishment of a coalition government. Second, the Soviet leader advised Hanoi leaders to develop a platform to win over the "Third Force" in South Vietnam. Finally, regarding Indochina, Kosygin urged improving relations with both Laotian princes, Souvanna Phouma and Souphanvoung, as well as with Sihanouk.[164]

The Soviets also tried to undermine any potential rapprochement between the United States and China and to prevent Nixon from exploiting the Sino-Soviet split. Throughout 1970, Moscow tried to create tension between Washington and Beijing by relaying information that would increase antagonism between the two countries. At the same time, the Soviets considered bettering relations with the Chinese by using the

Indochinese revolution as a rallying point for joint action. First, Moscow planned to share intelligence with Beijing regarding Nixon's intentions to expand the war in Laos; second, the Soviets considered approaching the Chinese to plan Sino-Soviet actions to aid Vietnam.[165] Soviet efforts, in the end, proved futile. Sino-American rapprochement could not be stopped and the Sino-Soviet split could not be mended.

As VWP leaders consulted their great-power patrons, the Nixon administration went on the diplomatic offensive. Although the United States refused to comply with the DRV-PRG demand for the removal of Thieu, the South Vietnamese president believed he had much to fear. In preparation for the unveiling of a "major initiative for peace," through a televised address scheduled for 7 October, Nixon needed the U.S. ambassador to South Vietnam, Ellsworth Bunker, to gain Thieu's acquiescence. Although Bunker tried to impress on Thieu that Nixon's proposal would not affect the political outcome, which was for the South Vietnamese to determine, Thieu feared that Nixon's new initiative of a "cease-fire in place" had replaced Washington's demand for mutual withdrawal.

Fortunately for Thieu, the North Vietnamese had already rejected Nixon's offer when informed of it in during the secret meeting in September. On 7 October, Nixon nonetheless outlined to American viewers his five-point proposal, which did call for a "cease-fire in place." Since Nixon was aware that Hanoi had already rejected his offer in secret, he aimed his "major initiative for peace" not at the Vietnamese but at the U.S. public, which was about to go to the polls in the midterm elections. Whether this effort to defuse the war issue produced success is hard to say. Republicans gained modestly in the Senate and lost modestly in the House, and few of the races pivoted on Vietnam.

After Nixon's televised address, Xuan Thuy telegrammed Le Duc Tho, Nguyen Duy Trinh, and the Politburo indicating that he would continue to push Hanoi's demand that the United States withdraw its support for the Thieu-Ky-Khiem clique in Paris. On 15 October, *Nhan Dan* published the DRV Foreign Ministry's rejection and criticism of Nixon's five-point proposal.[166] Although Bruce, the U.S. delegate to the Paris negotiations, suggested the creation of four-party secret meetings to hash out a settlement based on Binh's eight points and Nixon's five points, Thuy advised the Politburo that these talks would be fruitless since Bruce held no power in the Nixon administration.[167] He did not need to remind his bosses that there were already significant secret meetings taking place with Kissinger.

As public and private negotiations floundered in Paris, Nixon decided to launch attacks on DRV territory and thus restart the air war over North Vietnam. In late November, he ordered a raid on the Son Tay prison camp, located around twenty-three miles west of Hanoi, in order to rescue American POWs.[168] The raid failed since the North Vietnamese had moved the prisoners in July; however, Nixon's approval ratings improved because the American people supported his aims for the raid. At the same time, but with less fanfare, Nixon launched two days of "protective reaction" strikes against North Vietnamese radar and missile sites, claiming that they were in retaliation for Hanoi's firing at unarmed American reconnaissance planes.[169] North Vietnamese leaders, of course, neither accepted Nixon's reasoning for the Son Tay raid nor the air attacks and instead viewed them as his desire and capability to resort to military means to punish Hanoi for intransigence in Paris.[170] Nixon's air war would reach new heights over the next few years and surpass Johnson's Rolling Thunder in its ferocity.

While Nixon exerted military pressure, the Vietnamese communists continued to work on world opinion. On 12 December, Binh released a statement from Paris that included three preconditions for a cease-fire, which she and her comrades knew would be a nonstarter for Washington: U.S. troop withdrawal by 30 June 1971; the removal of the Thieu-Ky-Khiem regime; and discussion by concerned parties of the measures to ensure the respect and implementation of the cease-fire.[171] Her three points suggest that the VWP was leaning closer to Moscow given the tense relationship with Beijing over Indochina; Soviet leaders had just advised leaders in Hanoi to merge the DRV's peace initiatives with the PRG's.[172] Although *Hoc Tap* published an article that painted a rosy picture of the international scene in 1970, particularly the contributions from Moscow and Beijing, events in 1971 would reveal that Hanoi could rely on neither ally.[173]

## CONCLUSION

The war in 1970 must have confounded Le Duan. Not only were his enemies proving wilier, but his Asian allies were acting suspicious. While Sihanouk and the Cambodian communists seemed to resent Vietnamese aid, leaders in Beijing engaged in double talk. Chinese leaders, who began to view the Vietnamese communists less as allies in Indochina and more as competitors, began to reach out to the United States in their dangerous game with the Soviets. As foreign relations proved unwieldy, domestic support for the war began to dwindle as the socialist revolution appeared on hold indefinitely while opposition to the war increased. Once again relying on Tran Quoc Hoan, Le Duan's police state became more adept at cracking down on potential dissent. Nevertheless, the first secretary, a leader who had devoted himself to waging war in the South, found himself having to refocus on the North. Le Duan turned to the diplomatic sphere of the war, the sphere that he least wanted to rely on, which presented both obstacles and opportunities. Secret negotiations with the United States now included a tough negotiator on par with his trusted deputy, Le Duc Tho. Ordering Tho to stand firm in Paris against Kissinger while communist forces stood at a disadvantage vis-à-vis American soldiers on the Indochinese battlefield, Le Duan employed a powerful new weapon in his diplomatic arsenal: Nguyen Thi Binh. Although Le Duan and his comrades in the Politburo did not believe that diplomacy could take the place of military victory, Binh proved to them that it could most definitely buy much-needed time for forces to regroup, offset Sino-Soviet rivalry, and, most important, damage the enemies' war efforts.

Meanwhile, on the other side of the Pacific as 1970 drew to a close, neither Nixon nor Kissinger could see an imminent end to the Vietnam War. Particularly for the national security advisor, negotiations with Hanoi had yielded frustratingly little success, leading him to start considering a "decent interval" solution.[174] Kissinger looked to ending the war with American credibility intact but not necessarily to preserve the Saigon regime in the long term. Nixon, in contrast, had not yet abandoned hope of victory. He believed that by resuming the air war over North Vietnam and internationalizing the peace process, he could find Hanoi's breaking point and thus guarantee the survival of an independent, noncommunist South Vietnam. Even though the president did not hold out much hope for Vietnamization, he had not yet implemented two principal elements of his strategy—major military action and superpower diplomacy—that might yield results. The final two years of America's conflict would actually prove Nixon right, at least in the short term.

Cambodia and Laos, of course, bore the tragic consequences of Le Duan and Nixon's prolongation of the war for peace. While these two countries were never divorced from the conflict in Vietnam, 1970 marked a pivotal year in the nations' postcolonial development. Particularly for Cambodia, the events of this year set into motion what would become the most horrific period in that nation's history. Although it would have been impossible to predict in 1970 that Pol Pot would have the opportunity later in the decade to promote his brand of revolution, resulting in the deaths of millions of Cambodians, and to provoke war with his neighbor and one-time ally, Vietnam, so too was it unfathomable that China and Vietnam would sever relations in 1979 so soon after defeating the United States. However, the seeds for the destruction of the Asian communist alliance were laid in 1970, bringing about what would become the post–Cold War era in Southeast Asia.

*The year 1971 proved the political maxim that one should never despair until the votes have been cast and counted. Something can always turn up, often from an unexpected source or quarter, that utterly transforms one's situation and one's prospects. —Richard Nixon*[1]

chapter six

# TALKING WHILE FIGHTING

On 12 June 1971, Nixon gave away his daughter, Tricia, in a stunning ceremony in the White House Rose Garden. Although it had rained all morning, the president had it on good authority that the sun would come out late in the afternoon, in time for the bride to make a grand entrance in front of 400 guests. Looking dapper and relaxed in his long tuxedo jacket, Nixon could breathe easily: Tricia's wedding went off without a hitch. Weeks before, he had authorized his national security advisor to make an important concession at a secret meeting in Paris with the North Vietnamese that would seal the fate of the RVN. Although Nixon and Kissinger had retracted the demand for mutual withdrawal and accepted that North Vietnamese forces would stay in South Vietnam after the signing of any peace agreement, they believed they still possessed the upper hand. On 15 July 1971, Nixon announced to the world that he would visit the PRC. Like the ray of sunshine that dispelled the rain for the rest of Tricia's wedding day, Nixon's opening with China offered a bright solution to America's war in Vietnam. At least that's how it appeared to Nixon in the summer of 1971.

Since the start of North Vietnam's war in 1959, the Sino-Soviet split presented both advantages and disadvantages for leaders of the VWP in their war for national liberation and reunification. Although Hanoi was able to play Beijing and Moscow off one another and thus maintain strict autonomy over its war effort, the Sino-Soviet split also created logistical problems regarding aid and weapons transport and precluded the possibility of a unified diplomatic and political internationalist front. Enter the United States into the communist triangle. By late 1970, the United States and China began to take tentative steps toward one another, and in 1971 these steps culminated in the announcement of Nixon's trip to Beijing scheduled for early the next year. At the same time, Moscow, fearing isolation in the wake of Sino-American breakthrough, pushed forward with détente by scheduling Nixon's visit to Moscow to follow his Beijing visit a few months later.

The impact of Nixon's triangular offensive on Hanoi's war effort has been a topic of much debate and scholars, not surprisingly, have not arrived at a consensus. Historian Lorenz Lüthi argues that Sino-American rapprochement and Soviet-American détente did not have a negative impact on the North Vietnamese war effort because both allies remained loyal to the Vietnamese cause.[2] In Lüthi's estimation, the Soviet Union was more willing than the PRC to help Nixon and betray the Vietnamese cause. China scholars Li Danhui and Shen Zhihua use recently declassified materials from China to reveal that Beijing's contribution to Hanoi's war effort did not decline as a result of Sino-American rapprochement but in fact increased as relations between the United States and China improved.[3] Historian Qiang Zhai, on the other hand, sees more friction in Sino-Vietnamese relations following the Tet Offensive and the initiation of negotiations in 1968 as well as greater competition following the anti-Sihanouk coup in 1970.[4] Regarding the Soviet Union, the late historian Ilya Gaiduk, who had the most extensive access to CPSU archives, argues that Moscow was more or less left in the dark regarding North Vietnamese strategy. According to Gaiduk, Beijing exerted more pressure than the Soviets, but in the end, neither ally was successful in forcing the VWP to bend to its will.[5] Stephen Morris describes Soviet-Vietnamese relations in the 1970s as "one of public amity coexisting with private enmity."[6] Finally, official histories from Vietnam are overtly presentist: they vary depending on the course of Sino-Vietnamese and Russian-Vietnamese relations at the time of publication in Hanoi or Ho Chi Minh City.[7]

Based on previously closed Vietnamese-language materials as well as recently declassified documents from the Nixon Presidential Materials Project, this chapter shows that Nixon's superpower diplomacy had a significant impact on Le Duan and Le Duc Tho's war effort. Although the year began well for the leaders Le with the communist victory over the South

Vietnamese army in Laos, Nixon and Kissinger were able to diminish Hanoi's victory on the Indochinese battlefield by turning to superpower diplomacy. Throughout the summer of 1971, while Hanoi leaders vacillated between the two prongs of their policy of "talking while fighting," Nixon ensured that the VWP inclined toward the latter with his triangular offensive. As China and the Soviet Union moved closer to the United States, thereby threatening North Vietnam with a "big-power sellout," North Vietnam's military hubris, resulting from its stunning victory over South Vietnamese forces in Laos, prompted Hanoi leaders into choosing war over negotiating peace by late 1971.

## THE SPRING OF NEW STRATEGIES

The beginning of 1971 found Le Duan in a more desperate position than the previous year. The Party's efforts to boost North Vietnamese support for the war at the Eighteenth Plenum in January 1970 had failed to produce results. The DRV home front continued to suffer from sagging morale and economic problems. Under these circumstances, the Hanoi leadership convened its Nineteenth Plenum and designated the North Vietnamese economy as the most critical issue facing the Party in 1971. Even though sustained bombing over North Vietnam had ceased after 1968, with the brief flare-up in late 1970 of Nixon's Son Tay raids, VWP leaders noted that infrastructure and industries had only been partially restored. As a result, they devised a state plan that paid greater attention to manpower issues, supply of raw materials, and production.[8] Meanwhile, the war in South Vietnam, as well as in Cambodia and Laos, dragged on.

Even the most hardened "South-first" militants, who consistently placed North Vietnamese economic development on the backburner in favor of escalation and expansion of the war in the South, were forced to reckon with the domestic ills that confronted the DRV. Le Duan devoted his Nineteenth Plenum to addressing domestic policy by outlining three crucial tasks that faced the DRV in the upcoming year: advancing socialist reforms, evaluating the current economic situation, and maintaining the correct Marxist-Leninist path.[9] Le Duc Tho then echoed Le Duan's speech by exhorting Party members to devote greater attention to building the North Vietnamese economy in 1971.[10]

With the drop in the DRV's war productivity and the rising discontent among the North Vietnamese masses in 1971, at least one communist official benefited. Minister of Public Security Tran Quoc Hoan's stature rose as the Party deemed his ministry's work of the utmost importance. During a conference to address the "Catholic problem," a group that Hoan considered the most "outstanding lackeys of the imperialists and also representatives of the most reactionary feudalist and traitorous capitalist classes," the minister attempted to distinguish between the impressionable Catholic masses and the dangerous reactionary elements that exploited the Catholic religion.[11] The latter sought to expand the power of the church and use the banner of "protecting the faith" as a means to brainwash the religious, keeping them "backward and in the dark, to the point of becoming fanatics whom they could incite to oppose the revolution."[12] Hoan's solution was reminiscent of French colonial officials or American proponents of nation building who sought to maintain order and promised uplift. He urged more operations "aimed at mobilizing and educating the Catholic masses, improving their political and cultural education levels, and improving their standard of living."[13] This would be the way to defeat counterrevolution in the long term in this "most reactionary" community.

Catholics were not the only suspect group. Looking back on their imprisonment, three musicians accused of playing "yellow music," arrested in 1968, and tried in January 1971, recalled being charged with "poisoning the young generation with pessimistic and reactionary songs, promoting a retrogressive and sex-oriented lifestyle."[14] Although Minister Hoan had targeted "yellow music" in his speeches before 1971, the three-day trial of singer Phan Thang Toan (or "Hairy" Toan), guitarist Tran Van Thanh, and guitarist Nguyen Van Loc, was the first court case against the "spreading of imperialistic depraved culture and antirevolutionary propaganda."[15] The three young men, who began a band in 1965, confessed to playing this forbidden music that included prewar and foreign love songs at weddings and parties. "Hairy" Toan, the leader of the band and the "yellow music" movement, was sentenced to fifteen years and was finally released in 1980, while the others received lesser punishment including guitarist Loc, who received a ten-year sentence with four years' probation. Although Loc later claimed that the band was apolitical and that their love for this illicit music trumped the dangers involved, the Ministry of Public Security and newspapers in Hanoi that covered the trial found the band's performances to be subversive and dangerous as war ravaged the country.[16] There was no room for love or nostalgia in music when the country was fighting for its survival. At the time, Hoan admitted that, as with the Revisionist Anti-Party Affair, he should have handled the "yellow music" movement earlier, since "Hairy" Toan was formerly an enemy psychological warfare officer.[17]

Hoan elaborated on other suspect groups besides Catholics and musicians. With growing discontent in North Vietnam, Hoan prepared his forces for more crackdowns. During a discussion session with the Committee to Review the Handling of Cases, he delineated the differences between criminal and political cases. Within the latter, he noted the distinctions separating sleeper agents, commando spies, and foreign agents stationed in North Vietnam.[18] The minister urged his security officers to refrain from treating these cases in a singular manner and fitting them into one mold. "You need to look at how the Americans do it," Hoan stated. "They are very practical."[19] Noting that relations with allies in 1971 had become more fraught, Hoan pointed out that a potential threat could come in friendly guise. "There are some of our [socialist] 'brothers' who come to our country to conduct intelligence activities," Hoan warned his officers.[20] Or, the threat could come from students who studied abroad in ostensibly friendly countries and returned home as "sleeper spies," often "lying dormant for a long time, and then after fifteen or twenty years they finally become active."[21] For these cases, security forces had to remain patient and practice constant vigilance. Most ominously, Hoan predicted that the "class struggle, the struggle against counterrevolutionaries," would be a long-term one that would not end with the war.

> For example, in South Vietnam right now there are targets on whom we need to establish an operational case right now, but even later, after we completely liberate South Vietnam, we cannot just drop the case and cease to monitor these targets. . . . There are some types of people who, even though they are members of the NLF, we still need to keep an eye on. There are a number of people whom the CIA has gained control over and whom the CIA had deployed into position to let them appear to be opposed to the United States and Thieu in order to trick us so that they can sneak into our NLF organization in order to serve the enemy's long-term political schemes after South Vietnam is liberated, North and South Vietnam are reunified, and our entire nation is advancing toward the socialist revolution.[22]

With these words, Hoan created the conditions for perpetual struggle. Since it became more difficult by 1971 to distinguish friend from foe, Hoan and Le Duan's police state redefined the terms of Hanoi's war so that it could persist indefinitely.

As Hoan dealt with potential internal and external threats, other Hanoi leaders went abroad in search of aid in order to bolster North Vietnam's flagging war economy. Following on the success of DRV delegations in negotiating economic and military aid packages in 1970, the government appointed Vice Premier and Politburo member Le Thanh Nghi, a veteran of aid negotiations, to head such a mission in the first half of 1971. In early January, Nghi and his delegation set out to visit Hungary, Poland, and East Germany. The Vietnamese delegates spent approximately two and a half weeks in each country and concluded not only aid packages but also agreements on economic, scientific, and technical cooperation.[23] Eastern Europe was not the only region where the DRV proved successful. On 21 January, Havana and Hanoi signed an agreement for nonrefundable aid while the premier of Mongolia promised the same package via a letter to DRV prime minister and Politburo member Pham Van Dong.[24] By 1971, twelve communist countries had reaffirmed the importance of North Vietnam's war effort by contributing economic, military, scientific, and technical aid.

In addition to procuring material aid, Hanoi's international strategy also included "influencing U.S. domestic opinion to increase pressure on American leaders to end the war."[25] On 5 January 1971, the Vietnamese Women's Movement Demanding the Right to Live and the American Women's International League for Peace and Freedom (WILPF) organized an International Women's Congress in Saigon. In addition to signing a "peace agreement," the participants fulfilled the previous congress's resolution calling on every member to send a card to Nixon demanding an end to the war. At the conclusion of the congress, the Vietnamese organization joined the WILPF to influence their activities and help promote the cause of the restoration of peace through the league's network of national associations.[26]

Although North Vietnamese delegations scored economic successes abroad and people's diplomacy made inroads in the global arena, the diplomatic struggle in Paris yielded little gain.[27] In late fall of 1970, both the secret talks and the public sessions broke off amid escalating tensions and insurmountable disagreement. When the public talks resumed in mid-January 1971, DRV negotiator Xuan Thuy cabled his "special advisor" and DRV foreign minister Trinh in Hanoi with his frank assessment of the meeting. The Nixon administration, in Thuy's estimation, was putting forward its Five-Point Proposal from a position of military and diplomatic strength. Even though VWP leaders recognized that Nixon's peace initiative was hollow and intended only to deceive U.S. and world public opinion, Thuy claimed that it was nonetheless effective. The DRV negotiator identified two factors that gave Nixon strength in his diplomatic strategy in Paris in early 1971. First, fewer Americans were dying in Southeast Asia because troop withdrawal was progressing unhindered; second, the Nixon administration had successfully exploited the POW issue in negotiations. Thuy, however, had no idea how to combat Nixon's Five-Point Plan. He proposed that the Party continue holding both public and private meetings with the Americans and adhere rigidly to the original strategic objectives while adopting a flexible tactical posture.[28]

Hanoi's uninspired stance came as no surprise. North Vietnam's negotiating strategy was predicated on how its forces were doing militarily; the lack of movement in Paris in early 1971 reflected the stalemated battlefield picture in Indochina. Despite the lack of unity among the revolutionary parties—particularly the Vietnamese and Khmer communists—the VWP felt confident that its counteroffensives in mid-1970 had succeeded in at least turning the military tide in favor of the Indochinese revolutionary forces, albeit slowly. In southeastern Laos, North Vietnamese and Pathet Lao forces were able to liberate the crucial areas around Attopeu by early May 1970. Communist forces were thus able to link the liberated zones in the north and south of the country. Meanwhile in Cambodia, Saigon and Phnom Penh troops continued to conduct operations in Khmer Republic territory, but they failed to threaten communist strongholds. Instead, American bombs, which fell with more frequency and covered more ground, were able to inflict damage on the resistance and the country more generally. Nonetheless, the crucial northeast provinces in Cambodia remained in communist hands. As a result, by the summer of 1970, Hanoi leaders were hopeful that their forces had begun the slow process of recovery following the disastrous 1968 Tet Offensive.[29] Hanoi's optimism, however, was guarded. Even though VWP leaders claimed that the liberated territories in South Vietnam, Cambodia, and Laos "constituted a firm base area for revolutionary forces of Indochina," linking the "strategic transportation corridor throughout Indochina," the remaining communist supply route—the famous Ho Chi Minh Trail—was still vulnerable. For this reason, the VWP's ability to continue its war for liberation and reunification in the foreseeable future remained precarious, making a negotiated settlement impossible.

Meanwhile, American military leaders located in "Pentagon East," the popular moniker given to the headquarters of MACV at Tan Son Nhut Airbase in Saigon, arrived at the same conclusion as leaders in Hanoi. The Ho Chi Minh Trail proved the linchpin of Hanoi's ability to wage war in the South. In late 1970, MACV Commander General Creighton Abrams, under pressure from Washington, put forth a military plan based on a South Vietnamese initiative for the 1971 dry season that included interdicting the flow of resources down the main artery of the Ho Chi Minh Trail running through Laos by launching a large-scale operation with ARVN ground soldiers under the protection of U.S. air power.[30] If successful, the United States and its allies in Saigon would be able to prevent communist troops from launching an offensive in 1972. Since the previous year witnessed the closing of the communist water trail through Port Sihanouk with the regime change in Phnom Penh, the sole remaining infiltration route ran overland through southern Laos. Working on multiple fronts starting in June 1970, the Hanoi Politburo prepared to meet the eventual attack on its transportation and logistics line to the South by ordering reinforcements to fortify communist strongholds in three main areas alongside Route 9 in southern Laos, around the DMZ, and in northeastern Cambodia.[31] By the end of the year, Abrams and MACV had begun to receive disturbing intelligence of the North Vietnamese buildup in the first area around southeastern Laos.

Just as in the pre-Tet war, members of the U.S. civilian and military leadership often butted heads, as military planning for 1971 underscores. Over the protests of Abrams, Nixon decided to announce the removal of 100,000 troops from South Vietnam during the latter half of the year, leaving only 175,000 American troops by 1972.[32] Optimistic about his ability to force the North Vietnamese to settle in Paris by stepping up the air war and exerting diplomatic pressure before de-Americanization could fatally undermine Vietnamization, Nixon accelerated troop withdrawals in order to placate public opinion at home. By doing so, Nixon and Kissinger not only hindered Abrams but also placed greater pressure on RVN president Thieu. The Saigon leader was to assemble his South Vietnamese forces to make what civilian leaders in Washington called "a show of strength" in 1971 while there were still a sufficient number of American combat troops to provide effective support. It was in this context that Abrams implemented his military plans in a three-phase operation code-named Lam Son 719, harking back to a famous Vietnamese battle in 1427 against the Chinese.[33] Phase 1 of the operation included American troops clearing the area around Route 9 west to the Laotian border and readying air support for the South Vietnamese troops. Phase 2 involved an ARVN strike lasting four to five days along Route 9 toward Tchepone in southern Laos, and Phase 3 included a three-month attack on the PAVN logistics complex located in Tchepone and interdiction of the supply trails around the area.[34] In conjunction with the Laotian operations, the ARVN forces from Military Region III would mount an attack on Cambodia's Kompong Cham province to destroy communist forces and logistics facilities there in Operation Toan Thang 1–71.[35] In addition to constituting a major "show of strength" to prove the success of Vietnamization to the world, Nixon also hoped Lam Son 719 would prove to the Hanoi leadership that he was not afraid to expand the war to Laos in dramatic fashion. However, the stakes were high. If Lam Son 719 failed, it would not only inflict major damage to South Vietnamese morale but also bolster the North Vietnamese and try the patience of the American public.

Nonetheless, Nixon and Kissinger believed the gamble was worth taking on Thieu's behalf in early 1971, even though the political and military situation was not ideal. In the United States, the joint U.S.-ARVN "incursion" into Cambodia in 1970 continued to cause political problems for the Nixon administration during the planning for Lam Son 719. Resolutions to curtail the expansion of the war and to bring about an end to American military involvement proliferated in Congress. In the House, representatives proposed to cut off U.S. air and sea support for operations in Cambodia, while in the Senate, George McGovern and Mark Hatfield reintroduced a revised Disengagement Act that would require the withdrawal of all American forces by the end of 1971. In an attempt to avoid the mistakes of Cambodia, Nixon and Kissinger this time tried to involve Secretary of State William Rogers and Secretary of Defense Melvin Laird in the decision making, at least to a point. When State and Defense balked, particularly after Rogers discovered that the enemy may have acquired the military plans for Lam Son 719 and was prepared to counter the operation by amassing soldiers in the area, Nixon paid them no need. As usual, Kissinger supported the president's decision. Despite the internal bickering, Nixon gave the green light for Phase 1 to begin on 31 January 1971.[36]

Immediately following the start of Phase 1, however, news of Lam Son 719 leaked to the American media, endangering the ARVN's chances for success—however limited—in Phases 2 and 3. Although network television and newspaper editorials revealed aspects of the Laotian operation not only to the American public but also to North Vietnamese military planners, Nixon and Kissinger concluded that they should not be dissuaded from launching Phase 2.[37] As a result, on 7 February, despite anger in Saigon at the leaks, the South Vietnamese armed forces crossed the Laotian border. By the end of the month, the Saigon regime's worst nightmare became a reality. On 9 February, the Politburo put COSVN leadership on alert that victory on Highway 9 was essential.[38] Although the South Vietnamese, with American air support, were able to inflict heavy casualties and great damage on the numerically superior North Vietnamese army, Lam Son 719 was a public relations defeat for the RVN. As cameras caught the ARVN's hasty retreat on film, images of the failure of Vietnamization were broadcast around the world.[39]

There were many reasons for the failure of Lam Son 719. First, instead of possessing numerical superiority, 17,000 South Vietnamese troops encountered 22,000 North Vietnamese soldiers who were equipped with tanks and heavy artillery, and by the end of the operation, the numerically inferior ARVN fought against 60,000-strong PAVN troops.[40] Second, South Vietnamese president Thieu made a controversial decision to change the military plans in the midst of battle. Instead of holding on to Tchepone, the logistical center of the North Vietnamese Army, for an extended period, Thieu ordered his general to abandon the empty village after a day. Third, language barriers impeded effective coordination between the South Vietnamese and the Americans. What is clear is that both sides fought a conventional battle with arms and heavy weaponry supplied by their superpower patrons and thus suffered heavy casualties.

Nixon and Kissinger's gamble on South Vietnam's behalf not only severely undermined the standing of the Thieu regime, but it also coincided with the resurgence of antiwar activity in the United States. As Nixon declared Vietnamization "a success" in April, Vietnam Veterans against the War (VVAW) launched its "Winter Soldier Investigation" into U.S. war crimes in Vietnam. In late March, one of those responsible for these crimes was brought to justice when Lieutenant William Calley was found guilty of the murder of twenty-two Vietnamese civilians in Son My village in 1968. On 2 April 1971, however, Nixon intervened by freeing Calley from jail, placing him under house arrest, and initiating the process for reviewing the verdict. Nixon's intervention in the Calley case, along with the 7 April announcement of additional troop withdrawals, failed to defuse the veterans' anger at the administration's perpetuation of the un-winnable war. Throughout the spring, the VVAW staged effective demonstrations in the nation's capital. For five days in April, select veterans, such as VVAW leader John Kerry, testified against the war in a Senate committee hearing while 700 others laid down their medals and ribbons on the steps of the Capitol. The veterans unnerved Nixon, who feared that they, more than the antiwar hippies and radicals, would turn public opinion against the war.[41]

Nixon's domestic woes did not abate in the late spring and summer.[42] Following the veterans' demonstrations, hundreds of thousands of protestors gathered in Washington in an attempt to shut down the government. Although Nixon left town during the "May Day" actions, he went on the offensive against the antiwar Left by ordering the arrests of thousands of demonstrators on questionable grounds. Then, on 13 June, another bombshell dropped. The *New York Times* began printing the first of a series of articles based on top-secret documents given to the paper by a former Pentagon official and consultant to Kissinger, Daniel Ellsberg. These documents, which became known as the Pentagon Papers, were part of a multivolume study of U.S. decision making regarding Vietnam from 1945 to 1968 commissioned by former secretary of defense Robert S. McNamara. Nixon's policies were not part of the study, and several advisers urged him to refrain from intervening. Nixon, however, had other ideas; with Kissinger's enthusiastic support, he took the offensive. He ordered an injunction against the *New York Times*, obtained an indictment against Ellsberg, and formed a group known as the "Plumbers" to break into the offices of real and potential domestic adversaries. Nixon's war at home, however, would eventually bring down his presidency. The *Washington Post* and various other newspapers continued to print the Pentagon Papers, and all charges against Ellsberg would eventually be dropped when the Plumbers' illegal activities were exposed in the ensuing Watergate scandal.[43]

Nixon continued to play for time, and fortunately for him, all did not bode ill for the United States in 1971. Although Lam Son 719 was a military and political debacle for the RVN, the United States reaped the lion's share of diplomatic advantage in early 1971. In particular, the Chinese and Soviets issued only mild criticism of American expansion of the war into Laos, not wanting to endanger the progress made toward rapprochement and détente with Washington. In the month preceding Lam Son 719, Zhou Enlai expressed Beijing's interest in inviting Nixon to China via the Romanians, while Soviet ambassador Anatoly Dobrynin indicated to Kissinger that Moscow accepted the U.S. proposal for a Brezhnev-Nixon meeting to negotiate a Strategic Arms Limitation Talks (SALT) agreement.[44]

Despite these positive signals from Beijing and preliminary talks with Moscow, Nixon did not exercise the same caution as his Chinese and Soviet counterparts. By turning up the heat in Indochina, he seemingly endangered all of this progress in Sino-American rapprochement and U.S.-Soviet détente in late February 1971. Although he appeared not to care if Lam Son 719 derailed the planning for the upcoming U.S.-Soviet summit, he did undertake minimal steps to protect the tentative contacts with China by assuring Beijing that the Laotian operation was not directed against the PRC.[45] Apparently, Mao was satisfied with Nixon's public statement, since Beijing issued only moderate criticism of the ARVN invasion of Laos in February 1971, especially when compared to Beijing's heavy condemnation of the U.S.-ARVN invasion of Cambodia in May 1970. At the same time, U.S. officials noted the Soviets' restraint in their condemnation of the United States.[46]

Even though both of Hanoi's patrons refrained from heavily criticizing U.S. aggression in Laos, they were far from unified on the Indochina issue. In early March, Soviet officials in Hanoi recommended that the Chinese and Soviets agree to "joint or parallel actions in support of the struggle of peoples in Indochina."[47] Taking advantage of an upcoming scheduled meeting between Chinese and North Vietnamese leaders in Hanoi, the Soviets asked the North Vietnamese to convey Moscow's proposal to the Chinese. For the Soviets, it was a win-win situation: if Beijing agreed to joint action, Sino-American relations would suffer, and if Beijing refused, the North Vietnamese would see China's uncooperative policy. On 7 March, Premier Zhou Enlai tried to convince Le Duan and Pham Van Dong that the Soviet offer was not in their best interests: "If we take the Soviets' side, they will control us. And if there is disagreement between us, we should talk it out on the basis of independence and self-reliance. If we establish a world-wide people's front that includes the Soviets, they will control this front. . . . The Soviets wish to establish a united front in which we have to listen to them." At this point, Le Duan turned the tables on Zhou Enlai by suggesting the formation of a united internationalist front with China at the forefront. The Vietnamese first secretary employed a common tactic of forcing Beijing's hand with flattery: "The world's people wish to oppose the 'Nixon doctrine,' which also means opposing the U.S.-Japan alliance. The questions, therefore, are how we establish this front, who is capable of doing this. Only China and no one else. Everyone knows that the Indochinese Summit took place in China. So in the future, it will be more influential if a conference of the world's people is held in China."[48] Zhou Enlai begged off by saying that China would "need more time to think" about leading a people's front to oppose the United States and Japan.[49] Compared to China's enthusiasm in the previous year at hosting a summit following the anti-Sihanouk coup, the VWP first secretary could not help but read Beijing's reluctance in early 1971 as further evidence that relations with the United States were now more important than the Indochinese cause. On 16 March, after Chinese leaders left Hanoi, the Soviet ambassador to the DRV, Ilya Scherbakov, told Prime Minister Pham Van Dong that the Soviets had consistently approached China for joint action in Vietnam and that the Chinese Foreign Ministry's rejection of the Soviet offer this time was based on "dissimilar positions" regarding American actions in Indochina.[50] At the end of the month, Le Duan attended the Twenty-Fourth Congress of the CPSU. To Brezhnev's dismay, the Vietnamese leader informed him that Hanoi's military strategy for 1972 would echo some of the same objectives of the 1968 Tet Offensive.[51] Even though Moscow did not want Hanoi to escalate the war, the Soviets were ecstatic that North Vietnamese leaders confided in them. The Soviet embassy in Hanoi reported to Moscow that it was convinced that Soviet-Vietnamese relations were growing stronger just as "new frictions" arose in the Sino-Vietnamese alliance.[52] Le Duan's four-week stay in the Soviet Union prompted Nixon and Kissinger to hope that a settlement was imminent. "Something may come out of this Le Duan visit to Moscow," Kissinger stated during a phone conversation with Nixon. "It's three weeks . . . and they may be getting ready to settle it."[53]

Chinese leaders were convinced that their moderate response to American military actions in Laos and their suspicions regarding Soviet proposals for joint action in Vietnam were correct for two reasons. First, the CCP believed that Sino-Vietnamese relations would not be badly damaged. Due to the increase of Chinese aid and support for the North Vietnamese war effort in 1970–71, Beijing thought that Hanoi was confident of the PRC's stalwart support. Chinese leaders made a concerted effort early in the year to improve Sino-Vietnamese relations by endorsing the PRG proposal for peace, approving Hanoi's negotiating stance, and planning a high-level visit to North Vietnam in the spring. Prior to the February visit to Beijing of a delegation led by Minister of Finance Le Thanh Nghi, Chinese leaders approved a generous supplementary economic and military aid package.[54] Second, Beijing had its own geostrategic objectives. Chinese leaders wanted to protect their tentative steps toward Washington since they did not fully trust the North Vietnamese and, of course, distrusted the Soviets completely. Hanoi's growing dependence on Soviet weaponry and its military success in Laos meant that Chinese influence was on the wane in Vietnam and that North Vietnamese strength, under Soviet tutelage, was on the rise in Indochina. And, unlike in Cambodia, where Pol Pot's faction of the Communist Party detested the Vietnamese, the Pathet Lao and the VWP were closely aligned, leaving the Chinese with little room to maneuver in Laos.

North Vietnamese disappointment with the inability of the Chinese and Soviets to bridge their differences and establish a unified internationalist front in March was replaced with utter despair when each of Hanoi's allies took steps that drastically improved relations with Washington in April and May.[55] Two months following Beijing's pro forma denunciations of U.S. imperialist aggression in Laos and one month after Zhou Enlai's visit to Hanoi, Mao issued an invitation to the American table tennis team to visit Beijing in early April. Following this "ping pong diplomacy," Zhou Enlai sent Nixon a message through Pakistani president Yayha Khan that sealed Sino-American rapprochement: China was ready to accept a special envoy of the U.S. president.[56] On 9 May, Nixon decided to send Kissinger to Beijing for a secret meeting with Zhou Enlai. At a three-day CCP Central Committee meeting in late May, Chinese leaders placed the withdrawal of American troops from Indochina as the lowest priority. Beijing reasoned that bettering relations with the United States would somehow help the Vietnamese cause.

Regarding the Soviet Union, Nixon appeared hopeful in March that a high-level meeting between himself and Brezhnev would take place in the fall of 1971. By May, a major breakthrough had occurred regarding a procedural issue that smoothed the way for an eventual SALT agreement.[57] The groundwork for Nixon's triangular offensive had begun to take shape and would force the Hanoi Politburo to again revise its strategy by the end of the summer of 1971, downgrading diplomacy in favor of a military offensive the next year.

### THE SUMMER OF OPPORTUNITIES

According to historian Jeffrey Kimball, both the United States and North Vietnam viewed the spring and summer 1971 round of negotiations following Lam Son 719 as the last chance to arrive at a settlement and avoid military escalation.[58] In actuality, however, both sides deemed a settlement impossible in 1971. Rapprochement with China and détente with the Soviet Union had strengthened Nixon's resolve in Vietnam. The U.S. president was convinced that he could force the North Vietnamese to settle on American terms either by using superpower diplomacy or by again dramatically escalating the war. Although there is debate as to whether Nixon had adopted a "decent interval" strategy at this point, Kissinger had resigned himself to negotiating an honorable exit for the United States that would not precipitate an immediate collapse of the RVN. At the same time, the Vietnamese communist victory over the ARVN in the Lam Son 719 debacle boosted the Party leadership's confidence in scoring a major military victory in 1972. Not only did the "puppet forces" fail to interdict the flow of men and matériel down the Ho Chi Minh Trail, but Vietnamese and Lao revolutionary forces were able to deliver what they—and the rest of the world—viewed as a crushing blow to Vietnamization. This military success, combined with troubling events at the international level including Sino-American rapprochement and Soviet-American détente, led Hanoi leaders to conclude that the time was not ripe to reach a negotiated settlement.

In mid-April, Kissinger informed the American ambassador to South Vietnam, Ellsworth Bunker, that he intended to reopen the "special forum" in Paris in order to deliver a "concrete package" to the North Vietnamese, and he asked Bunker whether the United States should inform Thieu of the probe. Kissinger feared that informing the South Vietnamese president might shake his morale following so close on the heels of the Lam Son 719 debacle.[59] When Bunker recommended informing Thieu, Kissinger suggested that the ambassador tell the South Vietnamese president that the North Vietnamese were the ones who had initiated contact because they feared the implications of "the ping-pong and SALT developments" on Saigon's confidence.[60] Nearly three weeks after the American initiative, and after an eight-month hiatus, the North Vietnamese finally relented and agreed to a meeting between Kissinger and Xuan Thuy on 31 May. Delivering Nixon's last-ditch effort at peace in the form of a seven-point proposal, Kissinger concluded that the meeting was a success since the North Vietnamese negotiator "displayed uncertainty" for the first time and since he omitted his usual claim that Kissinger had proposed nothing new.[61] In essence, the U.S. seven-point proposal asked the North Vietnamese to accept Thieu as the leader of the RVN in exchange for a fixed date for U.S. withdrawal, a cease-fire, and prisoner release. However, Kissinger could not help but needle Thuy by indicating that the "post–Ho Chi Minh leadership may be too divided" to make a decision about the seven-point proposal and that they would "also have to clear their position with Moscow and Peking."[62] What is clear is that in all of the machinations leading up to the 31 May meeting about whether or not to inform Thieu, the South Vietnamese president was left ignorant of the fact that the United States was offering the pivotal concession that would eventually seal the RVN's fate: Washington now accepted the presence of the PAVN in South Vietnam even after a cease-fire.

In response to Kissinger's proposal, Xuan Thuy insisted on three points that he had made at the mid-January 1971 four-party public forum: all U.S. forces must be withdrawn by 30 June 1971; a government must be established in Saigon without President Nguyen Van Thieu, Vice President Nguyen Cao Ky, and Prime Minister Tran Thien Khiem; and the United States should definitively stop all violations of the sovereignty and security of the DRV. Regarding the seven-point proposal, the North Vietnamese negotiator complained that the United States still insisted on separating the military and political issues and only wanted to address the former but not the latter.

However, in his postmeeting assessment to Le Duc Tho and Nguyen Duy Trinh, Xuan Thuy noted that Kissinger's seven-point proposal represented a major breakthrough, since it was the first time the United States presented a solution addressing all of Indochina, was willing to set a time limit for troop withdrawal, and, most important, did not insist on mutual withdrawal from the South. In contrast to his January report following the public four-party talks, where he concluded that the U.S. five-point proposal came from a position of strength in October 1970, the North Vietnamese negotiator surmised that Kissinger's seven-point proposal in April 1971 came from a position of weakness. Not only did the failure of Lam Son 719 weaken the American negotiating position, Thuy concluded, but both Washington and Saigon hoped to reach an agreement and thus score a public relations victory in anticipation of their respective presidential elections (October 1971 in South Vietnam and November 1972 in the United States).[63] If Hanoi responded positively to the seven-point proposal and appeared flexible during the peace talks, Party leaders believed that the United States would be willing to negotiate an acceptable solution by the end of 1972. If Hanoi seemed unwilling to compromise and seek a viable solution, however, the United States would continue Vietnamization and stop negotiating seriously in 1972.[64] Given Hanoi's reading of the importance of the seven-point proposal and what VWP leaders saw as a critical juncture in negotiations, the DRV Foreign Ministry announced that Le Duc Tho would return to Paris after being away for more than a year. Le Duan's Politburo wanted to convey to the Americans that Tho's return signaled that Hanoi was ready to negotiate seriously in the secret meeting set for 26 June. Nixon and Kissinger followed Tho's movements with interest since in their estimation he was the "third man in the hierarchy[,] . . . the only man who can take independent decisions on negotiations," and a man who "travels only when there are crucial matters."[65]

In mid-June, the Politburo instructed Xuan Thuy to deliver a new nine-point peace plan at the 26 June secret meeting.[66] In an effort to appear flexible, North Vietnamese leaders even changed the décor of the usual meeting place by spreading a green tablecloth on top of the normally drab working table. Kissinger read into the gesture that the North Vietnamese were serious about working toward a solution.[67] Most important, Tho's return to the secret meetings after a year's absence was not lost on the national security advisor, even if it also meant that he was treated to another lecture on American perfidy that dominated the first half of the meeting. During the customary break, however, the usually frosty Tho led Kissinger around the garden for a walk, while Xuan Thuy ostensibly worked on North Vietnam's response to the U.S. seven-point proposal from the previous meeting. When the meeting recommenced, Thuy presented Kissinger with the DRV's nine-point plan.[68] In an effort to appear more conciliatory, Hanoi extended the deadline for U.S. troop withdrawal to 31 December 1971 (the original deadline of 30 June was coming up in four days), requested that rather than call for the outright removal of the Thieu-Ky-Khiem clique, the United States simply end support for the Saigon regime (which amounted to the same thing), and asked for war reparations from the United States (causing Kissinger to object immediately, even though Washington had expressed willingness to offer economic aid). Although the 31 May and 26 June meetings produced major breakthroughs, too many differences remained. At the conclusion of the 26 June meeting, both parties agreed to meet again on 12 July.[69]

At the same time that Tho met Kissinger in Paris, war leaders in Hanoi held a military conference to assess the gains made in the victory on Highway 9 in southern Laos. The conference report differentiated the communist victory in early 1971 from previous victories in Indochina in many ways. First, Hanoi concluded that its forces had scored a decisive victory over the Nixon Doctrine and its Vietnamization policy since they were able

to defeat the elite forces of the U.S.-trained South Vietnamese army. Previous communist victories over the "puppet forces" of Indochina, including Lon Nol's army and Vang Pao's soldiers, were important but paled in
comparison to defeating Thieu's crack troops, including paratroopers and
marines. Second, Hanoi considered its victory on Highway 9 of monumen-
tal importance because it had a resounding effect not only on the Laotian
battleground but also on the Cambodian and South Vietnamese fronts.
The conference report emphasized the need to convert the military success into a political one in light of the upcoming presidential elections in
South Vietnam.[70] In two telegrams to the COSVN chief, Pham Hung, and
other southern leaders written around the same time as the conference,
Le Duan elaborated on capitalizing on the success in southern Laos by increasing the political struggle in the cities.[71] In the first telegram, dated 24
June, the first secretary outlined an urban political offensive strategy in
preparation for the RVN's presidential and Lower House elections. It included four tasks: (1) mobilizing propaganda campaigns while coordinating the public struggle with the secret negotiations; (2) bringing to power
a more amenable regime in Saigon; (3) exploiting political divisions in the
RVN; and (4) integrating the political struggle in the urban centers with
that in the countryside.[72] In the second and more detailed telegram to
Pham Hung and COSVN, Le Duan elaborated on the military tasks confronting the Vietnamese revolution. After concluding that the fighting in
Cambodia and Laos now decisively favored the revolution, the first secretary emphasized the necessity to refocus on the most important theater:
South Vietnam. Specifically, he identified three "main strategic blows [*ba
qua dam chien luoc*]": (1) using main force units to defeat the puppet army
in South Vietnam; (2) combining military and political forces in the delta
region; and (3) increasing political activity in the urban areas.[73]

The results of the military conference and Le Duan's orders to COSVN
shed light on why the Vietnamese communist position in Paris hardened following what had seemed to be two productive secret meetings
with Kissinger in May and June. At the military conference, war leaders
in Hanoi were convinced that communist forces had dealt a devastating
blow to Vietnamization with the victory along Highway 9 in southern Laos.
As a result, Le Duan advocated increasing political agitation in the cities
of South Vietnam in order to capitalize on the military victory, especially
in order to influence the upcoming RVN presidential elections. In other
words, the first secretary once again saw an opportunity to redeem his
risky strategy. In an attempt to vindicate his General Offensive and Gen-

eral Uprising strategy that had failed in 1964 and in 1968, Le Duan ordered the first step to heighten the political blow that a military attack aimed at urban centers could have on South Vietnam. Political agitation in 1971 would lay the groundwork for another grand slam attempt to topple the Saigon regime in 1972.[74]

In early July, then, Hanoi took steps to antagonize the United States in Paris and to undermine the progress made during the secret meetings of May and June. At the 119th public forum on 1 July, PRG foreign minister Madame Nguyen Thi Binh presented her government's seven-point proposal.[75] The PRG's public peace plan was inspired by Le Duan's instruction to "combine the public struggle and the secret negotiations" and only differed from the DRV's secret nine points by dealing more explicitly with the Thieu problem.[76] Increased activity by the U.S. antiwar movement in the spring both in Congress and on the streets, controversy over the Calley trial, and the publication of the Pentagon Papers, convinced the VWP it could press harder at negotiations.[77] The PRG called on the United States to refrain from supporting any rigged elections in South Vietnam and instead to assist in setting up a three-part national government. The United States, however, regarded the PRG's seven points and the DRV's nine points as purposely inconsistent because the Vietnamese communists were trying to appear flexible in public while remaining intransigent in private.[78] Moreover, in early July, Le Duc Tho granted an interview to Anthony Lewis of the *New York Times* in which he announced that the DRV was ready to exchange American troop withdrawals for prisoners of war.[79] Like Binh's seven points, Nixon and Kissinger believed that Tho's public proposal was a Vietnamese communist "duplicitous stunt," since in private the North Vietnamese negotiator had consistently tied such a settlement to other provisions.[80] They believed Hanoi was not interested in negotiating a solution in 1971 but rather was only trying to increase U.S. domestic opposition to war by feigning flexibility. In any case, Nixon would not yet agree to withdraw U.S. forces merely in return for the release of American prisoners.

Hanoi's diplomatic campaign in July was in fact part of a broader strategy to influence the October presidential elections in South Vietnam. On 8 July, Le Duan sent instructions to southern leaders regarding the proper urban strategy to follow in order to defeat Thieu in the upcoming elections. The first secretary, who had long been an advocate for pushing the political struggle in the urban centers, chastised southern leaders for not putting adequate pressure on the Saigon regime. Not only should there be demands for freedom of the press, freedom of assembly, and overall opposition to the repressive tactics of the Thieu clique, Le Duan wanted southern leaders to incorporate the call for complete American troop withdrawal into the overall demand for peace. He reasoned that these issues needed to be brought to the forefront of the political struggle in Saigon.[81] A few days later, Le Duan telegrammed Tho and Thuy in Paris twice with urgent instructions. The first telegram emphasized the need to coordinate the three spheres of the VWP's war effort: the military, political, and diplomatic struggles.[82] In the second telegram, the first secretary went into more concrete detail by identifying the two objectives of the diplomatic struggle as, first, inciting the antiwar movement in Congress and on the streets in order to force Nixon to withdraw troops from Vietnam and, second, toppling the puppet Saigon government.[83]

Meanwhile, in Washington, developments in Sino-American relations presented Nixon with potential diplomatic leverage over the North Vietnamese. From 9 to 11 July, Kissinger met with Zhou Enlai in Beijing to discuss Nixon's visit to Beijing set for 1972, but Vietnam was addressed as well.[84] At the first day of meetings, Kissinger informed Zhou of Nixon's offer to withdraw all American troops, presented at the 31 May secret meeting. Since Hanoi had stopped keeping Beijing abreast of developments at the private talks, Zhou Enlai expressed interest in learning more about the American offer of total troop withdrawal and must have been happy to hear that Kissinger promised to keep him updated on the upcoming meeting with the North Vietnamese set for 12 July. However, when the U.S. national security advisor tried to link Chinese help with an honorable withdrawal from Vietnam to the Taiwan issue and PRC representation in the United Nations, Zhou did not acquiesce. In response to Kissinger's statement that the United States wanted to preserve American honor in Vietnam, the Chinese premier recommended complete withdrawal from Indochina as the "greatest honor and glory for the United States."[85] However, on the morning of Kissinger's departure from Beijing, the Chinese premier wished him success at the upcoming secret meeting with Le Duc Tho in Paris and suggested that he might even find the North Vietnamese "more generous" than the United States "believed."[86] In Kissinger's report to Nixon, the former was so optimistic at Zhou's parting words to him that he wrote: "This means he will talk to the North Vietnamese and may be able to exert some influence. The mere fact of his talking to them is likely to compound the shock of your announced visit to Beijing. In any case, he knows that the very fact we and Peking [Beijing] are moving closer will have an impact in Hanoi."[87] When Zhou Enlai briefed Mao Zedong on his meetings with Kissinger, the two Chinese leaders decided not to comply with Kissinger's request to pressure Hanoi to change its position in Paris.[88]

On 13 July, Zhou Enlai flew to Hanoi in what was most likely a very difficult trip. The Cold War International History Project (CWIHP) located only a brief statement by Le Duan, saying that Kissinger's visit to Beijing had been designed to offset "surprises" that the Vietnamese have been able to inflict.[89] Historian Luu Van Loi includes a lengthier synopsis of Zhou Enlai's comments.[90] We now have from recently released Vietnamese sources a fuller transcript of Hanoi's summary of Zhou Enlai's meeting with Le Duan and Pham Van Dong. This transcript reveals that the Chinese premier began the meeting by giving a detailed history of the Nixon administration's strenuous efforts to reestablish communication with China. Presenting the United States as being "more keen" on advancing Sino-American rapprochement, Zhou downplayed Beijing's role in facilitating contact in late 1970 and described the "ping pong talks" as products of "chance [*ngau nhien*]."[91] The Chinese premier then spoke at length regarding Beijing's unwavering support of Hanoi's war. In recounting his meeting with Kissinger, Zhou Enlai informed Le Duan and Pham Van Dong that he let the American know that China did not have any soldiers in Vietnam, aside from engineering troops, since Hanoi never requested any forces. Regarding diplomatic strategy, Zhou reminded his Vietnamese interlocutors that Chairman Mao had approved of North Vietnam's decision to hold negotiations with the United States in Paris as early as the previous year. For this reason, the Chinese premier tried to reassure the VWP leaders that Beijing's policy was to avoid discussing the Indochina issue with the Americans. Zhou even stated, "We sincerely believe that next year, sometime leading up to the U.S. presidential elections, a settlement will be concluded in Paris. Only after that will Nixon come to visit China."[92] After informing the North Vietnamese of Kissinger's intention to couple U.S. withdrawal from Indochina with Beijing's support for political continuity in Saigon and American withdrawal from Taiwan, the Chinese leader also tried to dispel any Vietnamese doubts. "At this time, Indochina is the crucial issue, while the Taiwan issue will be resolved sooner or later—it does not matter."[93] Le Duan and Pham Van Dong were extremely upset with Zhou Enlai and the Beijing leadership's decision to invite Nixon to China. North Vietnamese leaders believed that Sino-American rapprochement was Nixon's attempt to "save himself" in Vietnam, and they forbade Chinese leaders to negotiate on their behalf. Even though Chinese leaders did not exert the type of pressure Kissinger had hoped for, according to Hanoi, the damage had already been done.

As a result of Kissinger's trip to Beijing, Nixon found more resolve to stand his ground in Paris and ordered his national security advisor to reject North Vietnamese demands for Thieu's ouster during the secret meetings that took place in the summer of 1971. With the South Vietnamese presidential elections in early October, Nixon could not risk losing his staunch ally in Saigon, and, with Beijing's help, he believed he could force Hanoi to accept that condition. On 12 July, Le Duc Tho and Xuan Thuy met with a smug Kissinger in Paris. Neither Vietnamese leader knew about the American negotiator's recent trip to Beijing, since they thought that Kissinger had only met with Thieu in Saigon. Kissinger began the meeting by "sharply attacking" Binh's publication of the PRG's seven points as well as North Vietnamese leaders' recent press interviews, telling the VWP that it had to choose between propaganda and negotiations.[94] Xuan Thuy shot back that Binh had no choice but to go public with the seven points because Kissinger had turned down her request for a meeting and because the PRG's deadline for American troop withdrawal by 30 June 1971 had passed. Moreover, Xuan Thuy pointed out that the United States should choose between escalating the war and negotiating the peace, since American military actions in Indochina increased after the June meeting.[95] After both sides aired their discontent, Le Duc Tho suggested that they outline the remaining areas of agreement and disagreement.

Kissinger viewed the meeting as "very positive" since the United States and DRV were in disagreement only on one issue: Thieu.[96] The U.S. negotiator believed that the North Vietnamese would think seriously about compromising on this remaining issue before the next secret meeting set for 26 July. Tho and Thuy also considered the meeting a success but for different reasons. Over the past three secret contacts, the North Vietnamese sensed a weakening of the Nixon administration's position in Paris. Although Kissinger had stated that the U.S. seven points were nonnegotiable at the 31 May meeting, Tho and Thuy pointed out to their comrades in the Politburo that the United States had compromised on many points by the 13 July meeting, especially in dropping the demand for mutual withdrawal. The North Vietnamese read U.S. acceptance of a cease-fire on the signing of the agreement rather than on withdrawal as a sign of weakness. Regarding Thieu, the VWP leaders were confident that if they stuck firm to their demand for his removal, the Nixon administration would come to see his head as an acceptable price for peace.[97]

On 15 July, however, before the next secret meeting, Nixon delivered a major diplomatic bombshell by announcing his intention to visit China before May 1972, prompting a thorough reanalysis of VWP strategy by North Vietnamese leaders. The Politburo decided that this was an inopportune time for the DRV to negotiate a settlement in Paris. Nixon wanted to settle quickly since a cease-fire and peace agreement would place Thieu in a better position. As a result, Le Duan advised the negotiators in Paris to advance the nine points and not present any new proposals.[98] Tho and Thuy, however, tried to soften this hard-line position by revising the nine points, in light of the gains made at the 12 July meeting, into a new eleven-point proposal. In particular, the two negotiators suggested three changes, including a clearer statement that prisoner releases would take place simultaneously with American troop withdrawal in point 1; the removal of Nguyen Van Thieu only and not Nguyen Cao Ky and Tran Thien Khiem in point 3 (there would be an election in the fall that would change the face of the Saigonese government in any case, especially given the split between Thieu and Ky); and the change from "war reparations" to "U.S. agreement to help rebuild North and South Vietnam" in point 6.[99] However, when the DRV and PRG negotiators received more information from Chinese leaders regarding the state of Sino-American relations, their stance became more rigid in Paris. In late July, Le Duc Tho, Xuan Thuy, and Nguyen Thi Binh were given a full report on Sino-American talks by the Chinese ambassador to France, Huang Zhen.[100] The ambassador said that according to Kissinger there were only two remaining obstacles to peace: Hanoi's refusal to drop the demand for the removal of Thieu and to observe a cease-fire as American troops exited the region.

On 26 July, Le Duc Tho and Xuan Thuy held a meeting with Kissinger that did not produce a breakthrough as the latter had expected. The U.S. negotiator attributed the DRV's lack of a clear decision regarding Thieu to the "shock of [the] China trips and [the] reported illness of Pham Van Dong."[101] Or, as Kissinger more bluntly put it, Tho and Thuy were giving it "one last college try on getting us to dump Thieu while clearly revealing their ambivalence."[102] In fact, the North Vietnamese negotiators had made two demands and issued a warning. The demands included the complete withdrawal of American troops and Thieu's removal, and the warning to Kissinger was that he should not entertain illusions that an agreement on Vietnam could be reached in Beijing rather than Paris.[103] Kissinger responded to Hanoi's first demand by indicating that the Nixon administration would not be able to withdraw in 1971 but only within nine months after an agreement. Regarding Thieu, Kissinger reported to Nixon that during the meeting, he had flatly refused to remove the South Vietnamese president and threatened to break off talks if the North Vietnamese did not "rethink their political position and consider new formulations."[104] According to Luu Van Loi's transcript of the event, Kissinger feigned sincerity when he responded to Hanoi's warning. "We know that the solution to the Vietnam war should be found in Paris. . . . We respect and admire the spirit of independence that you have always shown. . . . We do not want to find a solution anywhere other than here."[105] With little reconciled, the two sides agreed on 16 August as the date for the next meeting, which Kissinger predicted would be "climactic."[106]

After the meeting, Tho and Thuy broke from normal protocol by not sending a joint report to the Politburo. Instead, Tho wrote a personal letter to Le Duan on 27 July assessing VWP diplomatic strategy, while Xuan Thuy cabled the rest of the Politburo the next day regarding the content of the secret meeting with Kissinger. Tho asked the first secretary for instructions on how to distinguish between the "open struggle" for world opinion and the secret struggle in the private talks in order to achieve the two aims of complete U.S. troop withdrawal and Thieu's removal. In Tho's estimation, the two aims should never be separated. In closing, he agreed with Le Duan's advice that the Foreign Ministry in Hanoi should not waste time developing a strategy for the public talks but should instead focus on the secret meetings. In Xuan Thuy's postmeeting synopsis, he merely reported that Kissinger had finally accepted to discuss political issues as well as military ones.[107]

Since the diplomatic struggle was at a crucial turning point, Le Duc Tho set out to return to Hanoi, making a brief stop first in Beijing. On 1 August, he met with Zhou Enlai, who tried to reassure the North Vietnamese leader that Beijing had no intentions of selling out its comrades. Adopting the posture of an imperial ruler allocating local responsibility, he called the North Vietnamese the "heads of their household [*chu nha*]" and promised that the Chinese would not interfere in how they ran their home. After three years of negotiations, Zhou Enlai reasoned that the DRV had garnered a lot of experience, more than even the PRC, and as a result Beijing solidly supported the VWP and PRG's seven points.[108] Meanwhile, Kissinger and Dobrynin discussed the North Vietnamese in Washington on 29 July. The Soviet ambassador informed the national security advisor that there were only two remaining issues according to Hanoi: "setting a deadline and overthrowing the Thieu Government." All other issues, Dobrynin claimed, could be settled.[109]

With Le Duc Tho absent from Paris, only Xuan Thuy met with a tardy Kissinger on 16 August.[110] Although Kissinger believed that Tho's absence was a stalling tactic on the VWP's part, he presented Thuy with a new eight-point counterproposal that combined the U.S. seven points and the DRV nine points.[111] Essentially, the eight-point counterproposal offered four new elements: (1) U.S. neutrality in the upcoming presidential elections in South Vietnam; (2) a demand for an Indochina-wide cease-fire and not just one for Vietnam; (3) a withdrawal deadline for U.S. forces by 1 August 1972 as long as a final agreement was signed by 1 November 1971; and (4) a prisoner release to be made two months before the completion of troop withdrawal.[112] Before commenting on the U.S. counterproposal, Xuan Thuy launched into a severe indictment of the Nixon administration for the recent intensification of the war and for compromising the secret meetings. After Kissinger strenuously denied both allegations, Thuy tentatively commented on the U.S. eight points. He indicated that the time timetable for troop withdrawal was "too long" and that Thieu's removal was nonnegotiable.[113] Since the two sides could not reconcile their differences, they decided to meet again on 13 September.

Although Sino-American rapprochement threw Hanoi's negotiating strategy off kilter, Saigon did not welcome the warming of relations between Washington and Beijing either. Following Nixon's 15 July announcement of Kissinger's secret trip to China, Thieu began to doubt his allies. According to Nguyen Tien Hung, who served as special assistant to the RVN president, Thieu was highly suspicious of Nixon and Kissinger's diplomatic strategy to end the Vietnam War: "Had Kissinger made a secret deal with Zhou Enlai? Did he stop in Hanoi before Beijing? What role would South Vietnam play in America's new strategy after the normalization of relations with Beijing?"[114] Thieu even told his advisors that "America has been looking for a better mistress and now Nixon has discovered China. He does not want to have the old mistress hanging around. Vietnam has become ugly and old."[115] In other words, since U.S. policy toward Vietnam had been predicated at least in part on stopping Chinese expansionism, what would happen to South Vietnam now that China no longer was seen as a threat?

In the six months leading up to Nixon's visit, Saigon leaders tried to prevent the United States from offering the RVN as a sacrificial lamb to Sino-

American rapprochement. Thieu dispatched his special advisor for foreign affairs, Nguyen Phu Duc, to meet with various American officials in order to obtain a clearer picture of U.S. intentions. Although the officials Duc met insisted that Beijing did not desire increased North Vietnamese influence in Indochina, his report to Thieu still advised caution.[116] Duc's warning reaffirmed Thieu's belief that the communist side of Indochina, which in his estimation included not only the North Vietnamese but also the Chinese and Soviet parties, regarded any settlement short of total conquest as only a "strategic pause."[117] Eliciting the opinions of South Vietnamese elected officials, Thieu's foreign minister, Tran Van Lam, met with the RVN Senate Foreign Relations Committee in Saigon on 26 August to discuss Nixon's upcoming trip to Beijing and its impact on the RVN.[118] The Vietnamese senators raised concerns regarding the lack of a coherent policy toward Sino-American rapprochement. Compared with the other Asian nations, including South Korea, Taiwan, Philippines, and Thailand, that responded quickly with new policies, South Vietnam's lack of direction, the senators warned, placed the RVN in danger of being left behind and isolated. Particularly since issues between the United States and South Vietnam had not been settled regarding a peace initiative, the senators advised Thieu to address those issues with Nixon before his visit to Beijing.[119] Thieu, however, would not get the chance to incorporate the input of his advisors and the RVN Senate Foreign Relations Committee. He had to ensure his own reelection before he could worry about the survival of South Vietnam.

## THE FALL OF DEMOCRATIC ELECTIONS

In the summer before the South Vietnamese presidential elections, Thieu forced an electoral law through his National Assembly that required candidates to obtain signatures from either 40 Assembly members or 100 provincial or municipal councilors. Only Duong Van Minh (known as "Big Minh" to the Americans) was able to obtain the requisite signatures; Nguyen Cao Ky, the vice president and Thieu's long-time rival, could not.[120] On 20 August, Ky dropped out of the race; three days later Big Minh called it quits even though the CIA tried to bribe him to stay on. Thieu's tampering with electoral laws and his ability to manipulate the system ensured that he would run unchallenged in October.[121] Thieu now stood as the only candidate for president. Kissinger claimed that Rogers and the State Department viewed the fall election as an "a God-sent opportunity to get rid of" Thieu, but both he and Nixon were firmly against this.[122] "Turn on him?

Never, never. . . . I hope never," Nixon stated to Kissinger. "No, we must never do that. It's like what they did in killing Diem."[123]

On 31 August, Le Duan wrote to southern revolutionary leaders to expose the single-candidate elections in South Vietnam as a "farce [*tro he*]."[124] As Le Duan dealt with the political struggle in the urban centers, Le Duc Tho addressed how the recent developments in Saigon affected the diplomatic struggle in Paris. Tho identified to Thuy on 7 September what Hanoi saw as a split in the Nixon administration regarding Thieu. While U.S. ambassador Bunker wanted to keep Thieu in power, Kissinger preferred to remove him, since Thieu was the remaining obstacle to a settlement with Hanoi. In addition to the embarrassment suffered by the United States and Thieu as a result of Ky and Minh's withdrawal from the presidential race, Hanoi was convinced that the United States was also beset with economic problems that the Sino-American rapprochement media blitz could not make go away. As a result, Tho believed that the Party's diplomatic struggle had reached an important juncture. Under no circumstances, he warned Thuy, should the DRV reach a settlement with the United States at this point. Instead, Le Duc Tho counseled dragging out the talks in Paris.[125]

At the 13 September meeting with Kissinger, Xuan Thuy carried out Le Duc Tho's instructions. Although Kissinger had hoped for a "climactic" meeting, Thuy's critical response to the U.S. eight-point counterproposal dashed these hopes. Thieu's certain "reelection" in South Vietnam, in Hanoi's estimation, cast a dark shadow over the talks. In the shortest meeting to date, Thuy and Kissinger exchanged veiled and not-so-veiled insults, directed at each other and at their respective governments, over the course of a brief two-hour meeting. Given the impasse regarding Thieu and the overall breakdown of discussions, neither side suggested a date to meet again.[126] Xuan Thuy's postmeeting report to Le Duc Tho and Foreign Minister Trinh was pessimistic. Kissinger engaged in insincere tactics, including bringing up the possibility of Big Minh as RVN president, even though the world knew that the United States had more or less chosen Thieu as their man in Saigon. In short, Thuy concluded, the United States wanted to settle quickly because that was in their—and Thieu's—best interests, and therefore detrimental to Hanoi.[127] Kissinger's postmeeting assessment was just as bleak. Writing to Ambassador Bunker in Saigon, Kissinger described the meeting as "thoroughly unproductive and frosty." Compared to the summer when Hanoi had seemed close to an agreement, Kissinger concluded that "they must have calculated that Thieu might look stronger a year from now and it was not worth trying to shake him with a settlement."[128]

On 3 October, Nguyen Van Thieu won reelection with 94.3 percent of the vote.[129] Nonetheless, Thieu believed his—and his nation's—survival was still in jeopardy. As for Le Duan, tensions with superpower patrons threatened Thieu's ability to continue the war. Thieu's default strategy in dealing with the Americans had been based on extorting as much aid from Nixon as possible before Kissinger sold him out. For instance, Thieu consistently sent Ambassador Bui Diem detailed instructions on how to negotiate with the Americans to get more aid under Vietnamization, but he only issued vague orders on how to evade American intrusion into South Vietnamese politics. "Leave this initiative alone for the time being," Thieu would say to Diem whenever the United States introduced the notion of political change in the RVN. "Restrict yourself to talking about Vietnamization." When the South Vietnamese ambassador informed Thieu that deflection did not always work and that the U.S. State Department had become increasingly vocal about the need for significant democratic reforms, Thieu would get angry. "Do not let Rogers preempt me on this either," the Saigonese leader vented to his ambassador. "It annoys me. He should respect me on this."[130] In his memoirs, Ambassador Diem characterized Thieu's modus operandi for deflecting American pressure to curb South Vietnamese corruption and to institute political reforms: "For his part, Thieu never refused anything. His usual way was to agree, acquiesce and make promises, then to wait and see what would happen. As long as he sensed that the American position was not being pressed with great force or energy, which was the case most of the time, he would procrastinate, waiting for issues to disappear by themselves or to lose their urgency as other, more demanding matters piled up."[131] But by late 1971, Thieu feared that Kissinger's second trip to China that October had already paved the way for the United States to strike a secret deal behind South Vietnam's back, making it ever more urgent to procure sufficient funds and equipment for the Republic of Vietnam Armed Forces (RVNAF).[132]

Since Thieu suspected Kissinger of hiding from him crucial developments about the secret meetings with Le Duc Tho, the South Vietnamese president wanted to establish two additional reserve divisions, believing that the RVN did not possess enough reserves to counter any thrust by the PAVN across the DMZ. In addition, the pace of U.S. troop withdrawal proceeded much faster than Thieu was led to believe it would at the outset. From the more than a half million U.S. troops in 1969, 65,000 were with-

Left to right: *Secretary of State William Rogers, Nguyen Van Thieu, and Foreign Minister Tran Van Lam (Douglas Pike Photograph Collection, Vietnam Center and Archive, Texas Tech University)*

drawn by the end of that year, 50,000 in 1970, and 250,000 in 1971, leaving 139,000 troops in 1972. With the upcoming U.S. presidential elections, Thieu knew that 1972 was a pivotal year to get as much for South Vietnam as possible as American ground troop numbers dwindled.

Despite his electoral victory, Thieu felt the American noose tightening around his neck. During his visit to Saigon before the elections in late September, General Alexander Haig, Kissinger's deputy, presented America's new negotiating position, which contained a provision for a new presidential election in South Vietnam within six months of signing a peace treaty that would mandate Thieu's resignation one month before the internationally supervised election.[133] Since Thieu knew that the communists would never agree to a presidential election, he did not oppose the proposal to step down one month before. Communicating directly with Nixon via personal letters, Thieu warned the American president not to agree to any coalition government with the communists and insisted that regardless of any formal settlement, the key to peace lay in South Vietnam's ability to defend itself. These letters did nothing to ameliorate Thieu's anxiety. South Vietnam had become a tiresome old hag that needed to be gotten rid of in order to ensure the success of Nixon's trip to visit his new mistress in Beijing.

### THE WINTER OF NORTH VIETNAM'S DISCONTENT

The Paris talks, both public and private, predictably stalled in the aftermath of the "elections" in South Vietnam. On 4 October, General Vernon Walters, U.S. military attaché in Paris, contacted Vo Van Sung, DRV delegate-general and Mai Van Bo's deputy, to set up a meeting between Kissinger and Xuan Thuy so that the former could present a revised eight-point proposal. The North Vietnamese chief delegate refused to meet, forcing Walters to present Kissinger's new peace proposal to Sung on 11 October.[134] The revised eight points offered two new terms. They shortened the duration of troop withdrawal (all American troops out by 1 July 1972 provided that an agreement be signed by 1 December 1971), and, more important, they promised the resignation of Thieu one month before a new election supervised by an electoral commission. According to political scientist Larry Berman, Nixon needed to dampen U.S. domestic criticism of Thieu by offering a new peace plan that would show Thieu's commitment to peace. The American president was able to procure Saigon's acquiescence by convincing Thieu that the North Vietnamese would summarily reject the revised peace plan so the RVN president would never actually have to step down.[135] Although VWP leaders were not optimistic that negotiations would yield anything new and they indeed rejected Kissinger's revised eight-point plan, Hanoi indicated that that Tho and Thuy were willing to meet Kissinger on 20 November. However, neither that meeting nor any other took place in Paris for the remainder of 1971.[136]

Thieu's controversial "reelection" alone did not cause the breakdown in negotiations. Nixon's triangular offensive also ensured that no settlement would be reached that year. If there was any hesitation in Party leaders' minds between pursuing a diplomatic solution or preparing for a military victory in 1971, the Sino-American opening and Soviet-American détente both pushed the North Vietnamese toward the latter. Following Kissinger's July trip to Beijing and Nixon's announcement of his forthcoming visit to China in 1972, developments in Soviet-American relations compounded Hanoi's sense of urgency to change the balance of power on the ground militarily before events at the international level could fatally weaken the VWP war effort.

The zero-sum game of the Sino-Soviet split reached a critical juncture in the latter half of 1971. As Sino-American rapprochement progressed, Moscow immediately took steps to improve its relations with Washington even though this meant alienating Hanoi. On 10 August, Moscow sent a formal invitation to Nixon to visit the Soviet Union in the late spring and early summer of the following year. The United States accepted the invitation shortly thereafter, but it did not announce the president's trip to the Soviet Union until 12 October. Before Nixon's announcement, however, Soviet leaders took steps to assuage the North Vietnamese in the exact same fashion as the Chinese had done earlier in the year. Brezhnev told East European leaders that Moscow wanted to send a high-ranking delegation to Hanoi in order to deliver the news of Nixon's visit, given how "poorly Vietnam took to the news" of Nixon's trip to Beijing.[137] In 1971, Moscow signed two agreements on supplemental aid and provided artillery that VWP leaders deployed to the Laotian battlefield.[138] In addition to providing economic and military aid, Soviet chairman Nikolai Podgorny visited Hanoi from 3 to 8 October. During his visit, Podgorny informed the North Vietnamese of Nixon's upcoming visit, urged Hanoi to reach a settlement in Paris, and sought to dissuade VWP leaders from launching a military offensive in 1972.[139] During their talks, North Vietnamese officials let Podgorny know that although Chinese leaders promised not to sacrifice Vietnamese interests, Hanoi feared that Beijing believed it was the PRC's right to solve the Indochinese problem. Left unspoken was Hanoi's belief that the same could be said for Moscow. In the end, VWP leaders did not publicly express their displeasure at Nixon's upcoming visit to the Soviet Union directly to Podgorny, but instead they showed their disdain by later dismissing the Soviet leader's advice.

Meanwhile, Beijing leaders also tried to quell North Vietnamese fears of betrayal as Sino-American relations continued to improve; like the Soviets', Chinese efforts proved futile.[140] Historical lessons played a part. In the early autumn of 1971, some of the deterioration of Sino-Vietnamese relations can be seen in a conversation between Le Duc Tho and Cambodian leader Ieng Sary: "We will always remember the experience in 1954. Comrade Zhou Enlai admitted his mistakes in the Geneva Conference of 1954. Two or three years ago, Comrade Mao did so. In 1954, because both the Soviet Union and China exerted pressure, the outcome became what it became. We have proposed that the Chinese comrades admit their mistakes and now I am telling you, the Cambodian comrades, about this problem of history."[141] From Tho's perspective, the 1954 Geneva Conference represented a dark moment in communist history when Beijing and

Moscow pressured the Vietnamese communists to accept less-than-stellar terms from the French at the end of the First Indochina War. By 1971, he must have experienced déjà vu. On 20 October, eight days after Nixon's announcement of his upcoming visit to the Soviet Union in 1972, the U.S. administration declared that Kissinger intended to make a second trip to Beijing. From the transcripts of the conversations there between Kissinger and Zhou Enlai, it is apparent that the United States and China were in agreement on the situation in Indochina. First, both Kissinger and Zhou hoped that a negotiated settlement on Vietnam could be reached before Nixon's visit to China. Although the Chinese premier paid lip service to not "interfering in the internal affairs" of the Vietnamese, Beijing was prepared to help the United States and would let the North Vietnamese leaders know that Beijing wanted to see an early settlement.[142] In addition, both Chinese and American leaders conveyed frustration in dealing with the North Vietnamese. Although Kissinger stated that he had respect for his adversaries, he launched into a bitter critique: "The North Vietnamese are so suspicious. . . . There is a certain egocentricity about them."[143] Chinese leaders echoed Kissinger's characterization of the North Vietnamese by describing them as "proud" and unwilling to take advice. When Zhou Enlai tried to justify Hanoi's suspicious nature by invoking North Vietnam's experience at the 1954 Geneva Conference, Kissinger interjected that the United States also drew a lesson from that experience. If the North Vietnamese felt cheated at talks, they would continue fighting. Finally, Kissinger and Zhou seemed to be in agreement that Soviet intentions ran counter to Chinese and American interests. When Kissinger mentioned that "outside countries" far away wanted the war to continue, Zhou Enlai stated, "We know. They hope you can be tied down to that place," prompting Kissinger to respond, "And that you can be embarrassed."[144]

Although October was a difficult month for VWP leaders on the international front, DRV foreign minister Trinh published an article in the major Party journal, *Hoc Tap* (The Study), thanking the Marxist-Leninist states, particularly the Soviet Union and China, for all of their support.[145] He emphasized the importance of the diplomatic struggle and the strength of the unified internationalist front that would lead Vietnam to victory against the United States. Aside from China and the Soviet Union, relations between the DRV and other socialist nations were as strong as ever. When Binh visited Cuba, Fidel Castro proclaimed to her, "For Vietnam, Cuba is prepared to offer its blood."[146] In the fall of 1971, Politburo member Hoang Van Hoan traveled to Eastern Europe to ensure that the VWP still enjoyed the support of the communist nations in the region.[147] In the weeks lead-ing up to Nixon's visit to the PRC, DRV trade with the Warsaw Pact nations continued to rise.[148]

As the situation in the communist world became more complex, Le Duan and the Hanoi Politburo moved on the negotiations and military fronts. On 11 November, the Politburo sent orders to Xuan Thuy to meet with Kissinger if the Americans still desired to talk. Initially, Le Duc Tho was to be present at the meeting, but since Nixon had not yet unveiled his Vietnam policy, the Politburo believed it prudent for only Xuan Thuy to go to the 20 November meeting. The DRV planned to offer a new counter-proposal and did not want to give Nixon the chance to undermine that offer publicly before a secret meeting. If the meeting did take place, Hanoi wanted Thuy to ask Kissinger about the new eight-point proposal and push even more aggressively the demand for the removal of Thieu.[149] The next day, Nixon announced that he would withdraw 45,000 troops by 1 February 1972. Although the U.S. president did not address any political issues, the North Vietnamese decided that Nixon appeared "very stubborn," and thus Hanoi would not offer its new counterproposal in Paris but instead would turn its attention to the battlefield.[150] When North Vietnamese leaders re-ceived a message via General Walters that the Nixon administration was uninterested in meeting if Le Duc Tho could not attend, secret meetings were shelved for the remainder of 1971.[151]

After Kissinger's second visit to Beijing, Pham Van Dong traveled to Beijing in November, having turned down a Chinese invitation to Beijing in July, after Kissinger's first visit.[152] From 20 to 25 November, the Viet-namese premier failed to persuade Mao Zedong and Zhou Enlai, just as he had failed to impress Soviet leaders, to cancel Nixon's upcoming visit in 1972.[153] On the first day of meetings Premier Dong brought up how North Vietnam contributed to the PRC's success in taking over Taiwan at the United Nations on 25 October, implicitly juxtaposing it with Beijing's be-trayal of the DRV. Since his Chinese hosts seemed unmoved by that rea-soning, the Vietnamese leader used the Soviet card by extolling Moscow's contribution to national liberation struggles worldwide.

Meanwhile, in Washington, Kissinger and Dobrynin discussed Vietnam over dinner on 18 November. While Kissinger wanted Dobrynin to deliver a threat to North Vietnamese leaders that the United States was prepared to "take strong action to bring about the release of our prisoners," Dobrynin redirected the conversation by inquiring whether the United States was disappointed in Chinese efforts to end the war.[154] "I had never expected any significant effort to end the Vietnamese war," Kissinger responded, but in fact he and Nixon did believe that their diplomacy would succeed in getting Beijing to intervene.[155] According to the Soviet ambassador, Hanoi was able to get Beijing to toe the line by "threatening a public attack on Peking's policies and by taking its case to the Communist Parties around the world, on the ground that Peking was betraying the revolution."[156]

However, Hanoi's attempts to blackmail and pressure Beijing and Moscow to present a united communist front against the United States failed; Nixon's superpower offensive trumped Le Duan's small-power diplomacy. Chinese and Soviet leaders justified their refusal to comply with North Vietnamese requests to cancel their upcoming summits with Nixon by claiming that bettering relations with the United States ultimately helped the Vietnamese cause. Hanoi saw through the double-talk. Since the United States continued to support Thieu and still maintained troops in Vietnam, Hanoi concluded that Beijing and Moscow's engagement with Washington had not helped North Vietnam's position at all. On 26 December, Nixon approved a five-day bombing campaign, Operation Proud Deep, over North Vietnam.[157] Although Beijing and Moscow issued public pronouncements on 30 and 31 December, respectively, condemning U.S. military activities in Vietnam, Hanoi had already concluded that its patrons had chosen to better relations with Washington for their own selfish interests rather than advance the communist cause.[158]

By the end of 1971, then, the breakdown of the Paris talks and the intensification of American bombing with Operation Proud Deep over North Vietnam reaffirmed the Hanoi Politburo's suspicions that the improvement of relations between the United States and China as well as the Soviet Union resulted only in a hardening of Nixon's position. Frustrated with their allies, VWP leaders set out to neutralize the effect of Nixon's upcoming visits to Beijing and Moscow by turning to the battlefield. On 29 November, one month before Nixon approved Operation Proud Deep, Le Duan sent orders to the South to prepare the urban centers for a large-scale offensive in 1972.[159]

## CONCLUSION

Over the course of the four seasons, the glimmer of peace that seemed to glow in the summer extinguished completely by the start of winter. The year 1971 witnessed fundamental changes in the military, political, and diplomatic spheres of the war. As the tide of war seemingly turned in

Hanoi's favor with the defeat of ARVN forces in Laos, international diplomatic events appeared to undo these military gains. Since the VWP predicated its ability to settle in Paris on a superior position on the Indochinese battlefield, peace never had a chance in 1971.

Although both Le Duan and Nixon encountered domestic opposition to their war efforts and public pressure to end the war in 1971, they prolonged the fighting and ordered their deputies to stall in Paris. Each leader believed he could find the other's breaking point and win the war for peace. While Le Duan was convinced that mounting a major military offensive — based on his General Offensive and General Uprising — could end the war by toppling the Thieu regime, Nixon relied on furthering relations with the Soviet Union and China and launching a devastating air campaign over North Vietnam to force Hanoi into submission in Paris. Developments in 1971 bolstered each side's foolhardy strategies to win the war for peace.

In retrospect, Lam Son 719 may have been a pyrrhic victory for the Vietnamese communists. At the start of the year, North Vietnamese leaders braced themselves for a difficult period militarily and politically, but the U.S.-RVN defeat in Laos gave Hanoi the morale boost it needed. Communist forces thwarted the enemy's objective to interdict the Ho Chi Minh Trail. Although the military victory on Highway 9 in southern Laos proved important politically and psychologically for the VWP, it may have led Hanoi leaders to assume incorrectly that communist forces had dealt a decisive blow to Vietnamization. The easy victory in Laos thus blinded VWP leaders to the resistance they would encounter in South Vietnam in 1972.

At the same time, events on the world stage hastened Hanoi's ambitious military planning for 1972. Not only was the moment ripe for communist forces to attempt a decisive victory in South Vietnam given the ARVN's losses in 1971, Politburo members believed, but Nixon's superpower diplomacy also now threatened relations with Beijing and Moscow, whose assistance was vital to continuing the war. In other words, the time had come for communist forces to tip the balance of power in their favor, while the ARVN appeared weak and before socialist funds ran out. As news of Nixon's scheduled visits to China and the Soviet Union traveled the globe, Beijing and Moscow separately tried to reason with Hanoi that bettering relations with Washington would ultimately advance communist Vietnam's cause. Their justifications did not convince Le Duan and his comrades; North Vietnamese leaders not only stiffened their resolve in Paris and focused their energies on a major military offensive, but they also set out to undermine rapprochement and détente in 1972.

part four

# THE MAKING OF A FAULTY PEACE

*You are murderers. There is blood of old people, women, and*
*children on your hands. When will you finally end this senseless war?*
                        —*Leonid Brezhnev to Richard Nixon*[1]

## chapter seven

# WAR AGAINST DÉTENTE

Nixon and Kissinger sat awkwardly as Brezhnev hurled insults at them at
his dacha in Novo Ogarevo, west of Moscow. As the first American president to visit the Soviet Union, Nixon's trip to Moscow in May 1972 during a
beautiful Russian spring was just as momentous as his visit to Beijing a few
months earlier. Although the historic encounter began uncomfortably at
the Soviet leader's summer estate, it included a more pleasant river cruise
down the Moscow River. As American leaders took in the historic splen-
dors of Moscow, including the Kremlin, the Cathedral of Christ the Savior,
Gorky Park, and the giant statue of Peter the Great, the Soviet leader's bel-
licose tone softened. Soon the mood became downright boisterous as Russian and American leaders dined and drank, toasting détente until both
delegations became undeniably drunk. Meanwhile, nearly 4,000 miles
away in Hanoi, Le Duan and his comrades in the Politburo ducked into
bomb shelters as Nixon increased the air war over North Vietnam.

As the United States, the PRC, and the Soviet Union rejoiced over the
ratcheting down of Cold War tensions embodied in Nixon's visits to Beijing and Moscow, North Vietnam braced itself for betrayal by its big-power
patrons. Throughout its "anti-American resistance struggle for reunification and national salvation," the DRV extracted maximum military and
economic aid from its feuding great-power patrons. Although Hanoi had

been successful in navigating the Sino-Soviet split during the first half of its war, the VWP realized that socialist funds would soon run out for the Vietnamese cause. Even as the Chinese and Soviets increased weapons shipments, economic support, cooperation in technical fields, and signed more protocols and supplementary aid packages in 1971, Hanoi read these measures as palliatives for détente and rapprochement. And with good reason. By 1972, Beijing and Moscow struggled for influence with Hanoi not only out of desire to stand at the vanguard of international proletarian movement but also, and more important, as a way to gain leverage with the Americans. Although Hanoi's patrons promised that they would not sell out the Vietnamese cause or "deal over the heads of their friends," at the end of 1971, Moscow and Beijing were conforming to Nixon's plans. As the Soviets urged VWP leaders to refrain from launching an offensive and to concentrate instead on the diplomatic initiative for 1972, Chinese leaders tried to pressure the North Vietnamese to relent on demanding South Vietnam's President Nguyen Van Thieu's ouster by invoking Beijing's toleration of Chiang Kai-shek. On the eve of the summits, then, VWP leaders prepared their forces to launch a major military action in Indochina aimed at undercutting Nixon's triangular offensive in China and the Soviet Union.

Like the planning of the 1968 Tet Offensive, the origin of the 1972 Easter Offensive, which Vietnamese communists referred to as "Chien dich Xuan he 1972 [1972 Spring–Summer Offensive]," is unclear. According to the official PAVN history, the Politburo issued the direction for the 1972 campaign on 14 May 1971.[2] However, the 1987 history of the offensive in the Tri-Thien region, which encompasses the two northernmost provinces of South Vietnam, dates the key decision by the Politburo, the National Defense Council, and the Ministry of Defense to July 1971.[3] This is reaffirmed in the official classified history of the 1972 Spring–Summer Offensive in the eastern Mekong Delta, published in 1988, which states that the communist forces prepared in two stages: from July to December 1971 and from January to March 1972.[4] Former foreign minister Nguyen Co Thach told historian Jeffrey Kimball after the war that the Hanoi Politburo had begun preparation for a 1972 offensive as early as 1970, but that key decisions were made between May and October 1971.[5] This is confirmed in historian Stephen Randolph's study of the Nixon administration and the Easter Offensive.[6]

The origins of the planning for the 1972 offensive thus can be located in the events of the previous year. Although 1971 began well for the VWP, with the communist victory over the South Vietnamese armed forces in the Lam

Son 719 campaign, Nixon and Kissinger had countered Hanoi's victory on the Indochinese battlefield by turning to superpower diplomacy. Throughout the summer of 1971, while Hanoi leaders vacillated between talking and fighting, Nixon ensured that the VWP inclined toward the latter with his triangular offensive. By the end of 1971, the belief that Vietnamization had been defeated in Lam Son 719, Nixon's successful courtship of China and the Soviet Union, and Nguyen Van Thieu's sham elections in South Vietnam all reinforced the VWP's decision to hold off on negotiations and instead plan for major military action in 1972.

Equally important to the origins and timing surrounding the 1972 offensive are the questions of who devised strategy and for what ends. During the war, American analysts assumed that the Politburo member and President of the National Assembly Truong Chinh was the main strategist, since he delivered a key speech during the Third Congress of the Viet Nam Fatherland Front on 17 December 1971 that foreshadowed communist strategy for 1972.[7] In his speech, Truong Chinh called for using main force units to deliver a crushing blow to the enemy troops. During the war, Foreign Service Officer Douglas Pike argued that Truong Chinh could not have devised VWP strategy for 1972 since the Politburo leader had long been an advocate of protracted struggle.[8] Instead, Pike suggested that the offensive was the brainchild of Defense Minister General Vo Nguyen Giap, the hero of Dien Bien Phu, who had long preferred high-technology, big-unit battles. Historian Dale Andrade, however, insists that General Giap's brief "ascendancy," as a result of the 1971 victory in Laos, was insufficient to gain him command of PAVN operations and that instead it was General Van Tien Dung who was in charge of planning the 1972 communist offensive.[9] Major-General Nguyen Dinh Uoc, former head of the Vietnam Institute of Military History, claimed the Politburo collectively devised strategy and aimed only to change the balance of power militarily on the ground and not to alter the international picture.[10]

This chapter suggests, on the basis of cables, letters, and reports that have recently been declassified, that VWP first secretary Le Duan and his right-hand man, Le Duc Tho, were in firm control of strategy in 1972, and that General Van Tien Dung made operational their military plans. The militant leaders held two distinct aims for the offensive. At the international level, they wanted to neutralize the diplomatic blow dealt by Nixon's impending visits to China and the Soviet Union. In the lead-up to both summits and after, Beijing and Moscow pressured Hanoi to end the war and seek a negotiated settlement that would allow the Americans to withdraw their forces. A smashing military victory in South Vietnam would inoculate North Vietnam from superpower manipulation at the Paris peace talks: if the ARVN collapsed, the United States would have no choice but to settle on Hanoi's terms. At the domestic level, Le Duan and Le Duc Tho wanted to redeem their Tet Offensive strategy, which relied on a spectacular coordinated military attack that would create the conditions for a general political uprising, in 1972. According to Pike, there was a struggle within the Party on the eve of the Easter Offensive between those who wanted to continue protracted struggle and those who preferred to wage big-unit war. However, new evidence reveals there was more general consensus regarding the 1972 offensive, and disagreements were only minor ones over tactics. Le Duan and Le Duc Tho were pushing for a dramatic, large-scale offensive using Soviet tanks to cross the DMZ followed by greater coordination between the military activity of the troops with the revolution in the countryside and the political struggle in the cities. Believing that the failure of the 1968 offensive lay in the lack of coordination between the military and political spheres after the surprise attack, they hoped not repeat their past mistakes in 1972. Once again Giap objected to Le Duan and Le Duc Tho's military plans by urging greater caution, but he failed to alter their strategy.

This chapter traces the evolution of North Vietnamese decision making from January to June 1972, when DRV leaders focused on the armed conflict over the diplomatic struggle as a means to prevent superpower diplomacy from derailing the VWP's war effort. The first section addresses Nixon's visit to Beijing while the second section analyzes the launching of the 1972 offensive and the VWP leadership's decision to abandon its strategy of the "economy of forces" that had been in effect since the disastrous Tet Offensive. Nixon's visit to Moscow and the DRV's frustration with the lack of diplomatic support from China and the Soviet Union are the subject of the third section while the final part of this chapter traces the limits of Hanoi's small-power diplomacy as a means to offset superpower machinations.

## THE VIETNAM WAR IN BEIJING AND MOSCOW

On the eve of the Year of the Rat, Le Duc Tho conveyed his and Le Duan's anxiety over the Beijing and Moscow summits to COSVN commander Pham Hung. Tho confided to his long-time colleague in a secret telegram that the current international pressure on the revolution could only be alleviated by seizing the military initiative in South Vietnam. Hung needed to prepare his forces for a large-scale offensive that could thwart big-power collusion to force Hanoi's hand.[11] Tho exhorted the COSVN leader not to allow international developments to preoccupy him, however; Hung's primary task was to mobilize the southern cadres to lay the groundwork for the upcoming offensive by focusing on the "three strategic blows." Defined in the summer of 1971, these tactics included using main force units to defeat the puppet army in South Vietnam, combining military and political forces in the delta region, and increasing political activity in the urban areas.

"Past experiences over the last few years," Tho wrote to Hung, "have shown that the resistance has paid too much attention to the movements of main force units and too little attention to the activities of guerrilla troops. In our focus on large battles, we forget about pacification as well as the political struggle." Although Tho's instructions to Hung seemed to run counter to his and Le Duan's hawkish concentration on "large battles" and appeared to echo some of General Giap's military policies, the "comrades Le" had not abandoned their desire to launch their ambitious strategy. Tho also instructed Hung to advance the political struggle in the cities in the period leading up to the military offensive since, in Tho's estimation, this was the key reason why 1968 did not succeed. By increasing the number of special guerrilla troops and commando forces in urban centers prior to a large-scale attack on the cities and towns of South Vietnam in 1972, Le Duan and Le Duc Tho were confident they could ignite a mass insurrection that could topple the Saigon regime.[12]

The Party's military plan to achieve a "decisive victory" in early 1972 was an attempt not only to break the stalemate on the battleground but also to change the course of "international trends" that threatened the communist resistance. A letter from a midlevel functionary in the VWP reveals the Party's desperation in the face of Nixon's triangular offensive. On 19 January, Le Toan Thu penned an extremely disgruntled letter to Le Duan, Le Duc Tho, and Nguyen Duy Trinh, voicing his frustration at the Party's lack of progress on the international diplomatic front. At the beginning of 1968, the Politburo established the International Works Committee (Ban Cong Tac Quoc Te, IWC) to advise the CEC on matters relating to Hanoi's international strategy.[13] The Politburo designated Foreign Minister Trinh as head of the IWC, with Xuan Thuy, Nguyen Van Kinh, and Thu as his deputies. By 1972, however, Thu pointed out that the committee had only met twice since its inception, and in a rather risky move the midlevel functionary blamed the lack of progress on his boss, Foreign Minister Trinh. Since it is rare to find testaments to failure or assignations of blame in Party documents, Thu's letter is invaluable since it settles the debate over whether or not the Party in Hanoi controlled the southern resistance movement. Thu complained to his superiors including Le Duan, Tho, and the guilty Trinh that the IWC was shut out of its role in ensuring that the VWP retain an "iron clad grip" over the diplomatic work of the NLF-PRG. Since 1969, Thu pointed out, Trinh had consistently given the IWC little notice of the Politburo's decisions to unveil various peace plans through southern diplomats, including the declaration of the NLF's ten points in 1969 and the PRG's seven points in 1971.

Thu's letter also reveals a midlevel official's impatience with the inner workings of the Party leadership—a perspective seldom seen or heard. "It was as if," Thu lamented in his letter, "the DRV foreign minister had forgotten about the existence of the IWC." The deputy conceded that although secrecy and restrictive access were necessary evils since there had been cases where CEC members had leaked classified information in the past (an allusion to the Revisionist Anti-Party Affair), there were instances when the closed nature of the Party leadership had hindered policy making. Throughout the letter, Thu expressed his fears at speaking so boldly with his superiors, but he excused his audacity by emphasizing the urgency of the present diplomatic situation and asked only that he be given the opportunity to serve the Party.[14]

As the VWP experienced problems with its "international work" among midlevel cadres, the Nixon administration eagerly advanced its triangular offensive. In early January, Deputy Assistant for National Security Affairs Alexander Haig traveled to Beijing to meet with Premier Zhou Enlai. The "atmosphere" surrounding Sino-American talks had worsened slightly since Kissinger's October 1971 visit as a result of Nixon's bombing campaign in Vietnam at the end of the year.[15] At the first meeting, Haig justified the bombing as an appropriate response to Hanoi's escalation of military activities in Laos. Playing on Beijing's hatred and fear of Moscow, Haig stated his hosts, "I hope that before I leave, we can further exchange opinions regarding the recent increase of Soviet influence in Hanoi, and the Soviet strategy to surround directly the People's Republic of China."[16] On the second day of talks, the Chinese premier turned the tables on the United States by indicating that the only party that had benefited from Nixon's military escalation was the Soviets, who had exploited the bombing to gain more influence over North Vietnam.[17]

While Haig failed to sway Zhou Enlai with the Soviet threat, Kissinger was equally unsuccessful in his attempts to play the China card with Dobrynin. Over "slugs of vodka and cans of caviar," the four-hour meeting "was conducted in an atmosphere of effusive cordiality," even if it did not produce the results that Kissinger desired.[18] When the national security advisor expressed disappointment with Moscow's inability to influence Hanoi, the Soviet ambassador blamed Hanoi's military escalation and intransigence in Paris on Beijing.[19] Indeed, the Chinese and Soviets were competing not only for Washington's attention but also for Hanoi's favor. Reports from the Soviet embassy in Hanoi to Moscow indicate that Chinese leaders had tried to gain Hanoi's acquiescence to their discussing a settlement for Indochina with Washington. The PRC even tried to bribe North Vietnamese leaders by signing a military agreement with the DRV on 22 January. Fortunately for Moscow, Hanoi refused Beijing's request for permission to negotiate with Washington.[20]

Nixon also pursued a combination of public and private diplomacy to pressure Hanoi to decrease its military activities in Indochina and to negotiate seriously in Paris. Although the upcoming summits had boosted Nixon's approval ratings as the presidential election year began, he still wanted to assuage antiwar sentiments in the United States. On 13 January, Nixon announced the withdrawal of 70,000 additional troops, leaving 69,000 American ground forces in Vietnam after 1 July.[21] On 25 January, Nixon sought to place Hanoi on the defensive by making public the secret negotiations and announcing a new peace plan in order to show the American people that Hanoi was to blame for the breakdown of the peace talks.[22] When VWP Politburo leaders received Nixon's request that the private meetings continue even though he had exposed existence of the secret talks, they were understandably livid.[23] Even though Nixon's public announcements regarding Vietnam aimed more at winning over American domestic opinion than at changing Hanoi's negotiating stance, his private threats to Soviet and Chinese leaders that the United States might have to resort to military escalation, such as his late 1971 air raids with Operation Proud Deep, were meant to intimidate North Vietnam. On the same day of his television appearance, Nixon issued a stern warning to Brezhnev that he would have "no choice but to react strongly" if the North Vietnamese continued to increase its attacks on South Vietnam's northern panhandle.[24] The president also sent a similar message to Chinese leaders, saying that Hanoi's military actions threatened to "complicate the international situation."[25]

The United States also dealt brusquely with Saigon. A few days before Nixon's January address, Ambassador Ellsworth Bunker gave South Vietnamese president Thieu the contents of president's speech, and as usual demanded Thieu's immediate acquiescence. This time, however, Thieu objected and thereby delayed Nixon's plans to unveil his peace plan by more than a week.[26] In the end, Thieu still had to support Nixon's proposals publicly but privately he was "deeply disturbed" by the shift from mutual to unilateral withdrawal in a manner described as "cavalier" by Thieu's private secretary and cousin, Hoang Duc Nha.[27] Resolving to go along with the United States as long as Nixon increased the amount of aid to South Vietnam, Thieu sent Nixon another personal letter on the eve of the president's trip to China that regardless of Thieu's resignation or any signed peace, the ability of the RVN to defend itself was the key to lasting peace in the area. By the time South Vietnamese foreign minister Lam declared, "We fully approve of Mr. Nixon's trip. No one can deny that it helped create an atmosphere of eased tensions," he was not referring to the atmosphere around U.S.-RVN relations.

The DRV responded to Nixon's disclosure of the secret talks on 31 January by publishing the text of its nine-point peace proposal that Tho and Thuy had presented to Kissinger at a quasi-friendly secret meeting in June of the previous year.[28] In an attempt to foist the blame for the breakdown of the secret talks onto Washington, North Vietnamese diplomats gave journalists copies of the correspondence between the United States and the DRV surrounding a meeting set for 20 November 1971 that never transpired.[29] The result of the finger-pointing and mudslinging doomed the potential for any further private contacts between the United States and the DRV in February and hindered the public sessions as well.[30] When North Vietnamese leaders rejected Nixon's televised peace offer, Kissinger turned to the Chinese for assistance on 5 February. Beijing leaders opted not to pressure the North Vietnamese to meet with the Americans.[31] Moscow, however, did. During a lengthy meeting between Kissinger and Dobrynin on 7 February, the latter offered to "facilitate overcoming the difficulties" at the Paris talks.[32]

As international developments continued to worsen for the North Vietnamese, Party leaders convened the Twentieth Plenum in Hanoi from 27 January to 2 February to define and delineate the Party's grand strategy for 1972.[33] Prior to the publication of the resolution, the Politburo circulated two lengthy declarations regarding the plenum's findings and conclusions.[34] The first declaration addressed the Indochinese battlefield and

was divided into two sections that elaborated on the military and economic situations. The military outlook was positive. The Party extolled
the victories of the resistance forces in Vietnam, Cambodia, and Laos and
tracked the many defeats of the "neoimperialists" and their Indochinese
"lackeys" up to 1972. With the failure of Nixon's policy of Vietnamization
and pacification since at least mid-1970, Party leaders concluded, the tide
had turned in the favor of the revolution.[35]

The second declaration set forth the 1972 State Economy Plan and was
surprisingly candid. Due to Nixon's intensification of the air war over
North Vietnam, VWP leaders concluded that although the northern economy had improved, it was impossible both to build socialism in the North
and wage war in the South. Although Le Duan had highlighted the pressing economic tasks in 1971, he concluded that socialist transformation of
the northern economy would have to take a back seat once again in 1972.
Nonetheless, Party leaders congratulated themselves at the plenum for increasing agricultural output, attributing the success to major gains in collectivization, the mechanization of the communes, and electrification in
rural areas. Regarding communication and transportation, DRV leaders
called for the development of more routes leading to and from Hanoi and
for the protection of Hai Phong harbor.[36] Amid the calls for celebration,
there was a distinct tone of desperation.

Most important, the Twentieth Plenum marked a major turning point
in Hanoi's war since it signified the Party's official decision, under Le
Duan's direction, to abandon its strategy of "economy of forces" implemented in the post-Tet war.[37] Regarding the home front, VWP leaders concluded that socialist transformation of the economy had to wait not only
because the southern war demanded more attention but because the resumption of U.S. bombing once again threatened the North's survival. As a
result, VWP leaders decided to accelerate the military struggle in the South
and build defenses in the North. In reality, the Party's decision to make a
stab for complete military victory over the RVN reflected its concerns not
only with the domestic situation but, more important, with the distressing
international picture.

Following the plenum, the Party's military decision-making group,
the CMC, convened a conference in February to work out the details for
1972 offensive. During the previous summer, Le Duan and Le Duc Tho re-
shuffled Party, military, and government positions in order to marginalize
Giap, whose victories on the Laotian battlefield prompted the leaders Le to
cut down the general once again as important decisions were being made

*Vo Nguyen Giap (second from left) and Le Duan (in white shirt) with military cadres*
*(Douglas Pike Photograph Collection, Vietnam Center and Archive, Texas Tech University)*

for the upcoming attacks. The first secretary changed the composition of the National Defense Council (NDC), the government's military planning body, when he appointed himself and Truong Chinh—two civilian leaders—to the NDC and demoted Giap, who had previously been cochair, to third-ranking member. Le Duan's membership in the NDC was his first state position; prior to this, the first secretary had been confident enough of his power in the Party and in the DRV that he did not feel the need to hold a government post. The reshuffling of the NDC reveals the ways Le Duan sought to gain the lion's share of praise if the 1972 offensive proved successful as well as to minimize Giap's role in military affairs. Meanwhile, the Party's military planning committee, the CMC, a more substantial decision-making body, kept its civilian membership unknown. It is most likely that the key members of the Politburo, including Le Duan, Le Duc Tho, Truong Chinh, and Pham Van Dong, were on the CMC as well as the even more important Politburo subcommittee for military affairs. Officially, General Giap served as the secretary while Senior General Van Tien Dung was the deputy secretary of the commission.[38] Even that, however, would soon change.

At the same time that Hanoi leaders focused on the military sphere of the war, Nixon achieved a stunning victory in the diplomatic theater.

Vietnam was the most important issue on Nixon's agenda when he became the first American president to visit the People's Republic of China
from 21 to 28 February.[39] Nixon toured the Great Wall and Shanghai and
was feted by his Chinese hosts with great banquets, in a visit that was a
historic event in not only the Vietnam War but the Cold War generally.[40]
During the second day of meetings, Zhou Enlai summarized the position
Beijing had held on Vietnam since the start of Sino-American rapprochement: "Only the Indochinese [have] the right to speak, to negotiate with
you [the United States]. But as the Indochinese area is a concern to us we
should have the right to raise our voice on that matter. What's more we
have the obligation to give the Indochinese peoples assistance and support."[41] Turning to Nixon, Zhou Enlai asked if the president had any views
differing from Kissinger's regarding the Indochinese situation. Nixon reaffirmed that both the United States and China desired peace for Southeast Asia, while the Soviet Union only wanted to prolong America's war.
Nevertheless, Nixon insisted that the United States intended to end its role
in the war through Vietnamization. To show that Washington would not
just abandon its ally in Saigon, Nixon also issued a threat to the North Vietnamese via his Chinese hosts. If Hanoi persisted in escalating the war, the
United States would have no choice but to close down diplomatic channels
and respond militarily. Zhou carefully dealt with Nixon's threat by encouraging the U.S. president to choose his friends more wisely in the future.[42]

After the United States and the PRC signed the Shanghai Communiqué,
Zhou Enlai flew to Hanoi on 3 March to repair Sino-Vietnamese relations.
During his talks with Le Duan and Le Duc Tho, the Chinese premier tried
to reassure the North Vietnamese leaders that Beijing did not betray the
Indochinese cause during Nixon's visit. Instead, Zhou claimed that he told
the United States that Vietnam was more important than Taiwan and that
Nixon needed to negotiate based on the DRV's nine points. The meeting
was not all about damage control; Zhou Enlai also did Nixon's bidding
during his stay in Hanoi. The Chinese premier pressured VWP leaders to
work toward a negotiated solution rather than seek a military victory, despite Beijing's awareness of Hanoi's plans for a large-scale military offensive. If the DRV did not negotiate on the basis of the U.S. seven points,
Zhou warned, then Nixon would punish the North Vietnamese after his
reelection.

VWP leaders were visibly upset at the meeting and did not attempt to
restrain their anger. Le Duan told Zhou Enlai that the PRC had saved a
"drowning" Nixon by inviting him to visit China. Moreover, the VWP first

secretary predicted that Nixon would hit Vietnam harder as a result of the Beijing summit. Invoking the Geneva Conference, Le Duan warned Chinese leaders not to betray Hanoi in 1972 as they had in 1954. Historian Lorenz Lüthi's research in the former East German archives also suggests that the Vietnamese Politburo was greatly distressed by Nixon's trips. In particular, Hanoi feared that Beijing and Moscow would drastically reduce economic and military aid to the VWP war effort after the summits. In their observations of daily life in the DRV, GDR officials concluded that the North Vietnamese people were exhausted by the war, while foreign support did little to alleviate the internal situation. According to East German diplomats, war weariness was so acute because the DRV had exhausted its resources in preparation for the 1972 offensive, to the point that North Vietnam might not possess sufficient reserves to last beyond the year. "The internal situation in the DRV is under tension. The life of the people has not improved in the past years," GDR officials reported. "The military struggle has exhausted the country, despite [foreign] support. In the national average, the working-class population consists of 75 percent of women and 25 percent of men. Productivity is very low. Parts of the population physically are not able to work for more than 4–5 hours per day."[43]

At the same time, CIA Director Richard Helms recommended that the agency "develop a series of deception and disinformation operations against North Vietnam to compound the problems of North Vietnam's leaders and simultaneously increase the attractiveness in their eyes, of a negotiated settlement."[44] Although the United States had already attempted such deception programs on a limited basis around the Cambodian incursion and Lam Son 719, the "negotiating situation" among the United States, DRV, PRC, and the Soviet Union meant that these operations could yield more success. Helms recommended promoting five "proposed legends." The first two included spreading rumors that Nixon had worked out a deal with Chinese and Soviet leaders that included the cessation of Sino-Soviet military aid to the DRV. The third proposal suggested exploiting the "Hoang Minh Chinh affair of 1967" by claiming that a "faction inside the DRV Politburo [was] planning a coup motivated by the belief that increased emphasis should be placed on rebuilding the DRV economy as opposed to the primacy of the war policies" that had the backing of Chinese or Soviet support in 1972.[45] The final two proposals included planting stories that Soviet and Chinese officials separately conveyed to third parties their apprehension that a North Vietnamese victory actually threatened long-term Soviet and Chinese interests in the region.[46]

## 1972 AS 1968 REDUX

Nixon's visit to Beijing lent urgency to the task set forth by Party leaders at the Twentieth Plenum and the Party's CMC conference in February. Throughout the month of March, Politburo leaders in Hanoi sent a steady stream of directives and reports to southern commanders. On 10 March, Le Duan instructed southern leaders to adopt his three-stage plan for the political struggle in the cities.[47] Seeking to create the conditions for a general uprising in the urban centers, the first secretary warned southern commanders that the implementation of his three-stage plan might encounter complications, but that sure victory over Thieu required stepping up the political struggle. The next day, the Politburo and the military brass met to hammer out the final details for the upcoming offensive. At the end of the month, Le Duc Tho cabled Pham Hung and other southern leaders with the results of this meeting.[48] Even though the enemy's pacification efforts had succeeded in increasing occupied areas and decreasing liberated zones, particularly in the Tri-Thien region located in the northern provinces of South Vietnam, DRV war leaders had concluded that Nixon's troop withdrawal had reached a level where communist forces possessed a clear superiority on the battlefield.[49] Vietnamization had strengthened the South Vietnamese armed forces, but they were still not as effective as American troops. The major losses of the "reactionary armies" in South Vietnam, Cambodia, and Laos threw the "puppet governments" into political turmoil. Nixon's policy of Vietnamization, and more generally "Indochinization," had failed. Convinced that communist forces had destroyed the backbone of the ARVN in Laos in 1971, Tho believed victory would be within Hanoi's grasp in 1972.[50] Moreover, the U.S. administration, beset with its own domestic problems as a result of the war, had turned to the international arena to improve the military situation in Vietnam. However, Tho predicted, Nixon's international strategy was doomed to failure "because no other party can replace us to resolve the problem [*vi khong ai co the thay the ta ma giai quyet duoc*]," undeniably a reference to Chinese and Soviet leaders, who wanted North Vietnam's permission to discuss resolution of the war with Nixon.[51] Preoccupied with his historic visits, Nixon, North Vietnamese leaders believed, would be unable to respond militarily to Hanoi's offensive.[52]

Regarding military strategy, Tho predicted that the upcoming communist offensive would differ from previous ones in 1970 and 1971 in duration. Like the 1968 offensive, the 1972 attacks would extend beyond the dry season and into the spring and summer. Communist forces would not allow the enemy any respite. However, in order to carry out a lengthy military campaign and to translate battlefield success into total victory, the Party needed to coordinate the military offensive with the political movement in the cities and the countryside as well as the diplomatic struggle in Paris. Tho exhorted Hung and the other COSVN commanders to be vigilant and to follow the situation carefully in the South to ensure that the "offensive and uprising" was successful in 1972.[53]

On 28 March, the Politburo convened another meeting with the CMC and cabled the results to the heads of all the regional Party committees and military theaters in the South. Since D-Day was fast approaching, the Politburo provided a more detailed assessment of the enemy's intelligence regarding the upcoming offensive and possible American retaliation.[54] According to the Party, Washington knew that communist forces were going to attempt a major military action in early 1972.[55] As a result, the Politburo predicted that if the puppet forces appeared on the verge of defeat, the United States might redeploy its forces or at the very least, concentrate its remaining troops in the Tri-Thien region to save the Saigon regime. In addition, the report stated that Nixon might even undertake a public relations campaign to portray the DRV as the aggressor in order to launch a bombing campaign against the North, targeting Noi Bai airport, Hai Phong harbor, major bridges, petroleum depots, and large industries. The Politburo warned the leaders of the resistance to brace their forces for such eventualities.

On 30 March 1972, tens of thousands of PAVN troops, armed with Soviet and Chinese tanks and weaponry, crossed the DMZ toward Quang Tri province.[56] The Spring–Summer Offensive targeted Tri-Thien military region in northern South Vietnam, the eastern Mekong Delta, and the Tay Nguyen area in the Central Highlands. Contrary to the 1968 Tet Offensive, which relied heavily on southern units to launch a surprise attack on all of the major cities and towns in the RVN (at least in phase 1), the 1972 Spring–Summer Offensive primarily utilized the North Vietnamese army to strike on three fronts.[57] Alongside the spectacular PAVN crossing of the DMZ, North Vietnamese troops marched from Laos and Cambodia toward Kontum in the western Central Highlands and from bases in the Fishhook region of eastern Cambodia toward South Vietnamese towns located north of Saigon.[58]

At first, Party leaders intended communist forces to concentrate on the eastern Mekong Delta with secondary attacks across the DMZ in the extreme north of Tri-Thien and in the Central Highlands, but at the last minute, operations in Tri-Thien assumed greater importance than operations in the other two regions.[59] In a rare instance of transparency, Vietnamese officials now claim that Giap was against only a full-frontal attack across the DMZ to the Tri-Thien theater that was preferred by Le Duan, Le Duc Tho, and General Van Tien Dung, but once again he lost out to these more powerful leaders.[60] According to the official history of the Combat Operations Department, "Comrade Vo Nguyen Giap suggested that we build a road to the west to enable us to conduct a 'campaign-level flanking attack' in combination with our frontal attack."[61] In fact, Giap called for building roads to the west in all three locations—the eastern Mekong, the Central Highlands, and Tri-Thien—to launch attacks around the enemy's flank. As in 1968, however, Giap left the country for "medical treatment" before the military planning firmed up.[62] During his absence, the roads were not completed in time for an attack on the enemy's rear; instead, Le Duan and Tho saw to it that crossing the DMZ would gain the lion's share of resources. The "group that advocated making Tri Thien our primary offensive sector" won, even though "it would be a frontal attack into the teeth of the enemy's defenses," official historians later recorded.[63]

Nonetheless, the communist offensive scored stunning victories within the first month and a half with the fall of Quang Tri City in the north, the Dak To and Loc Ninh district capitals, and the area north of Saigon. PAVN soldiers surged forward to threaten the former imperial capital of Hue and two provincial capitals, Kontum and Binh Long. During May, U.S. bombs were able to slow the North Vietnamese onslaught, resulting in what Hanoi considered a period of "equilibrium."[64] By early June, the South Vietnamese Army had blunted the attack on Hue and had turned the tide of the fighting in the RVN's favor following the battle for An Loc, the capital of Binh Long located near the Cambodian border, and Kontum, in the Central Highlands, during which massive PAVN attacks were decisively repelled. By the late summer, the ARVN launched counterattacks and was able to recapture Quang Tri City. The 1972 offensive once again failed to bring about a general insurrection to topple the Saigon regime.

During the first few weeks of the offensive, Le Duan and Le Duc Tho were convinced that victory was within their grasp. In fact, the launching of the attacks constituted an early birthday gift for the VWP first secretary. As PAVN forces encountered little resistance in the first week of operations, Le Duan happily received well-wishes on his sixty-fifth birthday from all of his allies in the communist camp—an honor normally reserved for the DRV president.[65] Buoyed by the acknowledgement of his leadership abroad and ecstatic about the easy victories in the South, Le Duan believed that conditions were ripe for a mass insurrection. Here was the opportunity, the first secretary believed, to vindicate his strategy. On 9 April, he telegrammed COSVN to push the political struggle forward in the cities since communist forces were scoring victories on the battlefield while the masses continued to rise up in the countryside. Wary of reliving the setbacks of 1968, when the communist forces were unable to exploit the surprise attacks and the revolutionary fervor in the countryside, Le Duan took pains to emphasize the need for coordination between the victories on the battlefront, the increase of activity in the countryside, and political agitation in the urban centers.[66] The following day, the Politburo convened a meeting that echoed Le Duan's exhortations.[67] In mid-April, Le Duc Tho cabled Pham Hung to urge the southern leaders to maintain pressure on ARVN forces in Binh Long province. Tho wanted Hung to tie down ARVN troops in Binh Long so that communist forces might threaten Saigon.[68]

### BIG-POWER BETRAYAL

As North Vietnamese tanks rolled across the DMZ, leaders in Beijing and Moscow found themselves caught between Hanoi and Washington. Although Hanoi's official statement at the time (and after) claimed that the offensive was strictly to alter the military balance of power on the ground, VWP leaders timed the launching between the Beijing summit (21–28 February) and the Moscow summit (22–30 May).[69] Both allies issued public declarations of support, but privately, Soviet and Chinese leaders were extremely frustrated with their North Vietnamese ally for not heeding their advice in seeking victory through negotiations rather than military escalation. Given the timing of the attacks, the Soviets were more upset since they were convinced that Hanoi purposely aimed to sabotage détente but refrained from harming Sino-American rapprochement.[70] In fact, Brezhnev told the Americans that the Chinese were behind the North Vietnamese offensive and that both Asian powers wanted to see the Moscow summit canceled. The Chinese, in contrast, could afford to appear more supportive of the North Vietnamese since the Beijing summit had already taken place. Nevertheless, CCP leaders probably were still annoyed with their intractable ally.[71] Beijing might even have been pursuing a policy of pushing the North Vietnamese into the Soviet camp on the eve of the

Easter Offensive.[72] Although Chinese leaders reasoned that greater inter-action between Moscow and Hanoi would produce greater friction, an argument can be made that Beijing also wanted to sabotage Soviet-American relations and to distance itself from Hanoi's war in order to protect Sino-American relations.

Before punishing the North Vietnamese for their military transgressions, Nixon and Kissinger issued threats to Hanoi via its allies. On 3 April, Kissinger sent a secret letter to Beijing warning Chinese leaders that Nixon had no choice but to respond militarily to the DRV's offensive.[73] With the Soviets, the United States carried on a more complicated "diplomatic game," combining both public statements and private channels to convey its threats.[74] In addition to enlisting the Soviets and Chinese to pressure the North Vietnamese to end the offensive and return to the negotiating table, Nixon authorized military strikes against the DRV and sent requests to resume the secret meetings.[75] On 4 April, he approved the use of B-52 bombers for the first time against the DRV and less than a week later, he ordered air and sea attacks around Hanoi.[76] At the same time that Nixon approved these military measures, he tried to pin down the DRV on a date to resume public and private talks in Paris. In fact, both sides realized the necessity to keep negotiations alive.[77] Although Party leaders refused Washington's offer to meet privately on 24 April, the DRV delegation in Paris proposed that plenary sessions resume on 27 April and that a private meeting take place on 6 May. Le Duc Tho and Nguyen Duy Trinh then tele-grammed Xuan Thuy in Paris with Hanoi's intentions:

> Although the US is stepping up attacks against the North, we still foresee the continuation of the Paris conference. . . . In the conditions of détente between China, the Soviet Union, and the US, an international conference aimed at settling the problem is not to our advantage. We should maintain the Paris conference as a propaganda forum for our benefit and for direct settlement with the US later. The maintenance of the Paris forum is not because of our weakness, but because we need it in concert with the battlefield in the struggle against the US.[78]

The Soviet Union played a key role as intermediary between the United States and the DRV. On 14, 15, and 17 April, Soviet ambassador to the DRV Ilya Scherbakov met respectively with Pham Van Dong, Nguyen Duy Trinh, and Le Duan in order to convey America's proposal—and the Soviet Union's willingness—to set up a meeting between Kissinger and Le Duc

Tho in Moscow during the former's visit to the Soviet Union from 21 to 23 April. VWP leaders rejected this arrangement since it suited Washington and Moscow more than it did Hanoi. Nixon, they claimed, wanted to "enhance" the Soviet Union's role as intermediary in order to exploit détente for American ends in Vietnam, while Brezhnev wanted to offer his services as a go-between in order to gain leverage with Nixon during his visit to Moscow.[79] During Kissinger's first day in the Soviet Union in late April, the U.S. national security advisor complained bitterly to Brezhnev about Hanoi's "insolent" refusal to meet him in Moscow.[80] On the second day of talks, Kissinger continued to focus his remarks on Vietnam and conveyed Nixon's demands to his Soviet hosts. The DRV must withdraw all of its troops sent south during the Easter Offensive, respect the DMZ, and accept the U.S. demand for the return of all POWs before any settlement could be reached.[81] After Kissinger was satisfied that he had exhausted the Vietnam issue with Brezhnev, he ignored Nixon's orders and addressed the upcoming summit.[82] On 25 April, Moscow sent Konstantin Katushev, head of the foreign relations commission of the CPSU Central Committee, to Hanoi in order to debrief the North Vietnamese. After presenting Nixon's terms, which included the demand for the DRV to cease all attacks and respect the DMZ as well as specific negotiating issues, Katushev conveyed Nixon's threats as well. If Hanoi did not negotiate seriously, especially in a presidential election year, Nixon was prepared to take resolute measures to expand the war. Pham Van Dong registered his disapproval of Nixon's demands and expressed his astonishment at Nixon's hubris to the Soviet messenger.[83] Nonetheless, after an exchange of notes between the United States and the DRV, North Vietnamese leaders agreed to convene a plenary session in late April and to meet Kissinger privately in early May.[84]

Although the negotiating track was kept alive, Nixon was still unhappy with the results of his superpower diplomacy. Upset with an "arrogant" Kissinger who gave the Soviets everything they wanted—discussions on the summit and a Kissinger visit to Moscow that was longer than his visit to China—the president believed the United States had received nothing in return.[85] According to Nixon, the Soviets refused to pressure the North Vietnamese despite his threats. On the eve of Kissinger's departure for Paris to meet with Le Duc Tho, Nixon was reminded of the futility of his threats as communist forces stepped up their attacks in South Vietnam and captured Quang Tri City.[86] On 26 April, Nixon delivered his second address to the nation on Vietnam in 1972, informing the American people that he intended to withdraw 20,000 troops over the next two months, that

Ambassador William J. Porter, who had replaced Ambassador David K. E. Bruce in 1971 as head delegate to the Paris negotiations, would return to the plenary sessions on 27 April, and that he would continue air and naval attacks against military targets in North Vietnam.[87] Nixon's "tough" speech was intended to compel the North Vietnamese to end their offensive as the president escalated the war to new heights in the weeks to come.

On 2 May, an upset Kissinger met with a confident Le Duc Tho for a session that made little headway given the heavy fighting in South Vietnam. Since this was the first time that the negotiators had met since the secret talks were made public, Kissinger and Xuan Thuy exchanged heated words over the confidentiality of the meetings. Once both sides agreed to keep the private forum private, the conversation turned to substantive matters. Kissinger spoke first and made three demands on the DRV—to end the offensive, to abide by the 1968 understanding to wind down the war, and to negotiate seriously.[88] Tho objected to Kissinger's insinuations that the DRV had violated the 1968 promises, since Nixon's expansion of the war to Cambodia and Laos constituted the true violation. Exploiting growing antiwar sentiment in the United States, the North Vietnamese negotiator referred to Senator J. William Fulbright's comments on 8 April that defended the "patriotic forces' military activities" and even quoted recently printed excerpts from the Pentagon Papers to reveal the extent of U.S. meddling in Vietnam. A "pained" Kissinger did not respond to Tho's pointed comments regarding the American political scene, but instead he pushed North Vietnamese buttons by asking if Hanoi had a response to his questions regarding the U.S. eight-point peace proposal conveyed through the Soviets. An angry Le Duc Tho demanded that Kissinger ask these questions directly to the North Vietnamese rather than go through the Moscow.[89] The meeting ended with neither side proposing a date for the next session.

Three days later, Tho and Thuy cabled Hanoi that the United States had suspended the public talks on the Avenue Kléber.[90] The Politburo responded with an urgent message. Regarding Nixon's strategy, Hanoi leaders were of the opinion that the U.S. administration would hold out for another month until the wet season arrived since the Americans believed that the seasonal shift would signal the end of the communist offensive in South Vietnam. The VWP concluded that Nixon would probably not present anything new or different from the eight points during the month of May. Instead, Hanoi was convinced that the United States would use superpower diplomacy to bring Chinese and Soviet pressure to bear on the North Vietnamese at the negotiating table. The Politburo ruefully observed that now the Soviets joined the Chinese in exerting maximum pressure on the North Vietnamese to accept a resolution to the Vietnam problem in light of Nixon's upcoming visit to Moscow. As such, Hanoi concluded, Nixon and Kissinger would request a private meeting in Paris only after they had punished the DRV militarily.[91] According to historian Luu Van Loi's version of what was possibly the same telegram, Hanoi conveyed even more suspicion of potential Soviet betrayal: "There have been transactions between the US and the Soviet Union with regards to the Vietnam problem. Up to Nixon's trip to the Soviet Union, another visit (secret or public) by Kissinger to Moscow is not out of the question, to put pressure on the host country regarding Vietnam and to reduce US difficulties. We should be vigilant of the scheme for undermining the Paris conference and finding another way to settle the Vietnam problem, for instance by convening an international conference."[92] The telegram ended with instructions for Tho and Thuy to put off any American requests for a private meeting until after the Moscow summit.[93] Meanwhile, Kissinger, who had left the meeting disappointed, described his three hours with Tho and Thuy on 2 May as "thoroughly unproductive on substance" in his assessment to Nixon. North Vietnamese intransigence, Kissinger believed, was based on the fluid military situation and the belief that better terms were on the horizon. Nixon, who never had as much faith in negotiations with Hanoi as Kissinger, began to doubt his national security advisor's ability to gauge North Vietnamese actions.[94]

Although the upcoming summit with the Soviet Union and negotiations with North Vietnam would be put at risk, Nixon announced on 8 May the initiation of Operation Linebacker: the bombing of the area north of the twentieth parallel, including the vicinity around Hanoi and the mining of the North Vietnamese ports.[95] The U.S. president told Haig that he wanted the B-52 attacks against Hanoi and Hai Phong to increase during the Moscow summit, since Nixon believed he had made a mistake when he decreased sorties during the Beijing summit.[96] At the same time, the president stepped up the psychological warfare operations against the North Vietnamese. The CIA was ordered to knock out Radio Hanoi and then simulate broadcasts emphasizing great losses. Rumors were to be spread about the death of General Giap and the mental well-being of Le Duan.[97] Nixon's campaign was intended not only to send a message to the North Vietnamese to end their offensive but also to the Soviets and Chinese to put more pressure on the North Vietnamese to return to the nego-

*Destruction from Operation Linebacker in Nam Dinh, DRV (Douglas Pike Photograph Collection, Vietnam Center and Archive, Texas Tech University)*

tiating table rather than supply Hanoi with more tanks. At the same time that Nixon announced Operation Linebacker, he also dangled a carrot by putting forward a seemingly new peace proposal, including the release of all U.S. prisoners of war, internationally supervised elections, cessation of all U.S. acts of force throughout Indochina, and the complete withdrawal of U.S. forces from South Vietnam within four months after the signing of the agreement.[98] Even though Kissinger had already offered these terms to the North Vietnamese in private, the American public was kept unaware of this. In fact, Nixon had formally suspended the public talks on 4 May, and informed his representative to the Paris talks, Ambassador Porter, that he would not have anything to do in France and suggested that Porter stay in Washington instead.[99]

Nixon was ecstatic with the public's embrace of Linebacker. Even without the phony letters of support sent by the Committee to Re-elect the President (CRP, later nicknamed CREEP), public reaction to Nixon's firm military actions was positive. In July, when the Democratic Party selected an outspoken dove, South Dakota Senator George McGovern, as its party's nominee, Nixon's second term seemed all but assured. Linebacker I confirmed to Nixon that he could reap rewards by escalating the war. Nixon's good fortune was not limited to the home front. Although North Vietnam's allies protested the U.S. bombing and mining campaign, they also conveyed that these attacks should not derail rapprochement or détente. The Chinese, with greater room for maneuver than the Soviets, could afford to act more resolutely. On 12 May, Beijing condemned the U.S. mining of Hai Phong harbor and other North Vietnamese ports and pledged Chinese support for the Vietnamese until final victory.[100] During May, the

PRC sent mine-clearing teams to Hai Phong, planned for Chinese assistance in building pipelines, and transferred equipment to help the North Vietnamese rebuild bridges and roads.[101] However, Beijing's aid and support stopped short of granting Soviet ships crucial access to Chinese harbors.[102] In early May, Soviet premier Alexei Kosygin had sent a letter to Zhou Enlai via Xuan Thuy requesting Soviet access to Chinese ports and use of Chinese railroads in order to transport goods and supplies to North Vietnam. Although Hanoi leaders forwarded Moscow's request along with a note stating that they hoped China and the Soviet Union would be able to reach an agreement on this matter, Beijing remained obstinate. With Nixon's mining operations, North Vietnamese appeals for internationalist cooperation became more desperate. Throughout May, Zhou Enlai continued to put off North Vietnamese leaders, claiming that the Soviets could not be trusted.[103]

Initially, Moscow was divided on whether or not to hold the summit in light of Nixon's bombing and mining operations, but in the end, Brezhnev won the debate to proceed with the Soviet-American meeting.[104] As a result, Moscow's official response to Operation Linebacker appeared mild compared to Chinese protests. The Soviet Union condemned the U.S. government for "inadmissible" actions and protested any potential damage to Soviet ships.[105] The North Vietnamese grasped that it was more important to recognize what the Soviets did not say than what was actually said. Moscow made no announcement regarding the summit. According to Luu Van Loi, however, the VWP understood the constraints on Soviet foreign policy. "Vietnam understood that in any case the Vietnam problem was for the Soviet Union the problem of a remote region. The Soviet Union had to cope with many problems closer to home, such as those of China, the Middle East, and Europe. Therefore, when Nixon had achieved rapprochement with China, it was impossible for the Soviet Union not to continue détente with the US."[106] Vietnam scholar Gareth Porter, in contrast, argues that Hanoi did expect strong diplomatic support, particularly for its offensive and against American bombing, from Moscow and Beijing. What North Vietnamese leaders did not expect, according to Porter, was that Nixon would be able to escalate the war and escape any diplomatic or political setbacks.[107] According to a telegram from the Politburo to Le Duc Tho on the eve of Nixon's departure for Moscow, Hanoi leaders emphasized the deleterious effects of Soviet-American détente on the Vietnamese revolution.[108]

Regardless of North Vietnamese expectations, the Moscow summit was a repeat performance of the Beijing summit except with Russian rather than Chinese actors. From 22 to 30 May, Nixon scored his second stunning diplomatic victory with his visit to Moscow. Like Chinese leaders, the Soviets gave relations with the Nixon administration and détente with the United States priority over relations with the VWP and support for the fraternal communist cause. The Soviets were unwilling to "hand over" North Vietnam to the Chinese, however. Moscow gave reassurances that it would not to sell out the Vietnamese revolution and made promises to "help" Hanoi deal with Washington. On the first day of plenary meetings, Brezhnev raised the issue of Vietnam.[109] "The war which the United States has for many years now been waging in Vietnam," the Soviet general secretary stated, "has left a deep imprint in the soul of our people and in the hearts of all Soviet people. To take in these circumstances serious steps to develop Soviet-American relations was for us not at all an easy thing."[110] Rather than dwell on Vietnam at the start of talks, Brezhnev promised to return to the issue later in Nixon's visit. At the general secretary's dacha on 24 May, the time had come to discuss Vietnam. After stating his views on Vietnam and the Moscow-Hanoi alliance, Nixon tried to steer the conversation away from Southeast Asia, preferring to discuss it during a "small forum." Soviet leaders, however, seized the opportunity to condemn U.S. actions. "It would certainly be interesting to hear for the sake of what the U.S. invaded Vietnam," Brezhnev baited Nixon. "I am sure no nation could find any just explanation for what is being done. And that is probably why all countries call the U.S. the aggressor and probably rightly so. I don't want to hurl more epithets on you."[111] However, after "hurling" a few more epithets for good measure, Brezhnev and his crew shifted gears and toasted the American president and the improvement in U.S.-Soviet relations. Nixon later described Brezhnev's behavior as "Jekyll and Hyde" as the Soviet leader who could "laugh and slap him on the back" at one moment and "shout angrily" at him at the next.[112] Just like the Chinese, then, the Soviets voiced their disapproval in no uncertain terms to Nixon "for the record," but they did little to compel the United States to change its policy toward Vietnam. Instead, both allies hoped to convince Hanoi to settle the war based more or less on Washington's terms.

After the Moscow summit, Soviet chairman Nikolai Podgorny traveled to Hanoi to convince the North Vietnamese to return to the negotiating table, just as Zhou Enlai had done following the Beijing summit a few months earlier.[113] Prior to his visit, Hanoi leaders were deeply upset with the Soviets not only for receiving Nixon but also for trying to pressure

North Vietnam to meet privately with the United States.[114] As a result, the DRV demanded that a four-party public session occur before any private meeting between Kissinger and Tho took place.[115] On 13 June, Nguyen Duy Trinh and Xuan Thuy sent a letter to Le Duc Tho identifying what they believed to be the Soviet chairman's two objectives during his stay in Hanoi. "The Soviets will want to convey Nixon's position regarding Vietnam and then they will hope to explore our position regarding peace," the letter stated. Right before Podgorny's visit to the DRV from 14 to 16 June, VWP leaders expressed their indignation with the joint U.S.-U.S.S.R. communiqué and disappointment with their allies' failure to act strongly against U.S. bombing and mining operations.[116]

After Podgorny left Hanoi, Le Duc Tho flew to Beijing to request that Chinese leaders relent on the aid transport issue with the Soviets. On 18 June, the North Vietnamese leader's pleas proved successful. The PRC agreed to grant Soviet, Cuban, and East European ships access to Chinese harbors and to transport these goods via Chinese rail. However, the arrangement immediately encountered difficulties when Soviet goods arrived in Chinese harbors covered by torn blankets rather than sturdy tarpaulins. Beijing concluded that Moscow purposely wanted the U.S. satellites to see what it was sending to Hanoi.[117] Although Tho left Beijing satisfied that he gained Chinese cooperation regarding aid transport and greater aid packages, he could not have been happy to know that his departure was followed by Kissinger's arrival in China the following day.[118]

On 1 June, after Nixon's visit to Moscow but before Podgorny's trip to Hanoi, the VWP Politburo officially shifted the nation's resources and attention from the offensive in the South to the defense of the North.[119] By mid-month, U.S. bombing and South Vietnamese counteroffensives had rolled back the early communist victories. As a result, Le Duan and the Hanoi leaders reanalyzed and reformulated VWP strategy by taking stock of the Spring–Summer Offensive, Nixon's Operation Linebacker, and Sino-Soviet-American relations.[120] Although the performance of main force units had improved, problems still existed in organization as well as with command and control.[121] By June, communist leaders privately admitted to themselves that the high technology, big-unit warfare exemplified in the 1972 Spring–Summer Offensive had failed to attain its objectives.[122] In describing Hanoi's military assessment at the time, Luu Van Loi writes, "In a word, though a fundamental victory was not yet achieved, the situation on the battlefield had changed to the advantage of [North] Vietnam, creating conditions for the revolution in SVN to later develop its struggle in strength."[123] Once again, Le Duan's strategy proved unsuccessful as American bombs and South Vietnamese counterattacks cut short any burgeoning political struggle in the cities. The Hanoi Politburo as a whole had to accept that its objective for the 1972 Spring–Summer Offensive to alter the military balance of power on the ground and to thwart superpower obstruction from above had failed. For the remainder of the war, then, VWP leaders resigned themselves to struggle solely in the diplomatic arena.

### CONCLUSION

The first half of 1972 reveals that Beijing and Moscow were as much theaters of battle in the Vietnam War as the frontlines of Indochina, the Paris negotiations, and the beleaguered home fronts in the United States and Vietnam. As Nixon undertook his historic visits to China and the Soviet Union to lessen tensions in the Cold War and thus change the course of international relations in the postwar era, Le Duan—as well as Nguyen Van Thieu—tried to stop the intricate dance among the great powers as it threatened to stamp out their local struggles. Vietnamese leaders resorted to publicly shaming and privately manipulating their great-power allies to "toe the ideological line." Familiar Cold War scripts that Third World actors utilized to entice superpower patrons, however, were no longer as persuasive. Alliances in the Cold War by 1972 not only involved "servitude" but also treachery and double-dealing as the line between friend and foe became further blurred in the Vietnam War.

In this oppressive international climate, Hanoi attempted its third bid for victory. Just as in 1964 and 1968, Le Duan's General Offensive and General Uprising strategy in 1972 did not lead the VWP to certain triumph. Although PAVN forces began the Easter Offensive in brilliant fashion, the political and military conditions in South Vietnam by 1972 were different than they were in 1964 or even in 1968. According to Le Duan, a general uprising failed to materialize not only because the United States stymied the communist advance with its bombs but because "the puppet regime" was able to conscript more South Vietnamese men into its regional and provincial forces. With this admission, the VWP first secretary finally abandoned his goal of stirring the masses to rise up and join the communist troops in overthrowing the Saigon regime during the 1972 offensive.

Meanwhile, although Nixon and Kissinger had dealt a stunning diplomatic blow with the Beijing summit, they were prepared to risk these gains as well as détente to enact the military prong of their strategy. Resuscitating Operation "Duck Hook," Nixon's contingency military planning that was deemed too extreme in 1969, Operation Linebacker executed portions of those plans in the late spring of 1972. For the first time since the cessation of Operation Rolling Thunder, the United States launched a continuous large-scale aerial campaign—this time including B-52 bombers—over railroad lines leading to the Chinese border, military installations, as well as populated cities in North Vietnam. Moreover, Nixon ordered the mining of Hai Phong and other harbors in the DRV to cut off Hanoi's maritime supply lines, endangering Soviet vessels in the process. In other words, the president made good on his early madman threats.

Nixon's gamble paid off. Neither Beijing nor Moscow was willing to risk its relations with the United States for the Vietnamese cause. The Soviet Union proceeded with the Moscow summit, while Beijing only issued empty threats at Washington for escalating the war in Vietnam. As Vietnamese communist forces struggled to hold on to their initial victories in the South, Chinese and Soviet leaders pressured Hanoi to abandon its military offensive and return to the negotiating table. Equipping the DRV with defensive armaments against Operation Linebacker but not offensive weaponry to continue the communist campaign in South Vietnam, Beijing and Moscow could claim that they were providing assistance to their North Vietnamese ally. Le Duan and his comrades had little choice but to shift gears and pursue a new strategy in the war for peace.

*There was no precedent, either in Vietnamese*
*history or elsewhere in the world, for the kind of "talk-fight"*
*situation we had at that time. — Vo Van Sung*[1]

chapter eight

# WAR FOR PEACE

Each time Nga received a letter from her husband, Le Duan, telling her to remain strong and be a hero of the revolution, she passed it along to her colleagues, who felt similarly buoyed by his words. By 1972, Nga had become deputy head of the Women's Auxiliary Corps and a member of the Party Regional Committee. Although she held an important position and wanted to travel around the Mekong Delta to survey the war effort, her comrades insisted that Nga stay close to headquarters for fear that she be arrested by enemy forces. Her capture would not only be a blow to them, they pointed out, it could destroy Le Duan's spirit in Hanoi.[2] At first Nga bristled. As a journalist by training, she needed to be out observing and analyzing the situation around her, not remaining cloistered in one area listening to other people's war stories. When she had the occasion to travel to northern Can Tho, she jumped at the opportunity. The precariousness of her situation, however, immediately hit her as she stood staring at a picture of herself on a "wanted" poster on the docks of the port city. "Real name: Nguyen Thuy Nga, New name: Nguyen Thi Van. Wife of the Number 1 Communist Enemy in North Vietnam. Anyone who apprehends her or has information regarding . . ." Nga could read no more; she stood shivering in the hot, humid air of the Mekong Delta.[3]

Ignorant of the dangers confronting his wife, Le Duan already had enough to worry about in Hanoi. While his great-power friends wined and dined Nixon, they bullied and pressured him to end the war. Staking his reputation once again on his military strategy, Le Duan had launched the 1972 Spring–Summer Offensive. Though it began well, the first secretary was not so sure going into the summer phase of attacks. Despite his deep reservations, perhaps the time had come to consider negotiations. Throughout his career, Le Duan had tried to avoid repeating the mistakes of Ho, but in the end, he finally understood that diplomacy was necessary to stave off defeat.

This chapter analyzes the endgame of America's war in Vietnam. As Saigon forces slowly reversed Hanoi's gains made during the Spring–Summer Offensive, recapturing pivotal territory, Beijing and Moscow, urged on by Nixon, pulled out all the stops to pressure Hanoi to accept American terms. Le Duan finally admitted defeat. With the failure of his 1972 Spring–Summer Offensive to achieve a decisive victory, the first secretary, who long abhorred relying on diplomacy during the war, focused the Party's resources on the "talking" portion of his policy—"fighting" had failed to achieve the Party's goals.

Nixon, however, was not ready to end the fighting and to come to a resolution in the fall of 1972. Although Tho and Kissinger had hammered out a draft agreement in October, RVN president Thieu used his remaining weapon—his obstinacy—to sabotage the peace. Thieu's tactics paid off: Nixon abandoned the prospects for peace and instead unleashed one more devastating round of bombing over Hanoi. As B-52s brought death and destruction to North Vietnam, public outcry blunted Nixon's aggression and thwarted Thieu's obstruction. Although Le Duan and Le Duc Tho failed not only to win the war for peace but also to save the DRV from further destruction in 1972, their global offensive to garner world support did manage to tie Nixon's hand and dull Sino-Soviet betrayal. Nonetheless, these violent events on the eve of the 1973 Paris agreement boded ill for all parties, tearing apart any chance for a viable resolution to the war. Although American departure was imminent, peace did not return to Vietnam.

### LE DUAN'S ADMISSION OF DEFEAT:
### FROM GO-GU TO DIPLOMACY

By the summer of 1972, it was clear to Hanoi leaders that the Spring–Summer Offensive had failed to alter the military balance of power and to create conditions for a mass uprising in South Vietnam. Nixon's bombing and mining campaigns in Operation Linebacker had caused extensive damage to North Vietnamese industry and infrastructure, forcing the VWP Politburo to shift focus from its offensive in the South to defense of the North.[4] Once again, the North Vietnamese urban population relocated to the countryside, fleeing American bombs that disrupted daily life as they had under Johnson's Rolling Thunder. In South Vietnam, Saigon forces, supported by American air power, launched counterattacks to regain territory that communist troops had seized. On 2 May, President Thieu appointed General Ngo Quang Truong, who was in command of the I Corps when PAVN forces launched their first wave of attacks across the DMZ in March, to replace General Hoang Xuan Lam. The South Vietnamese president blamed Lam for the collapse of the northern provinces to communist forces and relieved him of duty by appointing him to head an anticorruption campaign in the Ministry of Defense. Under the leadership of General Truong, South Vietnamese paratroopers and marines launched Operation Lam Son 72 to recapture the city and province of Quang Tri.[5]

As a result of Saigon's counteroffensive and after much debate in Hanoi, the Party's CMC ordered its forces to cease the third wave of attacks and shift gradually to a defensive posture in the Quang Tri–Thua Thien region.[6] Under the command of General Giap, communist troops prevented General Truong's forces from recapturing Quang Tri City until September 1972.[7] Le Duan believed that the problem facing the communist offensive in 1972 was vastly different from the one it had confronted in 1968:

> Our strategy for the military offensive, which is now in its fourth month [August], remains to carry on the offensive and uprising and to annihilate and smash the puppet army. Even though we have defeated a large part of the puppet's main force units, the regional and popular forces have not been destroyed. Moreover, although the military offensive is progressing well, the masses have still not risen up in large portion. . . . Today, the situation in the countryside differs greatly from the one during the Tet Offensive. After years of pacification, the enemy's goal is to subjugate the masses and force them into military service. . . . Approximately 70–80 percent of families have a member who has been conscripted as a result.[8]

Le Duan's internal assessment confirmed U.S. General Creighton Abrams's public statements at the time that the United States and the RVN had been winning the war in the South Vietnamese countryside with the U.S. "one war" strategy.[9] Although the VWP first secretary continued to track the progress of the 1972 Spring–Summer Offensive from his headquarters in Hanoi, he no longer believed that communist forces could achieve a decisive victory on the battlefield that would produce a favorable agreement in Paris.[10] The first secretary finally reconciled himself to the failure of his GO-GU strategy for victory; instead, he would focus on the "talking" aspect of his talk-fight strategy. "If we want to speed up negotiations in Paris and sign an agreement before November 1972," Le Duan confided to his comrades in the Politburo after the ARVN retook Quang Tri City, "we must concentrate our efforts on doing whatever it takes to resolve our first objective, which is 'to fight to force the Americans to withdraw.' The achievement of our first objective will create the conditions necessary for us to subsequently attain our second objective, 'to fight to make the puppets collapse.'"[11] With this admission, Le Duan no longer sought to topple the Saigon regime to force Washington's hand in negotiations. Rather, he strove for more minimal terms in Paris and shelved his military plans until the Americans vacated Vietnam. For the remainder of the war against the United States, then, Le Duan and the Politburo relied primarily on diplomatic and political struggles and downgraded the military offensive, devising an international strategy aimed at thwarting Sino-Soviet obstruction, exploiting U.S. domestic opposition to the war during an election year, and negotiating seriously in Paris.

### THE PERPETUAL WAR

In late June and early July, Le Duc Tho hastily returned to Hanoi from Sofia, Bulgaria, for an urgent Politburo meeting to vote on a new strategy for the remainder of 1972.[12] The Politburo, according to Luu Van Loi, had positive reasons to "switch from a strategy of war to a strategy of peace."[13] Since the start of the Kissinger-Tho talks, the DRV had scored two victories at the negotiating table. The United States relented on mutual withdrawal and agreed to Thieu's resignation one month prior to any election in South Vietnam. With what Party leaders disingenuously hailed as communist victories on the battlefield and in light of the upcoming U.S. presidential election, Loi wrote, North Vietnamese leaders wanted to seize the opportunity to negotiate seriously from a position of strength.

In reality, neither the military balance of power on the ground nor the diplomatic struggle at the international level provided Party leaders with much reason for optimism. Militarily, South Vietnamese forces were able to prevent communist troops from taking Kontum and An Loc as well as to launch their own counterattacks to reclaim lost territory. Diplomatically, Nixon was successful in getting Chinese and Soviet leaders to exert pressure on the North Vietnamese to de-escalate the fighting and to settle the war through negotiations. Not only did Beijing and Moscow use every opportunity to lecture Hanoi on the need to negotiate more flexibly, but both powers also reduced aid to the DRV.[14] Although Hanoi's patrons continued to provide military and economic assistance, this only equipped the DRV to defend itself from American bombs and mines, not to maintain military pressure on the RVN.[15] As a result, the Hanoi Politburo's shift to a "strategy of peace" was an admission of failure, not a declaration of victory. In June, the DRV authorized its delegate-general, Vo Van Sung, to approach the U.S. Air Force attaché in Paris, Colonel Georges Guay, to set up a private meeting between Le Duc Tho and Kissinger for mid-July.[16] Although North Vietnamese leaders were keen to negotiate, they wanted to avoid meeting on or before the Democratic Party Convention set for 10 July. Hanoi did not want to convey the impression that it would interfere with the U.S. presidential election even if the VWP did plan to accelerate the political struggle for the hearts and minds of the American voters.[17] Instead, Party leaders preferred to use "people's diplomacy," including American actress Jane Fonda's two-week visit to survey the extent of damage done by Nixon's bombs in Operation Linebacker.[18] Both sides finally agreed on 13 July for the plenary session and 16 July for the private meeting.[19]

American politics was not the only factor weighing heavily on North Vietnamese minds; Hanoi's strategy deliberation also took place in the context of changes in the Party leadership. During the height of the Easter Offensive, Van Tien Dung and Minister of Public Security Tran Quoc Hoan were elevated to the Politburo, increasing membership from nine to eleven. After the Third Party Congress in 1960, there had been no new members inducted to the top echelon of party power even after the deaths of Nguyen Chi Thanh in 1967 and Ho Chi Minh in 1969.[20] The desire to present an image of stability and constancy, in addition to solidarity, probably influenced the decision to maintain the status quo. By 1972, Le Duan must have felt his grip on power weakening as a result of Nixon's diplomatic successes and the failure of his General Offensive and General Uprising earlier in the year.

The elevation of Dung and Hoan to the Politburo in the summer of 1972 thus deserves more analysis. Dung was not only inducted in the Politburo but also made a full general, perhaps reflecting Le Duan's desire to check Giap's growing influence after the failure of the 1972 Spring–Summer

Offensive. Even though Dung took over command of the war from 1968 onward and thus oversaw the Tet and Spring–Summer Offensives, General Giap's influence continued to increase in the PAVN, particularly after his success in defeating ARVN forces in Laos in 1971. Le Duan's inability to score a definitive military victory and create the conditions for a mass insurrection in 1972 may have prompted the first secretary to push for Dung's membership in the Politburo and thus act as a counterweight to Giap, who had assumed command of defensive operations in the South.[21]

Minister of Public Security Hoan's elevation to the Politburo was an expression of the Party leadership's desire to clamp down on growing unrest in the DRV. The failure of the Party to redress economic problems in 1971 and the return of the air war over the DRV in 1972 took a heavy toll on the North Vietnamese people. There were seventeen mass media articles on "counterrevolution [*phan cach mang*]" during May alone.[22] Party leaders attributed black marketing, the decrease in labor productivity, economic speculation, hoarding, the exploitation of urban evacuees, and the overall breakdown in the morale and discipline of the North Vietnamese people to counterrevolution. In two articles in *Hoc Tap*, Hoan outlined the Party's response to the decades of "counterrevolution" by launching a "counter-counterrevolutionary" movement in 1972.[23]

U.S. records reveal that the intensive U.S. psychological warfare campaign, which began during Linebacker, did make substantial inroads in 1972.[24] By the beginning of the summer, the United States entertained a plan, referred to as Operation Archie Bunker, to reach a large portion of the North Vietnamese population by destroying Radio Hanoi's transmitters shortly before the major evening news broadcast and replacing it instead with a fake "emergency transmission from Radio Hanoi" broadcast from the Coronet Solo aircraft.[25] Even though Secretary of Defense Melvin Laird vetoed the operation, questioning its military viability and citing its potential international and domestic drawbacks, the United States did continue dropping leaflets and spreading misinformation.[26] By mid-July, Kissinger believed that the psyops campaign was "*striking a raw nerve of the DRV leadership.*"[27] As Hanoi appeared more flexible in Paris throughout August, the Psychological Operations Group planned to introduce a fake Party resolution to let the "genie of peace . . . out of the bottle," one that VWP leaders would have a hard time putting back in.[28]

Despite America's best efforts, a counterrevolution in the DRV was unlikely given the extent of Party control over North Vietnam. Nonetheless, Le Duan and other Politburo members were concerned to prevent any dissent from arising as a result of their decisions during the remainder of 1972. This allowed Hoan to take an even harder line against those suspected of rightist deviationism since, in his view, loyal opposition or legitimate political grievances did not exist. Carrying out his campaign of "nipping in the bud" potential reactionary organizations, Hoan dismantled the World Proletarian League and Poor People's Liberation Front to Oppose Injustice, just to name a few, in the early summer of 1972.[29] Fine-tuning his speeches justifying the expansion of his and his ministry's power, Hoan described opposition to the will of the state and Party as a crime.[30] Early the following year, Hoan's labors paid off: Decree No. 32-ND/CP created the Counterreactionary Department, giving the Ministry of Public Security the legal document needed to continue its domestic war in the DRV indefinitely.[31]

Although the extent of inner-Party squabbles and DRV domestic unrest in 1972 remains unclear, the international response to North Vietnam's decision to resume private talks is well documented. Before the scheduled Kissinger-Tho meeting in July, Chinese leaders tried to persuade their North Vietnamese allies to settle in Paris. In particular, Beijing wanted Hanoi to drop the demand for the United States to cease its support of the current Saigon regime. Since the summer of 1971, Chinese leaders had cited Beijing's toleration of Chiang Kai-shek in Taiwan as a reason for Hanoi to accept Nguyen Van Thieu in South Vietnam. During Zhou Enlai's meeting with Pham Van Dong in Kunming on 6 and 7 July, the Chinese leader tried to convince Dong to settle any outstanding issues with the Americans first before turning to oust Thieu. In fact, the Chinese leader raised the idea of a three-way coalition government with the Vietnamese premier: "If the military and the political questions cannot be resolved in the Vietnamese-American talks, it is proper to establish a coalition government between the right, the neutrals, and the left in South Vietnam. A coalition government can directly be negotiated with Nguyen Van Thieu, it will take some time, if it does not work out fight again, the Americans will not return."[32] Immediately after his meeting with Dong, Zhou met with Xuan Thuy and DRV vice minister of trade Ly Ban in Beijing. During the meeting, Thuy briefed Zhou on Hanoi's strategy but did not reveal much to the Chinese leader. Thuy said the VWP was prepared to fight or negotiate based on reasonable terms.[33] A few days later, Zhou Enlai held a longer and more important meeting with Le Duc Tho, who remained unmoved by the Chinese leader's pleas to compromise in Paris. Zhou appealed to flattery (Hanoi was "correct" in 1968 to engage in negotiations with the

United States despite Chinese disapproval) and to China's vast experience (Beijing conducted "talking while fighting" during the Korean War as well as with Taiwan). The Chinese leader argued that the North Vietnamese had to negotiate with the "chieftain [*dau so*]." At some point it was best to deal with Thieu as representative of the "right" in a tripartite government, otherwise he might try to sabotage the peace.[34] Moreover, Zhou pointed out, after a coalition government was established, the DRV could resume fighting. "The question is to play for time with a view of letting North Vietnam recover, thus getting stronger while the enemy is getting weaker." Tho's response was unequivocal: "But we still think of a government without Thieu."[35] In Hanoi's estimation, Thieu was still unpalatable as one of three forces in a coalition government.[36]

## BATTLEGROUND: U.S. DOMESTIC POLITICS

As VWP leaders dealt with internal problems and external pressure, Senator George McGovern's nomination as the Democratic Party candidate for president gave the Politburo reason for optimism in an otherwise difficult period. McGovern's public declaration that if he were elected he would immediately end support for the Thieu regime, bring back American POWs, and conclude the U.S. war in Vietnam within ninety days was roundly applauded in Hanoi.[37] On 12 July, DRV leaders once again took note of McGovern's political solution for Vietnam. The Democratic nominee campaigned on ending America's war through the unconditional cessation of bombing over Indochina, the complete withdrawal of American troops within ninety days of the cessation of bombing, the cessation of military aid to the Thieu regime, and the promotion of diplomatic efforts to settle the POW issue.[38] On 17 July, Nguyen Duy Trinh cabled Tho and Thuy regarding the impact of McGovern's candidacy. "The new picture is favorable for our war effort," the DRV foreign minister wrote. "We now have more ways to exploit the contradictions between the two U.S. parties and to force Nixon to offer a settlement favorable to us."[39]

Two days after Foreign Minister Trinh's telegram arrived in Paris, Tho and Thuy met with Kissinger for six and a half hours at 11 Rue Darthé. Both sides were cordial, but neither offered any new terms.[40] Kissinger did, however, reiterate the administration's principles with respect to a settlement in Vietnam, including its flexibility in dealing with any present (and future) governments in Indochina. He hinted that Washington could do without Thieu since the United States neither was "wedded" to any particular personalities in South Vietnam (these words were deleted from Ambassador Ellsworth Bunker's postmeeting assessment for Thieu) nor deemed it necessary to have a pro-American government in Saigon when the United States interacted with governments that were "not pro-American in the largest of Asian nations"—an obvious reference to the PRC.[41] The U.S. negotiator also warned Hanoi that it should not try to influence American electoral politics. If the DRV did attempt to meddle, Kissinger warned, the Nixon administration would stop all negotiations until after the election. Unperturbed by Kissinger's threat, Tho and Thuy proceeded with their prepared lectures regarding the DRV's glorious tradition and long history of opposing foreign aggression. After the discussion turned to substantive matters, Kissinger presented a five-point plan, which he called America's "last effort" at peace.[42] Tho was not impressed; he described Kissinger's peace offer as vague and containing nothing new.[43] Both sides, however, agreed to meet again on 1 August.

According to Luu Van Loi, Le Duc Tho and Xuan Thuy sent a lengthy postmeeting synopsis to Hanoi.[44] The DRV negotiators believed that Kissinger's five-point plan "might have some significance" since it was less rigid than what the United States had offered at the previous private meeting in May.[45] Kissinger's "flexible" attitude at the meeting was undermined, however, by his insistence on negotiating "from a position of strength."[46] While the DRV's leverage had all but disappeared as a result of battlefield losses, America's bargaining position had grown stronger through superpower diplomacy. Nonetheless, Tho and Thuy insisted that the United States still had a weak point. Kissinger's warning to the DRV to refrain from trying to influence the U.S. presidential elections suggested to Hanoi that the Nixon administration was vulnerable to just such pressures.[47] VWP leaders thus opted to dismiss Kissinger's threat. According to Loi, the Hanoi Politburo stressed the importance of "taking advantage at present of the acute contradictions in the U.S. elections" and instructed Tho and Thuy to "make adequate use of these contradictions among the U.S. people and the political parties."[48]

On 27 July, the Politburo sent negotiating instructions to Paris not only for the upcoming private meeting but for the entire month of August. In the lead-up to the Republican National Convention on 23 August, Hanoi leaders predicted that the Nixon administration might try to convert progress in Paris into political gains at home. As a result, in order to extract a comprehensive settlement from Kissinger, Tho and Thuy should be inwardly uncompromising yet appear outwardly flexible. If Nixon and

Kissinger refused to budge before the convention, then the opportunity for a settlement would appear in October on the eve of the elections. The Politburo's conclusion struck a confident tone: "Do not let Nixon think that we are afraid of failing to negotiate a settlement when it is really him who is afraid that he won't be able to resolve Vietnam before the elections."[49] According to East German sources, Hanoi leaders were unwilling to make the necessary concessions in Paris because they nurtured "illusions" that McGovern might win at the polls.[50]

On 1 August, U.S. and DRV negotiators met for eight hours in their longest session to date. During the meeting, Kissinger presented a twelve-point plan that he later described as offering "nothing new" since it made only "cosmetic modifications."[51] However, Le Duc Tho and Xuan Thuy saw the American plan differently. Not only did the twelve-point plan discuss political and military issues, it conceded more than America's previous eight-point plan by being "softer in tone, clearer in expressing Washington's desire to come to a resolution, and more conciliatory."[52] After a brief discussion of Kissinger's plan and a short recess where "whiskey, wine, and tea" were offered to the U.S. team, Tho presented the DRV's new ten-point proposal that allowed the PRG to negotiate directly with the Thieu regime. Hanoi dropped the demand for Thieu's removal by proposing what Chinese leaders had suggested the North Vietnamese leaders accept in early July: a three-component national reconciliation government.[53]

Although both sides made compromises in their plans, major areas of disagreement still existed regarding political issues, making Hanoi leaders pessimistic about a settlement before the Republican National Convention. On 11 August, with few remaining options, the Politburo instructed the PRG to call on the support of the socialist nations, the American public, and the progressive people of the world to help break the diplomatic stalemate in Paris.[54] The VWP aimed to force Nixon's hand by increasing public pressure on administration before the convention. Meanwhile, in Washington, after listening to Kissinger's assessment of the meeting, Nixon began to contemplate what could happen militarily after his victory at the polls if Hanoi refused to settle. "After November 7, school's out," Nixon stated, "and we're going to take out the heart of installations in Hanoi. . . . We're going to take out the whole goddamn dock area, ships or no ships. Tell them: 'Clear out of there.' We'll stay away from the Chinese border. And frankly, Henry, we may have to take the dikes out not for the purpose of killing people, [but] to warn the people."[55] This seemed a much more attractive option to Nixon than settling prematurely in Paris.

Kissinger and Tho's private meeting on 14 August was a "holding action" by both sides, as the former needed to consult with Saigon and the latter intended to return to Hanoi for further instructions. Nonetheless, Kissinger used the opportunity to express his annoyance with Vietnam's ploy to portray the Paris talks as being deadlocked when there had been substantial progress in the private negotiations.[56] He thus presented a packet of materials that included a U.S. policy statement, a new ten-point plan, and a procedural document regarding the conduct of negotiations.[57] Tho heavily criticized the new terms presented in Kissinger's packet and presented one document in return.[58] In addition to demanding that military and political issues be discussed, the DRV negotiator reiterated the need for a three-component government of national reconciliation since there were, according to his count, two armies, two administrations, and three political forces in South Vietnam.[59] Even though the United States and North Vietnam continued to close the gap between their positions, Kissinger informed Tho that he could not discuss political issues until he met with Saigon leaders. Both sides agreed to meet again on 15 September.[60] Two days after the meeting, the DRV negotiators relayed the contents of the U.S. three-part packet to Hanoi.[61]

Meanwhile, Kissinger flew to Saigon to gain Thieu's support for the upcoming U.S.-DRV negotiating session in September through two days of intense meetings with South Vietnamese officials. When Saigon leaders understood that the joint electoral commission would not only organize an election but also stand to gain governmental authority, they understandably balked. Kissinger could not convince Thieu that the U.S.-proposed Committee of National Reconciliation would not become a coalition government. Kissinger reasoned that since each side would appoint half of the third segment, Saigon would possess a double veto. Thieu, however, was convinced that any tripartite body was the first step toward a coalition government.[62] Nonetheless, he understood that he was powerless to stop Kissinger, since Saigon's interests were not directly represented at the private negotiations. Given Nixon's additional abandonment of the demand for mutual withdrawal, the Thieu administration decided it was time to use the one remaining weapon in its diplomatic arsenal vis-à-vis its superpower patron: recalcitrance. Even though Thieu received a personal letter from Nixon promising that the United States would never abandon its "brave ally," he rejected the American proposal for the CNR two days before the 15 September private meeting.[63] Kissinger noted in his memoirs that Saigon was no different from Hanoi, and possibly even worse: "Insolence is the armor of the weak; it is a device to induce courage in the face of one's panic. . . . In September 1972 a second Vietnamese party—our own ally—had managed to generate in me that impotent rage by which the Vietnamese have always tormented physically stronger opponents."[64]

As Nixon accepted the Republican Party's nomination for reelection as president on 22 August, Hanoi leaders formulated a negotiating policy for the fall of 1972. According to Luu Van Loi, Tho and Thuy painted two pessimistic scenarios for the Politburo. If Nixon decided to settle the Vietnam problem before the elections, then the political struggle would be fierce and fighting would resume in the near future. If Nixon decided not to settle before the elections and was successful at the polls, then the situation would be very difficult for the DRV. The North Vietnamese negotiators identified late September and October as a crucial period during which VWP forces had to maintain the military initiative in South Vietnam and launch diplomatic and political offensives in order to force Nixon to settle before the elections. Although Le Duc Tho and Xuan Thuy now warned Hanoi not to "pin too much hope" on a McGovern victory, the VWP's military, diplomatic, and political struggles should still try to bring about Nixon's defeat at the polls.[65] Time was of the essence not only because of the upcoming U.S. presidential elections, but also because of the increasing demand for peace in North Vietnam. According to East European sources, DRV officials had admitted that the people were "tired of war" and that VWP leaders needed to work toward a negotiated solution even though disagreements existed within the leadership.[66] Combined with the spike in CIA psyops that year, the work of Minister of Public Security Hoan seemed to never end.

## "AMERICAN WITHDRAWAL—PUPPET COLLAPSE"

With September and October presenting a pivotal period in negotiations, Hanoi's diplomatic machinery worked overtime to prepare. VWP decision making in the diplomatic realm, just as in the military and political ones, remains a mystery. We now have a clearer picture of the foreign policy apparatus during the war thanks to the recent writings of former participants. With the start of peace talks in 1968, Bureau II, a special foreign affairs unit responsible for the analysis and study of the United States, became an important apparatus in the Foreign Ministry. Nguyen Co Thach, who would later become SRV foreign minister, and Phan Hien directed the bureau, which included three subcommittees, or "cells": "Administrative and Logistics Affairs" under Le Tan, "Settlement" under Dinh Nho Liem, and "Steps" under DRV delegate-general Vo Van Sung. In early 1971, Bureau II was transformed into the CP50, with an enlarged staff of director-level cadres and specialists. At that point, Phan Hien and Vo Van Sung were transferred to Paris, where they joined Le Duc Tho's team since the "special advisor" believed that the talks would soon "begin in earnest." According to Sung, the secret talks team from early 1971 to the end of the summer 1972 consisted of Tho, Xuan Thuy, Phan Hien, himself, and their interpreter, Nguyen Dinh Phuong. Sung does not place Luu Van Loi in France until the "draft agreement" stage, when virtually all CP50 cadres were transferred to Paris.[67]

Sung can remember clearly when he was called to direct the Steps cell under Bureau II. Le Duc Tho had summoned Sung to his office at 6 Nguyen Canh Chan Street, north of Ba Dinh Square, in Hanoi to give him his orders. Rather than lay out the responsibilities of Sung's new post, Tho "said nothing about the substance of the work I would be performing. Instead, he focused all of his comments on just one single issue: the responsibility of keeping secrets." Although they had worked together for many years and were friends, Tho warned Sung: "The cell that you will be in charge of is a place that possesses a tremendous number of our secrets in this struggle against the enemy—secrets ranging from strategy to specific matters—military, political, and diplomatic secrets. For that reason, you must always ensure that you maintain secrecy and security. If you leak a secret, I will not simply discipline you—I will recommend that you be thrown into prison!"[68] In fact, Tho told Sung that a previous director had been removed after he talked about the bureau's plans to someone outside the group. The tough words made a deep impression and helped Sung understand the gravity of his responsibilities. He later came to believe that the "historic clash between the Vietnamese revolution's fledgling diplomatic service and the veteran diplomats of a superpower" led to diplomatic victory in 1973 as well as total victory in 1975.[69]

The Steps cell Sung directed worked in tandem with the Settlement cell. While the latter determined what "scenarios" the DRV could accept, the former provided "initiatives," namely, the various peace proposals, which it called "diplomatic attacks."[70] Sung's team had to be aware of what the Settlement group defined as acceptable scenarios at any given time, without losing perspective of the Party's ultimate objective: "American withdrawal—Puppet collapse." The debate in the Party and Foreign Ministry centered on the order of these two goals. While some believed that since the "Americans and puppets were organically connected, [the Party] had to simultaneously shatter the will of both the master and the servant," others argued that U.S. withdrawal should be achieved first through negotiations. Le Duan sided with the former by focusing on "the puppet collapse" that would automatically result in American withdrawal. Only after his military plans failed with the ARVN's recapture of Quang Tri City did Le Duan accept that the diplomatic struggle had to prioritize "American troop withdrawal" first and foremost. At this point, Sung and his Steps cell had to recalibrate what concessions the Party could make in order to "clear the way" for the opponent to escape from the impasse and for the DRV delegation to shepherd the negotiations that would be most beneficial to the Party.

Another member of the CP50, Doan Huyen, who was assigned to a military advisory group, suggested to Director Nguyen Co Thach in the wake of Quang Tri that the Party should "lower our demands, to some extent at least, on the South Vietnamese political issue." Huyen's team debated the relative merits of a tripartite coalition government, a government of national reconciliation, and a committee for the peaceful reconciliation of the nation. As events would soon reveal, the exact wording of the political constitution of postagreement South Vietnam would prove extremely important.[71] While Saigon warned the United States not to accept any tripartite body that could become a Trojan horse for a coalition government, Washington naively believed that Saigon could dominate any watered-down commission created only to facilitate elections. Hanoi, of course, sought a stronger apparatus—preferably a governmental body—that would oversee, not just facilitate, elections and the transition. The subsequent war over the wording of the draft agreement proved no small skirmish; South Vietnam's political future was on the line.

Thus, new publications reveal that Hanoi's diplomatic struggle was carefully planned and coordinated. The DRV and PRG delegations followed orders resulting from the research of these secretive committees under the ultimate direction of Le Duc Tho and Le Duan. These new sources also reveal that the failure of the 1972 Spring–Summer Offensive to topple the Saigon regime—Le Duan's bid for victory using his improved GO-GU strategy—in the late summer of 1972 finally prompted the first secretary to negotiate seriously. This meant focusing on "American withdrawal" through negotiations and shelving "puppet collapse" by not only abandoning Hanoi's military aims to topple the Saigon regime but also eventually dropping the demand for Thieu's ouster in Paris.

While the various sectors in the CP50 compiled their analyses, Party leaders sought to increase the possibility of a negotiated settlement before the U.S. presidential elections by launching a public relations campaign aimed at increasing mobilization at home and generating sympathy abroad. Through radio and print, Hanoi leaders castigated Nixon for prolonging the war and for refusing to settle.[72] On 2 September, Pham Van Dong delivered a scathing speech on National Day calling on the United States to end its military activities in Indochina.[73] A week later, Le Duc Tho echoed Dong's speech in his public remarks on his arrival at the airport in Paris.[74] At the same time, the PRG issued a statement condemning the United States for its policy of Vietnamization in South Vietnam, expansion of the war to all of Indochina, and massive bombing of North Vietnam. In addition, the PRG reiterated its seven-point proposal, calling on the United States to abandon its support for Thieu and to recognize the reality of two governments, two armies, and three political forces in South Vietnam.[75] In order to increase pressure on Nixon, the DRV released three American prisoners of war to the antiwar movement and received McGovern's special envoy in Hanoi.[76]

As Hanoi focused on its public relations campaign, Washington sought to use superpower diplomacy. Prior to the September meeting, Kissinger met with Soviet leaders in Moscow, where he revealed that he would meet Le Duc Tho for the "final push," but that Hanoi had to "clinch the deal."[77] Although Brezhnev declined to mediate, claiming that it was not the position of the Soviet Union to get involved, Kissinger was still confident that the United States had successfully isolated the North Vietnamese from their allies. Comments made by PRG officials and editorials in *Nhan Dan* (The People's Daily) reveal that Kissinger was correct.[78] Vietnamese communist leaders indirectly blamed the Soviets and the Chinese for compounding the military losses sustained in the Spring–Summer Offensive. Without citing the parties directly, Hanoi castigated the CPSU and the CCP for sacrificing "proletarian internationalism to accommodate American imperialists and their policy of reconciliation."[79] Both the Soviet Union and the PRC had acted narrowly by placing their nations' geostrategic interests over their internationalist duties. Moreover, Hanoi required more action from Beijing and Moscow, not mere promises or hollow declarations. "The vitality of Marxism-Leninism and proletariat internationalism manifests itself in revolutionary deeds, not in empty words. Though that enhanced the strategic position of the Communist powers, it weakened the revolutionary movement and with it the 'heroic' cause of the Vietnamese people."[80] Just as the VWP entered the crucial fall season of negotiations, it increased the pressure on its allies to toe the Marxist-Leninist line and back North Vietnam militarily.

Kissinger, meanwhile, had ample reason to be confident when he walked into the seventeenth private meeting with Tho on 15 September. Not only was he convinced of the success of superpower diplomacy, but Saigon forces had just scored a major victory by retaking Quang Tri. Chiding the North Vietnamese for the recent public relations campaign that included releasing three American prisoners and for allowing the PRG to call for the ousting of Thieu, Kissinger warned Tho and Thuy that the window to settle on reasonable terms was about to close for Hanoi, since Nixon would be reelected in November. The national security advisor then presented a new ten-point peace plan that included the proposed Committee of National Reconciliation even though Thieu had rejected this idea, fearful that any tripartite body constituted a slippery slope to a coalition government.[81]

Rather than discuss Kissinger's proposal, however, Tho indicated that Hanoi was indeed ready to settle and put forth the DRV's new concessions. Instead of a tripartite government of national reconciliation that would call for the elimination of the PRG and the Saigon regime, the North Vietnamese proposed a government of national reconciliation (GNR). Existing alongside the PRG and the Saigon administrations, the GNR would only oversee compliance with the agreement and have limited control over internal affairs. Most important, Hanoi finally dropped its demand for Thieu's ouster. In addition to these momentous concessions regarding political matters in South Vietnam, Hanoi was prepared to extend the timeframe for U.S. troop withdrawal from thirty to forty-five days. Kissinger was flabbergasted by Hanoi's generosity and was now convinced that his enemies were serious about ending the war.[82] After a brief discussion regarding the possibility of Kissinger visiting Hanoi, the U.S. negotiator proposed that if a workable timetable could be agreed to by both parties, he envisioned a settlement by 15 October (if not before), but added that everything should be completely finished by the end of November. According to Luu Van Loi, Le Duc Tho and Xuan Thuy did not pay attention to the second part of Kissinger's statement and so immediately accepted the 15 October deadline. "From the bottom of their hearts," Loi wrote, "they were glad that they had cleverly pushed the other side to say what they themselves wished to hear."[83]

Prior to the next private meeting, set for the end of the month, Foreign

Minister Trinh updated Tho and Thuy on the Politburo's analysis of the DRV's negotiating options. Although the Politburo believed that the talks had reached the point of producing a settlement, the time to resolve the outstanding issues was short if 15 October remained the deadline. As a result, the Party leadership needed to reassess what issues it could exploit to procure a settlement. Moreover, the Politburo could not agree whether Kissinger's visit to Hanoi should take place before or after a settlement. Some members wanted to wait until an agreement was signed and sealed whereas others believed that an agreement on the fundamentals would be enough to host the U.S. national security advisor. Trinh only relayed Le Duan's opinion. The first secretary deemed it acceptable to invite Kissinger before signing an agreement in order to sound out his position regarding the scope of America's long-term strategy. Moreover, Le Duan argued that perhaps the United States was holding out on certain issues until Hanoi issued an invitation to Kissinger.[84] Two days later, Trinh indicated that he would send a draft of the protocol and agreement to Paris with Ha Van Lau and Luu Van Loi.[85] The final Politburo communication before the 26 September meeting included the VWP's proposal for Cuba and Hungary to be the nations represented in the new international commission to oversee implementation of the agreement and cease-fire.[86]

On 26 and 27 September, Tho and Kissinger met at a different locale, since the French and international media had discovered their regular meeting place. In his memoirs, Kissinger described the private residence of a French Communist Party member in the country town of Gif-sur-Yvette as "pleasant and elegant," a marked improvement from the dingy quarters at 11 Rue Darthé.[87] At the start of the first day of talks, Tho wanted clarification on the 15 October deadline that had begun to worry the North Vietnamese leadership since the 15 September private meeting. Did the United States really want to sign a comprehensive settlement on or before 15 October or did it intend to drag out negotiations until after the presidential elections? Kissinger, appearing less eager to settle, stated that November 1 was more realistic. Undeterred, Tho brought up the matter of the national security advisor's visit to Hanoi, allowing Kissinger to reiterate his desire to visit the DRV capital sooner rather than later. Tho then conveyed Le Duan's interest in having Kissinger visit Hanoi after the two sides reached an agreement on fundamental issues but before a formal treaty. Hanoi's eagerness for a settlement was evident when Tho presented what he called the DRV's final offer. After the second meeting on 27 September, the remaining issues included the nature of the tripartite political apparatus, the deadline for the withdrawal of American troops, the details regarding prisoner releases, reparations, and the military and political situation in Cambodia and Laos. Regarding the most important issue, Tho proposed a "Provisional Government of National Concord," which still excluded Thieu. Although Kissinger failed to get Tho to promise the withdrawal of North Vietnamese troops from the South, the Hanoi leader admitted for the first time that PAVN forces were present in Cambodia and Laos and promised, off the record, to withdraw those forces after a ceasefire. At the close of the meeting, Tho stated that he hoped the remaining issues could be worked out within the month and that Kissinger could come to Hanoi and work out the details there.[88]

After the meeting, the DRV delegation in Paris informed the Politburo that they would deliver the DRV's note to Kissinger expressing Hanoi's desire for both sides to view the upcoming three-day meeting as of "utmost importance [*vo cung quang trong*]." Moreover, Hanoi leaders conveyed their hope for constructive negotiations and a settlement based on the agreed timetable. If these were not produced, the North Vietnamese warned, the Nixon administration would have to accept the responsibility for prolonging the war.[89] Foreign Minister Trinh's private message to the DRV negotiators, according to Luu Van Loi, was less optimistic.[90] After meeting to assess the 26–27 September talks, the Politburo concluded that Nixon and Kissinger were not interested in signing an agreement until after the November elections and that the United States still intended to maintain the Saigon regime.[91]

Although Kissinger had been willing to accept a "decent interval" strategy since December 1970, he did not want Thieu to discover his plans in September 1972. Even though substantial progress had been made toward a settlement during the eleventh-hour meeting on 26–27 September, Kissinger instructed Ambassador Bunker to tell Thieu that "there was no significant progress and no agreements of any kind were reached."[92] The South Vietnamese president, however, no longer believed what he was told regarding the U.S.-DRV private talks. In late September, he launched a public relations campaign that accused the DRV of offering a "trick" solution in Paris. On 29 September, Thieu spoke at Saigon University, warning that the acceptance of a coalition government would sound the death knell for the RVN. In the former imperial city of Hue, the South Vietnamese president criticized a "small number of political speculators, lackeys, and exiles who call themselves a Third Force in South Vietnam," hoping to neu-

tralize the group that could act as a balance between the Saigon administration and the PRG.[93]

Nixon sent his deputy assistant for national security affairs to reason
with the South Vietnamese president. The first day of meetings on 2 October went well. Thieu listened quietly as Haig presented the offer that the
United States intended to propose at the 8 October meeting with the North
Vietnamese.[94] On the following day, however, Thieu and his retinue of advisors adopted a much less conciliatory posture.[95] The South Vietnamese
leaders proceeded to tear apart the American proposal, criticized Kissinger
for never requesting Saigon's input, and strongly advised the United States
to reject any Hanoi proposal that included a tripartite body.[96] Although
Nixon oscillated between sympathizing with Thieu and giving Kissinger
the green light to settle, on the eve of the 8 October meeting, the U.S. president opted to threaten his South Vietnamese counterpart by telling Ambassador Bunker to make veiled references to a coup.[97]

### PEACE WITHIN GRASP

Just as South Vietnamese leaders became more obstinate, North Vietnamese negotiators appeared ready to compromise. The period directly
before the upcoming private meeting scheduled for 8–10 October found
DRV leaders in a frenzy of activity. Exchanges between Le Duc Tho in
Paris and Le Duan in Hanoi reveal that the Party leadership was in agree-
ment regarding the DRV's need to conclude a settlement before the U.S.
presidential elections.[98] The CP50, under the direction of Foreign Minister Trinh, prepared several draft agreements and submitted them to the
Politburo for review; two were accepted: the Treaty to End the War and
Restore Peace in Vietnam and the Agreement on the South Vietnamese
People's Right to Self-Determination.[99] By the end of September, Luu Van
Loi and Doan Huyen of the CP50 were entrusted to personally deliver the
draft agreements to Tho in Paris.[100]

Based on the Politburo's instructions, Tho and Thuy intended to demand a cease-fire and American withdrawal and be prepared to compromise on political issues for South Vietnam. This constituted what the
United States had pushed for since the start of the war: a two-track negotiating policy of dealing with the military issues first and allowing the South
Vietnamese parties to settle internal issues later. Although Hanoi leaders
stated at the time and after the war that the DRV had finally arrived at a

position of strength to push forward a settlement in the fall of 1972, the DRV's position was in fact more ambiguous. By October, the military balance of power in South Vietnam, the domestic picture in North Vietnam, and the international situation placed the DRV in a disadvantageous position vis-à-vis the United States and the RVN. Hanoi leaders shifted to prioritizing their less ambitious objectives—a cease-fire and American withdrawal—and dropped their maximum aims—toppling or getting rid of the Thieu regime—in order to secure a settlement before Nixon's reelection, escape any greater damage to the communist war effort, and prevent Vietnamization from further strengthening Saigon and its forces.

In order to prepare for a settlement, the DRV increased its political activities at home and diplomatic campaign abroad. In preparation for a national "Call to Arms [*Loi keu goi*]" aimed at bringing the world's attention to the destructive nature of Nixon's war, the Party secretariat ordered VWP cadres to document all of the damage done to the cities, towns, and villages across the DRV as a result of American bombs.[101] Politburo member and the Minister of Propaganda To Huu, using his nom de guerre, Lanh, told South Vietnamese commanders to expect detailed instructions regarding preparations for the upcoming political struggle following a settlement in Paris.[102] While communist forces prepared themselves for a cease-fire, the DRV sent two separate delegations to "secure the support of the Soviet Union and China and to increase pressure on the U.S." by sharing the DRV's draft agreement that would be presented to Kissinger at the upcoming private meeting.[103] In early October, Trinh traveled to Moscow while Minister of Finance Le Thanh Nghi headed to Beijing. According to Luu Van Loi, both allies praised the North Vietnamese draft agreement, supported Hanoi's terms, and promised resolute support.[104]

On 8 October, Kissinger, along with General Haig, who had flown directly from Saigon, met with Le Duc Tho in Paris for what would become a four-day marathon of talks. The morning session on the first day of meetings began in the customary manner: Kissinger and Tho discussed the previous peace plans presented at the late September meeting and the new U.S. position, which addressed minor details in the modalities of the military issues and slight modifications to the political terms.[105] When the talks resumed in the afternoon, however, Tho veered from the usual script. Instead of launching into a lengthy diatribe on American perfidy, he began his comments with cheer and goodwill. Presenting the Agreement on Ending the War and Restoring Peace in Vietnam, Tho held Kissinger and Haig in rapt attention.[106] "We cannot allow the South Vietnamese political question to be the most difficult issue to prolong negotiations; we can quickly end the war."[107] With those words, Tho handed Kissinger the DRV's first ever comprehensive plan, based on the respective North Vietnamese and U.S. ten-point plans presented on 26 September 1972, which made two major concessions. Hanoi proposed an "administration of national concord," rather than a "government" and accepted the separation of military from political issues.[108] Kissinger immediately grasped the significance of Tho's proposal and later described that moment as the most thrilling in all his years of public service.[109] The remainder of the talks concentrated on hammering out a few minor details and forging a timetable for the signing of the agreement.

The following day, 9 October, Kissinger presented Xuan Thuy with a regimental necktie that he had promised the day before and Tho with the U.S. counterproposal. After Kissinger went through the counterproposal article by article, comparing it with Tho's draft, he directed most of the day's discussion to his impending visit to Hanoi.[110] Although the end of the second day of talks ended on a positive note as Kissinger indicated his desire to visit the Ho Chi Minh Trail, the U.S. delegation sent Nixon's new stringent demands to the North Vietnamese delegation later that night. The president wanted reassurance on military guarantees, including the permanence of the cease-fire, in return for the cessation of bombing. When the delegations met on 10 October, Tho criticized the U.S. delegation for trying to place greater pressure on the North Vietnamese and throwing up roadblocks to peace. "Yesterday night you sent us a message," Tho stated, "which complicated the settlement on the Vietnam problem."[111] Kissinger tried to placate Tho by recognizing that although Hanoi had gone to great lengths toward peace in its proposal, the United States still had many different parties who would carefully scrutinize the implementation of the agreement. "Mr. Special Advisor," Kissinger appealed to Tho, "when you get to know America better you will think that this will be a superhuman effort to get this accepted in Washington by everybody who will have to defend it. Because if we don't make a peace that has genuine support it will not last."[112] When the meeting ended, Kissinger sent pleading messages to Nixon and Chief of Staff H. R. Haldeman urging them to remain steady and not lose faith in the negotiating process.

After receiving an update from the negotiators on the progress of the talks, the Politburo sent instructions to Tho and Thuy in Paris on 10 October. Hanoi leaders urged the North Vietnamese delegation to remain vigilant and not to budge on the timetable in order to force the Americans to sign before the U.S. presidential election. If the DRV negotiators could convince the Americans to come to an agreement on fundamental issues before the end of the private meeting, then Kissinger could come visit Hanoi on 19 October. The Politburo proceeded to outline the DRV's final negotiating stance on the remaining military, political, reparations, and international issues. Hanoi wanted agreement on four issues: (1) a cease-fire in place rather than the withdrawal of North Vietnamese troops; (2) U.S. recognition of two administrations and two armed forces as well as an administration of national concord consisting of three forces; (3) a written statement regarding reparations; and (4) the rejection of an additional, fifth nation to any international control commission.[113]

Equipped with fresh instructions from Hanoi for the final session on 11 October, Le Duc Tho and Xuan Thuy negotiated with Kissinger for sixteen hours. The meeting did not end until 2:00 A.M. the following day. Much of the discussion centered on the situation in Cambodia and Laos. When Kissinger brought up the issue of the withdrawal of North Vietnamese troops from the neighboring countries, Tho spoke candidly about Hanoi's ability to produce a lasting cease-fire in Laos but not Cambodia. In the former, the Pathet Lao had already offered to enter into talks with the Royal Lao Government. Although Tho could not promise the withdrawal of Chinese forces from Laos, he indicated that one month after a cease-fire in Vietnam, North Vietnamese troops would put down their arms in Laos and withdraw eastward. "Objectively speaking, the problem of Cambodia," the Tho admitted, was "different from that of Laos."[114] The situation there was more "complicated," he confessed, since negotiations had not been broached by the either the Cambodian communists or the Lon Nol government.[115] In reality, Hanoi could not guarantee a cease-fire for Cambodia since Vietnamese and Khmer communist forces had stopped coordinating military activities.[116] Tho opted not to reveal the troubled state of Khmer-Vietnamese relations to Kissinger, who merely stated, "I understand that with relation to Cambodia your political situation is much more difficult than with relation to Laos, because your friends in Cambodia live in Peking."[117] The nineteenth private meeting concluded with Kissinger's proposed timetable, according to which the agreement would be signed by the end of the month.[118] "The real victory for both," Kissinger stated as the meeting adjourned, "will now be the durable relations we can establish with each other. . . . And we know you will be as dedicated to the pursuit of peace as you have been in the fighting of a war."[119] These words would prove premature, as the draft agreement confronted obstacles in the "war over the wording" on the bloody path to peace.

SABOTAGING PEACE

When Kissinger returned to Washington, he "somewhat exultantly" told Nixon that it appeared that the administration had been successful in scoring its three diplomatic goals for 1972: rapprochement with China, détente with the Soviet Union, and settlement of the Vietnam problem.[120] Nixon celebrated with filet mignon and a 1957 bottle of Lafite-Rothschild as he listened to Kissinger's proposed timetable but stopped long enough to point out the potential problem to Kissinger's plan: gaining Thieu's approval.[121] Meanwhile, Hanoi's excellent espionage apparatus had already detected the storm brewing over Saigon. While in private talks with Kissinger, Le Duc Tho and Nguyen Duy Trinh received an update on the Saigon political scene from "Anh Bay Cuong," otherwise known as COSVN commander Pham Hung. The message stated that COSVN had obtained inside information on Thieu's early October meetings with General Haig. Pham Hung reported that, according to Thieu's "political advisor and private secretary," after the tense meeting on 4 October the South Vietnamese president called an urgent meeting of his national security council to hash out a strategy to obstruct any American plan to agree to a cease-fire before the U.S. presidential election.[122]

At this juncture, U.S. leaders set out to prevent Thieu from repeating his 1968 performance. Although Thieu's defiance of Johnson during the 1968 presidential election had boosted Nixon's chances over Humphrey, Kissinger could not imagine that Thieu would do the same for McGovern, even if he was unhappy with Nixon. The greater fear, according to Kissinger, was that Thieu would try to hold out for better terms after Nixon's reelection. Since the national security advisor wanted to secure his position in the administration for the second term and make his mark on history, he sought to conclude the peace agreement before November. On 14 October, Ambassador Bunker met with Thieu, who still had not showed any sign of displeasure with the United States or any impending disobedience, to instruct the South Vietnamese leader to prepare for a cease-fire in place by regaining as much territory as possible. Two days later, President Nixon sent his South Vietnamese ally a letter of reassurance that any agreement would provide for the security of Thieu's government, armed forces, and political institutions.[123] In a telephone conversation with Nixon, Kissinger was more confident that Thieu would accept the agreement: "There's no sophisticate who will not see that this is the thinnest form of face-saver for the other [side]. . . . Thieu stays, there's no coalition government, the negotiations start. Then they form a sort of half-ass committee."[124] Just to be safe, however, Kissinger contemplated giving Thieu an earlier version of the settlement with worse terms to scare him into acquiescence. In the end, he waited until 18 October to send off the genuine draft agreement.[125]

After his arrival in Saigon, Kissinger was dismayed to learn that Thieu had already obtained the text of the draft agreement from South Vietnamese intelligence and that the text of the agreement and instructions on how it should be implemented were already being circulated to communist forces in South Vietnam down to the district level. Trembling with anger, Thieu could not believe that Kissinger had conceded so much to Hanoi. Not only had the United States allowed North Vietnamese troops to remain in South Vietnam after a cease-fire and granted them access through the demilitarized zone while Washington promised a total and complete American withdrawal with no residual forces, but Kissinger had agreed to a tripartite governmental commission with the National Council of National Reconciliation and Concord (NCNRC) that would oversee the election for a new government.[126] While the United States described the NCNRC in more ambiguous terms as an "administrative structure," in the English text, Hanoi had managed to strengthen that body in the Vietnamese text by referring to it as a "co cau chinh quyen," which translates as "governmental structure." "In anger and sadness," Thieu convened a high-level meeting of his closest advisors to discuss the extent of American betrayal and how best to deal with Kissinger's upcoming visit to Saigon.[127]

It was apparent that the U.S.-RVN alliance was on its last legs. When Kissinger arrived at the Independence Palace on 19 October, Thieu kept Kissinger and his entourage waiting for fifteen minutes in the reception room.[128] Received by an aloof Thieu, Kissinger presented a letter from Nixon indicating that he had full support of the president. After listening to Kissinger's summary of the private meetings with Tho and Thuy over the summer and fall, Thieu asked frankly if Nixon needed to sign the agreement before or after the presidential election. Kissinger responded by quoting Nixon's handwritten note: "Dear Henry, as you leave for Paris I thought it would be useful for you to have some guidance that we were talking about on paper. First, do what is right without regard to the election. . . . Secondly, we cannot let a chance to end the war honorably slip away."[129] By the afternoon session, however, American officials believed that Thieu was moving toward a settlement, since he seemed eager to discuss Enhance Plus, an accelerated program replacing Operation Enhance that began in late August 1972 to equip South Vietnamese forces with sufficient ground and air equipment to wage war against the Vietnamese communists after American withdrawal.[130] When Thieu's national security council joined the meeting, Kissinger finally handed over a single copy of the draft agreement in English, but did not inform his hosts that he was due in Hanoi immediately after his visit to Saigon in order to initial the agreement.[131]

According to Thieu's closest advisor and cousin, Hoang Duc Nha, it was immediately apparent to South Vietnamese leaders that the agreement was "tantamount to surrender" and that it confirmed the veracity of South Vietnam's captured intelligence.[132] Neither the RVN president nor his closest aide showed any sign of emotion at the time; Thieu later revealed that he wanted to punch Kissinger in the mouth.[133] Even without the original Vietnamese text, Saigon leaders proceeded to pick apart the draft agreement without conveying their doubts to the Americans. In particular, South Vietnamese officials feared that the reference to the National Council of National Reconciliation and Concord was in fact a coalition in disguise in the Vietnamese text. Since the Saigon leaders only had the English text, they later wrote in their memoirs that they believed Hanoi's translation of "administrative structure" in Vietnamese was "co cau chinh quyen" rather than "co cau hanh chanh."[134] Although similar, the latter expression is closer in meaning to the English word *administrative*, while the former could mean "governmental." North Vietnamese documents written at the time reveal that Hanoi leaders had taken advantage of the ambiguity to use the latter terminology, "co cau chinh quyen" — a governmental structure.

Without the Vietnamese text, Thieu only raised his long-standing objection to the presence of 140,000 North Vietnamese troops in South Vietnam at the 20 October meeting. Kissinger, confident that he had smoothed over these doubts, insisted that the draft was the best agreement possible for the RVN and left the meeting convinced that he had "made some progress."[135] Thieu was less confident and proposed a meeting for the following day between Kissinger and South Vietnamese foreign minister Tran Van Lam to discuss the original North Vietnamese version that was due to arrive in Saigon shortly.[136] On the morning of 21 October, Kissinger had an "extremely well tempered" meeting with Lam, who proposed twenty-three changes to the draft agreement. Kissinger deemed sixteen of them acceptable, while the seven unacceptable changes concerned North Vietnamese forces and political provisions. Kissinger tried to assuage RVN concerns regarding PAVN forces in the South by echoing General Abrams's comment, made during the previous day's meetings, that these weakened northern forces would soon wither away after the cease-fire for lack of reinforcement.[137]

Although Kissinger remained optimistic after his morning meeting with Lam, troubles began brewing when Thieu postponed their afternoon meeting. When South Vietnamese leaders received the Vietnamese text, their worst fears were confirmed, placing the remainder of the meetings with Kissinger in jeopardy. Merle Pribbenow, the CIA's Vietnamese expert in Saigon, recalls that RVN officials did not raise any vociferous objections until they were presented with the Vietnamese text. Pribbenow and his boss, the CIA chief of station in Saigon Thomas Polgar, were called into Ambassador Bunker's office so that Pribbenow could verify the South Vietnamese objections to the language in the Vietnamese draft agreement. There, Pribbenow confirmed that Hanoi had exploited the linguistic ambiguity concerning the tripartite commission by using "co cau chinh quyen," and thus differed from the English-language text agreed to at the October private meetings.[138] As a result, Hoang Duc Nha encouraged Thieu to cancel the meeting with Kissinger scheduled for later that day.[139] When Bunker and Kissinger learned of the cancellation, they immediately demanded to see the South Vietnamese president but were denied access by Thieu's advisors. Kissinger fumed on the phone to Nha: "I am the Special Envoy of the President of the United States of America. You know I cannot be treated as an errand boy."[140] Nha, unmoved by Kissinger's wrath, simply hung up the phone.

Kissinger's role in the "war over the wording" of the Vietnamese draft agreement is ambiguous. Comparing his memoir and the recent *FRUS* volumes, the national security advisor appears to have misled both parties on numerous occasions regarding this issue. On 20 October, Nixon and Kissinger had ordered U.S. Air Force attaché to France Colonel Guay, the middleman for relaying messages to the North Vietnamese in Paris, to inform the North Vietnamese that the text of the draft agreement could now be considered complete.[141] During the meetings with Thieu and other South Vietnamese officials, however, he claimed that the issue of translation of the terms in question was still up in the air and was to be resolved at a later date. Moreover, Kissinger claims in his memoir that U.S. officials were already aware of Hanoi's linguistic manipulation of the draft agreement and had rejected North Vietnamese attempts to use the stronger phrasing for the NCNRC at the technical meeting on 12 October.[142] However, either Kissinger never managed to relay that to Thieu and other South Vietnamese officials or the United States never detected Hanoi's manipulation in the first place.[143] Since Hanoi's modus operandi, carefully designed by the CP50, included treating the English and Vietnamese texts separately, North Vietnamese negotiators could concede terms in the English draft while maintaining its language in the Vietnamese version. Kissinger was perhaps unaware of Hanoi's sleight of hand at the negotiations.[144]

As U.S. and RVN officials engaged in a battle of wills in Saigon, North Vietnamese leaders moved on a diplomatic offensive to ensure the agreement. On 18 October, Prime Minister Dong granted an exclusive interview to Arnaud de Borchgrave of *Newsweek* in which he revealed that Hanoi considered the NCNRC to be a coalition and dismissed Thieu's role in the council.[145] At virtually the same time, although because of the time difference it was only 17 October in Paris, Xuan Thuy met with Kissinger, who had stopped in Paris on the way to meet Thieu in Saigon, in order to discuss the fate of 30,000 detainees.[146] On 19 October, Hanoi leaders agreed to concede to U.S. demands and accept the release of all prisoners except PLAF cadres. Two days later, the DRV relented on the final issues regarding Cambodia and Laos.[147] In order to buy time, the United States pushed back the original timetable and proposed the cessation of bombing and mining for 23 October, Kissinger's visit to Hanoi for 24 October, and the signing of the agreement on Halloween day. On 22 October, the U.S. delegation in Paris sent a note to the North Vietnamese stating that although Hanoi had met all of the U.S. demands, it warned the DRV not to take public actions and castigated Dong for his interview with de Borchgrave.[148] According to Luu Van Loi, "the US scheme to not sign the agreement according to the timetable became clear" to Hanoi leaders.[149]

Although it is hard to discern which Vietnamese party held Kissinger in greater contempt and disdain, Thieu's handwritten notes from his 22 October meeting with Nixon's ambitious "errand boy" might point toward South Vietnam. When Saigon leaders found out about the *Newsweek* interview early on the morning of the scheduled meeting, they had proof of U.S. duplicity. Kissinger, who was unaware that South Vietnamese leaders knew about Dong's interview, arrived for his early evening meeting with Thieu at the palace refreshed from his "toast to peace" with Lon Nol in

Phnom Penh.[150] Thieu began the meeting in a severe tone by saying, "I have a right to expect that the U.S. has connived with the Soviets and China to sell out South Vietnam. Now that you recognize the presence of [the] North Vietnamese here, the South Vietnamese people will assume that we have been sold out by the U.S. and that North Viet-Nam has won the war."[151] Personalizing the betrayal, Thieu believed that his "good friends had failed" him and that his greatest satisfaction would only be to sign a peace agreement. Kissinger, who did not possess a high regard for the South Vietnamese president, responded: "I admire the courage and heroism which have characterized your speech. However, as an American I can only deeply resent your suggestion that we have connived with the Soviets and Chinese. How can you conceive this possible when the President on May 8 [Linebacker] risked his whole political future to come to your assistance? When we talked with the Soviets and Chinese, it was to exert pressure on Hanoi."[152] Although he tried to convince Thieu that the United States did not intend on abandoning him, Kissinger ended the meeting on a bitter note. Stating that Thieu was parting on a "suicidal" course not only for himself but for his country, Kissinger reminded Thieu that the United States had fought for years, had "mortgaged" the entirety of U.S. foreign policy "to the defense of one country."[153]

As Kissinger spoke, Thieu's frantically scribbled down notes, mainly in Vietnamese but with the occasional French and English curse words, which went haphazardly in all different directions on the paper. Furious at what he saw was tantamount to America's "surrender and humiliation," Thieu could not believe that the United States had appeased the "invader" by withdrawing American troops and agreeing to a coalition government. The more Kissinger spoke, the more apparent it became to Thieu that the RVN's issues were never raised by the U.S. negotiator during his secret and private talks with Hanoi. Thieu fumed as he listed three main problems confronting Saigon: the continued presence of North Vietnamese troops in the South, the potential for the NCNRC to be a mere decoy for a coalition government, and the inability to establish the DMZ as a secure border. Thieu must not have been happy with Kissinger's response to his grievances since he roughly outlined an alternate strategy. In a rare glimpse of small-power subversion in the making, the final section of Thieu's notes as Kissinger droned on included detailed plans on how to outmaneuver Kissinger and kill his draft agreement by launching a major press campaign.[154] South Vietnam would use the media in order to wage a battle of wills against not just the Vietnamese communists but also, and more important, the United States.

Kissinger's fortunes continued to decline when he left Saigon. After the disastrous meeting with South Vietnamese leaders, Kissinger cabled Hanoi that the timetable was no longer functional as a result of the DRV's unreasonable scheduling demands, the disastrous influence of Dong's interview in *Newsweek* on Saigon leaders, the question of PAVN troops in South Vietnam, and a host of other reasons.[155] Although Kissinger knew that his last minute change of plans would be received poorly in Hanoi, he had not given up hope. Kissinger proposed a meeting for 30 October to produce a settlement with or without Saigon's approval. In order to gain Hanoi's acquiescence to the new timetable, Kissinger enlisted the help of the Soviet Union and China.[156] On 23 October, the DRV delegation rejected Kissinger's request for a 30 October meeting and warned the United States that it must bear full responsibility for the consequences of prolonging negotiations and delaying a settlement. On the following day, however, Hanoi softened its tone and indicated that since an agreement had been reached, the DRV was "prepared to welcome Kissinger to Hanoi for initialing the Agreement and to officially sign it on 31 October 1972."[157] Since both Moscow and Beijing insisted that Hanoi approve the agreement, VWP leaders appeared to have caved to allied pressure. On 25 October, Soviet ambassador Ilya Scherbakov met twice with DRV prime minister Pham Van Dong, once at 2:00 A.M., and stated, "The Soviet leadership wishes that you would do everything possible so that what has been achieved will not turn into smoke. Vietnam should dispatch Le Duc Tho to Paris."[158]

However, Chinese and Soviet leaders may have pushed the North Vietnamese too far. On 26 October, Hanoi went public with the chronology of the private talks, the key terms of the draft agreement, and the abandoned timetable. The DRV demanded that the United States abide by its commitments and sign the agreement on 31 October 1972.[159] Le Duan prepared VWP forces within Vietnam to take advantage of the announcement by pushing forward the political struggle. The first secretary advised his southern commanders to impress on the South Vietnamese masses as well as the Saigon "puppet" officers and officials that Thieu had managed to sabotage the agreement and prevent peace from returning to Vietnam. Le Duan ordered his troops to rally the people, particularly in Saigon and Cho Lon, to overthrow Thieu and thus the final obstacle to peace, independence, and liberation.[160] A few hours after the DRV's announcement,

Kissinger held a press conference proclaiming his belief that "peace was at hand" but that an agreement could not be signed because of Hanoi's unrealistic timetable.[161] As the American media began to question whether Kissinger's televised appearance was designed to manipulate the presidential election, Nixon began to distance himself from his national security advisor. Not only had Kissinger failed to deliver an agreement that he confidently promised and in the process angered Thieu, but he also had begun to receive more coverage than the president.[162]

## "TWELVE DAYS OF DARKNESS"

According to North Vietnamese sources, the 26 October public announcements resulted in an outpouring of world support for Hanoi as DRV and PRG officials held press conferences there and in Paris to advance their cause.[163] In Hanoi's assessment, the majority of the international media reported sympathetically on the DRV's negotiating plight and called on Nixon to sign the agreement.[164] At midnight on 26 October, Zhou Enlai received representatives from the DRV and the PRG to express China's support of the VWP's decision to publicize the agreement. Although the Vietnamese noticed that the Chinese leader spent more time criticizing Thieu than castigating Nixon, they agreed with his advice to coordinate their negotiating strategy.[165] On 27 October, Soviet premier Alexei Kosygin met with DRV and PRG representatives in Moscow to inform them of the CPSU Politburo's decision reached the night before. The Soviet Union was solidly behind the VWP's announcement. Moreover, Moscow was prepared to exert pressure on Washington to conclude the war, but not to the extent that it would endanger negotiations. It no longer mattered to Kosygin if the signing of the agreement took place before or after the U.S. presidential election, which it was apparent Nixon would win.[166] On 27 October, the United States indicated its desire to meet on 1 November, but it received an ambiguous response on 30 October from the DRV stating that its leaders needed time to study the request and would respond in a few days.[167] On 4 November, Hanoi finally proposed a meeting for 14 November in order to show that Hanoi did not "pin its hopes" on the U.S. election.[168] On 7 November, Politburo member To Huu cabled Hanoi's man in the South, Pham Hung, with detailed instructions on how to maximize the Vietnamese communist position in the upcoming round of talks. The communication shows that the North and South Vietnamese communists collaborated on a negotiating strategy and that the PRG-NLF might not have possessed the agency or autonomy to break from Hanoi's will at this crucial point in negotiations.[169]

On 7 November, the same day he was reelected in a landslide, thus winning an overwhelming mandate for his Vietnam policy, Nixon acknowledged the DRV's note but pushed the private meeting to 15 November.[170] Facing an increasingly dovish Congress that identified Thieu as the only obstacle to American withdrawal from Southeast Asia, Nixon needed to resolve the Vietnam problem by dealing with not only Hanoi but also Saigon.[171] On 9 November, Nixon sent General Haig back to Saigon with a personal letter to the South Vietnamese president.[172] Prior to Haig's arrival, Ambassador Bunker had already informed Thieu of Kissinger's intention to meet with Le Duc Tho in mid-November and had outlined the U.S. negotiating position. First, the United States ensured that the NCNRC would not become a coalition government by replacing the DRV's "co cau chinh quyen [governmental structure]" with the RVN's "co cau hanh chanh [administrative structure]" and by stipulating that the NCNRC's functions would include only "promoting" and not "supervising" the implementation of the agreement. Once again, Hanoi exploited the difficulties in translation; it used "don doc," meaning "supervise," not "promote," which the South Vietnamese protested.[173] Regarding military issues, the United States would insist on the withdrawal of North Vietnamese troops and respect for the DMZ.[174] The purpose of Haig's visit, then, was to gain Thieu's acquiescence to the U.S. position by providing carrots and wielding sticks. The carrots included the benefits of Enhance Plus, the expedited transfer of approved Vietnamization equipment programs that by November consisted of twenty-nine Army items and nine Air Force items, including military supplies and bases to the RVN, and the promise of retaliation against North Vietnam if communist forces violated the agreement.[175] The sticks were that if Thieu did not abandon his current dangerous course, including "self-defeating" public "distortions," the U.S.-RVN alliance would fall apart and that Nixon might have no choice but to take what historian Jeffrey Kimball terms "brutal action" against Saigon.[176]

Although shaken over the course of the two-day meeting on 11 and 12 November, Thieu did not back down and presented Haig with South Vietnam's own demands for the upcoming Kissinger-Tho meeting, including total PAVN withdrawal before any Vietnamese election.[177] "With respect to troops in the South," Thieu stated, "this is a life or death issue."[178] The South Vietnamese president reasoned that if the duplicitous Kissinger remained as the U.S. negotiator during these private meetings, then Thieu had to make his voice heard. According to Haig, Thieu could not "bring himself to an open break with us. On the other hand, he [would] exercise every ploy in his dictionary to achieve further delay, hopefully without commitment."[179] This was exactly what Thieu did. Two days before the private meeting between Kissinger and Tho, which had been delayed further to 20 November because of Le Duc Tho's illness, Thieu presented Bunker with Saigon's sixty-nine suggested modifications.[180] Moreover, Thieu organized a task force to follow the negotiations and beefed up the RVN's presence in Paris. Sending Hoang Duc Nha to Paris, the South Vietnamese president equipped his relative with blank stationary that included his signature and presidential seal. Thieu wanted to make sure that he had his men ready to draft an immediate letter of protest to Nixon in case Kissinger sold out South Vietnam at the meeting.[181]

In an exchange of notes, Hanoi and Washington agreed to hold three rounds of talks until the signing of an agreement. The first would take place from 20 to 25 November, the second from 4 to 13 December, and the third from 8 to 13 January. The VWP entered these discussions with little room for maneuver for three reasons.[182] First, Saigon had resolved to utilize its opposition to a settlement as a weapon to ensure that the United States not capitulate to Hanoi's demands.[183] Thieu would only accept an agreement if Nixon really intended to cut off aid and sign a separate agreement with the DRV. Second, with reelection no longer a concern, Nixon was inclined to try extreme military force to extract more concessions from Hanoi and to placate Saigon.[184] Nixon's bombing and mining campaign in the summer of 1972 had produced results in the fall round of negotiations. Nixon reasoned that if Hanoi was ready to sign an agreement in October before the election, now faced with four more years, Hanoi might be convinced to compromise further by a brutal bombing campaign. Third, the DRV had no guarantee from China or the Soviet Union that either would intervene on its behalf if Nixon opted to use his overwhelming military might to punish Hanoi for its purported intransigence in Paris. Although Beijing and Moscow increased aid to help Hanoi defend itself from Nixon's bombs and mines, they coupled aid with increased pressure on Hanoi to settle.

Although North Vietnamese leaders claimed that they were no longer operating under a rushed timetable to settle, the Politburo still desired a speedy settlement based on the October draft and did not intend to retract any concessions or revert back to "*dam va danh* [talking while fighting]." The VWP leadership's overriding concern was to escape further destruction and damage to its war effort by American bombs in order to preserve its forces for battle against South Vietnamese troops after U.S. withdrawal. Since Nixon was in a position to exploit détente with the Soviet Union and China and use South Vietnam as an excuse to prolong negotiations, the Hanoi Politburo wanted to prevent any decline in the VWP's position at the negotiating table in Paris and on the military front in South Vietnam.[185] Although North Vietnamese leaders ordered their forces to go on the offensive in the Central Highlands as well as the Mekong Delta in order to "liberate" more territory, these were not large-scale attacks that would threaten the negotiations in Paris.[186]

During the first day of negotiations on 20 November, Le Duc Tho unleashed his fury on Kissinger by reading a stinging five-page denunciation of Washington's deception regarding the October peace. Compared to Vietnam's past dealings with the fascist Japanese and colonial French, Tho claimed, Hanoi found U.S. duplicity even more flagrant. Attempting to bring some levity to the tense meeting, Kissinger remarked that he had at least succeeded in unifying North and South Vietnam in a common hatred for him.[187] His attempts at humor and even gift-giving—Kissinger had presented Tho with a picture book of Harvard in case the "special advisor" agreed to teach a seminar on Marxism-Leninism there and had given a Steuben glass horse's head to Xuan Thuy, known for his fondness of horse racing—could not break the tension.[188] Tho remained in bad spirits as Kissinger grudgingly presented a list of sixty-nine modifications, dictated by Saigon's demands, which appeared impossible to resolve by the end of the month.[189] The more substantive revisions included wording surrounding the DMZ that would render illegal North Vietnamese troops below the seventeenth parallel, withdrawal of PAVN troops simultaneous with the release of political prisoners, changes to weaken the NCNRC, and striking any mention of the PRG.[190]

Although the Saigon regime was not present at the private negotiations, it made its presence known there. Thieu took special precautions to ensure that Kissinger presented Saigon's sixty-nine demands for changes to the agreement at the negotiating sessions. Not only did he equip Nha, as well as his special assistant for foreign affairs, Nguyen Phu Duc, with pre-signed official letterhead to send word to Nixon if Kissinger betrayed Saigon, Thieu dispatched his Washington, London, and Paris ambassadors to oversee the talks as well. This diplomatic entourage was not enough. Thieu also sent the defense chairman of the National Assembly, General Tran Van Don, who had close ties with the expatriate Vietnamese community in Paris, as well as his economic advisor, Nguyen Tien Hung, to fine-tune any resulting agreement.[191] Kissinger resented Thieu's beefed-up presence in Paris, especially since the national security advisor had to update three South Vietnamese diplomats every night on the negotiations at his private residence. According to Kissinger, Thieu had instructed the diplomats to accept Hanoi's surrender on all sixty-nine modifications—and nothing less.[192]

With Saigon exerting external pressure on the private negotiations, the Politburo predicted two possible outcomes for the November round of talks. If Tho could force Kissinger to drop the ridiculous demands and negotiate seriously again, then the war could end before 20 January 1973. If the United States allowed its "puppets" to drag out the negotiations, Politburo leaders surmised, then the war would continue for another three years. After reviewing Thieu's list, Le Duan and the Politburo instructed Tho and Thuy to remain steadfast, to protect the core principles of the October draft, and to only be flexible with minor details.[193] When Tho met with Kissinger on 21 November, he lambasted the list of modifications and presented his own set of new demands including striking any mention of the withdrawal of PAVN forces from South Vietnam since, he claimed, these troops were in fact volunteer forces fighting on behalf of the PRG-NLF. A no-nonsense Kissinger dug in his heels as well. Although he had winnowed down the list of Saigon's demands so that they accorded with Nixon's promises to Thieu, Tho's retraction of previous concessions on prisoners allowed Kissinger to abandon all "understanding" of Hanoi's tricky position with its Cambodian allies, with which he had feigned sympathy at the breakthrough 11 October meeting. Kissinger now demanded that North Vietnam guarantee an immediate cease-fire for Cambodia and Laos to coincide with the one for South Vietnam. Moreover, Kissinger ignored Tho's demand not to mention the withdrawal of PAVN forces, exhorting the North Vietnamese negotiator that if Hanoi agreed to remove its troops from the South then the question of political prisoners would be more easily resolved.[194]

Hanoi leaders made a risky move at the 22 November meeting. Tho ignored the October agreement and demanded that all political prisoners in the South be freed simultaneously with American prisoners and the withdrawal of all foreign troops. In return, Hanoi would remove a number of PAVN troops around the DMZ.[195] Historian Robert Brigham has attributed Hanoi's retraction of the October agreement on civilian prisoners to increased NLF-PRG pressure on Hanoi leaders.[196] However, given the extent of control that the VWP possessed over southern affairs throughout the period of negotiations, it is unlikely that Nguyen Thi Binh and other southern revolutionaries became rogue diplomats breaking from the Party line by demanding the release of their comrades. Rather, the VWP most likely ordered the PRG to stand firm on this issue because Hanoi leaders could not. In other words, the VWP was using the good cop–bad cop tactic that Vietnamese communist leaders had employed since the start of negotiations. Perhaps the real objective in Le Duc Tho's demand was to hold on to American prisoners as leverage, since the United States was adamant that the release of POWs not be linked with any other issue. Instructions sent by the Politburo to Paris that day support the notion of a unified diplomatic front rather than tension between Hanoi and the PRG. Le Duan's Politburo instructed Tho and Thuy to coordinate the negotiating strategy of the private talks with the public forum while Hanoi stepped up its propaganda campaign to denounce U.S. Indochinization, particularly with increasing weapons transfers to Saigon and Phnom Penh. Since world opinion was leaning more heavily on the United States to uphold its promises to end the war, Politburo leaders concluded, Tho and Thuy would be able to reject U.S.-RVN demands that North Vietnam withdraw its troops from South Vietnam.[197]

The remainder of the talks in late November degenerated to stonewalling, pounding fists, and issuing threats. While Kissinger rejected the linking of the release of political prisoners to American POWs, Tho refused to countenance Washington's new demand that American advisers be allowed to remain in South Vietnam. Even when some issues were resolved, including the wording surrounding the DMZ, new issues sprung to the fore. When Washington insisted on Saigon's demands regarding the NCNRC, Tho slammed his fist on the table and said there was a limit to what Hanoi could endure, particularly after agreement had been reached between Washington and Hanoi on the October draft.[198] While the negotiating parties took a long lunch break and shared a Thanksgiving-themed meal on 23 November, it dawned on Hanoi leaders that North Vietnam would not be able to escape another round of American bombs before a settlement could be reached.[199] North Vietnamese fears were confirmed when Kissinger and Haig cornered Tho before a private meeting on 24 November to deliver Nixon's threat that if Hanoi refused to negotiate seriously and honorably, the United States would resume military activities.[200] Kissinger tried to soften Nixon's warning by saying that he would do his best to exert maximum pressure on Saigon but Hanoi had to show flexibility as well. When the formal negotiating session commenced, Kissinger reiterated the necessity of showing that Saigon's demands had been taken into account.[201] Tho, however, was neither moved by Nixon's threat nor sympathetic to Kissinger's position.[202] On the final day of meetings, Kissinger "decided to play for a week's delay before seeking final agreement with Le Duc Tho," since the South Vietnamese continued to be intransigent and the North Vietnamese insisted on their demand that South Vietnamese civilians be released. Tho grudgingly agreed to Kissinger's request for a delay, prompting Kissinger to believe that the United States had "reseized" the initiative with not only Hanoi but Saigon as well.[203]

While Kissinger sensed a weakening in Hanoi's position, particularly with regard to Cambodia and Laos and the wording surrounding the DMZ, Tho was convinced that he had emerged victorious in the late November round of meetings. In particular, Tho noted to Foreign Minister Trinh that Washington had retreated on three issues: the presence of North Vietnamese soldiers, the general nature of the NCNRC, and the recognition of the PRG's legitimacy.[204] Leaders in Hanoi, however, had a somewhat more somber assessment than Tho did in Paris. According to the Politburo, the United States must have sensed a weakening in North Vietnam's position. Not only had Washington retreated on the agreed October draft, Hanoi had only put up a show of resistance before it put forward a more flexible offer. The Politburo surmised that the Americans believed that they could conclude the war and negotiate the peace from a position of strength and thereby produce an agreement that would prove advantageous to the Saigon regime. The only recourse, in Hanoi's opinion, was to stick to the terms of the October draft in the upcoming December talks while the Politburo increased communist defenses around Hanoi and Hai Phong and prepared for the evacuation of its urban population to the countryside.[205]

Nonetheless, North Vietnamese negotiators in Paris cabled the Hanoi Politburo stating that even though Washington had entirely changed the substance of the October draft with its new demands, the DRV should still strive for an early solution.[206] As a result, VWP leaders entered the second round of talks pessimistic but still intent on producing an agreement. Meanwhile, Nixon dealt firmly with South Vietnamese leaders, including Thieu's special advisor, Nguyen Phu Duc, and South Vietnamese ambassador Tran Kim Phuong, who continued to mount objections to any U.S.-DRV settlement that allowed PAVN troops to remain in the South.[207] Vowing to "go it alone," these South Vietnamese officials tried the patience of their patrons. While Kissinger called Duc a "little bastard," Nixon explained that the "major trouble" in Saigon was Hoang Duc Nha, whom the president described as a "punk kid in the Palace, this 3-year-old suit—suitor, who is acting out a Wagnerian drama."[208]

On 4 December, the first day of the second round of talks, Kissinger and Le Duc Tho stuck firm to their respective demands regarding the preamble of the agreement, the Vietnamese text on the NCNRC, substantive issues involving North Vietnamese troops in the South, the release of political prisoners, and provisions concerning Cambodia and Laos. Kissinger concluded that Hanoi might be prepared "to break off negotiations and go another military round."[209] When the two sides reconvened on 6 December, Tho tried to gain Kissinger's sympathy by presenting the PRG as a potential obstacle regarding the NCNRC.[210] Kissinger evidently believed the North Vietnamese negotiator when he commented in his memoirs that Hanoi was "obviously under tremendous pressure from the Viet Cong on this issue."[211] On 7 December, in a last-ditch effort, Tho requested a return to the October draft. When Kissinger refused to budge, the DRV negotiator dropped all pretense of playing it cool and acceded to most of America's demands. In particular, Hanoi was ready to "abandon" the PRG, if in fact they ever disagreed, by dropping the demand for the release of political detainees in the South.[212] The next day, Kissinger gained more ground as Tho agreed to acquiesce to American demands regarding the DMZ in return for U.S. acceptance that the PRG be mentioned in the preamble.[213] Nonetheless, there were still many outstanding issues. When the 9 December meeting appeared as if it would end in stalemate, as both sides held their ground on various issues, Kissinger reported to Nixon that during the break, Tho took him aside and suggested that if Kissinger could "start the next phase of the meeting with a concession, he would make a big concession."[214]

On 10 December, Le Duc Tho, who had complained the day before that his blood pressure was high and that he was not feeling well, tried to end the grueling four-hour meeting forty-five minutes early.[215] According to Luu Van Loi, Tho was exhausted after he confessed to the Americans that he had overstepped his orders by conceding too much: "I have been harshly criticized. . . . Last week I repeatedly contacted Hanoi. The instructions received from my government are more rigid than the formula I gave you. The fact is that at the demarcation line, one side belongs to the North, the other is the liberated zone of the PRG. We should have had nothing to discuss about regulations for movement across the demar-

cation line, but endeavoring to settle with you, we have proposed this formula."[216] The Politburo had sent orders the day before telling the delegation to refuse the U.S. formula.[217] Although Tho understood the necessity
for compromise at this juncture, perhaps Le Duan and the Politburo did
not. The historical record remains silent on any disagreement between
the "comrades Le" on this matter. By 11 December, then, the only issue
that remained was the status of the DMZ. Kissinger continued to push for
the North and South Vietnamese to discuss the modalities of movement
across the demarcation line, thus prohibiting any movement—military or
civilian—until after the two Vietnamese settled the issue. At the 12 December meeting, however, Tho insisted that no reference be made to civilian
movement, which Kissinger construed as Hanoi's attempt to leave open
the possibility for military movement.[218] By this point, the Politburo expressed its frustration to its negotiators: "Signing now or later, timing is
no longer an issue."[219] With negotiators unable to settle the DMZ issue,
progress remained impossible for the remainder of the meetings.[220]

When Tho informed Kissinger that he was due to leave Paris for Hanoi
on 14 December and that he would be in touch by messages, Kissinger
concluded that Hanoi had "decided to play for time," because the North
Vietnamese leaders were too divided or they sought to exploit the split between Washington and Saigon.[221] With the Western holiday season imminent, the Politburo resolved to advance the diplomatic struggle and use
U.S. domestic pressure and world public opinion to force Nixon to sign
an agreement. North Vietnamese leaders believed international opinion
favored them over Washington.[222] At the final meeting on 13 December,
which Kissinger described as even more "ludicrous and insolent" than
the previous meetings, the negotiations remained deadlocked.[223] During the lunch break, Tho refused to relent on the two major outstanding issues—the DMZ and the signing procedure—because, as Kissinger
reported, "Hanoi's keeping him on a tight leash and overruling various
deals he made with me."[224]

As U.S.-DRV talks hit these bumps on the road to peace, Thieu launched
a major public relations campaign to try to derail the entire process and
kill off any chance for a settlement. Appearing before the RVN National
Assembly on 12 December, the South Vietnamese president denounced
Kissinger's efforts in Paris.[225] The next day, Thieu informed key politicians
and leaders in Saigon that he intended to reject any draft settlement.[226]
On 14 December, as Le Duc Tho left Paris for consultations with the Politburo, Nixon ordered a resumption of the bombing for 18 December, the

day that Tho was due to return to Hanoi, with Operation Linebacker II, otherwise known as the Christmas bombings. During the twelve-day campaign, known in Hanoi as the "twelve days of darkness [*moi hai ngay dem*]," 3,420 sorties carpet-bombed the Hanoi–Hai Phong area, inflicting severe physical and psychological damage on North Vietnam.[227] Nixon intended to convey a message to Hanoi and to Saigon that Washington was determined to force a peace and neither Vietnamese party could stand in the way.[228] In a personal letter to Thieu on the eve of the bombing, Nixon wrote, "These actions [bombing] are meant to convey to the enemy my determination to bring the conflict to a rapid end. . . . I do not want you to be left, under any circumstances, with the mistaken impression that these actions signal a willingness or intent to continue U.S. military involvement if Hanoi meets the requirements for a settlement which I have set."[229] While Thieu was "shaken" by Nixon's letter,[230] Hanoi remained silent. When Nixon announced a thirty-six-hour Christmas truce and halted the bombings, the DRV still did not exhibit any desire to resume negotiations.

Although the Chinese and Soviets issued strong condemnations of the fiercest bombing campaign in the war, both allies again privately pressured Hanoi to settle with the Americans.[231] On 23 December, Soviet ambassador Scherbakov listened sympathetically to Pham Van Dong's condemnation of Nixon's bombing campaign, but when the opportunity arose to push Hanoi toward accepting the American offer to resume talks, the Soviet official pounced. Not only did he encourage Dong to inform the Americans that Hanoi was ready to meet, but he also suggested that VWP leaders only demand the cessation of bombing. Four days later, during a discussion with Deputy Foreign Minister Hoang Van Tien, it was apparent to Scherbakov that Hanoi no longer needed any convincing to negotiate. The North Vietnamese official asked Moscow to persuade the United States to stop the bombing.[232]

Meanwhile, Chinese leaders also encouraged the North Vietnamese to return to negotiations. On 29 December, Mao Zedong criticized some "so-called 'Communists,'" who encouraged the Vietnamese not to negotiate and to "fight for another 100 years."[233] "This is revolution; otherwise it is opportunism," Chairman Mao said to PRG head delegate Nguyen Thi Binh, who represented the obstinate South Vietnamese comrades Mao viewed as bent on torpedoing the peace for their own selfish motives. In other words, if the PRG's demands regarding the release of political detainees prevented Hanoi from accepting the settlement in early December, then Mao was sending a thinly veiled warning to Binh not to engage

*Mao Zedong and Le Duc Tho (Douglas Pike Photograph Collection, Vietnam Center and Archive, Texas Tech University)*

in "opportunism."[234] Mao's warnings were unnecessary, however, Le Duan had kept a close eye on southern diplomats since the beginning of the war for peace.[235]

Binh, on the other hand, prefers to remember the powerful effect of people's diplomacy at this juncture in the war. With 27 U.S. aircraft shot down, including 15 B-52s (the North Vietnamese claimed 81 aircraft shot down, including 34 B-52s), 44 captured American pilots (one of whom died in captivity) and another 42 killed or missing in action, not to mention the damage wrought on North Vietnam, including more than 2,000 civilians killed and more than 1,500 wounded, public outrage forced Nixon to end the bombing campaign and his approval ratings plummeted.[236] Singer Joan Baez and VVAW members arrived in Hanoi when the bombings began and publicized the destruction of Bach Mai Hospital and the neighborhoods surrounding the capital city.[237] Meanwhile, VWP leaders took note of official pronouncements by statesmen as well as headlines worldwide, taking solace in the condemnation of Nixon's brutal campaign in the United States, the socialist bloc, Western Europe, and the Third World.[238] Influential American journalists decried Linebacker II as a barbaric act by a mad tyrant, an act that was unnecessary for the United States to get out of Vietnam.[239] In short, the Christmas bombings produced global outrage; rather than break the will of Hanoi, American bombs mobilized the international community to condemn the U.S. administration.[240]

On 31 December, Truong Chinh met with Zhou Enlai in Beijing and asked the Chinese leader his opinion on the DRV's negotiating prospects. Zhou tried to convince his Vietnamese guest to negotiate seriously with the aim of reaching an immediate agreement, since the Americans were definitely on their way out of Southeast Asia.[241] The Chinese leader repeated this advice to Le Duc Tho a few days later. "The most important [thing] is to let the Americans leave," Zhou stated. "The situation will change in six months or a year."[242] North Vietnamese leaders, however, did not have to be browbeaten into showing flexibility and approaching negotiations seriously; Nixon's bombs had done their damage. On 26 December, the heaviest day of bombing, Hanoi had notified Washington that it was ready to resume negotiations on 4 January.[243] Washington ended its bombing north of the twentieth parallel on 29 December, allowing Kissinger and Tho to meet in Paris early in the new year.

On 8 January 1973, the third and final round of Tho and Kissinger talks began and concluded with a settlement that some officials and scholars argue resembled the 1972 fall draft agreement.[244] They claim that the resultant January draft was essentially achieved on Thanksgiving Day 1972, incorporating some of the December and January compromises. Moreover, Nixon's brutal bombing campaign failed to break Hanoi's will and only resulted in Washington's accepting terms that it had rejected.[245] However, according to others, the final round of talks did produce differences. The DMZ provisions were strengthened, but "civilian" movement remained an issue for later negotiations. Nguyen Thi Binh's last-minute demands for the simultaneous release of civilian detainees were omitted, but PAVN troops were allowed to remain in South Vietnam and so were American advisers. In addition, the PRG remained in the preamble, but not in the document.[246]

Thieu, in contrast, after getting over Nixon's threats in mid-December, was greatly encouraged by the Christmas bombing and thus continued to hold out for PAVN withdrawals and other significant changes to the agreement. The U.S. president, however, could no longer appease Thieu. In early January, legislation to cut off all funds to Indochina contingent on the return of American POWs passed both the House and Senate. Thus, given the very real threat of an immediate cutoff of U.S. aid, the South Vietnamese president finally relented. Even though Nixon had forced Hanoi's—and Saigon's—hand, the American public and world opinion, which had become more sympathetic to the Vietnamese communists thanks to the DRV and PRG's adept international and transnational diplomacy, denounced the brutality of Nixon's aerial campaign.

After more than four years of acrimonious negotiations and bitter fighting, the Paris agreement and cease-fire signed in late January 1973 managed to end the American phase of the war but gave little respite to the Vietnamese. A new stage of fighting—the war of the flags—ensued as Hanoi and Saigon scrambled to stake out territory and ground while the Americans, Chinese, and Soviets watched. Although Le Duan may not have definitively won the war for peace, he managed to prevent Nixon and Thieu from gaining victory with a negotiated settlement that could have resulted in the permanent division of Vietnam. True victory, however, would have to wait.

## CONCLUSION

The 1973 Paris Agreement on Ending the War and Restoring the Peace did not end the Vietnam War. Instead, it was a penultimate finale, marking only the end of the bitter war for peace that began in the midst of the Tet Offensive and ended in the devastation of Operation Linebacker II. Most important, it was the endgame to America's war and heralded a new stage of fighting among the Vietnamese. Despite the fanfare surrounding the signing of the peace agreement and cease-fire in Paris in early 1973, then, no side believed the fight was over.

Although Le Duan finally abandoned his long-held desire to win the war through his General Offensive and General Uprising strategy in the summer of 1972, his decision to rely on diplomacy to end the war did not result in an immediate agreement. Distrustful of negotiations from the start of the southern struggle, Le Duan was perhaps fearful of suffering the same fate as Ho Chi Minh had during the French-Indochina War. Since he had shuffled around important Party, state, and defense positions earlier in the year, however, Le Duan did not have to fear that a rival Politburo member would take advantage of his missteps. Thus, with the admission that his 1972 Spring–Summer Offensive failed to score a decisive victory by toppling the Thieu regime, the first secretary shifted the Party's resources to achieve the goal of American withdrawal rather than that of "puppet collapse." Abandoning the plans to incite a general uprising and dropping the demand for Thieu's ouster, Le Duc Tho could still not manage to secure a settlement in Paris. The "puppet" ensured that its patron would not and could not settle in 1972.

Saigon's effective campaign to sabotage peace in 1972 reveals two important aspects of the internationalization of the war for peace. First, despite being bitter enemies, Saigon and Hanoi found themselves in similar positions in the 1970s with the reconfiguration of Sino-Soviet-American relations. RVN and DRV leaders utilized the tools available to junior allies in the Cold War, including obstruction, blackmail, and threats to influence their patrons' actions. Le Duan and his comrades, however, were not as successful as Thieu and his advisors, since the competition between the Chinese and the Soviets for America's favor neutralized their rivalry for influence over North Vietnam. Second, Thieu's ability to thwart a settlement in 1972 reveals that the United States was not in a position to unilaterally dictate the course of the war. Even though Kissinger had gone to great lengths to secure a draft agreement with Hanoi in the fall of 1972, he had not factored in Thieu's ability to influence Nixon's decisions.

Finally, Thieu's last-minute obstruction also bolstered Nixon's resolve to end the war for peace on his own terms by using the two remaining weapons in his arsenal: superpower diplomacy and military escalation. Convinced that the Beijing and Moscow summits as well as Linebacker I had forced Hanoi to negotiate seriously, Nixon once again launched a devastating bombing campaign and roped in the Chinese and the Soviets to pressure the North Vietnamese to return to the negotiating table in the winter of 1972. Since the Politburo's aim had been to arrive at an agreement without further damage to its war effort, even though Hanoi eventually prepared itself and was ready to accept the destruction, Linebacker II represented the failure to attain that goal. Thieu's intransigence in late 1972, in a sense, bought him approximately another three years until communist forces could recover militarily.

At the same time, international condemnation, facilitated by Hanoi's public relations campaign, surrounding the Christmas bombings ensured that Thieu could no longer put up any further roadblocks to peace and that Nixon could no longer utilize American air power in Vietnam. Regardless of what changes it may or may not have caused to the resulting peace agreement, especially since no side believed that the document would bind the belligerents, the final round of devastation and destruction only underscored the futility of negotiating peace for Vietnam.

# EPILOGUE

Under the command of General Van Tien Dung, PAVN troops entered Saigon on 30 April 1975, bringing the Ho Chi Minh Offensive to a successful close. As communist soldiers marched and rode atop Soviet tanks into the heart of RVN power, exuberant masses lined the streets of Saigon to welcome the troops as liberators. In the end, the Party did not need for the South Vietnamese people to rise up and help topple the Saigon regime; South Vietnam's leaders had more or less fled the country a week before. On 21 April, Nguyen Van Thieu had given a rambling resignation speech in which he blamed the imminent demise of South Vietnam on the United States and Washington's abandonment of its stalwart ally to the communists. Rumored to have taken copious amounts of gold on a CIA cargo plane to Taiwan, Thieu handed over the deteriorating situation to Vice President Tran Van Huong who, one week later, fobbed it off on General Duong Van Minh.[1] "Big Minh," who had no intention of continuing the fight, announced his intention to surrender to the PRG, but North Vietnamese forces dispensed with the formality and assumed direct power. The war in Vietnam had finally come to a close.

With the liberation of Saigon, Le Duan and Le Duc Tho celebrated the end of their fifteen-year struggle in Hanoi. After defeating rivals for power in the North to promote war in the South, the militant leaders had succeeded in negotiating the end of American involvement in 1973 and defeating Saigon forces on the battlefield more than two years later. Although the war had not always proceeded as they had planned, they emerged victorious nonetheless. The transition to peace and reunification after 1975, however, proved even more difficult for these revolutionaries. After a few years of peace, leaders of the unified country, renamed the Socialist Republic of Vietnam, were once again at war by the end of the decade, this time against their former allies, the PRC and the Khmer Rouge. Once again, Vietnamese forces proved successful on the battlefield. They pushed back Chinese troops who marched south to teach their "ungrateful" neighbor a lesson and, more important, ousted the murderous Pol Pot regime that had begun its attacks on Vietnam a year earlier. Although Vietnam's alliance with the Soviet Union had been solidified when Hanoi joined the Comecon in June 1978, the Third Indochina War and its aftermath brought about the international marginalization of Vietnam and plummeted the nation into economic stagnation and hyperinflation. The country entered its most difficult years during the winter of Le Duan's life.

The general secretary, who had battled French colonialists, Japanese imperialists, American neoimperialists, and Chinese chauvinists, continued to promote a Marxist view of the world as divided into the two camps of socialism and imperialism. This binary approach fit poorly with the realities of the late Cold War. While Vietnam battled both the PRC and the nations of ASEAN, it looked to the Soviet economic and political system for inspiration.[2] The latter proved disastrous for Vietnam's postwar reconstruction, as Hanoi sent former RVN officials and soldiers into reeducation camps and shuttled southern peasants into New Economic Zones. As a result, nation (re)building and regional problems in the 1980s prevented Hanoi from assuming an influential role in world affairs. Although the Vietnamese revolution had inspired national liberation struggles throughout the Global South, Hanoi could not become the "Havana of the East."[3] Even though Vietnam sent soldiers to train the Sandinistas in Nicaragua, advised the Red Army in Afghanistan, hosted students and officials from such disparate groups as the Palestine Liberation Organization and the People's Movement for Liberation of Angola, and had worldwide distribution of its translated pamphlets and manuals detailing the victories at the 1954 Dien Bien Phu Siege, the 1968 Tet Offensive, and the 1975 Ho Chi Minh Campaign to readers in El Salvador, South Africa, and Eritrea, to name just a few countries, the SRV could not capitalize on its global reputation as a small-power David who had defeated the U.S. Goliath.[4] With troops stationed in Cambodia, the Vietnamese transformed from the dar-lings of the progressive world media to the pariahs of Southeast Asia. Po-litical scientist and current deputy chief of mission Nguyen Vu Tung con-trasts the period before and after reunification: "Hanoi might be adept in diplomatic struggle for national liberation. But it did not have a contin-gent of well-trained diplomats for diplomacy in the nation-building period that followed."[5]

Winds of change, however, soon blew through Vietnam. Just prior to Le Duan's death, Nguyen Thuy Nga was able to visit her husband on his sickbed as he lay with a high fever caused by lung injuries sustained dur-ing his colonial prison terms decades before. Promising her that he would join her once he regained his health, Le Duan intended to retire to the Mekong Delta and urged Nga to prepare. He passed away before he could return to the south.[6] On 15 July 1986, 100,000 Hanoians lined the six miles between Ba Dinh Square and Mai Dich Cemetery to bid a final farewell to the leader who had guided them through most of the Cold War. While family members donned the traditional white or yellow headscarves of mourning, high-ranking attendees walking in the funeral procession wore armbands over their Mao-collared suits or military fatigues. The casket, drawn by an army vehicle, was draped in the national flag and flanked on both sides by soldiers marching in lock-step garbed in white uniforms. The Soviet Union, the People's Republic of Kampuchea, and the Lao People's Democratic Republic sent dignitaries to pay their respects, while the PRC remained conspicuously absent. Across the Pacific, U.S. president Ronald Reagan did not register Le Duan's passing as he urged the U.S. Congress to fund Nicaragua's "freedom fighters" and put to rest the "Vietnam syn-drome."[7]

Le Duan's death marked the beginning of the end of Vietnam's "America syndrome," as reformers pushed through the policies of Doi Moi (Renova-tion) in 1986. Although Vietnam's move to a market economy helped pull the country out of its economic crisis, glasnost did not accompany Viet-nam's perestroika. The promised social and political reforms at the grass-roots level never transpired, though there were changes at the top. At the Sixth Party Congress in December 1986, Le Duc Tho and Truong Chinh vol-untarily retired, while Van Tien Dung and To Huu were given a vote of no confidence by members of the Congress when they failed to be reelected to the Politburo. Dung's considerable ego, which came forth in his pub-lication extolling his role in the 1975 victory, and his conservative stance regarding Cambodia, led to his downfall.[8] Even though he became associated with the successful "blooming lotus" military strategy exemplified in the 1975 attack on Saigon and the 1979 assault on Phnom Penh, he lost his defense post and became the most visible casualty of the new wave of reforms. Likewise, To Huu lost power in the Party leadership when he became too closely aligned with the disastrous economic policies, including monetary reform, that had brought runaway inflation.

Although Le Duan's former allies retired from political life or fell from power, his enemies did not enjoy a resurgence. The changes sweeping through Vietnam after 1986 never salvaged the role of General Vo Nguyen Giap. Following reunification in 1976, Le Duan dropped all pretense of tolerating the famous general. Stripped of his position as secretary of defense in 1980 and later his seat in the Politburo in 1982, Giap continued to be the recipient of Le Duan's scorn and jealousy. Even after he had squeezed Giap out of state and Party positions, Le Duan still viewed the renowned general with unveiled suspicion. But Giap may get the last word. Managing to outlive the "comrades Le," Giap has eclipsed the obscure Le Duan to rank consistently as one of the greatest generals and grandest strategists in world history. Even though Le Duan managed to marginalize Giap within Vietnam, he never could suppress Giap's enduring influence abroad.

In country, however, Le Duan's legacy lives on. Even though Le Duc Tho and Pham Hung followed Le Duan to the grave two years later, the power structure they built lasted beyond their deaths. Their acolytes, including former COSVN officials such Nguyen Van Linh, Vo Chi Cong, Le Duc Anh, and Vo Van Kiet, to name a few, rose to the top Party positions in the 1980s and 1990s. Nonetheless, there were visible cracks in the Le Duan–Le Duc Tho foundation. The facade of a collective and stable leadership that masked the monopoly of power by Le Duan gave way to the emergence of a trilateral ruling government. After Le Duan's death, the positions of the president and prime minister rose in importance to rival that of the general secretary. The Party leadership no longer wanted collective decision making in name only.

As younger leaders were poised to take the helm in 1986, Vietnam was on the cusp of rejoining the world community. Even before the Velvet Revolution, the fall of the Berlin Wall, and the demise of the Soviet Union, Vietnam began to emerge from the Cold War in Asia when Hanoi announced its intention to withdraw all troops from the People's Republic of Kampuchea, to repair relations with Beijing, and to seek a friendlier policy toward ASEAN. As the PAVN ended its "internationalist duties" tour in neighboring Cambodia, the Cold War finally came to an end in Europe. This prompted a debate over grand strategy as the Hanoi triumvirate weighed the relative merits of what political scientist Alexander L. Vuving has termed following an "anti-imperialist" line (to protect the regime from domestic upheaval) versus an "integrationist" one (to join the Western-dominated world economy).[9] The latter appeared triumphant as Vietnam normalized relations with the United States and joined ASEAN in 1995, ascended to the World Trade Organization in 2006, and continues to draw closer to the United States in an effort to contain China. This newest chapter in Vietnam's international history would have been unimaginable nearly forty years ago during the signing of the Paris Agreement to End the War and Restore the Peace.

*Were there missed opportunities for each side to have achieved its geopolitical objectives without the terrible loss of life suffered in the war—missed opportunities either for avoiding the war before it started or terminating it before it had run its course?—Robert S. McNamara*[1]

# CONCLUSION

It has been nearly four decades since the fall of Saigon. In the intervening years, policymakers, journalists, and historians have battled over the question of what went wrong. How did the United States become mired in a disastrous war in Southeast Asia and why did Washington fail to achieve victory in Vietnam? While these crucial debates will continue, this study suggests that perhaps the time has come to formulate a new set of questions for insight into the old debates. How did North Vietnam manage to engage the United States in total war and why did Hanoi emerge victorious over the world's greatest superpower? In short, it is time for historians to develop a better understanding of the agents and structures behind Hanoi's victory in its fifteen-year struggle for the fate of Vietnam.

Too often, however, the Vietnam War is still viewed solely through the American lens. Leaders in Washington, U.S. soldiers on the battlefront, and American protestors on the streets take center stage while the Vietnamese disappear in the background, part of the terrain in which Americans became quagmired. However, the war was at least as much a Vietnamese conflict as it was an American one. Viewing the conflict from the perspectives of leaders in Hanoi, a new international history of the Vietnam War, and indeed of the wider Cold War, emerges. As historian Odd Arne Westad observes, "the most important aspects of the Cold War were neither military nor strategic, nor Europe-centered, but connected to the political and social development in the Third World."[2]

If the role of actors in the Global South remains an important and understudied dimension of the Cold War, why have more scholars not attempted to view the Vietnam War through the perspectives of the Vietnamese, if even elite ones?[3] Perhaps because the difficulties are many. Linguistic and archival challenges notwithstanding, methodological obstacles exist as well. It is not easy to demonstrate small-power autonomy and agency amid great-power squabbles. Moreover, there is also a danger in ascribing too much power to Third World players, since some could claim that it absolves superpowers of responsibility for the violence created by their interventions. The reality of the Cold War in the Third World, however, did consist of local elites "marrying their own domestic purposes to a faith in a common, international ideology, many [of whom] aimed at some form of superpower involvement from the revolutionary stage onwards."[4] But the bipolarity of the Cold War, which constituted the backdrop of Vietnam's postcolonial development, made the Vietnamese civil war was much bloodier, longer, and harder to resolve.[5]

By viewing the Vietnam War from Vietnamese perspectives, this study not only casts new light on local and regional events, but it also provides new insights into the global Cold War. It reveals that postcolonial development in the revolutionary Third World was derailed not only by the East-West rivalry but also by the Sino-Soviet split. The ideological struggle between Moscow and Beijing forced medium and small powers in the socialist bloc and revolutionary parties in the Global South to tread a careful line between peaceful coexistence and violent confrontation with the West. Opting to follow one path over the other not only could bring devastating domestic repercussions on the road to revolution for these postcolonial communist regimes, but it also held great consequences for their struggles to keep Western encroachment at bay. From the perspectives of these smaller powers, the Soviet Union and China were not above placing their own geostrategic interests in the Sino-Soviet competition before their junior allies' struggles, even if that meant putting the "internationalist" cause at peril in the face of the American "neoimperialist" threat.

Although international debates and fissures in the struggle between democratic capitalism and Marxism-Leninism as well as between Soviet and Chinese policies affected postcolonial development in the Global South, this study also reveals that the Third World actors still managed to manipulate the great powers invested in seeing their path of modernization flourish in the Third World. Pitting superpower rivals against one another ensured that Third World actors could maintain their independence and extract maximum military aid without relinquishing their autonomy. Postcolonial leaders did this directly by appealing to one side over another and by signaling their allegiances by manipulating their own domestic politics. However, America's realignment of superpower relations at the start of the 1970s threatened this system. Détente blurred ideological lines in the global Cold War. No longer could Third World nations rely on old Cold War scripts (the "threat of communist subversion" or the "necessity of internationalist solidarity") to elicit unadulterated great-power support for their local causes. Instead, regional enemies found themselves in the same abandoned boat, as their respective great-power patrons sailed off together in pursuit of détente.

Under these new geopolitical circumstances, Third World actors adapted the small-power tools at their disposal both to challenge their enemies and control their allies. The final contribution of this study is to show that the global Cold War witnessed a clash of contesting global visions not only between the United States and the Soviet Union and between the Soviet Union and China but also, and more important, between superpowers and small powers. In addition to outright wars, the struggles also took the form of diplomatic contestations in the international arena. Davids took on and defeated Goliaths by taking advantage of an international—and indeed transnational—space that opened up on the world stage. Harnessing the power of sympathetic public opinion to their cause, nonstate actors and smaller powers could level the playing field against economically and militarily stronger nations. America's enemies in the Third World utilized this revolutionary diplomacy, which included small-power diplomacy and transnational people's diplomacy, to weaken the United States in the global arena. Tapping into this global network of relations that bridged the radical segments of the West with the revolutionary parties of the Third World, these postcolonial regimes were able to bring great political pressure to bear on the United States to abandon its "neoimperialist" aims.

These North-South conflagrations took place not only between ideologically opposed powers but also within Cold War alliances. While the Nixon Doctrine signified the retrenchment of U.S. commitments and a retreat from unconditional defense guarantees in the Global South—a shift from a militarily "formal empire" to an "informal empire"—and as Nixon's superpower diplomacy sought a balance-of-power politics, the violent turn in the Sino-Soviet split prompted Beijing and Moscow to seek better relations with Washington. Third World allies of the United States, on the one side, and of the Soviet Union and China, on the other, fought back. The junior allies dragged their feet, coerced and cajoled, and resorted to outright blackmail to stymie their patrons from sacrificing their causes on the altar of great-power politics.

Thus, the global Cold War from the perspectives of small powers in the Third World reveals a vastly different conflict—with its own pitfalls, challenges, and stakes—from the one seen by the great powers. Since most of the violence perpetuated in the Cold War fell on the Global South, it is high time that scholars shift their focus to take into account these lesser known, but equally important, perspectives.

## TOWARD A NEW INTERNATIONAL HISTORY OF THE VIETNAM WAR

In addition to its contributions to our understanding of the global Cold War more generally, this book also has challenged much of the received wisdom concerning the Vietnam War more specifically. Although nothing is definitive until the Party, military, and Foreign Ministry archives open their doors, the extant historical record opens the way for new interpretations of Hanoi's struggle and the international history of the war for peace in Vietnam.

Hanoi's decision to go to war was not solely the product of southern pressure on northern leaders to save the resistance. Rather, the Party's resolution approving armed conflict in the South was intimately connected to the problems with state building in the North. In other words, revolutionary war provided effective means to deflect attention from domestic problems. After the French-Indochina War, the Party suffered severe blows to its prestige with the land reform debacle and never quite recovered during the travails of the 1950s. Recalling Le Duan to the North in 1957, Politburo leaders needed their comrade with the most experience in the South to implement the policy shift in Hanoi. In doing so, the Party sought to combine armed conflict with the southern political struggle and socialist transformation of the northern economy to rally the people behind the Party's policies. Instead, Le Duan, who had predicated his career on the South, was by 1963 advancing full-scale war at the expense of the socialist revolution in the North.

Politburo members were thus blindsided by the first secretary's monopolization of decision making. Although the Hanoi leadership is often portrayed as a collective decision-making body, the reality was vastly different. Le Duan drew on his revolutionary experience taking down formidable enemies and rivals in the Mekong Delta and had learned from the past mistakes of his predecessors, including Ho Chi Minh and Truong Chinh, who lacked strong bases of power to build a veritable communist empire. Placing his deputies in key positions within the Party and the state, Le Duan took advantage of the fluid nature of the Party hierarchy to solidify the power of the apparatchiks over the armed forces, government, and mass organizations.

Dominating the highest rungs of Party power, Le Duan identified Vietnam's most visible leaders—Vo Nguyen Giap and Ho Chi Minh—as the greatest threats to his authority. Although credited with leading Hanoi's war against the United States, Ho and Giap were sidelined by Le Duan and Le Duc Tho at nearly all key decision-making junctures. In 1963 and 1964, Le Duan blackmailed Ho into silence when the aged leader attempted to oppose the first secretary's decision to escalate the war and attempt all-out victory. In 1967 and 1968, Giap became the target of a large-scale purge when Le Duc Tho arrested the general's—and Ho's—deputies and friends. The two leaders thus paid dearly for voicing their disagreement with Le Duan's plans for what would become the Tet Offensive. On both occasions, however, Ho and Giap proved correct in their call for moderation: Le Duan's 1964 and 1968 offensives exacted enormous costs on the revolution. While Ho died in 1969, Giap continued to be the recipient of Le Duan's scorn. In 1972, the general found himself once again on the losing side of the military debate, this time over the Easter Offensive. It is worth contemplating how Hanoi's war would have been different had Ho and Giap been in charge.

Le Duan also extended his power beyond the Politburo by erecting a police state in the North and strengthening the Party apparatus in the South. The common notion of the Vietnamese struggle for national liberation as a unified war effort comprised of North and South Vietnamese patriots led by the Party conceals a much more complex truth. In reality, Le Duan constructed a national security state that devoted all of its resources to war and labeled any resistance to its policies as treason. Although there was vast support for the communist war effort on both sides of the seventeenth parallel, especially in the early years of the fighting, opposition and later war weariness also existed. Le Duan dealt with this domestic turmoil by increasing the powers of the internal security forces and ideological police to surveil North Vietnamese society and by strengthening COSVN in order to thwart rival southern communist leaders and subjugate their insurgency to the Party center. While "North-first" moderates in the DRV objected to Le Duan's southern war as a means to reunification, local southern communists resented orders from Hanoi that often put the insurgency in peril.

The internal debates within the Vietnamese Communist Party were not insular, however; they mirrored the wider ideological struggle encapsulated in the Sino-Soviet split. Although leaders in Hanoi at the time and now claim that decision making during the war responded directly to the enemy's war effort—namely, the military picture in the South and the political situation in the United States—the rivalry between Moscow and Beijing played a major role in Hanoi's strategy deliberation as well. Even though there were "pro-Chinese" and "pro-Soviet" factions within the VWP, nearly all Politburo leaders, including Le Duan, were never that partial to one side over the other. Instead, they used internationalist debates as justification for domestic repression. Beyond the impact on North Vietnamese domestic politics, Hanoi's relations with its larger allies greatly influenced the Vietnamese communist war effort as well. In 1964, China's emerging radical line allowed Le Duan to advance full-scale war in the South and to adopt a pro-Chinese tilt, though the DRV's international allegiances returned to equilibrium a year later with the onset of Soviet aid in response to the Americanization of the war. By 1968, the high-profile nature of Vietnam's struggle for sparked more intense competition between Beijing and Moscow for influence over Hanoi, prompting Le Duan to assert his autonomy and independence from both allies by launching the Tet Offensive.

The underlying strategy of the 1968 offensive, as well as the coordinated attacks launched in 1964 and 1972, was the ambitious—yet ultimately unattainable—notion of a General Offensive and General Uprising. The mistakes committed by the U.S. military in Vietnam under William Westmoreland and Creighton Abrams have their counterparts in the Vietnamese communist war effort under Nguyen Chi Thanh and Van Tien Dung. Although official Vietnamese histories, echoed by some Western studies, view the aim of these offensives as striking a political and psychological blow to the United States and its foreign policy, Hanoi's actual objective was to present Washington with a fait accompli by toppling the Saigon regime through a mass insurrection sparked by coordinated attacks aimed at urban centers. Le Duan, who remained wary of negotiations, relied on this controversial strategy to win the war rather than compromise for peace. Victory, however, eluded Le Duan and his generals as mass insurrection failed to materialize each time. Instead, the large-scale offensives exacted enormous casualties on the Vietnamese revolution. Nonetheless, Le Duan continued to seek his elusive goal of toppling the unstable Saigon regime, despite opposition from Ho, Giap, and the military brass who considered the GO-GU a reckless strategy.

Le Duan's war effort encountered not just military difficulties but also diplomatic ones as Nixon and Kissinger launched their triangular offensive in the 1970s. The extant Vietnamese historical record reveals that the Nixon administration's superpower diplomacy was far from ineffectual; on the contrary, it succeeded in squaring the Sino-Soviet-Vietnamese triangle. North Vietnamese leaders felt powerless in the face of Sino-American rapprochement and Soviet-American détente, and they allowed the realignment in great-power relations to affect their war in Indochina. Although both allies continued to provide military and economic aid to North Vietnam, DRV leaders viewed this aid as a holdover from Sino-Soviet competition for Hanoi's favor that would soon be replaced by the communist powers' rivalry for Washington's good graces. In other words, Le Duan perceived that the great powers were prepared to betray the Vietnamese revolution in 1972 as they had previously in 1954. He and his comrades acted on this perception by stiffening their resolve in Paris and by planning a military offensive. Furious with their allies, VWP leaders timed their 1972 coordinated attacks to take place in the midst of Nixon's historic visits to China and the Soviet Union. However, as Vietnamese forces struggled to hold on to their initial victories in the South, which required greater Soviet and Chinese diplomatic support and military aid, Beijing and Moscow betrayed Hanoi. The allies issued hollow condemnations of Nixon's bombing and mining campaigns, equipped Hanoi with assistance to defend the DRV but not to attack the RVN, and, most important, did Nixon's bidding by pressuring the North Vietnamese to abandon their offensive and return to the negotiating table.

Despite immense allied pressure to end the fighting and to accept American terms in Paris, Hanoi was able to blunt great-power machinations with its small-power diplomacy. The key to Hanoi's ultimate success in the war lay not in launching general offensives or even winning hearts and minds in South Vietnam; rather, it resided with its world relations campaign aimed at procuring the support of antiwar movements around the world. Hanoi's enemies, however, were not idle. While Saigon reached out to conservative neighboring regimes that shared the goal of suppressing revolutionary change in the region with the onset of American withdrawal, Washington aimed for a balance of power in international relations though détente with the Soviet Union and China. The Vietnam War, however, witnessed the pinnacle of power enjoyed by the revolutionary Third World on the international stage, and Vietnamese communist diplomacy during the war constituted the key catalyst to this "diplomatic revolution." Hanoi tapped into a revolutionary network of relations that managed to bridge the Global South with the progressive segments of the West. In the end, Hanoi's radical relations—fueled by the global antiwar movement taking place in the streets of Washington and Paris, Havana and Algiers, and even New Delhi and Tehran—as well as its shrewd small-power diplomacy, managed to blunt not only Saigon's regional relations but also, and more important, Washington's superpower diplomacy. This is perhaps the greatest legacy of Hanoi's war.

Vietnamese leaders were thus anything but puppets or passive players in the war for peace; they shaped American actions in Vietnam as well as the global Cold War order. As Le Duan and Le Duc Tho thwarted Nixon's objective of "peace with honor" and frustrated his superpower designs, Nguyen Van Thieu prolonged American withdrawal from his country and laid bare the problems with the Nixon Doctrine. Although Washington possessed its own internal and geostrategic reasons to intervene and stay in the Vietnamese conflict, it was leaders in Hanoi and Saigon who dictated the nature and pace of U.S. intervention. Domestic and Cold War pressures indeed played significant roles throughout American involvement in Vietnam, but Vietnamese elite actors created the context in which U.S. leaders operated. Hanoi and Saigon were not only active agents in their own destinies, but they also heavily influenced the terms of American intervention and ultimately the outcome of their war.

Viewing war from the perspectives of the "other" side is necessary in the exploration of our past; it is also essential to understanding our present. Failing to do so for the Vietnam War has led to a faulty understanding of the enemy's war as well as America's. The history of Washington's violent confrontation with the Third World during the Cold War demonstrates that there were undeniable losers; however, the history of Hanoi's war for peace reveals that there were no clear-cut victors, either. Instead, the dark side of victory in the Vietnam War is that leaders ensured peace could only be won through the barrel of a gun.

# Notes

ABBREVIATIONS

The following abbreviations are used throughout the notes and bibliography.

BNG    Bo Ngoai Giao (Ministry of Foreign Affairs)

BNV    Bo Noi Vu (Ministry of the Interior)

BQP    Bo Quoc Phong (Ministry of Defense)

BTTM-CTC    Bo Tong Tham Muu-Cuc Tac Chien (General Staff–Combat Operations Department)

CAND    Nha Xuat Ban Cong An Nhan Dan (People's Public Security Press)

CLV-AO    Cambodge-Laos-Vietnam, Asie-Océanie

CTQG    Nha Xuat Ban Chinh Tri Quoc Gia (National Publishing Press)

DCSV    Dang Cong San Viet Nam (Communist Party of Vietnam)

DPC    Douglas Pike Collection

DTNG    BNG, *Dai su ky chuyen de: Dau Tranh Ngoai Giao va van dong quoc te trong nhung chien chong My cuu nuoc* (Special Chronology: The Diplomatic Struggle and International Activities of the Anti-American Resistance and National Salvation), 5 vols., luu hanh noi bo (internal circulation only) (Hanoi, 1987)

FAMAE    Archives du Ministère des Affaires Etrangères (Ministry of Foreign Affairs Archives), Paris

FCO    Foreign Commonwealth Office

FRUS    U.S. Department of State, *Foreign Relations of the United States* (Washington, D.C.: Government Printing Office, 1862– )

GFL    Gerald Ford Presidential Library, Ann Arbor, Michigan

JDC    John Donnell Collection

MOL    Magyar Országos Levéltár (Hungarian National Archives), Budapest

NARA    National Archives and Records Administration, College Park, Maryland

NPM    Richard Nixon Presidential Project Materials

NSA    National Security Archive, Washington, D.C.

NSAF    National Security Agency Files

NSCF    National Security Council Files

NSCVIG    National Security Council Vietnam Information Group: Intelligence and Other Reports

PLT-BNG    Phong Luu Tru–Bo Ngoai Giao (Ministry of Foreign Affairs Archives), Hanoi

PTTDN    Phu Tong Thong De Nhi Viet Nam Cong Hoa (Office of the Second Republic of Vietnam)

QDND    *Nha Xuat Ban Quan Doi Nhan Dan* (People's Army Press)

QK7    Quan Khu 7 (Military Region 7)

TPHCM    Thanh Pho Ho Chi Minh (Ho Chi Minh City)
TTLTQG-2    Trung Tam Luu Tru Quoc Gia 2 (National Archives Center 2), TPHCM
TTLTQG-3    Trung Tam Luu Tru Quoc Gia 3 (National Archives Center 3), Hanoi
TVQD    Thu Vien Quan Doi (Military Library), Hanoi
UKNA    National Archives, Kew, United Kingdom
USDSC    U.S. Department of State Collection
VA-TTU    Virtual Archive, Texas Tech University, Lubbock
VKDTT    DCSV, *Van Kien Dang Toan Tap* (The Complete Collection of Party Documents), 54 vols. (Hanoi: CTQG, 1998– )
VLSD    Vien Lich Su Dang (Institute of Party History)
VLSQSVN    Vien Lich Su Quan Su Viet Nam (Institute of Military History)
VNDR    Viet-Nam Document and Research Notes
VPBCHTU    Van Phong Ban Chap Hanh Truong Uong (Office of the Central Executive Committee)
WDC    William Duiker Collection
WIEU    Weekly Intelligence Updates

## INTRODUCTION

1. Radio Hanoi, 10 July 1986, rpt. in "100,000 Mourn Vietnam's Le Duan," United Press International, 16 July 1986, http://articles.chicagotribune.com/198-07-16/news/8602200511_1_truong-chinh-party-leader-communist-party (accessed 28 Dec. 2010). On Le Duan's death, Truong Chinh took over briefly as the first secretary of the Vietnamese Communist Party.

2. The evacuation of the population is recounted in Burchett, *Grasshoppers and Elephants*, 162–94. Burchett interviewed Hanoi mayor Tran Duy Hung. See also Tran Luan Tin, *Duoc song va ke lai*, for an excellent memoir of the experiences faced by an evacuee (*so tan*).

3. "Mua phun" appears in the poem by Mai Khoa, "Hanoi va me" (Hanoi with Mother), about loss and the Christmas bombings. http://diendan.nguoihanoi.net/viewtopic.php?t=6132 (accessed 8 July 2011).

4. Pribbenow, *Victory in Vietnam*, 319. See also "In a Bombed Street," Vietnamese News Agency, 6 Jan. 1973.

5. Just as historian Chen Jian demonstrates the importance of understanding Mao for studies of China's foreign policy during the Cold War, it is as equally imperative to understand Le Duan for histories of the Vietnam War. See Chen Jian, *Mao's China and the Cold War*, 10.

6. The Vietnamese Communist Party used "first secretary" (*bi thu nhat*) during the war; after 1976, the proper title became "general secretary" (*tong bi thu*).

7. "Le Duan Dies; Was Successor to Ho Chi Minh," Associated Press, 10 July 1986, http://articles.latimes.com/1986-07-10/news/mn-22581_1 (accessed 28 Dec. 2010).

8. For an excellent discussion of an earlier period in Vietnamese Communist history when a cult of personality was advanced, see Holcombe, "De-Stalinization and the Vietnam Worker's Party."

9. For the enormity of the canon on the Vietnam War, see Herring, "The War That Never Seems to Go Away," 346.

10. This study answers the call put forth in Tony Smith, "New Bottle for New Wine."

11. See Connelly, *A Diplomatic Revolution*.

12. The Pentagon Papers, based on the *United States–Vietnam Relations, 1945–1967: A Study Prepared by the Department of Defense*, appeared in the *New York Times* in 1971. NARA announced the full release of the Pentagon Papers to the Richard Nixon Presidential Library and Museum in June 2011.

13. In particular, this study owes an enormous debt of gratitude to the pioneering works by Herring, *America's Longest War*; and Young, *The Vietnam Wars*; as well as to the informative syntheses in Bradley, *Vietnam at War*; Prados, *Vietnam*; Lawrence, *The Vietnam War*; Turley, *The Second Indochina War*; Anderson, *The Vietnam War*; Schulzinger, *A Time for War*; and Hess, *Vietnam and the United States*.

14. For the "recent resurgence," see Moyar, *Triumph Forsaken*, for the origins of American involvement; and Lewis Sorley, *A Better War*, for the second half of the conflict. See also Lind, *Vietnam, a Necessary War*; and Summers, *On Strategy*. For an earlier expression of the "revisionist" school, see Lewy, *America in Vietnam*. The Taylor-Buzzanco debate—Buzzanco, "Fear and (Self-)Loathing in Lubbock"; Taylor, "Robert Buzzanco's 'Fear and (Self-)Loathing in Lubbock'"; Miller, "War Stories," and "Roundtable on Mark Moyar's *Triumph Forsaken*"—provides a brief glimpse at the dangers and pitfalls of the field in recent years. For a great summary of the Vietnam War historiography and its debates, see Hess, *Vietnam*.

15. Kahin, *Intervention*; Rotter, *The Path to Vietnam*; Anderson, *Trapped by Success*; Lloyd Gardner, *Pay Any Price*; Logevall, *Choosing War*; Kaiser, *American Tragedy*. For studies that analyze the effects of U.S. nation-building in South Vietnam more closely and view the RVN as an American construct or as unviable, see Carter, *Inventing Vietnam*; and Jacobs, *Inventing Vietnam*.

16. For "quagmire," see Schlesinger, *The Bitter Heritage*; for "stalemate," see Gelb and Betts, *The Irony of Vietnam*; for "flawed containment," see Herring, *America's Longest War*.

17. For transatlantic pressures, see Lawrence, *Assuming the Burden*; and Statler, *Replacing France*. For domestic political considerations, see Logevall, *Choosing War*. For the importance of key officials and bureaucratic infighting, see Porter, *Perils of Dominance*; and Preston, *War Council*. For modernization, see Ekbladh, *The Great American Mission*.

18. Prados's recent comprehensive study is the exception. Although it covers the entirety of the Vietnam War, it focuses on the second half of the conflict. See Prados, *Vietnam*.

19. Kimball, *Nixon's Vietnam War*.

20. Berman, *No Peace, No Honor*.

21. See Herring, *America's Longest War*.

22. Allen, *Until the Last Man Comes Home*; Johns, *Vietnam's Second Front*, 195–324.

23. For a great description of the newer trend, see Miller and Tuong Vu, "The Vietnam War as a Vietnamese War." The exception includes a few senior scholars who have

long published in this field using Vietnamese-language sources or, if they did not read Vietnamese, using translated documents or French materials on the war period. See Duiker, *The Communist Road to Power in Vietnam*, and *Sacred War*; Marr, *Vietnam, 1945*; and Race, *War Comes to Long An*.

24. Brocheux, *Ho Chi Minh*; Currey, *Victory at Any Cost*; Duiker, *Ho Chi Minh*; Giebel, *Imagined Ancestries of Vietnamese Communism*; Pelley, *Postcolonial Vietnam*; Hoai Julie Pham, "Revolution, Communism, and History in the Thought of Tran Van Giau"; Quinn-Judge, *Ho Chi Minh*. The field of Vietnam War studies owes a debt of gratitude to Merle Pribbenow, who translated the official PAVN history, *Victory in Vietnam*.

25. For instance, see Kerkvliet, *The Power of Everyday Politics*; and Ninh, *A World Transformed*.

26. For the southern revolution, see Brigham, *Guerrilla Diplomacy*; David Elliott, *The Vietnamese War*; Hunt, *Vietnam's Southern Revolution*; and Thayer, *War by Other Means*. For the Republic of Vietnam, see Biggs, *Quagmire*; Elkind, "The First Casualties"; Tuan Hoang, "Ideology in Urban South Vietnam"; Stewart, "Revolution, Modernization and Nation-Building in Diem's Vietnam"; and Nu Anh Tran, "Contested Identities." For a more dated account, see Jamieson, *Understanding Vietnam*. For the ARVN, see Brigham, *ARVN*; Loicano, "Military and Political Roles of Weapons Systems in the Republic of Vietnam Armed Forces"; Wiest, *Vietnam's Forgotten Army*; and Willbanks, *Abandoning Vietnam*.

27. Bradley, *Imagining Vietnam and America*.

28. For the best account of a bilateral history of the peace negotiations, see Asselin, *A Bitter Peace*. See also Goodman, *The Lost Peace*; and Porter, *A Peace Denied*.

29. Catton, *Diem's Final Failure*; Chapman, *Debating the Will of Heaven*; Masur, "Hearts and Minds"; Miller, *Grand Designs*.

30. For an excellent anthropological study of the bloody nature of the Cold War in the postcolonial world, one that was anything but the "long peace" experienced in the West, see Kwon, *The Other Cold War*.

31. For Sino-Vietnamese relations, see Ang, *Vietnamese Communists' Relations with China and the Second Indochina Conflict, The Vietnam War from the Other Side*, and *Ending the Vietnam War*. See also Duiker, *China and Vietnam*; Chen Jian, *Mao's China and the Cold War*, esp. chaps. 5 and 8; Roberts, *Behind the Bamboo Curtain*; and Zhai, *China and the Vietnam Wars*. For Soviet-Vietnamese relations, see Gaiduk, *The Soviet Union and the Vietnam War*; Gaiduk, *Confronting Vietnam*; Olsen, *Soviet-Vietnam Relations and the Role of China*; Pike, *Vietnam and the Soviet Union*. For the role of East European countries during the Vietnam War, see Hershberg, *Marigold*.

32. For instance, see Ang, *Southeast Asia and the Vietnam War*; and Ruth, *In Buddha's Company*.

33. For an excellent study that places the Vietnam War in a larger global Cold War setting, see Westad, *The Global Cold War*. See also Suri, *Power and Protest*. Ralph B. Smith wrote three volumes of his pioneering *An International History of the Vietnam War*, but he passed away before he could take his study beyond 1966.

34. See the articles on *VKDTT* by Tuong Vu, Ken MacLean, Pham Quang Minh, Pierre Asselin, and Alec Holcombe in the Forum section of *Journal of Vietnamese Studies* 5, no. 2 (Summer 2010): 183–247.

35. The first volume covers the years 1924–30, while subsequent volumes span only a single (Western) calendar year.

36. *DTNG*. I would like to thank Jeffrey Kimball for providing me with an early translated copy of edited portions of this chronology.

37. This study also draws heavily from the chronologies of COSVN as well as the Ministry of Public Security. See VLSD, *Lich su bien nien*; BNV, *Luc luong chong phan dong*.

38. BQP-VLSQSVN, *Lich su khang chien chong My*. This study gives the figures for total Vietnamese casualties and devastation as 1.1 million soldiers killed; 600,000 wounded; 300,000 missing-in-action; approximately 2 million civilians killed; 2 million crippled or disabled; 2 million exposed to poisonous chemicals; 7.85 million tons of bombs and tens of millions of liters of herbicide dropped over the country; ibid., 8:463.

39. For example, see Vien Mac-Lenin, DCSV, *Le Duan*.

40. Nguyen Thuy Nga, *Ben nhau tron doi*.

41. Unfortunately, her memoir does not offer much detail after 1968.

42. Indeed, historian Hue-Tam Ho Tai writes, "Practically every southern family has members who fought on different sides of the Vietnam War." See Hue-Tam Ho Tai, "Faces of Remembrance and Forgetting," 190.

## CHAPTER ONE

1. Quoted in Le Kha Phieu, "Y chi," 31.

2. Vo Van Kiet, "Anh Le Duc Tho," 30.

3. Vu Quoc Khanh, *Tong Bi thu Le Duan*, 58.

4. Vo Van Kiet, "Anh Le Duc Tho," 30. I will refer to North Vietnam or the DRV as "the North" and South Vietnam or the RVN as "the South" only for the period after 1954.

5. See Ngo Vinh Long, "The Indochinese Communist Party and Peasant Rebellion in Central Vietnam," 15–34; and Luong, "Agrarian Unrest from an Anthropological Perspective." For an interesting article on the Yen Bai uprising and its impact on the Dai Viet in the 1930s and 1940s, see Guillemot, "La tentation 'fasciste' des luttes anticoloniales Dai Viet."

6. Zinoman, *Colonial Bastille*, 200. See also Nguyen Thi Huong and Nguyen Minh Hien, *Nho Anh Le Duc Tho*, 9–12; and Vo Quoc Khanh, *Tong Bi thu Le Duan*, 13–34.

7. See Zinoman, *Colonial Bastille*, esp. chap. 7.

8. See Jennings, *Vichy in the Tropics*.

9. Zinoman, *Colonial Bastille*, 299–300; Bui Tin, *Following Ho Chi Minh*, 32.

10. According to Bui Tin, however, Le Duan missed the August Revolution because the Party's top man in the South at the time, Tran Van Giau, forgot to pick him up; Bui Tin, *Following Ho Chi Minh*, 33. This is wrong: Le Duan was released in June or July 1945; Huynh Van Lang, "Cach mang thang 8 nam 1945," 62. For Le Duan's "revolutionary" education in Con Dao in 1945, see also Zinoman, "Reading Revolutionary Prison Memoirs," 32, 35.

11. Marr, "World War II and the Vietnamese Revolution," 129.

12. Vu Quoc Khanh, *Dong chi Truong Chinh*, 6–48.

13. Bui Tin, *Following Ho Chi Minh*, 30–31.

14. Bradley, *Imagining Vietnam and America*, 73–106.

15. Quinn-Judge, "Through a Glass Darkly."

16. For an excellent account, see Tonneson, *Vietnam, 1946.*

17. Bui Tin, *Following Ho Chi Minh*, 33.

18. For an excellent environmental history of the Mekong Delta in modern Vietnamese history, see Biggs, *Quagmire*. See McHale, "Understanding the Fanatic Mind?" For an alternate view, see Gilbert, "Persuading the Enemy."

19. See Bourdeaux, "Approches statistiques de la communauté du bouddhisme Hoa Hao."

20. Goscha, "A 'Popular' Side of the Vietnamese Army," 339.

21. See Tonneson, *The Vietnamese Revolution of 1945*, 340–44. During the Second World War, there was the *Tien Phong* (Vanguard) under Tran Van Giau and the *Giai Phong* (Liberation) under Pham Ngoc Thach. By the end of the war, Giau and his base of operations in Saigon took the lead and did not take instructions from Truong Chinh in the North in the summer of 1945.

22. See Goscha, *Thailand and the Southeast Asian Networks of the Vietnamese Revolution*, 143.

23. For an alternate but equally convincing interpretation that Nguyen Binh was in fact carrying out the orders of Ho Chi Minh and the Politburo in Hanoi, see Goscha, "A 'Popular' Side of the Vietnamese Army."

24. Comment made by Ngo Vinh Long at "Remembering Vietnam: The Last Memoir of the War in the Mekong Delta," workshop organized by the Center for the Study of Force and Diplomacy and the Center for Vietnamese Philosophy, Culture, and Society, Temple University, Philadelphia, 11 Nov. 2010.

25. Indeed, Nguyen Binh had already begun a campaign of terror and had assassinated many of the DRV's opponents within the Hoa Hao, Cao Dai, and Binh Xuyen in the South from 1945 to 1948. Undoubtedly, his success made him the foe of Le Duan and Le Duc Tho.

26. Nguyen Thuy Nga, *Ben nhau tron doi*, 41–44, 48–50. See also Xuan Ba, "Nguoi vo mien Nam cua co Tong bi thu Le Duan."

27. For the best study of the internationalization of the French Indochina War, a work that identifies 1950 as the turning point, see Lawrence, *Assuming the Burden.*

28. See Goscha, "Courting Diplomatic Disaster?"

29. The full list of inductees into the Politburo included Ho Chi Minh, Truong Chinh, Le Duan, Hoang Quoc Viet, Vo Nguyen Giap, Pham Van Dong, and Nguyen Chi Thanh. The alternate was Le Van Luong. At the congress, Ho was elected president and Truong Chinh was elected first secretary.

30. Goscha, "A 'Popular' Side of the Vietnamese Army," 347–49.

31. Ralph B. Smith, "China and Southeast Asia," 106.

32. Goscha, "A 'Popular' Side of the Vietnamese Army," 356.

33. Vo Nguyen Giap and Huu Mai, *Duong toi Dien Bien Phu*, 237–38.

34. Ralph B. Smith, "China and Southeast Asia," 103–4. In the middle region, Nguyen Son also launched costly attacks and in the South, Nguyen Binh, alluded to earlier, was in charge.

35. Le Hai Trieu, *Dai Tuong Nguyen Chi Thanh voi cuoc khang chien chong My, cuu nuoc*, 9–10.

36. Ibid., 11.

37. Ralph B. Smith, "China and Southeast Asia," 103–4.

38. Ban Bien Soan Lich Su Tay Nam Bo Khang Chien, *Lich su Tay Nam bo khang chien*, 1:304.

39. Vo Nguyen Giap, "Dong chi Le Duan."

40. There were an estimated 60,000 cadres at the time of the cease-fire, with 30,000 in the entire central region of the Mekong Delta. See Ban Bien Soan Lich Su Tay Nam Bo Khang Chien, *Lich su Tay Nam bo*, 1:352; and David Elliott, *The Vietnamese War*, 1:165.

41. According to some scholars, Le Duc Tho's becoming COSVN chair caused tension between him and Le Duan. According to Bui Tin, who defected to France in the 1990s and whose memoir must be read more as gossip, with perhaps a nugget of truth buried deep in its pages, their relationship was fraught with petty jealousy and distrust. Given the lack of documentation in Bui Tin's book, we can only speculate on the true nature of their relationship. If tensions did erupt between them during this period, these differences were smoothed over by the end of the French-Indochina War and in the new era of a shaky peace; Bui Tin, interview by author, Fairfax, Va., 12 April 2004. See also VNDR, Report 114, part 1, VA-TTU.

42. See David Elliott, *The Vietnamese War*, 1:163–211; and Hunt, *Vietnam's Southern Revolution*, 1–67. See also Vo Van Kiet, "Tong bi thu Le Duan."

43. Vo Van Kiet, "Tong bi thu Le Duan," 58.

44. Ibid., 58–59.

45. Quoted in DCSV, *Lich su Dang Cong san Viet Nam*, 2:80.

46. See Nguyen Thuy Nga, *Ben nhau tron doi*, 63–64.

47. Ban Bien Soan Lich Su Tay Nam Bo Khang Chien, *Lich su Tay Nam bo*, 1:353.

48. See Hansen, "Bac di cu."

49. VPBCHTU-DCSV, *Lich su Van phong*, 22. With Khuong's capture in late 1955, the headquarters of Territorial Committee 2 shifted to central Saigon.

50. Vo Van Kiet, "Tong bi thu Le Duan," 58.

51. David Elliott, *The Vietnamese War*, 1:219–22.

52. Le Kha Phieu, "Y chi," 44; Vo Chi Cong, "Dong chi co tong bi thu Le Duan," 30.

53. Vo Van Kiet, "Tong bi thu Le Duan," 58–59.

54. See VPBCHTU-DCSV, *Lich su Van phong*, 23.

55. David Elliott, *The Vietnamese War*, 1:220–21.

56. See Nguyen Thi Dinh, *No Other Road to Take*.

57. See VLSD, *Lich su bien nien*, 129–31.

58. Vo Van Kiet, "Anh Le Duc Tho," 30.

59. Estimates differ regarding how many casualties resulted from the campaign. Historian Edwin Moise estimates that 3,000 to 15,000 perished, while new Party documents hint that possibly more were killed. See "Chi thi cua Bo Chinh tri ve may van de dac biet trong phat dong quan chung, ngay 4 thang 5 nam 1953" (Politburo Directive on a Few Special Issues in Mass Mobilization, 4 May 1953), rpt. in *VKDTT*, 14:201–6.

60. The most famous uprising against agricultural collectivization took place in November 1956 in the predominantly Catholic community of Quynh Luu district in Nghe An province. The 325th PAVN Division reportedly put down the uprising, resulting in thousands of deaths and deportations. The RVN took advantage of the DRV's prob-

lems in Nghe An by publicizing the plight of hundreds of Quynh Luu survivors who managed to escape to the RVN, including the request for UN intervention. See Vietnam Chapter of the Asian Peoples' Anti-Communist League, *The Quynh Luu Uprisings*, n.d., Folder 12, Box 08, DPC: Unit 11—Monographs, VA-TTU.

61. *Nhan Dan*, 31 Oct. 1956. See also Holcombe, "The Complete Collection of Party Documents."

62. See *Nhan Dan*, 31 Oct. 1956.

63. See Ralph B. Smith, *An International History of the Vietnam War*, 1:89–95, for a very persuasive discussion on the lines of division among the factions in the Politburo and the shift in leadership following the Tenth Party Plenum of the VWP in the aftermath of the land reform campaign. See also Thayer, "Origins of the National Liberation Front for the Liberation of South Viet-Nam." Although the Tenth Plenum marked a major shift in the VWP leadership, the militants who used the Party apparatus needed to continue the consolidation of their power in the Politburo and the Party even after the 1956 Tenth Plenum, since their control was not yet absolute.

64. Nguyen Thi Huong and Nguyen Minh Hien, *Nho Anh Le Duc Tho*, 11.

65. Ninh, *A World Transformed*, 122–26.

66. Zinoman, "Nhan Van-Giai Pham and Vietnamese 'Reform Communism' in the 1950s."

67. See Ninh, *A World Transformed*, 126–31.

68. See Nguyen Chi Thanh, "Hay lao minh vao cuoc song va chien dau cua bo doi de sang tac phuc vu bo doi." Thanh presented this lecture at the Second National Cultural Conference in March 1957. See also Ninh, *A World Transformed*, 130–31.

69. Quoted in Ninh, *A World Transformed*, 131–32.

70. Ibid., 143.

71. The contributors to *Masterpiece of Spring*, meant to be a one-time publication, ended up compiling four volumes between August and November 1956. *Humanism* began with a circulation of 2,000 copies and grew to 12,000 by its fourth issue.

72. See Boudarel, *Cent fleurs écloses dans la nuit du Vietnam*; Ninh, *A World Transformed*, 154–63; Jamieson, *Understanding Vietnam*, 257–84; and Vo Minh, *Phan Tinh Phan Khang*.

73. With Le Duan's departure, Pham Huu Lau took over as head of the Territorial Committee. When Lau died on 16 December 1959, one of Le Duan's loyal deputies, Nguyen Van Linh (also known by his *nom de guerre*, Muoi Cuc), became head of operations in the South. See VPBCHTU-DSVN, *Lich su Van phong*, 21.

74. Nguyen Thuy Nga, *Ben nhau tron doi*, 66–84.

75. Ibid., 82.

76. Ibid., 83.

77. Ibid., 86–88. See also Xuan Ba, "Nguoi vo mien Nam."

78. Vo Nguyen Giap, "Dong chi Le Duan," 32–41.

79. See also Pribbenow, "General Vo Nguyen Giap," 7–8. Pribbenow claims that Giap held onto the draft until late 1958.

80. See Ninh, *A World Transformed*, 164–203.

81. See Kerkvliet, *The Power of Everyday Politics*, 67.

82. Ibid., 37–48.

83. Ibid., 54–56. Kerkvliet's theoretical approach seeks to synthesize the various approaches in the literature on Vietnam politics to understand the power dynamics in communist Vietnam, with "dialogical" approach being the one within which much of his research fits.

84. Ibid., 34–36.

85. "Bao cao Nhiem vu ke hoach ba nam (1958–1960) phat trien va cai tao kinh te quoc dan" (Report on the Mission of the Three-Year Plan [1958–60] to Develop and Economically Reeducate the Nation), rpt. in *VKDTT*, 19:451–524. See also "The Implementation of a Three-Year Plan of Socialist Reform and the Beginning of Economic and Cultural Development (1958–1960)," 1970, Folder 25, Box 07, DPC: Unit 06—Democratic Republic of Vietnam, VA-TTU.

86. Chapter 3 of Kerkvliet's study is devoted to the Party's collectivization policy from 1955 to 1961 and is titled "Building on Wobbly Foundations." According to Kerkvliet, although the state did not use violence to suppress resistance, coercion did help get villagers to join the cooperatives. Kerkvliet also points out other factors, such as villagers' trust in the Party and the promise of better living conditions, which he argues also contributed to the high participation. Although news of the literati dissidence in the capital spread to the countryside, on the whole, villagers did not openly protest the top-down process of collectivization.

87. Ibid., 70–72.

88. For example, see MacLean, "Manifest Socialism."

89. See Turley, "Urbanization in War," 377.

90. See Szalontai, "Selected Hungarian Documents on Vietnam."

91. Soviet deputy premier Anastas Mikoyan visited Hanoi in early April 1956, after the VWP approved the resolutions adopted at the Twentieth Congress of the CPSU. However, a joint statement did not result from the visit, suggesting that the Soviet and North Vietnamese leaders did not agree on all matters.

92. See Chen Jian, *Mao's China and the Cold War*.

93. Ibid., 74–84. See also Lüthi, *The Sino-Soviet Split*, 80–156; Radchenko, *Two Suns in the Heavens*, 23–70.

94. See Vu, "From Cheering to Volunteering"; and Vu, "Dreams of Paradise."

95. Ralph B. Smith, *An International History of the Vietnam War*, 1:103, 220. Beijing advised Hanoi "to concentrate on the socialist revolution and reconstruction in the North"; quoted in Chen Jian, *Mao's China and the Cold War*, 206.

96. *Nhan Dan*, 18 April 1958.

97. See Thomas Latimer, "Hanoi's Leaders and the Policies of War," pp. 2–4, n.d., Folder 18, Box 01, JDC, VA-TTU. See also David Elliott, *The Vietnamese War*, 1:216–24.

98. David Elliott, *The Vietnamese War*, 1:228.

99. Vo Nguyen Giap, "Dong chi Le Duan," 37.

100. Ibid.

101. Ralph B. Smith, *An International History of the Vietnam War*, 1:166.

102. "Bao Cao cua Bo Chinh tri tai Hoi nghi Ban Chap hanh Trung uong lan thu 15 (mo rong) hop tu ngay 12 den ngay 22-1-1959 ve tinh hinh mien Nam" (Politburo Report at the CEC Fifteenth Party Plenum [Enlarged] from 12 to 22 January 1959 on the Situation in the South), rpt. in *VKDTT*, 21:2–56. See also Brigham, *Guerrilla Diplomacy*, 1–18;

David Elliott, *The Vietnamese War*, 1:289–349; and Duiker, *The Communist Road to Power in Vietnam*, 179–214.

103. David Elliott, *The Vietnamese War*, 1:228.

104. See Nguyen Duy Trinh, "Thong tri cua Ban bi thu, So 232-TT/TU, ngay 16-5-1969 ve viec tiep tuc va mo rong phong trao dau tranh chong My-Diem tang cuong khung bo o mien Nam" (Secretariat Circular 232, 16 May 1969, Regarding the Continuation and Expansion of the Resistance Movement against the U.S.-Diem Advancement of Terrorism in South Vietnam), rpt. in *VKDTT*, 20:518–23.

105. BQP-VLSQSVN, *Lich su bo doi Truong Son Duong Ho Chi Minh*, 30–31; *Tu dien bach khoa Quan su Viet Nam*, 522. See also Hoang Vien, *Lich su Cong binh Duong Truong son*; and Phan Huu Dai and Nguyen Quoc Dung, *Lich su Doan 559 bo doi Truong son Duong Ho Chi Minh*.

106. David Elliott, *The Vietnamese War*, 1:215.

107. Ralph B. Smith, *An International History of the Vietnam War*, 1:157.

108. Mao's post-1958 shift in rhetoric toward supporting national liberation movements did not immediately translate into material support of Hanoi's war in the South.

109. Direct communication between Hanoi and the southern resistance through radio was not established until the summer of 1961. See David Elliott, *The Vietnamese War*, 1:229.

110. See "Bao cao tai Hoi nghi Ban Chap hanh Trung uong lan thu 16 (mo rong) hop ngay 16 den 30-4 va ngay 1 den ngay 10-6-1959 kien quyet dua nong thon mien Bac nuoc ta qua con duong hop tac hoa nong nghiep tien len chu nghia xa hoi" (CEC Report at the Sixteenth Party Plenum [Enlarged] of 16–30 April and 1–10 June 1959 on the Resolute Placement of Our Northern Countryside on the Road to Agricultural Collectivization to Advance Socialism), rpt. in *VKDTT*, 20:282–357.

111. David Elliott, *The Vietnamese War*, 1:229–30; 234–36. See also Hunt, *Vietnam's Southern Revolution*, 29–67.

CHAPTER TWO

1. Hoang Minh Chinh, interview with author, Cambridge, Mass., 28 Sept. 2005.

2. The VWP was organized under the principle of democratic centralization along five levels—central, regional, provincial, district, and village—with the national congress as the supreme body organ; however, real power lay with the Politburo. French colonial repression and the subsequent war for decolonization prevented the Party from holding regular congresses. Before the Third Party Congress in 1960, there were only two: the first took place in China in 1935 and the second in Hanoi in 1951. With the resumption of war, the Fourth Party Congress was postponed until 1976. After the 1960 congress delegates performed their tasks, which included electing forty-three full members and twenty-eight alternates to the Central Executive Committee, the congress was dissolved. The newly elected committee members, who served five-year terms, then elected eleven full members and two alternate members to the Politburo. The members of the Politburo were charged with carrying out decision making between the Party plenums. Although the CEC plenums were to take place twice a year, they averaged once a year during the war. See "Dien van khai mac Dai hoi dai bieu toan quoc lan thu

III do Chu tich Ho Chi Minh doc, ngay 10-9-1960" (President Ho Chi Minh's Opening Speech at the Third Party National Congress, 10 Sept. 1960), rpt. in *VKDTT*, 21:481–90. See also "Bao cao cua Ban tham bau cu doc tai Dai hoi toan quoc lan thu III" (Report of the Election Committee of the Third Party National Congress), rpt. in *VKDTT*, 21:491–94; Nguyen Van Canh, *Vietnam under Communism*, 56.

3. From 1960 until 1976, the position was officially called the "first secretary [*bi thu nhat*]"; it changed to "general secretary" after the war.

4. "Bao cao Chinh tri cua Ban Chap hanh Trung uong Dang tai Dai hoi dai bieu toan quoc lan thu III do dong chi Le Duan trinh bay, ngay 5-9-1960" (CEC Political Report at Third Party National Congress Delivered by Comrade Le Duan on 5 September 1959), rpt. in *VKDTT*, 21:495–656.

5. See Hunt, *Vietnam's Southern Revolution*, 29–46.

6. Ibid., 33.

7. See Truong Nhu Tang, *A Vietcong Memoir*; and Goscha, "Réflexions sur la guerre du Viet Minh dans le Sud-Vietnam." For the reestablishment of COSVN, see VLSD, *Lich su bien nien*, 240.

8. Nguyen Van Linh, n.d., Folder 08, Box 12, DPC: Unit 08—Biography, VA-TTU.

9. VLSD, *Lich su bien nien*, 246.

10. "Dieu le Dang (do Dai hoi dai bieu toan quoc lan thu III cua Dang thong qua)" (Party Statute [Ratified by the Third Party National Congress Representatives]) ("Dieu le Dang"), rpt. in *VKDTT*, 21:777–814. The Constitution of the DRV, ratified by the National Assembly in December 1959, also defined the structure of power in North Vietnam but is a less important document than the 1960 Party Statute. The only significant aspect of the 1959 Constitution can be seen in its departure from the 1946 Constitution: the latter was written by a National Assembly that included other nationalist parties in the DRV, while the preamble of the 1959 Constitution only acknowledged the Communist Party.

11. The full list of members elected to the Politburo in 1960 includes Ho Chi Minh, Le Duan, Truong Chinh, Pham Van Dong, Pham Hung, Vo Nguyen Giap, Le Duc Tho, Nguyen Chi Thanh, Nguyen Duy Trinh, Le Thanh Nghi, Hoang Van Hoan, and two alternates, Tran Quoc Hoan and Van Tien Dung.

12. "Dieu le Dang," rpt. in DCSV, *VKDTT*, 21:777–814. See also Nguyen Duy Trinh, "Chi thi cua Ban Bi Thu ve viec tang cuong lanh dao cong tac to chuc, ngay 20-7-1959" (Secretariat Directive on the Elevation of the Organization Leadership's Tasks, 20 July 1959), rpt. in *VKDTT*, 20:613–19. See also Thomas Latimer, "Hanoi's Leaders and the Policies of War," p. 8, n.d., Folder 18, Box 01, JDC, VA-TTU.

13. "Dieu le Dang," rpt. in *VKDTT*, 21:790.

14. Le Hai Trieu, *Dai Tuong Nguyen Chi Thanh*, 18.

15. "Dieu le Dang," rpt. in *VKDTT*, 21:790–91. The other members in the Politburo subcommittee were Vo Nguyen Giap, Nguyen Chi Thanh, and Van Tien Dung. See BTTM-CTC, *Lich su Cuc tac chien*, 396.

16. See Tran Quoc Hoan, "Loi khai mac tai Hoi nghi xay dung luc luong Cong an, thang 5 nam 1962" (Opening Speech at the Conference on Building the Security Forces, May 1962), rpt. in Tran Quoc Hoan, *Mot so van de xay dung luc luong Cong An Nhan Dan*, 7–19.

17. I would like to thank Merle Pribbenow for his insights into the far-reaching na-

ture of the VWP's security apparatus. One of the first occasions when the Bao Ve worked directly with the Cong An was in 1959, when they put down the rebellion, led by tribal chieftain Vuong Chi Sinh, of an entire ethnic minority community in Dong Van, Ha Giang province. See BNV, *Luc luong chong phan dong*, 110–12.

18. Tran Quoc Hoan, *Mot so van de xay dung luc luong Cong An Nhan Dan*, 11.

19. "Tang cuong cong tac dau tranh chong phan cach mang de bao dam thang loi cho cach mang xa hoi chu nghia" (Escalating the Work in the Struggle against Counter-revolution to Protect the Victory of the Socialist Revolution), rpt. in Trinh Thuc Huynh, *Dong chi Tran Quoc Hoan*, 525–38. See also Conboy and Andrade, *Spies and Commandos*.

20. BNV, *Luc luong chong phan dong*, 130–35.

21. She claims that he only married Le Thi Suong to appease his parents. Xuan Ba, "Nguoi vo mien Nam."

22. Nguyen Thuy Nga, *Ben nhau tron doi*, 99–100.

23. Quoted in Xuan Ba, "Nguoi vo mien Nam."

24. Nguyen Thuy Nga, *Ben nhau tron doi*, 110–12.

25. See Zhai, *China and the Vietnam Wars*, 86–88.

26. Following the failure of the Great Leap Forward (1958–60), which aimed to separate China from the Soviet model of economic development, the chairman had to cast Khrushchev and the Soviet Union as a threat to China, for domestic as well as external reasons. In response, Khrushchev reneged on the Soviet Union's agreement to share its nuclear weapons technology with China, and he withdrew all Russian technicians from the PRC in the summer of 1960. Prior to this point, Beijing and Moscow sparred indirectly by castigating other's communist satellites, with the Chinese condemning Yugoslavia and the Soviets criticizing Albania.

27. Gaiduk, *Confronting Vietnam*, 114.

28. Zhai, *China and the Vietnam Wars*, 83; Ralph B. Smith, *An International History of the Vietnam War*, 1:210.

29. For instance, Hanoi stated that its foreign policy was driven by the need to secure Chinese and Soviet aid for North Vietnam's first Five-Year Plan (1961–65).

30. See Yang Kuisong, *Changes in Mao Zedong's Attitude toward the Indochina War*, 26. Mao established schools and bases for secret military training in Asia, Africa, and Latin America, with special attention to the burgeoning revolutionary scene in Southeast Asia. He had learned from the Korean War, however, and never let his sponsorship take the form of active military involvement. In the early 1960s, Mao encouraged the Perserikatan Komunis di Indonesia (Indonesian Communist Party) to undertake a revolution, but he stood by in 1965 and 1966 as right-wing elements slaughtered unarmed PKI members in Java and Bali and General Suharto overthrew the PKI's ally, President Sukarno.

31. Gaiduk, *Confronting Vietnam*, 209.

32. See Stuart-Fox, *A History of Laos*, 99–126. According to Vietnamese sources, although the Soviets publicly promised to pressure the DRV to cease its military activities, they continued to supply North Vietnam and the Pathet Lao, sending a large air transport unit with Soviet crew to participate in the fighting up to the signing of the 1962 Geneva Agreement on Laos.

33. For the Chinese contribution to the Pathet Lao's attack on Nam Tha in May 1962, see Zhai, *China and the Vietnam Wars*, 104.

34. According to historian Christopher E. Goscha, the overland route only through Laos delivered only 317 tons of weapons in 1961, half of its goal, forcing the DRV to create Doan 759 to oversee a maritime route through the South China Sea. See Goscha, "Towards a Geo-history of the Wars for Vietnam."

35. At first, the Kennedy administration raised the hopes of the VWP's moderate faction, which hoped that the United States would agree to a coalition government in a neutralized South Vietnam as it did in Laos. For a brief period, diplomatic and political means rather than military ones once again gained ascendancy in the Party, as diplomatic feelers probed the possibility of neutralism and southern cadres reached out to noncommunist elements in Saigon society in preparation for a coalition government. The talks led nowhere, however. McNamara, Blight, and Brigham, *Argument without End*, 99–15; Herring, *America's Longest War*, 94–102.

36. See Herring, *America's Longest War*, 89–96.

37. For PAVN estimates, see BTTM-CTC, *Lich su Cuc tac chien*, 401–2; for the PLAF and irregular troops as well as ARVN strength, see Mai Ly Quang, *The Thirty-Year War*, 2:81, 85; and BQP-QK7, *Lich su Bo chi huy mien*, 89–90. For U.S. troop numbers, see "Total U.S. Military Personnel in South Vietnam," rpt. in Herring, *America's Longest War*, 182.

38. Quoted in Mai Ly Quang, *The Thirty-Year War*, 2:79.

39. See VLSD, *Lich su bien nien*, 242–43.

40. See BQP-K7, *Lich su Bo chi huy mien*, 94.

41. VLSD, *Lich su bien nien*, 279–81.

42. See Ralph B. Smith, *An International History of the Vietnam War*, 2:37; and Grossheim, "Revisionism in the Democratic Republic of Vietnam," 454–58.

43. See Stowe, "'Révisionnisme' au Vietnam," 58.

44. DCSV, *Lich su Dang cong san Viet Nam*, 2:175–76.

45. "Report Written on 6 May 1963 by the Hungarian Embassy in the DRV. Subject: The Results and Problems of the DRV's 1962 Economic Plan, and the Main Objectives of the 1963 Economic Plan," XIX, J-1-j, Box 8, 24/b, 004321/1963, MOL, Budapest. I would like to thank Balasz Szalontai for the document and its translation. See also Le Van Luong, "Chi thi cua Ban bi thu ve viec khan truong tap trung luc luong chong han, day manh vu san xuat Dong-Xuan 1962–1963" (Secretariat Directive on the Tense Work of the Combined Forces, Pushing forward Production of 1962–1963 Winter–Spring Term), So 58-CT/TU, ngay 31, thang 1 nam 1963 (31 Jan. 1963), rpt. in *VKDTT*, 24:70–75.

46. Le Duan's stance on the path to socialist revolution in the DRV was moderate compared to Truong Chinh's. By the early 1960s, Le Duan reversed Truong Chinh's emphasis on collectivization and called instead for industrial development first. He placed a higher priority on increasing production than on ideological purity in agricultural affairs. See Le Duan, "Cai tien quan ly hop tac xa, cai tien ky thuat, day manh san xuat nong nghiep" (Improving Cooperatives Management, Improving Technique, Stepping Up Agricultural Production), *Hoc Tap* 85, no. 2 (1963): 4–12, rpt. as Politburo Resolution So 70-NQ/TU, ngay 19 thang 2 nam 1963 (19 Feb. 1963), in *VKDTT*, 24:96–114.

47. Thanh oversaw the collectivization efforts from 1960 to 1962, traveling to Quang Binh province in the southern DRV to evaluate the Dai Phong cooperative. See Le Hai Trieu, *Dai Tuong Nguyen Chi Thanh*, 19–20.

48. See Mai Ly Quang, *The Thirty-Year War*, 2:94. The communist victory at Ap Bac in early 1963 boosted the VWP's confidence that it could defeat Ngo Dinh Diem's forces in a larger battle.

49. In 1963, Beijing and Moscow solidified their ideological positions in a final open exchange: the CCP published *The Chinese Communist Party's Proposal Concerning the General Line of the International Communist Movement*, and the Soviets responded with *Open Letter of the Communist Party of the Soviet Union*. See Lüthi, *The Sino-Soviet Split*; and Radchenko, *Two Suns in the Heavens*, 71–119.

50. See Asselin, "Revisionism Triumphant."

51. See BQP-QK7, *Lich su Bo chi huy mien*, 134–35. See also Pribbenow, *Victory in Vietnam*, 120. For an alternate view of Ap Bac, see Moyar, *Triumph Forsaken*, 186–205.

52. Logevall, "De Gaulle, Neutralization, and American Involvement in Vietnam."

53. For an excellent discussion of Diem and Nhu's motivations behind their dealings with the communists, see the 1963 chapter in Miller, *Grand Designs*.

54. Gnoinska, "Poland and Vietnam."

55. According to Luu Van Loi, the Diem regime turned down the NLF's proposal for a Laos-style neutralization for South Vietnam. It is unclear whether Loi was referring to Diem's opposition to the public proposal made in 1962 or to a secret initiative in 1963. Vietnamese communist studies neither confirm nor deny that secret contacts took place in 1963. See transcript of interview with Luu Van Loi by Merle Pribbenow, Hanoi, 4 June 2007, 42–43, http://vietnaminterviewsusc.org/wp-content/uploads/2009/07/Luu-Van-Loi-Oral-History-Interview.pdf (accessed 4 June 2011).

56. See Jones, *Death of a Generation*.

57. For decision making at the end of 1963, see David Elliott, *The Vietnamese War*, 1:430. For an alternate view, see Duiker, *The Communist Road to Power in Vietnam*, 221–22, which argues that Hanoi leaders needed to escalate the conflict because the post–Ngo Dinh Diem government under Duong Van Minh was popular and morale was low among resistance fighters.

58. Logevall, *Choosing War*.

59. See Ralph B. Smith, *An International History of the Vietnam War*, 2:348; and Duiker, *The Communist Road to Power in Vietnam*, 221–23.

60. Stowe, "'Révisionnisme' au Vietnam," 56–58.

61. "Quan triet thuc hien Chi thi cua Trung uong Cuc mien Nam va Bo cong an ve dau tranh chong phan dong sau dao chinh Diem-Nhu" (Studying and Implementing Directives from COSVN and the Ministry of Public Security on the Struggle against Reactionaries Following the Coup against Diem and Nhu), rpt. in BNV, *Luc luong chong phan dong*, 197–98.

62. See transcript of interview with Luu Doan Huynh by Merle Pribbenow, Hanoi, 6 June 2007, 42–43, http://vietnaminterviewsusc.org/wp-content/uploads/2009/07/Luu-Doan-Huynh-Oral-History-Interview.pdf (accessed 4 June 2011).

63. The Czech and Polish party lines, however, were not as neutral as Hoang Minh Chinh might have remembered them to be.

64. Hoang Minh Chinh, interview by author, Cambridge, Mass., 28 Sept. 2005. According to Hoang Minh Chinh, Truong Chinh had "coaxed and cajoled [*vuot ve, mua chuoc*]" him into preparing a report that he knew would be rejected.

65. For example, a COSVN cable to the National Reunification Committee on the South Vietnamese Buddhist protests held in the aftermath of the Venerable Thich Quang Duc's funeral ceremony emphasizes that the masses "had demonstrated a high level of hatred and revolutionary spirit and had been prepared to combat the enemy repression and terrorism," but COSVN still had "not quickly and fully understood the spirit and the revolutionary potential of the masses" enough to direct the movement; VLSD, *Lich su bien nien*, 377.

66. Ibid., 405–6.

67. David Elliott, *The Vietnamese War*, 1:613.

68. "Nghi quyet cua Hoi nghi lan thu chin Ban chap hanh Trung uong Dang: Ra suc phan dau, tien len, gianh nhung thang loi moi o mien Nam" (CEC Ninth Party Plenum Resolution: Escalating the Resistance, Advance, and Scoring New Victories in the South) ("NQ9: Ra suc"), Thang 2 nam 1963 (Feb. 1963), rpt. in *VNDTT*, 24:823, 829.

69. Pribbenow, *Victory in Vietnam*, 124–28.

70. The public statement of Resolution 9 was broadcast in Vietnamese on Radio Beijing and appeared in *Nhan Dan* on 20 January 1964. For the full Vietnamese version, see "Nghi quyet cua Hoi nghi lan thu chin Ban chap hanh Trung uong Dang Lao Dong Viet Nam ve tinh hinh the gioi va nhiem vu quoc te cua Dang ta" (CEC Ninth Party Plenum Resolution Regarding the World Picture and International Duties of Our Party) ("NQ9: Tinh hinh"), rpt. in *VKDTT*, 24:716–810. See also Ralph B. Smith, *An International History of the Vietnam War*, 2:220.

71. Le Duan, "Mot vai van de trong nhiem vu quoc te" (A Few Issues in Our International Duty), *Hoc Tap* 97, no. 2 (1964): 1–20.

72. Ibid.

73. Yugoslavia's Marshal Josip Tito was the principal target named in North Vietnam's public condemnation of modern revisionism. Attacks on Khrushchev were circulated orally within the VWP. See Ralph B. Smith, *An International History of the Vietnam War*, 2:226.

74. See Le Duc Tho, "Phat huy truyen thong cach mang, tang cuong suc manh chien dau cua Dang" (Bringing in the Revolutionary Tradition and Strengthening the Party's Resistance)," *Nhan Dan*, 2 Sept. 1963; Nguyen Chi Thanh, "Ai se thang ai o mien Nam Viet Nam?" (Who Will Emerge Victorious in South Vietnam?), *Hoc Tap* 90, no. 7 (1963): 18–21; "Nang cao lap truong, tu tuong vo san, doan ket, phan dau gianh thang loi" (Raising Our Position, Proletarianism, Unity, Striving for Victory), *Hoc Tap* 93, no. 10 (1963): 1–13.

75. Hoang Minh Chinh, interview by author, Cambridge, Mass., 28 Sept. 2005. For instance, Pham Van Dong continued to advocate peaceful coexistence; Pham Van Dong, "Mot so van de y thuc tu tuong doi voi hai cuoc van dong cach mang lon hien dang tien hanh" (A Few Issues Regarding Ideological Consciousness Regarding Two Major Revolutionary Movements under Way), *Hoc Tap* 94, no. 11 (1963): 11–16.

76. Quoted in Grossheim, "Revisionism in the Democratic Republic of Vietnam," 454.

77. Ibid., 454–55.

78. See Stowe, "'Révisionnisme' au Vietnam," 57; and Grossheim, "Revisionism in the Democratic Republic of Vietnam," 457–58.

79. Grossheim, "Revisionism in the Democratic Republic of Vietnam," 457.

80. Hoang Minh Chinh, interview by author, Cambridge, Mass., 28 Sept. 2005.

81. Le Duan alludes to the sensitive elements of Resolution 9 that could not be written down during his speech to the Twelfth Party Plenum in December 1965; see Le Duan, "Bai noi cua dong chi Le Duan, Bi thu thu nhat Ban Chap hanh Trung uong Dang tai Hoi nghi Trung uong lan thu 12 cua Trung uong" (First Secretary Le Duan's Speech at the Twelfth CEC Plenum) ("Bai noi Le Duan 12"), rpt. in *VKDTT*, 26:609. See also Hoang Minh Chinh, interview by author, Cambridge, Mass., 28 Aug. 2005.

82. Hoang Minh Chinh, interview by author, Cambridge, Mass., 28 Sept. 2005.

83. "NQ9: tinh hinh," rpt. in *VKDTT*, 24:716–810; "NQ9: Ra suc," rpt. in *VKDTT*, 24:811–62.

84. Nguyen Phuc Hoai, *Lich su Cuc Bao ve*. See also Le Duc Tho, "Nghi quyet cua Bo chinh tri ve viec phan cong nhiem vu giua Quan doi Nhan dan va luc luong Cong an nhan dan vu trang trong viec bao ve tri an o mien Bac va dieu chinh to chuc luc luong Cong an nhan dan vu trang" (Politburo Resolution Regarding the Assignment of Duties between PAVN and the Peoples' Public Security Forces in the Defense of Security in the North and the Correct Organizational Stance of the Peoples' Security Forces), So 116-NQ-TU, ngay 28 thang 4 nam 1965 (28 April 1965), rpt. in *VKDTT*, 26:150–58.

85. Nguyen Phuc Hoai, *Lich su Cuc Bao ve*.

86. Hoang Minh Chinh, interview by author, Cambridge, Mass., 28 Sept. 2005. In his 1993 "Open Letter [*Thu Ngo*]," Chinh identified Le Duc Tho as the main person responsible for his illegal incarceration; "Thu Ngo cua Cong dan Hoang Minh Chinh," rpt. in Thanh Tin (Colonel Bui Tin), *Mat that*, 371–88.

87. Nguyen Phuc Hoai, *Lich su Cuc Bao ve*. See also Grossheim, "Revisionism in the Democratic Republic of Vietnam," 456–57.

88. Nguyen Phuc Hoai, *Lich su Cuc Bao ve*.

89. According to Bui Tin's political memoir, the period from 1964 to 1966 witnessed a repressive movement called the "Military Revisionist Affair [*Vu xet lai trong quan doi*]." Bui Tin's account of this affair is based on information provided by retired General Kinh Chi, chief of the Bao Ve from 1958 to 1976. See Thanh Tin, *Mat that*, 189–90. The quote appeared in Bui Tin, *Following Ho Chi Minh*, 54.

90. See Vu Thu Hien, *Dem giua ban ngay*, 274–87; Grossheim, "Revisionism in the Democratic Republic of Vietnam," 460–61. Duong Bach Mai's mysterious death led European diplomats to speculate that he had been murdered because of his views.

91. By 1964, approximately 1,000 North Vietnamese studied at Soviet institutions. Although the vast majority followed the Party line, approximately fifty applied for asylum in the Soviet Union. See Stowe, "'Révisionnisme' au Vietnam," 58; and Grossheim, "Revisionism in the Democratic Republic of Vietnam," 464–68.

92. Grossheim, "Revisionism in the Democratic Republic of Vietnam," 461–62.

93. Nguyen Phuc Hoai, *Lich su Cuc Bao ve*.

94. Ibid.

95. Nguyen Thuy Nga, *Ben nhau tron doi*, 133.

96. For the Politburo's directive to strengthen the Party's leadership throughout the South, see VLSD, *Lich su bien nien*, 242–43. See also David Elliott, *The Vietnamese War*, 1:281–349.

97. See Truong Minh Hoach, *Quan Khu 9*, 369. The "Orient Group" (Doan Phuong Dong) was named after Moscow's successful launching of the "Vostok" (Orient) space-craft that coincided with the departure of North Vietnamese military and political cadres for the South in early May 1961. This was the largest group of high-ranking cadres sent to reinforce the South. See VLSD, *Lich su bien nien*, 259.

98. See Tran Van Tra, *Ket thuc cuoc chien tranh 30 nam*. For the English translation, see *Concluding the Thirty Years of War*.

99. Tran Van Tra, *Goi nguoi dang song*, 52.

100. Ibid., 59. See also BQP-QK7, *Lich su Bo chi huy mien*, 150–51.

101. Truong Minh Hoach, *Quan Khu 9*, 369. Thanks to Merle Pribbenow for the reference and translation.

102. Initially, Nga intended to sail on the same ship as General Thanh, a vessel provided by the Chinese and destined for the port of Sihanoukville. Sihanouk objected to Nga's presence, however, believing it bad luck to have a woman onboard. In the end, she took a smaller boat on a much more perilous journey, accompanying a shipment of weapons to the South. See Nguyen Thuy Nga, *Ben nhau tron doi*, 134.

103. BQP-QK9, *Lich su Bo chi huy mien*, 156. See also VPBCHTU-DCSV, *Lich su Van phong*, 46.

104. Le Van Tuong, "Tam Nhin Chien Luoc Sac Sao," 148. Thanks to Merle Pribbenow for the reference and citation.

105. BQP-QK7, *Lich su Bo chi huy mien*, 190.

106. Ibid., 150–67; VPBCHTU-DCSV, *Lich su Van phong*, 46–52. See also Duiker, *The Communist Road to Power in Vietnam*, 245.

107. BQP-QK7, *Lich su Bo chi huy mien*, 145–67; for Plan X, see 167–77. See also Pribbenow, "General Vo Nguyen Giap." At the same time, the VWP tried to launch a campaign in the South similar to the 1950s land reform and organizational rectification program. However, the Motivating the Peasants campaign was eclipsed by the military picture and the arrival of American troops. The Party needed to appeal to a broader base and thus played down the class-based nature of the revolution. See David Elliott, *The Vietnamese War*, 2:737–95.

108. Quoted in Pribbenow, *Victory in Vietnam*, 142.

109. Although Hanoi prepared for American intervention when the VWP Central Committee passed Resolution 9 in late 1963, the Politburo did not think the United States would actually expand its war effort. See David Elliott, *The Vietnamese War*, 1:612–13.

110. We now know that the attack on 4 August did not take place. See Prados, *The Gulf of Tonkin Incident*. For the full extent of declassifications on the Gulf of Tonkin incident by the National Security Agency, 30 Nov.–30 May 2006, see http://www.nsa.gov/vietnam/index.cfm (accessed 30 May 2006). See also Moise, *The Tonkin Gulf Incident of the Vietnam War*.

111. See Logevall, *Choosing War.*

112. See Zhai, *China and the Vietnam Wars*, 128–31. According to Zhai, Soviet heavy machinery and construction materials in 1964 dropped by 20 percent from 1962. In April, Le Duan requested that China send volunteer pilots and soldiers to North Vietnam. See "Conversation between Liu Shaoqi and Le Duan," 8 April 1965, Beijing, rpt. in Westad et al., *77 Conversations*, 85.

113. See Gaiduk, *The Soviet Union and the Vietnam War*, 33.

114. Radchenko, *Two Suns in the Heavens*, 141.

115. By mid-1965, the Soviet Union had replaced the United States as China's main enemy. See Khoo, "Breaking the Ring of Encirclement," 5.

116. Radchenko, *Two Suns in the Heavens*, 141–44.

117. See Cao Hung, *Lich su Binh Chung Thiet Giap Quan Doi Nhan Dan Viet Nam*, 37.

118. Le Duan to General Nguyen Chi Thanh, Feb. 1965, in Le Duan, *Thu vao Nam*, 74. Although Le Duan informed General Thanh that he would soon receive the contents of the Politburo's resolution of early 1965 outlining the strategy that COSVN should adopt, the first secretary gave his personal opinion on the proper application of the resolution.

119. BQP-QK7, *Lich su Bo chi huy mien*, 193–205.

120. Le Duan to General Nguyen Chi Thanh, May 1965, rpt. in Le Duan, *Thu vao Nam*, 96–114. This letter is a response to a series of questions that COSVN sent to the Politburo. Although Le Duan's tone is less optimistic than in the February letter, he continues to advocate aggressive war and to reject negotiations.

121. "Nghi quyet Hoi nghi Trung uong lan thu 11 (dac biet) ve tinh hinh va nhiem vu cap bach truoc mat, ngay 25–27 thang 3 nam 1965" ([Special] Resolution 11 Regarding the Current Picture and Pressing Duty, 25–27 March 1965), rpt. in *VKDTT*, 26:102–18.

122. Cao Van Luong, *Lich su Viet Nam*, 18.

123. Quoted in Pribbenow, "General Vo Nguyen Giap," 5. See Le Duan, *Thu Vao Nam*, 90–91, for the original quote.

124. See Herring, *America's Longest War*, 173, 182.

125. U.S. intelligence estimates concluded that North Vietnam was "taking punishment in its own territory, but a price it can afford and one it probably considers acceptable in light of the political objectives it hopes to achieve." See "The Vietnamese Communists' Will to Persist—Summary and Principal Findings Only," 26 Aug. 1966, in National Intelligence Council, *Estimative Products on Vietnam*, 366.

126. Herring, *America's Longest War*, 174.

127. "Capabilities of the Vietnamese Communists for Fighting in South Vietnam," Special National Intelligence Estimate, 13 Nov. 1967, in National Intelligence Council, *Estimative Products on Vietnam*, 434. According to U.S. estimates, approximately 500,000 to 600,000 civilians in the DRV had been diverted to part- and full-time war-related activities.

128. War Experiences Recapitulation Committee, *The Anti-U.S. Resistance War for National Salvation*, 68–69. Le Duan sounded the death knell for North Vietnam's socialist revolution in late 1964 when he cited the shortcomings of the VWP's agenda in the DRV, but he redoubled his exhortation of Party members to focus on the war in the South; Le Duan, "Nam vung quy luat kinh te va thuc te trong nuoc de lam tot cong tac

xay dung va quan ly nen kinh te xa hoi chu nghia (Bai noi cua dong chi Le Duan, Bi thu thu nhat Ban Chap hanh Trung uong Dang tai Hoi nghi Trung uong lan thu 10 ngay 26 thang 12 nam 1964)" (Firmly Grasping the Nation's Economic Law and Reality in order to Enact Good Development and Management Tasks for an Economic Socialist Foundation [First Secretary Le Duan's Speech at the Tenth Party Plenum on 26 December 1964]), rpt. in *VKDTT*, 25:509–57.

129. See Tran Thu, *Tu tu xu ly noi bo*, 276.

130. Hoang Minh Chinh, interview by author, Cambridge, Mass., 28 Sept. 2005. The militant leaders launched a campaign decrying Johnson's first bombing pause of December 1965 and January 1966 as a "dirty trick." See *Nhan Dan*, 3 Jan. 1966; and *Quan Doi Nhan Dan*, 12 Jan. 1966. See also Luu Van Loi, *Cuoc tiep xuc bi mat*, 124–38. We now know that the Johnson administration initiated the bombing pause to prove that Hanoi would not agree to talks. See Herring, *The Secret Diplomacy of the Vietnam War*, 110.

131. See Le Duc Tho's articles in *Nhan Dan*, 3–4 Feb. 1966, which were broadcast over Radio Hanoi, 6 Feb. 1966.

132. See also Le Duc Tho's article in *Nhan Dan*, 5–6 Feb. 1966.

133. George Washington University Cold War Group and Cold War History Research Center, *New Central and Eastern European Evidence on the Cold War in Asia*.

134. Hershberg, *Marigold*, prologue; Hershberg, *Who Murdered "Marigold"?* (2000). According to Cecil Currey, Giap was opposed to Hanoi's decision to pass up on the opportunity for direct negotiations in 1965; Currey, "Giap and Tet Mau Than 1968," 81. According to Hoang Minh Chinh, it was common knowledge in the VWP that the Poles were working to set up peace talks between Hanoi and Washington; Hoang Minh Chinh, interview by author, Cambridge, Mass., 28 Sept. 2005.

135. Vu Quoc Khanh, *Thu tuong Pham Van Dong*, 7–129; BNG, *Pham Van Dong va Ngoai giao Viet Nam*.

136. Le Duan, "Bai noi cua Le Duan 12," rpt. in *VKDTT*, 26:594–95.

137. Quoted in Pribbenow, "General Vo Nguyen Giap," 20–21.

138. Ibid., 11.

139. See Vo Nguyen Giap, "Ca nuoc mot long day manh cuoc chien tranh yeu nuoc vi dai kien quyet danh thang giac My xam luoc" (The Will of the Entire Country Strongly Pushes the Great Liberation Struggle to Defeat the Invading Americans), *Hoc Tap* 120, no. 1 (1966): 1–30.

140. Nguyen Chi Thanh, "Cong tac tu tuong trong quan va dan mien Nam ta voi chien thang mua kho 1965–1966" (Ideological Tasks of the Army and the People of the South and the Victories of the 1965–1966 Dry Season), *Hoc Tap* 126, no. 7 (1966): 1–10.

141. *Nhan Dan*, 22 Dec. 1965.

142. Le Duan wrote to COSVN in November 1965 that the struggle would have to be protracted (Le Duan, *Thu vao Nam*, 115–57). See also "Translation of Absolutely Secret (Declassified) Letter Possibly Written by Le Duan, First Secretary of the Lao Dong Party Central Committee (Captured by Units of the 173rd Airborne Brigade)," pp. 21–22, 15 March 1967, Folder 18, Box 06, DPC: Unit 02—Military Operations, VA-TTU.

143. BQP-QK7, *Lich su Bo chi huy mien*, 281–82. See also McGarvey, *Visions of Victory*, 7–16.

144. McGarvey, *Visions of Victory*, 16–17.

145. BTTM-CTC, *Lich su Cuc tac chien*, 455–56. See also Pribbenow, "General Vo Nguyen Giap," 12.

146. "Bai noi Le Duan 12," rpt. in *VKDTT*, 26:564–621.

147. Radchenko, *Two Suns in the Heavens*, 144–48.

148. Over 320,000 Chinese soldiers served in Vietnam during the course of the war. On PRC aid, see Zhai, *China and the Vietnam Wars*, 132–39; and Chen Jian, "Personal-Historical Puzzles about China and the Vietnam War," in Westad et al., *77 Conversations*, 26. See also Bui Tin, *From Enemy to Friend*, 99–100. On Soviet aid, see Gaiduk, *The Soviet Union and the Vietnam War*, 57–64, 79. The involvement of Soviet antiaircraft artillery increased with the intensification of America's air war in April, when B-52s were used against North Vietnam for the first time.

149. Regarding China's pressure on Vietnam to apply Mao's military strategy, see "Conversation between Zhou Enlai and Pham Van Dong, Hoang Tung," Beijing, 23 Aug. 1966, and "Conversation between Mao Zedong and Pham Van Dong, Vo Nguyen Giap," Beijing, 11 April 1967, rpt. in Westad et al., *77 Conversations*, 98–99; 104–7. For Soviet military aid and assistance, see Gaiduk, *The Soviet Union and the Vietnam War*, 59–63.

150. Luong Viet Sang, *Qua trinh Dang lanh dao dau tranh ngoai giao*, 34.

151. See "Conversation between Zhou Enlai, Chen Yi, and Nguyen Duy Trinh," Beijing, 18 Dec. 1965; "Conversation between Zhou Enlai and Le Duan," Beijing, 23 March 1966; "Conversation between Zhou Enlai and Pham Van Dong," Beijing, 10 April 1967; "Conversation between Vietnamese and Chinese Delegations," Beijing, 11 April 1967; and "Conversation between Chinese Deputy Foreign Minister Qiao Guanhua and Vietnamese Ambassador Ngo Minh Loan," Beijing, 13 May 1967; all rpt. in Westad et al., *77 Conversations*, 89–91, 93–94, 101–4, 107–14, 121–23.

152. The Chinese agreed only to a system whereby Hanoi had to pick up Russian shipments at the Soviet-Chinese border and escort the goods through PRC territory. When the Soviets asked for permission to transport planes to Vietnam by flying over Chinese airspace, the Chinese refused and accused the Soviets of wanting to pass secrets to the Americans. See "Conversation between Chinese Deputy Foreign Minister Qiao Guanhua and Vietnamese Ambassador Ngo Minh Loan," Beijing, 13 May 1967, rpt. in Westad et al., *77 Conversations*, 121–23.

153. See Vietnamese News Agency, 25 April 1966, for Pham Van Dong's speech to North Vietnamese National Assembly.

154. Document V, "Record of Czechoslovak Delegation Talks in Moscow Following Late September 1966 Visit to North Vietnam," Central State Archive, Prague; CC CPCz Archive, fond 02 11, Sv. 10, Ar. J. 11, List. 20, b. 18, file Novotny, Foreign Affairs—Vietnam. Document provided by Oldrich Tuma and translated by Francis Raska, in George Washington University Cold War Group and Cold War History Research Center, *New Central and Eastern European Evidence on the Cold War in Asia*.

155. Yang Kuisong, *Changes in Mao Zedong's Attitude toward the Indochina War*, 32–34; Zhai, *Beijing and the Vietnam Peace Talks*.

156. Quoted in Gaiduk, *The Soviet Union and the Vietnam War*, 80.

157. Ibid., 96–97.

158. According to Hoang Minh Chinh, Soviet and East European officials would regu-

larly come to see him both officially and informally at the Nguyen Ai Quoc Party School to ascertain the VWP revolutionary line; Hoang Minh Chinh, interview by author, Cambridge, Mass., 28 Sept. 2005.

159. See Le Kha Phieu, "Y chi," 31.

CHAPTER THREE

1. "Alleged Coup d'Etat Plot in Hanoi: 1967, December 1967," Folder 20, Box 1, DPC: Unit 06, VA-TTU. The excerpt appeared in the captured notebook of a squad leader named Truong of the Eleventh Company, Thirtieth Battalion, of the PAVN Capital Regiment, found in South Vietnam in February 1970. The excerpt, based on Le Duc Tho's classified report that was ratified at the end of 1967, appears to have been recorded by Truong while he was on active duty in Hanoi on 21 December 1967.

2. To Huu, "Nho Anh" (Remembering You), 7 July 1967, rpt. in Le Hai Trieu, *Dai Tuong Nguyen Chi Thanh*, 42–43.

3. Le Hai Trieu, *Dai Tuong Nguyen Chi Thanh*, 35–37.

4. For the most comprehensive discussion of the contemporary and postwar debates and disagreements regarding Hanoi's Tet strategy, see Pribbenow, "General Vo Nguyen Giap"; and David Elliott, *The Vietnamese War*, 2:1054–62. See also Ngo Vinh Long, "The Tet Offensive and Its Aftermath."

5. The vast preponderance of the literature on the Tet Offensive in the West focuses on the military, political, and psychological impact of the offensive on the U.S. war effort. Regarding Hanoi's motivations for launching the Tet Offensive, Western studies generally echo the Vietnamese ones. Given the absence of official documents and other primary evidence from the Vietnamese side, this is understandable. A few studies stand as exceptions, however. See David Elliott, *The Vietnamese War*, 2:1036–125; Asselin, "Revisionism Triumphant"; Brigham, "The NLF and the Tet Offensive," 63–69; Duiker, *The Communist Road to Power in Vietnam*, 255–99; and Ang, "Decision-Making Leading to the Tet Offensive."

6. David Elliott, *The Vietnamese War*, 2:1055.

7. See Ho Khang, *The Tet Mau Than 1968 Event*, 13–19. According to Ho Khang, Operations Attleboro, Cedar Falls, and Junction City failed to attain their objective of destroying the insurgency, while the ARVN made little headway in its pacification efforts, controlling only 13 percent of the countryside.

8. BQP-VLSQSVN, *Lich su khang chien chong My*, vol. 5, *Tong tien cong va noi day nam 1968*, 29. See also Ho Khang, *The Tet Mau Than 1968 Event*, 23.

9. See *Lich su khang chien chong My*, 5:9–28.

10. See Pham Gia Duc, *Lich su Quan chung Phong khong*, 2:77–126.

11. Tran Van Tra, "Tet," 39.

12. BQP-VLSQSVN, *Huong tien cong va noi day*, 5. For the English translation, see Destatte and Pribbenow, *The 1968 Tet Offensive and Uprising in the Tri-Thien-Hue Theater*, i.

13. According to the official history, there were three phases to the General Offensive and General Uprising, which took place from the winter of 1967 to the fall of 1968. See BQP-VLSQSVN, *Lich su khang chien chong My*, 7.

14. Lien-Hang T. Nguyen, "The War Politburo," 4–55.

15. David Elliott, *The Vietnamese War*, 2:1056.

16. Pribbenow, "General Vo Nguyen Giap," 11.

17. VLSD, *Lich su bien nien*, 573–74.

18. Luu Van Loi, *Nam muoi nam ngoai giao Viet Nam*, 1:259. See also Pribbenow, "General Vo Nguyen Giap," 9–11.

19. Pribbenow, "General Vo Nguyen Giap," 15.

20. "Nghi quyet Hoi nghi lan thu 14 cua Trung Uong Dang" (Resolution 14), rpt. in *VKDTT*, 29:41–68.

21. The Hoang Minh Chinh Affair is actually a part of the Revisionist Anti-Party Affair since the latter refers to the entire period from 1963 to 1967 while the former usually refers only to the arrests that took place in 1967.

22. Hoang Minh Chinh, interview by author, Cambridge, Mass., 28 Sept. 2005.

23. Bui Tin, interview by author, Fairfax, Va., 12 April 2004; Hoang Minh Chinh, interview by author, Cambridge, Mass., 28 Sept. 2005.

24. Le Van Luong, "Thong tri cua Ban Bi thu ve viec tich cuc thi hanh Chi thi 145 cua Ban Bi thu" (Secretariat Circular Regarding the Execution of Secretariat Directive 145), so 197-TT/TU, ngay 7 thang 8 nam 1967 (7 Aug. 1967), rpt. in *VKDTT*, 28:382–86.

25. See Vu Thu Hien, *Dem giua ban ngay*. For a more comprehensive list of the suspects in the Anti-Party Affair from 1963 to 1967, see Hoang Minh Chinh, "Thu ngo cua cong dan Hoang Minh Chinh" (Open Letter of Citizen Hoang Minh Chinh), Hanoi, 27 Aug. 1993, rpt. in Thanh Tin, *Mat that*, 387–88.

26. Transcript of Hanoi Intelligence Figure's News Conference, pp. 1–3, 17 April 1969, Folder 04, Box 02, DPC: Unit 06, VA-TTU.

27. By 1967, Major General Song Hao, director of the GPD, and Le Van Luong, a member of the Secretariat, had joined the Investigation Guidance Committee (ibid., 2).

28. Nguyen Phuc Hoai, *Lich su Cuc Bao ve*.

29. Tran Quoc Hoan, "Bai noi cua dong chi Bo truong ve nhiem vu cong tac tuyen huan (thang 7 nam 1967)" (Comrade Minister's Speech on the Responsibilities and Tasks of Propaganda Instruction [July 1967]), rpt. in Tran Quoc Hoan, *Mot so van de xay dung luc luong Cong An Nhan Dan*, 559.

30. In 1970, the head of the Bao Ve, Tran Kinh Chi, submitted his report to Tho and Hoan's Investigation Guidance Committee. In 1972, the committee submitted its report to the Politburo and CEC. In the end, legal action was taken against eight mid- to high-level officers. See Nguyen Phuc Hoai, *Lich su Cuc Bao ve*.

31. "Alleged Coup d'Etat Plot in Hanoi."

32. Stowe, "'Révisionnisme' au Vietnam," 59.

33. The only work that does briefly mention a connection between the arrests and the Tet Offensive is Oberdorfer, *Tet!*, 65–66. For a great discussion of the legal ramifications of the affair, see Quinn-Judge, "The Ideological Debate in the DRV and the Significance of the Anti-Party Affair."

34. According to Hoang Minh Chinh, the only way to debate the war in the South was through invoking Marx and Lenin in abstract terms; Hoang Minh Chinh, interview by author, Cambridge, Mass., 28 Sept. 2005.

35. This is a literal translation of the title of Vu Thu Hien's memoir about the affair, *Dem giua ban ngay.*

36. See Westad et al., *77 Conversations*, 66–97.

37. China's control over the valve of socialist aid to North Vietnam can be seen in Pham Van Dong's early April 1967 request to Chinese leaders to allow more Soviet aid to pass through to the DRV; "Conversation between Zhou Enlai and Pham Van Dong, Vo Nguyen Giap," Beijing, 7 April 1967, rpt. in Westad et al., *77 Conversations*, 97. A few days later, Zhou responded by informing the North Vietnamese that the Soviets wanted access to China's ports not only to aid the Vietnamese revolution but for "ulterior motives as well"; "Conversation between Zhou Enlai and Pham Van Dong," Beijing, 10 April 1967, rpt. in Westad et al., *77 Conversations*, 99. In May, the issue of Soviet use of Chinese airspace emerged; "Conversation between Deputy Foreign Minister Qiao Guanhua and Vietnamese Ambassador Ngo Minh Loan," Beijing, 13 May 1967, rpt. in Westad et al., *77 Conversations*, 119–20.

38. "Conversation between Zhou Enlai and Pham Van Dong, Vo Nguyen Giap," Beijing, 7 April 1967, 3:30 P.M.–6:30 P.M., rpt. in *77 Conversations*, 98.

39. Ibid., 100. See also Zhai, *China and the Vietnam Wars*, 170–71, 178.

40. "Conversation between Mao Zedong and Pham Van Dong, Vo Nguyen Giap," Beijing, 11 April 1967, rpt. in Westad et al., *77 Conversations*, 105.

41. See Ho Khang, *The Tet Mau Than 1968 Event*, 27–29.

42. For the Kremlin's activities prior to 1968, see Gaiduk, *The Soviet Union and the Vietnam War*, 52–56, 73–107.

43. Ibid., 128.

44. Stowe, "'Révisionnisme' au Vietnam," 60–61. See also Gaiduk, *The Soviet Union and the Vietnam War*, 108–10. According to Gaiduk, Soviet observers noted that by the spring of 1967, Hanoi had made its policy more militant, and the previous interest in negotiations had declined.

45. Gaiduk, *The Soviet Union and the Vietnam War*, 130–32; and Quinn-Judge, "The Ideological Debate in the DRV and the Significance of the Anti-Party Affair," 485. The headway made after the Glassboro meeting abruptly stopped in August.

46. "Alleged Coup d'Etat Plot in Hanoi."

47. Not only was Hoang Minh Chinh accused of passing state secrets to the Soviet Union, but General Nguyen Van Vinh, vice minister of defense and director of the National Reunification Committee, also discussed the extent of Chinese aid to Vietnam during a meeting with Soviet ambassador Scherbakov on 13 June 1967. On the Vietnamese Communist Party's 1994 evidence, compiled in a report titled "Hoat dong cua mot so the luc thu dich va chong doi" (The Activities of a Number of the Influential Hostile Opposition), which included Hoang Minh Chinh's passing secret Sino-Vietnamese transcripts and preparing traitorous theses, see Stowe, "'Révisionnisme' au Vietnam," 66; and Quinn-Judge, "The Ideological Debate in the DRV and the Significance of the Anti-Party Affair," 482. East German documents reveal that Duong Bach Mai was an informant before his death in 1964, and Polish documents allude to a Vietnamese informant's providing intelligence regarding Hanoi and Beijing's positions on negotiations. See Grossheim, "Revisionism in the Democratic Republic of Vietnam," 451–52; Polish

cyphergrams nos. 16274 and 16288, in George Washington University Cold War Group and Cold War History Research Center, *New Central and Eastern European Evidence on the Cold War in Asia*; and Hershberg, *Marigold*.

48. See Hoang Van Hoan, *A Drop in the Ocean*, 420.

49. See Oberdorfer, *Tet!*, 44.

50. Bui Tin, *Following Ho Chi Minh*, 64.

51. See Nguyet Tu, *Chuyen tinh cua cac chinh khach Viet Nam*, 68–84. See also Pribbenow, "General Vo Nguyen Giap," 13–14.

52. Nghi quyet Hoi nghi lan thu nam Trung uong Cuc, thang 5 nam 1967" (Resolution of the Fifth COSVN Plenum, May 1967), rpt. in *VKDTT*, 28:485–559. See also Nguyen Chi Thanh, "Dong–Xuan thang lon" (Winter–Spring Decisive Victory), and "Chien thang Dong–Xuan 1966–1967 va nam bai hoc thanh cong ve chi dao chien luoc quan su" (1966–1967 Winter–Spring Decisive Victory and the Successful Lessons and Teachings of Military Strategy), rpt. in Le Hai Trieu, *Dai tuong Nguyen Chi Thanh*, 575–615. See also BQP-QK7, *Lich su Bo chi huy mien*, 283.

53. BTTM-CTC, *Lich su Cuc Tac chien*, 468.

54. Ibid., 469.

55. "Gui Khu uy Sai Gon–Gia Dinh, ngay 1 thang 7 nam 1967" (Le Duan to the Saigon–Gia Dinh Zone Party Committee, 1 July 1967), rpt. in Le Duan, *Thu vao Nam*, 158–88. At the Fourteenth Plenum in January 1968, Le Duan emphasized the ability of the revolution to hold on to Da Nang for seventy days during the uprisings as proof that urban centers were ripe for a general uprising; "Bai phat bieu cua Dong chi Le Duan tai Hoi nghi lan thu 14 Ban chap hanh Trung uong Dang Lao dong Viet Nam" (Comrade Le Duan's Speech at the Fourteenth Plenum of the Central Committee of the VWP), Jan. 1968, in *VKDTT*, 29:29–31. For a good account of the uprisings in the summer of 1966, see Topmiller, *Lotus Unleashed*.

56. Oberdorfer (*Tet*, 65–66), writing only in 1971, concluded that had General Thanh lived past 1967, the Tet Offensive would not have been as violent. See also Turley, *The Second Indochina War*, 102. At the time, the Soviet embassy in Hanoi did not have an accurate reading of the roles played by Thanh and Giap in the military debate. It believed that Thanh, being "pro-Chinese," would have been against a major military offensive in 1968. See Gaiduk, *The Soviet Union and the Vietnam War*, 139. For a different interpretation of Giap's contributions to the 1968 offensive and the fault lines between military commanders in Hanoi versus Tri-Thien, see Prados, *Vietnam*, 190–96.

57. Bui Tin has claimed that Le Duan, Le Duc Tho, and Pham Hung tried to neutralize Ho Chi Minh, Pham Van Dong, and Vo Nguyen Giap. The "professional revolutionaries," such as Le Duc Tho, who possibly had "class" skeletons in the closet, may have had personal reasons for resorting to intimidation. See Bui Tin, *Following Ho Chi Minh*, 32–34; and Thanh Tin, *Mat that*, 187–93.

58. BTTM-CTC, *Lich su Cuc Tac chien*, 456.

59. Ho Khang, *The Tet Mau Than 1968 Event*, 30.

60. "VWP-DRV Leadership, 1960–1973, Part 1—The Party," 35–36, Document no. 114, VNDR, WDC, VA-TTU.

61. Pribbenow, "General Vo Nguyen Giap."

62. BTTM-CTC, *Lich su Cuc Tac chien*, 473. See also Pribbenow, "General Vo Nguyen Giap," 16.

63. BQP-QK7, *Lich su Bo chi huy mien*, 287.

64. Quinn-Judge, "Through a Glass Darkly," 128.

65. The formal paperwork was not concluded until 1972, but the legal ramifications persisted even after 1976. In 1970, the head of the Bao Ve sent a complete report of the investigation to the Party's CMC and to Tho and Hoan's Investigation Guidance Committee. In 1972, Tho and Hoan submitted their report on the arrests and made recommendations on how to handle the suspects to the Politburo and the CEC, both of which unanimously approved the report and its recommendations. See Nguyen Phuc Hoai, *Lich su Cuc Bao ve*.

66. Tran Quoc Hoan, "Bai noi cua dong chi Bo truong trong Hoi nghi phan gian lan thu 3 ban ve chuyen de phong chong gian diep hoat dong theo phuong thuc an nap 1966" (Minister's Speech during the Third Counterespionage Conference Focused on Combating Enemy Spies Hiding within Our Country, 1966), rpt. in Tran Quoc Hoan, *Mot so van de ve dau tranh chong phan cach mang*, 269–315.

67. Ibid., 277–82.

68. Ibid., 282.

69. Ibid., 304.

70. Hoang Minh Chinh, interview by author, Cambridge, Mass., 28 Sept. 2005.

71. Pribbenow, "General Vo Nguyen Giap," 22–23.

72. Ibid., 17–18.

73. BQP-VLSQSVN, *Lich su khang chien chong My cuu nuoc*, 5:32–34.

74. Hoang Minh Chinh, interview by author, Cambridge, Mass., 28 Sept. 2005.

75. According to Pribbenow, Giap asked a journalist in 2004 to contact Le Trong Nghia, whom the general described as "an old and loyal subordinate." Giap said that Le Trong Nghia had "been close to him from the Battle of Dien Bien Phu up to just before the Tet Offensive but [that he] had then been 'separated' from him for reasons impossible to resist"; Pribbenow, "General Vo Nguyen Giap," 23.

76. Pribbenow, "General Vo Nguyen Giap," 18.

77. David Elliott, *The Vietnamese War*, 2:1064.

78. Ho Khang, *The Tet Mau Than 1968 Event*, 31.

79. Tran Van Tra, "Tet," 53. See also Tran Bach Dang, "Mau Than—Sau 30 Nam Nhin Lai" (1968 Tet—Thirty Years Later in Retrospect), in VLSQSVN, *Cuoc tong tien cong*, 101. According to a postwar study, the need to maintain strict secrecy caused the delay in transmission. The PAVN general staff first sent a set of fake battle plans to southern battlefield commanders. In October and November, to prevent the real Tet battle plans from falling into enemy hands, key commanders traveled to Hanoi or special envoys from PAVN High Command traveled South to pass on the plans orally. See Ho Khang, *The Tet Mau Than 1968 Event*, 53. However, this explanation does not account for the delay in transmission, since DRV war leaders could have simultaneously carried on their deflectionary tactics and briefed southern commanders as early as July.

80. Pribbenow, "General Vo Nguyen Giap," 23.

81. One notable exception is Hoang Van Hoan, who defected to the PRC in 1979.

82. See Le Duc Tho, "Xay dung Dang kieu moi mac-xit-le-ni-nit vung manh cua giai cap cong nhan" (Building the Party in a New Marxist-Leninist Manner That Continues to Strengthen the Role of the Worker), *Hoc Tap* 145, no. 2 (1968): 31. See also Truong Chinh, "Doi doi nho on Cac Mac va di con duong Cac Mac da vach ra" (We Are Eternally Grateful to Karl Marx and the Path He Opened), part 1, *Hoc Tap* 152, no. 9 (1968): 1–12; and ibid., part 2, *Hoc Tap* 153, no. 10 (1968): 10–53. See also "Notes on DRV Leaders Views on the Issues of War in the South and Reconstruction in the North: The Limited Possibility of Internal Dispute," pp. 8–15, n.d., Folder 18, Box 01, JDC, VA-TTU.

83. Quinn-Judge, "The Ideological Debate in the DRV and the Significance of the Anti-Party Affair," 486.

84. "Alleged Coup d'Etat Plot in Hanoi."

85. Pribbenow, "General Vo Nguyen Giap," 19.

CHAPTER FOUR

1. Quoted in Nguyen Thi Binh, "Le Duc Tho," 351.

2. Tran Thi Lien (former resident of 62/195 Ly Chinh Thang, Quan 3, Phuong 8), interview by author, Springfield, Penn., 30 Jan. 2008.

3. Nguyen Thuy Nga, *Ben nhau tron doi*, 166.

4. Ibid., 169–70.

5. Luu Van Loi, *Nam muoi nam ngoai giao Viet Nam*, 1:321.

6. For the writing of history in postwar Vietnam, see Pelley, *Postcolonial Vietnam*. See also Giebel, *Imagined Ancestries of Vietnamese Communism*. See also Lien-Hang T. Nguyen, "Vietnamese Perceptions of the French-Indochina War."

7. For a recent official estimate of "111,306 cadres and enlisted men of our armed forces and political in South Vietnam were killed or wounded and tens of thousands of members of the revolutionary masses," see DCSV, *Lich su Dang cong sang Viet Nam*, 2:441. See also VLSQSVN, *Cuoc tong tien cong*. The story behind the conference that led to the publication of this essay collection is in Colonel Bui Tin's memoir published under his pseudonym (Thanh Tin, *Mat that*, 171–81), which includes critical remarks on Le Duan's leadership. See also Tran Van Tra, "Tet," 37–65.

8. Ho Khang, *The Tet Mau Than 1968 Event*, 1.

9. Official estimates place civilian casualties at 3,000 to 6,000. For contemporaneous analyses of the "Hue Massacre," see Porter and Ackland, "Vietnam"; and Pike, *The Viet Cong Strategy of Terror*, 23–42. On 16 October 1968, Le Duan issued a Politburo resolution that announced the change in leadership of the Tri-Thien-Hue region. See "Nghi quyet cua Bo Chinh tri ve viec kien toan to chuc va lanh dao cua Khu uy Tri-Thien-Hue" (Politburo Resolution Regarding Strengthening the Organizational Leadership of the Tri-Thien-Hue Zone Party Committee), 16 Oct. 1968, rpt. in *VKDTT*, 29:478–91.

10. David Elliott, *The Vietnamese War*, 2:1101–19, 1126–45.

11. See Zhai, *China and the Vietnam Wars*, 178.

12. According to historian Ilya Gaiduk, the Soviets may have tried to tip off the Americans indirectly regarding the ambitious scope of the Tet Offensive by issuing a communiqué, "unprecedented for Moscow in its relations with its allies and proxies,"

to reveal the "extent and scope" of Soviet assistance to the North Vietnamese in 1967; Gaiduk, *The Soviet Union and the Vietnam War*, 139–40.

13. "President Lyndon B. Johnson's Address to the Nation," 31 March 1968, rpt. in *Public Papers of the Presidents of the United States: Lyndon B. Johnson, 1968–69*, vol. 1, entry 170, 469–76.

14. See Le Duan, "Bai noi Le Duan 12," rpt. in *VKDTT*, 26:594–95. See also document 209, "Summary of a Speech by Chairman of the Lao Dong Party Reunification Department: Gen. Nguyen Van Vinh at a COSVN Congress, April 1966," rpt. in Porter, *Vietnam*, 329–30.

15. For a discussion of Johnson's policies in March and April 1968, see Herring, *America's Longest War*, 251.

16. According to Bui Tin, Le Duan's arrogance and hubris caused him to launch subsequent waves of attack to achieve the chimerical general uprising in South Vietnam. See Thanh Tin, *Mat that*, 177–81.

17. At the start of the second wave of attacks, enthusiasm in the countryside was quite high. However, a few weeks into May, when it appeared that revolutionary forces would fail to take Saigon, the cadres returned to the villages and refused to resume the fight. See David Elliott, *The Vietnamese War*, 2:1113–14.

18. Luu Van Loi and Nguyen Anh Vu, *Cac cuoc thuong luong*, 260.

19. In one interview, Loi claims he was cultural and press attaché at the DRV embassy in Moscow (Chinh Dinh, "Ky uc ve Hoi nghi Paris"). In his memoir, he claims to have served concurrently at the Foreign Ministry in Hanoi and as Ho Chi Minh's secretary for his foreign correspondence before being sent to Africa in early 1968 (Luu Van Loi, *Gio bui Duong hoa*, 231, 247). In an interview with Merle Pribbenow, Loi claims he was in Hanoi as assistant to the foreign minister (*tro ly BNG*); see transcript of interview with Loi Van Loi by Merle Pribbenow, Hanoi, 4 June 2007, 42–43, http://vietnaminterviewsusc.org/wp-content/uploads/2009/07/Luu-Van-Loi-Oral-History-Interview.pdf (accessed 4 June 2011).

20. Chinh Dinh, "Ky uc ve Hoi nghi Paris."

21. See Zhai, *Beijing and the Vietnam Peace Talks*, for Chinese obstruction of peace initiatives prior to 1968. On the Soviet Union's role in setting up peace talks, see Herring, *The Secret Diplomacy of the Vietnam War*.

22. "Meeting between Zhou Enlai and Pham Van Dong," Beijing, 13 April 1968, rpt. in Westad et al., *77 Conversations*, 122.

23. "Meeting between Zhou Enlai and Pham Van Dong," Beijing, 19 April 1968, rpt. in ibid., 124–27.

24. For the discussion of the Cultural Revolution, see "Meeting between Zhou Enlai, Kang Sheng, and Pham Van Dong," Beijing, 29 April 1968, rpt. in ibid., 129–34. For Zhou Enlai's comments regarding Hanoi's war strategy, see "Hoi dam cap cao Trung-Viet, 29-4-1968" (High-Level Sino-Vietnamese Meetings, 29 April 1968), rpt. in *DTNG*, 4:152–53.

25. Gaiduk, *The Soviet Union and the Vietnam War*, 140.

26. Ibid., 152–55.

27. Van kien cua nuoc VNDCCH (DRV Country Files), 3 May 1968, tap 18a (vol. 18a), PLT-BNG.

28. Luu Van Loi, *Nam muoi nam ngoai giao Viet Nam*, 273.

29. Ang, *Ending the Vietnam War*, 11.

30. "Meeting between Zhou Enlai, Chen Yi, and Xuan Thuy," Beijing, 7 May 1968, rpt. in Westad et al., *77 Conversations*, 126–29.

31. See "Meeting between Zhou Enlai and Pham Hung," Beijing, 29 June 1968, rpt. in ibid., 137–38.

32. Northern security forces clashed with ethnic minority tribesmen in early February 1968 when a rumor had spread that a Meo king would soon replace Ho Chi Minh, prompting Meo youth to become draft dodgers. Around the Lunar New Year, there were reports that Meo tribesmen held "spirit possession ceremonies and seances" to avoid being commandeered into service after the holiday. A few weeks later, stories had spread that the king had arrived in Xa Nhe village and that he possessed magic powers that could kill all his enemies. He and his soldiers engaged security forces in battle but lost. Following the episode, the Ministry of Public Security resolved to improve the Party's ethnic minority policy. See BNV, *Luc luong chong phan dong*, 259–65.

33. See Thanh Tin, *Mat that*, 177–81, for Le Duan's role in decision making. For the official version of the decision to approve the second wave of attacks, see BQP-VLSQSVN, *Lich su khang chien chong My*, 5:159–62.

34. Bui Tin, *From Enemy to Friend*, 68–69.

35. Luu Van Loi and Nguyen Anh Vu, *Cac cuoc thuong luong*, 264.

36. See chapter 2 for a lengthier discussion of how Le Duan marginalized Ho Chi Minh and of Le Duan's report to the southern revolutionaries after Geneva.

37. In an interview with the *Journal of Military History*, Le Duc Tho said he regretted leaving his position as director of the Party's Organizational Department. See "Dong chi Le Duc Tho noi ve mot so van de tong ket chien tranh va bien soan lich su quan su" (Comrade Le Duc Tho Discusses the End of the War and the Writing of Military History), *Tap Chi Lich su Quan su* 4 (28) 1988, 105.

38. Stowe, "'Révisionnisme' au Vietnam," 59.

39. Although the arrestees who survived their confinement were released in 1972 and some later in 1976, lingering stigma made their reentry into society difficult. In 1981, prior to the Fifth Congress of the Vietnamese Communist Party, Hoang Minh Chinh and General Dang Kim Giang submitted a statement that they were victims of injustice. Under the orders of Le Duc Tho, both men were sent back to prison, where General Dang Kim Giang died for lack of medical attention. Hoang Minh Chinh was released in 1987 and again wrote statements regarding the abuses committed by the VWP in the 1960s, resulting in his being placed under house arrest for another nine years. In 1993, Hoang Minh Chinh wrote an open letter to Party and government organs on behalf of himself and others who were incarcerated in 1967, demanding restitution and the posthumous assignment of guilt to Le Duc Tho. On 14 June 1996, Hoang Minh Chinh was finally released after spending another year in jail. See Hoang Minh Chinh, "Thu ngo," rpt. in Thanh Tin, *Mat that*, 371–88. See also chap. 3, note 65.

40. Gaiduk, *The Soviet Union and the Vietnam War*, 157.

41. Ibid., 170.

42. BQP-VLSQSVN, *Lich su khang chien chong My*, 208.

43. Ibid., 208–9.

44. Ibid., 206–7.

45. Ang, *Ending the Vietnam War*, 12.

46. See "Nghi quyet cua Bo Chinh Tri: Ve tong khoi nghia, tong cong kich o mien Nam" (Politburo Resolution: Toward a General Uprising, General Offensive in South Vietnam), Aug. 1968, rpt. in *VKDTT*, 29:393–444.

47. Luu Van Loi and Nguyen Anh Vu, *Cac cuoc thuong luong*, 268–69.

48. Ibid., 271. See "Gap rieng ta va My, 8-9-1968" (Private Meeting between Us and the Americans, 8 Sept. 1968), Set 1, vol. E, rpt. in *DTNG*, 4:162; "Telegram from the Embassy in France to the Department of State," Paris, 7 Sept. 1968, Document 7, rpt. in *FRUS*, vol. VII, Vietnam, Sept. 1968–Jan. 1969.

49. "Telegram from the Embassy in France to the Department of State," Paris, 20 Sept. 1968, Document 24, rpt. in *FRUS*, vol. VII, Vietnam, Sept. 1968–Jan. 1969. See also Luu Van Loi and Nguyen Anh Vu, *Cac cuoc thuong luong*, 278–81.

50. Luu Van Loi and Nguyen Anh Vu, *Cac cuoc thuong luong*, 281.

51. "Anh Tho va anh Xuan Thuy gui den Bo chinh tri" (Incoming Telegram from Le Duc Tho and Xuan Thuy to the Politburo), Dien den, 20 Sept. 1968, rpt. in *DTNG*, 4:166.

52. "Anh Tho va anh Xuan Thuy gui anh Trinh, 28-9-1968" (28 September 1968 Telegram from Le Duc Tho and Xuan Thuy to Nguyen Duy Trinh), rpt. in *DTNG*, 4:168–69.

53. Luu Van Loi and Nguyen Anh Vu, *Cac cuoc thuong luong*, 282.

54. "Bo chinh tri gui Anh Tho va anh Xuan Thuy, 3-10-1968" (3 Oct. 1968 Telegram from the Politburo to Le Duc Tho and Xuan Thuy), rpt. in *DTNG*, 4:170–71.

55. See "Bo chinh tri gui Anh Tho va anh Xuan Thuy, 8-10-1968" (8 Oct. 1968 Telegram from the Politburo to Le Duc Tho and Xuan Thuy), rpt. in ibid., 4:172–73.

56. Luu Van Loi and Nguyen Anh Vu, *Cac cuoc thuong luong*, 284.

57. See "Dien mat cua Bo Chinh tri gui Trung uong Cuc" (Secret Politburo Telegram to COSVN), 10 Oct. 1968, rpt. in *VKDTT*, 29:468–74.

58. "Telegram from Embassy in France to the Department of State," Paris, 11 Oct. 1968, Document 58, rpt. in *FRUS*, vol. VII, Vietnam, Sept. 1968–Jan. 1969.

59. Luu Van Loi and Nguyen Anh Vu, *Cac cuoc thuong luong*, 285–86.

60. Ibid., 287.

61. "Information Memorandum from the President's Special Assistant (Rostow) to President Johnson," Washington, D.C., 16 Oct. 1968, Document 76, rpt. in *FRUS*, vol. VII, Vietnam, Sept. 1968–Jan. 1969.

62. If a meeting transpired between Le Duc Tho and Soviet leaders, it would have been tense. Since late September and early October, the Soviets were working hard backstage to convince Hanoi to accept Saigon's participation in the negotiations. The Hanoi Politburo's new demands, then, would not have been received well by Moscow leaders. See Gaiduk, *The Soviet Union and the Vietnam War*, 180–81.

63. "Meeting between Chen Yi and Le Duc Tho," Beijing, 17 Oct. 1968, rpt. in Westad et al., *77 Conversations*, 139.

64. Ibid.

65. "Bo chinh tri gui anh Xuan Thuy, 20-10-1968" (20 Oct. 1968 Telegram from the Politburo to Xuan Thuy), rpt. in *DTNG*, 4:180–81. See also Luu Van Loi and Nguyen Anh Vu, *Cac cuoc thuong luong*, 290.

66. "Dien mat cua Bo Chinh tri gui Trung uong Cuc" (Secret Politburo telegram to COSVN), 20 Oct. 1968, rpt. in *VKDTT*, 29:484–87.

67. Additional issues included the description and announcement of the enlarged talks. Regarding the description, the North Vietnamese preferred to call the enlarged talks a four-party conference, whereas the United States, not wanting to give equal stature to the NLF, insisted it was a two-sided conference. As for the announcement, the DRV wanted the United States to issue a special communiqué declaring the unconditional cessation of bombing.

68. "Situation Report by the Executive Secretary of the Department of State," Washington, D.C., 21 Oct. 1968, Document 95, rpt. in *FRUS*, vol. VII, Vietnam, Sept. 1968–Jan. 1969.

69. Gaiduk, *The Soviet Union and the Vietnam War*, 183.

70. "Information Memorandum from the President's Special Assistant (Rostow) to President Johnson," Washington, D.C., 25 Oct. 1968, Document 122, rpt. in *FRUS*, vol. VII, Vietnam, Sept. 1968–Jan. 1969.

71. See Zhai, *China and the Vietnam Wars*, 179.

72. Bui Diem, "Phuc trinh: Mot vai nhan xet ve chinh sach cua Hoa-Ky doi voi Viet Nam Sau ngay bau cu Tong Thong 1968 (mat)" (Report: Analysis of U.S. Policy toward Vietnam after the 1968 Presidential Elections [classified]), 3, Folder 1599, PTTDN, TTLTQG-2. The Nixon camp also obtained crucial information via Nelson Rockefeller's man, Henry Kissinger, who had contacts within the Democratic Party. Kept in the loop by his former student from Harvard who graduated to become Harriman's aide, Kissinger was able to warn Nixon that a diplomatic breakthrough was afoot in early October and thus secure his position in the new administration. With this information, Nixon then accused Humphrey of sabotaging peace negotiations in Paris and endangering the lives of American troops in Vietnam with his 30 September announcement. See Kimball, *Nixon's Vietnam War*, 57–58. See also Dallek, *Nixon and Kissinger*, 69.

73. For the Anna Chennault affair, see Berman, *No Peace, No Honor*, 32–36; and Bundy, *A Tangled Web*, 35–38. Chennault, chair of the Republican Women for Nixon, passed on communication from the Nixon camp to RVN ambassador Bui Diem telling Thieu to "hold out" on negotiations in late 1968, thereby guaranteeing the election of Nixon, who, following Johnson's October speech, was trailing Humphrey in the polls.

74. Ang, *Ending the Vietnam War*, 20–22.

75. "Nghi quyet hoi nghi Trung uong Cuc lan 9 (7/1969)" (COSVN Resolution 9 [July 1969]), T355V(09), 12559, TVQD. COSVN Resolution 9 has also been seen as Hanoi's decision to scale back its attacks from 1968 and to emphasize low-level "guerrilla warfare," but the Party would not revert to a defensive posture until 1970. See Lewis Sorley, *A Better War*, 155–57; and Davidson, *Vietnam at War*, 597.

76. Pribbenow, *Victory in Vietnam*, 244–52.

77. For the official casualty statistics, see Vo Van Kiet and Tran Bach Dang, *Lich su Nam bo Khang chien*, 2:673. According to these statistics, Regions 8 and 9 of Nam Bo suffered 5,983 killed in action and 8,199 wounded.

78. Nga, *Ben Nhau Trong Doi*, 171–78.

79. "Bo Chinh Tri gui anh Tho + X. Thuy" (Outgoing Telegram from the Politburo to Le Duc Tho and Xuan Thuy), Dien di, 1 Jan. 1969, rpt. in *DTNG*, 4:202.

80. Ibid.

81. See Burr and Kimball, *Nixon White House Considered Nuclear Options against North Vietnam.*

82. *New York Times*, 2 Aug. 1968; Berman, *No Peace, No Honor*, 45.

83. Kimball, *Nixon's Vietnam War*, 75.

84. Nixon, *No More Vietnams*, 103–7.

85. Quoted in Prados, *Vietnam*, 290. Nixon predicated his "madman" approach on what he saw as Eisenhower's success in ending the Korean War.

86. See Perlstein, *Nixonland.*

87. See Berman, *No Peace, No Honor*, 35.

88. See Hanhimaki, *The Flawed Architect*; and Del Pero, *The Eccentric Realist.*

89. Suri, *Henry Kissinger and the American Century.*

90. Dallek, *Nixon and Kissinger.*

91. See "Telegram from the Embassy in Vietnam to the Department of State," Saigon, 24 Jan. 1969, Document 7, rpt. in *FRUS, 1969–1976*, vol. VI, Vietnam, Jan. 1969–July 1970. It is clear that Nixon and Kissinger opted to ignore Ambassador Ellsworth Bunker's recommendations to keep Saigon in the loop.

92. Revised Summary of Responses to NSSM 1: The Situation in Vietnam, 22 March 1969, pp. 6–7, Box H-122, NSC Institutional Files (H-Files), NSCF, NPM, NARA.

93. See Kimball, *Nixon's Vietnam War*, 97, and *The Vietnam War Files*, 11.

94. Dallek, *Nixon and Kissinger*, 110.

95. Burr, *Kissinger Conspired with Soviet Ambassador to Keep Secretary of State in the Dark*. See also Keefer, *Soviet-American Relations*, 20–25.

96. "Meeting between Presidential Assistant Kissinger and Ambassador Dobrynin: Memorandum of Conversation," Washington, D.C., 21 Feb. 1969, rpt. in ibid.

97. Kissinger, *White House Years*, 171.

98. See Kimball, *Nixon's Vietnam War*, 146–76.

99. See "Memorandum from the President's Assistant for National Security Affairs (Kissinger) to President Nixon," Washington, D.C., 19 Feb. 1969, Document 22, rpt. in *FRUS, 1969–1976*, vol. VI, Vietnam, Jan. 1969–July 1970. Nixon approved Kissinger's memorandum on 22 February. See "Memorandum from the President's Assistant for National Security Affairs (Kissinger) to Secretary of Defense Laird," Washington, D.C., 22 Feb. 1969, Document 23, rpt. in *FRUS, 1969–1976*, vol. VI, Vietnam, Jan. 1969–July 1970.

100. "Memorandum for the Record," Washington, D.C., 15 March 1969, Box 136, Viet-Nam Country Files, Vietnam, vol. 1 through 3/19/69, NSCF, NPM, NARA.

101. Nixon, *RN*, 381; Kissinger, *White House Years*, 246–47.

102. Kimball, *Nixon's Vietnam War*, 135.

103. In late 1967, Soviet and Chinese border guards engaged in a few squabbles, but no deaths resulted. The first loss of life occurred when Soviet vehicles crushed four Chinese fishermen in January 1968.

104. See Yang Kuisong, "The Sino-Soviet Border Clash of 1969."

105. See Luu Van Loi and Nguyen Anh Vu, *Cac cuoc thuong luong*, 55.

106. Kissinger, *White House Years*, 172.

107. "Memorandum from the President's Assistant for National Security Affairs

(Kissinger) to President Nixon," 15 April 1969, Box 489, President's Trip Files, Dobrynin/HAK, 1969 (part 2), NSCF, NPM, NARA.

108. Kimball, *Nixon's Vietnam War*, 143–44.

109. "Memorandum from President Nixon to Secretary of State Rogers," Washington, D.C., 10 April 1969, Document 57, rpt. in *FRUS, 1969–1976*, vol. VI, Vietnam, Jan. 1969–July 1970.

110. Bui Diem, "Mot vai nhan xet va de nghi de trinh Tong Thong va Chinh Phu VNCH (thang 1 nam 1969) (toi mat)" (A Number of Issues and Resolutions for the President and Government [Jan. 1969] [absolutely classified]) ("Mot vai nhan xet"), p. 3, Folder 1666, PTTDN, TTLTQG-2. Bui Diem quotes directly from this confidential report in his memoirs without citation; Bui Diem, *In the Jaws of History*, 249.

111. Bui Diem, *In the Jaws of History*, 230–31.

112. Diem, "Mot vai nhan xet," 7–9.

113. Bui Diem, *In the Jaws of History*, 258.

114. "Memorandum from the President's Assistant for National Security Affairs (Kissinger) to President Nixon," Washington, D.C., 11 June 1969, Document 83, rpt. in *FRUS, 1969–1976*, vol. VI, Vietnam, Jan. 1969–July 1970.

115. Nguyen Thi Binh, "Le Duc Tho," 349.

116. Hung and Schecter, *The Palace File*, 37.

117. Ibid., 33–34. See also "Memorandum from the President's Assistant for National Security Affairs (Kissinger) to President Nixon," Washington, D.C., 4 June 1969, Document 79, rpt. in *FRUS*, 1969–1976, vol. VI, Vietnam, Jan. 1969–July 1970.

118. According to Ambassador Bunker, Thieu had accepted on 21 May that troop reduction would be on the agenda at Midway; "Backchannel Message from the Ambassador to Vietnam (Bunker) to the President's Assistant for National Security Affairs (Kissinger)," Washington, D.C., 21 May 1969, Document 70, rpt. in *FRUS, 1969–1976*, vol. VI, Vietnam, Jan. 1969–July 1970.

119. Hung and Schecter, *The Palace File*, 33.

120. Quoted in ibid., 34.

121. See Bui Diem, *In the Jaws of History*, 256. Ambassador Diem viewed the flurry of diplomatic activity in the United States as "a sudden deluge of delegations visiting Washington from South Vietnam. Somehow Vietnamese assemblymen, senators, judges, and members of an astonishing number of government agencies had discovered the concept of 'fact-finding' junkets."

122. "Phieu trinh cua Tran Chanh Thanh gui den Nguyen Van Thieu va Tran Thien Khiem v/v v/v tinh hinh chinh tri tai Hoa-Ky trong 1 dl 1969, 31-1-1969 (mat, khan)" (Report by Tran Chanh Thanh to Nguyen Van Thieu and Tran Thien Khiem on the U.S. Political Picture, 31 Jan. 1969 [Confidential and Urgent]), Folder 1666, PTTDN, TTLTQG-2.

123. "Tran Van Lam, Bang tong ket nhung thuc hien cua Chinh phu trong lanh-vuc ngoai giao, 3-9-1969" (Comprehensive Summary of the State of the Government's Foreign Relations, 3 Sept. 1969), Folder 1616, PTTDN, TTLTQG-2.

124. For an excellent study of the NLF-PRG's diplomacy, see Brigham, *Guerrilla Diplomacy*.

125. "Trinh bay Tong Cuc Chien Tranh Chinh Tri, thang 7 nam 1969" (Political War Department Policy Report, July 1969), Folder 479, PTTDN, TTLTQG-2.

126. "Van thua cua Nguyen Van Thieu den Tran Thien Khiem, 20-1-1970" (Letter from Thieu to Khiem, 20 Jan. 1970), Folder 1690, PTTDN, TTLTQG-2.

127. See "Memorandum from the President's Assistant for National Security Affairs (Kissinger) to President Nixon; Subject: Your Meeting with Sainteny, Tuesday, July 15, 1969, 10:30 A.M.," Washington, D.C., 14 July 1969, Document 97, rpt. in *FRUS, 1969–1976*, vol. VI, Vietnam, Jan. 1969–July 1970.

128. See *Public Papers of the President of the United States, Richard Nixon, 1969*, 544–56.

129. Hung and Schecter, *The Palace File*, 40.

130. See "Memorandum of Conversation," Saigon, 30 July 1969, Document 103, rpt. in *FRUS, 1969–1976*, vol. VI, Vietnam, Jan. 1969–July 1970.

131. "Memorandum from the President's Assistant for National Security Affairs (Kissinger) to President Nixon; Subject: Meeting in Paris with North Vietnamese," Washington, D.C., 6 Aug. 1969, Document 106, rpt. in *FRUS, 1969–1976*, vol. VI, Vietnam, Jan. 1969–July 1970.

132. Ibid., 333.

133. See attachment, 25 Aug. 1969, Ho Chi Minh to Nixon, in "Memorandum from the President's Assistant for National Security Affairs to President Nixon," Box 106, Country Files, Vietnam, "S" Matter, vol. I, Kissinger Office Files, NSCF, NPM, NARA.

134. Nixon and Kissinger considered Le Duan and Truong Chinh to have the "inside track" as the candidates most likely to succeed as Ho, although it was noted that Le Duan was on the decline. Pham Van Dong and Vo Nguyen Giap were also considered feasible candidates. "Memorandum from the President's Assistant for National Security Affairs (Kissinger) to President Nixon," Washington, D.C., 5 Sept. 1969, Document 116, rpt. in *FRUS, 1969–1976*, vol. VI, Vietnam, Jan. 1969–July 1970.

135. "Memorandum of Conversation of the Ambassador to the USA A. F. Dobrynin with Kissinger, Aide to President Nixon to A. Gromyko," 12 July 1969, Communist Party of the Soviet Union Central Committee Archive, *CWIHP Bulletin*, no. 3 (Fall 1993): 65–66.

136. Ibid., 65.

137. Zhai, *China and the Vietnam Wars*, 181–82.

138. Kissinger to Nixon, 5 Sept. 1969, Box 139, Vietnam Country Files, Vietnam, vol. X, Sept. 1969, NSCF, NPM, NARA.

139. Kimball, *Nixon's Vietnam War*, 164.

140. See "Memorandum from the President's Assistant for National Security Affairs (Kissinger) to President Nixon; Subject: Vietnam Options," Washington, D.C., 11 Sept. 1969, Document 119, rpt. in *FRUS, 1969–1976*, vol. VI, Vietnam, Jan. 1969–July 1970. Option D: "Escalation" and Point 3: "Military Tactics" outline the Duck Hook strategy. See also "Memorandum from the President's Assistant for National Security Affairs (Kissinger) to President Nixon; Subject: Contingency Military Operations against North Vietnam," Washington, D.C., 2 Oct. 1969, Document 129, rpt. in *FRUS, 1969–1976*, vol. VI, Vietnam, Jan. 1969–July 1970.

141. See Burr and Kimball, *Nixon's Nuclear Ploy*. See also Burr and Kimball, "Nixon's Secret Nuclear Alert."

142. See Kimball, *Nixon's Vietnam War*, 164. See also "Memorandum for Record; Sub-

ject: JCS Meeting with the President," Washington, D.C., 11 Oct. 1969, Document 136, rpt. in *FRUS, 1969–1976*, vol. VI, Vietnam, Jan. 1969–July 1970.

143. Thompson, *Peace Is Not at Hand*, 71–72. See also "Memorandum of Conversation; Subject: Remarks to Sir Robert Thompson Concerning the Vietnam Situation," Washington, D.C., 17 Oct. 1969; "Memorandum of Conversation; Subject: Sir Robert Thompson's Report on Conditions in Vietnam," Washington, D.C., 1 Dec. 1969, Document 153, both rpt. in in *FRUS, 1969–1976*, vol. VI, Vietnam, Jan. 1969–July 1970.

144. For the "Silent Majority" speech, see *Public Papers of the Presidents of the United States: Richard Nixon, 1969*, 901–9.

145. Greenberg, "Nixon as Failed Statesman," 53.

146. In his preface to DCSV, *President Ho Chi Minh's Testament*, the first secretary of the Central Committee of the Communist Party of Vietnam, Nguyen Van Linh, writes that in 1969 the Political Bureau of the Third Party Central Committee decided to declare the time of Ho Chi Minh's death to be at 9:47 A.M. on 3 September so that it would not coincide with the national celebration on 2 September.

147. The CEC published President Ho Chi Minh's testament, which he composed on 10 May 1969. The testament has been posted online by the DCSV: http://www.cpv.org.vn/cpv/Modules/News_English/News_Detail_E.aspx?CN_ID=89253&CO_ID=30036 (accessed 29 Nov. 2011).

148. "La France et le Vietnam (voyage de M. Alphand à Moscou)" (France and Vietnam, Alphand's trip to Moscow), 31 Dec. 1969, Box 288, Sud-Vietnam (SV), CLV-AO, FAMAE. The Soviet Union's shift in policy was more noticeable than China's since Moscow's policies were more in line with Washington's. Particularly in the realm of negotiations, Moscow's active participation stopped with the death of Ho Chi Minh.

149. "Rencontre entre Kosygin et Chou En Lai" (Meeting between Kosygin and Zhou Enlai), 12 Sept. 1969, Box 70, Nord-Vietnam (NV), CLV-AO, FAMAE.

150. Tran Do, "Tet mau than: Tran tap kich chien luoc" (Tet 1968: A Strategic Offensive), *Tap chi Lich su Quan su* (Feb. 1988): 47.

CHAPTER FIVE

1. Kissinger, *White House Years*, 442.

2. See Suri, *Henry Kissinger and the American Century*.

3. Nguyen Thi Binh, "Le Duc Tho," 354.

4. Henry Kissinger's comments to author, Institute of Military History associate director Nguyen Manh Ha, and Ambassador Tran Van Tung at "The American Experience in Southeast Asia, 1946–1975," conference at U.S. Department of State, Bureau of Public Affairs, Office of the Historian, Washington, D.C., 29 Sept. 2010.

5. The speech appeared in *Nhan Dan* and *Quan Doi Nhan Dan* on 14 February, and in the second issue of *Hoc Tap* in 1970.

6. See "VWP-DRV Leadership, 1960–1973," part 1: "The Party," Document 114, VNDR, July 1973, Folder 32, Box 01, WDC, VA-TTU.

7. "Nghi quyet cua Bo Chinh Tri ve cuoc van nang cao chat luong dang vien va ket nap dang vien Lop Ho Chi Minh" (Politburo Resolution Regarding Raising the Quality

of Cadres and Admission of the Ho Chi Minh Class), So 195-NQ/TU, 3 June 1970, rpt. in *VKDTT*, 31:129–38.

8. "Yellow music" was considered reactionary since it included songs from the pre-1954 era, foreign countries, and the Republic of Vietnam. See Nga Pham, "Risking Life for Pop Music in Wartime Vietnam."

9. BNV, *Luc luong chong phan dong*, 266–68.

10. Tran Quoc Hoan, "Ket luan cua dong chi Bo truong ve cong tac suu tra va xac minh hiem nghi (1969)" (The Minister's Concluding Speech on Investigative Operations and Determining Suspected Threats) ("Ket luan cua dong chi Bo truong"), rpt. in Tran Quoc Hoan, *Mot so van de ve dau tranh chong phan cach mang*, 339–60.

11. BNV, *Luc luong chong phan dong*, 268.

12. Hoan, "Ket luan cua dong chi Bo truong," 353.

13. BNV, *Luc luong chong phan dong*, 281–83.

14. At the same time that Hoan launched his "nipping in the bud" campaign, the CIA began a program of actions against the DRV, including attacks by fire against targets on supply depots as well as rocket attacks against truck parks and pipelines. By early 1972, twenty-two operations were carried out, but the director of the CIA, Richard Helms, deemed the program of "questionable value" since the United States lacked reliable reconnaissance photography to assess the operations' effectiveness. See "Memorandum from the Director of Central Intelligence Helms to the President's Assistant for National Security Affairs; Subject: Operations against North Vietnam," Washington, D.C., 10 March 1972, Document 37, rpt. in *FRUS, 1969–1976*, vol. VIII, Vietnam, Jan.–Oct. 1972.

15. See "Bao cao cua Bo Chinh Tri tai Hoi nghi la thu 18 Ban chap hanh trung uong" (The Politburo Report at the CEC Eighteenth Plenum), 27 Jan. 1970, rpt. in *VKDTT*, 31:27–92.

16. "II. Am muu va chu truong chien luoc cua dich" (II. The Enemy's Military Plan and Position), in "Nghi quyet Hoi nghi lan thu18 Ban chap hanh trung uong" (Resolution 18) ("NQ18"), So 196-NQ/TU, 10 March 1970, in *VKDTT*, 31:106–16.

17. "III. Nhiem vu truoc mat cua ta" (III. Our Immediate Tasks), in "NQ18," So 196-NQ/TU, 10 March 1970, rpt. in *VKDTT*, 31:116.

18. Mai Ly Quang, *The Thirty-Year War*, 2:197.

19. See subsection titled "Tien cong ngoai giao va dau tranh quoc te" (Diplomatic Offensive and International Struggle), in "NQ18," So 196-NQ-TU, 10 March 1970, rpt. in *VKDTT*, 31:121–22.

20. See "Nghi quyet cua Bo Chinh Tri ve cuoc van dong phat huy dan chu, tang cuong che do lam chu tap the cua quan chung xa vien o nong thong, day manh san xuat nong nghiep phat trien toan dien, manh me va vung chac" (Politburo Resolution Regarding the Democratization Movement, the Acceleration of Collectivization Process in the Countryside, and the Increase in Agricultural Production Levels), So 197-NQ-TU, 15 March 1970, rpt. in *VKDTT*, 31:143–66.

21. "Van thua cua Tran Van An den Nguyen Van Thieu, de-muc: Chung quanh van de Tong Thong cong du Nhut Bon, 10-6-1970 (mat)" (Letter from Tran Van An to Thieu, Subject: General Issues Regarding the President's Trip to Japan, 10 June 1970 [Confidential]), p. 1, Folder 1713, PTTDN, TTLTQG-2.

22. Ibid., 3.

23. In mid-1967, the Political War Department placed a high priority on a joint effort with Taiwan and South Korea in waging a psychological war against the communists (Hop Tac Tam Ly Chien). See "Dien cua Cao Van Vien v/v Hop Tac Tam Ly Chien, 4-1-1968" (Telegram from General Cao Van Vien regarding Joint Psychological Warfare), 4 Jan. 1968, Folder 336, PTTDN, TTLTQG-2. On 22 January 1968, they expanded the meetings to Thailand and the Philippines in the same manner. See "Van thua cua Nguyen Van Huong den Tong truong Phu Thu-tuong, 7-31-1968 (mat)" (Letter from Nguyen Van Huong [Secretary at Office of the President] to the Chief of Staff of the Prime Minister's Office, 31 July 1968 [Confidential]), Folder 336, PTTDN, TTLTQG-2.

24. "Thua van cua Tran Van Lam den Tran Thien Khiem trich yeu: v/v Quoc-Vu-Khanh Phan Quang Dan di vieng cac Quoc-Gia vung Dong-Nam-A, 8-11-1969 (toi mat)" (Letter from Tran Van Lam to Tran Thien Khiem Regarding Minister of State Phan Quang Dan's Visit to the Countries of the Southeast Asian Region, 8 November 1969 [Highly Confidential]) ("Thua van v/v Quoc-Vu-Khan Phan"), Folder 1653, PTTDN, TTLTQG-2. See also Telegram from Moreton to Foreign Commonwealth Office (FCO), 20 Jan. 1970, Folder 1338, FC015, UKNA.

25. Thua van v/v Quoc-Vu-Khan Phan, Folder 1653, PTTDN, TTLTQG-2.

26. "Thua van cua Phan Quang Dan den Tran Thien Khiem trich yeu: vai nhan xet cac nhiem so Ngoai giao VNCH o cac quoc gia toi vieng tham trong chuyen cong du 11-11-1969–25-12-1969, 12-1-1970 (mat)" (Letter from Phan Quang Dan to Tran Thien Khiem Regarding Points of Issue for the RVN Diplomacy in the Countries I Visited during My Official Visit from 11 November 1969 to 25 December 1969, 12 January 1970 [Confidential]), Folder 1774, PTTDN, TTLTQG-2.

27. "Thua van cua Le Nhung den Tran Van Lam v/v cac muc tieu chinh can hoat dong manh tai Nam Vang, 3-3-1970" (Letter from Le Nhung at the Office of the Overseas Vietnamese Committee in Phnom Penh to Tran Van Lam Regarding Important Issues That Need Strong Action in Phnom Penh, 3 March 1970), Folder 1726, PTTDN, TTLTQG-2, Le Nhung summarizes "them ban, bot thu" as "la nen tim cach lien-ket voi nhieu Quoc-gia tren the gioi cung cai to va hoat dong manh tai cac Quoc gia ma VNCH tuy co mat nhung chua duoc cong nhan chanh thuc hoat dong vi ly do chinh tri bi gian doan bang giao [to find a way to align with more countries and to reorganize and increase activities in countries in which the RVN has a diplomatic presence but has not yet recognized the acting head of state, resulting in the political reason for the interrupted state of relations]."

28. Luu Van Loi and Nguyen Anh Vu, *Cac cuoc thuong luong*, 339.

29. "Anh Xuan Thuy gui den Bo chinh tri" (Telegram from Le Xuan Thuy to the Politburo), Dien den, 14 Jan. 1970, Q. 182, PLT-BNG), rpt. in *DTNG*, 4:245; "Transcript of Telephone Conversation between President and His Assistant for National Security Affairs (Kissinger)," Washington, D.C., 14 Jan. 1970, Document 169, rpt. in *FRUS, 1969–1976*, vol. VI, Vietnam, Jan. 1969–July 1970.

30. "Memorandum for Record; Drafted by Walters," Paris, 17 Feb. 1970, Document 185, rpt. in *FRUS, 1969–1976*, vol. VI, Vietnam, Jan. 1969–July 1970; Luu Van Loi and Nguyen Anh Vu, *Cac cuoc thuong luong*, 342.

31. In 1970, Le Duc Tho maintained his title of special advisor to Xuan Thuy, which Kissinger viewed as full of "conceit," since Le Duc Tho outranked Xuan Thuy by "several levels"; Kissinger, *White House Years*, 440.

32. Ibid., 440–42.

33. Defense Secretary Laird and General Wheeler, who oversaw Vietnamization, compiled an optimistic report of the situation in South Vietnam based on their trip; "Memorandum from the Secretary of Defense Laird to President Nixon; Subject: Trip to Vietnam and CINCPAC, February 10–14, 1970," Washington, D.C., 17 Feb. 1970, Document 187, rpt. in *FRUS, 1969–1976*, vol. VI, Vietnam, Jan. 1969–July 1970.

34. "Memorandum of Conversation," Paris, 21 Feb. 1970, 9:40 A.M., Document 189, rpt. in ibid.

35. Luu Van Loi and Nguyen Anh Vu, *Cac cuoc thuong luong*, 118. See also "Memorandum of Conversation," Paris, 21 Feb. 1970, 4:10 P.M., Document 190, rpt. in ibid.

36. Kissinger, *White House Years*, 444.

37. Ibid. See "Anh Tho va anh Xuan Thuy gui Bo chinh tri" (Telegram from Le Duc Tho and Xuan Thuy to the Politburo), Dien den, 25 Feb. 1970, Q. 182, PLT-BNG, rpt. in *DTNG*, 247–48.

38. "Memorandum of Conversation," Paris, 21 Feb. 1970, 4:10 P.M., Document 190, p. 660, rpt. in *FRUS, 1969–1976*, vol. VI, Vietnam, Jan. 1969–July 1970; Luu Van Loi and Nguyen Anh Vu, *Cac cuoc thuong luong*, 122. RVN president Nguyen Van Thieu speculated that Hanoi's change in negotiating position was related to Laos; "Meeting with President Thieu," pp. 2–3, March 11, 1970, Box 11, SGN-DC, 12/15/69–12/16/71(1), NSAF, NSCVIG, GFL.

39. See BQP-VLSQSVN, *Chien dich phong ngu*.

40. See Le Duan, *Thu Vao Nam*, 53–55. In the letter from Le Duan to COSVN in July 1962, the first secretary stresses the importance of Vietnamese aid to the Laotian movement, the need for continued cooperation, and the lessons the Vietnamese should learn from the Laotian struggle.

41. Following the 1962 Geneva Agreements, the Vietnamese maintained a force of 5,000 troops in southeastern Laos. The Americans also violated Laotian neutrality through Air America, the Hmong forces, and the CIA.

42. With the arrival of the U.S. Seventh Fleet in 1965, the DRV's use of the South China Sea to transport men and arms below the Seventeenth Parallel became impossible. As a result, the DRV relied solely on land routes—the Truong Son trail (Ho Chi Minh Trail) that cut through southern Laos and eastern Cambodia—and a new sea route with access to the port of Sihanoukville (Kompong Som) in the Gulf of Thailand. See Goscha, "Towards a Geo-history of the Wars for Vietnam."

43. "Memorandum from the President's Assistant for National Security Affairs (Kissinger) to President Nixon; Subject: National Security Council to Consider Public Posture on Laos," Washington, D.C., 27 Feb. 1970, Document 193, and "Minutes of the National Security Council Meeting," Washington, D.C., 27 Feb. 1970, Document 194, both rpt. in *FRUS, 1969–1976*, vol. VI, Vietnam, Jan. 1969–July 1970.

44. Pribbenow, *Victory in Vietnam*, 254.

45. See Stuart-Fox, *A History of Laos*, 142. Alongside 35,000 Pathet Lao and "Patriotic

Neutralist" forces, the North Vietnamese waged war against 60,000 soldiers in the Royal Lao Army, 10,000 neutralists under Kong Le, and 40,000 troops in Vang Pao's Secret Army.

46. See Vo Nguyen Giap, "Chi thi nhan ro tinh hinh moi, day manh tan cong va noi day, phoi hop chat che voi quan doi Campuchia-Lao gianh thang loi moi" (Instructions Regarding the New Picture, Pushing forward the Offensive and Uprising, Closely Collaborating with Khmer-Laotian Forces in Order to Achieve Victory in the New Era) (n.d.), tuyet mat (top secret), 355V(09)/T12.289–90, TVQD.

47. Luu Van Loi and Nguyen Anh Vu, *Cac cuoc thuong luong*, 341.

48. For Nixon's 6 March statement, see "About the Situation in Laos," in *Public Papers of the President: Nixon, 1970*, 244–49. For Nixon's dispatch of Thai forces, see *FRUS*, vol. VI, Vietnam, Jan. 1969–July 1970, 685–739.

49. Luu Van Loi and Nguyen Anh Vu, *Cac cuoc thuong luong*, 350.

50. "Memorandum of Conversation," Paris, 16 March 1970, 9:40 A.M., Document 201, rpt. in *FRUS, 1969–1976*, vol. VI, Vietnam, Jan. 1969–July 1970; Telegram from Kissinger to Bunker, pp. 4–5, 19 March 1970, Box 11, DC-SGN, 12/15/69–12/16/71(1), NSAF, NSCVIG, GFL.

51. "Bo chinh tri gui Anh Tho va anh Xuan Thuy" (Telegram from the Politburo to Le Duc Tho and Xuan Thuy), Dien den, 3 March 1970, Q. 182, PLT-BNG, rpt. in *DTNG*, 249.

52. "Anh Tho va Xuan Thuy gui BCT" (Telegram from Le Duc Tho and Xuan Thuy to the Politburo), Dien den, 20 March 1970, Q. 182, LT-BNG, rpt. in *DTNG*, 249–50.

53. Pribbenow's translation of the official history of the PAVN (Pribbenow, *Victory in Vietnam*, 255) reveals that communist forces experienced supply problems with the advent of the rainy season after the Thai-Lao counterattack rescued Vang Pao's forces. However, by the end of the joint PAVN–Pathet Lao campaign on 25 April, the North Vietnamese claimed victory in the Plain of Jars–Xieng Khoang region, because Vang Pao lost thirteen battalions consisting of 7,800 Hmong soldiers. See also Thanh Son, "Cang mo rong chien tranh dac biet o Lao, de quoc My va tay sai cang that bai nang ne" (The Expansion of the 'Special War' in Laos by the Americans and Their Puppets Suffers Heavy Losses)," *Hoc Tap* 3 (1970): 77–83, 95.

54. See Owen and Kiernan, "Bombs over Cambodia."

55. Kiernan, *How Pol Pot Came to Power*, 169–282.

56. Chandler, *The Tragedy of Cambodian History*, 189.

57. "Memorandum from the President's Assistant for National Security Affairs (Kissinger) to President Nixon; Subject: MACV Cambodia Assessment," Washington, D.C., 17 March 1970, Document 202, rpt. in *FRUS, 1969–1976*, vol. VI, Vietnam, Jan. 1969–July 1970.

58. Chandler, *The Tragedy of Cambodian History*, 194–95.

59. Zhai, *China and the Vietnam Wars*, 187.

60. "Nguoi phat ngon BNG nuoc VNDCCH ra tuyen bo" (DRV Government Declaration), Van kien cua nuoc VNDCCH (DRV Government Documents), 21 March 1970, tap 20a, PLT-BNG, rpt. in *DTNG*, 4:251. For the American response, see "Memorandum from the President's Assistant for National Security Affairs (Kissinger) to President Nixon; Subject: Recognition of the New Government in Cambodia," Washington, D.C.,

20 March 1970, Document 206, rpt. in *FRUS, 1969–1976*, vol. VI, Vietnam, Jan. 1969–July 1970.

61. Do Thon, "Sai lam ve chien luoc cua De Quoc My trong viec dao chinh Xi-Ha-Nuc" (U.S. Imperialist Wrongdoings in the Anti-Sihanouk Coup), *Tap Chi Lich Su Quan Su* 8 (1986), 32–38, 94.

62. "Conversation between Zhou Enlai and Pham Van Dong," Beijing, 21 March 1970, rpt. in Westad et al., *77 Conversations*, 162.

63. Ibid.

64. Ibid.

65. Zhai, *China and the Vietnam Wars*, 189. According to Nay Valentin, Cambodian ambassador to China, Pham Van Dong told Sihanouk's wife, Princess Monique, that Vietnamese forces could help Sihanouk regain power within a day; see Chandler, *The Tragedy of Cambodian History*, 200.

66. Chandler, *The Tragedy of Cambodian History*, 194–95.

67. Ibid., 200.

68. Pol Pot's first victim may have been Tou Samouth, the leading revolutionary figure in the Khmer Workers' Party (KWP), the forerunner to the CPK. Following Tou Samouth's murder, Pol Pot was able to assume leadership of the KWP. After student demonstrations in Siem Reap in February 1963, Sihanouk cracked down on the Left, forcing Pol Pot and his deputy Ieng Sary to flee Phnom Penh for the jungles in order to wage the communist struggle. By the end of 1963, the CPK's entire Central Committee lived in the countryside. See Kiernan, *How Pol Pot Came to Power*, 197–98.

69. The French colonial project in Cambodia did not create animosity and hostility between the Khmer and the Vietnamese (tensions as well as cooperation between them predated French colonialism), but the French did enforce and reify the ethnic divide in order to convince the Khmer that French protection was crucial to Cambodia's survival. By reviving historic tensions between the two Indochinese nations, the French played on Cambodians' fears of being "swallowed" up by their more powerful neighbor. While the French tried to instill Khmer self-confidence by romanticizing the height of Khmer power on the mainland, manifested in the ruins of Angkor Wat, the colonial power also pointed out that Vietnamese "manifest destiny" to expand southward came at the cost of weakened Khmer Krom in the Mekong Delta. See Kiernan, *How Pol Pot Came to Power*, ix–xvii.

70. Goscha, "Vietnam and the Meltdown of Asian Internationalism," 166. See also Kiernan, "The American Bombardment of Kampuchea."

71. "Conversation between Zhou Enlai and Pham Hung," Beijing, 19 June 1968, rpt. in Westad et al., *77 Conversations*, 135–37. However, Kiernan (*How Pol Pot Came to Power*, 219–24) found records of a visit by Pol Pot to Beijing in 1965.

72. "Conversation between Zhou Enlai and Pham Hung," Beijing, 19 June 1968, rpt. in Westad et al., *77 Conversations*, 136.

73. See Lien-Hang T. Nguyen, "The Sino-Vietnamese Split and the Indochina War."

74. Chandler, *The Tragedy of Cambodian History*, 206–7.

75. Ibid., 201–3.

76. Luu Van Loi, *Nam muoi nam ngoai giao Viet Nam*, 292. See also "Cuoc dao chinh

o Cam-pu-chia mot hanh dong xam luoc moi cua de quoc My" (Coup d'Etat in Cambodia: A New Act of American Imperialist Aggression), *Hoc Tap* 3 (1970): 84–87.

77. "Conversation between Zhou Enlai and Prince Sihanouk," Beijing, 28 March 1970, rpt. in Westad et al., *77 Conversations*, 163.

78. The VWP viewed France's 1 April declaration as a hostile act: Paris's call for an international conference aimed to legitimize the Lon Nol regime, isolate North Vietnam, and define the neutralization of Cambodia as the removal of PLAF troops from the country. See "Anh Trinh gui anh Xuan Thuy va cac co quant a o ngoai nuoc" (Telegram from Nguyen Duy Trinh to Xuan Thuy and DRV Diplomatic Missions Abroad), Dien di, 12 April 1970, Q. 183, PLT-BNG, rpt. in *DTNG*, 251–52.

79. See "Conversations franco-soviétiques sur l'Indochine" (Franco-Soviet Conversations Regarding Indochina), 22 May 1970, Carton 178, CLV-AO, FAMAE. U.N. first secretary U Thant also called for an international conference on Cambodia.

80. Ibid.

81. See Zhai, *China and the Vietnam Wars*, 190–91, 260n66.

82. Duiker, *China and Vietnam*, 57.

83. Zhai, *China and the Vietnam Wars*, 191.

84. "May 2, 1970 Telegram from French Embassy in Beijing to Paris," Folder 289, CLV-AO, AAE.

85. BNG nuoc VNDCCH (DRV Ministry of Foreign Affairs), "Van kien cua nuoc VNDCCH" (DRV Country Records), 27 April 1970, tap 20a, PLT-BNG, rpt. in *DTNG*, 253.

86. "Thua van cua Tran Van Lam den Tran Thien Khiem, v/v Ngoai-Truong Indonesia Adam Malik de nghi trieu tap Hoi Nghi cac quoc-gia A-Chau de thao luan ve van de Cam-Bot, 4-5-1970 (mat, khan) (Letter from Tran Van Lam to Tran Thien Khiem Regarding Indonesian Foreign Minister Adam Malik's Proposal for a Conference of Asian States on the Cambodian Issue, 4 May 1970 [Confidential and Urgent]), p. 3, Folder 1768, PTTDN, TTLTQG-2.

87. "3 Suy nghi cua Bo Ngoai Giao, So luoc ve Hoi Nghi Djakarta, phan 3: Nhung kho khan cua VNCH, thang 5 nam 1970" (Foreign Ministry Think-Piece Regarding the Djakarta Conference, Section 3: RVN's Difficulties, May 1970), Folder 1768, PTTDN, TTLTQG-2.

88. 13 April 1970 telegram from Laurent Giovangrandi to Paris, "Réactions et suite de la déclaration du 1er avril 1970" (Immediate Reactions to the 1970 1 April Declaration), Folder 289, CLV-AO, FAMAE.

89. 22 May 1970 telegram from Laurent Giovangrandi to Paris, "a/s Conférence de Djakarta" (re: Djakarta Conference), Folder 298, CLV-AO, FAMAE.

90. "BCT gui anh Tho + Anh Xuan Thuy" (Telegram from the Politburo to Le Duc Tho and Xuan Thuy), Dien den, 30 March 1970, Q. 182, PLT-BNG, rpt. in *DTNG*, 250.

91. See "Telegram from Kissinger to Bunker," 1–3, 4 April 1970, Box 11, DC-SGN, 12/15/69–12/16/71(2), NSAF, NSCVIG, GFL. See also Luu Van Loi and Nguyen Anh Vu, *Cac cuoc thuong luong*, 358.

92. See "Minutes of Washington Special Actions Group Meeting; Subject: Laos and Cambodia," Washington, D.C., 24 March 1970, Document 209, rpt. in *FRUS, 1969–1976*, vol. VI, Vietnam, Jan. 1969–July 1970.

93. "Memorandum of Conversation," Paris, 4 April 1970, 9:30 A.M., Document 222, p. 812, rpt. in *FRUS, 1969–1976*, vol. VI, Vietnam, Jan. 1969–July 1970.

94. Telegram from Kissinger to Bunker, 1–3, 4 April 1970, Box 11, DC-SGN, 12/15/69–12/16/71(2), NSAF, NSCVIG, GFL.

95. Luu Van Loi and Nguyen Anh Vu, *Cac cuoc thuong luong*, 362.

96. "Memorandum of Conversation," Paris, 4 April 1970, 9:30 A.M., Document 222, pp. 817–26, rpt. in *FRUS, 1969–1976*, vol. VI, Vietnam, Jan. 1969–July 1970.

97. "Memorandum from the President's Assistant for National Security Affairs (Kissinger) to President Nixon; Subject: Meeting on Cambodia, Sunday, April 26, 1970, at 4:30 P.M. in the President's EOB Office," Washington, D.C., 26 April 1970, Document 259, rpt. in ibid. For Rogers and Laird's objections, see "Notes of a Meeting; Subject: Mtg-Rogers-Laird-K[issinger]-[Nixon-and Haldeman] in EOB," Washington, D.C., 27 April 1970, rpt. in ibid.

98. See "Editorial Note," Document 239, pp. 831–44, and "Editorial Note," Document 248, pp. 849–50, in ibid.

99. "Telegram from the Commander of the U.S. Military Assistance Command in Vietnam (Abrams) to the Chairman of the Joint Chiefs of Staff (Moorer); Subject: COSVN Headquarters, Saigon, 18 May 1970, Document 296, rpt. in ibid.

100. Perlstein, *Nixonland*, 497.

101. Dallek, *Nixon and Kissinger*, 133–34, 208. In the end, J. Edgar Hoover scaled back much of the Huston Plan since he did not want to share domestic spying with a White House aide.

102. Herring, *America's Longest War*, 295.

103. See Berman, *Perfect Spy*, 34–37, for *Time* magazine correspondent Robert Sam Anson's account of his role during the massacres. See also Anson, *War News*.

104. "Phieu trinh cua Le Nhung den Tran Van Lam ve tinh-hinh tai Phnom-Penh thuong tuan thang 5/1970, 10-5-1970 (mat)" (Report by Le Nhung at the Office of the Overseas Vietnamese Committee in Phnom Penh to the Tran Van Lam on the Weekly situation report in Phnom Penh, May 1970, 10 May 1970 [Confidential]), Folder 1726, PTTDN, TTLTQG-2.

105. "Telegram from the Department of State to the Embassy in Cambodia," Washington, D.C., 21 May 1970, Document 301, and "Telegram from the Embassy in Vietnam to the Department of State," Saigon, 27 May 1970, Document 301, both rpt. in *FRUS, 1969–1976*, vol. VI, Vietnam, Jan. 1969–July 1970.

106. Cambodia would divide Ky and Thieu. Following the anti-Sihanouk coup, Ky assumed charge of RVN policy toward Cambodia, indicating that Saigon would assume full responsibility for the defense of Cambodia and that the South Vietnamese leadership desired an Indochinese military pact with Phnom Penh. Thieu, who disagreed, relieved Ky of his responsibility for Cambodia policy.

107. 17 June 1970 confidential Diplomatic Report no. 332/70 from British Embassy in Saigon to London, Folder 1353, FCO 15, UKNA.

108. "Thua van cau Tran Van Lam den Tran Thien Khiem, v/v quan-nhan VNCH pham phap tai Kampuchia, 16-12-1970 (toi mat khan)" (Letter from Tran Van Lam to Tran Thien Khiem Regarding Abuses by ARVN in Cambodia, 16 December 1970 [Extremely Urgent and Classified]), Folder 1725, PTTDN, TTLTQG-2.

109. "Phieu trinh cua Tran Van Lam den Tran Thien Khiem, trich yeu: Thai do cua Chanh-phu Kampuchea va van de quan phi cua Quan-luc VNCH tai Kampuchea, 9-4-1971 (mat)" (Report by Tran Van Lam to Tran Thien Khiem Regarding Cambodia's Position on Military Expenditures of ARVN in Cambodia, 9 April 1971 [Classified]), p. 4, Folder 381, PTTDN, TTLTQG-2.

110. Ibid., 5.

111. "Thua van cua Tran Thien Khiem den Nguyen Van Thieu, 21-4-1971 (mat)" (Letter from Tran Thien Khiem to Nguyen Van Thieu, 21 April 1971 [Classified]), Folder 381, PTTDN, TTLTQG-2. The letter includes Thieu's handwritten notes in the margins. On 4 April 1971, the Cambodian ambassador to Japan, Sim Var, gave an interview to a Sankei Shimbum reporter in which he stated that the RVN was refusing to lift a blockade of National Highway 4 in order to force Cambodia to address the military expenditure issue. See "Thua van cua Tran Kiem Phuong den Su quan VNCH o Nam Vang v/v Ong Sim Va, Dai-su Khmer tai Tokyo tuyen bo ve nhung cuoc hanh quan cua VNCH tai Kampuchea, 10-6-1971 (mat)" (Letter from Tran Kim Phuong at Asia-Pacific Office to RVN Embassy in Phnom Penh Regarding Statements by Cambodian Ambassador to Tokyo, Mr. Sim Va, about ARVN Soldiers in Cambodia, 10 June 1971 [Confidential]), Folder 420, PTTDN, TTLTQG-2.

112. "13 December 1971 Restricted Report by F. D. Robins at the British Embassy in Saigon to London," Folder 1480, FCO 15, UKNA. See also "23 December 1971 Restricted Report by A. J. Williams at British Embassy in Phnom Penh to E. C. Glover at SEAD, FCO," Folder 1480, FCO 15, UKNA, for more on South Vietnamese arrogance as a source of "Cambodian irritation."

113. "Phieu trinh cua Cao Van Vien den Nguyen Van Thieu, v/v Chinh-phu Khmer xin huy bo hanh lang hanh-quan 16 cay so doc theo bien gioi, 10-9-1971 (mat)" (Report by Cao Van Vien to Thieu Regarding Cambodian Government's Request to Stop ARVN Border Activities at Sixteen Kilometers, 10 Sept. 1971 [Confidential Report]), Folder 413, PTTDN, TTLTQG-2.

114. "Phieu trinh cua Tran Van Lam den Tran Thien Khiem v/v Thu-Tuong Lon Nol de nghi thay doi che do Hanh quan cua Quan luc VNCH tren lanh tho Kampuchea, 22-9-1971 (mat)" (Report by Tran Van Lam to Tran Thien Khiem Regarding Prime Minister Lon Nol's Proposal to Change the System of ARVN Border Activity in Cambodia, 22 Sept. 1971 [Confidential]), Folder 420, PTTDN, TTLTQG-2.

115. "Phieu trinh cua Tran Van Lam den Bo truong quoc phong v/v Su Quan VNCH tai Kampuchea de nghi mot chien thuat moi ve hanh quan va dong quan tai Kampuchea, 2-12-1971 (mat, khan)" (Report by Tran Van Lam to Defense Minister Regarding RVN Embassy to Cambodia's New Proposal Regarding Our Military Activity in Cambodia, 2 December 1971 [Urgent and Confidential]), Folder 420, PTTDN, TTLTQG-2.

116. "Dien cua Ban Bi Thu ve mot so dien bien moi cua tinh hinh ba nuoc Dong Duong va nhiem vu cu the truoc mat" (Telegram from the Secretariat Regarding Developments in Indochina and the Duties Facing Us), So 147/MD, 2 May 1970, rpt. in *VKDTT*, 31:207–9.

117. "Nghi quyet cua Bo chinh tri ve tinh hinh moi o ban dao Dong Duong va nhiem vu moi cua chung ta" (Politburo Resolution Regarding the New Picture in Indochina and Our New Duties), So 107/QU, 19 June 1970, rpt. in *VKDTT*, 31:221–59.

118. Pham Dinh Am, *Mot Thoi De Nho*, 207–8, 215–16.

119. Chandler, *The Tragedy of Cambodian History*, 207.

120. Vo Chi Cong, *Tren Nhung Chang Duong Cach Mang*, 247. Cong's memoir indicates that he was assigned to COSVN headquarters to serve as an "advisor" to the CPK Central Committee but he was transferred to take over Region 5 in the Central Highlands in 1964 and remained there until 1975. See also Goscha, "Vietnam and the Meltdown of Asian Internationalism," 166.

121. See Goscha, "Vietnam and the Meltdown of Asian Internationalism," 166.

122. Kiernan, *How Pol Pot Came to Power*, 309–10.

123. Le Duan, *Thu Vao Nam*, 234.

124. Vo, *Khmer-Viet Relations and the Third Indochina Conflict*, 68.

125. Goscha, "Vietnam and the Meltdown of Asian Internationalism," 168; Chandler, *The Tragedy of Cambodian History*, 209–10.

126. Kiernan, *How Pol Pot Came to Power*, 318–20.

127. Quoted in ibid., 329.

128. Vo, *Khmer-Viet Relations and the Third Indochina Conflict*, 69.

129. The provinces were Kratie, Stung Streng, Ratankiri, Mondukiri, and Preah Vihear.

130. See BQP-VLSQSVN, *Lich su Quan Su Nhan Dan Viet Nam*, 354.

131. Kiernan, *How Pol Pot Came to Power*, 349–68; Kiernan, "The American Bombardment of Kampuchea." See also Shawcross, *Sideshow*, 264–97.

132. American sources indicate that Le Duan spent three weeks in Moscow but "left without any fanfare. This suggests that he and the Soviets did not reach a common understanding as to what to do at this point." "Memorandum from the President's Assistant for National Security Affairs (Kissinger) to President Nixon; Subject: Pressure on Hanoi," Washington, D.C., 19 May 1970, Document 299, rpt. in *FRUS, 1969–1976*, vol. VI, Vietnam, Jan. 1969–July 1970. See also Ang, *Ending the Vietnam War*, 53–54.

133. "Conversation between Mao Zedong and Le Duan," Beijing, 11 May 1970, rpt. in Westad et al., *77 Conversations*, 163–69.

134. Ibid.

135. Brigham, *Guerrilla Diplomacy*, 90.

136. Nguyen Thi Binh, "Truong thanh," 481–84.

137. Ibid., 484–86. See also Nguyen Thi Binh, *Mat tran*.

138. Nguyen Thi Binh, *Mat tran*, 38.

139. Nguyen Thi Binh, "Truong thanh," 486–87.

140. Nguyen Thi Binh, *Mat tran*, 47–48. In contrast, the other delegations were not as gender-balanced: the RVN appointed only one woman, Nguyen Thi Vui, to its delegation for a short period of time while the American delegation included only a woman translator.

141. "Conversation between Zhou Enlai and Nguyen Thi Binh," Beijing, 17 June 1970, rpt. in Westad et al., *77 Conversations*, 169–70.

142. See Nguyen Thi Binh, *Mat tran*, 60–61. See also "Thu tu Van phong Bo ngoai giao den Van phong Bo Truong v/v thuyet trinh cua Bo Ngoai giao truoc Uy ban ngoai giao Thuong nghi vien va Uy ban ngoai giao Ha nghi vien" (Telegram from the Foreign Ministry to the Ministry of Defense Regarding the Foreign Ministry's Hearing be-

fore the Senate Foreign Relations Committee and the Lower House Foreign Relations Committee), 22 Aug. 1970, Folder 1719, PTTDN, TTLTQG-2. In January 1972, the Indian consulate-general in Hanoi was raised to the status of embassy. The RVN's immediate response was to deal only with the Canadian and Polish delegations to the ICC and to refuse the Indian chairman of the ICC entry into Saigon.

143. Nguyen Ngoc Dung, "Co gai mien Nam tai Hoi nghi Khong lien ket," 494–95.

144. Quoted in ibid., 295.

145. See Luu Van Loi, *Nam muoi nam ngoai giao Viet Nam*, 20.

146. On 7 May 1970, a North Vietnamese delegate to the Paris negotiations, Mai Van Bo, sent a telegram to Foreign Minister Nguyen Duy Trinh to let Hanoi know that Kissinger desired another secret meeting while in Paris, but Hanoi declined; "Anh Mai Van Bo gui anh Trinh" (Telegram from Mai Van Bo to Nguyen Duy Trinh), Dien den, 7 May 1970, Q. 184, PLT-BNG, rpt. in *DTNG*, 255. Hanoi turned down another U.S. request for a private meeting in early June ("Memorandum from Richard Smyser of the Operations Staff of the National Security Council to the President's Assistant for National Security Affairs (Kissinger); Subject: Message from General Walters regarding Meeting with Le Duc Tho," Washington, D.C., 8 June 1970, Document 320, rpt. in *FRUS, 1969–1976*, vol. VI, Vietnam, Jan. 1969–July 1970.

147. "Memorandum from the President's Assistant for National Security Affairs (Kissinger) to President Nixon; Subject: NSC Meeting July 21, 1970—Negotiating Strategy and Paris Talks," Washington, D.C., n.d., Document 346, rpt. in ibid.

148. "Memorandum of Conversation," Paris, 7 Sept. 1970, 9:30 A.M.–2:30 P.M., Document 34, rpt. in *FRUS, 1969–1976*, vol. VII, Vietnam, July 1970–Jan. 1972.

149. "Paris gui Bo Chinh Tri" (Telegram from Paris to the Politburo), Dien den, 7 Sept. 1970, Q. 184, PLT-BNG, rpt. in *DTNG*, 260–61. See also Luu Van Loi and Nguyen Anh Vu, *Cac cuoc thuong luong*, 373–74.

150. Telegram from Kissinger to Bunker, 1–2, 10 Sept. 1970, Box 11, SGN-DC, 9/15/69–9/16/71, NSAF, NSCVIG, GFL.

151. "Anh Tho va Anh Trinh gui anh Xuan Thuy" (Telegram from Le Duc Tho and Nguyen Duy Trinh to Xuan Thuy), Dien di, 10 Sept. 1970, Q. 183, PLT-BNG, rpt. in *DTNG*, 261.

152. See "Anh Xuan Thuy gui Bo Chinh Tri" (Telegram from Xuan Thuy to the Politburo), Dien den, 17 Sept. 1970, Q. 184, LT-BNG, rpt. in *DTNG*, 162–63.

153. Telegram from Kissinger to Bunker, 1, 23 Sept. 1970, Box 11, DC-SGN, 12/15/69–12/16/71, NSAF, NSCVIG, GFL; "Memorandum from the President's Assistant for National Security Affairs (Kissinger) to President Nixon; Subject: My Meeting with Xuan Thuy, September 7, 1970," Washington, D.C., 7 Sept. 1970, Document 35, rpt. in *FRUS, 1969–1976*, vol. VII, Vietnam, July 1970–Jan. 1972.

154. "Memorandum from the President's Assistant for National Security Affairs (Kissinger) to President Nixon; Subject: A Longer Look at the New Communist Peace Proposal," Washington, D.C., 22 Sept. 1970, Document 43, rpt. in *FRUS, 1969–1976*, vol. VII, Vietnam, July 1970–Jan. 1972. According to historian Jeffrey Kimball, Nixon and Kissinger may have changed war aims from the preservation of a noncommunist South Vietnam to a negotiated settlement that would allow the United States to extri-

cate from Vietnam. See Kimball, *Nixon's Vietnam War*, 233–34; and Kimball, "The Case of the 'Decent Interval.'"

155. "Memorandum from the President's Assistant for National Security Affairs (Kissinger) to President Nixon; Subject: My September 27 Meeting with the North Vietnamese," Washington, D.C., 28 Sept. 1970, Document 45, rpt. in *FRUS, 1969–1976*, vol. VII, Vietnam, July 1970–Jan. 1972. See also Luu Van Loi and Nguyen Anh Vu, *Cac cuoc thuong luong*, 376–77.

156. See "Conversation between Zhou Enlai and Pham Van Dong," Beijing, 17 Sept. 1970, and "Conversation between Mao Zedong and Pham Van Dong," Beijing, 23 Sept. 1970, rpt. in Westad et al., *77 Conversations*, 174–75, 177–78.

157. "Conversation between Zhou Enlai and Pham Van Dong," Beijing, 17 Sept. 1970, rpt. in ibid., 174–75.

158. Ibid., 175.

159. "Conversation between Zhou Enlai and Pham Van Dong," Beijing, 19 Sept. 1970, rpt. in ibid., 176.

160. "Conversation between Mao Zedong and Pham Van Dong," Beijing, 23 Sept. 1970, rpt. in ibid., 178.

161. See Kissinger, *White House Years*, 684.

162. See Memcon, "Meeting between the President and Pakistan President Yahya," 25 Oct. 1970, Top Secret/Sensitive, Box 1032, Cookies II, Chronology of Exchanges with PRC, Feb. 1969–April 1971, NPM, NARA. See also Burr, *The Beijing-Washington Back-Channel and Henry Kissinger's Secret Trip to China*.

163. See Gaiduk, *The Soviet Union and the Vietnam War*, 219–22.

164. "Bo Chinh Tri gui anh Xuan Thuy" (Telegram from the Politburo to Xuan Thuy), Dien di, 19 Nov. 1970, Q. 184, PLT-BNG, rpt. in *DTNG*, 268.

165. Gaiduk, *The Soviet Union and the Vietnam War*, 228.

166. *Nhan Dan*, 15 Oct. 1970.

167. "Anh Xuan Thuy gui anh Tho, anh Trinh" (Telegram from Xuan Thuy to Le Duc Tho and Nguyen Duy Trinh), Dien den, 17 Nov. 1970, Q. 184, PLT-BNG, rpt. in *DTNG*, 268.

168. "Memorandum from the President's Assistant for National Security Affairs (Kissinger) to President Nixon; Subject: Meeting with Secretaries Rogers and Laird, Chairman of Joint Chiefs of Staff Moorer, and Henry Kissinger at 11:30 A.M., November 18, 1970," Washington, D.C., 18 Nov. 1970, Document 71, rpt. in *FRUS, 1969–1976*, vol. VII, Vietnam, July 1970–Jan. 1972.

169. See "Memorandum from the President's Deputy Assistant for National Security Affairs (Haig) to the President's Assistant for National Security Affairs (Kissinger); Subject: Your Meeting with Secretary Laird and Chairman of the Joint Chiefs of Staff Moorer at 10:30 A.M., Friday, November 13, 1970—Room 3E 880, Pentagon," Washington, D.C., 13 Nov. 1970, Document 66, rpt. in ibid.

170. "Anh Xuan Thuy gui Bo Chinh Tri, Ban Bi Thu" (Telegram from XT to the Politburo and the Secretariat), Dien den, 5 Dec. 1970, Q. 184, PLT-BNG, rpt. in *DTNG*, 269–70.

171. "3 diem cua Chinh phu CMLT CHMNVN" (The PRG's Three Points), *Van kien ve DTNG cua VN* (Records of the Diplomatic Struggle), 10 Dec. 1970, PLT-BNG, rpt. in *DTNG*, 270.

172. See "Nguyen Van Huyen gui Thu Tuong" (Letter from DRV Ambassador to Germany Nguyen Van Huyen to the Office of the Prime Minister), 11 July 1970, *Phu Thu Tuong* (Collection of the Office of the Prime Minister), TTLTQG-3.

173. "Nam 1970, Tinh hinh the gioi phat trien tot va thuan cho cuoc chien dau chong My, cuu nuoc ta" (1970: The World Picture Develops Positively for Our Anti-American Resistance Struggle for National Salvation), *Hoc Tap* 1, no. 181 (1971): 82–89.

174. Kissinger to Nixon, 22 Sept. 1970, "Sub: A Longer Look at the New Communist Proposal on Vietnam," Folder: Paris Talks, July–Sept. 1970, Box 3, WH/NSC: POW-MIA, NPM, NARA. See also Kissinger, *White House Years*, 972.

### CHAPTER SIX

1. Nixon, *RN*, 498.

2. Lüthi, "Beyond Betrayal."

3. Li Danhui, "The Sino-Soviet Dispute over Assistance for Vietnam's Anti-American War"; Shen Zhihua, "Sino-U.S. Reconciliation and China's Vietnam Policy."

4. Zhai, *China and the Vietnam Wars*, 157–215, and "China and the Cambodian Conflict, 1970–1975."

5. Gaiduk, *The Soviet Union and the Vietnam War*, 133–245.

6. Morris, "The Soviet-Chinese-Vietnamese Triangle in the 1970s," 425.

7. Lien-Hang T. Nguyen, "Vietnamese Perceptions of the French-Indochina War."

8. "Bao cao trinh Hoi Nghi Ban Chap Hanh Trung Uong Dang ve tinh hinh va phuong huong, nhiem vu kinh te truoc mat (1971–1973) va nhiem vu ke hoach nha nuoc nam 1971" (Report of the CEC Plenum Regarding the New Direction and Current Economic Responsibilities [1971–1973] and the 1971 State Plan), Dec. 1970, rpt. in *VKDTT*, 32:1–114. See also "Thong cao ve Hoi Nghi Lan Thu 19 Ban Chap Hanh Trung Uong Dang Lao Dong Viet Nam" (Declaration of the CEC Nineteenth Party Plenum), *Hoc Tap* 2, no. 182 (1971): 1–5. For the published resolution that was circulated on 1 March 1971, see "Nghi quyet Hoi nghi lan thu 19 cua Ban chap hanh trung uong Dang" (CEC Nineteenth Party Plenum Resolution), So 214-NQ-TU, 3 Jan. 1971, rpt. in *VKDTT*, 32:192–243.

9. "Bai phat bieu cua dong chi Le Duan, Bi Thu Nhat tai Hoi Nghi Lan Thu 19 Ban Chap Hanh Trung Uong Dang" (First Secretary Le Duan's Speech at the CEC Nineteenth Party Plenum), rpt. in *VKDTT*, 32:115–91.

10. "Nghi quyet cua Bo Chinh Tri ve viec tang cuong su lanh dao cua Trung uong Dang va Chinh phu doi voi cac mat cong tac cua Dang va Nha nuoc" (Politburo Resolution Regarding the Elevation of the Leadership of the Party Central Committee and the Government to Confront All Party and State Tasks), So 213-NQ-TU, 2 Feb. 1970, rpt. in *VKDTT*, 32:259–65.

11. BNV, *Luc luong chong phan dong*, 285. See also Tran Quoc Hoan, "Bai noi Bo truong o Hoi nghi Tong ket 15 nam cong tac cong an dau tranh chong bon phan dong loi dung dao Thien chua" (The Minister's Speech to the Conference Reviewing the Public Security Branch's Fifteen-Year Battle against Reactionaries Who Exploit the Catholic Religion), rpt. in Tran Quoc Hoan, *Mot so van de ve dau tranh chong phan cach mang*, 432–62.

12. BNV, *Luc luong chong phan dong*, 285.

13. Ibid., 287.

14. Quoted in Nga Pham, "Risking Life for Pop Music in Wartime Vietnam."

15. Ibid.

16. Ibid. According to Loc, "yellow music" has experienced a recent renaissance in Vietnam. It is performed at his successful Café Loc Vang—Golden Vang, in Hanoi.

17. Tran Quoc Hoan, "Ket luan cua Dong Chi Bo Truong ve Cong tac Suu tra va Xac minh hiem nghi" (The Minister's Concluding Speech on Investigative Operations and Determining Suspected Threats), rpt. in Tran Quoc Hoan, *Mot so van de ve dau tranh chong phan cach mang*, 352.

18. See "Memorandum for the Forty Committee; Subject: Periodic Report on the Covert Psychological Warfare Operations against North Vietnam and the National Liberation Front of South Vietnam," Washington, D.C., 27 Nov. 1970, Document 77, rpt. in *FRUS, 1969–1976*, vol. VII, Vietnam, July 1970–Jan. 1972. According to this memo, psychological operations included black radio broadcasts to North Vietnam and South Vietnam as well as the distribution of black leaflets and fabricated enemy documents delivered by armed reconnaissance teams in the RVN.

19. Tran Quoc Hoan, "Mot so y kien cua Dong chi Bo Truong ve mot so van de co ban khi tong ket cong tac chuyen an" (A Few Opinions Expressed by the Minister on Several Basic Issues during the Overall Review of the Handling of Cases), rpt. in Tran Quoc Hoan, *Mot so van de ve dau tranh chong phan cach mang*, 366.

20. Ibid., 365.

21. Ibid., 370.

22. Ibid., 371.

23. "Trends & Highlights: Aid between North Vietnam and Communist Countries by Organización del Tratado de Asia del Sureste (OTASE or SEATO)," 4 Jan. 1971, Box 69, Folder PE-31-23, Nord Vietnam (NV), CLV-AO, FAMAE.

24. Ibid.

25. Ngo Ba Thanh, "Phong trao do thi va luc luong chinh tri thu ba voi dam phan va dau tranh thi hanh Hiep dinh Pari," 276.

26. Ibid., 275–76.

27. Trinh Ngoc Thai, "Mat tran nhan dan the gioi ung ho Viet Nam giai doan dam phan Hiep dinh Paris." See also La Con, "Su phat trien manh me cua Phong trao Nhan dan The gioi ung ho Viet Nam danh thang de quoc My xam luoc" (The Strong Development of the International People's Movement to Support Vietnam's War against the Imperialist America's Invasion), *Hoc Tap* 8 (1968): 84–89.

28. "Anh Xuan Thuy gui Anh Tho, anh Trinh" (Telegram from Xuan Thuy to Le Duc Tho), Dien den, 19 Jan. 1970, Q. 184, PLT-BNG, rpt. in *Dau tranh ngoai giao*, 4:275.

29. Ang, *Ending the Vietnam War*, 52.

30. "Backchannel Message from the President's Deputy Assistant for National Security Affairs (Haig) to the President's Assistant for National Security Affairs (Kissinger)," Saigon, 15 Dec. 1970, Document 89, rpt. in *FRUS, 1969–1976*, vol. VII, Vietnam, July 1970–Jan. 1972. See also Sorley, *A Better War*, 232–41.

31. See BQP-VLSQSVN, *Chien dich phan cong*, 26–37.

32. "24 October 1970: Commanders Weekly Intelligence Updates (WIEU)," rpt. in Sorley, *Vietnam Chronicles*, 498. See also "Backchannel Message from the President's Assis-

tant for National Security Affairs (Kissinger) to the Ambassador to Vietnam (Bunker)," Washington, D.C., 27 March 1971, Document 170, rpt. in *FRUS, 1969–1976*, vol. VII, Vietnam, July 1970–Jan. 1972.

33. "6 Feb. 1971: WIEU," rpt. in *Vietnam Chronicles*, 529–32. See also Kimball, *Nixon's Vietnam War*, 242.

34. "Memorandum for the President's File by the President's Deputy Assistant for National Security Affairs (Haig); Subject: Meeting with the President, Dr. Kissinger, Admiral Moorer and General Haig on Tuesday, January 26, 1971, in the Oval Office, 12:25 P.M.–1:03 P.M.," Washington, D.C., 26 Jan. 1971, Document 109, rpt. in *FRUS, 1969–1976*, vol. VII, Vietnam, July 1970–Jan. 1972. See also Sorley, *A Better War*, 243–60.

35. "Memorandum for the Record; Subject: Minutes of the WSAG Meeting," Washington, D.C., 19 Jan. 1971, Document 105, rpt. in *FRUS, 1969–1976*, vol. VII, Vietnam, July 1970–Jan. 1972; BQP-VLSQSVN, *Chien dich phan cong*, 14–15. Operation Toan Thang 1/71 in Cambodia was as disastrous as Lam Son 719 but not as well-known. Although it began well under the planning and command of III Corps Commander Lieutenant General Do Cao Tri, his premature death during phase 2 of the operation left ARVN forces without an able leader and they suffered heavy losses. See Ha Mai Viet, *Steel and Blood*, 56–67.

36. Kissinger, *White House Years*, 997–1000.

37. "Diary Entry by the White House Chief of Staff (Haldeman)," Washington, D.C., 3 Feb. 1971, Document 117, rpt. in *FRUS, 1969–1976*, vol. VII, Vietnam, July 1970–Jan. 1972.

38. "Dien cua Bo Chinh Tri gui Dong chi Bay Cuong (Pham Hung), Trung uong Cuc, Anh Muoi Khang (Hoang Van Thai) va Quan uy Mien ve cuoc tan cong lon cua dich vao duong hanh lang cua ta va nhiem vu cua cac chien truong" (Telegram from the Politburo to Pham Hung, COSVN, Hoang Van Thai, and the Military Regional Committee Regarding the Enemy's Offensive on Our Corridor and All Battlefield Tasks), So 322, 9 Feb. 1971, rpt. in *VKDTT*, 32:266–68.

39. For the postwar assessment of the VWP's victory on Highway 9, see Tran Ha, "1971: Nam phan cong thang loi gianh quyen chu dong chien truong" (1971: The Year of the Successful Counteroffensive to Reseize the Battlefield Initiative), *Lich Su Quan Su* 4, no. 52 (1991): 1–5; Ngo The Nung, "Tu cua khau hanh lang chien luoc den duong 9–Nam Lao" (From the Border Corridor on Highway 9–Southern Laos), *Lich Su Quan Su* 4, no. 52 (1991): 13–16; and Ngoc Thang, "Chi vien ve khong quan va hau can cua My cho quan nguy Saigon trong cuoc hanh quan Lam Som 719" (American Air Support for the Saigon Puppet Troops during Lam Son 719), *Lich Su Quan Su* 4, no. 52 (1991): 44. See also BQP-VLSQSVN, *Chien dich phan cong*.

40. See Nguyen Viet Phuong and Tu Quy, *Cong tac chien dich duong 9 Nam Lao 9*, 8–134.

41. Prados, *Vietnam*, 420–25.

42. "Conversation between President Nixon and His Assistant for National Security Affairs," Washington, D.C., 23 April 1971, Document 190, rpt. in *FRUS, 1969–1976*, vol. VII, Vietnam, July 1970–Jan. 1972. Nixon and Kissinger complained about a demonstration scheduled for Saturday, 24 April 1971, about how "90 percent" of the media wanted the United States to lose the war, and about the troubling outlook on college campuses.

43. See Ellsberg, *Secrets*, esp. part 3. See also Prados, *Vietnam*, 425–38.

44. "Memorandum of Conversation; Participants: Dr. Kissinger and Ambassador Dobrynin," Washington, D.C., 22 Feb. 1971, Document 121, rpt. in *FRUS, 1969–1976*, vol. XIII, Soviet Union, Oct. 1970–Oct. 1971; See also Kimball, *Nixon's Vietnam War*, 244; and Zhai, *China and the Vietnam Wars*, 193.

45. Kissinger, *White House Years*, 706–7.

46. "Memorandum of Conversation," Washington, D.C., 26 Feb. 1971, Document 138, esp. p. 421, rpt. in *FRUS, 1969–1976*, vol. VII, Vietnam, July 1970–Jan. 1972.

47. Quoted in Gaiduk, *The Soviet Union and the Vietnam War*, 228.

48. "Conversation between Zhou Enlai with Le Duan and Pham Van Dong," 7 March 1971, Beijing, rpt. in Westad et al., *77 Conversations*, 179.

49. Ibid., 180.

50. "Dai su Serbakov gap thu tuong Pham Van Dong" (Ambassador Scherbakov's Meeting with Prime Minister Pham Van Dong), 16 March 1971, Dai su ky Viet-Xo 60–73, trang 371, Luu tai Vu Lien Xo (Soviet Bureau Files), rpt. in *DTNG*, 4:280.

51. "Trong loi chao mung doc tai Dai hoi lan thu XXIV cua Dang cong san Lien Xo" (Salutations for the Twenty-Fourth Party Congress of the CPSU), 31 March 1971, VN-LX-30 nam quan he, tr. 265 (Soviet-Vietnamese Relations, p. 265), rpt. in *DTNG*, 4:281. On his way back from Moscow, Le Duan stopped in Beijing, where he emphasized the importance of China's role in the Indochinese cause.

52. "The Policy of the Lao Dong Party Regarding a Solution of the Indochina Problem and Our Tasks Arising from the Decisions of the Twenty-Fourth Congress of the CPSU," translation of Scherbakov Report, 21 May 1971, Embassy of the U.S.S.R. in the DRV. I would like to thank Sophie Quinn-Judge for the document and translation.

53. When Nixon asked Kissinger if Le Duan was the "big man," Kissinger replied, "Yeah, he's the Party—he's the number one man." "Conversation between President Nixon and His Assistant for National Security Affairs," Washington, D.C., 10 May 1971, Document 200, p. 611, rpt. in *FRUS, 1969–1976*, vol. VII, Vietnam, July 1970–Jan. 1972.

54. Ang, *Ending the Vietnam War*, 68.

55. "Memorandum from the President's Assistant for National Security Affairs (Kissinger) to President Nixon; Subject: Hanoi's Reaction to the Ping Pong Visit," Washington, D.C., 17 April 1971, Document 183, rpt. in *FRUS, 1969–1976*, vol. VII, Vietnam, July 1970–Jan. 1972.

56. See "Message from Premier Chou En Lai," 21 April 1971 (Delivered to Mr. Kissinger, 6:15 P.M., 27 April 1971), Box 1031, Exchanges Leading Up to HAK Trip to China—Dec. 1969–July 1971(1), NSA.

57. Kimball, *Nixon's Vietnam War*, 261.

58. Ibid., 264.

59. Telegram from Kissinger to Bunker, 13 April 1971, Box 11, DC-SGN, 12/15/69–12/16/71(2), NSAF, NSCVIG, GFL.

60. See "Telegram from Kissinger to Bunker," 25 May 1971, in same folder, ibid. See also Bunker, "Meeting with President Thieu, May 27, 1972," in same folder, ibid.

61. See "Memorandum of Conversation," Pars, 31 May 1971, 10:00 A.M.–1:30 P.M., Document 207, rpt. in *FRUS, 1969–1976*, vol. VII, Vietnam, July 1970–Jan. 1972.

62. See "Telegram from Kissinger to Bunker," 1 June 1971, Box 11, DC-SGN, 12/15/69–12/16/71 (2), NSAF, NSCVIG, GFL.

63. "Anh Xuan Thuy gui anh Tho + anh Trinh" (Telegram from Xuan Thuy to Le Duc Tho and Nguyen Duy Trinh), Dien den, 2 June 1971, Q. 185, PLT-BNG, rpt. in *DTNG*, 4:284–85.

64. Luu Van Loi and Nguyen Anh Vu, *Cac cuoc thuong luong*, 391.

65. "Conversation between President Nixon and His Assistant for National Security Affairs," Washington, D.C., 12 June 1971, Document 218, p. 718, rpt. in *FRUS, 1969–1976*, vol. VII, Vietnam, July 1970–Jan. 1972.

66. "Anh Xuan Thuy gui anh Trinh" (Telegram from Xuan Thuy to Nguyen Duy Trinh), Dien den, 16 June 1971, Q. 185, PLT-BNG, rpt. in *DTNG*, 286.

67. Kissinger, *White House Years*, 1021.

68. The DRV's nine-point plan included (1) complete U.S. troop withdrawal by the end of 1971, (2) release of all military and civilian detainees simultaneous with U.S. troop withdrawal, (3) stopped U.S. support for the Thieu-Ky-Khiem regime, (4) full U.S. financial responsibility for losses caused to the whole of Vietnam, (5) U.S. respect for the Geneva Agreements of 1954 on Cambodia and of 1962 on Laos, (6) settlement of problems relating to Indochinese countries by the Indochinese parties alone, (7) observation of cease-fire by parties after signing of the agreements, (8) establishment of international supervision, and (9) international guarantee of the fundamental national rights of the Indochinese. See Luu Van Loi and Nguyen Anh Vu, *Cac cuoc thuong luong*, 396.

69. "Memorandum of Conversation," Paris, 26 June 1971, 10:45 A.M.–3:05 P.M., Document 223, rpt. in *FRUS, 1969–1976*, vol. VII, Vietnam, July 1970–Jan. 1972.

70. "Bao cao cua Quan Uy Trung Uong trong cuoc hoi nghi tong chien dich duong 9" (The Party's Central Military Commission [CMC] Report Regarding the Conference on the Highway 9 Counteroffensive), 26 June 1971, 355V(09) T22.12440–41, TVQD.

71. See "VWP-DRV Leadership, 1960 to 1973," 96–96, 30 June 1973, Folder 32, Box 01, WDC, VA-TTU.

72. "Dien cua dong chi Le Duan gui Anh Bay Cuong va cac dong chi Khu uy Saigon–Gia Dinh, Khu uy V, Khu uy Tri-Thien ve phuong huong cong tac o Saigon va cac tinh trong dip bau cu Tong thong va Ha nghi vien cua chinh quyen nguy" (Cable from Comrade Le Duan to Pham Hung and Comrades of the Saigon–Gia Dinh Party Regional Committee; Zone 5 Party Regional Committee; Tri-Thien Party Regional Committee), So 44, 24 June 1971, rpt. in *VKDTT*, 32:356–61.

73. "IV. Phuong huong va nhiem vu sap toi" (IV. The Upcoming Direction and Tasks), in "Dien cua dong chi Le Duan gui Anh Bay Cuong va Trung uong Cuc ve tinh hinh cach mang mien Nam va phuong huong, nhiem vu trong thoi gian toi" (Cable from Comrade Le Duan to Pham Hung and COSVN Regarding the Revolutionary Situation in the South and the Direction and Tasks in the Upcoming Period) ("Dien cua dong chi Le Duan"), So 00, 29 June 1971, rpt. in *VKDTT*, 32:380–90.

74. "Phai lam cho phong trao dau tranh chinh tri o thanh thi va nong thon gan chat voi nhau" (The Necessity of Coordinating the Political Struggles in the Cities and Countryside), in "Dien cua dong chi Le Duan," 32:386–90.

75. "7 diem cua Chinh phu CMLT CHMNVN (Dua ra tai hoi nghi Paris phien 119)" (The PRG's Seven-Point Proposal [Presented at the 119th Plenary Session]), 1 July 1971,

Van kien co ban ve dau tranh ngoai giao cua VN (Fundamental Vietnamese Diplomatic Struggle Records), PLT-BNG, rpt. in *DTNG*, 4:289–90.

76. See Nguyen Thi Binh, *Mat tran*, 73.

77. Luu Van Loi and Nguyen Anh Vu, *Cac cuoc thuong luong*, 398. See also "Anh Tho + Xuan Thuy gui Bo Chinh Tri: Nhan xet va dot tan cong 7 diem cua ta" (Telegram from Le Duc Tho and Xuan Thuy to the Politburo: Reanalysis of Our Seven-Point Proposal), Dien den, 8 July 1971, Q. 185, LT-BNG, rpt. in *DTNG*, 291.

78. "Memorandum from W. Richard Symser of the National Security Council Staff to the President's Assistant for National Security Affairs (Kissinger); Subject: Mme. Binh's 'Seven Points,'" Washington, D.C., 1 July 1971, Document 226, rpt. in *FRUS, 1969–1976*, vol. VII, Vietnam, July 1970–Jan. 1972.

79. *New York Times*, 7 July 1971; "Co van dac biet Le Duc Tho noi chuyen voi Ong Anthony Lewis (*New York Times*)" (Special Interview of Le Duc Tho by Anthony Lewis of the *New York Times*), 7 July 1971, Tai lieu ve dau tranh ngoai giao-tuyen truyen voi dich nam 1971 (Diplomatic Struggle and Enemy Propaganda Documents 1971), PLT-BNG, rpt. in *DTNG*, 290.

80. See Kimball, *Nixon's Vietnam War*, 269.

81. "Dien cua dong chi Le Duan gui Dong chi Tu Anh (Tran Bach Dang), Thuong vu Trung uong Cuc mien Nam, Thuong vu Khu uy Khu V, Khu uy Tri-Thien ve khau hieu dau tranh va hinh thuc tap hop quan chung o Saigon trong dip chinh quyen nguy bau cu Tong thong" (Cable from Comrade Le Duan to Tran Bach Dang; COSVN; Zone 5 and Tri-Thien Party Regional Committees Regarding the Slogan for the Struggle and the Form of the GMass Movement in Saigon Leading Up to the Puppet Regime's Presidential Elections), So 245, 8 July 1971, rpt. in *VKDTT*, 32:399–406.

82. "Dien cua dong chi Le Duan kinh gui Anh Tho, ve viec phoi hop ba mat dau tranh: quan su, chinh tri, ngoai giao" (Cable from Comrade Le Duan to Le Duc Tho Regarding the Coordination of the Three Struggles: Military, Political, Diplomatic), So 00, 7 Oct. 1971, rpt. in *VKDTT*, 32:407–8.

83. "Dien cua dong chi Le Duan ve nhung yeu cau truoc mat trong Dau tranh ngoai giao" (Cable from Comrade Le Duan Regarding the Upcoming Requirements Regarding the Diplomatic Struggle), n.d., rpt. in *VKDTT*, 32:409–10.

84. See Memcon, Kissinger and Zhou, 9 July 1971, 4:35–11:20 P.M., Box 1033, China HAK Memcons, July 1971, NSCF, NPM, NARA.

85. Ibid. See also Zhai, *China and the Vietnam Wars*, 196.

86. Memcon, Kissinger and Zhou, 11 July 1971, 10:30 A.M.–11:55 A.M., Box 1033, China HAK Memcons, July 1971, NSC, NPM, NARA.

87. Kissinger to Nixon, "My Talks with Chou En-lai," 14 July 1971, Box 1033, Miscellaneous Memoranda Relating to HAK Trip to PRC, July 1971, NSCF, NPM, NARA.

88. Zhai, *China and the Vietnam Wars*, 196.

89. "Conversation between Zhou Enlai and Le Duan," Beijing, 13 July 1971, rpt. in Westad et al., *77 Conversations*, 180.

90. Luu Van Loi and Nguyen Anh Vu, *Cac cuoc thuong luong*, 406–7.

91. "Noi dung Chu An Lai thong bao dong chi Le Duan va Pham Van Dong ve cuoc trao doi Chu An Lai–Kissinger" (Contents of Zhou Enlai's Report to Comrades Le Duan

and Pham Van Dong on the Zhou Enlai–Kissinger Talks), Dien den, 13 July 1971, Q. 185, PLT-BNG, rpt. in *DTNG*, 32:291–92.

92. Ibid.

93. Ibid.

94. "Memoradum from the President's Assistant for National Security Affairs (Kissinger) to President Nixon; Subject: My Meeting with the North Vietnamese, July 12, 1971," Washington, D.C., 14 July 1971, Document 233, rpt. in *FRUS, 1969–1976*, vol. VII, Vietnam, July 1970–Jan. 1972.

95. Luu Van Loi and Nguyen Anh Vu, *Cac cuoc thuong luong*, 399–400.

96. Telegram from Kissinger to Bunker, 17 July 1971, Box 11, DC-SGN, 12/15/1969–12/16/1971(2), NSAF, NSCVIG, GFL.

97. "Anh Tho, anh Thuy gui Bo Chinh Tri" (Telegram from Le Duc Tho and Xuan Thuy to the Politburo), Dien den, 14 July 1971, Q. 185, PLT-BNG, rpt. in *DTNG*, 32:292–94.

98. "Bo Chinh Tri gui anh Trinh, anh Tho va anh Xuan Thuy" (Telegram from the Politburo to Nguyen Duy Trinh, Le Duc Tho, and Xuan Thuy), Dien di, 17 July 1971, Q. 185, PLT-BNG, rpt. in *DTNG*, 32:294–95. See also Luu Van Loi and Nguyen Anh Vu, *Cac cuoc thuong luong*, 408.

99. "Anh Tho, anh Xuan Thuy gui Bo Chinh Tri" (Telegram from Le Duc Tho and Xuan Thuy to the Politburo), Dien den, 19 July 1971, Q. 185, PLT-BNG, rpt. in *DTNG*, 32:295. See also Kimball, *Nixon's Vietnam War*, 272.

100. "Anh Tho, Xuan Thuy gui anh Trinh" (Telegram from Le Duc Tho and Xuan Thuy to Nguyen Duy Trinh), Dien den, 25 July 1971, Q. 185, LT-BNG, rpt. in *DTNG*, 32:296. See also Ang, *Ending the Vietnam War*, 78.

101. "Memorandum of Conversation," Paris, 26 July 1971, 10:30 A.M.–4:00 P.M., Document 236, rpt. in *FRUS, 1969–1976*, vol. VII, Vietnam, July 1970–Jan. 1972.

102. Telegram from Kissinger to Bunker, 28 July 1971, Box 11, DC-SGN, 12/15/69–12/16/71(2), NSAF, NSCVIG, GFL.

103. Luu Van Loi and Nguyen Anh Vu, *Cac cuoc thuong luong*, 408–14.

104. "Memorandum from the President's Assistant for National Security Affairs (Kissinger) to President Nixon; Subject: My Meeting with the North Vietnamese, July 26, 1971," Document 237, p. 840, rpt. in *FRUS, 1969–1976*, vol. VII, Vietnam, July 1970–Jan. 1972.

105. Quoted in Luu Van Loi, *Le Duc Tho–Kissinger Negotiations in Paris*, 198.

106. Telegram from Kissinger to Bunker, 28 July 1971, Box 11, DC-SGN, 12/15/69–12/16/71(2), NSAF, NSCVIG, GFL.

107. "Anh Xuan Thuy gui Bo Chinh Tri + anh Trinh ve cuoc gap Kiss." (Telegram from Xuan Thuy to the Politburo and Nguyen Duy Trinh regarding meeting with Kissinger), Dien den, 28 July 1971, Q. 185, PLT-BNG, rpt. in *DTNG*, 4:297.

108. "Chu an Lai noi voi dong chi Le Duc Tho" (Zhou Enlai's conversation with Le Duc Tho), Dai su ky Vu Trung quoc, 1 Aug. 1971, rpt. in ibid., 4:297.

109. "Memorandum of Conversation; Participants: Henry A. Kissinger, Ambassador Dobrynin," Washington, D.C., 29 July 1971, Document 239, p. 843, rpt. in *FRUS, 1969–1976*, vol. VII, Vietnam, July 1970–Jan. 1972.

110. Kissinger was late due to the meeting because his meeting with Chinese ambas-

sador Huang Zhen ran longer than scheduled. See Luu Van Loi and Nguyen Anh Vu, *Cac cuoc thuong luong*, 416.

111. Memo, Kissinger to Nixon, 16 Aug. 1971, Box 4(6), Camp David Folder, NSC: POW/MIA, NPM, NARA.

112. "Meeting with President Thieu," 6 Sept. 1971, Box 11/SGN-DC, 12/15/1969–12/16/1971(2), NSAF, NSCVIG, GFL; "Memorandum from the President's Assistant for National Security Affairs (Kissinger) to President Nixon; Subject: My Meeting with the North Vietnamese, August 16, 1972," Washington, D.C., 16 Aug. 1972, Document 245, rpt. in *FRUS, 1969–1976*, vol. VII, Vietnam, July 1970–Jan. 1972.

113. Luu Van Loi and Nguyen Anh Vu, *Cac cuoc thuong luong*, 415–19. See also "Anh Xuan Thuy gui Bo Chinh Tri + anh Trinh ve cuoc gap Kiss." (Telegram from Xuan Thuy to the Politburo and Nguyen Duy Trinh Regarding Meeting with Kissinger), Dien den, 17 Aug. 1971, Q. 185, LT-BNG, rpt. in *DTNG*, 4:298.

114. Hung and Schecter, *The Palace File*, 9.

115. Ibid., 10.

116. See Nguyen Phu Duc's confidential report, "Thai do cua Nga va Trung-Cong doi voi thoi cuoc Dong-Duong" (Soviet and Chinese Attitudes Regarding Indochina), 2 June 1971, File no. 1890, PTTDN, TTLTQG-2.

117. Hung and Schecter, *The Palace File*, 49.

118. "Viec Tong Thong Nixon di Bac Kinh va anh huong doi voi Viet Nam Cong Hoa" (The Business of President Nixon's Trip to Beijing and the Impact on the RVN) appeared in a report by Cao Van Tuong, who held the position equivalent to a White House chief of staff. Tuong's role was focused on relations with the National Assembly. See "Phieu trinh cua Tong thong Viet Nam Cong Hoa cua Bo Truong Dac Trach Lien Lac Quoc Hoi v/v y kien cua cac Nghi-Si ve the ngoai giao cua Viet Nam" (Report for RVN President from Ministry of National Assembly Relations regarding the opinions of the Senate Foreign Relations Committee), File no. 1773, PTTDN, TTLTQG-2.

119. Ibid. According to Hung, Thieu had invited him back to Saigon in response to his letter that had urged the South Vietnamese president to begin his own peace initiative toward North Vietnam before Nixon's China trip. See Hung and Schecter, *The Palace File*, 10.

120. It is not known whether Ky had learned that Hanoi no longer called for his removal.

121. For Thieu's tampering with electoral laws in the summer of 1971, see Berman, *No Peace, No Honor*, 92. For CIA officials' trying to bribe "Big Minh" into staying in the race in order to give the elections a veneer of legitimacy, see Ahern, *CIA and the Generals*.

122. "Transcript of a Telephone Conversation between President Nixon and His Assistant for National Security Affairs," Washington, D.C., 19 Aug. 1971, Document 248, p. 920, rpt. in *FRUS, 1969–1976*, vol. VII, Vietnam, July 1970–Jan. 1972.

123. Ibid.

124. "Dien cua dong chi Le Duan gui Anh Bay Cuong, Thanh uy Sai-Cho, Khu uy V, Khu uy Tri-Thien ve van de lien minh mat tran trong thoi gian chinh quyen Saigon bau cu Tong thong" (Cable from Comrade Le Duan to Pham Hung; Saigon-Cho Lon City Party Committee; Zone 5 Party Regional Committee; Tri-Thien Party Regional Commit-

tee Regarding the Issue of the Allied Front in the Upcoming Saigon Regime's Presidential Elections), So 367, 31 Aug. 1971, rpt. in *VKDTT*, 32:420–24.

125. "Anh Tho va anh Trinh gui anh Xuan Thuy" (Telegram from Le Duc Tho and Nguyen Duy Trinh to Xuan Thuy), Dien di, 7 Sept. 1971, Q. 185, PLT-BNG, rpt. in *DTNG*, 4:299–300.

126. "Memorandum of Conversation," Paris, 13 Sept. 1971, 11:25 A.M.–1:30 P.M., Document 254, rpt. in *FRUS, 1969–1976*, vol. VII, Vietnam, July 1970–Jan. 1972. See also Luu Van Loi and Nguyen Anh Vu, *Cac cuoc thuong luong*, 419–20.

127. "Anh Xuan Thuy gui anh Tho va anh Trinh" (Telegram from Xuan Thuy to Le Duc Tho and Nguyen Duy Trinh), Dien den, 15 Sept. 1971, Q. 185, PLT-BNG, rpt. in *DTNG*, 4:300.

128. Telegram from Kissinger to Bunker, 15 Sept. 1971, Box 11, DC-SGN, 12/15/1969–12/16/1971(2), NSAF, NSCVIG, GFL.

129. Bui Diem, *In the Jaws of History*, 292–94.

130. Bui Diem, interview by author, Lubbock, Texas, 17–18 March 2006. See also Bui Diem, *In the Jaws of History*, 266–67.

131. Bui Diem, *In the Jaws of History*, 276.

132. Hung and Schecter, *The Palace File*, 48–49.

133. "Memorandum from the President's Assistant for National Security Affairs (Kissinger) to President Nixon; Subject: General Haig's Talk with President Thieu," Washington, D.C., 6 Oct. 1971, Document 268, rpt. in *FRUS, 1969–1976*, vol. VII, Vietnam, July 1970–Jan. 1972.

134. "Message from the United States to the Democratic Republic of Vietnam," Washington, D.C., 11 Oct. 1971, Document 269, rpt. in ibid. See also Luu Van Loi and Nguyen Anh Vu, *Cac cuoc thuong luong*, 421.

135. Berman, *No Peace, No Honor*, 97–100.

136. See "Editorial Note," pp. 985–87, in *FRUS, 1969–1976*, vol. VII, Vietnam, July 1970–Jan. 1972.

137. Quoted in Lüthi, "Beyond Betrayal," 70.

138. Ang, *Ending the Vietnam War*, 82.

139. Gaiduk, *The Soviet Union and the Vietnam War*, 232.

140. According to Lüthi, when Chinese Politburo member Li Xiannian traveled to Hanoi in late September 1971, the two sides agreed on a major economic and military aid package. See Lüthi, "Beyond Betrayal," 70.

141. "Conversation between Le Duc Tho and Ieng Sary," Beijing, 7 Sept. 1971, rpt. in Westad et al., *77 Conversations*, 180–81.

142. Memcon, Kissinger and Zhou, "UN and Indochina," p. 9, 21 Oct. 1971, Box 1034, Polo II—HAK China Trip, Oct. 1971 Transcript of Meetings, NSCF, NPM, NARA.

143. Ibid., 18.

144. Ibid.

145. Nguyen Duy Trinh, "Cong tac ngoai giao phuc vu cuoc khang chien chong My, cuu nuoc" (The Support of Diplomatic Work in the Salvation Struggle against the Invading Americans), *Hoc Tap* 10 (1971): 9–20.

146. Nguyen Thi Binh, *Mat tran*, 78.

147. See "Confidential Telegram from Le Van Loi, Permanent Delegate to the UN, to the RVN Foreign Ministry in Saigon, 'Contacts secrets avec les délégués des pays socialistes de l'Europe de l'Est'" (Secret Contacts with Socialist Diplomats from Eastern Europe), 15 Sept. 1971, Folder 1121, PTTDN, TTLTQG-2.

148. "Confidential Saving Telegram from British Consulate-General to SEAD/FCO," 1 Nov. 1972, FCO 15/1674, UKNA.

149. "Bo Chinh Tri gui anh Xuan Thuy" (Telegram from the Politburo to Xuan Thuy), Dien di, 11 Nov. 1971, Q. 185, PLT-BNG, rpt. in *DTNG*, 4:303.

150. Nixon and Kissinger received intercepts that Hanoi's military assessments at this juncture were pessimistic; "Transcript of a Telephone Conversation between President Nixon and His Assistant for National Security Affairs (Kissinger)," Washington, D.C., 13 Nov. 1971, 10:38 A.M., Document 276, rpt. in *FRUS, 1969–1976*, vol. VII, Vietnam, July 1970–Jan. 1972.

151. "Anh Xuan Thuy dien anh Tho, anh Trinh" (Telegram from Xuan Thuy to Le Duc Tho and Nguyen Duy Trinh), Dien den, 19 Nov. 1971, Q. 185, PLT-BNG, rpt. in *DTNG*, 4:304.

152. *Nhan Dan*, 27 Nov. 1971.

153. Zhai, *China and the Vietnam Wars*, 198–99.

154. "Memorandum of Conversation; Participants: Ambassador Anatoliy F. Dobrynin and Henry A. Kissinger," Washington, D.C., 18 Nov. 1971, 8:30 P.M., Document 277, p. 999, rpt. in *FRUS, 1969–1976*, vol. VII, Vietnam, July 1970–Jan. 1972.

155. Ibid., 1000.

156. Ibid.

157. See Asselin, *A Bitter Peace*, 29. See also Kimball, *Nixon's Vietnam War*, 293.

158. See "BNG Trung Quoc ra tuyen bo ve viec My lai nem bom Bac VN" (Chinese Ministry of Foreign Affairs Makes a Declaration Regarding U.S. Bombing of North Vietnam), 31 Dec. 1972, rpt. in *DTNG*, 4:306. See also "Chinh phu Lien Xo ra tuyen bo ve nhung hanh dong xam luoc cua My chong nuoc VNDCCH" (Soviet Government Makes a Declaration Regarding Military Hostilities Committed by the American Invasion against the DRV), 31 Dec. 1971, VN-Lien Xo—30 nam quan he, trang 283 (Vietnam-Soviet Union—Thirty Years of Relations, p. 283), rpt. in *DTNG*, 4:306.

159. "Dien cua dong chi Le Duan gui Anh Bay Cuong, Trung uong cuc, dong gui Khu uy Saigon ve danh gia tinh hinh phong trao dau tranh chinh tri o Saigon va nhiem vu nam 1972" (Cable from Comrade Le Duan to Pham Hung; COSVN; Saigon Regional Party Committee Regarding an Assessment of the Political Struggle in Saigon and Upcoming Tasks for 1972), So 485, 29 Nov. 1971, rpt. in *VKDTT*, 32:450–74.

## CHAPTER SEVEN

1. Quoted in Gaiduk, *The Soviet Union and the Vietnam War*, 239.

2. See Pribbenow, *Victory in Vietnam*, 283.

3. See BQP-VLSQSVN, *Huong tien cong chien luoc Tri-Thien nam 1972*, 13–14.

4. See BQP-VLSQSVN, *Chien dich tien cong Nguyen Hue*, 10, 21–29.

5. See Kimball, *Nixon's Vietnam War*, 284.

6. Randolph, *Powerful and Brutal Weapons*, 4–39.

7. See "VWP-DRV Leadership, 1960 to 1973," 18, 30 June 1973, Folder 32, Box 01, WDC, VA-TTU.

8. Pike, "North Vietnam in the Year 1972," 50.

9. See Andrade, *Trial by Fire*, 36–37. See also "VWP-DRV Leadership, 1960 to 1973," 97, 30 June 1973, Folder 32, Box 01, WDC, VA-TTU.

10. PAVN senior general Nguyen Dinh Uoc, interview by author, Hanoi, 15 Oct. 2002.

11. "Dien cua dong chi Sau Manh gui anh Bay Cuong" (Cable from Le Duc Tho to Pham Hung), So 77, 12 Jan. 1972, rpt. in *VKDTT*, 33:1–4.

12. Ibid., 2.

13. "Nghi quyet cua Bo Chinh Tri (Le Duc Tho) ve thanh lap Ban cong tac Quoc te cua Trung uong Dang" (Politburo Resolution, Drafted by Le Duc Tho, Regarding the Creation of the International Works Committee [IWC] of the VWP Central Committee), So 173-NQ/TU, 16 Jan. 1968, rpt. in *VKDTT*, 29:160–61. The IWC's responsibilities to the Central Committee were fourfold: (1) to research and report on the correct path, policy, and position regarding international work; (2) to research and report on the international work of the party, government, mass organizations, and reunification committee; (3) to research policy and the bureaucratic system on matters relating to diplomatic delegations and their conduct abroad; and (4) to follow the progress of the party and government's international strategy.

14. "Le Toan Thu gui den anh Trinh, anh Ba, anh Tho, anh Luong, anh Kinh" (Letter from Le Toan Thu to Nguyen Duy Trinh, Le Duan, Le Duc Tho, Le Van Luong, Nguyen Van Kinh), 19 Jan. 1972, Box 4, Folder 461, Phong Uy ban thong nhat chinh phu" (National Reunification Committee Files), TTLTQG-3.

15. Memcon, Haig and Zhou, 7 Jan. 1972, Box 1037, China—A. M. Haig January Visit, Jan. 1972, NSCF, NPM, NARA. See also "Memorandum from the President's Assistant for National Security Affairs (Kissinger) to President Nixon; Subject: Results of Our Recent Bombing of North Vietnam," Washington, D.C., 10 Jan. 1972, Document 288, rpt. in *FRUS, 1969–1976*, vol. VII, Vietnam, July 1970–Jan. 1972.

16. Memcon, Haig and Zhou, 3 Jan. 1972, Box 1037, China—A. M. Haig January Visit, Jan. 1972, NSCF, NPM, NARA.

17. "Haig's Preparatory Mission for Nixon's Visit to China in January 1972," Diplomatic History Institute of the Chinese Ministry of Foreign Affairs, *Xin zhongguo wenjiao fengyun* (New China's Diplomatic Experience) (Beijing: Shijie Zhishi, 1991), vol. 3, 71–82 (trans. Zhao Han, History Department, University of Virginia), NSA.

18. "Memorandum of Conversation; Participants: Ambassador Anatoli Dobrynin and Dr. Henry A. Kissinger," Washington, D.C., 21 Jan. 1972, 8:00 P.M.–midnight, Document 293, p. 1045, rpt. in *FRUS, 1969–1976*, vol. VII, Vietnam, July 1970–Jan. 1972.

19. Ibid., 1045–46.

20. Gaiduk, *The Soviet Union and the Vietnam War*, 232.

21. *Public Papers of the President of the United States, Richard Nixon, 1972*, 30.

22. Ibid., 100–106. See also 1 and 3 Jan. 1972 entries, Haldeman, *The Haldeman Diaries*.

23. Luu Van Loi and Nguyen Anh Vu, *Cac cuoc thuong luong*, 424. See also "Message

from the United States to the Democratic Republic of Vietnam," Washington, D.C., n.d., Document 295, rpt. in *FRUS, 1969–1976*, vol. VII, Vietnam, July 1970–Jan. 1972.

24. Kimball, *Nixon's Vietnam War*, 294.

25. Ibid.

26. On 10 January, Ambassador Bunker showed Thieu the U.S. proposal to reveal the secret talks and the new peace initiative, which the president hoped to announce on 18 January. When Thieu refused his approval on 15 January, Nixon decided to wait until 25 January in order to gain Thieu's acquiescence ("Editorial Note," pp. 1047–51, in *FRUS, 1969–1976*, vol. VII, Vietnam, July 1970–Jan. 1972).

27. Quoted in Hung and Schecter, *The Palace File*, 49–50. See also "Joint United States and Republic of Vietnam Proposals," Washington, D.C., 27 Jan. 1972, Document 8, rpt. in *FRUS, 1969–1976*, vol. VIII, Vietnam, Jan.–Oct. 1972.

28. "Trong cuoc hop bao" (Press Conference), 31 Jan. 1972, Bao nhan rpt. in *DTNG*, 4:311.

29. Luu Van Loi and Nguyen Anh Vu, *Cac cuoc thuong luong*, 425.

30. Hanoi leaders rejected U.S. attempts to meet privately when General Vernon Walters approached Vo Van Sung to arrange a meeting between Kissinger and Le Duc Tho for 20 February, and they refused to attend the public forum on 16 March 1972. For the rejection of the private meeting, see "Anh Xuan Thuy gui anh Tho + anh Trinh" (Telegram from Xuan Thuy to Le Duc Tho and Nguyen Duy Trinh), Dien den, 18 Feb. 1972, Q. 185, PLT-BNG, rpt. in *DTNG*, 4:315; for the refusal to attend the public session, see "Anh Xuan Thuy gui anh Tho, anh Trinh" (Telegram from Xuan Thuy to Le Duc Tho and Nguyen Duy Trinh), Dien den, 9 March 1972, Q. 185, PLT-BNG, 9 March 1972, in *DTNG*, 4:315.

31. Xia Yafeng, *Negotiating with the Enemy*, 184–85.

32. "Meeting between Presidential Assistant Kissinger and Ambassador Dobrynin," 7 Feb. 1972, rpt. in Keefer, *Soviet-American Relations*.

33. "Nghi quyet Hoi Nghi lan thu 20 Ban Chap Hanh Trung Uong Dang ve cuoc khang chien chong My, cuu nuoc" (Resolution of the CEC Twentieth Party Plenum Regarding the Anti-American Resistance Struggle for National Salvation), So 219-NQ/TU, 4 April 1972, rpt. in *VKDTT*, 33:139–47.

34. For the general resolution, not just its statements on the war, see "Nghi quyet Hoi Nghi lan thu 20 Ban Chap Hanh Trung Uong Dang" (Resolution of the CEC Twentieth Party Plenum), 355(V)/T125.17, TVQD. The resolution was also reprinted in *VKDTT*, 33:148–66. The VWP circulated the official resolution of the plenum on 4 April 1972.

35. "Bao cao cua Bo Chinh Tri tai Hoi nghi Ban chap Hanh Trung Uong Dang lan thu 20 ve tinh hinh cuoc khang chien chong My, cuu nuoc va nhiem vu can kip cua chung ta" (Politburo Report of the CEC Twentieth Party Plenum Regarding the Anti-American Resistance Struggle for National Salvation and the Pressing Tasks Facing Us), rpt. in *VKDTT*, 33:14–54.

36. "Bao cao cua Bo Chinh Tri trai Hoi nghi Ban chap Hanh Trung Uong Dang lan thu 20 ve phuong huong, nhiem vu, ke hoach nha nuoc nam 1972 va so kiem tra ke hoach nam 1973" (Politburo Report of the CEC Twentieth Party Plenum Regarding the Direction, Tasks, and Plans for the 1972 State Plan and Inspecting for a 1973 Plan), rpt. in *VKDTT*, 33:55–138.

37. Ibid., 33:42–51. See also David Elliott, *The Vietnamese War*, 2:1298–99.

38. See "Bases of Power in the DRV," pp. 6–8, 4 Sept. 1972, Folder 30, Box 01, WDC, VA-TTU.

39. See Kimball, *The Vietnam War Files*; and MacMillan, *Nixon and Mao*.

40. See MacMillan, *Nixon & Mao*.

41. "Memorandum of Conversation, Tuesday, 22 Feb. 1972, 2:10 P.M.–6:00 P.M.," Box 87, Memoranda for the President Beginning 20 February 1972, President's Office Files (POF), White House Special Files (WHSF), NPM, NARA.

42. For the full transcript of talks with Chinese leaders during Nixon's visit, see "Memorandum of Conversation," 21–28 Feb. 1972, Documents 194–204, rpt. in *FRUS, 1969–1976*, vol. XVII, China, 1969–1972.

43. Quoted in Lüthi, "Beyond Betrayal," 81.

44. "Memorandum from Director of Central Intelligence Helms to the President's Assistant for National Security Affairs; Subject: Operations against North Vietnam," Washington, D.C., 10 March 1972, Document 37, p. 128, rpt. in *FRUS, 1969–1976*, vol. VIII, Vietnam, Jan.–Oct. 1972.

45. Ibid., 129.

46. Nixon approved Helms's recommendations; "Memorandum from the President's Assistant for National Security Affairs (Kissinger) to President Nixon; Subject: Operations against North Vietnam," Washington, D.C., 5 April 1972, Document 62, rpt. in ibid.

47. "Thu cua dong chi Le Duan gui Trung uong cuc va cac Khu uy Mien nam" (Letter from Comrade Le Duan to COSVN and All Regional Party Committees in the South), 10 March 1972, rpt. in *VKDTT*, 33:186–93.

48. "Dien (Sau Manh) gui Anh Bay Cuong, anh Nam Cong (Vo Chi Cong), anh Bay Tien (Tran Van Quang), anh Tu Thuan (Truong Chi Cuong) ve chu truong cua Bo Chinh Tri mo cuoc tong tan cong tren ba mat tran quan su, chinh tri, ngoai giao de lam that bai chinh sach 'Viet Nam hoa chien tranh' cua dich" (Cable from Le Duc Tho to Pham Hung, Vo Chi Cong, Tran Van Quang, and Truong Chi Cuong Regarding the Politburo's Position on the Opening of the General Offensive on All Three Fronts, Including the Military, the Political, and the Diplomatic in Order to Defeat the Enemy's Plan of Vietnamization) ("Dien Sau Manh"), So 119, 27 March 1972, rpt. in *VKDTT*, 33:206–23.

49. BQP-VLSQSVN, *Chien dich tien cong Nguyen Hue*, 7.

50. See Randolph, *Powerful and Brutal Weapons*, 24. Randolph cites a conversation between Le Duc Tho and French Communist Party members in May 1972 in which Tho admits to the importance of Lam Son 719 for the 1972 Easter Offensive: it "showed us that, contrary to what was being published, Vietnamization could not pose any obstacle." According to Randolph, this prompted the Politburo to conduct "an extended debate, finally deciding to order the full-scale offensive by a majority vote."

51. "Dien Sau Manh," rpt. in *VKDTT*, 33:208.

52. Randolph, *Powerful and Brutal Weapons*, 25.

53. "Dien Sau Manh," rpt. in *VKDTT*, 33:223.

54. "Dien cua Bo Chinh Tri gui Trung uong Cuc va Quan uy Mien; Khu uy va Quan khu uy Tri-Thien, Khu uy V; dong dien Dang uy B3; Anh Dung va Dang uy B5; Anh Thien ve tinh hinh dich, ta va phuong an tac chien quan su tren chien truong mien Nam" (Cable from the Politburo to COSVN; Regional Party Committees; Tri-Thien Party and

Military Committees, Zone 5 Party Regional Committee; B3 Theater; Van Tien Dung and the B5 Theater Regarding the Military Picture in South Vietnam), So 182/B, 29 March 1972, rpt. in *VKDTT*, 33:224–28.

55. This is confirmed in U.S. sources: General Abrams and the MACV noted an "impending enemy offensive against the RVN," in late January 1972 ("Message from the Commander, Military Assistance Command, Vietnam (Abrams) to the Commander in Chief, Pacific (McCain), Saigon, 20 Jan. 1972, Document 1, and "Memorandum from the President's Assistant for National Security Affairs (Kissinger) to President Nixon; Subject: Vietnam Authorities," Washington, D.C., 29 Jan. 1972, Document 10, both rpt. in *FRUS, 1969–1976*, vol. VII, Vietnam, July 1970–Jan. 1972.

56. It is well-known that the North Vietnamese troops rode Soviet tanks across the DMZ, but the Chinese also provided a large number of tanks and armored vehicles to the DRV in 1972. See Zhai, *China and the Vietnam Wars*, 135.

57. See BQP-VLSQSVN, *Cac chien dich trong khang chien chong My, cuu nuoc*, 274–87.

58. BQP-VLSQSVN, *Chien dich tien cong Nguyen Hue*, 30–58.

59. The Party's decision to target the eastern Mekong Delta took place in April 1971; the shift to the Tri-Thien region occurred in March 1972. Ibid., 10. See also BQP-VLSQSVN, *Huong tien cong chien luoc Tri Thien nam 1972*, 14; and Pribbenow, *Victory in Vietnam*, 289.

60. Nguyen Khac Huynh, DRV delegation member to the Paris negotiations, interview by author, Paris, 14 May 2008.

61. BTTM-CTC, *Lich su Cuc tac chien*, 564.

62. See transcript of interview with Senior Colonel Tran Trong Trung by Merle Pribbenow, Hanoi, 19 June 2007, 39–43, http://vietnaminterviewsusc.org/wp-content/uploads/2009/07/Tran-Trong-Trung-Oral-History-Interview.pdf (accessed 4 June 2011).

63. BTTM-CTC, *Lich su Cuc tac chien*, 563.

64. See BQP-VLSQSVN, *Chien dich phong ngu*.

65. Phan Thien Chau, "Leadership in the Viet Nam Workers Party," 777. Ton Duc Thang became the president of the DRV after Ho Chi Minh's death.

66. "Dien cua dong chi Le Duan gui Trung uong Cuc mien Nam, Thanh uy Sai Gon—Cho Lon, Khu uy V, Tri-Thien ve phong trao dau tranh chinh tri o thanh pho" (Cable from Comrade Le Duan to COSVN; Sai Gon—Cho Lon City Party Committee; Zone 5 and Tri-Thien Regional Party Committees Regarding the Political Struggle in the Urban Centers), 9 April 1972, rpt. in *VKDTT*, 33:233–34.

67. "Dien cua Bo Chinh Tri gui Trung uong Cuc, Quan uy Mien, Khu uy va Quan khu uy Tri-Thien, Khu uy V, Dang uy B3" (Cable from the Politburo to COSVN; All Regional Party Committees; Zone 5 and Tri-Thien Party and Military Regional Committees; B3 Theater), So 222/TK, 12 April 1972, rpt. in *VKDTT*, 33:235–41. According to Politburo leaders, the United States and Republic of South Vietnam had been fooled into thinking that communist forces aimed to launch a short offensive and as a result concentrated only on the northern region of South Vietnam.

68. "Dien (Sau Manh) gui Anh Bay Cuong, dong gui anh Muoi Khang (c) ve danh pha 'binh dinh' va cung co vung giai phong" (Cable from Le Duc Tho to Pham Hung and Hoang Van Thai on Attacking "Pacification" and Holding onto the Liberated Zones), So 149, 15 April 1972, rpt. in *VKDTT*, 33:242–44.

69. Major-General Nguyen Dinh Uoc claims that the offensive did not factor on the international scene because the Soviets and Chinese were North Vietnam's allies. He emphasized the military balance of power on the ground, namely, that the Americans had a remaining force of 90,000 with only 30,000 fighting troops; Nguyen Dinh Uoc, interview by author, Hanoi, 15 Oct. 2002. However, see David Elliott, *NLF-DRV Strategy and the 1972 Offensive*, which argues that Soviet and Chinese considerations did play a part in Vietnamese calculations.

70. Lüthi, "Beyond Betrayal," 82; Zhai, *China and the Vietnam Wars*, 203–4.

71. See "Conversation between Zhou Enlai and Nguyen Tien," Beijing, 12 April 1972, rpt. in Westad et al., *77 Conversations*, 181–82.

72. Li Danhui, "The Sino-Soviet Dispute over Assistance for Vietnam's War," 305–6.

73. See Shen Zhihua, "Sino-U.S. Reconciliations and China's Vietnam Policy," 357.

74. Kissinger, *White House Years*, 1119.

75. "Conversation among President Nixon, the President's Assistant for National Security Affairs (Kissinger), and the Chairman of the Joint Chiefs of Staff (Moorer)," Washington, D.C., 3 April 1972, Document 52, rpt. in *FRUS, 1969–1976*, vol. VIII, Vietnam, Jan.–Oct. 1972.

76. "Conversation between President Nixon and the President's Assistant for National Security Affairs (Kissinger)," Washington, D.C., 4 April 1972, Document 58, and "Message from the Chairman of the Joint Chiefs of Staff (Moorer) to the Commander in Chief, Pacific (McCain) and Command, Military Assistance Command, Vietnam (Abrams)"; Washington, D.C., 8 April 1972, Document 71, both rpt. in ibid.

77. "Memorandum from John D. Negroponte of the National Security Council Staff to the President's Assistant for National Security Affairs; Subject: Vietnam Negotiations," Washington, D.C., 14 April 1972, Document 78, rpt. in ibid.

78. Luu Van Loi, *Le Duc Tho–Kissinger Negotiations in Paris*, 220. See also "Dien gui Trung uong Cuc, Khu uy V, Khu uy Tri-Thien va Dang uy B3, Dong gui anh Xuan Thuy ve chu truong cua Bo Chinh Tri doi pho voi viec dich tang cuong danh pha mien Bac" (Cable to COSVN, Zone 5 Party Regional Committee; Tri-Thien Regional Party Committee; B3 Theater; Xuan Thuy Regarding the Politburo's Position to Fight Back against the Enemy's Attacks on the North), So 154/A6, 18 April 1972, rpt. in *VKDTT*, 33:250–52.

79. Luu Van Loi and Nguyen Anh Vu, *Cac cuoc thuong luong*, 431–32.

80. "Memorandum from the President's Assistant for National Security Affairs (Kissinger) to President Nixon; Subject: My Trip to Moscow," Washington, D.C., 24 April 1972, Document 94, rpt. in *FRUS, 1969–1976*, vol. VIII, Vietnam, Jan.–Oct. 1972. See also Kissinger, *White House Years*, 1144–45.

81. Kissinger, *White House Years*, 1146–48.

82. Gaiduk, *The Soviet Union and the Vietnam War*, 236.

83. Luu Van Loi and Nguyen Anh Vu, *Cac cuoc thuong luong*, 434.

84. Kimball, *Nixon's Vietnam War*, 306. See also ibid., 431.

85. Gaiduk, *The Soviet Union and the Vietnam War*, 236–37.

86. "Memorandum from the President's Assistant for National Security Affairs (Kissinger) to President Nixon; Subject: General Abrams Personal Assessment," Washington, D.C., 26 April 1972, Document 98, rpt. in *FRUS, 1969–1976*, vol. VIII, Vietnam, Jan.–Oct. 1972.

87. *Public Papers of the President of the United States, Richard Nixon, 1972*, 550–54.

88. "Memorandum of Conversation," Paris, 2 May 1972, 10:00 A.M.–1:00 P.M., Document 109, rpt. in *FRUS, 1969–1976*, vol. VIII, Vietnam, Jan.–Oct. 1972.

89. "Anh Tho + anh Xuan Thuy gui BCT" (Telegram from Le Duc Tho and Xuan Thuy to the Politburo), Dien den, 2 May 1972, Q. 185, PLT-BNG, rpt. in *DTNG*, 4:319–20. See also Luu Van Loi and Nguyen Anh Vu, *Cac cuoc thuong luong*, 439.

90. "Tho + Xuan Thuy gui BCT" (Telegram from Le Duc Tho and Xuan Thuy to the Politburo), Dien den, 5 May 1972, Q. 185, PLT-BNG, rpt. in *DTNG*, 4:320. The two negotiators interpreted Nixon's insistence on conveying messages via the Soviets and not talking to the North Vietnamese directly as indications that the enemy believed communist forces would be unable to sustain the offensive.

91. "BCT gui anh Tho + Xuan Thuy" (Telegram from the Politburo to Le Duc Tho and Xuan Thuy), Dien di, 7 May 1972, Q. 185, PLT-BNG, rpt. in *DTNG*, 4:320–21.

92. Luu Van Loi, *Le Duc Tho–Kissinger Negotiations in Paris*, 233.

93. Luu Van Loi and Nguyen Anh Vu, *Cac cuoc thuong luong*, 440.

94. "Memorandum from the President's Assistant for National Security Affairs (Kissinger) to President Nixon; Subject: My May 2 Meeting with the North Vietnamese," Washington, D.C., 2 May 1972, Document 110, rpt. in *FRUS, 1969–1976*, vol. VIII, Vietnam, Jan.–Oct. 1972.

95. Secretary of State William Rogers and Secretary of Defense Melvin Laird were left out of the decision making. Nixon, who hoped to announce the news of military plans over the first weekend of May, did not want Rogers called to the White House until the following Monday. Meanwhile, Laird was not informed of the 4 May decision to mine Hai Phong Harbor. "Memorandum for the President's Files; Subject: National Security Council Meeting," Washington, D.C., 8 May 1972, 9:00 A.M.–12:20 P.M., Document 131, rpt. in ibid.; *Public Papers President of the United States, Richard Nixon, 1972*, 583–87. See also Randolph, *Powerful and Brutal Weapons*, 153–213; and Kimball, *Nixon's Vietnam War*, 324.

96. "Memorandum from President Nixon to the President's Deputy Assistant for National Security Affairs," Washington, D.C., 20 May 1972, Document 172, rpt. in *FRUS, 1969–1976*, vol. VIII, Vietnam, Jan.–Oct. 1972.

97. "Memorandum from the Special Assistant for Vietnamese Affairs, Central Intelligence Agency (Carver), to John H. Holdridge of the National Security Staff; Subject: Brainstorming Sessions Results," Washington, D.C., 18 May 1972, Document 161, and "Memorandum from the President's Assistant for National Security Affairs (Kissinger) to President Nixon; Subject: Psychological Warfare Operations against North Vietnam and North Vietnamese Forces in South Vietnam," Washington, D.C., 18 May 1972, Document 162, both rpt. in ibid.

98. *Public Papers President of the United States, Richard Nixon, 1972*, 583–87.

99. See "Editorial Note," pp. 701–3, and "Conversation among President Nixon, the President's Assistant for National Security Affairs (Kissinger) and the Head of the U.S. Delegation to the Paris Peace Talks (Porter)," Washington, D.C., 19 May 1972, Document 164, rpt. in *FRUS, 1969–1976*, vol. VIII, Vietnam, Jan.–Oct. 1972.

100. Zhai, *China and the Vietnam Wars*, 203.

101. Shen Zhihua, "Sino-U.S. Reconciliation and China's Vietnam Policy," 357–58.

102. See "Télégramme á l'arrivée, diffusion réservée: 'Visite de M. Katuchev à Hanoi'" (Telegram Regarding Katuchev's Visit to Hanoi), May 1972, Carton 69, Nord Vietnam (NV), CLV-AO, FAMAE.

103. Li Danhui, "The Sino-Soviet Dispute over Assistance for Vietnam's War," 308–9.

104. Podgorny advocated canceling the summit, while Brezhnev, supported by Kosygin and Gromyko, wanted to proceed with it; Kimball, *Nixon's Vietnam War*, 316.

105. "Chinh phu Lien Xo ra tuyen bo ve nhung hanh dong xam luoc moi cua My o VN" (Soviet Government's Declaration Regarding American Hostilities against Vietnam), 13 May 1972, VN-LX—30 nam quan he, trang 296 (Vietnam–Soviet Union—Thirty Years of Relations, p. 296), rpt. in *DTNG*, 4:323.

106. Luu Van Loi, *Le Duc Tho–Kissinger Negotiations in Paris*, 236.

107. See Porter, *A Peace Denied*, 112–13.

108. "BCT gui anh Tho, Paris" (Telegram from the Politburo to Le Duc Tho, Paris), Dien di, 19 May 1972, Q. 185, PLT-BNG, rpt. in *DTNG*, 4:324–25.

109. "Memorandum of Conversation," Moscow, 22 May 1972, 6:15–8:10 P.M., Document 257, rpt. in *FRUS, 1969–1976*, vol. XIV, Soviet Union, Oct. 1971–May 1972.

110. Ibid.

111. "Memorandum of Conversation," Moscow, 24 May 1972, 7:50–11 P.M., Document 271, rpt. in *FRUS, 1969–1976*, vol. XIV, Soviet Union, Oct. 1971–May 1972.

112. Nixon, *RN*, 613.

113. Gaiduk, *The Soviet Union and the Vietnam War*, 240–41.

114. On 11 June, the United States requested a private meeting with the DRV for the end of the month.

115. "BCT gui anh Tho, Paris" (Telegram from the Politburo to Le Duc Tho, Paris), Dien di, 7 June 1972, Q. 185, PLT-BNG, rpt. in *DTNG*, 4:325.

116. "Anh Trinh + Xuan Thuy gui anh Tho" (Telegram from Nguyen Duy Trinh and Xuan Thuy to Le Duc Tho), Dien di, 13 June 1972, Q. 185, LT-BNG, rpt. in *DTNG*, 4:326. See also Gaiduk, *The Soviet Union and the Vietnam War*, 241.

117. Li Danhui, "The Sino-Soviet Dispute over Assistance for Vietnam's War," 306–7, 309.

118. Kissinger was in Beijing from 19 to 23 June.

119. Although the VWP leadership circulated a report or declaration (*bao cao*) that defense of the North would become important as a result of Nixon's bombing campaign, the Politburo articulated the full shift in its 1 June resolution (*nghi quyet*). See "Bao cao ve chu truong chuyen huong cac mat hoat dong va nhiem vu cong tac cap bach de doi pho voi tinh hinh moi hien nay" (Report Regarding the Shift in Position of All Activity, Tasks, and Pressing Work to Battle the Present Situation), 1 June 1972, rpt. in *VKDTT*, 33:272–305. See also "Nghi quyet cua Bo Chinh Tri" (Politburo Resolution), So 220-NQ/TU, 1 June 1972, rpt. in *VKDTT*, 33:308–18.

120. Ibid., 33:272–305. By mid-June, Le Duan stopped any mention of advancing the political struggle in the cities; "Dien cua dong chi Le Duan gui Anh Bay Cuong, Anh Muoi Khang, Anh Tu Nguyen" (Cable from Comrade Le Duan to Pham Hung, Hoang Van Thai, and Tran Van Tra), 16 June 1972, so 453, rpt. in *VKDTT*, 33:329–33.

121. See Ang, *Ending the Vietnam War*, 100.

122. As a result of Nixon's bombing campaign, the Politburo mobilized the VWP's final reserves. Asselin, *A Bitter Peace*, 53.

123. Luu Van Loi, *Le Duc Tho–Kissinger Negotiations in Paris*, 239.

## CHAPTER EIGHT

1. Vo Van Sung, "Cau chuyen ngoai giao."

2. Nguyen Thuy Nga, *Ben nhau tron doi*, 154.

3. Xuan Ba, "Nguoi vo mien Nam."

4. By the fall of 1972, the Nixon administration had dropped more than 155,000 tons of bombs on North Vietnam. Asselin, *A Bitter Peace*, 66–67.

5. See Ngo Quang Truong, *The Easter Offensive of 1972*.

6. Mai Ly Quang, *The Thirty-Year War*, 2:233–34. The third wave of attacks from 20 to 27 June was the least successful phase. Commander Nguyen Huu An of the 308th Division in Quang Tri said he had wanted to shift over to the defensive stage earlier; however, his superiors insisted that communist forces "attack" or "counterattack" and not "defend." Commander An, however, realized the futility of the situation after the early attacks had failed; launching a "counterattack" would just waste manpower. However, Van Tien Dung and Le Duan were not ready to throw in the towel until the end of the summer. When Giap asked Commander An, who had returned to Hanoi after the campaign, if An could have held the citadel if Giap had approved a shift to a defensive position earlier, An responded, "I can't guarantee that with 100 percent certainty, but I can tell you that I am 90 to 95 percent certain that we could have held it"; Nguyen Huu An, *Chien Tranh Moi* (New Battlefield), 2nd ed. (Hanoi: *QDND*, 2002), 170–175; quote on 175.

7. Mai Ly Quang, *The Thirty-Year War*, 2:234.

8. "Dien cua dong chi Le Duan gui Anh Bay Cuong Trung uong Cuc" (Cable from Le Duan to Pham Hung and COSVN), So 603/B, 13 Aug. 1972, rpt. in *VKDTT*, 33:352–53.

9. See Sorley, *Vietnam Chronicles*.

10. See "Dien cua dong chi Le Duan gui Anh Bay Cuong Trung uong Cuc, Dong gui Anh Muoi Khang, Anh Tu Nguyen (Tran Van Tra); anh Nam Cong (Vo Chi Cong); anh Hai Manh (Chu Huy Man); anh Hoang (Hoang Minh Thao); anh Mon (Tran The Mon); anh Bay Tien (Tran Van Quang)" (Cable from Comrade Le Duan to Pham Hung and COSVN; Hoang Van Thai; Tran Van Tra; Vo Chi Cong; Chu Huy Man; Hoang Minh Thao; Tran The Mon; Tran Van Quang), So 453, 16 June 1972, rpt. in *VKDTT*, 33:329–32; "Dien cua dong chi Le Duan gui Anh Bay Cuong, anh Muoi Khang, anh Tu Nguyen (Tran Van Tra), anh Chin Vinh (Tran Quoc Vinh), Tran Do" (Cable from Comrade Le Duan to Pham Hung, Hoang Van Thai, Tran Van Tra, Tran Quoc Vinh, Tran Do), So 582/B, 4 Aug. 1972, rpt. in *VKDTT*, 33:339–43.

11. Quoted in Doan Huyen, "Thang My," 139.

12. Le Duan circulated the Politburo's revised strategy in September; "Dien cua dong chi Le Duan gui Thuong vu Trung uong Cuc, Thuong vu Khu uy Khu V, Thuong vu Khu uy Tri-Thien ve nhung cong tac cap bach o mien Nam" (Cable from Comrade Le Duan to COSVN; Zone 5 Regional Party Committee), 28 Sept. 1972, rpt. in *VKDTT*, 33:365–86.

13. Luu Van Loi, *Le Duc Tho–Kissinger Negotiations in Paris*, 240. U.S. intelligence re-

ceived indications of a shift in the VWP position in late June, including the abandonment of the demand for Thieu's removal; "Memorandum from the Special Assistant to the Ambassador (Polgar) to the Ambassador to South Vietnam; Subject: Indications of a Possible Change in Communist Negotiating Position," Saigon, 27 June 1972, Document 192, and "Note from the President's Deputy Assistant for National Security (Haig) to the President's Assistant for National Security Affairs (Kissinger), Washington, D.C., 28 June 1972, both rpt. in *FRUS, 1969–1976*, vol. VIII, Vietnam, Jan.–Oct. 1972.

14. See Luu Van Loi and Nguyen Anh Vu, *Cac cuoc thuong luong*, 446.

15. Ibid., 445–48. According to Chinese scholars, Beijing increased the level of aid from 1971 to 1973. Following Nixon's Operation Linebacker, the PRC sent minesweeping teams and helped increase coastal defense. Zhai, *China and the Vietnam Wars*, 203; Shen Zhihua, "Sino-U.S. Reconciliation and China's Vietnam Policy," 357–59.

16. See "Anh Vy gui anh Tho, Trinh, Xuan Thuy" (Telegram from Nguyen Van Vy to Le Duc Tho, Nguyen Duy Trinh, and Xuan Thuy), Dien di, 20 June 1972, Q. 185, PLT-BNG, rpt. in *DTNG*, 4:326; "Editorial Note," pp. 733–35, in *FRUS, 1969–1976*, vol. VIII, Vietnam, Jan.–Oct. 1972.

17. Luu Van Loi and Nguyen Anh Vu, *Cac cuoc thuong luong*, 444.

18. Nguyen Thi Binh, *Mat tran*, 86–87; Fonda, *My Life So Far*, 291–303.

19. "Anh Vy gui anh Tho, Trinh, Xuan Thuy" (Telegram from Nguyen Van Vy to Le Duc Tho, Nguyen Duy Trinh, and Xuan Thuy), Dien di, 26 June 1972, Q. 185, PLT-BNG, 26 June 1972, rpt. in *DTNG*, 4:326. In addition, Xuan Thuy returned to Hanoi from Paris.

20. From 1969 to 1972, the nine members of the Politburo included Le Duan, Le Duc Tho, Pham Van Dong, Vo Nguyen Giap, Truong Chinh, Pham Hung, Nguyen Duy Trinh, Le Thanh Nghi, and Hoang Van Hoan. The exact timing of Van Tien Dung and Tran Quoc Hoan's induction into the Politburo is unknown. For the U.S. assessment of the Politburo, see "Memorandum from John H. Holdridge of the National Security Council Staff to the President's Assistant for National Security Affairs; Subject: Hanoi's Decision-Making Process," Washington, D.C., 5 Aug. 1972, Document 229, rpt. in *FRUS, 1969–1976*, vol. VIII, Vietnam, Jan.–Oct. 1972.

21. See Pike, "North Vietnam in the Year 1972," 46–49, for a different take on the inner-party struggle as a result of the failure of the Easter Offensive. However, some accounts date Dung's promotion to full general in 1974.

22. Ibid., 53.

23. Tran Quoc Hoan, "Nam vung duong loi cua Dang trong cuoc dau tranh chong phan cach mang, quyet tam bao ve an ninh cua To quoc va hanh phuc cua nhan dan" (Struggling against Counterrevolution), *Hoc Tap* 195 (March 1972); and "Dau tranh chong phan cach mang la su nghiep cua quan chung duoi su lanh dao cua Dang" (The Party Line against Counterrevolution), *Hoc Tap* 197 (May 1972).

24. "Memorandum from the President's Assistant for National Security Affairs (Kissinger) to President Nixon; Subject: Psychological Warfare Campaign," Washington, D.C., 12 June 1972, rpt. in *FRUS, 1969–1976*, vol. VIII, Vietnam, Jan.–Oct. 1972.

25. "Memorandum from the Director, Joint Staff (Seignious) to the Assistant Secretary of Defense for International Security Affairs (Nutter); Subject: Proposed Radio Operation," Washington, D.C., 30 June 1972, Document 197, in ibid.

26. "Memorandum from Richard T. Kennedy and John H. Holdridge of the National Security Council Staff to the President's Assistant for National Security Affairs (Kissinger); Subject: Plan to Knock Out Radio Hanoi and Preempt Its Frequencies (Operation Archie Bunker)," Washington, D.C., 17 July 1972, Document 206, rpt. in ibid.

27. "Memorandum from the President's Assistant for National Security Affairs (Kissinger) to President Nixon; Subject: Psyops Campaign against North Vietnam," Washington, D.C., 15 July 1972, Document 205, rpt. in ibid.; emphasis in original.

28. "Memorandum from Secretary of Defense Laird to President; Subject: Special Operations," Washington, D.C., 10 Aug. 1972, Document 232; and "Memorandum from the Deputy Special Assistant for Vietnamese Affairs, Central Intelligence Agency (Horgan) to Osborne Day of the National Security Staff; Subject: Points to Be Covered in Report to the President about PPOG Activities," Washington, D.C., 11 Aug. 1972; both rpt. in ibid.

29. BNV, *Luc luong chong phan dong*, 293–96.

30. See Pike, "North Vietnam in the Year 1972," 53.

31. BNV, *Luc luong chong phan dong*, 296–97.

32. Quoted in Lüthi, "Beyond Betrayal," 93.

33. "Conversation between Zhou Enlai and Xuan Thuy, Ly Ban," Beijing, 7 July 1972, rpt. in Westad et al., *77 Conversations*, 182.

34. "Trong buoi tiep d/c Le Duc Tho tai Bac Kinh" (Le Duc Tho's Reception in Beijing), 12 July 1972, Ho so bien ban tiep xuc cua phong LT, Van phong Trung uong Dang (Central Committee Office Collection Archives), rpt. in *DTNG*, 4:328.

35. "Conversation between Zhou Enlai and Le Duc Tho," Beijing, 12 July 1972, rpt. in Westad et al., *77 Conversations*, 182–84.

36. In mid-July, the GDR also applied pressure on the DRV by urging Hanoi to heed Soviet chairman Podgorny's advice. During a meeting between East German head of state Erich Honecker and North Vietnamese ambassador to the GDR Nguyen Song Tung, Honecker pledged East Germany's support for the Vietnamese war effort but urged the DRV to find a negotiated settlement. Kimball, *Nixon's Vietnam War*, 319.

37. "Thuong nghi si My McGovern ra tuyen bo" (Senator McGovern's Declaration), 11 July 1972, Tai lieu ve dau tranh NG-Tuyen truyen voi dich, 3 thang 7, 8, 9/72 (Materials Concerning the Diplomatic and Propaganda Struggles in July, August, and September 1972), PLT-BNG, rpt. in *DTNG*, 4:328.

38. Ibid.

39. "Anh Trinh gui anh Tho va Xuan Thuy" (Telegram from Nguyen Duy Trinh to Le Duc Tho and Xuan Thuy), Dien di, 17 July 1972, Q. 185, PLT-BNG, rpt. in *DTNG*, 4:329.

40. Kissinger tried separating military and political issues, while Le Duc Tho insisted on one comprehensive plan.

41. "Memorandum of Conversation," Paris, 19 July 1972, 9:52 A.M.–4:25 P.M., Document 207, p. 761, rpt. in *FRUS, 1969–1976*, vol. VIII, Vietnam, Jan.–Oct. 1972.

42. The new terms included a cease-fire in place, the withdrawal of U.S. forces within four months of the cease-fire and prisoner exchange, and agreement on some issues with Hanoi regarding the political future of South Vietnam (ibid., 774–75).

43. Luu Van Loi and Nguyen Anh Vu, *Cac cuoc thuong luong*, 455.

44. Ibid., 458–61. For a more concise summary, see "Anh Tho gui BCT" (Telegram

from Le Duc Tho to the Politburo), Dien den, 23 July 1972, Q. 185, PLT-BNG, rpt. in *DTNG*, 4:329.

45. Luu Van Loi and Nguyen Anh Vu, *Cac cuoc thuong luong*, 451.

46. Ibid., 456.

47. Ibid., 455–56.

48. Luu Van Loi, *Le Duc Tho–Kissinger Negotiations in Paris*, 255.

49. "BCT gui anh Tho va anh Xuan Thuy" (Telegram from the Politburo to Le Duc Tho and Xuan Thuy), Dien di, 27 July 1972, Q. 185, PLT-BNG, rpt. in *DTNG*, 4:330.

50. See Lüthi, "Beyond Betrayal," 95.

51. The plan was based on "concrete proposals" that Nixon and Brezhnev worked out. "Conversation between President Nixon and the President's Assistant for National Security Affairs (Kissinger)," Washington, D.C., 2 Aug. 1972; and "Memorandum from the President's Assistant for National Security Affairs (Kissinger) to President Nixon; Subject: My August 1 Meeting with the North Vietnamese," Washington, D.C., 3 Aug. 1972; both rpt. in *FRUS, 1969–1976*, vol. VIII, Vietnam, Jan.–Oct. 1972. See also Kissinger, *White House Years*, 1315–16.

52. "Anh Tho + Xuan Thuy gui anh Trinh" (Telegram from Le Duc Tho and Xuan Thuy to the Politburo), Dien den, 1 Aug. 1972, Q. 185, PLT-BNG, rpt. in *DTNG*, 4:330–31.

53. "Conversation between President Nixon and the President's Assistant for National Security Affairs (Kissinger)," Washington, D.C., 2 Aug. 1972, rpt. in *FRUS, 1969–1976*, vol. VIII, Vietnam, Jan.–Oct. 1972. Kissinger had tacitly agreed to accept that a tripartite electoral commission, first proposed in October 1971, could transition to a coalition government during talks with Soviet leaders in late May 1972.

54. "BCT gui anh Tho va Anh Xuan Thuy" (Telegram from the Politburo to Le Duc Tho and Xuan Thuy), Dien di, 11 Aug. 1972, Q. 185, PLT-BNG, rpt. in *DTNG*, 4:331–32.

55. "Conversation between President Nixon and the President's Assistant for National Security Affairs (Kissinger)," Washington, D.C., 2 Aug. 1972, p. 835, rpt. in *FRUS, 1969–1976*, vol. VIII, Vietnam, Jan.–Oct. 1972.

56. "Memorandum from the President's Assistant for National Security Affairs (Haig) to President Nixon; Subject: Today's Paris Meeting," Washington, D.C., 14 Aug. 1972, Document 237, and "Memorandum from the President's Assistant for National Security Affairs (Kissinger) to President Nixon; Subject: My August 14 Meeting with the North Vietnamese," Washington, D.C., 19 Aug. 1972, Document 246, both rpt. in ibid.

57. "Paper Presented by the President's Assistant for National Security Affairs (Kissinger) to the Special Adviser to the North Vietnamese Delegate to the Paris Peace Talks (Le Duc Tho)," Paris, n.d., Document 238; and "Paper Presented by the President's Assistant for National Security Affairs (Kissinger) to the Special Adviser to the North Vietnamese Delegate to the Paris Peace Talks (Le Duc Tho); Subject: Procedures Regarding the Conduct of Negotiations," Paris, n.d., Document 239; both rpt. in ibid.

58. Luu Van Loi and Nguyen Anh Vu, *Cac cuoc thuong luong*, 468–72.

59. "Anh Tho + Xuan Thuy gui anh Trinh" (Telegram from Le Duc Tho and Xuan Thuy to Nguyen Duy Trinh), Dien den, 14 Aug. 1972, Q. 185, PLT BNG, rpt. in *DTNG*, 4:332–33.

60. Kissinger, *White House Years*, 1317–20; Luu Van Loi and Nguyen Anh Vu, *Cac cuoc thuong luong*, 472.

61. "Anh Tho + Xuan Thuy gui BCT" (Telegram from Le Duc Tho and Xuan Thuy to the Politburo), Dien den, 16 Aug. 1972, Q. 185, PLT-BNG, rpt. in *DTNG*, 4:333–34.

62. "Memoranda of Conversation," Saigon, 17 Aug. 1972, 4:35–6:40 P.M., Document 243; and Saigon, 18 Aug. 1972, 10:00 A.M.–1:30 P.M., Document 245; both rpt. in *FRUS, 1969–1976*, vol. VIII, Vietnam, Jan.–Oct. 1972.

63. "Memorandum from the President's Deputy Assistant for National Security Affairs (Haig) to President Nixon; Subject: Issue between US and GVN in New US Peace Proposal," Washington, D.C., 14 Sept. 1972, rpt. in ibid. Hung and Schecter, *The Palace File*, 68.

64. Kissinger, *White House Years*, 1327.

65. Luu Van Loi and Nguyen Anh Vu, *Cac cuoc thuong luong*, 472–78.

66. Quoted in Lüthi, "Beyond Betrayal," 95.

67. Vo Van Sung, "Cau chuyen ngoai giao."

68. Quoted in ibid.

69. Ibid.

70. These diplomatic attacks were the results of "products." "Strategic" products included documents, announcements, and proposals (such as the NLF's ten-point peace program, the PRG's seven-point plan, and the DRV's nine-point plan); "small step attack" products consisted of changing time limits on demands presented to the United States; and "miscellaneous" products were those that carried through on promises made by the delegation. Ibid.

71. Doan Huyen, "Thang My," 138.

72. Luu Van Loi and Nguyen Anh Vu, *Cac cuoc thuong luong*, 478.

73. "Thu tuong Pham Van Dong doc dien van nhan dip quoc khanh nuoc" (Prime Minister Pham Van Dong's Speech on National Day), 2 Sept. 1972, Tai lieu dau tranh ngoai giao—Tuyen truyen voi dich, 3 thang 7, 8, 9/72 (Diplomatic Struggle—Enemy Propaganda Documents, July–Sept. 1972) ("Tai lieu 3 thang"), PLT-BNG, rpt. in *DTNG*, 4:334.

74. "Dong chi Le Duc Tho ra tuyen bo tai san bay khi den Pari" (Comrade Le Duc Tho's Announcement at the Paris Airport), 11 Sept. 1972, Tai lieu (Documents), PLT-BNG, rpt. in *DTNG*, 4:335.

75. "Chinh phu CMLT CHMNVN ra tuyen bo" (PRG Announcement), 11 Sept. 1972, Tai lieu 3 thang (Three Months' Documents), PLT-BNG, rpt. in *DTNG*, 4:335. See also Luu Van Loi and Nguyen Anh Vu, *Cac cuoc thuong luong*, 478–79.

76. Luu Van Loi and Nguyen Anh Vu, *Cac cuoc thuong luong*, 478–79.

77. Quoted in Lüthi, "Beyond Betrayal," 96.

78. Asselin, *A Bitter Peace*, 66.

79. Quoted in ibid.

80. Quoted in Ang, *Ending the Vietnam War*, 108.

81. "Memorandum from the President's Assistant for National Security Affairs (Kissinger) to President Nixon; Subject: My Meeting with the North Vietnamese, September 15, 1972," Washington, D.C., 19 Sept. 1972, Document 263, rpt. in *FRUS, 1969–1976*, vol. VIII, Vietnam, Jan.–Oct. 1972.

82. During a conversation with Nixon after the 15 September meeting, Kissinger said

he believed Hanoi was "ready to cave" and noted that the Soviets had treated Le Duc Tho poorly during his 10–11 September visit to the Soviet Union. The North Vietnamese leader only met with First Deputy Premier Kiral Mazurov, "number 14 in the Politburo," while Brezhnev refused to meet him. In contrast, Kissinger, who was also in Moscow, saw Brezhnev for twenty-five hours during his visit from 10 to 13 September; "Conversation among President Nixon, the President's Assistant for National Security Affairs (Kissinger), and the President's Deputy Assistant for National Security Affairs," Washington, D.C., 15–16 Sept. 1972, Document 262, p. 964, rpt. in ibid.

83. Luu Van Loi, *Le Duc Tho–Kissinger Negotiations in Paris*, 289. Kissinger was vague on who proposed the deadline: "We settled on October 15"; Kissinger, *White House Years*, 1333.

84. "Anh Trinh gui anh Tho + Xuan Thuy" (Telegram Nguyen Duy Trinh to Le Duc Tho and Xuan Thuy), Dien di, 21 Sept. 1972, Q. 185, PLT-BNG, rpt. in *DTNG*, 4:338.

85. "Anh Trinh gui anh Tho + Xuan Thuy" (Telegram Nguyen Duy Trinh to Le Duc Tho and Xuan Thuy), Dien di, 23 Sept. 1972, Q. 185, PLT-BNG, rpt. in *DTNG*, 4:338–39. Nguyen Duy Trinh indicated that Ha Van Lau had long worked on military matters and that Luu Van Loi had been appointed the person responsible to transport the draft.

86. "Bo chinh tri gui anh Tho, anh Xuan Thuy" (Telegram from the Politburo to Le Duc Tho and Xuan Thuy), Dien di, 24 Sept. 1972, Q.185, PLT-BNG, rpt. in *DTNG*, 4:339. The Politburo wrote to its negotiators that if the United States refused to the current makeup of International Commission for Supervision and Control (ICSC), including Poland, Canada, and India, then the DRV was willing to accept that each side propose two countries for a new international body consisting of four countries total.

87. Kissinger, *White House Years*, 1335.

88. See "Memorandum from the President's Assistant for National Security Affairs (Kissinger) to President Nixon; Subject: My Meetings with the North Vietnamese September 26–27, 1972," Washington, D.C., 28 Sept. 1972, Document 267, rpt. in *FRUS, 1969–1976*, vol. VIII, Vietnam, Jan.–Oct. 1972; "Anh Tho, Xuan Thuy gui Bo Chinh Tri" (Telegram from Le Duc Tho and Xuan Thuy to the Politburo), Dien den, 26 Sept. 1972, Q. 185, PLT-BNG, rpt. in *DTNG*, 4:339.

89. "Anh Tho, Xuan Thuy gui Bo Chinh Tri" (Telegram from Le Duc Tho and Xuan Thuy to the Politburo), Dien den, 29 Sept. 1972, Q. 185, PLT-BNG, rpt. in *DTNG*, 4:440. See also Kimball, *Nixon's Vietnam War*, 335.

90. This cable does not appear in the chronology.

91. Luu Van Loi and Nguyen Anh Vu, *Cac cuoc thuong luong*, 491.

92. Telegram from Kissinger to Bunker, 27 Sept. 1972, Box 11, DC-SGN-9/16–10/17/1972(1), NSAF, NSCVIG, GFL.

93. Quoted in Berman, *No Peace, No Honor*, 149.

94. "Backchannel Message from the President's Deputy Assistant for National Security Affairs (Haig) to the President's Assistant for National Security Affairs (Kissinger)," Saigon, 2 Oct. 1972, Document 276, rpt. in *FRUS, 1969–1976*, vol. VIII, Vietnam, Jan.–Oct. 1972.

95. "Memorandum of Conversation," Saigon, 4 Oct. 1972, 9:00 A.M.–12:50 P.M., Document 277, rpt. in ibid.

96. Hung and Schecter, *The Palace File*, 72. See also Berman, *No Peace, No Honor*, 150–51.

97. "Transcript of a Telephone Conversation between President Nixon and the President's Assistant for National Security Affairs (Kissinger)," 4 Oct. 1972, 10:20 A.M., Document 279; and "Backchannel Message from the Ambassador to South Vietnam (Bunker) to the President's Assistant for National Security Affairs," Saigon, 5 Oct. 1972, Document 280; both rpt. in *FRUS, 1969–1976*, vol. VIII, Vietnam, Jan.–Oct. 1972. See also Kimball, *Nixon's Vietnam War*, 337. For Thieu's fear of an assassination attempt, see Hung and Schecter, *The Palace File*, 74–82.

98. Le Duan and the Politburo sent Tho and Thuy a telegram on 4 October emphasizing the need to end the war before the U.S. presidential election by seizing the initiative at negotiations. See Doan Huyen, "Thang My," 141.

99. Tran Hoan, "Thoa thuan," 161.

100. See Doan Huyen, "Thang My," 140–41. According to Luu Van Loi, the draft agreement he and Huyen brought from Hanoi was presented by Tho at the 27 September meeting.

101. "Dien cua Ban bi thu (Le Van Luong) gui cac khu, thanh, tinh uy ve day manh dau tranh len an My tren the gioi va o nuoc My" (Cable from the Secretariat to the Regional, Provincial, and City Party Committees Regarding Pushing Forward the Struggle against the United States at the International Level and in the United States), So 477, 1 Oct. 1972, rpt. in *VKDTT*, 33:391–92. See also "Cac Chu tich thanh pho Hanoi, Hai Phong, cac thanh pho khac va cac thi xa cua nuoc VNDCCH da ra loi keu goi" (The Declaration of the Mayors of Hanoi, Hai Phong, and Other Towns as well as from Heads of Villages of the DRV), 3 Oct. 1972, Tai lieu dau tranh ngoai giao—Tuyen truyen voi dich—thang 10/72 (Diplomatic Struggle Enemy Propaganda Documents, Oct. 1972), Tai lieu 10/72, PLT-BNG, rpt. in *DTNG*, 4:340.

102. "Dien cua Ban bi thu gui Anh Nam Cong, anh Hai Manh, Khu uy V ve van de chinh tri o mien Nam" (Cable from the Secretariat to Vo Chi Cong, Hai Manh, and Zone 5 Party Regional Committee Regarding Politics in South Vietnam), So 456, 10 Oct. 1972, rpt. in *VKDTT*, 33:395.

103. Luu Van Loi, *Le Duc Tho–Kissinger Negotiations in Paris*, 306.

104. See "Anh Trinh gui Bo chinh tri" (Telegram from Nguyen Duy Trinh to the Politburo), Dien den, 9 Oct. 1972, Q. 185, PLT-BNG, rpt. in *DTNG*, 4:341.

105. "Memorandum of Conversation," Paris, 8 Oct. 1972, 10:30 A.M.–7:38 P.M., Document 1, rpt. in *FRUS, 1969–1976*, vol. IX, Vietnam, Oct. 1972–Jan. 1973.

106. Ibid., 58–59; Luu Van Loi and Nguyen Anh Vu, *Cac cuoc thuong luong*, 502.

107. Quoted in Doan Huyen, "Thang My," 141.

108. Luu Van Loi and Nguyen Anh Vu, *Cac cuoc thuong luong*, 501–6.

109. Kissinger, *White House Years*, 1344–45.

110. "Memorandum of Conversation," Paris, 9 Oct. 1972, 3:58–6:08 P.M., Document 3, rpt. in *FRUS, 1969–1976*, vol. IX, Vietnam, Oct. 1972–Jan. 1973.

111. "Memorandum of Conversation," Paris, 10 Oct. 1972, 4:00–9:55 P.M., Document 5, p. 44, rpt. in ibid.

112. Ibid., 62.

113. "Bo chinh tri gui anh Tho, Xuan Thuy" (Telegram from the Politburo to Le Duc Tho and Xuan Thuy), Dien di, 10 Oct. 1972, Q. 185, PLT-BNG, rpt. in *DTNG*, 4:341.

114. "Memorandum of Conversation," Paris, 11–12 Oct. 1972, 9:50 A.M.–2:00 A.M., Document 6, p. 76, rpt. in *FRUS, 1969–1976*, vol. IX, Vietnam, Oct. 1972–Jan. 1973.

115. Luu Van Loi and Nguyen Anh Vu, *Cac cuoc thuong luong*, 515–16.

116. See Kiernan, *How Pol Pot Came to Power*, 341–47; and Engelbert and Goscha, *Falling Out of Touch*, 103–17.

117. "Memorandum of Conversation," Paris, 11–12 Oct. 1972, 9:50 A.M.–2:00 A.M., Document 6, p. 77, rpt. in *FRUS, 1969–1976*, vol. IX, Vietnam, Oct. 1972–Jan. 1973. The Vietnamese version of Kissinger's comment is nearly identical: "I believe that politically you have more difficulty in Cambodia than in Laos because your friends have their residence in Beijing, which makes the situation more complicated. I understand you"; Luu Van Loi, *Le Duc Tho–Kissinger Negotiations in Paris*, 329.

118. See "Anh Tho + Xuan Thuy gui BCT" (Telegram from Le Duc Tho and Xuan Thuy to the Politburo), Dien den, 10 Oct. 1972, Q. 185, PLT-BNG, rpt. in *DTNG*, 4:343.

119. "Memorandum of Conversation," Paris, 11–12 Oct. 1972, 9:50 A.M.–2:00 A.M., Document 6, p. 114, rpt. in *FRUS, 1969–1976*, vol. IX, Vietnam, Oct. 1972–Jan. 1973.

120. Kissinger, *White House Years*, 1360.

121. See 12 Oct. 1972 entry in Haldeman, *The Haldeman Diaries*.

122. "Anh Bay Cuong TU Cuc gui anh Tho + Trinh" (Telegram from Pham Hung of COSVN to Le Duc Tho and Nguyen Duy Trinh), Dien den, 11 Oct. 1972, Q. 185, PLT-BNG, rpt. in *DTNG*, 4:342–43.

123. "Letter from President Nixon to South Vietnamese president Thieu," Washington, D.C., 16 Oct. 1972, Document 20, rpt. in *FRUS, 1969–1976*, vol. IX, Vietnam, Oct. 1972–Jan. 1973.

124. "Telephone Conversation between President Nixon and the President's Assistant for National Security Affairs (Kissinger)," 15 Oct. 1972, Document 16, p. 147, rpt. in *FRUS, 1969–1976*, vol. IX, Vietnam, Oct. 1972–Jan. 1973.

125. See Berman, *No Peace, No Honor*, 160–61.

126. One account states that Thieu acquired the text of the agreement when South Vietnamese forces captured an underground communist bunker south of Da Nang on 17 October. See Hung and Schecter, *The Palace File*, 83. According to a CIA historical study declassified in 2009, however, the information in fact came from an espionage agent inside the Vietnamese communist ranks who was being run jointly by the CIA and South Vietnamese intelligence. When Kissinger was shown this report after his arrival in Saigon, he reportedly commented, "This has the unpleasant smell of truth." See Ahern, *CIA and the Generals*, 119. Regardless of how Thieu procured the text of the draft agreement, it is worth contrasting Hanoi's assiduous attention to keeping its lower echelons informed with Nixon and Kissinger's strenuous efforts to hide the truth from its ally in Saigon.

127. Hung and Schecter, *The Palace File*, 85.

128. Kissinger, *White House Years*, 1368.

129. "Memorandum of Conversation," Saigon, 19 Oct. 1972, 9:10 A.M.–12:20 P.M., Document 27, p. 198, rpt. in *FRUS, 1969–1976*, vol. IX, Vietnam, Oct. 1972–Jan. 1973.

130. "Memorandum from the President's Deputy Assistant for National Security Af-

fairs (Haig) to President Nixon; Subject: Second Meeting with President Thieu," Washington, D.C., Oct. 1972, rpt. in ibid. See also Kissinger, *White House Years*, 1371. At the meeting, Thieu was particularly happy to receive 150 planes along with other U.S. military equipment. By late October, Enhance Plus had rushed the delivery of tanks, artillery, helicopters, and other heavy weaponry before a cease-fire.

131. According to Kissinger's memoirs, he did mention to Saigon leaders that if they accepted the draft agreement, he would stop in Hanoi. See Kissinger, *White House Years*, 1371. However, South Vietnamese versions of the events indicate that Kissinger did not inform them of his timetable. See Hung and Schecter, *The Palace File*, 88.

132. Hung and Schecter, *The Palace File*, 88.

133. Ibid., 88.

134. South Vietnamese officials may have exaggerated in their memoirs that they knew for a fact that Hanoi would manipulate the terminology in the Vietnamese draft agreement.

135. "Memorandum from the President's Assistant for National Security Affairs (Kissinger) to the White House," Saigon, 20 Oct. 1972, Document 32, p. 216, rpt. in *FRUS, 1969–1976*, vol. IX, Vietnam, Oct. 1972–Jan. 1973.

136. Hung and Schecter, *The Palace File*, 89–90.

137. "Backchannel Message from the President's Assistant for National Security Affairs (Kissinger) to the President's Deputy Assistant for National Security Affairs (Haig)," Saigon, 21 Oct. 1972, Document 36, rpt. in *FRUS, 1969–1976*, vol. IX, Vietnam, Oct. 1972–Jan. 1973.

138. Merle Pribbenow, e-mail to author, 24 May 2008. Pribbenow dates his orders to show up at Bunker's office as 28 October, after Kissinger had departed from Vietnam, which indicates that the South Vietnamese officials did not receive the Vietnamese text until that time. If Saigon already possessed a version of the Vietnamese draft from the captured VC document, however, Nha could have pushed Thieu to cancel his meeting with Kissinger for other reasons.

139. "Backchannel Message from the President's Assistant for National Security Affairs (Kissinger) to the President's Deputy Assistant for National Security Affairs (Haig)," Saigon, 21 Oct. 1972, Document 36, rpt. in *FRUS, 1969–1976*, vol. IX, Vietnam, Oct. 1972–Jan. 1973.

140. Hung and Schecter, *The Palace File*, 100.

141. "Message from the President's Deputy Assistant for National Security Affairs (Haig) to the Air Attaché at the Embassy in France (Guay)," Washington, D.C., 20 Oct. 1972, Document 30, rpt. in *FRUS, 1969–1976*, vol. IX, Vietnam, Oct. 1972–Jan. 1973.

142. See Kissinger, *White House Years*, 1363–64.

143. Since Ambassador Bunker had to call in the CIA's linguistic expert to verify the terminology, it appears that perhaps the United States never detected Hanoi's manipulation. See Pribbenow, e-mail to author, 24 May 2008.

144. The 11–12 October meeting provides an example of Hanoi's modus operandi. After Kissinger asked Le Duc Tho to address both the English and Vietnamese drafts, Tho agreed to describe the National Council of National Reconciliation and Concord as an "administrative structure" (not governmental) that would have the task of "promoting" (not supervising) the two South Vietnamese parties' implementation of the

agreement, in both languages. However, the Vietnamese draft left the stronger wording, "governmental structure [*chinh quyen*]" and "supervising [*don doc*]," in tact. See "Memorandum of Conversation," Paris, 11–12 Oct. 1972, 9:50 A.M.–2:00 A.M., Document 6, pp. 89–94; "Message from John D. Negroponte of the National Security Council Staff to the President's Assistant for National Security Affairs (Kissinger)," Paris, 14 Dec. 1972, Document 174, pp. 633–34; and "Conversation among President Nixon, the President's Assistant for National Security Affairs (Kissinger), and the President's Deputy Assistant for National Security Affairs (Haig)," Washington, D.C., 14 Dec. 1972, p. 645, all rpt. in *FRUS, 1969–1976*, vol. IX, Vietnam, Oct. 1972–Jan. 1973.

145. "Thu tuong Pham Van Dong tra loi phong van Arnaud de Borchgrave" (Prime Minister Pham Van Dong's Interview with Arnaud de Borchgrave), Tai lieu 10/72, PLT-BNG, 18 Oct. 1972, rpt. in *DTNG*, 4:344; "Exclusive from Hanoi," *Newsweek*, 21 Oct. 1972.

146. "Memorandum from the President's Deputy Assistant for National Security Affairs (Haig) to President Nixon," Washington, D.C., Document 22, 17 Oct. 1972, rpt. in *FRUS, 1969–1976*, vol. IX, Vietnam, Oct. 1972–Jan. 1973.

147. "Transcript of a Telephone Conversation between President Nixon and the President's Deputy Assistant for National Security Affairs (Haig)," 21 Oct. 1972, 5:10 P.M., Document 37, rpt. in ibid.

148. "Message from the President's Deputy Assistant for National Security Affairs (Haig) to the Air Attaché at the Embassy in France (Guay)," Washington, D.C., 22 Oct. 1972, Document 51; and "Backchannel Message from the President's Assistant for National Security Affairs (Kissinger) to the President's Deputy Assistant for National Security Affairs (Haig)," Saigon, 23 Oct. 1972, Document 60; both rpt. in ibid.

149. Luu Van Loi, *Le Duc Tho–Kissinger Negotiations in Paris*, 344.

150. Berman, *No Peace, No Honor*, 167.

151. "Backchannel Message from the Ambassador to Vietnam (Bunker) to the President's Deputy Assistant for National Security Affairs (Haig)," Saigon, 22 Oct. 1972, Document 49, p. 261, rpt. in *FRUS, 1969–1976*, vol. IX, Vietnam, Oct. 1972–Jan. 1973.

152. Ibid., 262.

153. Ibid., 263.

154. Although there is no date and Thieu does not include his signature, it is apparent that the handwritten notes were his. I have compared the handwriting in other archival documents that Thieu signed or initialed, as well as the documents that appear in *The Palace File*. Regarding the date, and given the content of the notes, it is obvious that they refer to Kissinger's comments made during his late October 1972 visit to Saigon. Most important, Hoang Duc Nha confirms that the notes belong to his cousin, Nguyen Van Thieu, and were taken on 22 October 1972. See untitled, n.d., file 458, PTTDN, TTLTQG-2.

155. Luu Van Loi and Nguyen Anh Vu, *Cac cuoc thuong luong*, 528.

156. Ibid., 531.

157. Quoted in Luu Van Loi, *Le Duc Tho–Kissinger Negotiations in Paris*, 348.

158. Ibid.

159. "Chinh phu nuoc VNDCCH ra tuyen bo" (DRV Government Declaration), 26 Oct. 1972, Tai lieu 10/72, PLT-BNG, rpt. in *DTNG*, 4:344.

160. "Dien cua Ban bi thu gui Trung uong Cuc, Khu uy V, Khu uy Tri-Thien ve tap

trung mui nhon dau tranh chong Thieu" (Cable from Secretariat to COSVN; Zone 5 Regional Party Committee; Tri-Thien Regional Party Committee), So 484, 26 Oct. 1972, in *VKDTT*, 33:402–3.

161. For the full transcript, see *New York Times*, 27 Oct. 1972. See also Kissinger, *White House Years*, 1392–401.

162. Kimball, *Nixon's Vietnam War*, 345–46.

163. For example, see "Bo truong Xuan Thuy hop bao tai Pari" (Chief Delegate Xuan Thuy's Press Conference in Paris), Tai lieu 10/72, PLT-BNG, 26 Oct. 1972, rpt. in *DTNG*, 4:345.

164. Luu Van and Nguyen Anh Vu, *Cac cuoc thuong luong*, 532–33.

165. "Chu An Lai tiep dai dien 2 mien" (Zhou Enlai Receives Both Delegations), Thong bao so 5, trang 4, Vu Tong hop, PLT-BNG, 26 Oct. 1972, rpt. in *DTNG*, 4:345.

166. "D/c Kossygine tiep dai dien 2 mien Nam-Bac" (Comrade Kosygin Receives Representatives from North and South Vietnam), 27 Oct. 1972, Thong bao so 4, trang 4, Vu tong hop, PLT-BNG, rpt. in *DTNG*, 4:345.

167. "Backchannel Message from the President's Assistant for National Security Affairs (Kissinger) to the Ambassador to Vietnam (Bunker)," Washington, D.C., 30 Oct. 1972, Document 83, rpt. in *FRUS, 1969–1976*, vol. IX, Vietnam, Oct. 1972–Jan. 1973.

168. Luu Van Loi and Nguyen Anh Vu, *Cac cuoc thuong luong*, 537.

169. "Dien cua Ban bi thu kinh gui Anh Bay Cuong ve cong tac cua Chinh phu Cach mang Lam thoi va Mat tran Dan toc giai phong" (Cable from the Secretariat to Pham Hung Regarding the PRG's and NLF's Tasks), So 492, 7 Nov. 1972, rpt. in *VKDTT*, 33:404–6. For an alternate viewpoint that southern revolutionaries had their own agenda and obstructed Hanoi's will and that tensions existed between the VWP and PRG-NLF in November 1972, see Brigham, *Guerrilla Diplomacy*, 108–10.

170. See "Editorial Note," p. 365, in *FRUS, 1969–1976*, vol. IX, Vietnam, Oct. 1972–Jan. 1973. Nixon beat McGovern in forty-nine of fifty states, receiving 60.7 percent of the popular vote.

171. In 1972, the Democrats controlled the House of Representatives, while the Republicans lost three more seats in the Senate.

172. See "From President Nixon to South Vietnamese President," Washington, D.C., 8 Nov. 1972, Document 96, rpt. in *FRUS, 1969–1976*, vol. IX, Vietnam, Oct. 1972–Jan. 1973. See also Hung and Schecter, *The Palace File*, 383–85.

173. This second linguistic issue involved the first sentence in section b of Article 12. The South Vietnamese had told Bunker that "*don doc*" meant to supervise or direct. Despite Thieu's protests, "*don doc*" stayed in the final version of the agreement. See "Backchannel Message from the Vice Chief of Staff of the Army (Haig) to the President's Assistant for National Security Affairs (Kissinger)," Saigon, 17 Jan. 1973, Document 285, rpt. in *FRUS, 1969–1976*, vol. IX, Vietnam, Oct. 1972–Jan. 1973. See also chap. 8, n. 144.

174. "Backchannel Message from the Ambassador to Vietnam (Bunker) to the President's Assistant for National Security Affairs (Kissinger)," Saigon, 7 Nov. 1972, Document 94, rpt. in *FRUS, 1969–1976*, vol. IX, Vietnam, Oct. 1972–Jan. 1973. See also Hung and Schecter, *The Palace File*, 383–85.

175. See "Memorandum from Secretary of Defense Laird to President Nixon; Subject: Expedited Delivery of Matériel to the RVNAF (Project Enhance Plus)," Washington,

D.C., 17 Nov. 1972, Document 111, rpt. in *FRUS, 1969–1976*, vol. IX, Vietnam, Oct. 1972–Jan. 1973.

176. Kimball, *Nixon's Vietnam War*, 349.

177. "Backchannel Message from the President's Deputy Assistant for National Security Affairs (Haig) to the President's Assistant for National Security Affairs (Kissinger)," Saigon, 10–11 Nov. 1972, Documents 97 and 99, rpt. in *FRUS, 1969–1976*, vol. IX, Vietnam, Oct. 1972–Jan. 1973.

178. Ibid., 378.

179. Ibid., 274.

180. See "Changes Proposed by the Government of the Republic of Vietnam in the Draft Agreement Revised by the Government of the United States on November 14, 1972," n.d., Box 104, Country Files, Far East, South Vietnam, GVN Memcons, 20 Nov. 1972–3 April 1973 [1 of 3], Kissinger Office Files, NSCF, NPM, NARA.

181. Hung and Schecter, *The Palace File*, 127–29.

182. See Luu Van Loi and Nguyen Anh Vu, *Cac cuoc thuong luong*, 537–38. For an alternate view that Hanoi entered the final round of negotiations in a stronger position, see Ang, *Ending the Vietnam War*, 116.

183. See Nguyen Phu Duc, *The Viet-Nam Peace Negotiation*, 2005), 340–66.

184. See Kimball, *Nixon's Vietnam War*, 347–48, 352–53.

185. See "Thong bao cua Ban bi thu (Le Van Luong) ve cuoc gap giua ta va My o Pari va nhung cong viec cap bach" (Secretariat Circular Regarding Our Meeting with the Americans in Paris and the Important Pressing Tasks Ahead), So 287-TT/TU, 27 Nov. 1972, rpt. in *VKDTT*, 33:407–9; "Dien cua Ban bi thu (Le Van Luong) gui Cac Tinh uy Nghe An, Ha Tinh, Quang Binh, Thanh Hoa va Khu uy Vinh Linh, Quan khu uy Quan khu IV ve san sang danh thang chien tranh pha hoai cua de quoc My" (Cable from Secretariat to the Party Provincial Committees of Nghe An, Ha Tinh, Quang Binh, Thanh Hoa and the Vinh Linh Party Regional Committee, and Zone 4 Military Regional Committee Regarding Preparations for Our Victory over the Imperialist Americans), So 569, 9 Dec. 1972, rpt. in *VKDTT*, 33:410–12.

186. Asselin, *A Bitter Peace*, 110.

187. "Memorandum of Conversation," Paris, 20 Nov. 1972, folder: For the President's Files (Winston Lord)—China Trip/Vietnam, Sensitive Camp David, vol. 21, box 858, Minutes of Meetings, WH/NSCF, NPM, NARA.

188. Kissinger, *White House Years*, 1417.

189. Kissinger admitted in his memoirs (ibid., 1417) that the list of amendments was unreasonable. See also Luu Van Loi and Nguyen Anh Vu, *Cac cuoc thuong luong*, 543–44.

190. Minutes of Meeting, 21 Nov. 1972, folder: Camp David—Briefings of South Vietnamese, Paris, 20–25 Nov. 1972, vol. 21, box 4 (17A), WH/NSCF: POW/MIA, NPM, NARA. See also Kissinger, *White House Years*, 1416–22.

191. Hung and Schecter, *The Palace File*, 127–28. See also Tran Van Don, *Our Endless War*, 213–26.

192. Kissinger, *White House Years*, 1418.

193. "Bo Chinh Tri gui anh Tho, anh Thuy" (Telegram from Politburo to Tho and Thuy), Dien di, Q. 185, PLT-BNG, 22 Nov. 1972, rpt. in *DTNG*, 4:349.

194. Minutes of Meeting, Paris, 21 Nov. 1972, folder: For the President's Files (Winston Lord)—China Trip/Vietnam, Sensitive Camp David, vol. 21, box 858, WH/NSCF, NPM, NARA; "Anh Tho va anh Xuan Thuy gui Bo chinh tri" (Telegram from Tho and Thuy Telegram to Politburo), Dien den, Q.185, PLT-BNG, 21 Nov. 1972, rpt. in *DTNG*, 4:350.

195. Minutes of Meeting, Paris, 22 Nov. 1972, folder: For the President's Files (Winston Lord)—China Trip/Vietnam, Sensitive Camp David, vol. 21, box 858, WH/NSCF, NPM, NARA.

196. Brigham, *Guerrilla Diplomacy*, 110–11.

197. "Bo chinh tri gui anh Tho, anh Xuan Thuy" (Telegram from Politburo to Tho and Thuy), Dien di, 22 Nov. 1972, Q. 185-PLT-BNG, rpt. in *DTNG*, 4:350.

198. "Anh Tho, Xuan Thuy gui Bo chinh tri: Ngay 23-11-1972" (Telegram from Tho and Thuy to Politburo on 23 Nov. 1972), Dien den, 24 Nov. 1972, Q.185, PLT-BNG, rpt. in *DTNG*, 4:350.

199. Kissinger, *White House Years*, 1420.

200. "Message from President Nixon to the President's Assistant for National Security Affairs (Kissinger) in Paris," Washington, D.C., 24 Nov. 1972, Document 123, rpt. in *FRUS, 1969–1976*, vol. IX, Vietnam, Oct. 1972–Jan. 1973.

201. Minutes of Meeting, Paris, 23 Nov. 1972, folder: For the President's Files (Winston Lord)—China Trip/Vietnam, Sensitive Camp David, vol. 21, box 858, WH/NSCF, NPM, NARA.

202. "Memorandum of Conversation," Paris, 24 Nov. 1972, 11:00 A.M.–12:20 P.M., Document 122, and "Message from the President's Assistant for National Security Affairs (Kissinger) to President Nixon," Paris, 24 Nov. 1972, Document 124, rpt. in *FRUS, 1969–1976*, vol. IX, Vietnam, Oct. 1972–Jan. 1973.

203. "Message from the President's Assistant for National Security Affairs (Kissinger) to President Nixon," Paris, 25 Nov. 1972, Document 126, rpt. in ibid.

204. "Anh Tho va anh Xuan Thuy gui anh Trinh" (Telegram from Tho and Thuy to Trinh), Dien den, T. 187, PLT-BNG, 1 Dec. 1972, rpt. in *DTNG*, 4:352.

205. "Bo chinh tri gui anh Tho va anh Xuan Thuy" (Telegram from Politburo to Tho and Thuy), Dien di, T. 187, PLT-BNG, 1 Dec. 1972, rpt. in *DTNG*, 4:352. See also Asselin, *A Bitter Peace*, 122; and Ang, *Ending the Vietnam War*, 117.

206. Luu Van Loi and Nguyen Anh Vu, *Cac cuoc thuong luong*, 561–62.

207. "Backchannel Message from the President's Assistant for National Security Affairs (Kissinger) to the Ambassador to Vietnam (Bunker)," Washington, D.C., 30 Nov. 1972, rpt. in *FRUS, 1969–1976*, vol. IX, Vietnam, Oct. 1972–Jan. 1973.

208. "Conversation among President Nixon, the Assistant to the President (Haldeman), and the President's Assistant for National Security Affairs (Kissinger)," Washington, D.C., 30 Nov. 1972, Document 133, pp. 491–92, rpt. in ibid.

209. "Message from the President's Assistant for National Security Affairs (Kissinger) to President Nixon," Paris, 4 Dec. 1972, Document 139, p. 510, rpt. in ibid.

210. See "Bo chinh tri gui anh Tho va anh Xuan Thuy" (Telegram from Politburo to Tho and Xuan Thuy), 5 va 6-12-1972; 7-12-1972 (5–7 Dec. 1972); Dien di, T. 187, PLT-BNG, rpt. in *DTNG*, 4:355.

211. "Message from the President's Assistant for National Security Affairs (Kissinger) to President Nixon," Paris, 6 Dec. 1972, Document 144, p. 530, rpt. in *FRUS, 1969–1976*, vol. IX, Vietnam, Oct. 1972–Jan. 1973.

212. "Message from the President's Assistant for National Security Affairs (Kissinger) to President Nixon," Paris, 7 Dec. 1972, Document 147, rpt. in ibid.

213. "Message from the President's Assistant for National Security Affairs (Kissinger) to President Nixon," Paris, 8 Dec. 1972, Document 151, rpt. in ibid.

214. "Message from the President's Assistant for National Security Affairs (Kissinger) to President Nixon," Paris, 9 Dec. 1972, Document 152, p. 546, rpt. in ibid.

215. "Message from the President's Assistant for National Security Affairs (Kissinger) to the President's Deputy Assistant for National Security Affairs (Haig)," Paris, 11 Dec. 1972, Document 156, p. 559, rpt. in ibid.

216. Luu Van Loi, *Le Duc Tho–Kissinger Negotiations in Paris*, 405.

217. Luu Van Loi and Nguyen Anh Vu, *Cac cuoc thuong luong*, 577.

218. "Message from the President's Assistant for National Security Affairs (Kissinger) to the President's Deputy Assistant for National Security Affairs (Haig)," Paris, 12 Dec. 1972, Document 163, rpt. in *FRUS, 1969–1976*, vol. IX, Vietnam, Oct. 1972–Jan. 1973.

219. "BCT gui anh Tho + Xuan Thuy" (Telegram from Politburo to Tho + Xuan Thuy), Dien di, 10 Dec. 1972, Q. 186, PLT-BNG, rpt. in *DTNG*, 4:358–59.

220. "Tho + Xuan Thuy gui BCT" (Telegram from Tho and Xuan Thuy to Politburo), Dien den, 12 Dec. 1972, T. 187, PLT-BNG, rpt. in *DTNG*, 4:360. See also Asselin, *A Bitter Peace*, 127–39.

221. "Message from the President's Assistant for National Security Affairs (Kissinger) to the President's Deputy Assistant for National Security Affairs (Haig)," Paris, 12 Dec. 1972, Document 163, p. 594, rpt. in *FRUS, 1969–1976*, vol. IX, Vietnam, Oct. 1972–Jan. 1973.

222. "BCT gui anh Tho + Xuan Thuy" (Telegram from Politburo to Tho + Xuan Thuy), Dien di, 12 Dec. 1972, Q. 186, PLT-BNG, rpt. in *DTNG*, 4:361.

223. "Message from the President's Assistant for National Security Affairs (Kissinger) to the President's Deputy Assistant for National Security Affairs (Haig)," Paris, 13 Dec. 1972, Document 171, p. 620, rpt. in *FRUS, 1969–1976*, vol. IX, Vietnam, Oct. 1972–Jan. 1973.

224. Ibid., 621.

225. "Memorandum from the President's Deputy Assistant for National Security Affairs (Haig) to President Nixon; Subject: Vietnam Negotiations," Washington, D.C., 12 Dec. 1972, Document 160, rpt. in *FRUS, 1969–1976*, vol. IX, Vietnam, Oct. 1972–Jan. 1973.

226. "Tong thong VNCH Nguyen Van Thieu" (RVN President Nguyen Van Thieu), 12 Dec. 1972, Tai lieu ve dau tranh NG, Tuyen truyen voi dich—thang 12 (Diplomatic Struggle Documents, Propaganda with Enemy [Dec. 1972]), PLT-BNG, rpt. in *DTNG*, 4:361–62.

227. See Clodfelter, *The Limits of Air Power*, 177–202.

228. "Transcript of a Telephone Conversation between President Nixon and the President's Assistant for National Security Affairs (Kissinger)," Washington, D.C.,

17 Dec. 1972, 10:45 A.M., Document 187, rpt. in *FRUS, 1969–1976*, vol. IX, Vietnam, Oct. 1972–Jan. 1973.

229. "Letter from President Nixon to South Vietnamese President Thieu," Washington, D.C., 17 Dec. 1972, Document 189, rpt. in ibid. The letter was delivered to Thieu on 19 December 1972 by Haig and Bunker; "Memorandum of Conversation," Saigon, 19 Dec. 1972, Document 1972, rpt. in ibid.

230. "Backchannel Message from the President's Deputy Assistant for National Security Affairs (Haig) to the President's Assistant for National Security Affairs (Kissinger)," Saigon, 19 Dec. 1972, Document 198, p. 198, rpt. in ibid.

231. See Zhai, *China and the Vietnam Wars*, 206; and Gaiduk, *The Soviet Union and the Vietnam War*, 244.

232. Gaiduk, *The Soviet Union and the Vietnam War*, 244–45.

233. "Conversation between Mao Zedong and Nguyen Thi Binh," 29 Dec. 1972, Beijing, rpt. in Westad et al., *77 Conversations*, 185.

234. "Conversation between Mao Zedong and Nguyen Thi Binh," 29 Dec. 1972, Beijing, rpt. in ibid., 185.

235. Former DRV delegate general Vo Van Sung phrased it best: "Today, everyone knows that, even though on the surface this was a Four-Party Conference, the talks in fact were between two groups, two opposing sides. Political realities demanded that the DRV play up the role of the NLF, and later of the PRG, in order to counter the Saigon government, which was propped up by the Americans. Naturally, on our side, this was a 'two but actually only one' situation. The delegations of the DRV and of the PRG were in fact just two names used to enable us to work together jointly to carry out 'diplomatic attacks' under the unified and direct leadership of the Politburo." Vo Van Sung, "Cau chuyen ngoai giao."

236. Kimball, *Nixon's Vietnam War*, 365–66. See also Doan Huyen, "Thang My," 144; Wayne Thompson, *To Hanoi and Back*, 280; and Hobson, *Vietnam Air Losses*, 242–46.

237. Prados, *Vietnam*, 511–12.

238. *DTNG*, 4:363–69; 5:371.

239. Berman, *No Peace, No Honor*, 219; Kimball, *Nixon's Vietnam War*, 366.

240. Nguyen Thi Binh, *Mat tran*, 86–87.

241. "Conversation between Zhou Enlai and Truong Chinh," 31 Dec. 1972, Beijing, rpt. in Westad et al., *77 Conversations*, 185.

242. "Conversation between Zhou Enlai and Le Duc Tho," 3 Jan. 1973, Beijing, rpt. in ibid., 185–86.

243. "Message from the Air Attaché at the Embassy in France (Guay) to the President's Deputy Assistant for National Security Affairs (Haig)," Paris, 26 Dec. 1972, Document 224, rpt. in *FRUS, 1969–1976*, vol. IX, Vietnam, Oct. 1972–Jan. 1973.

244. "Anh Tho va anh Xuan Thuy gui Bo Chinh tri" (Telegram from Tho and Xuan Thuy to the Politburo), Dien den, 8 Jan. 1973, T. 187, PLT-BNG, rpt. in *DTNG*, 5:373; "Message from the President's Assistant for National Security Affairs (Kissinger) to President Nixon," Paris, 8–12 Jan. 1973, Documents 255, 256, 258, 263, 271; and "Memorandum of Conversation," Paris, 13 Jan. 1973, 9:48 A.M.–4:55 P.M., Document 274; both rpt. in ibid.

245. According to John Negroponte, NSC staffer under Kissinger, Nixon's bombing

only managed to make Hanoi accept American concessions (Ambrose, *Nixon*, 50), while Haig insisted in 2006 that the Christmas bombings were precisely the type of operations that could have won the Vietnam War (comments by Alexander Haig at the "Vietnam and the Presidency" conference, John F. Kennedy Presidential Library, Boston, 10–11 March 2006). See Kimball, *Nixon's Vietnam War*, 352, 367; Porter, *A Peace Denied*, 40; Prados, *Vietnam*, 513–14; and Tran Hoan, "Thoa thuan," 168–73.

246. Asselin, *A Bitter Peace*, 155–80, esp. 164–66, 175–80.

## EPILOGUE

1. See Nguyen Xuan Phong, *Hope and Vanquished Reality*.

2. Dosch and Vuving, "The Impact of China on Governance Structures in Vietnam," 9.

3. See Gleijeses, *Conflicting Missions*, for the influence of the Cuban Communist Party in international affairs.

4. Huu Ngoc (director of Gioi Publishers), interview by author, 15 Dec. 2008, 30 April 2010, Hanoi. See Lien-Hang T. Nguyen, "The Vietnam Decade." See also Chamberlin, *The Global Offensive*.

5. Nguyen Vu Tung, "Vietnam-ASEAN Cooperation after the Cold War," 174.

6. Xuan Ba, "Nguoi vo mien Nam."

7. Bothmar, *Framing the Sixties*, 87.

8. Van Tien Dung, *Dai thang mua xuan*. Translated into English as *Our Great Spring Victory: An Account of the Liberation of South Vietnam* (New York: Monthly Review Press, 1977).

9. Vuving, "Grand Strategic Fit and Power Shift"; Vuving, "Vietnam: Arriving in the World"; Vuving, "Vietnam: A Tale of Four Players."

## CONCLUSION

1. McNamara, Blight, and Brigham, *Argument without End*, 15–17.

2. Westad, *The Global Cold War*, 396.

3. For a useful study that focuses on Third World perspectives on a global level, see Prashad, *The Darker Nations*.

4. Westad, *The Global Cold War*, 397.

5. Ibid., 398.

# Bibliography

### ARCHIVES

Archives de la Ministère des Affaires Etrangères (Archives of the Ministry of Foreign Affairs), Paris
Gerald Ford Presidential Library, Ann Arbor, Michigan
Luu Tru Bo Ngoai Giao (Archives of the Ministry of Foreign Affairs), Hanoi
Magyar Országos Levéltár (Hungarian National Archives), Budapest
National Archives, Kew, United Kingdom
National Archives and Records Administration, College Park, Maryland
National Security Archives, Washington, D.C.
Richard M. Nixon Presidential Materials, National Archives and Records Administration, College Park, Maryland (now located in Yorba Linda, California)
Thu Vien Bo Ngoai Giao (Foreign Ministry Library), Vien Quan He Quoc Te (Institute for International Relations, now Diplomatic Academy of Vietnam), Hanoi
Thu Vien Quan Doi (Military Library), Hanoi
Trung Tam Luu Tru Quoc Gia 2 (Vietnam National Archives 2), Phu Tong Thong De Nhi Cong Hoa series, Ho Chi Minh City
Trung Tam Luu Tru Quoc Gia 3 (Vietnam National Archives 3), Hanoi
Vietnam Archive, Texas Tech University, Lubbock, Texas

### INTERVIEWS CONDUCTED BY THE AUTHOR

Bui Diem, 17–18 March 2006, Lubbock, Texas
Bui Tin, 12 April 2004, Fairfax, Virginia
Hoang Minh Chinh, 28 September 2005, Cambridge, Massachusetts
Huu Ngoc, 15 December 2008, 30 April 2010, Hanoi
Luu Doan Huynh, 21 June 2005, Philadelphia
Luu Van Loi, 29 August 2008, Hanoi
Nguyen Dinh Uoc, 15 October 2002, Hanoi
Nguyen Khac Huynh, 14 May 2008, Paris
Nguyen Ngoc Dung, 13 December 2008, Ho Chi Minh City
Tran Thi Lien, 30 January 2008, Springfield, Penn.

### INTERVIEWS CONSULTED

Luu Doan Huynh, interview with Merle Pribbenow, 6 June 2007, Hanoi
Luu Van Loi, interview with Merle Pribbenow, 4 June 2007, Hanoi
Tran Trong Trung, interview with Merle Pribbenow, 19 June 2007, Hanoi

PUBLISHED AND UNPUBLISHED COLLECTIONS OF GOVERNMENT
DOCUMENTS AND CHRONOLOGIES AND OFFICIAL HISTORIES

Ban Bien Soan Lich Su Tay Nam Bo Khang Chien (Editorial Committee of the History
of the Western Mekong Delta Resistance). *Lich su Tay Nam bo khang chien* (History
of the Western Mekong Delta Resistance). 3 vols. Hanoi: CTQG: 2010.

BNG. *Chan dung nam co Bo truong Ngoai giao* (Portraits of Five Great Foreign
Ministers). Hanoi: CTQG, 2005.

―――. *Dai su ky chuyen de: Dau Tranh Ngoai Giao va van dong quoc te trong nhung
chien chong My cuu nuoc* (Special Chronology: The Diplomatic Struggle and
International Activities of the Anti-American Resistance and National Salvation).
Luu hanh noi bo (internal distribution only). 5 vols. Hanoi, 1987.

―――. *Pham Van Dong va Ngoai giao Viet Nam* (Pham Van Dong and Vietnam Foreign
Relations). Hanoi: CTQG, 2006.

BNV. *Luc luong chong phan dong: Lich su bien nien (1945–1975)* (Anti-
counterrevolutionary Forces: Historical Chronology [1945–1975]). Luu hanh noi bo
(internal distribution only). Hanoi: CAND, 1997.

BQP-QK7. *Lich su Bo chi huy mien (1961–1975)* (History of the Regional Command
[1961–1975]). Hanoi: CTQG, 2004.

BQP-VLSQSVN. *Bo Quoc Phong, 1945–2000 (Bien nien su kien)* (Ministry of Defense,
1945–2000 [Historical Chronology]). Hanoi: *QDND*, 2003.

―――. *Cac chien dich trong khang chien chong My, cuu nuoc* (The Offensives in the
Anti-American Struggle for Salvation), 1954–1975. Hanoi: *QDND*, 2003.

―――. *Chien dich phan cong: Duong 9 Nam Lao 1971* (Counteroffensive: Highway 9 in
Southern Laos, 1971). Hanoi: Vien Khoa Hoc Quan Su, 1976.

―――. *Chien dich phong ngu: Canh Dong Chum–Xieng Khoang, mua mua 1972*
(Defensive Operation: Plain of Jars–Xieng Khoang in the 1972 Rainy Season). Luu
hanh noi bo (internal distribution only). Hanoi, 1987.

―――. *Chien dich tien cong Nguyen Hue (Nam 1972)* (The 1972 Nguyen Hue Offensive).
Luu hanh noi bo (internal distribution only). Hanoi, 1988.

―――. *Chien tranh nhan dan dia phuong trong khang chien chong My, cuu nuoc* (The
People's War on the Homefront during the Anti-American Resistance for National
Salvation) Hanoi: *QDND*, 1998.

―――. *Huong tien cong chien luoc Tri-Thien nam 1972* (The Direction of the 1972
Offensive in Tri-Thien). Luu hanh noi bo (internal distribution only). Hanoi, 1987.

―――. *Huong tien cong va noi day: Tet Mau Than o Tri-Thien-Hue (Nam 1968)*
(Direction of the General Offensive and General Uprising: The Lunar New Year in
Tri-Thien-Hue). Luu hanh noi bo (internal distribution only). Hanoi: VLSQS, 1988.

―――. *Lich su bo Doi Truong son Duong Ho Chi Minh* (The History of the Truong Son
Soldiers on the Ho Chi Minh Trail). Hanoi: *QDND*, 1994.

―――. *Lich su khang chien chong My cuu nuoc, 1954–1975.* Vol. 1, *Nguyen Nhan Chien
Tranh* (The Reasons for War); vol. 2, *Chuyen chien luoc* (Changing Strategy); vol. 3,
*Danh thang chien tranh dac biet* (Beating the Special War); vol. 4, *Cuoc dung dau lich
su* (On the Cusp of History); vol. 5, *Tong tien cong va noi day nam, 1968* (The History
of the Anti-American Resistance for National Salvation: General Offensive–General

Uprising, 1968); vol. 6, *Thang My tren chien truong ba nuoc Dong Nam A* (Defeating the Americans on the Indochinese Battlefield); vol. 7, *Thang loi quyet dinh nam 1972* (Decisive Victory in 1972); vol. 8, *Toan Thang* (Total Victory). Hanoi: CTQG, 2001–8.

———. *Lich su Quan Su Nhan Dan Viet Nam* (History of the People's Army of Vietnam). Hanoi: QDND, 1977.

BTTM-CTC. *Lich su Cuc tac chien (1945–2005)* (History of the Combat Operations Department [1945–2005]). Hanoi: QDND, 2005.

*Cold War International History Project.* Washington, D.C.: Woodrow Wilson Center Press.

DCSV. *Lich su Dang cong san Viet Nam (1954–1975)* (The History of the Communist Party of Vietnam, 1954–1975). 2 vols. Hanoi: CTQG, 1995.

———. *President Ho Chi Minh's Testament.* Hanoi: The Gioi, 1989. http://www.cpv .org.vn/cpv/Modules/News_English/News_Detail_E.aspx?CN_ID=89253&CO_ID =30036. Accessed 29 November 2011.

———. *Van Kien Dang Toan Tap* (The Complete Collection of Party Documents). 54 vols. Hanoi: CTQG, 1998–.

George Washington University Cold War Group and Cold War History Research Center. *New Central and Eastern European Evidence on the Cold War in Asia.* Compact disc. Budapest, 2003.

Keefer, Edward, ed. *Soviet-American Relations: The Détente Years, 1969–1972.* Washington: U.S. Department of State, 2007.

Ministry of Foreign Affairs of Democratic Kampuchea. *Black Paper: Facts and Evidence of the Acts of Aggression and Annexation of Vietnam against Kampuchea.* Phnom Penh, 1978.

Ministry of Foreign Affairs of the Socialist Republic of Vietnam. *The Truth about Vietnam-China Relations over the Last Thirty Years.* Hanoi, 1979.

National Intelligence Council. *Estimative Products on Vietnam, 1948–1975.* Pittsburgh: Government Printing Office, 2005.

*Public Papers of the Presidents of the United States.* Washington, D.C.: U.S. Government Printing Office.

U.S. Department of Defense. *United States–Vietnam Relations, 1945–1967: A Study Prepared by the Department of Defense.* 12 vols. Washington, D.C.: U.S. Government Printing Office, 1971.

U.S. Department of State. *Foreign Relations of the United States.* Washington, D.C.: U.S. Government Printing Office, 1862–.

Vien Mac-Lenin (Marxist-Leninist Institute), DCSV. *Le Duan: Tuyen Tap (1950–1975)* (The Collected Works of Le Duan, Vol. 1, 1950–1975). Hanoi: Su That, 1987.

VLSD. *Lich su bien nien: Xu uy Nam Bo Trung uong cuc mien Nam (1954–1975)* (Historical Chronology: Southern Territorial Committee and the Central Office of South Vietnam [1954–1975]). Hanoi: CTQG, 2002.

VLSQSVN. *Cuoc tong tien cong va noi day Mau Than—1968* (The Mau Than General Offensive and Uprising—1968). Hanoi: QDND, 1998.

VPBCHTU-DCSV. *Lich su Van phong Trung uong Cuc mien Nam (1961–1975)* (The History of the COSVN Office). Hanoi: CTQG, 2005.

War Experiences Recapitulation Committee of the High-Level Military Institute. *The Anti-U.S. Resistance War for National Salvation, 1954–1975: Military Events.* Translated by Joint Publication Research Services. Hanoi: People's Army Publishing House, 1980.

### NEWSPAPERS AND PERIODICALS

*Dien Dan* (The Forum)
*Giai Phong* (Liberation)
*Hoc Tap* (The Study)
*Nhan Dan* (The People's Daily)
*Radio Hanoi*
*Tap chi Lich su Quan su* (Military History Magazine) (later *Lich su quan su* [Military History])
*Tien Phong* (Vanguard)
Vietnamese News Agency (Viet Nam Thong Tin Xa)

### VIETNAMESE-LANGUAGE SECONDARY SOURCES

Bui Diem. *Gong Kim Lich Su: Hoi ky chinh tri* (In the Jaws of History: A Political Memoir). Paris: Co so Pham Quang Khai, 2000.
Bui Tin. *Mat that: Hoi ky chinh tri cua Bui Tin* (Their True Colors: The Political Memoir of Bui Tin). Irvine, Calif.: Saigon, 1993.
Cao Hung, ed. *Lich su Binh Chung Thiet Giap Quan Doi Nhan Dan Viet Nam (1959–1975)* (The History of the Armored Forces of the PAVN [1959–1975]). Hanoi: *QDND*, 1982.
Cao Van Luong, ed. *Lich su Viet Nam, 1965–1975* (The History of Vietnam, 1965–1975). Hanoi: Khoa Hoc Xa Hoi, 2002.
Chinh Dinh. "Ky uc ve Hoi nghi Paris cua mot nhan chung lich su" (A Memoir of the Paris Conference by a Historical Participant). *VNExpress* (*Tin Nhan Viet Nam*) (January 2003) http://www.vnexpress.net/GL/The-gioi/2003/01/3B9C4A7A. Accessed 4 February 2009.
Doan Huyen. "Thang My: Danh va Dam" (Defeating the Americans: Fighting and Talking). In *Mat tran ngoai giao voi Cuoc dam phan Paris ve Viet Nam* (The Diplomatic Front during the Paris Talks on Vietnam), edited by Nguyen Dinh Bin, 135–46. Hanoi: CTQG, 2004.
Ha Huu Khieu. *Dai Tuong Nguyen Chi Thanh: Nha Chinh Tri Quan Su Loi Lac* (General Nguyen Chi Thanh: An Outstanding Military Political Figure). Hanoi: *QDND*, 1997.
Hoang Vien, ed. *Lich su Cong binh Duong Truong son* (The History of the Truong Son Workers). Hanoi: *QDND*, 1999.
Huynh Van Lang. "Cach mang thang 8 nam 1945" (1945 August Revolution). *Saigon Nho* (Little Saigon), no. 1274, 14 December 2010.Le Duan. *Mot vai van De trong nhiem vu quoc te* (A Few Issues in Our International Duty). Hanoi: Su That, 1964.
———. *Thu vao Nam* (Letters to the South). Hanoi: Su That, 1985.
Le Hai Trieu, ed. *Dai Tuong Nguyen Chi Thanh voi cuoc khang chien chong My, cuu*

*nuoc* (General Nguyen Chi Thanh and the Anti-American Struggle for National Salvation). Hanoi: *QDND*, 2004.

Le Kha Phieu. "Y chi, niem tin cua dong chi Le Duan la bai hoc nong hoi cho nha hom nay" (The Will and Beliefs of Comrade Le Duan Are the Pressing Lessons of Our Nation's Present). In *Le Duan: Mot nha lanh dao loi lac, mot tu duy sang tao lon cua cach mang Viet Nam* (Le Duan: A Lost Leader and Great Thinker of the Vietnamese Revolution), edited by Le Van Yen et al., 29–31. Hanoi: CTQG, 2002.

Le Van Tuong. "Tam Nhin Chien Luoc Sac Sao, Tac Phong Khiem Ton, Sau Sat Cua Dai Tuong Nguyen Chi Thanh" (The Keen Strategic Vision and the Modest but Profound Attitude of General Nguyen Chi Thanh). In *Dai Tuong Nguyen Chi Thanh: Nha Chinh Tri Quan Su Loi Lac* (General Nguyen Chi Thanh: An Outstanding Military Political Figure), edited by Ha Huu Khieu, 144–49. Hanoi: *QDND*, 1997.

Le Van Yen, Nguyen Duy Cat, Dam Van Tho, Nguyen Thanh Binh, and Thai Trong Vinh, eds. *Le Duan: Mot nha lanh dao loi lac, mot tu duy sang tao lon cua cach mang Viet Nam* (Le Duan: A Lost Leader and Great Thinker of the Vietnamese Revolution). Hanoi: CTQG, 2002.

Luong Viet Sang. *Qua trinh Dang lanh dao dau tranh ngoai giao: Tai Hoi nghi Pari ve Viet Nam (1968–1973)* (The Party Leadership Process in the Diplomatic Struggle: At the Paris Negotiations on Vietnam [1968–1973]). Hanoi: CTQG, 2005.

Luu Van Loi. *Cuoc tiep xuc bi mat Viet Nam–Hoa Ky truoc Hoi Nghi Pari* (Secret Exchanges between Vietnam and the United States before the Paris Conference). Hanoi: Vien Quan He Quoc Te, 1990.

———. *Gio bui Duong hoa* (Dusty Wind, Flowered Road). Hanoi: CAND, 2006.

———. *Nam muoi nam ngoai giao Viet Nam, 1945–1995* (Fifty Years of Vietnamese Diplomacy, 1945–1995). 2 vols. Hanoi: Cong An Nhan Dan, 1996.

Luu Van Loi and Nguyen Anh Vu. *Cac cuoc thuong luong Le Duc Tho–Kissinger tai Paris* (Le Duc Tho–Kissinger Negotiations in Paris). 2nd ed. Hanoi: CTQG, 2002.

Ngo Ba Thanh. "Phong trao do thi va luc luong chinh tri thu ba voi dam phan va dau tranh thi hanh Hiep dinh Pari" (The Urban Movement and the Third Political Force in Connection with the Negotiations and the Struggle to Implement the Paris Agreement). In *Mat tran ngoai giao voi Cuoc dam phan Paris ve Viet Nam* (The Diplomatic Front during the Paris Talks on Vietnam), edited by Nguyen Dinh Bin, 270–80. Hanoi: CTQG, 2004.

Nguyen Chi Thanh. "Hay lao minh vao cuoc song va chien dau cua bo doi de sang tac phuc vu bo doi" (Let's Immerse in the Life and Struggle of the Soldier to Compose Support for the Soldier). In *Dai Tuong Nguyen Chi Thanh voi cuoc khang chien chong My, cuu nuoc* (General Nguyen Chi Thanh and the Anti-American Struggle for National Salvation), edited by Le Hai Trieu, 189–93. Hanoi: *QDND*, 2004.

Nguyen Dinh Bin, ed. *Mat tran ngoai giao voi Cuoc dam phan Paris ve Viet Nam* (The Diplomatic Front during the Paris Talks on Vietnam). Hanoi: CTQG, 2004.

Nguyen Huu An. *Chien Tranh Moi* (New Battlefield). 2nd ed. Hanoi: *QDND*, 2002.

Nguyen Ngoc Dung. "Co gai mien Nam tai Hoi nghi Khong lien ket" (A Southern Girl at the Non-aligned Conference). In *Ky uc nhu huyen thoai* (Legendary Memoirs), 2 vols., edited by Nguyen Thi Duoc, 1:491–97. TPHCM: Tre, 2006.

Nguyen Phuc Hoai. *Lich su Cuc Bao ve—An ninh Quan Doi Nhan Dan Viet Nam (1950–2000)* (History of the Ministry of Security of the PAVN [1950–2000]). Hanoi: QDND, 2003. http://www.quansuvn.net/index.php?topic=3826.0. Accessed 16 Nov. 2008.

Nguyen Phuc Luan. *Ngoai Giao Viet Nam: Trong cuoc dung dau lich su* (Vietnamese Diplomacy: On the Cusp of History). Hanoi: CAND, 2005.

Nguyen Thanh Le. *Cuoc dam phan Pari ve Viet Nam (1968–1973)* (Paris Negotiations on Vietnam [1968–1973]). Hanoi: CTQG, 1998.

Nguyen Thi Binh. "Le Duc Tho: Nha thuong thuyet tam co lon" (Le Duc Tho: A Beloved Great Theoretician). *Nho Anh Le Duc Tho* (Remembering Le Duc Tho), edited by Nguyen Thi Huong and Nguyen Minh Hien, 349–54. Hanoi: CTQG, 2006.

———. "Truong thanh tu cong tac phu nu sang hoat dong ngoai giao" (From Women's Work to Diplomatic Activity). In *Ky uc nhu huyen thoai* (Legendary Memoirs), 2 vols., edited by Nguyen Thi Duoc, 1:481–90. TPHCM: Tre, 2006.

———, ed. *Mat tran Dan toc Giai phong Chinh phu Cach mang lam thoi tai Hoi nghi Paris ve Viet Nam* (The National Liberation Front and the Provisional Revolutionary Government at the Paris Conference on Vietnam). Hanoi: CTQG, 2001.

Nguyen Thi Huong and Nguyen Minh Hien, eds. *Nho Anh Le Duc Tho* (Remembering Le Duc Tho). Hanoi: CTQG, 2006.

Nguyen Thuy Nga. *Ben nhau tron doi (hoi ky)* (Together Always [A Memoir]). TPHCM: Self-published, 2000.

Nguyen Viet Phuong and Tu Quy, eds. *Cong tac chien dich duong 9 Nam Lao 9 (tu 23/2 den 23/3/1971)* (Route 9–Southern Laos Campaign Rear Services [28 February–23 March 1971]). Hanoi: Tong Cuc Hau Can, 1987.

Pham Binh Minh, ed. *Cuoc dam phan lich su: Ky niem 35 nam Hiep dinh Paris 1973–2008* (Historic Negotiations: Thirty-fifth Anniversary of the Paris Agreement, 1973–2008). Hanoi: CTQG, 2009.

Pham Dinh Am. *Mot Thoi De Nho: Hoi Ky* (A Time to Remember: A Memoir). Hanoi: QDND, 2002.

Pham Gia Duc. *Lich su Quan chung Phong khong* (The History of the Anti-aircraft Defense). 3 vols. Hanoi: QDND, 1991–94.

Phan Huu Dai and Nguyen Quoc Dung, eds. *Lich su Doan 559 bo Do Truong son Duong Ho Chi Minh* (The History of Group 559). Hanoi: QDND, 1999.

Tran Bach Dang. "Mau Than—Sau 30 Nam Nhin Lai" (1968 Tet—Thirty Years Later in Retrospect). In *Cuoc tong tien cong va noi day Mau Than—1968* (The Mau Than General Offensive and Uprising—1968), by VLSQSVN, 97–104. Hanoi: QDND, 1998.

Tran Hoan. "Thoa thuan thang muoi 1972 va Hiep dinh thang gieng" (The October 1972 Agreement and the January 1973 Treaty). In *Mat tran ngoai giao voi Cuoc dam phan Paris ve Viet Nam* (The Diplomatic Front during the Paris Talks on Vietnam), edited by Nguyen Dinh Bin, 159–74. Hanoi: CTQG, 2004.

Tran Luan Tin. *Duoc song va ke lai* (To Survive and Retell). TPHCM: Self-published, 2008.Tran Quoc Hoan. *Mot so van de ve dau tranh chong phan cach mang* (A Number of Issues Regarding the Struggle against Counterrevolutionaries). Hanoi: Vien Nghien Cuu Khoa Hoc Cong An, December 1975.

———. *Mot so van de xay dung luc luong Cong An Nhan Dan* (A Number of Issues

Regarding the Building of the People's Security Forces). Luu hanh noi bo (internal distribution only). Hanoi: CAND, 2004.

Tran Thu. *Tu tu xu ly noi bo* (Sentenced to Death, Internal Settlement). Stanton, Calif.: Van Nghe, 1996.

Tran Van Tra. *Concluding the Thirty Years of War*. Vol. 5 of *History of the Bulwark B2 Theatre*. Southeast Asia Report no. 1247, 2 February 1983. Springfield, Va.: Joint Publications Research Service.

———. *Goi nguoi dang song* (To the Living). TPHCM: Tre, 1996.

———. *Ket thuc cuoc chien tranh 30 nam* (Concluding the Thirty Years of War). Vol. 5 of *Nhung Chang Duong Lich Su cua B2–Thanh Dong* (History of the Bulwark B2 Theater). Stanton, Calif.: Van Nghe, 1982.

Tran Xuan Nhi, Nguyen Minh Quang, and Dang Quoc Bao, eds. *Nguyen Thi Binh: Con nguoi va su nghiep Giao duc* (Nguyen Thi Binh: The Person and the Education). Hanoi: Giao Duc, 2004.

Trinh Ngoc Thai. "Mat tran nhan dan the gioi ung ho Viet Nam giai doan dam phan Hiep dinh Paris" (The Support of the World's People's Front for Vietnam during the Period of Negotiations for the Paris Agreement). In *Cuoc dam phan lich su: Ky niem 35 nam Hiep dinh Paris 1973–2008* (Historic Negotiations: Thirty-fifth Anniversary of the Paris Agreement, 1973–2008), edited by Pham Binh Minh, 157–66. Hanoi: CTQG, 2009.

Trinh Thuc Huynh, ed. *Dong chi Tran Quoc Hoan: Chien si cach mang trung kien cua Dang, Nha lanh dao xuat sac cua Cong An Viet Nam* (Comrade Tran Quoc Hoan: Steadfast Revolutionary Fighter, Excellent Leader of Vietnam's Security Forces). Hanoi: CTQG, 2006.

Truong Minh Hoach, ed. *Quan Khu 9: 30 Nam Khang Chien (1945–1975)* (Military Region 9: Thirty Years of Resistance [1945–1975]). Hanoi: QDND, 1996.

*Tu dien bach khoa Quan su Viet Nam* (Military Dictionary-Encyclopedia). Hanoi: QDND, 1996.

Tu Nguyet. *Chuyen tinh cua cac chinh khach Viet Nam* (Love Stories of Elder Vietnamese Statesmen). Hanoi: Phu Nu, 2006.

Van Tien Dung. *Dai thang mua xuan* (Our Great Spring Victory). Hanoi: QDND, 1976.

Vo Chi Cong. "Dong chi co tong bi thu Le Duan nha chien luoc kiet xuat, nha lanh dao loi lac cua cach mang mien Nam" (Comrade the Great First Secretary Le Duan, Towering Fighter and Lost Leader of the Southern Revolution). In *Le Duan: Mot nha lanh dao loi lac, mot tu duy sang tao lon cua cach mang Viet Nam* (Le Duan: A Lost Leader and Great Thinker of the Vietnamese Revolution), edited by Le Van Yen et al., 42–54. Hanoi: CTQG, 2002.

———. *Tren Nhung Chang Duong Cach Mang (Hoi Ky)* (On the Revolutionary Road [A Memoir]). Hanoi: CTQG, 2001.

Vo Minh. *Phan Tinh Phan Khang* (Self Criticism—Protest). Southern California: Thong Vu Tai Ban, 2004.

Vo Nguyen Giap. "Dong chi Le Duan—nguoi Cong San trung kien, nha lanh dao xuat sac cua cach mang Viet Nam" (Comrade Le Duan—A Steadfast Communist, Excellent Leader of the Vietnamese Revolution). In *Le Duan: Mot nha lanh dao loi lac, mot tu duy sang tao lon cua cach mang Viet Nam* (Le Duan: A Lost Leader and

Great Thinker of the Vietnamese Revolution), edited by Le Van Yen et al., 32–41. Hanoi: CTQG, 2002.

Vo Nguyen Giap and Huu Mai. *Duong toi Dien Bien Phu* (The Road to Dien Bien Phu). 3rd ed. Hanoi: *QDND*, 2001.

Vo Van Kiet. "Anh Le Duc Tho—mot chien si cong san nhiet thanh, mot nha lanh dao tai nang" (Le Duc Tho—A Fervent Communist Fighter and Talented Leader). *Nho Anh Le Duc Tho* (Remembering Le Duc Tho), edited by Nguyen Thi Huong and Nguyen Minh Hien, 27–32. Hanoi: CTQG, 2006.

———. "Tong bi thu Le Duan—Nha lanh dao kiet xuat cua cach mang Viet Nam, nguoi hoc tro xuat sac cua Bac Ho" (First Secretary Le Duan—A Towering Leader of the Vietnamese Revolution, An Excellent Study of Uncle Ho). In *Le Duan: Mot nha lanh dao loi lac, mot tu duy sang tao lon cua cach mang Viet Nam* (Le Duan: A Lost Leader and Great Thinker of the Vietnamese Revolution), edited by Le Van Yen et al., 55–68. Hanoi: CTQG, 2002.

Vo Van Kiet and Tran Bach Dang, eds. *Lich su Nam bo Khang chien (1954–1975)* (History of the Resistance in Cochinchina [1954–1975]). 2 vols. Hanoi: CTQG, 2010.

Vo Van Sung. "Cau chuyen ngoai giao 40 nam truoc bay gio moi ke" (A Forty-Year-Old Diplomatic Story That Is Now Being Told). *VietnamNet* (January 2008) http://www .vietnamnet.vn/chinhtri/2008/01/766176/. Accessed 28 January 2008.

Vu Quoc Khanh, ed. *Dong chi Truong Chinh* (Comrade Truong Chinh). TPHCM: Thong Tan, 2007.

———. *Thu tuong Pham Van Dong* (Prime Minister Pham Van Dong). TPHCM: Thong Tan, 2006.

———. *Tong Bi thu Le Duan* (General Secretary Le Duan). TPHCM: Thong Tan, 2007.

Vu Thu Hien. *Dem giua ban ngay: Hoi ky chinh tri cua mot nguoi khong lam chinh tri* (Nightmare in the Daytime: A Political Memoir Written by a Non-politician). Westminster, Calif.: Van Nghe, 1997.

Xuan Ba. "Nguoi vo mien Nam cua co Tong bi thu Le Duan" (The Great First Secretary Le Duan's Southern Wife). *Tien Phong*, 25 June 2006, http://www.tienphong.vn/ Phong-Su/51254/Nguoi-vo-mien-Nam-cua-co%C2%A0Tong-Bi-thu%C2%A0oLe-Duan.html. Accessed 10 July 2010.

### WESTERN-LANGUAGE SECONDARY SOURCES

Ambrose, Stephen E. *Nixon*. Vol. 3, *Ruin and Recovery*. New York: Simon and Schuster, 1991.

Ahern, Thomas, Jr. *CIA and the Generals: Covert Support to Military Government in South Vietnam*. CIA History, released 19 February 2009. http://www.foia.cia.gov/ vietnam/1_CIA_AND_THE_GENERALS.pdf. Accessed 15 June 2011.

Allen, Michael. *Until the Last Man Comes Home*. Chapel Hill: University of North Carolina Press, 2009.

Anderson, David. *Trapped by Success: The Eisenhower Administration and Vietnam, 1953–1961*. New York: Columbia University Press, 1991.

———. *The Vietnam War*. New York: Palgrave MacMillan, 2005.

Anderson, David, and John Ernst, eds. *The War That Never Ends: New Perspectives on the Vietnam War*. Lexington: University Press of Kentucky, 2007.

Andrade, Dale. *Trial by Fire: The 1972 Easter Offensive, America's Last Vietnam Battle*. New York: Hippocrene, 1995.

Ang, Cheng Guan. "Decision-Making Leading to the Tet Offensive (1968)—The Vietnamese Communist Perspective." *Journal of Contemporary History* 33, no. 3 (July 1998): 345–53.

———. *Ending the Vietnam War: The Vietnamese Communists' Perspective*. New York: Routledge, 2004.

———. *Southeast Asia and the Vietnam War*. London: Routledge, 2010.

———. *Vietnamese Communists' Relations with China and the Second Indochina Conflict, 1956–1962*. Jefferson, N.C.: McFarland, 1997.

———. *The Vietnam War from the Other Side: The Vietnamese Communists' Perspective*. London: RoutledgeCurzon, 2002.

Anson, Robert Sam. *War News: A Young Reporter in Indochina*. New York: Simon and Schuster, 1989.

Asselin, Pierre. *A Bitter Peace: Washington, Hanoi, and the Making of the Paris Agreement*. Chapel Hill: University of North Carolina Press, 2002.

———. "Choosing Peace: Hanoi and the Geneva Agreement on Vietnam, 1954–1955." *Journal of Cold War Studies* 9, no. 2 (Spring 2007): 95–126.

———. "Revisionism Triumphant: The Tet Offensive and the Death of Ultra-Leftism in Vietnam." Paper presented at Society for Historians of American Foreign Relations annual meeting, Chantilly, Virginia, 22–25 June 2007.

———. "Using the Van Kien Dang Series to Understand Vietnamese Revolutionary Strategy during the Vietnam War, 1954–1975." *Journal of Vietnamese Studies* 5, no. 2 (Summer 2010): 219–24.

Berman, Larry. *Lyndon Johnson's War: The Road to Stalemate in Vietnam*. New York: W. W. Norton, 1989.

———. *No Peace, No Honor: Nixon, Kissinger, and Betrayal in Vietnam*. New York: Free Press, 2001.

———. *Perfect Spy: The Incredible Double Life of Pham Xuan An, "Time" Magazine Reporter and Vietnamese Communist Agent*. New York: Smithsonian Books/Collins, 2007.

———. *Planning a Tragedy*. New York: W. W. Norton, 1982.

Biggs, David. *Quagmire: Nation-Building and Nature in the Mekong Delta*. Seattle: University of Washington Press, 2010.

Bothmar, Bernard von. *Framing the Sixties: The Use and Abuse of a Decade from Ronald Reagan to George W. Bush*. Amherst: University of Massachusetts Press, 2010.

Boudarel, Georges. *Cent fleurs écloses dans la nuit du Vietnam* (A Hundred Flowers Blooming in the Vietnam Night). Paris: Jacques Bertoin, 1991.

Bourdeaux, Pascal. "Approches statistiques de la communauté du bouddhisme Hoa Hao." In *Naissance d'un Etat-Parti: Le Vietnam depuis 1945* (The Birth of a Party-State: Vietnam since 1945), edited by Christopher E. Goscha and Benoît de Tréglodé, 277–304. Paris: Indes Savantes, 2004.

Bradley, Mark Philip. *Imagining Vietnam and America: The Making of Postcolonial Vietnam, 1919–1950*. Chapel Hill: University of North Carolina Press, 2000.

———. *Vietnam at War*. New York: Oxford University Press, 2009.

Bradley, Mark Philip, and Marilyn Young, eds. *Making Sense of the Vietnam Wars: Local, National, and Transnational Perspectives*. New York: Oxford University Press, 2008.

Brigham, Robert. *ARVN: Life and Death in the South Vietnamese Army*. Lawrence: University Press of Kansas, 2006.

———. *Guerrilla Diplomacy: The NLF's Foreign Relations and the Vietnam War*. Ithaca, N.Y.: Cornell University Press, 1998.

———. "The NLF and the Tet Offensive." In *The Tet Offensive*, edited by Marc Jason Gilbert and William Head, 63–72. Westport, Conn.: Praeger, 1996.

———. "Revolutionary Heroism and Politics in Postwar Vietnam." In *After Vietnam: Legacies of a Lost War*, edited by Charles H. Neu, 85–104. Baltimore: Johns Hopkins University Press, 2000.

Brocheux, Pierre. *Ho Chi Minh: A Biography*. Translated by Claire Duiker. Cambridge: Cambridge University Press, 2007.

Brown, MacAlister, and Joseph J. Zasloff. *Apprentice Revolutionaries: The Communist Movement in Laos, 1930–1985*. Stanford, Calif.: Hoover Institution Press, 1986.

Bui Diem with David Chanoff. *In the Jaws of History*. Boston: Houghton, Mifflin, 1987.

Bui Tin. *From Enemy to Friend: A North Vietnamese Perspective on the War*. Annapolis, Md.: Naval Institute Press, 2002.

———. *Following Ho Chi Minh: The Memoirs of a North Vietnamese Colonel*. London: Hurst & Company, 1995.

Bundy, William. *A Tangled Web: The Making of Foreign Policy in the Nixon Presidency*. New York: Hill and Wang, 1999.

Burchett, Wilfred. *The China Cambodia Vietnam Triangle*. London: Zed, 1981.

———. *Grasshoppers and Elephants: Why Vietnam Fell*. New York: Urizen, 1977.

Burr, William, ed. *The Beijing-Washington Back-Channel and Henry Kissinger's Secret Trip to China, September 1970–July 1971*. National Security Archive Electronic Briefing Book no. 66, http://www.gwu.edu/~nsarchiv/NSAEBB/NSAEBB66/#docs. Accessed 5 March 2008.

———, ed. *Kissinger Conspired with Soviet Ambassador to Keep Secretary of State in the Dark: U.S. State Department and Russian Foreign Ministry Publish Record of Dobrynin-Kissinger "Back Channel" Meetings, Based on First-time Access to Classified Soviet-Era Documents*. National Security Archive Electronic Briefing Book no. 233, http://www.gwu.edu/~nsarchiv/NSAEBB/NSAEBB233/index.htm. Accessed 5 November 2008.

———, ed. *The Kissinger Transcripts: The Top Secret Talks with Beijing and Moscow*. New York: Free Press, 1999. Burr, William, and Jeffrey Kimball. "Nixon's Nuclear Ploy." *Bulletin of the Atomic Scientists* 59, no. 1 (January–February 2003): 28–37, 72–73.

———. "Nixon's Secret Nuclear Alert: Vietnam War Diplomacy and the Joint Chiefs of Staff Readiness Test, October 1969." *Cold War History* 3, no. 2 (January 2003): 113–56.

———, eds. *Nixon's Nuclear Ploy: The Vietnam Negotiations and the Joint Chiefs of Staff*

*Readiness Test, October 1969.* National Security Archive Electronic Briefing Book no. 81, http://www.gwu.edu/~nsarchiv/NSAEBB/NSAEBB81/index2.htm. Accessed 15 January 2003.

———, eds. *Nixon White House Considered Nuclear Options against North Vietnam, Declassified Documents Reveal: Nuclear Weapons, the Vietnam War, and the Nuclear Taboo.* National Security Archive Electronic Briefing Book no. 195, http://www.gwu.edu/~nsarchiv/NSAEBB/NSAEBB195/index.htm#note. Accessed 1 September 2006.

Buttinger, Joseph. *Vietnam: A Political History.* New York, Praeger, 1968.

Buzzanco, Robert. "Fear and (Self-)Loathing in Lubbock, Texas, or How I Learned to Quit Worrying and Love Vietnam and Iraq." *Passport*, Dec. 2005.

Caldwell, Malcolm, and Lek Hor Tan. *Cambodia in the Southeast Asian War.* New York: Monthly Review Press, 1973.

Carter, James. *Inventing Vietnam: The United States and State Building, 1954–1968.* Cambridge: Cambridge University Press, 2008.

Catton, Phillip. *Diem's Final Failure: Prelude to America's War in Vietnam.* Lawrence: University Press of Kansas, 2002.

Chamberlin, Paul T. *The Global Offensive: The United States, the PLO, and the Making of the New International Order.* New York: Oxford University Press, forthcoming.

Chandler, David. *Brother Number One: A Political Biography of Pol Pot.* Boulder, Colo.: Westview, 1992.

———. *The Tragedy of Cambodian History: Politics, War, and Revolution since 1945.* New Haven, Conn.: Yale University Press, 1991.

Chapman, Jessica. *Debating the Will of Heaven: South Vietnamese Politics and Nationalism in International Perspective, 1953–1956.* Ithaca, N.Y.: Cornell University Press, forthcoming.

———. "The Sect Crisis of 1955 and the American Commitment to Ngo Dinh Diem." *Journal of Vietnamese Studies* 5, no. 1 (February 2010): 37–85.

———. "Staging Democracy: South Vietnam's 1955 Referendum to Depose Bao Dai." *Diplomatic History* 30, no. 4 (September 2006): 671–703.

Chen Jian. *Mao's China and the Cold War.* Chapel Hill: University of North Carolina Press, 2001.

Clodfelter, Mark. *The Limits of Air Power: The American Bombing in North Vietnam.* New York: Free Press, 1989.

Colvin, John. *Giap: Volcano under the Snow.* New York: Soho, 1996.

Conboy, Kenneth, and Dale Andrade. *Spies and Commandos: How America Lost the Secret War in Vietnam.* Lawrence: University Press of Kansas, 2001.

Connelly, Matthew. *A Diplomatic Revolution: Algeria's Fight for Independence and the Origins of the Post–Cold War Era.* New York: Oxford University Press, 2002.

Currey, Cecil. "Giap and Tet Mau Than 1968: The Year of the Monkey." In *The Tet Offensive*, edited by Marc Jason Gilbert and William Head, 73–88. Westport, Conn.: Praeger, 1996.

———. *Victory at Any Cost: The Genius of Vietnam's Gen. Vo Nguyen Giap.* Washington, D.C.: Brassey's, 1997.

Dallek, Robert. *Nixon and Kissinger: Partners in Power.* New York: HarperCollins, 2007.

Davidson, Philip B. *Vietnam at War: The History, 1946–1975*. Novato, Calif.: Presidio, 1988.

Del Pero, Mario. *The Eccentric Realist: Henry Kissinger and the Shaping of American Foreign Policy*. Ithaca, N.Y.: Cornell University Press, 2009.

Destatte, Robert J., and Merle L. Pribbenow for the U.S. Army Center for Military History, Histories Division. *The 1968 Tet Offensive and Uprising in the Tri-Thien-Hue Theater*. Fort McNair, Washington, D.C.: 2001.

Dommon, Arthur. *The Indochinese Experience of the French and Americans: Nationalism and Communism on Cambodia, Laos, and Vietnam*. Indianapolis: Indiana University Press, 2001.

Dosch, Jörn, and Alexander L. Vuving. "The Impact of China on Governance Structures in Vietnam." In *The Impact of Russia, India and China on Governance Structures in the Regional Environment*, Deutsches Institut für Entwicklungspolitik Research Project, http://www.die-gdi.de/CMS-Homepage/openwebcms3.nsf/(ynDK_content ByKey)/ANES-7GNEGJ/$FILE/DP%2014.2008.pdf. Accessed 15 July 2010.

Duiker, William J. *China and Vietnam: The Roots of Conflict*. Berkeley: Institute of East Asian Studies, University of California at Berkeley, Indochina Research Monograph 1, 1986.

———. *The Communist Road to Power in Vietnam*. 2nd ed. Boulder, Colo.: Westview, 1996.

———. *Ho Chi Minh: A Life*. New York: Hyperion, 2001.

———. *The Rise of Nationalism in Vietnam*. Ithaca, N.Y.: Cornell University Press, 1976.

———. *Sacred War: Nationalism and Revolution in a Divided Vietnam*. New York: McGraw-Hill, 1995.

Ekbladh, David. *The Great American Mission: Modernization and the Construction of an American World Order*. Princeton, N.J.: Princeton University Press, 2010.

Elkind, Jessica. "The First Casualties: American Nation Building Programs in South Vietnam, 1955–1965." Ph.D. diss., University of California, Los Angeles, 2005.

Elliott, David. *NLF-DRV Strategy and the 1972 Offensive*. Ithaca, N.Y.: Cornell University Press, 1974.

———. *The Vietnamese War: Revolutionary and Social Change in the Mekong Delta, 1930–1975*. 2 vols. Armonk, N.Y.: M. E. Sharp, 2003.

Elliott, Mai. *RAND in Southeast Asia: A History of the Vietnam War Era*. Santa Monica, Calif.: RAND Corporation, 2010.

Ellsberg, Daniel. *Secrets: A Memoir of Vietnam and the Pentagon Papers*. New York: Penguin, 2002.

Engelbert, Thomas, and Christopher E. Goscha. *Falling Out of Touch: A Study on Vietnamese Communist Policy toward an Emerging Cambodian Communist Movement, 1930–1975*. Clayton, Australia: Monash Asia Institute, 1995.

Fall, Bernard. *Anatomy of a Crisis: The Laotian Crisis of 1960–1961*. New York: Doubleday, 1969.

———. *Last Reflections on a War*. New York: Doubleday, 1967.

———. *The Two Vietnams: A Political and Military Analysis*. London: Pall Mall, 1967.

———. *Vietnam Witness, 1953–1966*. London: Pall Mall, 1966.

Fitzgerald, Frances. *Fire in the Lake: The Vietnamese and the Americans in Vietnam.* New York: Vintage, 1973 [1972].

Fonda, Jane. *My Life So Far.* New York: Random House, 2005.

Ford, Ronnie. *Tet 1968: Understanding the Surprise.* London: Frank Cass, 1995.

Gaddis, John Lewis. *Strategies of Containment: A Critical Appraisal of American National Security Policy during the Cold War.* New York: Oxford University Press, 2005.

———. *The Long Peace: Inquiries into the History of the Cold War.* New York: Oxford University Press, 1989.

Gaiduk, Ilya V. *Confronting Vietnam: Soviet Policy toward the Indochina Conflict, 1954–1963.* Stanford, Calif.: Stanford University Press, 2003.

———. *The Soviet Union and the Vietnam War.* Chicago: Ivan R. Dee, 1996.

Gardner, Lloyd. *Pay Any Price: Lyndon Johnson and the Wars for Vietnam.* New York: Ivan R. Dee, 1997.

Gardner, Lloyd C., and Ted Gittinger, eds. *Vietnam: The Early Decisions.* Austin: University of Texas Press, 1997.

Gelb, Leslie H., and Richard K. Betts, *The Irony of Vietnam: The System Worked.* Washington, DC: Brookings Institution Press, 1979.

Gettleman, Marvin, et al., eds. *Conflict in Indochina: A Reader to the Widening War in Laos and Cambodia.* New York: Random House, 1970.

Giebel, Christoph. *Imagined Ancestries of Vietnamese Communism: Ton Duc Thang and the Politics of History and Memory.* Seattle: University of Washington Press, 2004.

Gilbert, Marc Jason. "Persuading the Enemy: Vietnamese Appeals to Non-White Forces of Occupation, 1945–1975." In *Vietnam and the West: New Approaches*, edited by Wynn Wilcox, 107–42. Ithaca, N.Y.: Cornell University Press, 2010.

Gilbert, Marc Jason, and William Head, eds. *The Tet Offensive.* Westport, Conn.: Greenwood, 1996.

Gilks, Anne. *The Breakdown of the Sino-Vietnamese Alliance, 1970–1979.* Berkeley: Institute of East Asian Studies, University of California, 1992.

Gleijeses, Piero. *Conflicting Missions: Havana, Washington, and Africa, 1959–1976.* Chapel Hill: University of North Carolina Press, 2002.

Gnoinska, Margaret. "Poland and Vietnam, 1963: New Evidence on Secret Communist Diplomacy and the 'Maneli Affair.'" CWIHP Working Paper 45. Washington, D.C.: Woodrow Wilson Center, 2005: 1–78.

Goodman, Allan E. *The Lost Peace: America's Search for a Negotiated Settlement of the Vietnam War.* Stanford, Calif.: Hoover Institution Press, 1978.

Goscha, Christopher E. "Courting Diplomatic Disaster? The Difficult Integration of Vietnam into the Internationalist Communist Movement (1945–1950)." *Journal of Vietnamese Studies* 1, nos. 1–2 (February–August 2006): 59–103.

———. "A 'Popular' Side of the Vietnamese Army: General Nguyen Binh and the Early War in the South (1910–1951)." In *Naissance d'un Etat-Parti: Le Vietnam depuis 1945* (The Birth of a Party-State: Vietnam since 1945), edited by Christopher E. Goscha and Benoît de Tréglodé, 325–53. Paris: Indes Savantes, 2004.

———. "Réflexions sur la guerre du Viet Minh dans le Sud-Vietnam de 1945 à 1951"

(Reflections on the Viet Minh's War in South Vietnam between 1945 and 1951).
*Guerres mondiales et conflits contemporains* (World Wars and Contemporary
Conflicts) 206 (2002): 29–57.

———. *Thailand and the Southeast Asian Networks of the Vietnamese Revolution, 1885–
1954*. London: Routledge/Curzon, 1999.

———. "Towards a Geo-history of the Wars for Vietnam." Paper presented at the
International and Global History Seminar, Harvard University, 6 April 2004.

———. "Vietnam and the Meltdown of Asian Internationalism." In *The Third
Indochina War: Conflict between China, Vietnam, and Cambodia, 1972–1979*, edited
by Odd Arne Westad and Sophie Quinn-Judge, 152–86. New York: Routledge, 2006.

———. *Vietnam or Indochina? Contesting Concepts of Space in Vietnamese Nationalism*.
Copenhagen: INAS, 1995.

Greenberg, David. "Nixon as Failed Statesman: The Failed Campaign." In *Nixon and
the World: American Foreign Relations, 1969–1977*, edited by Fredrik Logevall and
Andrew Preston, 45–66. New York: Oxford University Press, 2008.

Grossheim, Martin. "Revisionism in the Democratic Republic of Vietnam: New
Evidence from the East German Archives." *Journal of Cold War History* 5, no. 4
(November–December 2005): 451–77.

Guillemot, François. "La tentation 'fasciste' des luttes anticoloniales Dai Viet:
Nationalisme et anticommunisme dans le Viet-Nam des années 1932–1945."
*Vingtième siècle* 4, no. 104 (2009): 45–66.

Ha Mai Viet. *Steel and Blood: South Vietnamese Armor and the War for Southeast Asia*.
Annapolis, MD: Naval Institute Press, 2008.

Haldeman, H. R. *The Haldeman Diaries: Inside the White House*. New York: G. P.
Putnam, 1994.

Hanhimaki, Jussi. *The Flawed Architect: Henry Kissinger and American Foreign Policy*.
New York: Oxford University Press, 2004.

Hansen, Peter. "Bac di cu: Catholic Refugees from the North of Vietnam, and Their
Role in the Southern Republic, 1954–1959." *Journal of Vietnamese Studies* 4, no. 3
(2009): 173–211.

Herring, George. *America's Longest War: The United States and Vietnam, 1950–1975*.
4th ed. New York: McGraw Hill, 2002.

———. *LBJ and Vietnam: A Different Kind of War*. Austin: University of Texas Press,
1994.

———. "The War That Never Seems to Go Away." In *The War That Never Ends: New
Perspectives on the Vietnam War*, edited by David Anderson and John Ernst, 335–50.
Lexington: University Press of Kentucky, 2007.

———, ed. *The Secret Diplomacy of the Vietnam War: The Negotiating Volumes of the
Pentagon Papers*. Austin: University of Texas Press, 1983.

Hershberg, James G. *Marigold: The Lost Chance for Peace in Vietnam*. Stanford, Calif.:
Stanford University Press and Woodrow Wilson Center Press, 2012.

———. "Peace Probes and the Bombing Pause: Hungarian and Polish Diplomacy
during the Vietnam War, December 1965–January 1966." *Journal of Cold War
Studies* 5, no. 2 (Spring 2003): 32–67.

———. *"Who Murdered "Marigold"?—New Evidence on the Mysterious Failure of Poland's Secret Initiative to Start U.S.–North Vietnamese Peace Talks, 1966.* Washington, D.C.: CWIHP, Woodrow Wilson Center, 2000.

———. *Who Murdered "Marigold"?—New Evidence on the Mysterious Failure of Poland's Secret Initiative to Start U.S.–North Vietnamese Peace Talks, 1966.* Stanford, Calif.: Stanford University Press and Woodrow Wilson Center Press, forthcoming.

Hess, Gary. *Vietnam and the United States: Origins and Legacy of War.* Boston: Twayne, 1990.

———. *Vietnam: Explaining America's Lost War.* Oxford, U.K.: Wiley-Blackwell, 2008.

Ho Khang. *The Tet Mau Than 1968 Event in South Vietnam.* Hanoi: The Gioi, 2001.

Hoang, Tuan. "Ideology in Urban South Vietnam, 1950–1975." Ph.D. diss., University of Notre Dame, 2011.

Hoang Van Hoan. *A Drop in the Ocean: Hoang Van Hoan's Revolutionary Reminiscences.* Beijing: Foreign Languages, 1988.

Hobson, Chris. *Vietnam Air Losses: United States Air Force, Navy, and Marine Corps Fixed-Wing Aircraft Losses in Southeast Asia, 1961–1973.* Hinckley, UK: Midland Publishing, 2001.

Hodgkin, Thomas. *Vietnam: The Revolutionary Path.* New York: St. Martin's, 1981.

Holcombe, Alec. "The Complete Collection of Party Documents: Listening to the Party's Official Internal Voice." *Journal of Vietnamese Studies* 5, no. 2 (Summer 2010): 225–42.

———. "De-Stalinization and the Vietnam Worker's Party." Paper presented at the Association of Asian Studies Annual Meeting, Philadelphia, 25–28 March 2010.

Honey, P. J. *Communism in North Vietnam: Its Role in the Sino-Soviet Dispute.* Westport, Conn.: Greenwood, 1973.

Hung, Nguyen Tien, and Jerrold Schecter. *The Palace File.* New York: Harper & Row, 1986.

Hunt, David. *Vietnam's Southern Revolution: From Peasant Insurrection to Total War, 1959–1968.* Amherst: University of Massachusetts Press, 2009.

Huynh, Kim Khanh. *Vietnamese Communism, 1925–1945.* Ithaca, N.Y.: Published under the auspices of the Institute of Southeast Asian Studies, Singapore, by Cornell University Press, 1982.

Jacobs, Seth. *Inventing Vietnam: The United States and State Building, 1954–1968.* Cambridge: Cambridge University Press, 2008.

Jamieson, Neil. *Understanding Vietnam.* Berkeley: University of California Press, 1993.

Jennings, Eric. *Vichy in the Tropics: Pétain's National Revolution in Madagascar, Guadeloupe, and Indochina, 1940–1944.* Palo Alto, Calif.: Stanford University Press, 2001.

Jian, Chen. *Mao's China and the Cold War.* Chapel Hill: University of North Carolina Press, 2001.

Johns, Andrew. *Vietnam's Second Front: Domestic Politics, the Republican Party, and the War.* Lexington, KY: University Press of Kentucky, 2010.

Jones, Howard. *Death of a Generation: How the Assassinations of Diem and JFK Prolonged Vietnam.* New York: Oxford University Press, 2003.

Journoud, Pierre. *De Gaulle et le Vietnam: 1945–1969—La réconciliation* (De Gaulle and Vietnam: 1945-1969—The Reconciliation). Paris: Tallendier, 2011.

———. "Le Quai d'Orsay et le processus de paix au Vietnam" (The French Foreign Ministry and the Vietnam Peace Process). In *L'Europe et la guerre du Vietnam, 1963–1973* (Europe and the Vietnam War, 1969–1973), edited by Maurice Vaïsse and Christopher Goscha, 385–400. Paris: Bruylant, 2003.

Kahin, George McTurnan. *Intervention: How America Became Involved in Vietnam.* New York: Knopf, 1986.

Kaiser, David. *American Tragedy: Kennedy, Johnson, and the Origins of the Vietnam War.* Cambridge: Belknap Press of Harvard University Press, 2000.

Keefer, Edward, David C. Geyer, and Douglas D. Selvage, eds. *Soviet-American Relations: The Détente Years, 1969–1972.* Washington, D.C.: U.S. Department of State, 2007.

Kerkvliet, Benedict J. *The Power of Everyday Politics: How Vietnamese Peasants Transformed National Policy.* Ithaca, N.Y.: Cornell University Press, 2005.

Khoo, Nicholas. "Breaking the Ring of Encirclement: The Sino-Soviet Rift and Chinese Policy toward Vietnam, 1964–1968." *Journal of Cold War Studies* 12, no. 1 (Winter 2010): 3–42.

Kiernan, Ben. "The American Bombardment of Kampuchea, 1969–1973." *Vietnam Generation* 1, no. 1 (Winter 1989): 4–41.

———. *How Pol Pot Came to Power: Colonialism, Nationalism, and Communism in Cambodia, 1930–1975.* 2nd ed. New Haven, Conn.: Yale University Press, 2004.

Kimball, Jeffrey. "The Case of the 'Decent Interval': Do We Now Have a Smoking Gun?" *Passport,* September 2001, http://www.shafr.org/publications/newsletter/september-2001/. Accessed 18 March 2008.

———. *Nixon's Vietnam War.* Lawrence: University Press of Kansas, 1998.

———. *The Vietnam War Files: Uncovering the Secret History of the Nixon-Era Strategy.* Lawrence: University Press of Kansas, 2004.

Kirk, Donald. *Wider War: The Struggle for Cambodia, Thailand and Laos.* New York: Praeger, 1971.

Kissinger, Henry. *White House Years.* Boston: Little, Brown, 1979.

Kolko, Gabriel. *Vietnam: Anatomy of War, 1940–1975.* London: Unwin Hymman, 1987.

Kwon, Heonik. *After the Massacre: Commemoration and Consolation in Ha My and My Lai.* Berkeley: University of California Press, 2006.

———. *Ghosts of War in Vietnam.* Cambridge: Cambridge University Press, 2008.

———. *The Other Cold War.* New York: Columbia University Press, 2010.

Lacouture, Jean. *Ho Chi Minh.* Harmondsworth, U.K.: Penguin, 1968.

Laderman, Scott. *Tours of Vietnam: War, Travel Guides, and Memory.* Durham, N.C.: Duke University Press, 2009.

Langer, Paul F. *The Soviet Union, China and the Pathet Lao: Analysis and Chronology.* California: Rand Corporation, n.d.

Langer, Paul F., and J. Joseph Zasloff. *North Vietnam and the Pathet Lao.* Cambridge: Harvard University Press, 1970.

Lawrence, Mark A. *Assuming the Burden: Europe and the American Commitment to the War in Vietnam.* Berkeley: University of California Press, 2005.

———. *The Vietnam War: A Concise International History.* New York: Oxford University Press, 2008.

Lewy, Guenter. *America in Vietnam*. New York: Oxford University Press, 1978.

Li Danhui. "The Sino-Soviet Dispute over Assistance for Vietnam's Anti-American War, 1965–1972." In *Behind the Bamboo Curtain: China, Vietnam, and the World beyond Asia*, edited by Priscilla Roberts, 289–318. Washington, D.C.: Woodrow Wilson Center Press, 2006.

Lind, Michael. *Vietnam, a Necessary War: A Reinterpretation of America's Most Disastrous Military Conflict*. New York: Free Press, 1999.

Logevall, Fredrik. *Choosing War: The Lost Chance for Peace and the Escalation of the Vietnam War*. Berkeley: University of California Press, 1999.

———. "De Gaulle, Neutralization, and American Involvement in Vietnam, 1963–1964." *Pacific Historical Review* 61, no. 1 (February 1992): 69–102.

Logevall, Fredrik, and Andrew Preston, eds. *Nixon and the World: American Foreign Relations, 1969–1977*. New York: Oxford University Press, 2008.

Loicano, Martin. "Military and Political Roles of Weapons Systems in the Republic of Vietnam Armed Forces, 1966–1972." Ph.D. diss., Cornell University, 2008.

Lowe, Peter, ed. *The Vietnam War*. London: Macmillan, 1998.

Luong, Hy Van. "Agrarian Unrest from an Anthropological Perspective: The Case of Vietnam." *Comparative Politics* 17, no. 2 (January 1985): 53–175.

Lüthi, Lorenz. "Beyond Betrayal: Beijing, Moscow, and the Paris Negotiations, 1971–1973." *Journal of Cold War Studies* 11, no. 1 (Winter 2009): 57–107.

———. *The Sino-Soviet Split: Cold War in the Communist World*. Princeton, N.J.: Princeton University Press, 2008.

Luu Van Loi. *Le Duc Tho–Kissinger Negotiations in Paris*. Hanoi: The Gioi, 1996.

MacLean, Ken. "The Collected Works of the Communist Party: The Possibilities and Limits of Official Representations of Actually Existing Government." *Journal of Vietnamese Studies* 5, no. 2 (Summer 2010): 195–207.

———. "Manifest Socialism: The Labor of Representation in the Democratic Republic of Vietnam (1956–1959)." *Journal of Vietnamese Studies* 2, no. 1 (February 2007): 27–79.

MacMillan, Margaret. *Nixon and Mao: The Week That Changed the World*. New York: Random House, 2007.

Mai Ly Quang, ed. *The 30-Year War (1945–1975)*. 2 vols. Hanoi: The Gioi, 2001.

Marr, David. *Vietnam, 1945: The Quest for Power*. Berkeley: University of California Press, 1995.

———. *Vietnamese Anticolonialism, 1885–1925*. Berkeley: University of California Press, 1971.

———. *Vietnamese Tradition on Trial, 1920–1945*. Berkeley: University of California Press, 1981.

———. "World War II and the Vietnamese Revolution." In *Southeast Asia under Japanese Occupation*, edited by Alfred W. McCoy, 104–31. New Haven, Conn.: Yale University Southeast Asia Monograph Series, no. 22 (1980).

Martini, Edwin. *Invisible Enemies: The American War in Vietnam*. Amherst: University of Massachusetts Press, 2007.

Masur, Matthew. "Hearts and Minds: Cultural Nation-Building in South Vietnam, 1954–1963." Ph.D. diss., Ohio State University, 2004.

McGarvey, Patrick. *Visions of Victory: Selected Vietnamese Communist Military Writings, 1964–1968*. Stanford, Calif.: Hoover Institution on War, Revolution, and Peace, 1969.

McHale, Shawn. "Understanding the Fanatic Mind? The Viet Minh and Race Hatred in the First Indochina War (1945–1954)." *Journal of Vietnamese Studies* 4, no. 3 (2009): 98–138.

McMahon, Robert. *The Limits of Empire: The United States and Southeast Asia since World War II*. New York: Columbia University Press, 1999.

———, ed. *Major Problems in the History of the Vietnam War*. 4th ed. Boston: Houghton Mifflin, 2008.

McNamara, Robert S., James G. Blight, and Robert Brigham. *Argument without End: In Search of Answers to the Vietnam Tragedy*. New York: PublicAffairs, 1999.

Menétrey-Monchau, Cécile. *American-Vietnamese Relations in the Wake of War: Diplomacy after the Capture of Saigon, 1975–1979*. Jefferson, N.C.: McFarland, 2006.

Miller, Edward. *Grand Designs: Vision, Power and Nation Building in America's Alliance with Ngo Dinh Diem*. Cambridge: Harvard University Press, forthcoming.

———. "Roundtable on Mark Moyar's *Triumph Forsaken: The Vietnam War, 1954–1965*." *Passport*, December 2007, http://www.shafr.org/publications/newsletter/december-2007/. Accessed 18 March 2008.

———. "War Stories: The Taylor-Buzzanco Debate and How We Think about the Vietnam War." *Journal of Vietnamese Studies* 1, nos. 1–2 (February–August 2006): 453–84.

Miller, Edward, and Tuong Vu, eds. "The Vietnam War as a Vietnamese War: Agency and Society in the Study of the Second Indochina War." *Journal of Vietnamese Studies* 4, no. 3 (2009): 1–16.

Moise, Edwin. "Land Reform and Land Reform Errors in North Vietnam." *Pacific Affairs* 49, no. 1 (Spring 1976): 70–92.

———. *The Tonkin Gulf Incident of the Vietnam War*. Chapel Hill: University of North Carolina Press, 1996.

Morris, Stephen. "The Soviet-Chinese-Vietnamese Triangle in the 1970s." In *Behind the Bamboo Curtain: China, Vietnam, and the World Beyond Asia*, edited by Priscilla Roberts, 405–32. Washington, D.C.: Woodrow Wilson Center Press, 2006.

Moyar, Mark. *Triumph Forsaken: The Vietnam War*. Cambridge: Cambridge University Press, 2006.

Nixon, Richard. *No More Vietnams*. New York: Avon Books, 1994.

———. *RN: The Memoirs of Richard Nixon*. New York: Grosset & Dunlap, 1978.

Ngo Quang Truong. *The Easter Offensive of 1972*. Washington, D.C.: U.S. Army Center of Military History, 1984.

Ngo Vinh Long. *Before the Revolution: Vietnamese Peasants under the French*. Cambridge: MIT Press, 1973.

———. "Communal Property and Peasant Revolutionary Struggles in Vietnam." *Peasant Studies* 17 (Winter 1990): 121–40.

———. "The Indochinese Communist Party and Peasant Rebellion in Central Vietnam, 1930–1931." *Bulletin of Concerned Asian Scholars* 10, no. 4 (Dec. 1978): 15–34.

———. "The Tet Offensive and Its Aftermath." *Indochina Newsletter*, no. 49 (January–February 1988): 1–5.

Nguyen, Lien-Hang T. "1968: Negotiating while Fighting or Just Fighting?" In *Vietnam, 1968–1976: Exiting a War*, edited by Pierre Journoud and Cécile Menétrey-Monchau, 37–49. Brussels: Peter Lang, 2011.

———. "The Sino-Vietnamese Split and the Indochina War, 1968–1975." In *The Third Indochina War: Conflict between China, Vietnam, and Cambodia, 1972–1979*, edited by Odd Arne Westad and Sophie Quinn-Judge, 12–32. New York: Routledge, 2006.

———. "The Vietnam Decade: Global Shock of the War." In *Shock of the Global: The 1970s in Perspective*, edited by Niall Ferguson, Charles Maier, Erez Manela, and Daniel Sargent, 310–40. Cambridge: Harvard University Press, 2010.

———. "Vietnamese Historians and the First Indochina War." In *The First Vietnam War: Colonial Conflict and Cold War Crisis*, edited by Mark Lawrence and Fredrik Logevall, 41–55. Cambridge: Harvard University Press, 2006.

———. "Vietnamese Perceptions of the French-Indochina War." In *Indochina in the Balance: New Perspectives on the First Vietnam War*, edited by Fredrik Logevall and Mark Lawrence, 41–55. Cambridge: Harvard University Press, 2006.

———. "The War Politburo: Hanoi's Diplomatic and Political Road to the Tet Offensive." *Journal of Vietnamese Studies* 1, nos. 1–2 (January–February 2006): 4–55.

Nguyen, Phu Duc. *The Viet-Nam Peace Negotiation: Saigon's Side of the Story*. Christiansburg, Va.: Dalley Book Services, 2005.

Nguyen, Thi Dinh. *No Other Road to Take: Memoir of Mrs. Nguyen Thi Dinh*. Translated by Mai V. Elliott. Ithaca, N.Y.: Southeast Asia Program, Cornell University, no. 102, 1976.

Nguyen, Van Canh. *Vietnam under Communism, 1975–1982*. Palo Alto, Calif.: Hoover Institution Press, 1985.

Nguyen, Vu Tung. "Vietnam-ASEAN Cooperation after the Cold War." Ph.D. diss., Columbia University, 2004.

Nguyen, Xuan Phong. *Hope and Vanquished Reality*. Washington, D.C.: ICIS Center for a Science of Hope, 2001.

Ninh, Kim N. B. *A World Transformed: The Politics of Culture in Revolutionary Vietnam, 1945–1965*. Ann Arbor: University of Michigan Press, 2002.

Oberdorfer, Don. *Tet!* New York: Doubleday, 1971.

Olsen, Mari. *Soviet-Vietnam Relations and the Role of China, 1949–64: Changing Alliances*. London: Routledge, 2006.

Owen, Taylor, and Ben Kiernan. "Bombs over Cambodia." *Walrus* (October 2006), http://www.yale.edu/cgp/Walrus_CambodiaBombing_OCT06.pdf.

Papp, Daniel S. *Vietnam: The View from Moscow, Peking and Washington*. Jefferson, N.C.: McFarland, 1981.

Pelley, Patricia. *Postcolonial Vietnam: New Histories of the National Past*. Durham, N.C.: Duke University Press, 2002.

Perlstein, Rick. *Nixonland: The Rise of a President and the Fracturing of America*. New York: Scribner's, 2008.

Pham, Hoai Julie. "Revolution, Communism, and History in the Thought of Tran Van Giau." Ph.D. diss., Cambridge University, 2008.

Pham, Nga. "Risking Life for Pop Music in Wartime Vietnam." *BBC News, Asia-Pacific* (16 June 2010), http://www.bbc.co.uk/news/10312758. Accessed 31 July 2011.

Pham, Quang Minh. "The Meaning of the Complete Collection of Party Documents." *Journal of Vietnamese Studies* 5, no. 2 (Summer 2010): 208–18.

Phan Thien Chau. "Leadership in the Viet Nam Workers Party: The Process of Transition," *Asian Survey* 12, no. 9 (September 1972): 772–82.

Pike, Douglas. *History of Vietnamese Communism, 1925–76*. Stanford, Calif.: Hoover Institution Press, 1978.

———. "North Vietnam in 1971." *Asian Survey* 12, no. 1 (January 1971): 16–24.

———. "North Vietnam in the Year 1972." *Asian Survey* 13, no. 1 (January 1973): 46–59.

———. *PAVN: People's Army of Vietnam*. Novato, Calif.: Presidio, 1986.

———. *Viet Cong: The Organisation and Techniques of the National Liberation Front of South Vietnam*. Cambridge: MIT Press, 1968.

———. *The Viet Cong Strategy of Terror*. Saigon: U.S. Mission, 1970.

———. *Vietnam and the Soviet Union: Anatomy of an Alliance*. Boulder, Colo.: Westview, 1987.

———. *War, Peace, and the Viet Cong*. Cambridge: MIT Press, 1969.

Porter, Gareth. *A Peace Denied: The United States, Vietnam, and the Paris Agreement*. Bloomington: Indiana University Press, 1975.

———. *Perils of Dominance: Imbalance of Power and the Road to War in Vietnam*. Berkeley: University of California Press, 2004.

———, ed. *Vietnam: A History in Documents*. New York: New American Library, 1981.

Porter, Gareth, and Len E. Ackland. "Vietnam: The Bloodbath Argument." *Christian Century* (5 November 1969): 1414–17.

Prados, John. *Vietnam: The History of an Unwinnable War, 1945–1975*. Lawrence: University Press of Kansas, 2009.

———, ed. *The Gulf of Tonkin Incident: 40 Years Later—Flawed Intelligence and the Decision for War in Vietnam*. National Security Archive Electronic Briefing Book no. 132, http://www.gwu.edu/~nsarchiv/NSAEBB/NSAEBB132/. Accessed 18 March 2008.

Prashad, Vijay. *The Darker Nations: A People's History of the Third World*. New York: New Press, 2007.

Preston, Andrew. *The War Council: McGeorge Bundy, the NSC, and Vietnam*. Cambridge: Harvard University Press, 2006.

Pribbenow, Merle. "General Vo Nguyen Giap and the Mysterious Evolution of the Plan for the 1968 Tet Offensive." *Journal of Vietnamese Studies* 3, no. 2 (Summer 2008): 1–33.

———, trans. *Victory in Vietnam: The Official History of the People's Army in Vietnam, 1954–1975*. Lawrence: University Press of Kansas, 2002.

Quinn-Judge, Sophie. *Ho Chi Minh: The Missing Years, 1919–1941*. Berkeley: University of California Press, 2002.

———. "The Ideological Debate in the DRV and the Significance of the Anti-Party Affair, 1967–68." *Journal of Cold War History* 5, no. 4 (November–December 2005): 479–500.

———. "Through a Glass Darkly: Reading the History of the Vietnamese Communist Party, 1945–1975." In *Making Sense of the Vietnam Wars*, edited by Mark Philip Bradley and Marilyn B. Young, 111–34. New York: Oxford University Press, 2008.

Race, Jeffrey. *War Comes to Long An: Revolutionary Conflict in a Vietnamese Province*. Berkeley: University of California Press, 1972.

Radchenko, Sergey. *Two Suns in the Heavens: The Sino-Soviet Struggle for Supremacy*. Washington, D.C.: Woodrow Wilson Center Press; Stanford, Calif.: Stanford University Press, 2009.

Randolph, Stephen P. *Powerful and Brutal Weapons: Nixon, Kissinger, and the Easter Offensive*. Cambridge: Harvard University Press, 2007.

Roberts, Priscilla, ed. *Behind the Bamboo Curtain: China, Vietnam, and the World beyond Asia*. Washington, D.C.: Woodrow Wilson Center Press, 2006.

Rotter, Andrew. *The Path to Vietnam: Origins of the American Commitment to Southeast Asia*. Ithaca, N.Y.: Cornell University Press, 1987.

Ruth, Richard. *In Buddha's Company: Thai Soldiers in the Vietnam War*. Honolulu: Hawaii Pacific, 2011.

SarDesai, D. R. *Vietnam: Struggle for National Identity*. 2nd ed. Boulder, Colo.: Westview, 1992.

———. *Vietnam: Trial and Tribulations of a Nation*. Long Beach, Calif.: Long Beach Publications, 1988.

Schlesinger, Arthur M., Jr. *The Bitter Heritage: Vietnam and American Democracy, 1941–1966*. Boston: Houghton Mifflin, 1967.

Schulzinger, Robert. *A Time for War: The United States and Vietnam, 1945–1975*. New York: Oxford University Press, 1999.

Schwartz, Thomas. *Lyndon Johnson and Europe: In the Shadow of Vietnam*. Cambridge: Harvard University Press, 2003.

Schwenkel, Christina. *The American War in Contemporary Vietnam: Transnational Remembrance and Representation*. Bloomington: Indiana University Press, 2009.

Shawcross, William. *Sideshow: Kissinger, Nixon, and the Destruction of Cambodia*. New York: Simon & Schuster, 1987.

Shen Zhihua. "Sino-U.S. Reconciliation and China's Vietnam Policy." In *Behind the Bamboo Curtain: China, Vietnam, and the World Beyond Asia*, edited by Priscilla Roberts, 349–68. Washington, D.C.: Woodrow Wilson Center Press, 2006.

Smith, John T. *The Linebacker Raids: The Bombing of North Vietnam, 1972*. London: Cassell, 1998.

Smith, Ralph B. "China and Southeast Asia: The Revolutionary Perspective, 1951." *Journal of Southeast Asia Studies* 19, no. 1 (March 1988): 97–110.

———. *An International History of the Vietnam War*. Vol. 1, *Revolution versus Containment, 1955–61*. London: Macmillan, 1983. Vol. 2, *The Struggle for Southeast Asia, 1961–65*. London: Macmillan, 1985. Vol. 3, *The Making of a Limited War, 1965–66*. London: Macmillan, 1991.

Smith, Tony. "New Bottle for New Wine: A Pericentric Framework for the Study of the Cold War." *Diplomatic History* 24, no. 4 (Fall 2000): 567–91.

Smyser, W. R. *The Independent Vietnamese: Vietnamese Communism between Russia and China, 1956–1969*. Athens: Ohio University Center for International Studies, 1980.

Sorley, Lewis. *A Better War: The Unexamined Victories and Final Tragedy of America's Last Years in Vietnam*. New York: Harcourt Brace, 1999.

———, ed. *Vietnam Chronicles: The Abrams Tapes, 1968–1972*. Lubbock: Texas Tech University Press, 2004.

Spector, Ronald H. *After Tet: The Bloodiest Year in Vietnam*. New York: Vintage, 1993.

Statler, Kathryn. *Replacing France: The Origins of American Intervention in Vietnam*. Lexington: University Press of Kentucky, 2007.

Stewart, Geoffrey. "Revolution, Modernization and Nation-Building in Diem's Vietnam: Civic Action, 1955–1963." Ph.D. diss., University of Western Ontario, 2010.

Stowe, Judy. " 'Révisionnisme' au Vietnam" ("Revisionism" in Vietnam). *Approche Asie* (Approach Asia), no. 18 (2003): 53–67.

Stuart-Fox, Martin. *A History of Laos*. Cambridge: Cambridge University Press, 1997.

Summers, Harry G. *On Strategy: A Critical Analysis of the Vietnam War*. New York: Dell, 1984.

Suri, Jeremi. *Henry Kissinger and the American Century*. Cambridge: Belknap Press of Harvard University Press, 2009.

———. *Power and Protest: Global Revolution and the Rise of Détente*. Cambridge: Harvard University Press, 2005.

Szalontai, Balasz. "Political and Economic Crisis in North Vietnam, 1955–1956." *Journal of Cold War History* 5, no. 4 (November–December 2005): 395–426.

———. "Selected Hungarian Documents on Vietnam, 1954–1966," Document 7, MOL. Paper presented at the conference "New Central and Eastern European Evidence on the Cold War in Asia," Cold War History Research Center, Budapest, 30 Oct.– 2 Nov. 2003.

Szoke, Zoltan. "Delusion or Reality: Secret Hungarian Diplomacy during the Vietnam War." *Journal of Cold War Studies* 12, no. 4 (Fall 2010): 119–80.

Tai, Hue-Tam Ho. "Faces of Remembrance and Forgetting." In *The Country of Memory: Remaking the Past in Late Socialist Vietnam*, edited by Hue-Tam Ho Tai, 167–95. Berkeley: University of California Press, 2001.

———. *Millenarianism and Peasant Politics in Vietnam*. Cambridge: Harvard University Press, 1983.

———. *Vietnamese Radicalism and the Origins of the Vietnamese Revolution*. Cambridge: Harvard University Press, 1992.

———, ed. *The Country of Memory: Remaking the Past in Late Socialist Vietnam*. Berkeley: University of California Press, 2001.

Tai, Sung An. *The Vietnam War*. Madison, N.J.: Fairleigh Dickinson University Press, 1998.

Taylor, Keith. "Robert Buzzanco's 'Fear and (Self-)Loathing in Lubbock.' " *Journal of Vietnamese Studies* 1, nos. 1–2 (Feb.–August 2006): 436–52.

Thai, Quang Trung. *Collective Leadership and Factionalism: An Essay on Ho Chi Minh's Legacy*. Singapore: Institute of Southeast Asian Studies, 1985.

Thayer, Carlyle. "Origins of the National Liberation Front for the Liberation of South Viet-Nam, 1954–1960: Debate on Unification within the Viet-Nam Workers' Party."

Paper presented at Sixteenth Conference of the Australasian Political Studies Association, Brisbane, Australia, July 1974.

———. *War by Other Means: National Liberation and Revolution in Vietnam, 1954–1960*. Sydney: Allen & Urwin, 1989.

Thompson, Robert. *Peace Is Not at Hand*. London: Chatto & Windus, 1974.

Thompson, Wayne. *To Hanoi and Back: The U.S. Air Force and North Vietnam, 1966–1973*. Washington, D.C.: Smithsonian Institution Press, 2000.

Tonneson, Stein. *Vietnam, 1946: How the War Began*. Berkeley: University of California Press, 2009.

———. *The Vietnamese Revolution of 1945: Roosevelt, Ho Chi Minh and de Gaulle in a World at War*. Oslo: International Peace Institute, 1991.

Topmiller, Robert. *Lotus Unleashed: The Buddhist Peace Movement in South Vietnam, 1964–1966*. Lexington: University Press of Kentucky, 2002.

Trachtenberg, Marc. "The French Factor in U.S. Foreign Policy during the Nixon-Pompidou Period, 1969–1974." *Journal of Cold War Studies* 13, no. 1 (Winter 2011): 4–59.

Tran, Nu Anh. "Contested Identities: Nationalism in the Republic of Vietnam, 1954–1963." Ph.D. diss., University of California at Berkeley, forthcoming.

———. "South Vietnamese Identity, American Intervention, and the Newspaper *Chinh Luan* (Political Discussion), 1965–1969." *Journal of Vietnamese Studies* 1, nos. 1–2 (January–February 2006): 169–209.

Tran Van Don. *Our Endless War: Inside Vietnam*. Novato, Calif.: Presidio, 1978.

Tran Van Tra. "Tet: The 1968 General Offensive and General Uprising." In *The Vietnam War: Vietnamese and American Perspectives*, edited by Jayne S. Werner and Luu Doan Huynh, 37–65. Armonk, N.Y.: M. E. Sharpe, 1993.

Truong Nhu Tang, with David Chanoff and Doan Van Toai. *A Vietcong Memoir: An Inside Account of the Vietnam War and Its Aftermath*. New York: Vintage, 1985.

Turley, William S. *The Second Indochina War: A Short Political and Military History*. 2nd ed. Lanham, Md.: Roman & Littlefield, 2008.

———. "Urbanization in War: Hanoi, 1946–1973." *Pacific Affairs* 48, no. 3 (Autumn 1975): 370–97.

Veith, George J. *Code-Name Bright Light: The Untold Stories of U.S. POW Rescue Efforts during the Vietnam War*. New York: Free Press, 1998.

Vickerman, Andrew. *The Fate of the Peasantry: Premature Transition into Socialism in the Democratic Republic of Vietnam*. New Haven, Conn.: Yale University Southeast Asia Studies, Yale Center for International and Area Studies, c1986.

Vo, Thu-Huong Nguyen. *Khmer-Viet Relations and the Third Indochina Conflict*. Jefferson, N.C.: McFarland, 1992.

Vu, Tuong. "Dreams of Paradise: The Making of a Soviet Outpost in Vietnam." *Ab Imperio* 2 (2008): 255–85.

———. "From Cheering to Volunteering: Vietnamese Communists and the Arrival of the Cold War, 1940–1951." In *Connecting Histories: Decolonization and the Cold War in Southeast Asia, 1945–1962*, edited by Christopher Goscha and Christian Ostermann, 172–204. Stanford, Calif.: Stanford University Press, 2010.

———. "Van Kien Dang Toan Tap: The Regime's Gamble and Researchers' Gain." *Journal of Vietnamese Studies* 5, no. 2 (Summer 2010): 183–94.

———. "Vietnamese Political Studies and Debates on Vietnamese Nationalism." *Journal of Vietnamese Studies* 2, no. 2 (Summer 2007): 175–230.

Vuving, Alexander L. "Grand Strategic Fit and Power Shift: Explaining Vietnam-China Relations." In *Living with China: Regional States and China through Crises and Turning Points*, edited by Shiping Tang, Mingjiang Li, and Amitav Acharya, 229–46. New York: Palgrave Macmillan, 2009.

———. "Vietnam: Arriving in the World—and at a Crossroads." *Southeast Asian Affairs*, 2008: 375–93.

———. "Vietnam: A Tale of Four Players." *Southeast Asian Affairs*, 2010: 361–91.

Wehrle, Edmund F. *Between a River and a Mountain: The AFL-CIO and the Vietnam War*. Ann Arbor: University of Michigan Press, 2005.

Weigersma, Nancy. *Vietnam: Peasant Land, Peasant Revolution*. New York: St. Martin's, 1988.

Werner, Jayne S., and David Hunt, eds. *The American War in Vietnam*. Ithaca, N.Y.: Cornell University Press, 1993.

Werner, Jayne S., and Luu Doan Huynh, eds. *The Vietnam War: Vietnamese and American Perspectives*. New York: M. E. Sharp, 1993.

Westad, Odd Arne. *The Global Cold War: Third World Interventions and the Making of Our Times*. New York: Cambridge University Press, 2005.

Westad, Odd Arne, et al., eds. *77 Conversations between Chinese and Foreign Leaders on the Wars in Indochina, 1964–1977*. Washington, D.C.: Woodrow Wilson Center Press, 1998.

Wiest, Andrew. *Vietnam's Forgotten Army: Heroism and Betrayal in the ARVN*. New York: New York University Press, 2008.

Willbanks, James H. *Abandoning Vietnam: How America Left and South Vietnam Lost Its War*. 2nd ed. Lawrence: University Press of Kansas, 2008.

Wirtz, James. *The Tet Offensive: Intelligence Failure in War*. Ithaca, N.Y.: Cornell University Press, 1991.

Woodside, Alexander. *Community and Revolution in Modern Vietnam*. Boston: Houghton, Mifflin, c1976.

Xia Yafeng. *Negotiating with the Enemy*. Bloomington: Indiana University Press, 2006.

Yang Kuisong. *Changes in Mao Zedong's Attitude toward the Indochina War, 1949–1973*. Washington, D.C.: Woodrow Wilson Center Press, 2002.

———. "The Sino-Soviet Border Clash of 1969: From Zhenbao Island to Sino-American Rapprochement." *Cold War History* 1, no. 1 (2000): 21–52.

Young, Marilyn. *The Vietnam Wars, 1945–1990*. New York: HarperCollins, 1999.

Zasloff, Joseph J., and MacAlister Brown. *Communism in Indochina: New Perspectives*. London: D. C. Heath, 1975.

———. *Indochina in Conflict: A Political Assessment*. Lexington, Mass.: Lexington, 1972.

———. *The Pathet Lao: Leadership and Organisation*. Toronto: Lexington, 1973.

Zhai, Qiang. *Beijing and the Vietnam Peace Talks, 1965–1968: New Evidence from Chinese Sources*. Washington, D.C.: Woodrow Wilson Center Press, 1997.

———. "China and the Cambodian Conflict, 1970–1975." In *Behind the Bamboo Courtain: China, Vietnam, and the World beyond Asia*, edited by Priscella Roberts, 369–404. Washington, D.C.: Woodrow Wilson Center Press, 2006.

———. *China and the Vietnam Wars, 1950–1975*. Chapel Hill: University of North Carolina Press, 2000.

Zinoman, Peter. *Colonial Bastille: A History of Imprisonment in Vietnam, 1862–1940, 1862–1940*. Berkeley: University of California Press, 2001.

———. "Nhan Van-Giai Pham and Vietnamese 'Reform Communism' in the 1950s: A Revisionist Interpretation." *Journal of Cold War Studies* 13, no. 1 (Winter 2011): 60–100.

———. "Reading Revolutionary Prison Memoirs." In *The Country of Memory: Remaking the Past in Late Socialist Vietnam*, edited by Hue-Tam Ho Tai, 21–45. Berkeley: University of California Press, 2001.

# Index

# THE NEW COLD WAR HISTORY

Lien-Hang T. Nguyen, *Hanoi's War: An International History of the War for Peace in Vietnam* (2012).

Tanya Harmer, *Allende's Chile and the Inter-American Cold War, 1970–1973* (2011).

Alessandro Brogi, *Confronting America: The Cold War between the United States and the Communists in France and Italy* (2011).

Gregg Brazinsky, *Nation Building in South Korea: Koreans, Americans, and the Making of a Democracy* (2007).

Vladislav M. Zubok, *A Failed Empire: The Soviet Union in the Cold War from Stalin to Gorbachev* (2007).

Stephen G. Rabe, *U.S. Intervention in British Guiana: A Cold War Story* (2005).

Christopher Endy, *Cold War Holidays: American Tourism in France* (2004).

Salim Yaqub, *Containing Arab Nationalism: The Eisenhower Doctrine and the Middle East* (2003).

Francis J. Gavin, *Gold, Dollars, and Power: The Politics of International Monetary Relations, 1958–1971* (2003).

William Glenn Gray, *Germany's Cold War: The Global Campaign to Isolate East Germany, 1949–1969* (2003).

Matthew J. Ouimet, *The Rise and Fall of the Brezhnev Doctrine in Soviet Foreign Policy* (2003).

Pierre Asselin, *A Bitter Peace: Washington, Hanoi, and the Making of the Paris Agreement* (2002).

Jeffrey Glen Giauque, *Grand Designs and Visions of Unity: The Atlantic Powers and the Reorganization of Western Europe, 1955–1963* (2002).

Chen Jian, *Mao's China and the Cold War* (2001).

M. E. Sarotte, *Dealing with the Devil: East Germany, Détente, and Ostpolitik, 1969–1973* (2001).

Mark Philip Bradley, *Imagining Vietnam and America: The Making of Postcolonial Vietnam, 1919–1950* (2000).

Michael E. Latham, *Modernization as Ideology: American Social Science and "Nation Building" in the Kennedy Era* (2000).

Qiang Zhai, *China and the Vietnam Wars, 1950–1975* (2000).

William I. Hitchcock, *France Restored: Cold War Diplomacy and the Quest for Leadership in Europe, 1944–1954* (1998).

Printed in the USA
CPSIA information can be obtained
at www.ICGtesting.com
CBHW030721090424
6581CB00011B/4

31